CONSUMERS
as
PROVIDERS
in

PSYCHIATRIC REHABILITATION

edited by

Carol T. Mowbray

David P. Moxley

Colleen A. Jasper

Lisa L. Howell

International Association of Psychosocial Rehabilitation Services

This book was prepared with partial support from the Center for Mental Health Services.

ISBN 0-9655843-1-3

Design and production management by ColburnHouse Publishing & Marketing

International Association of Psychosocial Rehabilitation Services
10025 Governor Warfield Parkway, #301
Columbia, MD 21044-3357

Printed in the United States of America

Contents

Section 1: Consumer Role Innovation in Psychiatric Rehabilitation and Community Support Systems: Contributions to Direct Service

Section 2: Consumers as Providers of Self-Help

Section 3: Consumer-Controlled Alternatives

Section 4: Consumer Initiatives

Section 5: Employment Roles for Consumers in Mental Health and Psychiatric Rehabilitation Services

Section 6: The Struggle for Identity as a Professional

Section 7: Organizational Issues

Section 8: Proactive Supports for Consumer Service Provision

Section 9: Perspectives on Consumers as Providers

Section 10: Conclusions

About the Editors

Carol T. Mowbray is associate professor and associate dean for research in the University of Michigan School of Social Work where she also serves as associate director of the Center for Poverty, Risk, and Mental Health. Her interests in psychiatric rehabilitation include women's issues, service innovation, and evaluation.

David P. Moxley is associate professor in the Wayne State University School of Social Work where he co-chairs the Concentration in Community Practice and Social Action. His interests in psychiatric rehabilitation include research and development, consumerism, and advocacy.

Colleen A. Jasper is director of consumer relations, behavioral health, in the Michigan Department of Community Health. Prior to this position, she was affiliated with the Justice in Mental Health Organization (JIMHO), in Lansing Michigan, where she offered training and technical assistance to consumer -run organizations. Ms. Jasper's interests in psychiatric rehabilitation include consumer leadership development and consumer advocacy.

Lisa L. Howell is executive director of the Justice in Mental Health Organization (JIMHO), a consumer-run advocacy organization in Lansing, Michigan. She is also director of Project Doors (Developing Our Own Rehabilitation Services). Ms. Howell's interests in psychiatric rehabilitation include consumer self-help and consumer activism.

Acknowledgments

A book is a difficult enterprise to complete. It not only takes substantial effort on the part of authors, but it also takes considerable support by others if success is to be realized. The editors want to acknowledge this support and thank those individuals and organizations who were so pivotal in bringing this book to fruition.

We want to acknowledge the support offered by Leroy Spaniol, Ph.D., of the Center for Psychiatric Rehabilitation at Boston University, who early in the conceptual stage of the project encouraged us to prepare a volume on consumerism which went well beyond a set of journal articles. Dr. Spaniol suggested we develop and submit a proposal for a book length manuscript to the Publications Committee of the International Association of Psychosocial Rehabilitation Services (IAPSRS). Without his involvement, we doubt that this book would have been planned and prepared. We want to thank the Publications Committee of IAPSRS for fostering and supporting publication. And, we want to recognize Ruth Hughes, executive director of IAPSRS, who was instrumental in steering this volume to publication. We want to thank Karen Colburn, ColburnHouse Publishing & Marketing, for her technical support and editorial competence.

Others deserve recognition. The support of the University of Michigan and Wayne State University Schools of Social Work was indispensable. This project would not have been possible without funding from the Center for Mental Health Services (SAMHSA) to the Ohio Department of Mental Health. This grant made it possible to assemble the resources needed for a project of this magnitude (including clerical support and editing), provide honoraria to chapter authors, and travel expenses for selected authors to participate in an IAPSRS Institute. Our thanks to Neal Brown of CMHS and Wilma Townsend of Ohio DMH for facilitating this funding, and for recognizing the importance of the theme and the project. Without these resources, we doubt whether this project could have been translated from plan to book—a volume that surveys consumers as providers of psychiatric rehabilitation.

As editors, we were quite fortunate in assembling a range of talented contributors who offered expertise, sensitivity, and commitment to the process. Chapter authors were deeply committed to preparing their work and to crafting statements that are as meaningful as they are practical.

Consumerism is a fundamental aspect of psychiatric rehabilition and its practice. As the policy environment of mental health service changes in the next several years, we hope that consumerism, consumer role innovation, and consumers as providers continue to be salient and continue to be a force for proactive change. This volume, we feel, can stimulate a dialogue concerning the role of consumers as providers in psychiatric rehabilitation. And, while we accept full responsibility for the quality and timeliness of the book's content, we want to thank those people and organizations who made this book possible.

The Authors

Foreword

I read this as a book of hope. Hope that in the foreseeable future we will be dealing with mental illness as just another of the long-term disabilities many of our fellow human beings are subject to—not as some frightening stigmatized derangements that are still present in much of our society's attitudes. We have a long way to go, but as the chapters of this book illustrate, there has come about a decided change in the attitudes of professionals in the treatment and rehabilitation of those with mental illness. How could we expect complete acceptance of their capabilities if we continue to register doubts about their ability to perform in our own fields of service?

It has taken nearly half a century to reach this point. In the 1940s, when the child guidance movement was in full sway, one aim was to keep youngsters from hospitalization. But the major psychoses and depressions occurred anyway and once the doors of the state institutions closed on the sufferer the cause was considered lost. Although many persons so incarcerated performed work functions and contributed to the maintenance of the hospitals in a variety of ways, very few clinicians or administrators recognized that these abiilities might be just those that could aid in the patient's return to living in the world outside.

Experiments abroad, particularly in Britain and Holland, led to the development of sheltered workshops and clubhouse programs in this country. One of the pioneers was John Beard, who, almost single handedly at first, demonstrated at Fountain House the feasibility of people with serious mental illness living and working in the community.

John knew this from his earlier work with patients in the back wards of a mental hospital. But he also knew it at the origin of Fountain House itself, for Fountain House was founded by a group of ex-patients of a mental hospital who, with the advice and guidance of a forward thinking psychiatrist, had formed the club for their own self-support. They felt the need for staff support, and chose John Beard to run their club. So, in a real sense, we have come full circle; psychosocial rehabilitation may be said to be bedded in consumer empowerment. In its peculiar way, too, the sheltered workshop, community-based programs manufacturing and selling in the open marketplace, like Altro Work Shops, were also consumer influenced, for their foremen and even managerial staff were recruited from the ranks. However, as with comments in a number of chapters in this book, we had to remind clinical staff that workshop personnel, too, were performing therapeutic tasks.

The advent of the psychosocial drugs started the movement of people with chronic mental illness out of the state hospitals, and then came the process of deinstitutionalization, that badly managed changeover to community services that has forever changed the framework of mental health policy in our society. As we know, mental health today is now more than a clinical program. It embraces housing, preparation for social living, attention to social and economic supports, as well as treatment and psychological support. One of the basic tenets of rehabilitation for any handicap or disability is that the patient (consumer) must be part of the treatment team. Plans must be done with, not for, the rehabilitant. Unfortunately, before the presence of the consumer movement, this principle was more often observed in the breech.

One very interesting demonstration that preceded deinstitutionalization, and aided in the movement of patients to community living, was the inauguration of what has come to be called the Fairweather Group. George Fairweather built his program in the Veterans Hospital out of experience and research and on the premise that small groups of mentally ill people could leave the hospital and set up enclaves that would prepare them to associate with the larger community, much as had been the experience with immigration from earlier European cultures. To a large extent this has worked, but it is telling to note that the first such group, once established, eliminated supervision and monitoring from Fairweather's staff and undertook management on their own. This practice has been followed in subsequent developments.

It is only fair in this brief summary of the beginnings of psychosocial rehabilitation, and the rise of a consumer movement, to mention a few people who, in my opinion, had much to do with obtaining footholds in professional and societal thinking. There was Richard Williams, a sociologist on the early staff of the then new National Institute of Mental Health, who saw the value of rehabilitation and who convinced the NIMH Mental Health Grants Committee to consider applications for support from agencies entering the field. He was followed by Allan Miller, M.D., later Commissioner of Mental Hygiene for New York State, who, as staff support for the Community Mental Health Grants Committee, encouraged grants for psychosocial club houses and other demonstrations in community mental health. That era, in the 1960s and early 1970s, provided the underpinnings for many of the foremost agencies and programs represented in IAPSRS today.

Two people deserve mention as contributing to the philosophy of consumer empowerment. We are all familiar with the concept of the "therapeutic community" as a clinical entity. However, the therapeutic community was rarely practiced as its founder, Maxwell Jones, M.D., envisioned. He considered the therapeutic community to be a means for patients to learn and take over management of large parts of their own lives. This was certainly the way he described it to me and the way I saw the therapeutic community in action at London's Belmont Hospital where it was first developed. The other person who deserves mention for his part in the patient/consumer development is the late Irving Blumberg. Irving should be well known to IAPSRS. He was a consumer advocate all his working life, and brought to the fields of mental health and mental disabilities marvelous abilities in stimulating, advising, supporting, and guiding the major national and international organizations in psychosocial rehabilitation.

When I started this foreword with the expression of hope, it is that the distinctions of "consumer" and "prosumer" will gradually vanish since persons with "mental illness" will be treated no differently than are people with any other form of disability. This had to start, as is amply described in these pages, with the field of mental health itself. And this has been a difficult challenge. As many writers in this book point out, there has been much resistance to allowing "restored patients" to share in the treatment process. I distinctly remember, just a generation ago, being taught the admonition "Stay out of their frame of reference."

It has taken the pressure of the consumer advocacy movement, the laws on rehabilitation, the Americans with Disabilities Act, and, most of all, the thoughtful behavior of supervisors, mentors and fellow professionals, so aptly described in this book, to bring us this far. This book should be must reading for all those who perform tasks in mental health.

Bertram J. Black, M.S.W.
Professor Emeritus of Psychiatry, Epidemiology and Social Medicine
Albert Einstein College of Medicine
Bronx, New York

Preface

The field of psychiatric rehabilitation has always been guided by hope: hope for the personal progress and success of people coping with the immediate and long-term consequences of serious mental illness, hope for the contributions staff can make to the improvement of the quality of life of people with serious mental illness, and hope for the field itself—that psychiatric rehabilitation will continue to be a competent and positive force in helping people with serious mental illness to achieve those goals they find personally valuable. The field itself has evolved from one dominated by illness and diagnostic perspectives to one that is now focusing on recovery through the development and implementation of proactive supports for community living and community involvement.

Consumers as Providers in Psychiatric Rehabilitation reflects the tremendous progress that has been made in psychiatric rehabilitation and it reflects the hope that the disabling consequences of serious mental illness can be obviated if not substantially reduced through innovations in the provision of support. The content is a testimony to the opportunities and benefits inherent in broadening our conceptualization and understanding of what constitutes support, who offers support, and the contexts within which support is offered. Consumers themselves are an important source of what is referred to in psychiatric rehabilitation as the provision of support. As we see in this volume, consumers as "providers" are often willing to undertake vital and important efforts to make supports accessible, usable, and effective. Both the consumer and ex-patients movements in psychiatric rehabilitation and mental health have demonstrated the profoundly important supports that consumers themselves can create, implement, and sustain.

The content of this volume demonstrates the critical roles assumed by people with serious mental illness as primary, committed, innovative, and motivated providers of a wide array of supports that are needed to make psychiatric rehabilitation a progressive, effective, and viable domain of human service practice. The content of the volume demonstrates the diversity of roles assumed by people with serious mental illness as providers of psychiatric rehabilitation supports. In addition, the volume highlights the evolution of psychiatric rehabilitation. Contemporary psychiatric rehabilitation programs and services are evolving into systems of transdisciplinary practice that value dynamic and flexible notions of professionalism—ones that are not rigidly bounded by credentialing or turf. As a transdisciplinary field, psychiatric rehabilitation is committed to forging knowledge and practice that reduces the negative social and personal consequences of serious mental illness, and that increases quality of life and standards of living.

Professionalism within our field calls for us to learn this knowledge and to put good practice to work whether as credentialed mental health professionals, professionals coming to the field from other domains (e.g., business or education), or as professionals whose knowledge base is founded on direct experience as consumers, ex-patients, or advocates. Within psychiatric rehabilitation, partnerships among members of different groups and different backgrounds and experiential bases are possible. Because of its transdisciplinary nature, psychiatric rehabilitation can take place in many different environments, under many different auspices, and with many different actors serving as providers. This book demonstrates the flexibility of psychiatric rehabilitation and documents the critical resources and gifts people with serious mental illness can offer to other people coping with the social and personal consequences created by psychiatric disability.

This book also illustrates the important role of consumers as innovators. A considerable portion of the book's content demonstrates that consumers are often on the leading edge of change and innovation in psychiatric rehabilitation. Indeed, some of the most important supports within contemporary mental health and rehabilitation systems were conceived and launched by consumers or ex-patients who now see that these innovations have become core elements of exemplary systems of service. Consumers and ex-patients often serve as advocates pushing for programmatic change so that practical supports designed to make positive effects on the quality of life of people become viable elements of mental health and rehabilitation systems. A number of the chapters within the text reflect innovation, creativity, and courage on the part of consumers or ex-patients working alone, in small groups, or in partnership with other advocacy groups. These consumers are themselves leaders offering inspiration and hope to all of us, and helping us to conceive of more supportive communities and situations.

Many of the chapters composing the volume offer a collection of ideas, know how, guidelines, principles, and practices for launching and sustaining supports offered by and for consumers. A number of chapters offer inspiration, and just plain common sense about how to proceed in this important yet emergent area of practice. And, some chapters highlight the pitfalls, barriers, and potentially negative situations that can arise when psychiatric rehabilitation systems and services identify new roles for consumers as providers of support, and seek to incorporate these roles as permanent features.

The book seeks to achieve several aims. First, it seeks to document the emergence of consumers as providers in psychiatric rehabilitation, and to honor the plurality and diversity of the various initiatives, programs, experiments, and innovations that actually take place under the rubric of "consumers as providers." Second, it seeks to identify the issues, challenges, and barriers that confront successful implementation of these various alternatives, and to identify the various supports that are needed to make their operation successful for the people who receive this support but also for the people who offer it. Third, it seeks to bring together know how, wisdom, and practices and the struggles and challenges that can be considered by readers when they establish their own alternatives and supports. And, fourth, it seeks to give a voice to people who are making this form of innovation within psychiatric rehabilitation happen.

This book is a product of those people who are at the forefront in making supports offered by and for consumers a reality within their communities, and they can contribute important knowledge to making this happen effectively.

This fourth aim offers the logic to the structure of the volume. There are many perspectives in this volume reflecting the diversity of approaches and alternatives that can emerge when consumers serve in roles as providers of support. The actual perspectives of the authors are confined primarily to the first section of the book which is devoted to establishing the rationale for consumers as providers, thinking about this area of psychiatric rehabilitation practice, and identifying issues that can emerge when consumers are engaged within psychiatric rehabilitation systems or services as providers of support. The perspectives composing the second section of the book are those of people who have been involved in the offer of self-help. These perspectives are those of consumers themselves, for the most part, who look at the variety of self-help alternatives that can be implemented within and outside of formal systems of service. Within this section, we learn about the promises and pitfalls of self-help when it is applied to meeting the support needs of people coping with issues created by bipolar illness, schizophrenia, or the combination of mental illness and substance use. Each of the chapters within this section tells stories about consumers working with one another as they make support happen within intimate groups and intimate communities.

The perspectives of the third section of the volume speak to consumer-controlled alternatives and the benefits that consumers can produce for one another through the operation of their own facilities and programs. The tone of these chapters is best captured by the title of Judi Chamberlin's now classic book, *On Our Own*. These chapter authors tell of the challenges and obstacles they needed to overcome in establishing, revitalizing, or sustaining consumer-controlled support alternatives. The diversity of these alternatives is reflected by the settings portrayed: a comprehensive community support system; a drop in center; a peer support facility that offers safety and nurturance to people coping with dissociative disorders; a network of supports integrating recreation, self-help, vocational development, and cultural enrichment; and consumer-run businesses. We learn from these authors that innovation among consumers in the creation and management of their own support systems is real, but so are the challenges that must be overcome.

Within the fourth section of the book, we hear the perspectives of those people who are forging new professional-consumer relationships within established mental health and rehabilitation services. This section recognizes the important roles consumers serve in defining the need for new supports, and then taking the leadership to create and implement these supports within established programs and organizations. Within this section, we learn about the leadership roles consumers can take in facilitating support groups, and in helping people to negotiate successfully critical role transitions (like going back to work, or going to school). We learn about how consumers contribute to outreach and to assisting peers to use existing psychiatric rehabilitation services and supports. We also learn about how a consumer can serve as a trainer who provides technical assistance in recovery, the aim of which is to help people gain skills to manage their symptoms and functioning. Since these change activities require leadership, we hear within this section about how consumers can learn leadership skills that are designed specifically to help them contribute to the strengthening of consumer-driven mental health and rehabilitation services and supports.

The perspectives composing sections five and six share a principal theme: What is involved in becoming an employee or professional within a mental health system when one is a consumer or has a history as a consumer? Contributors to section five discuss consumers as employees of mental health and psychiatric rehabilitation systems. Within this section we learn about programs specifically designed for consumers to serve in support roles as mentors, case managers, and housing support providers. We hear directly from consumers or ex-patients who work as employees within mental health programs and who examine and enumerate the benefits, stressors, and pitfalls of working within "the system." Several of the contributors to section six are themselves formally trained as mental health providers and we learn directly from them about the issues involved in reconciling their histories as consumers with their training and futures as credentialed mental health professionals. This revealing section suggests that people who are consumers, or who have backgrounds as consumers, can experience discrimination, stigma, and mistrust within established systems, even though they possess "bona fide" credentials.

The success of consumers as providers in psychiatric rehabilitation is the theme of section seven. These contributors examine success from the standpoint of those organizational arrangements that must be in place to sustain and perpetuate these programs and practices. Several of the chapters are devoted to the critical task of fostering successful transition after a period of innovation or demonstration. These transitions may take the form of moving from one status to another (e.g., moving from a self-help to a consumer-controlled organization), from one funding source to another, or from one way of offering services or support to another (e.g., from peer support to recreational support). Another organizational issue examined in this section involves the need to look at role dynamics that exist among traditionally trained mental health professionals and consumers who are serving in provider roles within established clinical or treatment settings.

These organizational issues highlight the need to identify and analyze the kinds of proactive supports that are required to foster the success of consumers as providers. Contributors to section eight offer a range of ideas concerning organizational, developmental, personal, programmatic, and practical supports found to be useful in fostering the professional development and well-being of consumers serving in roles as providers. Role modeling, supportive coaching and supervision, peer support, affirmative organizational policies and practices, staff training, and role change among formally trained mental health professionals are some of the supports examined by contributors to this section.

Section nine offers various perspectives on consumers as providers in psychiatric rehabilitation. A former commissioner of mental health and his colleagues reflect on how one state sought to promote consumer involvement in mental health services, and how roles for consumers as providers were subsequently developed within this state. An author active in the family movement identifies how family members and family advocates can encourage the implementation of consumer support alternatives, and discusses how family members can support the personal and career development of consumers who take on roles as providers. Another author active in the consumer movement crafts a statement about diversity and defines it in a rich manner so that the perspectives and voices of a variety of communities are considered and included when consumers serve as providers in psychiatric rehabilitation. Other authors present a rationale and set of practice tools for documenting and evaluating the supports offered by and for consumers in a chapter that incorporates many of the issues and themes from previous sections.

The conclusion of the book, in section ten, highlights some of the overarching themes found in the various sections and chapters of the volume. Addressing these themes in practice, we believe, will be fundamental to achieving an integration of consumer provided supports into existing and future rehabilitation systems. Given the vastly changing context of psychiatric rehabilitation systems, it is necessary that practitioners, consumers, family members, and advocates consider the numerous factors that can support or compromise the viability of consumers as providers.

As editors, we sought to craft an informative book—one that the members of the International Association of Psychosocial Rehabilitation Services find applicable to everyday practice and work. Whatever the reader's role may be within psychiatric rehabilitation, we believe that there is very useful content within this volume for thinking about consumers as providers and for creating practical initiatives to support the very important contributions consumers can make to the provision of high quality and high performance approaches to rehabilitation. As editors, we sought to craft a book that respects the diversity of approaches within this area, and that respects the many contributions made by the innovators: consumers, ex-patients, formally trained professionals, and advocates who endorse the idea that effective supports come in many different forms and from many different sources. The contents of this book recognize the diversity of supports that are needed for everyday community living, and the importance of including within our communities many different providers of these supports: for effective psychiatric rehabilitation occurs when there are strong and collaborative partnerships among a variety of people who can offer the precious gift of support.

It is in the spirit of this partnership that the editors came together to prepare this volume. All of us see ourselves as bringing to bear a different perspective on consumers as providers in psychiatric rehabilitation. And all of us see somewhat differently what constitutes effective support within this field. However, whether as researchers, administrators, academics, or advocates, we recognize the critical contributions that consumers are making to the support of people coping with the social and personal consequences of serious mental illness. And we see the untapped potential that exists among many consumers who can expand the variety of supports available. Thus, this book represents one effort to document these contributions by consumers, to help promote their inclusion as good practice within the field of psychiatric rehabilitation, and to expand their successful adoption in breadth and depth as an integral part of psychiatric rehabilitation practice.

SECTION 1

Consumer Role Innovation in Psychiatric Rehabilitation and Community Support Systems: Contributions to Direct Service

Consumers as Providers: Forces and Factors Legitimizing Role Innovation in Psychiatric Rehabilitation

David P. Moxley
Carol T. Mowbray

Considerable effort has been invested over the past two decades to involve consumers as providers in core rehabilitation activities involving service, support, and skill development within programs once dominated by only credentialed providers. Consumers as providers are somewhat new players in the psychiatric rehabilitation arena as their roles have been formalized and sometimes made permanent—although they were always informally involved, and indeed largely responsible for the considerable innovation that has occurred within the rehabilitation area we refer to as social support. Formalization is seen in demonstration projects, research initiatives, and progressive service systems and organizations that integrate consumer support alternatives, consumer operated programs, and consumer employment into their programmatic structures and operations.

The emphasis on consumerism in psychiatric rehabilitation has blurred the distinction between who is a consumer and who is a provider (Perry, Davis, & McVeigh, 1993), as demonstrated by the variety of alternatives described in this volume. No longer can it be said that a consumer is merely a recipient of services while a provider is a traditionally credentialed professional who offers and provides these services. Over the past twenty years, the field of psychiatric rehabilitation has witnessed the emergence of self-help and mutual support (Zinman, Howie the Harp, & Budd, 1987), as well as the most recent innovation of consumers serving in direct service roles, often times as employees (Mowbray, Moxley, Thrasher, et. al., 1996). The concept of provider has gone through a metamorphosis: a helper can pro-offer assistance to a person in need based on knowledge of serious mental illness that comes from sources other than professional training and education in the human services (Howie the Harp, 1987a; Zinman, 1987).

When it comes to the concept of professional, psychiatric rehabilitation has transversed much of the same ground as other related human service fields, like developmental disabilities. Interdisciplinary practice involving the blending of roles among credentialed professionals has given way to the notion of transdisciplinary practice in which professional identity, and even discipline, is seen as less important than the tangible skills, qualities, motivations, and competencies brought to various roles involved in service provision (Anthony,

Cohen, & Farkas, 1990; Farkas & Anthony, 1989; Flexer & Solomon, 1993). Consumerism can blend with professionalism within transdisciplinary practice as recipients themselves are seen as resources to the rehabilitation process (Baer, Goebel, & Flexer, 1993). Consumers can bring a bona fide experience and distinctive knowledge to rehabilitation given their understanding of mental health, mental illness, and service delivery often gained as direct participants in their own process of recovery (Perry et al., 1993).

Legitimizing what consumers bring to rehabilitation is not only a way of expanding resources sorely needed to improve community support for people, but it is also a way of recognizing that traditional professionals—even with their training, experience, and theoretical perspectives—simply do not have all of the answers to the innovative provision of care, support, and service (Unzicker, 1989). Consumers do bring something distinctive to service encounters. This distinctiveness is born from very personal experiences with serious mental illness, framed either from a medical (Low, 1950), consumer (Mental Health Association of Southeastern Pennsylvania, n. d.), liberationist (Chamberlin, 1990), or self-empowerment perspective (Unzicker, 1989).

What was once seen as an adjunct to service or as a curious innovation is now moving from the periphery of the field of psychiatric rehabilitation to its center as a regular service feature. This volume documents many of these alternatives and offers an opportunity to consumers, traditionally credentialed professionals, and service administrators to share their own perspectives, feelings, views, and data on "consumers as providers in psychiatric rehabilitation."

Our previous work, and the work of others, has demonstrated that the expansion of consumer roles in psychiatric rehabilitation service has at least five attributes. These are: (1) a deliberate expansion of a consumer's role beyond that of a user or recipient to include helping and support behaviors and activities (Mowbray et al., 1996); (2) an empowerment of the consumer role by recognizing that consumers can offer resources that traditional professionals either cannot offer or choose not to offer (Moxley, 1997); (3) an expansion of what we mean by credentials to legitimize the understanding, knowledge, skills, attitudes, and motivations consumers have gained through their encounters with service systems and their experiences as mental health clients; (4) a view that some kinds of service situations and roles (e.g. outreach) can be best fulfilled or led by providers who are consumers themselves (Howie the Harp, 1987b; Zinman, 1987); and (5) a perspective that the provision of help not only assists a user or recipient, but also can create tangible benefits for the helper whose identity can be strengthened by helping another person in need (Chamberlin, 1989; Zinman et al., 1987).

Expanding roles so that they incorporate these five attributes, however, can have a profound effect on the identity of the people holding them. In this book, we seek to focus, in part, on how serving in a provider role makes an impact, for better or worse, on the occupants of these rather novel positions.

Many of the contributors to this volume recognize both the rewards and limitations of serving as a provider, especially when organizational supports are not offered to promote role effectiveness, mobility, and career development.

This chapter begins the documentary journey taken in this book. We begin by looking at consumer role innovation in the field of psychiatric rehabilitation. We look at the social forces and factors that legitimize this form of innovation in psychiatric rehabilitation while we illustrate that the idea of consumers in service provision roles has precedent in several fields of human service. Psychiatric rehabilitation is neither alone nor unique in its efforts to expand the roles of consumers. The readers' appreciation of some of these innovations in other fields encourages a better understanding of what is happening in psychiatric rehabilitation, and what can be expected from an intentional expansion of the role of consumer beyond recipient to include peer support, consumer advocacy, and rehabilitation service activities. Finally, we end this chapter with a handful of observations about consumers as providers in order to illustrate the variety and richness of the alternatives that can be incorporated into psychiatric rehabilitation, and to prepare readers for what is to come.

Consumer Role Innovation in Rehabilitation Services

The empowerment of the consumer role in psychiatric rehabilitation, like in any field of human services, can be achieved in many different ways. Perhaps one of the most salient examples is that of the assertive consumer who holds high expectations for professional service and support. Many programs in psychiatric rehabilitation foster this kind of consumerism, relying on the involvement of consumers in service planning and on direct feedback from consumers about their satisfaction with the services and supports they receive. The consumer movement in psychiatric rehabilitation has produced numerous assertive recipients who want to share power with professionals, and who seek to become more involved in the direction and substance of their own care and support, as well as in the change of mental health systems (Chamberlin, Rogers, & Sneed, 1989).

Another form of consumerism involves rights protection and advocacy (Chandler, 1990). Here consumers, by virtue of their disabilities, are seen as highly vulnerable within the actual systems established to serve them (Weicker, 1987; Herr, 1983). This vulnerability comes, in part, from a heightened probability of abuse and neglect, bureaucratic obstacles to quality care (Sundram, 1987), the misuse of psychiatric medications (Breggin, 1991), diagnosis (Caplan, 1995), and interventions by dominant mental health professionals, particularly psychiatrists (Robitscher, 1980).

Vulnerability can also come from stigma and discrimination (Link, Cullen, Mirotznik, & Struening, 1992) evolving out of efforts to exert social control and the social production of diminished status (Wintersteen & Rapp, 1986). Systems of rights protection and advocacy have been established to protect the interests of people with serious mental illness, especially those served within restrictive settings like hospitals, long-term care facilities, and institutions (Freddolino & Moxley, 1988). Most of these systems of advocacy, however, focus on rights violations involving mental health care and do not focus on those violations that occur within everyday life and community living (Freddolino, Moxley, & Fleishman, 1989).

A third possibility of consumerism in psychiatric rehabilitation is to empower the consumer role so that consumers actually exercise more control over service providers and service encounters (Meenaghan, 1974; Meenaghan & Washington, 1980). Increasingly we see this form of consumerism discussed in policy and programmatic forums in which vouchers and other mechanisms of promoting consumer choice and control over service provision are considered (Meenaghan & Mascari, 1971; Rein, 1983). This form of consumerism is consistent with the microeconomic concept of market. An informed consumer, who has real choices and the resources to execute these choices, exerts influence and control in the market place (Gilbert, 1983). By virtue of their willingness to exercise these choices, and to look for service providers who will produce satisfaction for the "buyer," consumers themselves can be pivotal in the promotion of innovation, improvement, and quality. This approach to consumerism values dissent: the consumer's search for satisfaction, and a willingness to move to another provider if this satisfaction is not achieved, are seen as forces for change and innovation, and for provider accountability (Gilbert & Specht, 1974).

Yet this form of consumerism has been difficult to achieve both in psychiatric rehabilitation and in the larger domain of human services. For a variety of reasons, a market-like system of service that promotes information provision, provider competition, consumer choice, and consumer dissent has been more the ideal rather than the reality. But these concepts do indeed demonstrate that there is an ultimate form of consumer empowerment, and a more enlightened approach to consumerism in psychiatric rehabilitation that is consistent with the market system of the greater culture.

A conception of consumerism employed in this book is more midline, lying somewhere between an effort to enhance the consumer role by encouraging and facilitating involvement in the service process, and an approach to simulate a market system within psychiatric rehabilitation. Our midline conception is a fourth approach to consumerism. It focuses on the expansion of the traditional role of the consumer to include within this role (or role set) expectations, behaviors, and activities once thought to be reserved only for the role of professional (Mayer, 1972).

Role innovation in this approach means that consumers themselves are not merely recipients but are very important if not critical actors in the expansion of psychiatric rehabilitation services including advocacy, clinical care, skill development, and the provision of support. Consumerism here is expressed as a desire on the part of all stakeholders involved in the rehabilitation enterprise to legitimize the consumer role as containing not merely "recipient behaviors" but also "provider behaviors." These provider behaviors can include forming relationships with other consumers for the purposes of providing support and help, providing and sharing information about services and independent living options, and offering supports in community settings that enable people to be successful in everyday life.

Such role innovation at the provider level readily fits with other role innovations more oriented to policy and administration in which we see consumers increasingly involved in policy formulation and development, systems-level advocacy, goal and agenda setting in mental health programs, quality improvement, evaluation, and governance. In this fifth approach to consumerism, we may see consumers working in evaluation and research positions, serving on boards of directors, and undertaking quality improvement activities—roles previously reserved for other actors.

Reasons to Focus on Consumers as Providers

Today, we cannot merely characterize contemporary mental health systems as solely oriented to medical care, social services, or rehabilitation. We must also recognize that these systems are themselves complex collections of medical, social, rehabilitative, and consumer-oriented services. Consumerism is recognized as a fundamental aspect of recovery and as a fundamental element of progressive mental health systems (Anthony, 1994). We assert that role innovation is not only a progressive aim within informed psychiatric rehabilitation programs, but is needed to facilitate the healing or recovery process (Deegan, 1994; Moxley, 1994).

Despite the multiple forms of consumerism within psychiatric rehabilitation, we have chosen to focus on consumers as providers. So, when we subsequently refer to role innovation in this volume, we mean principally the expansion of the consumer role to include activities, behaviors, and expectations relating to the provision of direct rehabilitation support and service (Mayer, 1972).

"Consumers as providers" serves as the focus of this volume for several reasons. We recognize that consumer role innovation and expansion are occurring often at grass roots and programmatic levels even though such role change may not be fully or explicitly endorsed by the policies of mental health organizations and systems (Chamberlin, 1978). These changes, perhaps insignificant to some, signal that an evolution is occurring within psychiatric rehabilitation, especially at programmatic levels as well as within the context of provider-recipient interactions (Deegan, 1994). Professionals and consumers alike are recognizing that as recipients become increasingly aware of serious mental illness, and especially of its negative social consequences, they want more involvement in and control over the service process. These changes in consumer roles have important implications for how we think about rehabilitation help and support; for example, altering power structures, expanding the notion of support (Zinman et al., 1987), and changing the nature of the rehabilitation relationship (Mosher & Burti, 1994), to identify just a few.

We focus on consumers as providers because of a need to document these attempts, activities, and programmatic innovations not only to understand them, and to identify the variation we are seeing in consumers as providers, but also to identify implications they hold for how to organize rehabilitation services. Indeed, as editors of this volume, we are excited about the different forms consumer role innovation and expansion are taking in psychiatric rehabilitation, and the implications for service enhancement through the development and incorporation of consumers as employees in direct service roles, innovators in consumer-initiated services, self-help participants, and leaders in support alternatives they control themselves.

Another reason justifying our focus is that the emergence of consumers as providers in psychiatric rehabilitation recognizes the limits on service imposed by the number of professionally trained rehabilitation workers, and constraints produced by professional roles that may limit the range and availability of service and support offered by professionals, both of which are long standing problems in mental health (Albee, 1959, 1960; Levine, 1981; Zax & Specter, 1974). By documenting variations in consumers as providers, we recognize the possibility of extending the form and substance of rehabilitation supports and assistance without relying exclusively on professionals (Levine, 1981). Consumers as providers may operate differently in rehabilitative roles than professionals when it comes to the provision of support. Consumers can bring to service encounters different attitudes, motivations, insights, and behavioral qualities than can professionals (Budd, 1987).

The social consequences of serious mental illness, and the breadth of psychiatric rehabilitation, both suggest that professionals cannot satisfy all of the need, nor all of the demand for support (Albee, 1959). We must think in more innovative ways of extending supports that foster individual success and personally rewarding life styles in order to realize the mission of psychiatric rehabilitation: that of helping people to be successful in environments and roles of their own choosing with the least amount of ongoing professional assistance (Farkas, Anthony, & Cohen, 1989). Consumers as providers is certainly one way of achieving innovation in the expansion and elaboration of support.

And, finally, our focus on consumers as providers comes out of the reality that people not only need employment but also need to be engaged in productive activity (Ruffner, 1986). The emergence of consumers as providers within psychiatric rehabilitation comes at a time when our society is increasingly experiencing challenges if not difficulty in producing "good" jobs, ones that bring with them skill development, mobility, career ladders, and adequate pay (Reich, 1991; Rifkin, 1996). Our economy is producing these jobs in the service sector, and a principal source of job creation is found in the provision of personal service by nonprofit human service organizations. Offering people with serious mental illness viable employment in rehabilitation may help people to initiate careers. to obtain training, and to develop track records that are directly applicable to contemporary and future labor markets.

Role innovation can mean affirmative employment. The specter of unemployment among many of our citizens is a serious issue (Wilson, 1996). Role innovation can link naturally with the priority placed by psychiatric rehabilitation on involvement in work and career development.

By understanding this development within psychiatric rehabilitation, we can be more informed and critical about our efforts to expand and/or elaborate the roles of consumers. As suggested by the diversity of papers composing this volume, role enhancement and role innovation are not as easy as they appear. There are a number of issues, challenges, and concerns that must be addressed and resolved. By documenting these, we are in a better position to foster the success of consumers who become involved as providers of the services and supports that define psychiatric rehabilitation as a distinctive field of human service practice.

Background on Consumers as Providers

Historical Roots

The idea of consumers as providers is not a new concept. Within the field of mental health and psychiatric rehabilitation, we can trace an early stimulus for this innovation when mental health consumer Clifford Beers formed, in the early part of the century, the predecessor to what was to become state and local mental health associations (Dain, 1980). In collaboration with the psychiatrist Adolf Meyer, Clifford Beers sought to amplify the voice of the consumer and to promote citizen action to improve the plight of people receiving public psychiatric care—principally those individuals committed to state institutions (Dain, 1980). But Beers adopted an advocacy role and the perspective he set forth did not address the roles of consumers in self-help or direct service positions.

Beers, however, was instrumental in stimulating public interest in the care and treatment of people coping with mental illness, and in establishing through a collaboration with Meyer the concept of mental hygiene. Even though the advocacy undertaken by Beers failed to change the custodial character of state institutions, and it could not alter the cycle of abuse and neglect experienced by many of the people housed within these facilities, he was a modern exemplar of the activist consumer collaborating with mental health professionals.

One of the earliest programmatic expressions of consumers as providers of support was seen when Fountain House (and its predecessor WANA Society—We Are Not Alone) was established as a psychosocial support system for people leaving state institutions. Founded by people with serious mental illness as an innovative self-help approach, WANA and subsequently Fountain House, recognized the importance of encouraging supportive transactions among people with serious mental illness to help them stay out of hospitals and to sustain themselves in communities despite harsh isolation, loneliness, and material deprivation (Black, 1988).

The basic values and principles of peer support, mutual help, and transitional employment, put to practical use in the 1940s by the members of Fountain House to support one another, and to form a community among people struggling with serious mental illness, would become distinctive ideas of the clubhouse model (Beard, 1976; Doughty & Hayes, 1979; Beard, Propst, & Malamud, 1982; Beard, Schmidt, & Smith, 1963). And they would serve as important concepts animating the early development and diffusion of psychiatric rehabilitation programs in the 1960s and 1970s (Black, 1988).

As the basic ideas of public mental health and subsequently of community mental health were being formulated during the late 1950s and early 1960s, the beneficial effects of peer support for mental health patients was recognized by the Joint Commission on Mental Illness and Health, a commission established by federal legislation to make policy recommendations concerning mental health care in the United States (Cameron, 1989). The Joint Commission's 1961 report, *Action for Mental Health*, together with its principal monographs, argued for a dramatic expansion of mental health services, and it defined new approaches to care and support of people with serious mental illness (Brown, 1985).

Action for Mental Health recognized the role and work of ex-patient groups in the mental health system, although the report discounted the ability of these groups to be autonomous of professional direction or consultation:

> Many observers have noted that these organizations are remarkably unstable and short-lived, especially when no professional direction or consultation is involved. (It is interesting that a good majority of organizations in our study had a professional consultant or leader and were affiliated with a professional organization— a mental hospital or clinic, state or community agency, or some combination. A relatively large number were affiliated with mental health associations.) (Joint Commission on Mental Illness and Health, 1961, pp. 186-187)

The report did, however, identify four types of ex-patient alternatives based on the survey work of Wechsler (1960). Social clubs, whose membership was limited to people who were hospitalized for a mental illness, were organized to provide support, recreation, and social interaction while Mental Health Aid Societies provided social support to people who remained hospitalized and organized community action projects like parties, clothing drives, and advocacy efforts to address the needs of people who were institutionalized. Therapy groups were devoted to group discussion, addressing problems of community living, and creating supportive relationships. The model here was Recovery, Inc. (Low, 1943, 1950) which was organized as a self-help therapy and educational system, endorsing an illness model while also incorporating elements of socialization and recreation. And, social rehabilitation centers focused on helping members to develop social relationships within protected settings. Eight of these centers were identified by the commission with Fountain House the best known of these facilities.

All four of these efforts reflected a nascent movement to humanize the support of people with psychiatric problems especially through the expansion of social supports, work opportunities, social affiliation, and the provision of pragmatic resources like clothing. Collectively, several of these approaches identified by the Joint Commission would eventually fuse into an international movement to expand community support of people with serious mental illness that has come to be known as psychiatric or psychosocial rehabilitation. The supports and their agency sponsors were to be organized by umbrella organizations such as the International Association of Psychosocial Rehabilitation Services (IAPSRS) and the international clubhouse movement.

Within the context of *Action for Mental Health*, the Joint Commission viewed ex-patients as people who left psychiatric institutions and who needed supportive, rehabilitative, and psychiatric services in the community. The emphasis placed on ex-patients and their alternative support systems was an important element of a new mental health ideology emerging out of the framework of *Action for Mental Health*. Although the efforts of ex-patients were seen as important aspects of therapy and rehabilitation, the fact that mental health planners did not see ex-patients as autonomous of mental health professionals meant that these emergent practices were to be subordinate to medical and rehabilitation services delivered by professionals.

Yet there was a subtle contradiction here that would become more salient as the design of community mental health policy and programs ensued. While the epidemiology of mental disorders documented their high prevalence and incidence as well as the severe morbidity they induced (Srole and Associates, 1962), there was a recognition among policy and intellectual leaders of this field that the United States could not produce enough mental health professionals to address the perceived need (Albee, 1959, 1960; Gurin, Veroff, & Feld, 1960), especially the need in low income communities (Levine, 1981; Zax & Specter, 1974). Self-help and social support innovations would become more important in order to extend the assistance needed by people coping with serious mental illness or other mental health issues and to focus on prevention (Caplan, 1961a, 1961b, 1964, 1970, 1974). The literature of the 1960s and 1970s reflected the innovative involvement of indigenous nonprofessionals, informal helpers, lay people, clergy, teachers, and social support providers in the provision of mental health services in both rural and urban settings (Collins & Pancoast, 1976; Curtis, 1979; Zax & Specter, 1974).

These changes in role, and in the expansion of social support, were legitimized by research undertaken by social psychiatrists during World War II, the Korean conflict, and during the 1950s and 1960s. The knowledge of the importance of self-help to recovery from acute combat situations underscored the important role of the peer group as a provider of social support (Dean, Kraft, & Pepper, 1976), the critical role of supportive group interventions to the resolution of crises (Levine, 1981), and the importance of self-help to the provision of mental health care at front line hospitals. Social support gained further legitimacy through the work of Caplan (1974) whose pioneering theory of preventive psychiatry underscored the importance of using social supports to help people to negotiate successfully the stress created by crisis, role change, and social change.

The Ex-Patient Movement

The idea of ex-patient was to take a profoundly different turn in the 1960s and 1970s, as individuals grossly dissatisfied, even horrified, by their treatment within psychiatric institutions began to organize alternative support systems and a movement to express their dissent at the unrestricted dominance of psychiatrists and mental health professionals (Chamberlin, 1978). Within the general protest movements dominating the 1960s and early 1970s, the ex-patient movement took root and developed support systems that could serve as alternatives to established community mental health programs and psychiatric institutions.

Alternatives like drop-in centers, crash pads, drug free support systems, and consciousness raising support groups began to emerge across the United States and Canada. These programs and supports were infused with an anti-psychiatry ideology and were informed by ideologies developed by innovators in other protest movements like feminism (Ferree & Hess, 1985), civil rights (Blumberg, 1984), disability rights (Baker, 1993), and Gay rights (Adam, 1987). Unlike the original clubhouse programs and peer support alternatives identified by the Joint Commission, the participants in these ex-patient alternatives viewed themselves as part of a larger struggle for human rights. These organizations and their participants were vehemently anti-mental health and anti-psychiatry.

This ex-patient movement was not anticipated by the Joint Commission and by the authors of *Action for Mental Health*. Indeed, the Joint Commission was positing a passive consumer who needed the guidance, leadership, and mentorship of informed and progressive community mental health professionals. The peer supports documented by the Joint Commission were seen as secondary and supplemental to innovative psychiatric and mental health care controlled by professionals, mostly newly trained psychiatrists enlightened by public health principles and practices.

The contemporary ex-patient movement emerged out of a context of protest and conflict. Ex-patients saw themselves as assertive people rebelling against institutional and social oppression designed to make them passive and submissive. Their literature was one of criticism and critique—existing mental health arrangements and ideology were not merely labeled as problematic but as oppressive and evil. The prescription of ex-patients was one of separatism and mutual aid.

Thus, in the history of psychiatric rehabilitation, the label of ex-patient has double meaning—a situation that reflects the duality of this field when one focuses on the idea of consumerism. On the one hand, it literally means supporting people who are former patients of institutional care to live in the community. The image of the patient is shaped by biomedical constructs involving ill health, dependency, and disability. On the other hand, the label of ex-patient suggests an individual who stands in opposition to contemporary mental health arrangements and ideology. The image of the person here is shaped by social constructs involving discrimination, stigmatization, social intolerance, and repressive social norms.

The Consumer Movement and the Community Support Model

The evolution of the community support model and psychiatric rehabilitation during the late 1970s through the present has seen an increasing legitimization of role expansion that takes into consideration the duality of ex-patient and consumer. Some forms of role innovation try to build close working partnerships between professionals and consumers, while other forms of role innovation underscore the importance of separatist alternatives found in consumer-run and consumer-controlled support alternatives.

Psychiatric rehabilitation and community support have increasingly emphasized consumerism through the elaboration of the consumer role. There has been a great deal of attention paid to rights protection, active consumer involvement in rehabilitation, and more control by consumers of the service process (Anthony & Spaniol, 1994). According to the ideology or philosophy of psychiatric rehabilitation, consumerism seeks a more empowered consumer who is helped to overcome the personal issues and social consequences created by serious mental illness through their own action (Farkas, Anthony, & Cohen, 1989). From this perspective, serious mental illness is seen as a bona fide illness that has both disabling and handicapping implications for people.

But these negative consequences can be reduced in significance through self-care and self-help. And the active involvement of the consumer can help to offset these disabling and handicapping consequences. Much of the ideology of psychiatric rehabilitation emphasizes consumer role change through strategies involving the elaboration of supports for daily living, more proactive service delivery, self-help options, and the legitimization of self advocacy. Advocacy within this perspective, however, most likely focuses on achieving access to better and more appropriate service, expanding social support, and fostering consumer input and involvement rather than on helping recipients to control service provision or exercise dissent (Moxley & Daeschlein, 1997).

Yet from the perspective of many consumer advocates, the field does not go far enough. It still seeks submissive and obsequient recipients and this only results in the reinforcement of illness and disability and the emergence of learned helplessness. The ex-patient perspective can be seen in contemporary psychiatric rehabilitation and community support programs and services. This perspective recognizes the negative implications of labeling, the abuse that can be created through medicalization of service, the continuing dominance of the medical model, and the vested interests of mental health and rehabilitation professionals in maintaining power over people with serious mental illness.

The values of separatism and positive segregation, and a critical perspective on the "system," are distinctive contributions made to community support and psychiatric rehabilitation by the ex-patient movement. It is unlikely that many contemporary mental health systems would have implemented consumer-controlled and consumer-run support programs if it had not been for the anti-psychiatry posture taken by members of this movement. These systems often struggle with the form of advocacy introduced by an ex-patient perspective: people need support in resisting the intrusion of psychiatric professionals and their ideology into their personal lives and people can prosper through involvement in supports that they control along with their peers. According to this perspective, empowerment comes from this kind of personal and group control.

It is difficult to be certain about who has co-opted whom in the evolution of community support and psychiatric rehabilitation. One may argue that the Community Support Program of the National Institute of Mental Health sought to make consumers and ex-patients viable stakeholders within federal, state, and local community support efforts in order to reduce conflict and withdrawal of certain groups totally from involvement in mental health service delivery. Or, one may argue that consumer advocacy and the ex-patient movement co-opted community support and psychiatric rehabilitation programs by motivating these entities to adopt and legitimize more and more of their ideas, aims, and values. Suffice it to say, community support and psychiatric rehabilitation are substantively different now because of the involvement demanded by consumers and the conflict and alternatives created by ex-patients. Psychiatric rehabilitation has probably grown in popularity because it has sought to forge dialogues and alliances among these various stakeholders even though their perspectives can be quite different and often times conflictual.

There is rich variation in consumers as providers because different stakeholder groups have contributed different visions about what consumerism is all about in community support and psychiatric rehabilitation. The framework of community support as a model expands services over place, time, and location with an emphasis on the provision of services in the community, at all hours of the day, and in different locations under nontraditional auspices (Moxley, 1997). Requiring this heroic service delivery to be undertaken solely by professionals highlights the limitations in the availability of adequate numbers of staff, a willingness of these personnel to be flexible, and the ability of these personnel to offer the kinds of services that are relevant to community support and independent living (Moxley, 1997).

The original model of community support underscores the importance of incorporating social supports and family support into the provision of services (Turner & TenHoor, 1978). But the consumer as a peer helper or as a principal source of support to others was not really recognized as a primary attribute of the initial community support framework, although the recipient's social network was seen as a potential source of support.

By virtue of the enhancements in place, time, and location of support, implementation of the community support model within local communities expanded services with the aim of achieving more accessible, adequate, and appropriate systems for people with serious mental illness. Compared to the former aftercare, day treatment, and medication clinics embraced by traditional mental health centers, the community support model sought to increase service innovation and responsiveness. The different visions of consumerism introduced by rehabilitation professionals, consumers, and ex-patients, even though they may reflect conflicting perspectives on the nature of serious mental illness, find some compatibility since they foster the expansion and diversification of support of people in their everyday lives, an objective community support systems probably could not achieve if they relied only on professionals. Thus, achieving a linkage among these disparate visions appears to be a pragmatic strategy serving the interests of psychiatric rehabilitation and community support. The goal of expanding supports cannot be achieved without redefining the role of the direct recipient.

The liberalization of consumer involvement in community support programs took root in the 1980s and opened doors for consumers as rehabilitation and community support employees, and for expanded initiatives undertaken within the programs by consumers themselves. Increasingly, community support demonstrations began to incorporate the ideas of consumers and ex-patients as well as the actual programmatic initiatives formulated by these stakeholders. Liberalization within community support systems also meant that professionals needed to listen more attentively to what consumers wanted for themselves; be more sensitive and open to the creation of supports by consumers themselves; and see consumers as service providers who could add something different but nevertheless important to rehabilitation and support than what could be offered by professionals.

A semblance of cooperation among ex-patients and rehabilitation professionals has resulted in the emergence of consumer-run alternatives within established mental health systems. It has also resulted in the recognition of the unique and important role offered by mutual aid, peer support, and self-help when these are actually under the control of recipients. Within the fields of psychiatric rehabilitation and community support, we must recognize the alternative programmatic forms inherent in consumers as providers, and the broad conception of service provision that needs to be adopted in order to appreciate these different forms. Importance is also assigned to these alternative programmatic forms by the emerging concept of recovery. This idea underscores the necessity to organize a diversity of supports to help people achieve a life style they find rewarding (Anthony, 1994; Deegan, 1994).

The Dynamics of Consumer Role Innovation in Psychiatric Rehabilitation

Our examination of background illustrates the dual character of consumerism within psychiatric rehabilitation: mental health care can be seen as either remedy or as problem, depending on the perspective adopted by people identified as seriously mentally ill. For ex-patients, the social arrangements created by mental health systems are the problem. Resisting labeling, reframing mental illness as oppression, and engaging in mutual assistance among people who often experience the sting of marginalization become, from the ex-patient perspective, an essential aspect of healing (Chamberlin, 1990; Moxley, 1994). Self-help or mutual aid serves as an important vehicle for understanding the social construction of serious mental illness, for interpreting social reaction, and for encouraging healing realized through a more informed understanding of oppression than what could be achieved through participation in traditional mental health programs (Vinik & Levin, 1991; Zinman et al., 1987).

The transactional quality of self-help and mutual aid can be seen in the capacity of these forms of assistance to produce benefits for those receiving support and for those offering support (Cox, 1991). The fluid character of this form of help means that role change can occur in a flexible manner: the person serving as a helper in one meeting may return as a person seeking help at another meeting (Budd, 1987). Inflexible and rigid definitions separating the person serving as helper from the person receiving help was seen within protest movements as artificial and unnecessary (Chamberlin, 1978). Commonality is achieved through a mutual critique of the social dynamics reinforcing oppression and marginalization (Breton, 1991; Cox, 1991).

The distinction between professional role and client role is often portrayed as symptoms of hierarchy, paternalism, and oppression (Howie the Harp, 1987a). The emergence of consumers as providers can be seen in the desire for a flexibility assigned to helping and to recipient roles. This emergence counteracts an artificial separation of professionals and consumers using rigid and unnecessary role distinctions and role assignments, a separation that may be counterproductive in a community support model (Lewis, 1991).

The recognition of the power of self-help within progressive social movements is quite distinctive because it alters a prevailing societal commitment to the sanctity of professional dominance, and it validates the importance of self-help in reframing how people identified as seriously mentally ill can conceive of their status and role. It legitimizes social action on the part of people who are marginalized.

Self-help and mutual aid are ideas critical to the understanding of consumerism in psychiatric rehabilitation and community support. As previously discussed, the importance of the support offered by peers, that is, by people experiencing similar situations, harkens back to the observations made by psychiatrists of soldiers in combat and of the rehabilitation of soldiers experiencing serious and acute mental health reactions to the conditions of combat. The group offers a form of support that is not readily available in other approaches to care.

Self-help was further developed in the community mental health movement, and then subsequently in the community support model to, in part, supplement the scarce availability of services offered by rehabilitation professionals. However, we want to underscore that self-help and mutual aid stand as alternative approaches to care and support.

When we invoke the idea of consumers as providers, we can view it as possessing either a primary or secondary function in psychiatric rehabilitation. As a primary form, consumers as providers can involve consumer controlled services or self-help initiatives that are independent of the auspices or sponsorship of professional rehabilitation service, perhaps even replacing care or treatment offered by professionally-trained personnel. As a supplemental form, consumers as providers can be seen in consumers as employees (when they are seen as supplemental to professionals) and in what we refer to in a subsequent chapter as consumer initiatives—those projects undertaken by consumers to enhance professionally-controlled rehabilitation alternatives.

Certainly this portrayal may be seen as the presentation of polarities. But there is ample evidence in this volume for each pole. And there is evidence for the blending of alternatives into hybrid approaches to the integration of professional and consumer modes of service.

The idea of consumers as providers has not emerged within a vacuum but can be linked to a number of historical events and social movements. These are developments not only within mental health and psychiatry, but also within the greater society that have changed profoundly our contemporary conception of a consumer's role.

The Implications of Social Forces for Consumer Role Innovation in Psychiatric Rehabilitation

When viewed within the larger framework of social change, we see that the developments within psychiatric rehabilitation and community support are not unique but rather can be understood as expressions of changes and developments within the greater society, particularly within the human service sector. Consumer role innovation reflects many developments that have given new definitions and conceptions to consumerism and to the involvement of people in shaping their own interpretations and explanations for their social statuses and the roles they are assigned. To better understand consumer role innovation in psychiatric rehabilitation, this portion of the chapter looks at consumerism within the greater social system and the social changes that legitimize consumer role innovation.

Consumerism within the Greater Society

Empowerment of the consumer role can be seen throughout American society. Most relevant here is the advocacy work initiated by Ralph Nader who defined within our society the modern conception of active consumers who have rights to be both informed about the products and services they consume and protected against shoddy and dangerous business practices (Nader, Green, & Seligman, 1976). The activist role of Nader probably is under-appreciated within our society. His work anticipated the mushrooming of various protest movements and of self-help and mutual aid activities that emerged during the 1960s and which stretched into the 1970s. His work not only inspired the analysis and critique of the social arrangements within the burgeoning economy of the United States, it also stimulated the growth of a broad field of legal advocacy that would come to be known as public interest law (Abramowitz & Uva, 1987).

Beginning with his seminal work, *Unsafe at Any Speed*, revealing the dangers of the Chevrolet Corvair, Nader's organization proceeded to look at every area of the emerging consumer society including health care and mental health care. Most important to psychiatric rehabilitation was Nader's impact on mental health advocacy as an area of public interest law. Legal activists in mental health and developmental disabilities took on state governments in rectifying conditions within state psychiatric and mental retardation institutions, and battled not only to define minimal standards of adequate care in some cases, but perhaps, more importantly, actually spurred on the deinstitutionalization of facilities, and the closure of many state institutions. This legal advocacy, informed by social science that documented the horrors of institutional life, contributed to a growing concern with setting limits on psychiatric authority and control.

Nader's conception of an active, informed, and protected consumer is important to an appreciation of consumer role innovation in psychiatric rehabilitation. The rights perspective expounded by Nader underscored the negative aspects of submissive consumers who should not and do not question what they are getting from a provider. Nader's perspective brought into question the unrestricted autonomy often bestowed upon professionals by our society, especially medical professionals. And, he underscored the necessity for accountability of professionals to the public good and to the public interest.

Much of Nader's early legal advocacy work coincided with the emergence of a critical perspective in social research introduced by social scientists who were documenting the negative implications and consequences of labeling, and the contribution of stigma to discrimination, social marginalization, and social rejection (Goffman, 1961). This genre of social research sought to document the social construction of serious mental illness (Scheff, 1966), further undermining the hegemony of mental health professionals (Braginsky, Bragnisky, & Ring, 1969).

Although in the 1960s, psychiatric rehabilitation alternatives were just beginning to emerge, a Naderistic conception of consumer role suggested a more activist consumer who could question what was being received and how one was being treated. From our perspective, the consumer movement in the 1960s began to legitimize a more assertive consumer in all sectors of American society. And, this conception of consumer role offered people an opportunity to define their own expectations about products and services.

In light of the growing movement to question mental health policy and mental health service arrangements, in the 1970s the consumer movement under Nader's organizational leadership undertook a critique of the National Institute of Mental Health and of mental health systems and care (Chu & Trotter, 1974). This study underscored not merely the inadequacy of existing mental health care, but also documented deficits in the responsiveness of mental health systems to people with serious needs. This indictment also pushed into the public mind the inequitable treatment of people coping with serious disability as a result of mental illness, and the need for more appropriate responses to this population, an issue the Congress was examining in its evaluation of community mental health policy during the early to mid-1970s.

Certainly the work and perspective of Nader has been offset in contemporary society by a more conservative social ethos that has seen the erosion of consumer rights both within the court system and within the general economy. But market competition itself has given legitimacy to some of Nader's ideas about consumerism. The work of Deming and others committed to the enhancement of quality has given credence to the identification of the needs of consumers and the achievement of consumer satisfaction. Total Quality Management and Continuous Quality Improvement both underscore the critical (if not dominant) role of consumers in the determination of quality. Indeed, quality is now often operationalized as the discrepancy between consumer expectations and consumers' perceptions of what they actually get in a product or service. The diffusion of the ideas of Total Quality Management and Continuous Quality Improvement into psychiatric rehabilitation further reinforces the growing commitment of the field to the identification and fulfillment of those needs prioritized by consumers themselves, and to the monitoring of consumer satisfaction as a key performance indicator.

Developments within psychiatric rehabilitation parallel the emergence of consumerism within the greater society. The field has attempted to be responsive at least on ideological and theoretical levels to the legitimization and support of an assertive consumer. Consistent with a Naderistic conception of consumer role, as well as with the idea of an activist consumer within models of quality improvement, psychiatric rehabilitation has seen increasingly the development of more assertive consumers who are not afraid to critique existing service arrangements and to suggest ways that programs and services can attain higher levels of consumer satisfaction.

Such developments in consumer role definition have set a stage in which consumers as providers of psychiatric rehabilitation is a natural outgrowth of a system in which professional control is lessened and the status of professionals is somewhat reduced in importance. These developments have also shifted the notion of provider accountability. It is not only necessary for a professional to offer a "good service." The professional must also satisfy the consumer. To be accountable, a psychiatric rehabilitation professional must base the organization and provision of services on what consumers see as needed, and on how they want these supports to be offered or provided (Moxley & Freddolino, 1990), a perspective that is certainly consistent with the ethos of consumerism introduced by Nader and the advocates of quality improvement.

Social Movements and Mutual Aid

Nader's consumer movement did not evolve in isolation from other social movements. The many movements of the 1960s and early 1970s gave a conflictual and oppositional character to this period. They also helped define new roles for people who were often marginalized by strict and inflexible social norms. The "politics of identity" became an important focus of these movements as they articulated how their members were different from traditional conceptions of American society, and how these differences and resulting heterogeneity were good and legitimate (Aronowitz, 1992). The struggles of these movements offered members new identities and new sources of self esteem and positive self concept, attributes that members of these movements felt were too often denigrated by the greater society (Lane, 1992).

Some of the salient movements of this period, and whose legacy we see in the field of psychiatric rehabilitation even today, are those undertaken by Feminists, Gays, African Americans, and people with disabilities. Each of these movements made unique contributions to the rethinking of gender relations, race relations, sexual orientation, and disability within the greater society. The movements legitimized social critique and certainly offered models of protest to the emerging ex-patient and anti-psychiatry movements (Bayer, 1981). They reframed existing social relations and social arrangements and brought into question the dominance within society of people with certain characteristics and the legitimacy of the statuses they held (e.g., the hegemony of white males).

Most importantly, these movements demonstrated in graphic terms the violence the greater society could inflict on people of minority status, or on people whose situation in society was like that of a minority group (e.g., women) (Fortunato, 1982; Lane, 1992). These movements brought into public consciousness not only the strengths of the people composing them, but also their unique contributions to the development of culture within our society, often made under extreme circumstances. These movements produced considerable rethinking of American society, especially in relationship to human rights, the idea of social identity, and the proliferation of forms of helping and support conducive to assisting people who experience oppression, discrimination, and social marginalization.

Innovation in both helping and forms of social support by various social movements is particularly germane to our examination of consumers as providers in psychiatric rehabilitation (Shapiro, 1993). The disability rights movement demonstrated the viability of consumer-operated and consumer-controlled alternatives and pioneered a new form of community support found in the model of the independent living center.

The prototype of this programmatic form is seen in the Berkeley Independent Living Center. Originating on the campus of the University of California at Berkeley, it emerged out of a protest movement led by people with physical disabilities (Shapiro, 1993). Diffusion of this model was undertaken by consumers and their allies to address access, mobility, housing, social, and employment barriers faced by members of the disability community. The concept of an independent living center was based on self-help and mutual aid practices. And, people with physical disabilities were integral members of staff, leadership, and governance which reinforced the principle of consumer control. Expansion of independent living centers ensued and they have become established features of local and state rehabilitation systems.

The women's movement demonstrated the importance of mutual support and consciousness raising in its efforts to redefine the role of women in American society, and to reframe relationships between women and men. Identity politics played a crucial role in defining the struggle women faced in American society (Ferree & Hess, 1985). This struggle was placed in the context of sexism just like the disability rights, the civil rights, and the Gay rights movements placed the identities, plight, and struggle of their members in the context of handicapism, racism, or homophobia, respectively.

From the standpoint of mutual assistance, these movements legitimized the involvement of marginalized people in group efforts to raise their consciousness about their social situations and circumstances, and to reframe the "problems" they faced as ones perpetrated by culture, social structure, and the abuse of power. These group efforts underscored the plight of people experiencing sexism, racism, or handicapism and emphasized that their oppressive circumstances were not of their own making. Rather, they were seen as the result of social dynamics and a dysfunctional society—one that could not deal equitably with members of minority groups, or with people who were different from what was narrowly defined as normal or acceptable.

Consciousness raising reinforced the need to take action as a group. It offered group members opportunities to interpret and redefine prevailing reality through a group lens, and to offer nurturance and support through the group to members who shared a common experience or understanding of discrimination and stigmatization. While traditional mental health ideology identified the healing power of group therapy, identity politics and progressive social movements recognized the power of the group to resist oppression and to counteract "blaming the victim."

Perhaps a principal contribution of these social movements to psychiatric rehabilitation can be found in the metaphor of minority status applied to people struggling with the label of serious mental illness and its many negative social consequences (Gliedman & Roth, 1980). Like other minorities, people with serious mental illness needed to understand the social construction of their status and how society fostered and reinforced social marginalization. Like other minority groups, people with serious mental illness needed to form their own social structures and social organizations to resist this marginalization. Consciousness raising, social protest, legal advocacy, the establishment of alternative supports systems, and the creation of a media critical of established mental health and psychiatric practice—strategies used by larger and better established protest movements—were often adopted by ex-patients whose ideology was influenced by a construct of serious mental illness as a minority status (Chamberlin, 1978; Zinman et al., 1987).

Consumers as Providers in Other Human Service Sectors

As we noted earlier in this chapter, psychiatric rehabilitation is not unique in its efforts to recognize the important roles of recipients in service provision and the distinctive resources these individuals bring to the expansion of services and supports (Sobey, 1970). In fields as diverse as poverty and corrections, as well as in the sectors of substance abuse treatment and social services, we can observe efforts to expand service and to change service systems through consumer role innovation and elaboration (Atkinson, 1967; Brager, 1965; Gordon, 1965).

Consumer Service Provision in Corrections

Corrections, in the early part of the century, saw efforts by reform-oriented penologists and wardens to engage in institutional reform through the expansion of the roles of inmates. For example, as warden of Sing Sing in 1914, Thomas Mott Osborne introduced the idea of self-government through what was called the Mutual Welfare League (Friedman, 1993). Although this innovation was short lived since Osborne's tenure was cut short, his efforts sought to expand the typical role assigned to inmates by offering them opportunities to participate in the operation of the prison (Friedman, 1993).

Later in the century, a 1969 federal court decision eliminated a prison regulation that prevented the involvement of prisoners in helping one another to prepare court documents essential to legal defense and appeals (Friedman, 1993). If this regulation had prevailed, prisoners would have been prevented from accessing essential legal services through self-help and mutual aid and from using "jail house" legal skills to aid their peers. The jail house lawyer stands as an exemplar of how "recipients" can gain the skills and competencies typically reserved for professionals and exercise these in a potentially effective way. It also reflects the important role people can play in assisting their peers through mutual aid especially when professionals are unavailable or are not willing or motivated to lend assistance.

Consumer Service Provision in Social Service

Pearl and Riessman (1965) proposed consumer role changes in order to make social services more accessible and responsive to people in poverty. Recognizing the insufficient supply of professionals in inner city communities needing the most human services; access problems created by lack of sensitivity to social class, ethnicity, and race on the part of human service organizations; and vested interests on the part of professionals, Pearl and Riessman (1965) and Brager (1965) proposed the "indigenous nonprofessional" or the "helper therapist." This role was to be filled by a member of the local community or someone recruited from the target population served by an agency. Individuals in these positions would serve as advocates of the consumer whose "real needs" often could be overlooked by professionals who are more concerned with career and organizational interests than the interests and needs of the local community (Levinson & Schiller, 1966). "The effect of this role is to counterbalance the professional's tendency to conform to agency policy in determining eligibility for assistance. The nonprofessional identifies with the client"(Mayer, 1972, p. 76).

By being able to develop a strong identification with the consumer, the incumbent of this role could, according to Pearl and Riessman, model recovery, increase motivation of consumers to seek treatment, and communicate more effectively with recipients than professionals, thereby improving the performance of human services. Applications of this approach to consumer role innovation were also visible in Welfare Rights Organizations whose members often served as advocates for welfare recipients within social service bureaucracies (Mayer, 1972) as well as in Mobilization for Youth (Fishman, Pearl, & MacLennan, 1965; Moblization for Youth, 1961), child welfare (Costin, 1966), aging networks (Farrar & Hemmy, 1963), and community action agencies (Gordon, 1965).

Contemporary substance abuse treatment programs emphasize as a key credential for a service provider direct experience with the recovery process earned by successfully overcoming an addiction, suggesting that role modeling is assumed to be an essential feature of practice effectiveness. An aim here is to reduce the social distance that can separate the helper and the recipient. Mutual identification between the helper and the recipient (that is, the recipient sees the helper as someone who understands the "ropes," and the helper understands the real life obstacles that the recipient must negotiate) may actually be a defining characteristic of consumer role innovation. It is a characteristic that can be compromised in human service bureaucracies when professionals do not see consumers as a significant reference group (Lipsky, 1980).

Criticisms of Consumers as Providers

Criticisms of consumer role innovation identified in the 1960s and 1970s suggest that consumers or clients who engage in role innovation may actually become contaminated by organizational perspectives and professional aspirations, leading to a desire for upward mobility, less identification with consumers, and less value assigned to consumer advocacy (Mayer, 1972). Consumers undertaking these innovative roles may actually find themselves in ambiguous situations: they are neither consumer nor professional, and they are without a specific reference or peer group from which they can obtain behavioral, attitudinal, and cognitive guidance. There is the threat that the consumer provider can experience social marginalization from such ambiguity.

At the heart of these innovations is the hope for humanization—that indigenous nonprofessionals, consumer advocates, and helper therapists will treat consumers and members of an agency's target population as their principal reference group, taking their direction, cues, and aims from the needs and perspectives of these individuals. Unfortunately, examination of the behavior of social service organizations suggests that service providers tend to adopt other reference groups such as the employing organization, professional associations, and professional colleagues. Over time, professionals can begin to devalue and even disregard consumers as their loyalties become fused to career advancement, professional mobility, and acceptance by their peers (Lipsky, 1980). Recruiting people similar in background and experience to consumers is a strategy to remedy the realization that professionals may simply find service recipients unattractive. Such recruitment, however, is no guarantee that the new providers will identify with the circumstances of their clients—that is, their former peers.

In offering recommendations to address these criticisms, Mayer (1972) suggests that consumer role innovation may be more effective under two conditions—both of which are well documented in this volume. He suggests that role innovation may be more effective when it involves the movement of members into legitimate professional roles that offer viable career paths rather than into those roles characterized by ambiguity that may serve only to marginalize their incumbents (e.g. case management assistants), and confuse them about whose interests, values, and perspectives they should adopt and even champion. Yet, as identified above, the sponsoring program or agency may need to build in means for providers to strengthen and maintain their identification with recipients.

Mayer (1972) suggests the structuring of consumer control over service arrangements so that members of the target population or consumer group are actually in control of the administration and governance of human service organizations. The critical aim here is to enable those people who identify with the interests of the target population to be in control of the actual service apparatus.

Observations about Consumers as Providers

As our analysis suggests, the emergence of consumers as providers must be seen within a relatively complex framework of historical, social, and organizational forces that make this form of role innovation legitimate in psychiatric rehabilitation and other fields for the foreseeable future. In fact, the notion of consumer role innovation can be traced back almost fifty years in the field of psychiatric rehabilitation and for almost thirty years within many other human service fields. In this last principal section of the chapter we offer our observations about consumers as providers. These observations parallel the variation in consumers as providers documented by the content of this volume. They will assist readers to anticipate this variation and the specific options that compose our inquiry into consumers as providers.

There Are Multiple Forms of Consumer Service Provision

Each form of consumer service provision is influenced and shaped by different historical and social forces within the field of psychiatric rehabilitation and within the greater society. For example, while consumer employment may be linked to efforts to make human service organizations more responsive to consumers, consumer-controlled alternatives evolve out of efforts by people to deal with negative social forces and to what is perceived to be a paternalistic or abusive mental health system.

We cannot merely dismiss consumer service provision as supplemental services of lessor importance than those services offered by professionals. In some situations, they can form a primary service response for people who do not wish to affiliate or align themselves with formal systems of treatment or when there are serious inadequacies in existing community supports.

The multiple forms we identify in the next two chapters, and which are documented by other authors in later chapters, include a range of alternatives involving consumers as service providers employed by psychiatric rehabilitation agencies, consumers who develop their own self-help and mutual support options, consumers or ex-patients who create services and supports independent of formal systems, and consumers who take leadership within established programs to initiate and develop innovations in support.

Consumer Service Provision Can Occur Outside of Established Mental Health Systems

Over the relatively brief history of psychiatric rehabilitation, the efforts of consumers, and especially ex-patients, indicate that the provision of support and the offer of service are not confined to formal mental health systems. The history of consumers as providers suggests that consumers or ex-patients did not wait for professionals or for formal mental health systems to legitimize consumer service provision. People took social action to create supports. This history indicates that consumers or ex-patients often undertook innovation on their own, and indeed, often modeled program and service change for rehabilitation and mental health professionals.

Separate and independent systems of support can and do emerge within local communities that can offer people with serious mental illness real alternatives to participation in formal mental health services. The emergence of these alternatives outside of formal mental health services can be a signal of gross consumer dissatisfaction. Or, it can signal that consumers do not see participation in formal services to be very relevant or meaningful to their own recovery. The action these consumers take can be an expression of dissent regarding established service arrangements within formal mental health systems.

Thus, when we speak of mental health care, or mental health service, we may not be able to draw the line simply at what the formal system has to offer, and how the formal system is configured to offer services. We must look outside of these formal arrangements, and inquire into what consumers and ex-patients are doing for themselves, for each other, and for the community at large. We must consider the role of dissatisfaction and dissent among consumers, and look at the consequences these play in shaping alternative supports and services operated for and by consumers or ex-patients. The emergence and success of these "external" options raise the issue of "what is a mental health system?"

Consumer Service Provision Can Occur Within Established Mental Health Systems

Over the relatively brief history of psychiatric rehabilitation, the emergence of peer support activities through self-help and mutual assistance have extended formal mental health systems by capitalizing on social support and social networks. This form of consumer service provision offers consumers opportunities to assist one another without much emphasis placed on who offers and who receives help. It offers flexibility to arranging, locating, and providing supports. It can be seen as a way of extending formal services, although this extension can shift the burden of support from a system to consumers themselves. We must be vigilant to assure that consumer service provision is not adopted as a cost containment or a cost shifting strategy.

Self-help and mutual support are generally recognized as legitimate supplements to formal rehabilitation services, and they offer mental health systems a means to enrich service delivery both by providing more helping options to consumers and by expanding helping roles available to consumers. Certainly a supplemental role of self-help in professional care systems is seen in many areas of medical care when lay helping, support groups, and patient-led information and educational programs are added to expand and enhance services in order to address psychosocial issues created by medical concerns (Levin, Katz, & Holst, 1979).

These alternatives, as noted in a previous section of this chapter, are different than consumer-controlled service activities, since they do not stand as independent of the service system like consumer-controlled options do. Rather these options can be more readily integrated with formal service than consumer-controlled ones, and can be delivered in tandem with formal service when there is a mutually shared set of rehabilitation beliefs and practices (e.g., agreement on part of consumers and professionals that medication is good and that peer self-help can combine with medication to increase efficacy of outcome).

Consumer Employment Can Achieve Personal or System Aims

Consumer employment can help progressive mental health and rehabilitation systems to achieve two aims: one for the consumer and one for the system. For the system, it is a strategy to improve service delivery by personalizing, humanizing, and/or expanding it. Unfortunately, it may also constitute a strategy of substituting lower paid positions for higher paid ones.

For a consumer who is a candidate for a position as a service provider, consumer employment offers a new opportunity structure, one that was not readily available in the recent past. Creation of this opportunity structure means that consumers have employment opportunities on which to build new careers, new roles, and new identities within mental health systems. However, as we have seen historically, and as we see in subsequent chapters, consumer employment may not be so promising since it can be degraded by ambiguity, failure on part of organizations to develop and promote consumers, and the retreat of consumers themselves from representing the perspectives and concerns of their peers.

Consumers Can Be Service Innovators Within Established Programs

Service enhancements initiated by consumers within established programs (often undertaken on a self-initiated and voluntary basis, and offered informally) may be critical forms of consumer service provision that can expand service availability and improve service accessibility, responsiveness, and effectiveness. Consumers within programs can work together independent of professionals and their sponsorship or in collaborative arrangements to conceive of their own supports and service opportunities. They can organize themselves to offer these. These innovations may span the range of human development and interest and include, for example, the editing of a poetry journal, a job lead service, or an after hours recreational or hobby group.

Perhaps what is distinctive about these initiatives, and what differentiates them from other alternatives, is that they remain within the boundaries of professionally run programs and may not represent a structural alteration of these programs or of relationships among recipients and providers. Their emergence can be an expression of a need that goes unaddressed by professionals. Their emergence may indicate that a program is incomplete or inadequate.

A critical observation here is that consumers do not have to establish their own self-help approach, establish their own organization, or await the organization to hire them as service providers. They can come together within their own programs in the spirit of mutual aid to identify needs they have in common, service gaps, or desires for personal development, and they can fulfill or rectify these based on their own initiative. The product of this initiative can be service innovations that stand as models for programs and their sponsoring organizations, or they can be temporary arrangements and dissolve after their objectives are achieved by the innovators. Consumer-initiated innovation may be indicative of a vision and an energy that consumers bring to rehabilitation that is different than the vision and energy brought by professionals and their organizations.

These observations will be expanded in the following chapters as the various forms of consumer service provision are identified and as actual programs and efforts are described and analyzed by our contributors, many of whom are consumer service providers. Some contributors offer graphic personal accounts and examine the challenges, benefits, and pitfalls of consumers as providers in psychiatric rehabilitation. They offer us first-hand accounts of what consumer service provision means in practice, and what personal consequences these innovations hold for role incumbents.

Conclusion

What does consumers as providers and the role innovation it represents mean for psychiatric rehabilitation? This review of the social factors and forces legitimizing consumer role innovation in psychiatric rehabilitation illustrates the evolution of this idea. Self help, mutual aid, consumer-controlled alternatives, consumer-run programs, and collaboration between rehabilitation professionals and consumers have been enduring themes within the field of psychiatric rehabilitation and they persist to this day. The idea that rehabilitation services and supports cannot be confined to merely the provision of care by traditionally credentialed professionals may serve as a principal focus for preserving the substance and integrity of psychiatric rehabilitation in light of its integration into a health care framework.

In this conclusion to the first chapter of this volume, we reflect on the implications of our review for the substance and direction of contemporary mental health and rehabilitation services. More importantly, however, we assert that "consumers as providers in psychiatric rehabilitation" is not a passing fad. Rather it will continue to receive attention, to be the focus of experimentation, and to be developed programmatically.

Consumer Role Innovation in Changing Mental Health Systems

Consumerism in its many forms is an established feature of many progressive mental health systems and organizations, and empowered, articulate, and critical consumers and ex-patients do not appear to be backing down on their demands to make services and supports more participatory, democratic, and equitable for people with serious mental illness. Employment of consumers in service provision roles, and the incorporation of service innovations operated by and for consumers, are indicators that consumers are gaining a voice and influence in changing the very fabric of contemporary mental health systems.

We dare say that even with the rationalization of psychiatric rehabilitation achieved through managed care-like arrangements within mental health systems, diverse service options and staffing arrangements conducive to the ideas we present in this volume will become part of any reform occurring within state and local mental health systems. Why? The bad outcomes experienced by consumers that can, in turn, create tremendous costs for mental health systems, result most likely from a lack of practical support that enable people with psychiatric disabilities to fulfill productive roles, to overcome stress, and to achieve those outcomes they see as important to their quality of life.

The kinds of supports identified in this volume have a practical focus. They seek to help people achieve those outcomes that are conducive to quality of life, and may offset the negative, costly outcomes managed care systems seek to avoid. But there is another reason for inclusion of these options and alternatives. Are professionals innovative enough, motivated enough, and committed enough to offer the range of supports needed to help people to be successful in their day-to-day lives? Achieving the range, intensity, variety, and flexibility of supports that a "good" rehabilitation system requires demands new roles and new service options. Consumer service provision may be essential to the achievement of a good system of community support.

Consumer role innovation and consumers as providers may raise eyebrows of some health care administrators who are more accustomed to equating quality with medical credentials and with standards guiding medical procedures. Yet, we are confident that leaders and advocates within the field will put forth a convincing and compelling vision that illustrates just how essential consumer service provision is to an effective system of long-term mental health care and rehabilitation.

The Durability of Consumer Role Innovation

The durability of these innovations is seen in the background examined in this chapter. These innovations are simply not new. They can be observed over several decades, and lie at the heart of the history and culture of psychiatric rehabilitation as a field of human service practice. While health care is undergoing tremendous rationalization and proceduralization, the field of psychiatric rehabilitation is increasingly incorporating peer support, self help, and mutual assistance, the practice of which may be difficult to articulate and capture in concrete procedures and operationalize in service protocols. But nonetheless, if the current attention to the concept of recovery is to be taken seriously, we cannot dismiss the importance of these innovations. Activities that are intentionally undertaken to expand, elaborate, and empower the roles of consumers are seen as important elements of a framework of recovery (Moxley, 1994).

An indicator of the durability of consumer service provision is encapsulated in the table of contents to this volume. "Consumers as providers in psychiatric rehabilitation" is very real, and the range of contributions to this volume demonstrates that there are a diversity of ways of offering these services and supports. And, there are a diversity of people involved in making consumer service provision happen: from employment and peer support to consumer business development. The range is impressive. And the diversity of contributors, including their geographic locations, organizational affiliations, and their program settings suggest that consumers as providers is not a uniform or narrowly defined set of activities. This range shows that these innovations are serious business, and that they are moving from the periphery to the center of contemporary practice in psychiatric rehabilitation.

This is not to say that these forms of service and support are not without limitations. This volume attempts to document the many challenges, pitfalls, and negative experiences that can be generated by consumer service provision that is not well supported either organizationally or financially. We are not necessarily endorsing these innovations without caveats or without understanding. We are, however, asserting that consumerism has evolved to the point in psychiatric rehabilitation that we cannot ignore or dismiss these developments. The field as well as the purchasers of psychiatric rehabilitation services need to take consumer service provision seriously.

Consumer Role Innovation and Social Change

The salience of consumers as providers in psychiatric rehabilitation signals a significant change in the field—not merely change in organizational and service arrangements, but change in actual social roles. Any social system is composed of social relationships, and when change is created in the established pattern of social relationships, social change emerges within that system. Our characterization of the forces and factors influencing consumers as providers in psychiatric rehabilitation suggests that the pattern of social relationships and arrangements among professionals and consumers has been changing, especially over the past 20 years. These changes have been subtle and perhaps without clear salience. Nonetheless, today the field of psychiatric rehabilitation is characterized by a diversity of stakeholders involved in a variety of community and organizational settings. Describing oneself as either a consumer or ex-patient holds symbolic value for the identity of the person, and influences the kind of interaction the person expects with others.

There are a number of alternatives within psychiatric rehabilitation that people can choose among in order to identify oneself. And, these alternatives suggest change in the structural arrangements of psychiatric rehabilitation. No longer are traditionally credentialed professionals dominant within the field. Consumers as providers indicate new statuses, new roles, and new opportunities for people who are labeled as seriously mentally ill. Of course this is an idealized portrayal since a number of contributors indicate that consumers can be relegated to submissive and nominalistic service delivery roles. But other contributors indicate that real substantive change occurs when organizations take affirmative approaches to employment; when programs attempt to change from a culture of exclusion to one of inclusion; and when a consumer-run organization can achieve at least "detente" with the formal mental health system. Who ever suggested that social change is easy? And who ever said that changes in social structure are without challenge?

Before you move on in this volume, look at the table of contents. You will see many examples of experimentation, innovation, trial and error, failures, and successes. But perhaps these contributions all share one thing in common: they do not accept traditional social arrangements within psychiatric rehabilitation as a given. They see these arrangements as open to change, dynamic, and fluid, another sign that consumer service provision will be durable. This flexibility and openness may be one of the field's most important strengths.

This book is intended to serve as a resource for program development and program enhancement. We have attempted to capture the diversity of consumers as providers and the various forms that compose this innovation. Our objective is to document not only this variation, but the issues, challenges, and benefits experienced by contributors as well as to document successful practices that can guide others. However, our ultimate aim is to offer insight into the change in consumerism and the changes in roles that have been experienced by the field of psychiatric rehabilitation. For some this change may be perceived as nominalistic, but for us it reflects a significant alteration in what we now mean as "good" rehabilitation practice.

References

Abramovitz, J., & Uva, K. (1987). *Consumers and the law.* Baldwin, NY: Educational Activities Publishers.

Adam, B. D. (1987). *The rise of a gay and lesbian movement.* Boston, MA: Twayne.

Albee, G. (1959). *Mental health manpower trends.* New York, NY: Basic Books.

Albee, G. (1960). The manpower crisis in mental health. *American Journal of Public Health, 50*(12), 1895-1900.

Anthony, W. A. (1994). Recovery from mental illness: The guiding vision of the mental health service system in the 1990s. In W. Anthony & L. Spaniol (Eds.). *Readings in psychiatric rehabilitation.* (pp. 521-538). Boston, MA: Center for Psychiatric Rehabilitation.

Anthony, W., Cohen, M., & Farkas, M. (1990). *Psychiatric rehabilitation.* Boston, MA: Center for Psychiatric Rehabilitation.

Anthony, W. & Spaniol, L. (Eds.). *Readings in psychiatric rehabilitation.* Boston, MA: Center for Psychiatric Rehabilitation.

Aronowitz, S. (1992). *The politics of identity.* London: Routledge.

Atkinson, P. (1967). Alternative career opportunities for neighborhood workers. *Social Work, 12*(4), 81-88.

Baer, R., Goebel, G., & Flexer, R. W. (1993). An interdisciplinary team approach to rehabilitation. In R. W. Flexer & P. L. Solomon (Eds.). *Psychiatric rehabilitation in practice* (pp. 63-97). Boston, MA: Andover.

Baker, D. (1993). Human rights for persons with disabilities. In M. Nagler (Ed.), *Perspective on disability. Second Edition.* (pp. 483-494). Palo Alto, CA: Health Markets Research.

Bayer, R. (1981). *Homosexuality and American psychiatry: The politics of diagnosis.* New York, NY: Basic Books.

Beard, J. H. (1976). Psychiatric rehabilitation at Fountain House. In J. Meislin (Ed.). *Rehabilitation medicine and psychiatry.* Springfield, IL: Charles C. Thomas.

Beard, J. H., Propst, R. N., & Malamud, T. J. (1982). The Fountain House model of psychiatric rehabilitation. *Psychosocial Rehabilitation Journal, 5*(1), 47-53.

Beard, J. H., Schmidt, J. R., & Smith, M. M. (1963). The use of transitional employment in the rehabilitation of the psychiatric patient. *Journal of Nervous and Mental Disease, 136,* 507-514.

Black, B. J. (1988). *Work and mental illness: Transitions to employment.* Baltimore, MD: Johns Hopkins University Press.

Blumberg, R. (1984). *Civil rights: The 1960s freedom struggle.* Boston: Twayne.

Brager, G. (1965). The indigenous worker: A new approach for the social work technician. *Social Work,* 33-40.

Braginsky, B. M., & Braginsky, D. D. (1969). *Methods of madness: The mental hospital as a last resort.* New York, NY: Holt, Rinehart, and Winston.

Breggin, P. R. (1991). *Toxic psychiatry.* New York, NY: St Martin's Press.

Breton, M. (1991). Reflections on social action practice in France. In A. Vinik & M. Levin (Eds.). *Social action in group work.* (pp. 91-108). New York, NY: Haworth.

Budd, S. (1987). Support groups. In S. Zinman, Howie the Harp, & S. Budd (Eds.). *Reaching across: Mental health clients helping each other.* (pp. 41-55). Riverside, CA: California Network of Mental Health Clients.

Cameron, J. M. (1989). A national community mental health program: Policy initiation and progress. In D. A. Rochefort (Ed.), *Handbook on mental health policy in the United States.* (pp. 121-142). New York, NY: Greenwood Press.

Caplan, G. (1961a). *Prevention of mental disorders in children.* New York, NY: Basic Books.

Caplan, G. (1961b). *An approach to community mental health.* New York, NY: Grune & Stratton.

Caplan, G. (1964). *Principles of preventive psychiatry.* New York, NY: Basic Books.

Caplan, G. (1970). *Theory and practice of mental health consultation.* New York, NY: Basic Books.

Caplan, G. (1974). *Support systems and community mental health.* New York, NY: Behavioral Publications.

Caplan, P. J. (1995). *They say you're crazy: how the world's most powerful psychiatrists decide who's normal.* Reading, MA: Addision-Wesley.

Chamberlin, J. (1978). *On our own: patient-controlled alternatives to the mental health system.* New York, NY: McGraw-Hill.

Chamberlin, J. (1989). Ex-patient groups and psychiatric rehabilitation. In M. D. Farkas & W. A. Anthony (Eds.). *Psychiatric rehabilitation programs: Putting theory into practice.* (pp. 207-216). Baltimore, MD: Johns Hopkins University Press.

Chamberlin, J. (1990). The ex-patient's movement: Where we've been and where we're going. *Journal of Mind and Behavior, 11*(3, 4), 323-336.

Chamberlin, J., Rogers, J. A., & Sneed, C. S. (1989). Consumers, families, and community support systems. *Psychosocial Rehabilitation Journal, 12*(3), 93-106.

Chandler, S. (1990). *Competing realities: The contested terrain of mental health advocacy.* New York, NY: Praeger.

Chu, F. D., & Trotter, S.(1974). *The madness establishment: Ralph Nader's study group report on the National Institute of Mental Health.* New York, NY: Grossman.

Collins, A. H., & Pancoast, D. L. (1976). *Natural helping networks: A strategy for prevention.* Washington, DC: National Association of Social Workers.

Costin, L. (1967). *Training nonprofessionals for a child welfare service.* Children, 13(2), 63-68.

Cox, E. (1991). The critical role of social action in empowerment oriented groups. In A. Vinik & M. Levin, (Ed.). *Social action in group work.* (pp. 77-90). New York, NY: Haworth.

Curtis, W. R. (1979). *The future use of social networks in mental health.* Boston, MA: Social Matrix.

Dain, N. (1980). *Clifford W. Beers: Advocate for the insane.* Pittsburgh, PA: University of Pittsburgh Press.

Dean, A., Kraft, A., & Pepper, B. (1976). *The social setting of mental health.* New York, NY: Basic Books.

Deegan, P. E. (1994). Recovery: The lived experience of rehabilitation. In W. Anthony & L. Spaniol (Eds.). *Readings in psychiatric rehabilitation.* (pp. 149-161). Boston: Center for Psychiatric Rehabilitation.

Farkas, M. D., & Anthony, W. A. (1989). *Psychiatric rehabilitation programs: Putting theory into practice.* Baltimore, MD: Johns Hopkins University Press.

Farkas, M. D., Anthony, W. A., & Cohen, M. R. (1989). Psychiatric rehabilitation: The approach and its programs. In M. D. Farkas & W. A. Anthony (Eds.). *Psychiatric rehabilitation programs: Putting theory into practice.* Boston, MA: Center for Psychiatric Rehabilitation.

Farrar, M., & Hemmy, M. (1963). Use of nonprofessional staff in work with the aged. *Social Work,* 44-50.

Ferree, M., & Hess, B. B. (1985). *Controversy and coalition: The new feminist movement.* Boston, MA: Twayne.

Fishman, J. R., Pearl, A., & MacLennan, B. (1965). *New careers: Ways out of poverty for disadvantaged youth.* Report of Conference sponsored by Howard University, Center for Youth and Community Studies. Washington, DC.

Flexer, R. W., & Solomon, P. L. (1993). *Psychiatric rehabilitation in practice.* Boston, MD: Andover.

Fortunato, J. E. (1982). *Embracing the exile: Healing journeys of gay christians.* San Francisco, CA: Harper.

Freddolino, P., & Moxley, D. (1988). The states' role in fine tuning the new federal mandate for rights protection and advocacy for people labeled mentally ill. *New England Journal of Human Services,* 8(2), 27-33.

Freddolino, P., Moxley, D., & Fleishman, J. (1989). A field tested advocacy model for people coping with long-term psychiatric disabilities. *Hospital and Community Psychiatry,* 40(11), 1169-1174.

Friedman, L. M. (1993). *Crime and punishment in American history.* New York, NY: Basic Books.

Gilbert, N. (1983). *Capitalism and the welfare state: Dilemmas of social benevolence.* New Haven, CT: Yale University Press.

Gilbert, N., & Specht, H. (1974). *Dimensions of social welfare policy.* Englewood Cliffs, NJ: Prentice-Hall.

Gleidman, J., & Roth, W. (1980). *The unexpected minority: Handicapped children in America.* New York, NY: Harcourt Brace Jovanovich.

Goffman, E. (1961). *Asylums.* New York, NY: Doubleday.

Gordon, J. (1965). Project Cause: The federal antipoverty program and some implications of subprofessional training. *American Psychologist,* 20(5).

Gurin, G., Veroff, J., & Feld, S. (1960). *Americans view their mental health.* New York, NY: Basic Books.

Herr, S. S. (1983). *Rights and advocacy for retarded people.* Lexington, MA: Heath.

Howie the Harp (1987a). Philosophical models. In S. Zinman, Howie the Harp, & S. Budd (Eds.) *Reaching across: Mental health clients helping each other.* (pp. 19-24). Riverside, CA: California Network of Mental Health Clients.

Howie the Harp (1987b). Membership outreach. In S. Zinman, Howie the Harp, & S. Budd. (Eds.). *Reaching across: Mental health clients helping each other.* (pp. 63-78). Riverside, CA: California Network of Mental Health Clients.

Joint Commission on Mental Illness and Health (1961). *Action for mental health.* New York, NY: Basic Books.

Lane, H. (1992). *The mask of benevolence: Disabling the deaf community.* New York, NY: Knopf.

Levin, L. S., Katz, A. H., & Holst, E. (1979). *Self-care: Lay initiatives in health.* (second edition). New York, NY: Prodist.

Levine, M. (1981). *The history and politics of community mental helth.* New York, NY: Oxford University Press.

Levinson, P., & Schiller, J. Role analysis of the indigenous nonprofessional. *Social Work, 2*(3).

Lewis, E. (1991). Social change and citizen action: A philosophical exploration for modern social group work. In A. Vinik & M. Levin (Eds.). *Social action in group work.* (pp. 23-34). New York, NY: Haworth.

Link, B. G., Cullen, F. T., Mirotznik, J., & Struening, E. (1992). The consequences of stigma for persons with mental illness: Evidence from the social sciences. In P. J. Fink & A. Tasman (Eds.). *Stigma and mental illness.* Washington, D C: American Psychiatric Press.

Lipsky, M. (1980). Street-level bureaucracy: *Dilemmas of the individual in public services.* New York, NY: Russell Sage Foundation.

Low, A. (1943). *Lectures to relatives of former patients.* Boston, MA: Christopher.

Low, A. (1950). *Mental health through will-training: A system of self-help in psychotherapy as practiced by Recovery, Inc.* Winnetka, IL: Willett.

Mayer, R. R. (1972). *Social planning and social change.* Englewood Cliffs, NJ: Prentice-Hall.

Meenaghan, T. M. (1974). Role changes for the parents of the mentally retarded. *Journal of Mental Retardation, 12,* 48-49.

Meenaghan, T. M., & Mascari, M. (1971). Consumer choice, consumer control in service delivery. *Social Work, 10,* 50-57.

Meenaghan, T. M., & Washington, R. O. (1980). *Social policy and social welfare: Structure and application.* New York, NY: The Free Press.

Mental Health Association of Southeastern Pennsylvania (n.d.). *The National Mental Health Consumer Self-Help Clearinghouse.* Philadelphia, PA: Author.

Moblization for Youth (1961). Proposal for the prevention and control of delinquency by expanding opportunities. New York, NY: Author.

Mosher, L. R., & Burti, L. (1994). Relationships in rehabilitation: When technology fails. In W. Anthony & L. Spaniol (Eds.). *Readings in psychiatric rehabilitation.* (pp. 162-171). Boston, MA: Center for Psychiatric Rehabilitation.

Mowbray, C. T., Moxley, D. P., Thrasher, S. et. al. (1996). Consumers as community support providers: Issues created by role innovation. *Community Mental Health Journal, 32*(1), 47-67.

Moxley, D. (1994). *Serious mental illness and the concept of recovery: Implications for social work practice in psychiatric rehabilitation,* Community Support Monographic Series, 2(2), Boston University Center for Psychiatric Rehabilitation.

Moxley, D. (1997). *Case management by design: Reflections on principles and practices.* Chicago, IL: Nelson-Hall.

Moxley, D. & Daeschlein, M. (1997). Properties of consumer-driven forms of case management. In D. Moxley (ed.) *Case Management by Design: Reflections on Principles and Practice.* Chicago, IL: Nelson-Hall.

Nader, R., Green, M., & Seligman, J. (1976). *Taming the giant corporation*. New York, NY: Norton.

Pearl, A., & Reissman, F. (1965). *New careers for the poor*. New York, NY: The Free Press.

Perry, J. H., Davis, M. A., & McVeigh, J. (1993). Consumer perspectives on rehabilitation. In R. W. Flexer & P. L. Solomon (Eds.). *Psychiatric rehabilitation in practice* (pp. 3-15). Boston, MA: Andover.

Reich, R. B. (1991). *The work of nations: Preparing ourselves for 21st century capitalism*. New York, NY: Knopf.

Rein, M. (1983). *From policy to practice*. Armonk, NY: M. E. Sharpe.

Rifkin, (1996). The end of work. New York, NY: Knopf.

Robitscher, J. (1980). *The powers of psychiatry*. Boston, MA: Houghton, Mifflin.

Ruffner, R. H. (1986). The last frontier: Jobs and mentally ill persons. *Psychosocial Rehabilitation Journal, 9(1)*,

Scheff, T. J. (1966). *Being mentally ill: A sociological theory*. Chicago, IL: Aldine.

Shapiro, J. P. (1993). *No pity: People with disabilities forging a new civil rights movement*. New York, NY: Times Books.

Sobey, F. (1970). *The nonprofessional revolution in mental health*. New York, NY: Columbia University Press.

Srole, L., Langner, T. S., Michael, S. T., Kirkpatrick, P., Opler, M. K., & Rennie, T. (1978). *Mental health in the metropolis: The midtown Manhattan study*. New York, NY: New York University Press.

Sundram, C. J. (1985). Testimony before Joint Hearings of the Subcommittee on the Handicapped, Committee on Labor and Human Resources, and the Subcommittee on Labor, Health, and Human Services, Education, and Related Agencies, Commmittee on Appropriations, United States Senate.

Turner, J. D., & TenHoor, W. J. (1978). The NIMH Community Support Program: Pilot approach to a needed social reform. *Schizophrenia Bulletin, 4(3)*, 319-348.

Unzicker, R. (1989). On my own: A personal journey through madness and reemergence. *Psychosocial Rehabilitation Journal, 13(1)*, 71-77.

Vinik, A., & Levin, M. (1991). *Social action in group work*. New York: Haworth.

Wechsler, H. (1960). The self-help organization in the mental health field: Recovery, Inc., a case study. *Journal of Nervous and Mental Disease, 130*, 297.

Weicker, L. P. (1985). Opening Statement on the Joint Hearings on Care of Institutionalized Mentally Disabled Persons, United States Congress.

Wilson, W. J. (1996). *When work disappears: The world of the new urban poor*. New York, NY: Knopf.

Wintersteen, R. T., & Rapp, C. (1986). The young adult chronic patient: A dissenting view of an emerging concept. *Psychosocial Rehabilitation Journal, 9(4)*, 3-9.

Zax, M., & Specter, G. A. (1974). *An introduction to community psychology*. New York, NY: Wiley.

Zinman, S. (1987). Definition of self-help groups. In S. Zinman, Howie the Harp, & S. Budd (Eds.). *Reaching across: Mental health clients helping each other*. (pp. 7-15). Riverside, CA: California Network of Mental Health Clients.

Zinman, S., Howie the Harp, & Bud, S. (1987). *Reaching across: Mental health clients helping each other*. Riverside, CA: California Network of Mental Health Clients.

Chapter 2
A Framework for Organizing Consumer Roles as Providers of Psychiatric Rehabilitation

Carol T. Mowbray
David P. Moxley

In the previous chapter, we identified the multiple and heterogeneous forces influencing the development and legitimization of consumers as providers in psychiatric rehabilitation. We placed this mental health role innovation within the context of other rights and reform forces such as self-help, consumerism in the marketplace, welfare rights, affirmative action, and the empowerment of other social groups (who have organized according to gender, race, orientation, disability, etc.). We also discussed more specifically how consumer service provision relates to forces within the mental health service domain; for example, the Community Support Program, anti-psychiatry movement, rehabilitation services, etc. Given this diverse array of influences, it is not surprising that there is notable diversity in the ways that consumers are involved as service providers, with the actual programmatic expression of this diversity linked to these various movement forces. As should be expected, there are substantial differences in the roles consumers are playing and in the settings in which these roles are carried out. With such differences in roles and settings, there are also important differences in the issues which arise, the barriers to be overcome, the supports that are needed or desired, and successful resolutions to internal and external problems.

Unfortunately, the published literature concerning consumers in provider roles is oftentimes either too global, or too specific, or too prescriptive to assist in developing understandings and strategies which can be successfully used across settings. Thus, some reports describe their service/programs and their operations in detail, but lack any conceptualization of how their particular program fits into a broader framework. At the other extreme, some reports present global conclusions about the benefits of consumer involvement, or "how-to" approaches to program development, without recognizing the heterogeneity that exists among programs, which may make many of their conclusions irrelevant or inappropriate to much of what's going on.

What's needed are a framework and related typology to better understand the variations across different consumer/provider roles. A typology can serve as a heuristic device for conceptualizing the *important* versus trivial ways in which programs differ and thus can allow us to develop categorizations of programs which are similar on major dimensions. With a manageable typology—either theoretical or empirical, we are able to inductively derive similarities in problem solutions which should have greater power, since they have arisen from multiple cases.

The published literature contains some terms which might appear to represent various typologies: e.g., "consumer-run service," "self-help programs," "consumer-governed," etc. However, these terms have not been derived from a framework, and their use is idiosyncratic and without consistent definitions. Thus, for example, "consumer-run services" may be those which are controlled by and delivered through a consumer-governed organization, or they may represent services within professionally-operated mental health agencies which happen to employ consumers as staff. Similarly, the term "self-help" has been expanded from its usual definition of mutual help outside the formal service system or as an alternative to professional service to include any type of service provided to consumers by other consumers (Chamberlin, Rogers, & Ellison, 1996; Segal, Silderman, & Tomkins, 1993).

This chapter presents a framework and typology for describing and understanding the diverse ways in which consumers are involved in service provision in psychiatric rehabilitation. There are multiple purposes for this presentation. First, it serves to acknowledge the diversity and heterogeneity involved in this consumer role innovation. Second, and more importantly, it should allow us to better understand the barriers and problems associated with consumer service provision, as we can systematically analyze experiences and outcomes by type. Finally, with more systematic analysis and understanding, we should be better able to formulate problem solutions and policy responses that will enhance consumer service provision in the future.

Major Dimensions of the Framework

The framework and typology are presented in Figure 1. Two major dimensions have been used to produce the framework: (1) control of the consumer-based alternative and (2) the purpose of the consumer-based alternative. Within the first dimension, the levels of control are consumer versus nonconsumer. The control dimension was selected because of its historical importance in the consumer movement. Thus, Chamberlin's (1978) seminal work on consumers providing services to other consumers was explicit and outspoken in concluding that consumers working with professionals could *never* be in control of their services. The point was that with the uneven playing field which dominates mental health systems, consumers who attempt to work collaboratively with professionals will always end up being dominated by them. Of course, control is an important dimension in many other public and private arenas. When nontraditional programs or under-represented groups vie with the status-quo, the existing system, and/or the majority, their perspectives are often given lip-service, but have little significance, unless control is exerted through a governing board, executive leadership, publicity, or constituent pressure, for example.

The second dimension in the framework concerns the purpose of the alternative (i.e., formal service provision versus mutual support). This dimension actually represents a parsimonious grouping of several significant variables.

Figure 1: A Framework Organizing Consumer Alternatives in the Provision of Services or Supports in Psychiatric Rehabilition

<table>
<tr><td colspan="3">CONTROL OF ALTERNATIVE</td></tr>
<tr><td></td><td>Consumer</td><td>Nonconsumer</td></tr>
<tr><td rowspan="2">AIM OF THE ALTERNATIVE</td><td>SERVICE PROVISION</td><td>I. Consumer-Run Services</td><td>II. Consumers as Employees</td></tr>
<tr><td>MUTUAL SUPPORT</td><td>III. Self-Help</td><td>IV. Consumer Initiatives</td></tr>
</table>

Thus, formal service provision is usually extensively regulated; requires funding, exchange of fees, and formal contractual relationships; and is clearly intended to have benefits flow from the service provider to the recipient (consumer). On the other hand, mutual support is usually characterized as less formal, involving no funding or exchange of money, not subject to regulation, of a totally voluntary nature, and providing reciprocal benefits to the helper and the helpee.

This two-dimensional framework produces four types of consumer role innovation. Significant descriptors and characteristics of each type are presented below, along with some discussion of the unique benefits associated with that type.

1. Consumer-Run Alternatives

In this type, consumers serve as providers through organizations that they control—organizationally, administratively, and programmatically. Consumer control is usually carried out organizationally through the existence of a free-standing legal entity (not a division or service of a mental health or social services agency), with a board in which consumers are exclusive members or in the majority. Administration and operation of the program is usually exclusively by individuals who identify themselves as consumers, although nonconsumers may be temporarily employed, on an as-needed basis, and/or to fill highly technical functions. There is in place some formal operational structure designating governance, executive, and staff roles.

Service provision in consumer-controlled alternatives targets a group of consumers identified as having mental illness (past or current) and/or mental/emotional problems, although probably little effort is invested in any formal determination (diagnostically or otherwise). The service provision model should be specifically defined, with expectations stated concerning how the service will operate, for how long, with what intensity, and for what benefits. The service program requires formal resources in order to operate. It has in place a budget, at least to pay consumer administrators and consumer-employees; also, depending on the service, to pay operating expenses such as rent, utilities, supplies, travel, and other costs. The program's budget is financed through some combination of self-sustaining activities (such as fund-raising or grants), or through fee for service or contractual sources (i.e., under contract to a mental health agency). Usually, consumer-controlled alternatives will have performance and accountability expectations that the program must fulfill as determined by outside funders. In a survey of six consumer-run programs with a structure (selected for their diversity), Chamberlin et al.(1996) found yearly budgets ranging from $47,000 to $2.9 million per year.

Probably the most frequently described program within the consumer-controlled type is the drop-in center (Kaufmann, Ward-Colasante & Farmer, 1993; Meek, 1994; Mowbray & Tan, 1992, 1993). Other examples reported include consumer-run businesses (Cook, Jonikas & Solomon, 1991), companion services, case management, housing assistance (Harp, 1990), advocacy alternatives, vocational assistance (Rogers, 1994), and recreational programs (see also:

Long, 1988; Mowbray, Chamberlain, Jennings & Reed, 1988; Mowbray, Wellwood & Chamberlin, 1988; Toff, 1988). Opportunities offered can include employment options, problem solving, social and emotional support, socialization and social involvement, crisis intervention, role modeling, and supportive counseling. In the survey of consumer-run drop-in programs (selected for their diversity), Chamberlin et al., (1996) report that assistance with legal problems was the most common activity, followed by assistance with employment, general advocacy, social recreational services, and temporary shelter. In many sites, the program was used more as an adjunct than as an alternative to traditional services.

The rationale behind the consumer-controlled alternative is that consumers themselves have the ability to form creative, nontraditional, and more beneficial alternatives or adjuncts to formal mental health services. Having their own structure better enables them to implement these alternatives. Furthermore, since the consumer-controlled program is developed and delivered by consumers, it has the potential of contributing something that is very different to rehabilitation and community support than what individuals with professional training can do within existing structures.

2. Consumers as Employees

In this type, consumers are employed to provide services through a formal organization (social welfare, health, mental health, etc.) which they do not run or control. The organization is a legal entity and pays consumers for the services they provide. As a formal organization, it also has a budget and a structure for governance and administration—none of which are controlled by consumers, although "consumer interests" may be represented in governance. Funding can come from many sources; possibly direct service grants, fee for services, contractual, and/or self-sustaining activities (like production of piecework in a sheltered workshop). The organization will also have performance and accountability expectations determined by outside entities, like federal, state or local funding agencies, or third-party payers—entities that may not readily legitimize consumer employment.

The employing organization targets a specific group of consumers as service recipients and specifies interventions it provides to them, like clinical, community support, or rehabilitation services. Consumers are employed in some of these service positions. These consumer service roles can be created by either: (a) designating service roles exclusively for consumers (e.g., peer support specialists, consumer case management aides, etc.); or (b) affirmative employment practices that increase accessibility of consumers applying and being selected for these positions. In the latter case, the agency climate also promotes acceptance and recognition of the employee's dual role (consumer and provider) or supports disclosure of past consumer status. The most typical paid employment positions for consumers reported in the literature are those which are exclusively designated, and usually involve provision of support services, or extension of the services provided by a non-consumer professional; for example, consumers are employed to help individuals find jobs or housing

(Mowbray, Moxley, et al., 1996), to assist them to develop and practice the skills necessary to maintain their housing or get/keep their jobs (Besio & Mahler, 1993), to help solve problems, and to serve as role models, etc. (Sherman & Porter, 1991). Consumers have also been reportedly employed as case managers (Solomon, 1988; Solomon & Draine, 1995, 1996; Stoneking, Greenfield, Sundby & Boltz, 1991), on Assertive Community Treatment teams (Dixon, Krauss & Lehman, 1994; Wheaton, McLain & Powell, 1994), on mobile crisis teams (Lyons, Cook Ruth, & Karver, 1996), and in clinical positions (Fisher, 1994).

The rationale behind the consumer-employee model is that consumers have a right to employment as service deliverers within established mental health programs and that they can bring to these roles a motivation, sensitivity, empathy, and understanding that workers with only formal professional training, attitudes, and identities cannot. Furthermore, their involvement in service delivery is often seen as a reform strategy to make service delivery more accessible to various users. This can be achieved by matching consumer providers with recipient populations in terms of identity issues (e.g., sexual orientation), demographic characteristics, or presenting problems.

3. *Self-Help Alternatives*

This model follows that usually described through a vast literature on self-help services for diverse populations. These populations are defined by their common experience of a life problem or condition. Individuals from the identified population are involved in operating informal support groups and/or programs outside of formal systems of care, in which there is little distinction between those who provide help and support and those who receive it. Both providers and recipients are expected to benefit equally. In self-help alternatives for individuals with psychiatric disabilities, a mental illness is the life condition commonly experienced; otherwise, these groups are expected to operate like others with a self-help orientation (Kanaan, 1991).

In contrast to the formal organizations which provide services in Types 1 and 2, the self-help group itself is usually not characterized by significant role differentiation and hierarchical administrative structures (although some self-help groups are affiliated with large national organizations, which do have such structures). However, whether a small, grass-roots organization is involved, or a local group affiliated with a larger national organization, there is separation and independence from any formal mental health organization or system whose purpose is to treat psychiatric disability or its consequences. This alternative is "on its own."

The self-help alternative may or may not have some concrete or formal resources to support its operations and may or may not have any formal process to get resources in order to sustain itself. Usually if resources are part of the organization, they are self-generated (through member fees, user contributions, fund-raising, etc.) and not extensive. The self-help alternative may not even have a formal setting or meeting place in which services are provided. A final differentiating factor is that rather than adhering to formal performance and accountability demands of external entities (as with the formal organization), self-help alternatives usually follow norms governing the offer of help which may be quite broad. These norms and expectations are defined and formed by the members themselves. Oftentimes they incorporate friendship, social interaction, wider social contacts (outside the self-help alternative), and perhaps exchange of resources, like housing assistance.

Self-help alternatives for persons with psychiatric disabilities include local affiliates of formally developed models like Schizophrenics Anonymous, the National Manic-Depressive and Depressive Association (Kurtz, 1990), Recovery, Inc. (Galanter, 1988), GROW, etc. (Luke, Rappaport & Seidman, 1991; Young & Williams, 1988; Zimmerman et al., 1991), or local grass-roots groups that are independently started by consumers (Plumb, 1993) or, at times, by interested advocates and then turned over to the consumer-members (Caldwell & White, 1991; Emerick, 1990).

The rationale behind self-help alternatives for persons with psychiatric disabilities is that peers supporting peers and offering self-help and mutual support within informal structures enhance formal services by capitalizing on social support and social networks. This form offers consumers opportunities to assist one another with less emphasis on who offers and who receives help— to the enhancement of both parties. Self-help offers alternative communities, reference groups, new identities, and new or modified conceptions of mental illness based on various ideologies.

4. Consumer Initiatives

In this type, activities are initiated as informal components or elements of formal organizations offering community support, rehabilitation, or mental health clinical services to people identified as having a serious mental illness. Thus, the setting for the consumer-initiative fits all the previously described characteristics of a formal organization in terms of funding, governance, administration, formal staffing roles, external performance and accountability demands, etc. However, the consumer initiative within the formal organization is a program that was developed by consumers for consumers and is implemented by them, with some independence from the rest of the mental health establishment. Although, since it is a program contained within the formal organization, consumers do not have bottom-line responsibility for governance or management of the initiative.

The activity which is carried out through the consumer initiative is an informal helping arrangement where benefits come from mutual support and interaction among members. As in self-help alternatives, those offering help and those receiving help realize a benefit. While descriptions of consumer initiatives are infrequently seen in the published literature on mental health or psychiatric rehabilitation services, experientially most providers would agree that their existence is widespread and may represent a substantial resource to the formal mental health system and its service recipients. They often reflect innovation that bubbles up within agencies to suggest new programs, services, or opportunities. Examples include volunteer support arrangements within a community support program (Lieberman, Gowdy & Knutson, 1991), a buddy system within a Fairweather Lodge, a consumer-initiated support group within a clubhouse (for example, men's issues, women's issues, gay/lesbian support, abstinence/recovery), social/companionship activities (Petty, 1991), one-to-one support and friendly visiting (Armstrong, Korba, & Emard, 1995), or a support group (like a job club) within a vocational service.

While the formal organization hosting an initiative has a structure, a budget and accountability requirements, these same characteristics do not apply to the consumer initiative. As with self-help, the initiative may or may not have resources or a resource acquisition process to sustain itself over time. If there are resource allocations, they are usually minimal, since staffing is all based on voluntary provision of labor. Also, the norms governing the assistance, help, and/or support provided are probably broader than those of the formal organization and may not be explicit at all. There may or may not be performance and accountability expectations; if they exist they may be ambiguous. In some cases, they may be defined by the consumer-members; if resource allocations are involved, they may be defined by the formal organization.

The rationale behind the consumer-initiative type is that consumers and their first person experiences with serious mental illness can be translated into service and support innovations within existing service systems by the consumers themselves. Furthermore, these initiatives can actually expand service appropriateness, accessibility and effectiveness, by uniquely meeting needs that may otherwise go ignored by the formal organization and its programs.

Summary

This framework and the various "types" composing it help us to identify various programmatic alternatives and service arrangements making up the broad area of "consumers as providers in psychiatric rehabilitation." The four types offer an organizing scheme for many of the exemplars included in this volume. They also offer us a heuristic for organizing, documenting, and explicating the issues that are germane to a certain type. These issues and their clustering by type are the focus of the next chapter.

References

Armstrong, M.L., Korba, A.M., & Emard, R. (1995). Of mutual benefit: The reciprocal relationship between consumer volunteers and the clients they serve. *Psychiatric Rehabilitation Journal, 19*, 45-49.

Besio, S.W., & Mahler, J. (1993). Benefits and challenges of using consumer staff in supported housing services. *Hospital and Community Psychiatry*, May 44(5), 490-491.

Caldwell, S. & White, K.K. (1991). Co-creating a self-help recovery movement. *Psychosocial Rehabilitation Journal, 15*(2), 91-94.

Chamberlin, J. (1978). *On our own: Patient controlled alternatives to the mental health system.* New York, NY: Hawthorne Books.

Chamberlin, J., Rogers, E.S., & Ellison, M.L. (1996). Self-help programs: A description of their characteristics and their members. *Psychiatric Rehabilitation Journal, 19*(3), 33-42.

Cook, J.A., Jonikas, J.A., & Solomon, M.L. (1991). Models of vocational rehabilitation for youth and adults with severe mental illness. *American Rehabilitation, 17*(1), .

Dixon, L., Krauss, N., & Lehman, A. (1994). Consumers as service providers: The promise and challenge. *Community Mental Health Journal, 30*(6), 615-633.

Emerick, R.E. (1990). Self-help groups for former patients: Relations with mental health professionals. *Hospital and Community Psychiatry, 41*(4), 401-407.

Fisher, D.B. (1994). A new vision of healing as constructed by people with psychiatric disabilities working as mental health providers. *Psychosocial Rehabilitation Journal, 17*(3), 67-81.

Galanter, M. (1988). Zealous self-help groups as adjuncts to psychiatric treatment: A study of Recovery, Inc. *American Journal of Psychiatry, 145*(10), 1248-1253.

Harp, H. (1990). Independent living with support services: The goal and future for mental health consumers. *Psychosocial Rehabilitation Journal, 13*(4), 85-89.

Kanaan, S.B. (1991). The growing mental health self-help movement. *Policy in Perspective, Mental Health Policy Resource Center*, May, 1-3.

Kaufman, C.L., Ward-Colasante, C., & Farmer, J. (1993). Development and evaluation of drop-in centers operated by mental health consumers. *Hospital and Community Psychiatry, 44*(7), 675-678.

Kurtz, L.F. (1990). Measuring member satisfaction with a self-help association. *Evaluation & Program Planning, 13*(2), 119-124.

Lieberman, A.A., Gowdy, E.A., & Knutson, L.C. (1991). The mental health outreach project: A case study in self-help. *Psychosocial Rehabilitation Journal, 14*(3), 100-104.

Long, L. (1988). *Consumer-run self-help programs serving homeless people with a mental illness.* (Published under contract #304666, Division of Education and Service Systems Liaison, National Institute of Mental Health, June).

Luke, D.A., Rappaport, J., & Seidman, E. (1991). Setting phenotypes in a mutual help organization: Expanding behavior setting theory. *American Journal of Community Psychology, 19*(1), 147-167.

Lyons, J.S., Cook, J.A., Ruth, A.R., & Karver, M. (1996). Service delivery using consumer staff in a mobile crisis assessment program. *Community Mental Health Journal, 32*(1), 33-40.

Meek, C. (1994). Consumer-run drop-in centers as alternatives to mental health system services. *PRO/CON, 3*(1), 49-51.

Mowbray, C.T., Chamberlain, P., Jennings, M., & Reed, C. (1988). Consumer-run mental health services: Results from five demonstration projects. *Community Mental Health Journal, 24*(2), 151-156.

Mowbray, C.T., Moxley, D.P., Thrasher, S., Bybee, D., McCrohan, H., Harris, F., & Clover, G. (1996). Consumers as community support providers: Challenges created by role innovation. *Community Mental Health Journal*, 32(1), 47-67.

Mowbray, C.T., Wellwood, R., & Chamberlain, P.J. (1988). Project Stay: A consumer-run support service. *Psychosocial Rehabilitation Journal*, 12(1), 33-42.

Mowbray, C.T., & Tan, C. (1992). Evaluation of an innovative consumer-run service model: The drop-in center. *Innovations & Research*, March 1(2), 19-24.

Mowbray, C.T., & Tan, C. (1993). Drop-in centers run by and for psychiatric consumers: Evaluation of operations and impact. *Journal of Mental Health Administration*, 20(1), 8-19.

Petty, C. (1991). Consumer-driven programs gain momentum. *Insites*, 4(2), 1,10-11.

Plumb, A. (1993). The challenge of self-advocacy. *Feminism & Psychology*, 3(2), 169-187.

Rogers, S. (1994). Help wanted, available consumer/survivor services are helping with job training, placement and hope. *The Key*, 2(2), 5-16.

Sherman, P.S. & Porter, R. (1991). Mental health consumers as case management aides. *Hospital and Community Psychiatry*, 42(5), 494-498.

Segal, S. P., Silverman, C., & Temkin, T. (1993). Empowerment and self-help agency practice for people with mental disabilities. *Social Work*, 38(6), 705-712.

Solomon, P. (1988). Services to severely mentally disabled homeless persons and to emergency food and shelter providers. *Psychosocial Rehabilitation Journal*, 12(2), 3-13.

Solomon, P. & Draine, J. (1995). One-year outcomes of a randomized trial of consumer case management. *Evaluation and Program Planning*, 18(2), 117-127.

Solomon, P. & Draine, J. (1996). Perspectives concerning consumers as case managers. *Community Mental Health Journal*, 32(1), 41-46.

Stoneking, B.C., Greenfield, T., Sundby, E.B., and Boltz, S. (1991). *Adding trained consumers to case management teams as service coordinators: Program development, research design, and early outcomes.* 119th Annual Meeting of the American Public Health Association, Atlanta, GA, November 1991. (Published under NIMH Grant No. R18MH46146)

Toff, G.E. (1988). *Self-Help programs serving people who are homeless and mentally ill.* Proceedings of the Fourth Knowledge Development Meeting on Issues Affecting Homeless Mentally Ill People, The Intergovernmental Health Policy Project, The George Washington University. (With funding support from the Division of Education and Service Systems, National Institute of Mental Health contract number 278-86-0006).

Wheaton, J.A., McLain, J., & Powell, T.J. (1994). *Consumer worker contributions to ACT services.* Ann Arbor: The University of Michigan, School of Social Work.

Young, J. & Williams, C.L. (1988). Whom do mutual-help groups help: A typology of members. *Hospital and Community Psychiatry*, 39(11), 1178-1182.

Zimmerman, M.A., Reischl, T.M., Seidman, E., Rappaport, J., Toro, P.A., & Salen, D.A. (1991). Expansion strategies of a mutual help organization. *American Journal of Community Psychology*, 19(2), 251-278.

Chapter 3

Benefits and Issues Created by Consumer Role Innovation in Psychiatric Rehabilitation

Carol T. Mowbray

The movement towards consumer involvement in psychiatric rehabilitation and mental health service provision has grounding in the larger society's endorsement of consumerism and self-help in general, emerging in the late twentieth century, as well as in legal battles establishing human rights policies for disenfranchised groups, especially persons with disabilities. This involvement can be categorized into four models, which reflect its historical roots, to a certain extent: (1) self-help programs—controlled by consumers, where the aim is mutual support (versus formal service provision); (2) consumer-run services—also controlled by consumers, but with an aim of formal service provision; (3) consumers as employees — working in nonconsumer-controlled mental health or psychosocial programs, whose aim is formal service provision; and, finally (4) consumer-initiated services — whose aims are mutual support, but which operate within traditional service settings (not consumer-controlled). Correspondingly, the consumer roles that have evolved are heterogeneous (across and within models) and multi-faceted (encompassing governance, staffing, program development, and numerous other dimensions). The legitimacy of consumers playing roles in their own and others' service delivery has received confirmation from a variety of differing perspectives, including rehabilitation literature, professional associations (such as the National Association of State Mental Health Program Directors), and public policy.

Benefits and Opportunities

The benefits of consumer involvement in direct service provision have, perhaps, been best and most frequently articulated at the level of the individual receiving help from a consumer-provider. Much of this articulation has come from the self-help literature. For individuals with many types of problems and/or life experiences, including that of mental illness, consumers providing services offers an alternative source of help and support — one which differs markedly from that provided by professionals, and cannot be duplicated by them. The assistance available from peers is more normalized. It is also more empathic, concrete, and relevant, because it comes from someone "who's been there." Learning from peers can be more effective because it is less anxiety-producing for many individuals than dealing with professionals (who often present themselves as wishing to maintain a hierarchical relationship, and who also often have enormous power over the freedom and resources available to a person with mental illness). The process of communication with peer providers may also be easier to navigate than with professionals; more support and encouragement may be provided. Peers providing assistance can also serve as role models, having cognitive as well as emotional impacts. Cognitive, in that peers' suggested solutions have a great deal of credibility, because they have obviously worked for them; and emotional, in offering hope for recovery to persons who have otherwise been led to believe that their greatest possible aspiration should only be to stay out of the hospital. Studies assessing the operation of consumer vs. nonconsumer staff often find few differences between them (Lyons, Cook, Ruth, & Karver, 1996; Solomon & Draine, 1995).

Benefits have also been frequently cited for the individual consumers who provide the service. At the personal level, the opportunity to provide services and help to others is oftentimes experienced positively, especially by individuals who have been stigmatized and sometimes directly told that they have no value. Operating as a service provider can allow individuals to resume a sense of responsibility, to increase awareness of their own capabilities, and to pursue many other opportunities for personal growth and development. Furthermore, consumer-provided service involvement offers experiences which have often been identified as important to stabilization and recovery from mental illness according to clubhouse and assertive community treatment programs; that is, meaningful activities, valued roles and a structured day. At the vocational level, consumer involvement can give those individuals who are oriented towards human services and helping a unique opportunity for training and work, which otherwise would not exist. That is, most employment and volunteer activities available to individuals with psychiatric disabilities have involved "food and filth" or "hash and trash" — menial jobs in the food industry or janitorial services. Traditional jobs through vocational rehabilitation have often involved benchwork and/or clerical activities. Very few placements or training opportunities involved "people-oriented" positions. Even jobs in service establishments were seldom in serving people and were more often behind the counter, taking out trash, sweeping the floor, or other clean-up activities. On the other hand, consumers involved in service provision in their agencies have the unique opportunity to see if this line of work fits their preferences, and to help them develop a positive work history.

The benefits of consumer involvement in services can also be described at the program and system levels for psychiatric rehabilitation and mental health programs, although they have been less frequently cited. Acknowledging the meaningful roles that consumers can provide to clients of these programs makes explicit statements about the overall worth of consumers. That is, they are reliable and dependable enough to provide services. They are able to move away from their own symptoms and problems to help others. Because of the kinds of services consumers usually provide to others, there is also an implicit valuing of the subjective experience of persons with mental illness. Consumers helping others with their problems indicates that they can identify their subjective experiences, work with them and share them appropriately with others towards the end state of achieving rehabilitation goals. The fact that consumers can reliably report and apply their own experiences would probably have been seen as a nonsensical (or perhaps delusional) judgment as recently as twenty years ago (Davidson & Strauss, 1995). Reports from persons with diagnosed mental illnesses were historically subject to being ignored or refuted in criminal and civil matters; mental health personnel rarely sought input from their patients about side effects or functioning goals when making medication decisions. Some still don't.

Perhaps of even greater importance in terms of system impact is the fact that acknowledging the value of consumers providing services to others has implications for how the rest of service delivery takes place in an agency. Consumer services are delivered in a manner that is nonhierarchical, interactive, and collaborative. The basis for this service is often articulated according to ideological positions that value respect for other people and their wishes, while attempting to enhance their empowerment and self-determination. Since this is the basis for consumer-provided services and the agency or program endorses such services, does this not have implications concerning the desirability of such a service philosophy and practice across all programs and all service personnel?

The greatest potential impact of widescale endorsement and utilization of consumers as providers has to do with the opportunities it presents for advocacy through group solidarity. Consumer service provision means that individual consumers can no longer be isolated in their disability, negative identity, or stigma. Bringing individuals together provides the opportunity to share common perspectives and dissatisfactions concerning program and system mistreatments. Individuals have available to them a reference group from which they can model behavior, adopt values, and form attitudes toward professionals and "the system." Having a connection with a peer who has the acknowledged capacity to stand equal at some level with non-consumer providers gives their perspectives and dissatisfactions legitimate voice. Providers can no longer legitimately label individual complaints as pathological, manifestations of symptoms, denial of illness, and/or resistance to treatment when they are voiced by multiple others. Through the symbol and the reality of consumers who provide services, empowerment is actualized. Power is given away to those with a disability label — power to take control over their own outcomes and over system operations. As has been the case in other movements, this expression of common voice and experience of increased control can become operationalized in consumer-generated criteria (e.g., concerning successful outcome, satisfaction, respectful treatment, etc.) becoming legitimate and significant components for evaluating service delivery and agency performance.

The Consequences of Opportunities

Despite the real and potential benefits associated with consumer involvement in service, mental health critics contend that the extent of user involvement in psychiatric and/or rehabilitation services currently may be more theoretical than real (Church, 1989). Commitment to these initiatives is alleged to be only at the level of lip service and tokenism. For instance, in one survey of state mental health authorities, less than one-tenth of one percent of their total budgets supported consumer ex-patient projects, using a broad definition (Human Resource Association of the Northeast (HRAN), 1989). This probably comes as no surprise to most, since systems change in the mental health field has never been known for its rapidity or widespread occurrence. Thus, program innovations developed in the 1950's, such as Assertive Community Treatment, Fairweather Lodges, and clubhouses, which have demonstrable success and reduced costs, still do not constitute the majority of mental health expenditures. Indeed the Community Mental Health movement instituted in the 1960's probably never achieved its mandates. And some would contend that deinstitutionalization is still going on after more than the 40 years.

Yet despite these criticisms, we must look beyond "formal mental health services" supported through formal resources. As reflected by the many contributions made to this volume by consumers and professionals alike, consumers serve in a number of different roles as providers and many of these have evolved out of self-help or personal initiatives. The funding of these alternatives are frequently informal or do not get recorded within public mental health budgets; that is, through foundation grants, voluntary donations of time and effort, and probono contributions. The "real" budget of self-help and consumer initiatives is most likely not well understood. The funds used to initiate and implement consumer alternatives — especially in the early stages of development — may actually represent the informal or underground economy of rehabilitation, community support, and mental health service delivery. The realization of formal change in state mental health budgets, reflecting a more institutionalized commitment to funding and perpetuating consumer service alternatives may require a longer-term time frame.

The organizational change literature tells us that major alterations in policy, programming, or operations require complex and often lengthy adjustments — some taking generations. Innovation is not readily institutionalized by policy systems and organizations. In fact, many may resist it. Consumer role innovations definitely represent major alterations. They reflect a paradigm shift in our view of interventions for psychiatric illness: from a focus on maintenance and stabilization to one on rehabilitation, productive functioning, and recovery. Furthermore, they abandon hospital settings as the locus of intervention and psychiatric personnel as the key providers. More importantly, they reflect a changing view of the rights of mental health consumers to determine their own outcomes and treatments as well as of their capability to direct their own recovery.

Thus, signifying major organizational and policy changes, increased involvement of consumers in service provision is likely to confront multiple and complex issues. In the remainder of this chapter, we review the many issues and challenges which have so far been identified in mental health literatures related to this topic. Our aim in so doing is not to paint a bleak and discouraging picture of such innovations. The literature in this volume is a testimony to optimism and hope. However, we do want to improve understanding of what these role changes involve and increase awareness that their implementation is likely to have larger and more complex effects than might be anticipated. We believe that it is only with full knowledge that problems may be avoided and systems improved. The issues described will be seen throughout many of the programmatic chapters of this book. Sometimes these challenges have been overcome and issues resolved; sometimes they have not. However, it is only through understanding and acknowledgement of problems that advocates and system changers are likely to succeed. Armed with these weapons, they may be better able to prevent problems through the initial structuring of a service alternative, or by making available the response system and supports for early intervention which can mitigate otherwise unanticipated or negative outcomes. Thus, the reader is encouraged to process and think through the issues identified. Be alert to whether your own situation or agency could be involved in some of these same challenges; or perhaps is involved in similar challenges which have not, as yet, surfaced. Watch for these issues and challenges as they emerge in the programmatic and personal account chapters which follow. Their confrontation and resolution at local program levels appear in many chapters. Solutions to issues form the basis for the concluding sections of the book, in which we discuss changes in mental health policy and in the operations of mental health programs which need to be in place to address important issues and sustain these innovations. Remember, the purpose of our examining *Consumers as Providers in Psychiatric Rehabilitation* is not to simply provide testimonials to its positive effects; it is to make it work as a long-term and permanent alternative to traditional psychiatric rehabilitation and mental health services; and in so doing, to alter these traditional services towards the goals embodied in consumer involvement and perhaps in consumer control.

Challenges and Issues at Multiple Levels

In this chapter, we organize our discussion of issues according to the multiple levels of the service delivery system. That is, an organizational change framework recognizes that even though change ostensibly occurs only at one level, i.e., the program level with the availability of a new service model, changes are experienced at macro and micro levels as well. Thus, we will discuss the change ramifications of consumer role innovation in service delivery for: (1) the service recipients; (2) the service implementors which include (a) consumer-providers themselves in their new roles and (b) existing mental health professionals; (3) the program level of the innovation and its management; and

(4) the community, encompassing the larger mental health service delivery system and others. Finally, we conclude with a summary of ethical issues which have been identified.

Issues for Service Recipients

One of the benefits of greater involvement of consumers as direct service deliverers should be to decrease the distance between provider and client, thus increasing rapport, and to build on the similarity between provider and client, increasing understanding and improving services. However, some reports have indicated that service recipients, like society in general, accord stigma to mental illness and so may feel that only regular, "qualified" mental health professionals can help them — not people who have the same problems they do (Wheaton, McLain & Powell, 1994). Other consumers may be seen as not strong enough or capable enough to provide help (Simon, 1992). Thus, service recipients may avoid programs run by other consumers (self-help, consumer-run alternatives, or consumer initiatives) or refuse help from staff known to be current or former consumers.

Another problem is that some service recipients may view their peers differently once they assume a service provider role. That is, they see consumer-providers as one of the staff, no longer one of them and lose trust in them. This orientation also decreases utilization of consumer-provided services.

Other problems have also been noted. If a recipient does accept help from another consumer, his/her own problems and stress can increase if there has been a prior relationship, causing a blurring of the boundaries between friendship and helping; or if the consumer in the helping role is burdening the recipient with their own problems (rather than selectively disclosing information to be helpful) (HRAN, 1989). These issues are probably more intense when consumers are in more formal service provision roles, such as in consumer-controlled alternatives or consumer-employee models.

Related to recipient acceptance of peer helpers, it should be noted that the original rationale for self-help as an alternative to traditional services does not apply as well in the case of psychiatric disabilities. That is, one often-promoted basis for self-help is that help-receiving is a difficult role, but help-giving is a positive role. Receiving help through a self-help organization should be less difficult because the helpee has direct control over the help received, is a member of the group which is responsible for help provision, and furthermore the help receipt is embedded as part of training to be a helper oneself (Riessman, 1990). Furthermore, according to self-help theory, no stigma is attached because help is provided universally and help receipt is temporary. Obviously, some of these assumptions do not fit a population with psychiatric disabilities: that is, for them, help is not universal, but is offered because of the individual's mental illness and functioning; and probably less than a majority of psychiatric self-help group members consider themselves in training to be helpers. Noordsy, Schwab, Fox, and Drake (1996) report that individuals with psychiatric disabilities attending self-help groups had difficulty finding people they felt similar to. Thus, among persons with psychiatric disabilities, the self-help philosophy may be less appealing and participation in self-help groups and their derivatives therefore less probable.

Issues for Consumer-Providers

Consumers oftentimes perform roles as providers which are low status, low or no pay, and highly stressful — positions which are labeled as prone to burn-out when mental health professionals fill them. However, oftentimes the consumers who are in these roles have not had the advantage of training and/ or internships, as is the case for professionals, nor do they have specialized inservices or supervision that could compensate for this. Additionally, they have a number of personal issues to face because of their past history and the stigma associated with their ongoing mental illness label.

As individuals who have experienced long-term, severe mental illness, consumer-providers have often experienced multiple, past failures in vocational endeavors. Thus, a fear of failure may be crippling to their seeking out helping positions or carrying through once they attain them (Rogers, 1994). Consumers in paid positions (through consumer-run or established services) may additionally fear success: that is, that they will not be able to continue performing at the level required to keep their jobs. Furthermore, having attained some material success, such as a car, a better apartment, clothes, etc., the fear of losing their job can be increased because an improved lifestyle will be lost too (Rogers, 1994). Persons with psychiatric disabilities who get any kind of employment also have the justified fear of permanently losing the lifeline which disability benefits can provide, including health insurance, if they are successfully employed on more than a temporary basis (Rogers, 1994). Furthermore, while a job could end due to no fault of their own or a recurrence of their disability, the ability to retrieve the disability status may be gone forever. Worries about long-term financial stability can cause substantial anxieties for many consumers on SSI/SSDI (Church, 1989; Wheaton et al., 1994) or even cause them to abandon good jobs.

These anxieties over fear of failure or job loss, combined with consumers' close identification with their service-recipient-peers, can produce other emotional problems as well. Consumer-helpers may feel intensely and unreasonably responsible for clients assigned to them. They get frustrated when their clients fail to follow through (Armstrong, Korba, & Emard, 1995). They may overestimate their power as a helper, setting themselves up for failure (Lieberman, Gowdy & Knutson, 1991); or for burnout when their unrealistic expectations are inevitably quelched (Mowbray, Moxley, Thrasher et. al., 1996). Peer counselors sometimes get quite personally involved with assigned clients, causing excessive worry, sleeplessness, and lack of objectivity (Howie the Harp, 1991).

Consumer-helpers may find themselves in a "no man's land" (Shepherd, 1992) in terms of the social and emotional supports available to them. Helpers report feeling that they can't hang around with their consumer-friends anymore, intensifying their loneliness (Wheaton et al., 1994); or that the supports they used to have from other consumers are no longer available when they've switched roles (Fisher, 1994). At the same time, consumers in paid positions may find it difficult to open up and establish friendship relationships with nonconsumer mental health providers they work with (Fisher, 1994; Solomon & Draine, 1996), for fear that their problems may be seen as caused by their mental illness, increasing the stigma and discrimination they feel and their fears of job loss. Or, some may try to fit in too much with the existing staff, trading their clienthood for professionalism (Shepherd, 1992), to the detriment of their ties with consumers and self-help groups. Since consumer group connections are oftentimes the reasons why these consumers got their jobs, ironically, in aligning themselves too far with "professionalism, they may be sowing the seeds of their own unemployment. These dynamics may also lead to feelings of marginalized status, versus those associated with having a meaningful, stable role. Consumer-employees sometimes cope with doubts about their status or feelings of emotional isolation by constantly asking for feedback and guidance from supervisors in order to get reassurance (Shepherd, 1992). These behaviors are certainly understandable, but usually not well-received either; or, worse yet, framed as an expression of the consumer-provider's illness. Solomon and Draine (1996) suggest the need for support groups for consumer-staff, to minimize feelings of isolation.

Consumer-helpers may also have special needs directly related to their disabilities. Some of the problems identified have included: sensitivity to job stress (Carling, 1993; Howie the Harp, 1994), resulting in increased symptomatic behavior (Besio & Mahler, 1993); difficulty with distractions, requiring private work space (Howie the Harp, 1991); need for flexibility in scheduling hours (Shepherd, 1992), including markedly reduced work times for long durations when symptoms recur. In paid employment positions, persons with psychiatric disabilities can ask for reasonable accomodations for such difficulties. However, many consumers are reportedly reluctant to make these requests (Carling, 1993), often because this requires disclosure of the individual's psychiatric disability. While the ADA prevents an individual being fired due to a disability, disclosure and subsequent discriminatory treatment might affect an individual's performance and be less amenable to correction (Strauss & Davidson, in press).

However, there are other problems identified for potential consumer-helpers that cannot be addressed through the accommodations required by the ADA. These have to do with basic vocational skills and work behaviors demanded by a job. That is, many psychiatric consumers first experienced disabling episodes of mental illness at the time when their peers obtained their first vocational experiences, acquiring abilities to follow routines, be punctual, take supervision, work with other people, get organized, and be productive (Rogers, 1994). Having been stigmatized and forced into dependent positions, many consumers have no experience with taking responsibility or assuming authority; indeed, many have probably been punished by service providers for such behaviors. Thus, it is probably understandable for programs to report that consumers are reluctant to be active in governance positions, to set up rules for program operations or to enforce them. A response of "let the staff do it" may be too frequent (Long, 1988).

The ability of consumers to fill helper positions based only on their interests, their similarities to other consumers, and their past experiences in the mental health system, may become more and more of a problem. That is, managed care and other quality and efficiency initiatives are increasing demands for staff performance and often base staff evaluation solely on possessing formal credentials and clinical competencies. As described by Freund (1993), the ideal staff person in a psychiatric rehabilitation setting should be able to work with consumers in an empowering way, relating to them as friends who share many common experiences. However, these individuals need to be able to shift into formal roles during crises or other extraordinary situations. Additionally, they need a high tolerance for ambiguity and skill to facilitate development of empowered social networks for consumers. Certainly, these are skills that many mental health professionals with advanced degrees lack. Is it reasonable that many consumers without specialized training should be able to adequately fill such roles?

While raising this question, we should be reminded of the numbers of consumers who are successfully filling provider roles in psychiatric rehabilitation. The issue sometimes raised for these individuals by mental health professionals, however, is whether they really fit the criteria for mental health consumers; that is, were they really as "sick" as the individuals they're now working with (Simon, 1992)? Similarly, the question has been raised as to whether the majority of members in self-help groups focused on mental health problems fit the criteria of serious (a.k.a. "chronic") mental illness (Bond and DeGraaf-Kaser; 1990). The reality of this possibility has not been substantiated. Certainly at the point when they are functioning well as providers, these consumers do not appear like those individuals they are helping. However, many have described multi-problem backgrounds involving homelessness, hopelessness, psychotic states, and poor prognoses (see, for example, Harp, 1990).

Relationships with Mental Health Professionals

Consumer/ex-patient groups have often contended that mental health, among many human service systems, is markedly discriminating and stigmatizing towards those with psychiatric labels (HRAN, 1989). The self-help literature has noted the resistance experienced from traditional helpers (Riessman, 1990). With these factors alone, it is not surprising that consumer providers frequently report negative relationships with mental health professionals. Other explanations offered include staff fears of being replaced by consumer-based helpers (often touted as less expensive or no-cost services) (Stoneking, Greenfield, Sundby, & Boltz, 1991; Wheaton et al., 1994); and that staff resent the accommodations available to consumer-providers (Carling, 1993). The possible role strain experienced by traditional staff has also been discussed. That is, mental health professionals working with consumer-providers have to realign their relationships with and attitudes towards consumers (Church, 1989). They also have difficulty sorting out whether or how they should share personal feelings and perspectives with coworkers who were or still are clients of the program (Shepherd, 1992). Dixon, Krauss, & Lehman (1994) report that staff on an ACT team were tempted to inappropriately assume therapist roles for the team's two consumer advocates.

Consumer-providers working with mental health professionals have reported experiencing stigmatization and general distrust from staff members (Besio & Mahler, 1993). Behaviors towards them have been described as negative, fearful and exclusionary (Carling, 1993), and guarded and distant (Manos, 1993). It has also been alleged that professionals don't really want or trust consumer service providers or that they are accepted only as long as they stay away from systems change advocacy. In one program, mental health workers reportedly referred clients to a consumer-initiated service only when clients requested this (Lieberman et al., 1991). Another study found that social workers report making referrals to mental health self-help groups less frequently than to AA/NA (Kurtz & Chambon, 1987). Their referral patterns may reflect lack of information or increased competition where service provision domains are similar (Kurtz, Mann & Chambon, 1987). However, other reports indicate that consumer-providers also experience acceptance problems at other referral locations as well, i.e., the Social Security Administration (Solomon, 1988).

The professional behaviors towards consumer-providers that appear to cause the most consternation, however, are stigma and bias. Specifically, consumer providers report that mental health professionals they work with are continually looking for symptomatic behavior and attributing any behavioral problem as a manifestation of the individual's psychiatric label. Thus, an individual expressing justifiable anger or having a bad day is not dealt with in a normal manner, on a concrete level, but in terms of a patient expressing symptomatic behavior. Consumer-providers see such actions as the biggest barrier to working with existing professionals as equals (Howie the Harp, 1991; Shepherd, 1992).

Management Issues

A variety of issues have been identified at the level of program operations. These issues encompass many aspects of employment practices, including recruitment and placement, pay scales, fringe benefits, supervision, accommodations, role clarity, and training. The examples identified in the literature come primarily from mental health programs employing consumers and secondarily from consumer-run services. However, it would appear that issues related to training could also have relevance to other models of consumer-involvement.

Given the kinds of skills and abilities identified as desirable for psychiatric rehabilitation staff (Freund, 1993) and the problematic work skills possessed by many potential consumer workers (Solomon, 1988), recruitment of qualified and interested consumers for positions would appear to present multiple challenges. Consumer-run programs have reported problems in locating and keeping good staff, with applicants being either too self-involved or not having the skills or knowledge required (Long, 1988). Programs employing consumer-workers indicate gaps in being able to find individuals who have come to grips with their illness and have past experiences with paid work and with self-help and advocacy (Wheaton et al., 1994).

A number of reports have commented on suppressed pay scales and inadequate wages being paid to consumer-helpers (HRAN, 1989; Mowbray et al., 1996). Determining the extent to which this is a problem depends on whether consumers are being asked to do jobs similar to professionals (based on knowledge, skill, independence and judgement required, etc.). It also depends on perspectives as to the appropriate basis for salary; e.g.,whether consumers with life experiences should be paid the same as professionals with training; whether job performance should be the primary criteria for all employees, etc. For consumers moving off disability payments, having adequate health insurance is a necessity. This may mean changing agency practices to provide benefits for part-time workers, as well as expanding insurance coverage for psychiatric services (Carling, 1993; Petty, 1991). Agencies are fearful that these requirements will produce substantially higher operating costs (Carling, 1993), particularly if the expansion of benefits is available to all personnel.

A number of accommodations have been identified as typically required for consumer-workers; such as flexible scheduling; modifying duties which require driving an automobile (since many consumers lack drivers' licenses); providing more private office space; minimizing distractions from the physical environment, etc. (Carling, 1993; Wheaton et al., 1994). Agencies have expressed concern that providing coverage for absences during hospitalizations of consumer employees would create logistic problems (Carling, 1990), although the extent to which this has occurred is not documented. While agencies may express budgetary concerns (Shepherd, 1992), it is not clear that the accommodations requested by consumer workers are necessarily costly. Supervisory practices for consumer-providers may also need attention. Instructions and feedback may need to be individualized as some workers reportedly have difficulty with written communications and some with verbal. There may also be a need for increased clinical supervision (Solomon & Draine, 1996). Consumer-workers need to be assigned to supervisors who will appropriately interpret any problem behaviors (as job-produced vs. disability-produced)—provide support and direction rather than stigmatization or mental health treatment (Carling, 1993; Shepherd, 1992). Questions have arisen as to how much an employer should be expected to accommodate symptomatic behaviors of employees with psychiatric disabilities (Carling, 1993; Howie the Harp, 1991). For example, are yelling and angry outbursts in the workplace okay as long as they are not viewed by clients (even though they may disturb other employees)? How much inconsistency and unreliability in job performance, ostensibly due to the individual's mental illness, should be accommodated?

Providing training around work performance may be a solution to address such problematic behaviors; or perhaps these are pre-employment issues that need to be handled in rehabilitation or treatment. More specifically related to their job duties, perhaps more so than other workers, consumer-providers need training concerning confidentiality because of the greater pressures they may experience to reveal private and/or confidential information from other consumers as well as from mental health professionals (Besio & Mahler, 1993).

Employing consumers also raises policy issues at the agency level. Questions have been raised about the appropriateness of agencies creating special job slots to be filled only by consumers. This may have the advantage of expanding employment opportunities, but the disadvantage of stigmatizing and labeling an employee before he/she ever starts on the job (Mowbray et al., 1996). Concerns have also been expressed as to whether jobs labeled as "for consumers" are "make-work" jobs or real jobs, with appropriate levels of authority and responsibility. Mental health agencies allegedly follow a double standard: being willing to hire consumer employees, but only into the lowest level positions, e.g., clerical assistants for case managers or human service aides (see chapter by Allen in this volume). Consumer-provider positions may create problems for these employees and their coworkers by not having clearly conceptualized role descriptions (Solomon, 1994). Consumer employment also presents challenges for retention: should special career ladders be created just for consumers? or should positions tagged for consumers be considered training-level, after which individuals may move on to openly compete for other agency jobs? Questions have also arisen about whether consumer employees should be employed in the same program from which they receive services or in slots where they are likely to be familiar with service recipients. The former increases the likelihood that the consumer-employee will have relevant knowledge of issues; however, it also increases the probable role strain and the difficulties in confidentiality (Wheaton, et al., 1994).

Systemic Issues

As an innovation, any of the models of consumer service provision face challenges in how or even whether they fit in with existing systems designed to serve the same target clientele. The systemic issues that have been identified to date in the literature concern funding, contractual arrangements and agreements between programs involving consumer-providers, mental health authorities, and other systems.

As with payments to individual consumer providers, problems with inadequate resources to fund consumer-run, self-help and other consumer service provisions have been alleged (Church, 1989; HRAN, 1989). These small, innovative programs are competing with large, institutionalized services, to their detriment. Funding levels are felt to be far below what is acceptable for established programs with similar mandates (Long, 1988; Mowbray & Tan, 1993). While existing mental health programs may view consumer-provider innovations competitively, it is usually the case that these programs are targeting a clientele that has rejected traditional programs and/or that these programs have left alone. However, we are currently dealing with a shrinking, not expanding funding pot for services. In an era of managed care, innovative programs will probably fare poorly, lacking a track record to compete for service contracts, and/or lacking licensing and accreditation credentials.

Given these considerations and the competitive disadvantage which consumer-provider services face, additional assistance and consideration is often justifiably expected from mental health authorities. However, literature reports indicate that just the opposite may be occurring. For example, new programs have needed start-up funds before services were initiated, but could not obtain them from state funding sources (McLean, 1994). Other consumer-run programs reported that funding from public mental health authorities was often delayed (Long, 1988). These problems have required some agencies to take out loans, thus increasing their operating expenses. However, in some cases, new programs have found themselves unable to set up a credit line because they lacked a credit history (Long, 1988). In such cases, service delays and lay-offs of consumer workers can result. Consumer-provider programs have also reported difficulties in other aspects of arrangements with larger funding authorities. These involve expectations for their compliance with procedures and accountability demands established and in place for large-scale agencies; for example, for program audits that could cost nearly as much as their entire budgets; for client-level record-keeping systems to meet accountability standards; for financial and book-keeping systems beyond their needs or capabilities; for attendance and intake records on service participants that violate the non-treatment, mutual support orientation of the program, etc. (Mowbray, Chamberlin, Jennings, & Reed, 1988). Small innovative consumer-provider programs especially require different standards and expectations. Given their lack of familiarity with many business practices, and their difficulty in locating supporters or members with this kind of expertise, these consumer-provider programs will usually require technical assistance from mental health funders or other interest groups/organizations from the private or voluntary sector (such as Mental Health Associations).

Problems have occasionally been reported regarding relationships between consumer-provider programs and other systems. They have included accounts of traditional institutions (i.e., universities) not regarding consumer-run programs as legitimate, thus causing problems in the conduct of evaluation research with academic-based consultants (McLean, 1994); and of difficulties locating rental property for use by self-help and/or consumer-run services due to neighborhood resistance (Mowbray, Wellwood, & Chamberlain, 1988), e.g., "It was bad enough that the program was for people who were mentally ill, but it was run by people who were mentally ill, too" (Long, 1988, p. 58).

Of all the levels discussed, it would appear that systems level issues present the largest deterrent for expanding or even maintaining consumer-provider services. While greater levels of education, support and accommodation should be provided, instead large-scale obstacles, including inadequate funding levels, are often experienced.

Ethical Issues

Ethical issues emerge in situations where the legitimate rights, interests, or obligations of one party or their set of mandates are in direct conflict with those of another, and where there are no clear legal or professional standards for resolution. We see such ethical issues concerning consumer involvement in direct service provision at several levels. One that has often been identified revolves around the competing interests of a consumer/self-help organization with that of the mental health bureaucracy. The latter's interest involves maintenance and use of the existing way of doing business: standard procedures for contracting and personnel practices and routinized client treatment. Operations are hierarchical and product-oriented. In constrast, consumerism employs an empowerment and strengths-based philosophy and seeks to emphasize individualized, client-driven services, not treatment. While consumer service initiatives may need funding support from traditional mental health service programs and collaboration in serving clients, their own distinct identity and focus must be maintained. However, because mental health programs are larger, and have the money and longevity, concern arises that consumerism may become coerced or co-opted (HRAN, 1989; Long, 1988).

Some self-helpers allege that groups accept funds from government agencies at severe risk of losing their own autonomy (Kurtz & Chambon, 1987). Indeed, the funders and consumer organizations accepting the funds may experience conflict of interest when faced with an advocacy/systems change issue. If not anticipated in advance, consumer protests against objectionable policies can be interpreted by the funding agency and the public alike as "biting the hand that feeds." In reality, contracts can be written to allow freedom of expression, as long as lobbying and protest activities are not funded with direct service dollars.

In some analyses, just the expansion and consequent bureaucratization of consumer-based programs may present dangers to maintaining their missions. That is, it is alleged that groups which are successful in being funded may experience their objectives becoming skewed because of fiscal preoccupations and their spending patterns intensely scrutinized from competitive interests (Church, 1989). An organization's increase in size may inevitably lead to the adoption of hierarchical structures which move them away from their original mandates (Long, 1988).

A second set of ethical issues revolves around the informal, nonhierarchical direct service practices endorsed by consumer groups versus traditional professional standards of practice. Self-help and mutual support approaches are based, in part, on the value of caring and supportive relationships in helping individuals to identify their own goals and to succeed in attaining them. Reducing social distance between the helper and helpee is critical to this process. Traditional practice, however, emphasizes the need for boundaries, hierarchical relationships, nondisclosure and maintaining distance. Feminist therapies have adopted standards wherein disclosure, empathy and equal relationships are appropriate for professional practice. However, the need for some boundaries is still recognized. For example, the awareness that the relationship exists for the benefit of the client must be kept primary; contacts or disclosure for other purposes, such as for the therapist's personal interest, social support, enhancement of well-being, etc., cannot be tolerated at any level.

The issue of what boundaries are necessary when consumers provide services to their peers does not appear to have been well thought-out (Dixon, et al., 1994). Some consumer organizations advise peer-providers that, in terms of any individual with whom they have a prior relationship, supervision or direct service provision is strictly disallowed (Howie the Harp, 1991). Other programs do not appear to have developed policies to address such issues (Besio & Mahler, 1993; Mowbray et al., 1996). Some consumer service delivery programs and their staff describe themselves as providing friendship (Solomon & Draine, 1996). However, clarity is needed as to whether this is a two-way or one-way only proposition (i.e. from helper to helpee). Another related issue is whether the distancing practices usually followed by traditional service providers should be suspended when consumers provide services to each other; for example, prohibitions against interacting with clients outside of the professional relationship, giving out home phone numbers, and freely socializing with assigned clients in group situations, etc. In fact, to restrict these contacts would be isolating the consumer-providers from the organizations they were retained to represent. Fox and Hilton (1994) suggest that lack of professional distance may be the key to consumer-providers' greater success in engaging clients. However, in contrast, it might be argued that unclear boundaries and unclear role definitions may just exacerbate the stress that consumers already feel in service delivery positions. These boundary issues no doubt will operate differently across the four models, perhaps being most significant where consumers receive direct reimbursement for their services.

A related issue concerns confidentiality. Because they often come from the same circumstances and experiences as the service recipients they or their group works with, consumer-providers may have access to information that is not known to the formal service system. Thus, consumer workers have reported expectations from mental health professionals to divulge information that was obtained under personal circumstances concerning a member of the self-help group or information discovered outside the work role about a friend or acquaintance (Fisher, 1994; Wheaton, et al., 1994). Maintaining the trust of the service recipient versus loyalty to the employing organization are at stake, as well as the consumer-providers being true to themselves (separating out what is their own private business, versus job-related).

Given these reports where mental health professionals are in fact suggesting violations of personal confidentialities, it is ironic that one of the greatest fears expressed by programs employing consumers as direct service providers is whether they will be able to maintain confidentiality of information and records (Stoneking et al., 1991). Mental health staff question whether consumer-providers should be able to come to team meetings and hear open discussions of clients—some of whom may be friends or acquaintances. Wheaton et al. (1994) found that only in a minority of employment situations were consumer staff allowed to attend such meetings. In Mowbray et al.'s (1996) report of a Peer Support Specialist program, consumer workers said that they felt like second-class citizens due to such exclusions. Other more complicated issues have to deal with what to do about the team discussing the consumer-worker's case if indeed he/she can attend the meetings; should consumer workers have access to their own charts at the agency; and should the consumer-worker's job supervisor be able to talk to his/her case manager at the agency?

Finally, we might comment on some over-riding policy issues that may drive particular systems or operational issues which we have noted. That is, perhaps reflecting the multiplicity of forces which have driven the development of consumer involvement in direct service provision, there are multiple goals which are often associated with this innovation. Some of the main goals are: (1) to provide rehabilitation opportunities to consumers; (2) to increase the responsiveness of services; and (3) to effect organizational change. Perhaps all three could be operative, but the implications of the three may be quite different. Prioritizing the primary and secondary goal areas may assist in resolving or reducing the problematic consequences of some of the other issues. Related to this goal resolution is the policy issue of whether agencies and systems are making modifications in existing structures to accomodate consumer service provision, or whether this innovation is a step on the path towards a much larger policy of consumerism within a system and widespread changes in structures, policies, and operations.

In the next sections of the book, we will examine the variety of programs involving consumers as service providers as well as individual provider experiences, to see how these issues have been experienced and how some sites have successfully come to a resolution.

References

Armstrong, M.L., Korba, A.M., & Emard, R. (1995). Of mutual benefit: The reciprocal relationship between consumer volunteers and the clients they serve. *Psychiatric Rehabilitation Journal, 19,* 45-49.

Armstrong, M.L., Korba, A.M., & Emard, R. (1995). Of mutual benefit: The reciprocal relationship between consumer volunteers and the clients they serve. *Psychiatric Rehabilitation Journal*, 19, 45-49.

Besio, S.W., & Mahler, J. (1993). Benefits and challenges of using consumer staff in supported housing services, *Hospital and Community Psychiatry*, 44(5), 490-491.

Bond, G.R. & DeGraaf-Kaser, R. (1990). Group approaches for persons with severe mental illness: A typology. *Social Work with Groups*, 13(1), 21-36.

Carling, P.J. (1993). Reasonable accommodations in the work place for individuals with psychiatric disabilities. In J.E. O'Keefe & S.M. Bruyere, eds., *Implications of the Americans with Disabilities Act for psychology* (pp. 103-135). New York, NY: Springer Publishing Co.

Church, K. (1989). User involvement in the mental health field in Canada. *Canada's Mental Health*, June, 22-25.

Davidson, L. & Strauss, J.S. (1995). Beyond the biopsychosocial model: Integrating disorder, health, and recovery. *Psychiatry* 58, 44-55.

Dixon, L., Krauss, N., & Lehman, A. (1994). Consumers as service providers: The promise and challenge. *Community Mental Health Journal*, 30(6), 615-633.

Fisher, D. (1994). A new vision of healing as constructed by people with psychiatric disabilities working as mental health providers. *Psychosocial Rehabilitation Journal*, 17(3), 67-81.

Fox, L. & Hilton, D. (1994). Response to "Consumers as service providers: The promise and challenge." *Community Mental Health Journal*, 30(6), 627-629.

Freund, P.D. (1993). Professional role(s) in the empowerment process: "Working with" mental health consumers. *Psychosocial Rehabilitation Journal*, 16(3), 65-73.

Harp, H. (1991). *A crazy folks guide to reasonable accommodation and "psychiatric disability."* Burlington, VT: The Center for Community Change through Housing and Support, Institute for Program Development, Trinity College of Vermont.

Human Resource Association of the Northeast (HRAN). (1989). *Report of meeting of ad hoc committee on consumer/ex-patient involvement.* Holyoke, MA: HRAN.

Kurtz, L.F. & Chambon, A. (1987). Comparison of self-help groups for mental health. *Health and Social Work*, 12, 275-283.

Kurtz, L.F., Mann, K.B. & Chambon, A. (1987). Linking between social workers and mental health mutual-aid groups. *Social Work in Health Care*, 13(1), 69-78.

Lieberman, A.A., Gowdy, E.A., & Knutson, L.C. (1991). The mental health outreach project: A case study in self-help. *Psychosocial Rehabilitation Journal*, 14(3), 100-104.

Long, L. (1988). *Consumer-run self-help programs serving homeless people with a mental illness.* (Published under contract #304666, Division of Education and Service Systems Liaison, National Institute of Mental Health, June).

Lyons, J.S., Cook, J.A., Ruth, A.R., & Karver, M. (1996). Service delivery using consumer staff in a mobile crisis assessment program. *Community Mental Health Journal, 32*(1), 33-40.

Manos, E. (1993). Speaking out. *Psychosocial Rehabilitation Journal, 16*(4), 117-120.

McLean, A. (1994). *The role of consumers in mental health services research and evaluation: A report and concept paper.* Unpublished paper.

Mowbray, C.T., Chamberlain, P.J., Jennings, M. & Reed, C. (1988). Consumer-run mental health services: Results from five demonstration projects. *Community Mental Health Journal,* Summer 24(2), 151-156.

Mowbray, C.T., Moxley, D.P., Thrasher, S., Bybee, D., McCrohan, H., Harris, F., & Clover, G. (1996). Consumers as community support providers: Challenges created by role innovation. *Community Mental Health Journal, 32*(1), 47-67.

Mowbray, C.T., & Tan, C. (1993). Drop-In centers run by and for psychiatric consumers: Evaluation of operations and impact. *Journal of Mental Health Administration,* Spring 20(1), 8-19.

Mowbray, C.T., Wellwood, R., Chamberlain, P.J. (1988). Project Stay: A consumer-run support service. *Psychosocial Rehabilitation Journal, 12*(1), 33-42.

Noordsy, D.L., Schwab, B., Fox, L., & Drake, R.E. (1996). The role of self-help programs in the rehabilitation of persons with severe mental illness and substance use disorders. *Community Mental Health Journal, 32*(1), 71-82.

Petty, C. (1991). Consumer-driven programs gain momentum. *Insites,* 4(2), 1,10-11.

Riessman, F. (1990). Restructuring help: A human services paradigm for the 1990's. *American Journal of Community Psychology,* 18(2), 221-230.

Rogers, S. (1994). Help wanted: Available consumer/survivor services are helping with job training, placement and hope. *The Key,* 2(2), 5-16.

Simon, M. (1992). Making a difference: Ex-patients as staff. Resources, *Newsletter of the Human Resource Association of the Northeast.* Holyoke, MA, 9-10.

Shepard, L. (1992). *So you want to hire a consumer? Employing people with psychiatric disabilities as staff members in mental health agencies.* Burlington, VT: The Center for Community Change through Housing and Support, Institute for Program Development, Trinity College of Vermont.

Solomon, P. (1994). Response to "Consumers as service providers: The promise and challenge." *Community Mental Health Journal,* 30(6), 631-634.

Solomon, P. (1988). Services to severely mentally disabled homeless persons and to emergency food and shelter providers. *Psychosocial Rehabilitation Journal,* 12(2), 3-13.

Solomon, P. & Draine, J. (1995). One-year outcomes of a randomized trial of consumer case management. *Evaluation and Program Planning,* 18(2), 117-127.

Solomon, P. & Draine, J. (1996). Perspectives concerning consumers as case managers. *Community Mental Health Journal, 32*(1), 41-46.

Stoneking, B.C. & Greenfield, T. (1991). *Adding trained consumers to case management teams as service coordinators: Program development, research design, and early outcomes.* 119th Annual Meeting of the American Public Health Association, Atlanta, GA, November 1991. (Published under NIMH Grant No. R18MH46146).

Strauss, J. & Davidson, L. (In press). Mental disorders, work and choice. In R. Bonnie & J. Monahan, *Mental disorder, work disability and the law.* Chicago, IL: University of Chicago Press.

Wheaton, J.A., McLain, J. & Powell, T.J. (1994). *Consumer worker contributions to ACT services.* Ann Arbor, MI: The University of Michigan, School of Social Work.

Section 2

Consumers as Providers of Self-Help

Introduction to Section 2: Consumers as Providers of Self-Help

In this section, consumers are presented as providers within self-help organizations. The alternatives which the chapters describe are situated in a variety of settings and geographical locations. All are successfully providing help, although some settings (such as state hospitals) and some areas (i.e., rural) present more challenges than others. The groups represented also differ in structure and operations — from grass-roots efforts (Sciacca, Scott, Brink); to an expanding, multi-site movement (John P.); to an established national organization (Ackerman, Tracy).

Despite the diversity of the groups described, like other reports in the literature, these chapters emphasize the benefits of self-help. Authors underscore the importance of empathy (Tracy) and having friends who understand one's history and current situation (Scott). They also discuss informational assistance provided through self-help, i.e., knowledge about rights (Brink, John P.) and about disorders and treatment (Sciacca), and the value of the travel, social and other activities it offers. Whether it's through practical wisdom or philosophy for recovery which formally frames the group's mission (John P., Ackerman), or through sharing of individual stories and coping mechanisms, chapter authors describe how self-help groups provide members with insight, self-awareness, and strategies for life changes which significantly impact on recovery (Ackerman, Sciacca, Tracy). Members in the groups described have developed other skills as well. These go beyond interpersonal skills or personal development, to concrete skills, such as being able to plan activities and do fundraising (Scott), produce a newsletter (Brink), write, organize and start groups (John P., Sciacca).

The benefits of self-help are cited particularly in reference to how these groups can make up for the absence of support offered through mental health services. Thus, in their self-help groups, members feel free to talk about anything they want (Scott), to be assured confidentiality (John P.), and to be listened to and understood (Brink); not fearing that they will be judged (Sciacca, Scott), or experiencing the second-place status that is often a product of a hierarchical relationship with a professional (Tracy). Consumer-provider leaders of self-help describe how groups meet members' emotional needs (Scott, Brink, John P.) and how they may be tailored to address concrete individual needs of members. Through developing and maintaining their own group, members gain a sense of competence and independence and involvement in the community (Sciacca). In one case, the self-help group expanded its support into services, developing a 24-hour hotline and a supportive residence (Scott). Thus, in terms of structure, relationships and services, self-help addresses needs unmet by formal mental health services (where "if it couldn't be billed, it didn't need to exist"; Scott).

For all the model programs described in this section, self-help involvement is seen to contribute to staying out of the hospital, to reducing crises, and to avoiding bad situations in general. This may occur because self-help provides positive activities as substitutes for negative ones (Ackerman, Scott); or that contacts with other self-helpers act as early warning signals for intervention before crises worsen (Scott), or that self-help members provide outlets so that those having difficulty can reach out, talk, and/or provide problem-solving assistance (Tracy). These outcomes demonstrate the importance of self-help groups as alternative social networks for participants. In many of the chapters, self-help leaders indicate that through helping others they have frequently helped themselves even more — an outcome consistent with the literature on self-help. They have gained a supportive network of friends or acquaintances. Coping mechanisms and skills acquired through self-help involvement have spread benefits to spheres of family and work functioning (Tracy); self-help work has even been a focus to maintain life and well-being (John P.).

To the general public, it would probably be a marvel that individuals involved in self-help and labeled as "schizophrenic," "major affective disorder," "bipolar," or "dually diagnosed" are able not only to maintain themselves, but also to utilize their existing abilities to develop new skills to sustain their peers and their groups. For many, the descriptions of support and acceptance provided through self-help stand in sharp contrast to the stigma and rejection experienced from former friends and acquaintances who become knowledgeable about the individual's mental illness (Tracy).

The self-help models described and their leadership are not without challenges, however. Perhaps most frequently mentioned are individual stress and burn-out that can result from having too few leaders with too many responsibilities. Finding leadership is a pivotal, but usually difficult task (Scott, John P.). Personal setbacks of leaders are challenges described by chapter authors: some as a part of their illness; some, perhaps, in response to the stress of running their groups with less than adequate support. Groups have also had to confront their common fears and lack of confidence about dealing with psychiatric crises and extremely disturbed states of their members (Brink, Sciacca). Group turnover is also a constant challenge (Scott, Brink, John P.). Some turnover is positive, representing members moving on to other developmental tasks (going to school) or levels of competence (full-time work). Other turnover reflects a high percentage (perhaps half) of individuals who only attend one or two meetings and then drop out. Either way, for groups to continue in existence, new and stable membership must be found.

The chapters in this section also reflect the need to examine the embeddedness and context of self-help. None of the groups described have started or maintained self-help in a vacuum. They have received support from outside — larger organizations, government, or their communities. That help may have come in terms of donated goods (Scott), meeting space (John P., Sciacca), operational funds (Scott), administrative activities (John P., Brink), etc. But whatever its source or substance, it is help that is critical to the development and sustenance of the self-help group.

In some situations, help has been received from the mental health system in terms of funding, assistance with fiscal matters, moral support and encouragement, etc. For some groups, support from the local community mental health agency has been deemed critical in either their development or continued successful operation (Sciacca, Scott, John P.). Across the chapters, though, authors report diverse relationships with the mental health system and with therapists and psychiatrists. At the individual level, some mental health professionals have encouraged clients to pursue self-help and worked with them and their groups in formulating integrated plans for rehabilitation and recovery (Ackerman). At the systems level, some staff from mental health agencies have been supportive and helpful to self-help groups; others have shown resistance and rejection, frequently based on fears and distrust. The chapters provide evidence of how unfounded these fears are, however. Not one of the model self-help groups has taken an oppositional stand against medication usage or use of professional mental health services. In fact, most endorse the importance of their members obtaining the necessary treatment they need to stabilize their illness.

Thus, the chapters in this section frame an overall positive picture of the role of consumers as providers within a self-help approach to rehabilitation and support. There is apparently mixed support for such initiatives from mental health and rehabilitation systems. Self-help, however, is neither making nor attempting to make major demands in terms of its impact on the mental health system, nor in obtaining resources from it. Its biggest challenge appears to be human resources to start and maintain groups, material resources initially and on an ongoing basis, and the motivation of group members to continue affiliations and support their group's efforts.

While consumers who do affiliate with self-help groups are enthusiastic about participation and extol their benefits, it is noteworthy that these groups obviously attract only a minority of the mental health system's clients. This fact may reflect the stigma consumers themselves attach to mental illness and perhaps their failure to recognize the help consumers can provide to each other.

Chapter 4
The P.S. Project:
Together We Are Living the Miracle
Jackie Scott

The P.S. Project, Inc. was started in August of 1993 with a dream that I had to provide individuals in the mental health system a place in the community where they would feel free to talk about anything. I wanted a group that could be supportive, and also work toward recovery. I knew that recovery would never happen without a few key factors. These factors were the founding base for The P.S. Project support group.

I talked to some of the individuals who were being served at the local mental health center and asked them what they would need to get better. The answers were all about the same no matter how old the individuals were. "I need friends who understand," "I need to know that there is something in the community that I can do without a case manager," "I need to know what 'normal' is." With these factors in mind, I wrote the first grant for what was to become The P.S. Project.

It was a grass roots grant written to Chestnut Ridge Hospital in Morgantown, WV. I received $500 to start a community support group. The idea was to meet every two weeks and talk about what was going on in each others' lives and see if we could help each other. At the first meeting there were two individuals. In the next few months, the group would have anywhere from one to twelve people. There were times when it became very disheartening, while other times it was very rewarding to listen to members make decisions to make changes in their lives.

The first few members selected the name "The P.S. Project" for two reasons. One was that we were providing peer support. The other was that we saw what we were going to do as an add-on to what the local mental health agency was already doing. Like the "P.S." on a letter, we were to be the "P.S." on an individual's life. We also decided we would rather be called clients instead of consumers.

About one month into this project, the group members decided that they wanted to have a way to get in touch with someone who really understood and a person who they could say anything to 24 hours a day. The local mental health center had a 24 hour crisis line, but no one called that number because they were too afraid of being committed. Or sometimes they just wanted to chit-chat with someone about life or what they did that day, and the crisis line would not even deal with these calls. People were told, "Don't call unless you are having a real crisis." The group used what money was remaining from the grant to rent a beeper that stayed on 24 hours a day. Usually, as the Director, I had the beeper, but as other group members learned how to support each other, they all took turns carrying it. Having the beeper made them feel that there was always someone there to talk to.

As the group interacted, activities were suggested that members wanted to do. A majority of the group members did not have the experiences that most people take for granted such as going to the mall or to the park; some had never attended a parade in our own town. We began to see a correlation between the amount of time that an individual spent at the mental health center or in the hospital and the level of their involvement in the community. On this premise, we began to plan a variety of activities. The first concern was to figure out how to raise enough money to do the activities that the group wanted to do. Since we had no credentials and had no connection with the mental health center, we couldn't find conventional funding. So we held bake sales, car washes, and a big yard sale.

Our first activities were small. We went bowling, to the movies, to the local YMCA, and attended whatever community activities were going on. The activities quickly drew more people into the group. Soon the group planned a major trip; they decided that they wanted to go to Sea World in Ohio. This trip would cost about $400 and would take them further away from the mental health center than most had ever been. All of the group members banded together and worked hard to raise the money for the trip. We heard all kinds of remarks from the local mental health center about how we shouldn't take people so far away. We offered to take extra people with us since we had raised so much money, but the case managers never passed the word on to their clients. In the end, ten of us set out at 6 am and headed up to Ohio. It was a day that the group members would remember for a long time to come. And contrary to the belief of some people at the mental health center, everything went great.

The trip to Sea World was a catapult for members to work even harder at making this group go places. More activities and fund raisers were planned. The group also made more of an effort to reach out to other individuals served at the center and in the community. At one point our group reached over 20 active participants.

The next obstacle for the group was the problem of short-term housing and crisis housing. This was a problem faced by most of the people in our group at one time or another. I was living in a two-bedroom apartment with one of the bedrooms being an office. There were times when there were so many people sleeping at my apartment that a person could not walk through it. Our group was also asked by the local mental health center to help when a person was discharged from the hospital and had nowhere to go.

The group decided to take a huge leap of faith in January of 1995. We contacted a man who owned a lot of houses and property and shared with him our idea of having a house that our group members would control. After a lot of looking, we found the perfect house; it was big and located in a quiet neighborhood. We have the capability of assisting up to seven individuals at a time, and have been totally full on three different occasions to date. Two of the residents now have their own apartments and another has returned as the house manager. We also have a resident who has been able to stay there and out of the hospital for the longest period since first becoming ill.

Some of the things available in our home are sharing among the residents, having someone around 24 hours a day, and having available activities. But the most important thing for the residents is that they all know that they have a place that is their own where they can be themselves and have fun. Residents can do about anything that they want as long as things don't get violent. There is a lot of physical contact through hugging, wrestling, and just a caring touch when it is needed.

At this point, our long term goals include obtaining more houses to implement this type of program and also to have a couple of houses where it would just be group members living together and sharing expenses. We would even like to get into apartments. But of course, all of this takes money.

Why This Group was Formed

As a mental health client, there were many times that I needed someone to talk to about feelings of suicide, fear, self-destruction, my hopes and dreams — who I was as a person, not just a mental health client. I found this to be absent in our area. Attempts to get the local mental health center to start a group where people would feel free to share these thoughts were fruitless. I learned that the philosophy was that if it couldn't be billed, it didn't need to exist.

Organizational Structure

Since I was the one who started the group and continue to run the programs, I am the executive director. In this position, I am responsible for overseeing all of the programs that we run, writing grants to secure future funding, speaking to organizations about the project, dealing with the financial aspects of the organization, and being accountable to the Board of Directors. In the last few months the project has gotten so large that I have a volunteer assistant director who organizes and oversees most of the activities, and a house manager who takes care of the daily running of the house. Both of these individuals are currently mental health clients.

Last year a Board of Directors was formed to oversee the operations of The P.S. Project. This board is made up of six individuals who are mental health clients, three mental health professionals, and one housing specialist. We are actively seeking both a lawyer and an accountant to join our board. Our organizational structure is typical of a non-profit organization: the Board of Directors, followed by the executive director, assistant director, other staff, and members.

Membership

The P.S. Project has a policy of open membership; anyone who is experiencing any type of emotional or psychiatric problem is welcome in the group.

We will also allow people who have a genuine interest in helping individuals with these types of problems to join the group. We do not charge any membership dues, although we encourage members who have the means to contribute to a fund to provide snacks and drinks at the meetings.

Where We Have Obtained Money

Our first grant lasted about six months. When we got to the point where we were involved in a lot of activities, we applied for another grant from Chestnut Ridge Hospital. We received another $250. We used most of that money as a base to raise more money through bake sales and a car wash. Two of the bake sales were held at WalMart. The WalMart Corporation has a program that matches whatever funds are raised at their store. Between the two sales, the group raised almost $400. At this time, we approached our local mental health center and asked them to act as a fiscal agent for our group since they had 501(c) (3) status. With a little negotiating, the center agreed. We began writing various grants to different organizations; unfortunately since the whole idea of consumer-run programs was so new, we could not get accepted for funding. A local foundation, Parkersburg Area Community Foundation, did eventually give us a grant for $600 that was administered through the mental health center. We used this grant to pay for more activities, emergency medications and food, and transportation expenses. Soon after this, we received a grant from the state Office of Behavioral Health Services. Again this was through the mental health center. This grant was used for more activities, copying expenses, the cost of purchasing our beeper, and in the end, to pay the first month's rent for the house. Just before moving into our house, we got our own 501(c) (3) status from the IRS. When we moved into the house, the Salvation Army donated all of the bed frames and boxsprings for the residents. In February, we received a donation from a furniture store of an almost new couch and love seat. Since we did not have much furniture, this was a great help. In May, we received a grant for $3000 to install carpet in the house. The carpet company actually installed carpet of much better quality than what we could purchase through the grant. Also in May, we received another grant from Parkersburg Community Foundation for $2000 to buy furniture and other household items that we needed.

Our latest grant was from the U.S. Department of Housing and Urban Development in the amount of $88,200 which will pay 75% of our operating expenses for two years and 50% in the third year. This will be the first time in the program that we will have paid staff, as salaries for the executive director, a house manager, and other part time staff are included in the funding. All staff will be former or present mental health clients.

In addition to the grants that we have received, each of the residents are encouraged to pay $300 a month rent. We have had some individuals who were unable to pay anything or who could only pay a reduced rent. We are the only housing program in our area that will allow residents to pay what they can afford.

What People in the Program Can Expect

When individuals are referred to the group, either from the mental health center, state hospital, or through self-referral, they are offered the opportunity to be involved in all of the different activities that we do. This includes local activities such as parades, homecomings, festivals, and trips to places in the community. In exchange for helping in fundraising activities, they can go bowling, to the movies, to car races, and other fee-based activities. The biggest trip this year will be a trip to King's Island which will occur in August. Group members will have to raise about $600 for this trip and they are already well on their way.

In addition to the activities, an individual can expect to be involved in a group that will support them, be available just to talk, or to get together just for friendship. As a member in the group, they have access to the 24-hour beeper, and access to the house. Each member is a valuable part of the group and they know that their voice counts; this helps each of them to feel empowered. The group is also an educational experience for each member as they learn their rights, new coping skills, and life possibilities.

When an individual is referred to the housing program, they can expect their own space that will be respected and private. As a part of their rent, they are provided food, personal hygiene products, laundry facilities, and transportation. In cases of emergency when an individual does not have a medical card, we will purchase medications or help with other bills. When someone is in the program and goes into the hospital, they are always allowed to return to the home as long as they were not violent before entering the hospital.

Meeting the basic needs of group members is very important, but equally important in our program is how to meet their emotional needs. Each of our members can expect to have someone to talk to any time of the day or night, a caring shoulder to cry on, a hug if they need it, and crisis intervention if necessary. We require a meeting with the case manager before a prospective resident moves in to check background, but that is not the only factor that is taken into account. Instead of meeting preconceived expectations, each individual is greeted by open minded members who want to help them get further ahead in life. We remove a lot of the walls that individuals have faced in past living situations such as fear and a feeling of being alone.

Each resident meets with the Director on a regular basis to talk about any problems that they may be having and how to deal with them. This time is also used if someone needs to be confronted about a particular behavior that they have been displaying. An approach on how to deal with the problem is mutually agreed upon and reviewed at the next meeting. Any interventions that are undertaken at the house are discussed with the individual's case manager. Each case manager is also asked to actively suggest ideas for assisting each resident.

Other Programs That are Accessed

All of the individuals that we work with are encouraged to make going back to work one of their long-term goals. To assist with that goal, we work with the Department of Rehabilitation Services, the Social Security Office, and even employers if needed. Some of our members are now working on P.A.S.S. Programs arranged through Social Security. Several are in college working on degrees in different fields. We encourage members who need more pre-employment skills to become involved in the day programs at the mental health center. Those who don't have a high school diploma are encouraged to work toward their GED, and possibly some type of vocational training.

Advantages of Peer Support Programs

There are many advantages to a peer support group such as ours. Not only is the quality of life improved for the members, but the time demand and services needed from the mental health center are greatly reduced. Members are able to assist each other when they just need to talk, or when one of them needs to access a community resource and they don't know where to turn. Also by sharing the experiences that they have had, they are able to find new ways of dealing with little problems in life.

Because the members have a lot of daily contact with each other, they can tell when someone is beginning to have a crisis. With early intervention, many major crises are reduced or even eliminated all together. Members are available to offer support any time of the day or night, and they understand how hard weekends and holidays can be on a person who is alone. Having activities that members plan for the holidays cuts down on the crises that tend to happen at these times.

Having friends outside of the professionals at the mental health center, lets the members know that they don't need to depend solely on their case managers. The dependency that develops after years of being in the system makes it almost impossible to break away from the center. People feel that if they don't need mental health services anymore they can lose their only "friend." By showing them that they can have other friends, and how to make a success of those friendships, the individuals are less fearful of getting well. As we all know, having fun is a big part of what makes life worth living; and activities done with a friend are a lot more fun than the activities they could do with a case manager.

Honesty is an important part of recovery, but what happens when someone is afraid to share things that they are thinking or doing with a professional? In our group we cannot count the number of times that we have heard, "I can't believe you think that too." Having an environment where people can be open and honest about what they feel and knowing that no one is there to judge them, helps them to be much more honest about what is going on. Once they feel comfortable enough to talk about what is going on, they usually will share these thoughts or actions with their therapist.

Having a variety of activities in which members can become involved at different levels, gives them more reason to remain in the community and out of the hospital. By being active in the community, members feel more a part of the world around them. This helps avoid the feelings of loneliness and isolation that many individuals have had to face. The group focuses on activities where members have a good chance of achieving success. The group has been involved for two years in the American Cancer Society's Relay for Life and has won awards both years. Members are also developing interests and finding activities that they did not even know they would like, such as bowling, swimming, or camping. By working together as a group to raise the money, many more of these activities are available.

Disadvantages of a Peer Support Program

As with any program there are some disadvantages. The nice thing about the disadvantages that we found is that they can either be easily dealt with or even avoided altogether with the right steps. One of the disadvantages is burnout on the part of the main people running the program. When this program was first started, I was the only one who was doing the supporting, the fund raising, etc. As the group got larger, some of this let up; although when we got the house, the pattern repeated itself until more members again got involved. This is avoidable by having more people prepared in the beginning to be able to help others or for the mental health center to assist with the support of the key people in the program. When there are only a few people providing the major part of the support 24 hours a day, there is little "time off." In the mental health field, it is important to have time away to re-group, to be able to continue to provide the best possible services. By having more people prepared to step in to help, this problem can be managed.

Non-acceptance by mental health professionals is the biggest problem a peer group can face. Not only can it slow the growth of the members' self-esteem, but it can cause confusion by preventing good communication. When a mental health center is receptive to the idea of peer groups, and communication is open, members can receive the benefits of both the center and the group. The professionals have valuable information to share with the group and the group has valuable information to share with professionals. And there are times when we may be more available to provide a particular support service for a member than a case manager is.

It is obvious that with cooperation and—by having a joint venture with the local mental health center—a peer group has a much better chance of succeeding. What needs to be decided is exactly what that joint venture should entail. This can be accomplished through meetings between the proposed group and the professionals at the center.

Impact on the Mental Health System

There are different opinions at the local mental health center about our program. Some of the staff are very supportive and have even gone out of their way to help us with a member or problem. Other staff are not quite sure what we are doing and are a little afraid of a group of clients joining together. The worst obstacle has been those who are opposed to what we are trying to do. We have heard comments such as "you are nothing more than a support group," and "we are professionals, you are not." These comments are beginning to change as our group proves itself with the things we are doing. At the rate that we are gaining acceptance, we believe that before long, we will have the acceptance of the mental health community.

As far as the impact on the individuals served by the local mental health center, more of them now know what their rights are, they are involved in more ways with their treatment planning, and they know that there is someone around with whom they can discuss these issues.

We are still trying to get our members involved with the mental health center's Board of Directors and represented on planning committees at the center. At this time, no clients are permitted to be on any of these boards or committees, or to have any input into the center's operations.

Would We Do It All Again?

Given the trials and successes that the group has faced since August 1993, we agree that it has been worth it. The successes far outweigh the trials that we have faced. The pride we feel when we are able to wear a tee shirt or jacket with the group's name on it, or to walk up on a stage as a group when we win first place in a contest cannot be measured. We started as a small group of clients who had a dream; and now we live each day watching that dream and many new ones come true. As a group, we never stop dreaming about what we can do, and now we know that we can do whatever we set our minds and spirits to do. Day after day, we live our motto: Recovery is the miracle of the human spirit. Even our new tee shirts shout our victory with these words: LIVING THE MIRACLE.

We believe that any group of individuals with mental health problems can have the same success that we have had with some hard work and belief in themselves. The more support a group gets from the local mental health center and other consumer groups, the better their chances are; although even without such support success can be realized. Most areas now have a state consumer association that could be a valuable tool in helping to organize a local group such as ours. If a group can't get the support it needs in the beginning, they should keep working and hang in there and eventually it will happen. The most important part is to believe in what you and your group are capable of doing, and never give up.

Jackie Scott is the dreamer, founder, and present executive director of The P.S. Project, Inc.

Chapter 5

My Experience With Bipolar Support Groups
Kathy Brink

The Beginning

When I was first diagnosed as having manic-depression, over six years ago, I found it very beneficial to attend a lithium support group. I drove 50 miles one-way each week for the chance to be with people who understood what I was experiencing and how I was feeling. I believe I continued to attend the lithium support group in Broken Arrow, OK., during the two years I was in Tulsa for treatment and even until last year after I moved back to Bartlesville, but I have no memories to show that I attended regularly. My doctor tells me that I didn't want to go during the time I was in a partial hospitalization program in Tulsa, probably because I was already in various therapy groups all day. However, my doctors insisted that I attend and I guess that eventually, I started to like going because I have continued to attend, to derive benefit, and have recently begun to take a more active role, even to the point of assuming some leadership responsibilities. I do, however, remember that we used to have a yearly picnic/cookout and parties at Halloween and Christmas. I remember that after the meeting some members went out for a coke or coffee but I don't remember ever really saying much or participating very much. But back then I didn't feel that I had much to say except when I was manic and then you couldn't shut me up. I was on a roller coaster ride that my doctors say left them wondering what mood (state) I'd be in on almost an hourly basis. Still today I will swing either real high or real low and then snap out of it after an hour or two or I will reach out to someone — my doctors, mother or a group member and that generally helps avoid a crisis. I usually just get running too fast and take on too much and then crash. But being able to talk with someone who is sympathetic to what I am going through helps me to understand what's happening and I can generally come out of it without much trouble or having to change my medication.

General Experiences

The Broken Arrow group was facilitated by a professional until spring, 1994, when the group was turned over to the members. It was a slow transition and a very difficult one. At first we had no one who was willing to accept the role of facilitator. We finally had one person say he would do it for six months. There were also a lot of concerns about safety and what we would do if someone were psychotic or became violent. We were assured that there would be professionals in the building if such a situation should occur. The group also had some doubts about our ability to handle the situation if someone should start talking about being suicidal. We were afraid that we might say or do the wrong thing and send the person over the edge. As you can tell, there were a lot of fears about taking over control of our own group. I was out of touch with the group from mid-1994 to early 1995. When I checked on them then, I found out that the group was moving in three to four weeks and would not be meeting in the meantime. In their new location they would have a professional facilitator once again. The membership was down and had changed considerably; there were only a few people left that I knew. There also seemed to be a lot of confusion as to whether the group was just moving or disbanding altogether.

In 1991, we had formed our own lithium support group in Bartlesville, OK. It has always been consumer-led and the man who facilitates the group today is the same one who started it. There are very few of the original members left; however, most seemed to have benefited greatly from participating in the group. Some have gone on to finish their college degrees and some are working toward graduate degrees.

In the summer of 1994, I went to Georgia to visit my sister and to help her by watching her two children during the day so she wouldn't have to pay for child care. They were four and seven years old at the time — very active and very spoiled. They got on my nerves quite a bit and I was also having a great amount of difficulty sleeping, which didn't help the situation. Everything combined just made me crankier. After about two weeks, I could feel myself starting to cycle so I sought out a support group for those with manic-depression. It met in Savannah — approximately twenty-five miles from where my sister was living.

Attending the group in Savannah was extremely helpful. First, I was accepted immediately as if I'd been a member of their group for a long time. Second, I was given the opportunity to speak; to tell my story; to tell what was happening; and to tell how I was feeling. And, third, I was listened to and understood. They gave me names and phone numbers of group members that I could call if I felt overwhelmed again. After the meeting, I went out to a restaurant with some of them and talked more. It was strange because I felt so comfortable with them, as if I'd known them all my life and for me this is unusual because it normally takes me a very long time before I trust anyone — let alone a group — enough to share as I did that night.

The Inner Workings of a Group

During all the support group meetings I've attended, either in Bartlesville, Broken Arrow, or Savannah, the facilitator usually starts by asking if anyone has anything pressing they need to talk about or by introducing any new members. If there is not anything, then the facilitator will usually make any announcements or pass out new information. After this, we start going around the room talking about how we've been and what we have been doing since the last time we met. We generally talk about our moods, mood swings, events in our lives causing us stress — good and bad — medications or whatever else we feel we have to talk about. We share where we have come from, how we took control of our lives, and what we do to keep ourselves healthy. Sometimes, we encourage one another to seek professional help or just to use the group as a means of support; for example, calling a group member when we need to talk to someone or just getting together for some human contact — a walk, lunch, or other activity.

One night we chose to focus on a question: What can we do to help our families cope with our illness? We spent about an hour just brainstorming and writing every idea down, without discussion or comment. I felt that was one of the most productive meetings we've ever had. I got the feeling from talking to other group members that they felt the same. Later, we had this list copied and distributed to the group members. Some of the ideas and comments we came up with are:

1. Practice good communication skills.
2. Listen to the advice of families.
3. Accept family members' feelings when they are frustrated — it is justified for them to feel that way.
4. Be sensitive to others' feelings and moods.
5. Don't talk about illness all the time.
6. Take charge of your illness — tell your doctor, therapist and pharmacist what is happening, especially concerning side effects of medications.
7. Take your medication as prescribed and monitor it.
8. Take care of yourself — with proper nutrition, exercise, rest and meditation/relaxation.
9. Avoid things that stress you.
10. Apologize when appropriate.
11. Tell others when it is not their fault that it is not their fault.
12. Tell others that you appreciate their love and care.

My Personal Role

For the last year and a half, I have taken an active role in the lithium support group in Bartlesville. I participate much more during the meetings now than before by telling my personal experiences and how I've coped with or overcome them. I encourage others to speak about what is going on in their lives. We have a phone list and I encourage others to use it to call someone when things start to overwhelm them—to reach out for help. Sometimes it is just a matter of needing someone to talk to who will understand and either just listen or be able to provide encouragement and help in calming down.

I suggested that we put together a group newsletter every two to three months. I was willing to do it as long as the other group members were willing to help supply the material. I received a very negative response. Actually, there really wasn't any response when I spoke to the group about it; so another member and I spoke with a woman who publishes the newsletter for our local chapter of the Alliance for the Mentally Ill (AMI). She agreed to put the members of our support group on her mailing list. About that time, she asked me if I would like to start learning how to do the newsletter. As a result of starting to publish the AMI newsletter, I am also learning how to do computer word processing, which seems to be a prerequisite for almost any type of job. Therefore, I see it as a step toward the possibility of returning to work, if my doctor gives me the go ahead, even on a trial basis.

Not too long ago, instead of having our regular meeting, we decided to attend a lecture on anxiety disorders in Tulsa, OK., about 50 miles away. We did not have a very big turn out but we did come back with information and handouts to share with the rest of the group.

Recently, I suggested that we should have a cookout during our meeting time. I believe that activities such as this bond the group together, perhaps more so than just sitting around talking. There was a favorable response to this idea. At Christmas time, we did bring in snacks and drinks to share while we talked and that was a positive experience.

The Influence of the Group

I decided to speak with several of the members of our support group to get an idea of how the group has influenced their lives and the lives of their families. I asked questions such as: What benefits do you feel you and your family have received as a result of attending this group? What benefits do you think our community has derived as a result of this group's existence? What do you see as your role in this group? Do you feel that attending this group has helped you personally? What keeps you coming back? I asked these particular questions primarily because they were the same questions that I was asking myself. I felt that these questions would require everyone to think and reflect on their personal experience.

The answers I received from the group were mostly consistent with my own responses. It was felt unanimously that the bipolar support group in Bartlesville has been beneficial to each of us. Some of the benefits we received include: support, encouragement, education about manic-depression and its treatment, and advice on how to cope with the illness and deal with problems that arise. We also offer and exchange information about medications such as: what we take; what it is for; how it affects us; and whether or not we feel it has helped us. Generally, the group members see their role as supportive. This is the way I see my role today. I used to be more like a parasite — sitting back and absorbing all I could from other group members — but now I spend more time, in and out of group meetings, encouraging others and supporting others in any way I can. I try to listen without judgement or censorship as well as share similar experiences and how I got through them. One of the main ways that attending this support group has helped me personally is that I don't feel so isolated, like I'm the only one in the world dealing with this illness. It helps me realize that there are other people who experience the highs and the lows that characterize manic-depression or bipolar depression and that a lot of them do not handle stress too well either. Most of the group members feel that they would be a lot worse off—hospitalized more, institutionalized or perhaps even dead—without the support the group provides. I think what keeps me coming back, besides the support and encouragement I still receive, is the thrill I feel when someone else gets stabilized. They are then able, to a certain extent, to take control of their own lives.

My Personal Growth

Maybe all this just shows the personal growth of the past few years that was made possible by the encouragement and support of my mother, and of friends in my lithium support groups and the faith that my two very special doctors showed in me. They taught me to trust not only others but also myself and to believe in myself. I believe that this combined support is what has made it possible for me to stay out of the hospital and to keep the contract I made almost three years ago with my doctors not to attempt suicide or to engage in any self-destructive activity. This may not seem like much to a lot of people, but for someone who started in 1971 on a path of intentional self-destruction (I wanted to die but never told anyone because "good girls" didn't think that way) this is quite an accomplishment. I believe it shows that with the right amount of support and encouragement, as well as self-determination, we can overcome any self-defeating situation.

Acknowledgments

I give credit to these groups and their members for allowing me to rely on myself, accept my illness, take my medicine as prescribed, trust other members of the group and depend less on my psychologist and psychiatrist for support and encouragement. I want to thank all those who have helped make writing this possible, especially my mother, my doctors, my friends — both in and out of the support group; the staff at the hospitals in both Bartlesville and Tulsa and most importantly, my God, who's been with me the whole time, even when I doubted His existence.

Kathryn Brink is a consumer and editor of the newsletter for AMI of Washington County, OK.

Chapter 6

Peer Support for People Challenged by Dual Diagnosis: "Helpful People in Touch"

Kathleen Sciacca

People with dual/multiple diagnoses of mental illness, drug addiction and alcoholism experience the same severity of symptoms from substance disorders as do people who have alcohol and drug dependence but are not severely mentally ill. People who face these disorders and the issues they create often require daily support groups and networks at various stages of recovery. For some, on-going support may be necessary for years. Self-help support programs for people with dual disorders are very effective adjuncts to formal treatment. Such programs help participants attain and maintain recovery from substance abuse and addiction. The consumers who have developed and maintained the program, "Helpful People in Touch," have demonstrated that their programs are effective and beneficial for themselves and for their peers. As a result, they have provided a self-help program that was previously absent from both the mental health and substance abuse systems.

The development of treatment models and treatment programs for people with dual/multiple disorders (Sciacca,1987), has demonstrated that new and special program models are necessary. Correcting services that lack treatment resources for people with dual diagnoses requires a comprehensive approach, integrating mental health and addiction treatment into a single program design (Sciacca,1991). Traditional self-help programs have evolved to address singular, discrete disorders. Traditional twelve-step programs for alcoholism and drug dependence often neglect to address severe mental illness. People who have a severe mental illness often attempt to conceal this when attending such programs. Therefore, a self-help model that included all aspects of a person's symptoms and needs was developed. This program, "Helpful People in Touch," was developed by the participants; therefore, the format and content express what is important to these consumers within the realm of self-help.

This article begins with an overview of the profiles of people who participate in special MICAA (Mentally Ill Chemical Abusers Addicted) programs, in contrast to the profiles of people who participate in traditional addiction treatment services and self-help groups. Some aspects of traditional twelve-step programs will be reviewed, followed by a detailed outline of the development of the consumer-led program "Helpful People in Touch."

Description of Consumer Profiles

The term "Mentally Ill Chemical Abusers and Addicted" or MICAA was introduced by the New York State Commission on Quality of Care (1986). The

Commission's report clearly suggested the acronym MICAA to denote people who had a severe, persistent mental illness that exists independent of, yet is co-occurring with, chemical abuse and/or addiction. Characteristics associated with the MICAA label (Sciacca,1991) include the use of prescribed medication to control symptoms of mental illness; and substance abuse which exacerbates acute psychiatric symptoms and/or diminishes the effectiveness of medication. People who have MICAA generally access services in mental health programs. This term is in contrast to "Chemical Abusing Mentally Ill (CAMI)," which denotes people who have alcohol and/or drug dependence with co-occurring personality disorders (Axis 11, DSM-111) (Solomon, 1982), but do not have a severe mental illness.

The program described in this chapter is designed specifically for people with MICAA, not for people who are CAMI. People who are CAMI are most often appropriate for participation in traditional twelve-step self-help programs.

Traditional Twelve-Step Self-Help Recovery Programs

Traditional self-help programs for alcoholism, such as Alcoholics Anonymous (A.A.), are guided by twelve steps suggested as a program of recovery (A.A.,1976). Subsequent programs for drug addiction have also been developed around these steps and traditions, for example, Narcotics Anonymous (N.A.). The fourth step or tradition that guides A.A. espouses that "Each group should be autonomous except in matters affecting other groups or A.A. as a whole." For this reason, the composition of different groups may be more or less compatible with severe mental illness. For example, although A.A. literature clearly states that prescribed medication is strictly a matter between the participant and his/her physician, some A.A. groups include members who believe in abstinence from all chemicals, prescribed or not. When recommending A.A. meetings to people who take prescribed medication, it is important to advise them that some A.A. members may have such beliefs and, if possible, to locate groups where participants do not hold them.

One traditional A.A. concept that is adverse for MICAA consumers is that of "hitting bottom." In other words, participants must experience severe losses or deterioration in order to perceive that they need help for their addictions. This is not recommended for people who have a severe psychotic illness. Such deterioration is more often a traumatic experience that results in major setbacks in all areas of the person's functioning and stability. A MICAA consumer is best maintained at his/her level of stability, and increments of progress in substance abuse treatment should proceed from that level (Sciacca, 1987,1991).

An alternative to attending A.A. meetings in the community is the development of "institutional meetings." Institutional meetings are held in a variety of mental health settings, and led by an outside A.A. member. They are attended exclusively by consumers at the mental health facility. The success of these meetings depends upon the ability of the leader to modify A.A. steps and traditions and adapt the program to the needs of the participants.

Helpful People in Touch — A Consumer Self-Help Program for People Who Have a Severe Mental Illness and a Substance Disorder

In the treatment model for MICAA, the inclusion of A.A. guest speakers (Sciacca, 1987,1991) who visit groups and tell their stories and answer questions about twelve-step programs, serves as an introduction to A.A.This also serves to educate consumers about treatment approaches for substance disorders. Consumers with a severe mental illness who attend these programs must have an opportunity to discuss their positive and negative experiences with twelve-step programs in a setting that is accepting of all of their symptoms. In some instances, adjustments in one's participation will facilitate a beneficial involvement in a twelve-step program.

In recognition that traditional twelve-step programs are not always compatible or comprehensive for people who have a severe mental illness, the development of a self-help program to meet the needs of the participants was facilitated (Sciacca, 1991). This program was conceptualized to include participants community-wide versus institutional; therefore, it was open to all who wanted to attend.

MICAA program development for dual disorders yielded a community (in New York) where various hospitals, agencies, and community programs were addressing and/or providing treatment services for people with MICAA symptoms. Through the concept of interagency education and training that included consistent program materials and methods (Sciacca, 1990), numerous agencies appointed staff to participate and to develop program initiatives (Sciacca, 1987a). Programs included community residences, clinics, day treatment, shelters, hospital wards, continuing care programs, clubhouse programs, case management, addiction treatment programs, and others. These MICAA treatment programs differed from traditional substance abuse treatment in significant ways (Sciacca, 1991; Sciacca & Thompson,1996). In contrast to some traditional substance abuse programs that usually require consumers to be at treatment readiness that includes acknowledgement of a substance abuse problem and willingness to participate in treatment, MICAA programs began with consumers who were at various levels of readiness including denial of a substance abuse problem and lack of motivation or interest in treatment. Where traditional substance abuse treatment may include confrontational interventions to move consumers along the continuum of acceptance of substance disorders, MICAA treatment evolved with "non-confrontational" interventions in relationship to denial and readiness. MICAA consumers at various points of readiness and motivation along the continuum are free to explore education and information, give and receive support to group members, and decline to self disclose until they are comfortable doing so. This MICAA treatment philosophy readily transitioned into the development of the self-help program.

Discussion with consumers in the various MICAA programs about the potential usefulness of a new self-led, self-help model, produced enthusiastic responses. Consumers liked the idea of taking responsibility for running their own program including leading the groups. As a result, in the latter part of 1988, the plan to develop the program took shape.

An announcement of the intention to begin this program was sent to consumers, families and service providers. The notice clearly stated that the format, content, and philosophies of this program would be developed by the consumers in attendance. The meeting place was the MICAA Training Site, a New York State program which was directed and developed as a resource center for consumers, their families, and providers; other consumer groups such as MICAA-NON (Sciacca, Hatfield, 1995) were also held there. The training site served as a non-treatment oriented milieu. The role of the professional evolves from one of greater to lesser participation. A professional was in attendance throughout the planning stages, and then ceased to attend once the format was developed. The first meeting was held in January, 1989.

Structuring the Planning Meetings and Developing a Format

The meetings were scheduled in the evenings once a week, for one and one-half hours, since an assessment had found that support programs were most needed outside of treatment program hours.

The planning agenda, which took several meetings to cover, included the following:

1. Develop a *Statement of Purpose*: How should a MICAA self-help group be similar to or differ from traditional A.A., N.A.?
2. List *one goal*, activity: What would you like to get out of this group? What are the *common goals among participants*?
3. Determine how group members will *share the responsibility* for work.
4. List *tasks* that will help to achieve goals.
5. Develop *ground rules* for groups and participation.
6. Determine a *name for the group*.

The first meeting had five consumers in attendance. The consumers decided to limit the group size to twelve. A participant volunteered to write the responses on the board. A professional in attendance took the minutes. The group accomplished the statement of purpose and began to work on goals in the first meeting. Minutes were sent to the participants before the next meeting. They were also handed out to seven new participants at the second meeting.

The following are some excerpts from the summary of the first planning meeting:

"Everyone present agreed that the issues and areas they wanted to address were not limited to substance abuse issues. Therefore, this group would be open to any other concerns and issues."

Statement of Purpose. "This group was established to meet the needs of people who have a mental illness and some type of issue with the use of alcohol/drugs. It is meant to help people who have been unable to get help from traditional self-help groups such as A.A. or N.A.. In many ways this group would discuss topics and issues that are unrelated to other self-help groups and substance abuse treatments."

The consumers identified certain aspects of traditional self-help groups that they wanted to include in their group. This included: refreshments, fellowship/support, willingness to actively participate, rotating leadership and other roles, a nice way of ending meetings, and learning about the twelve steps. The decision to use speakers, films and literature for education came out of the experiences some members had in MICAA treatment groups. They also outlined aspects of the A.A. program that they did not want to include: requirements about medications, about attending ninety meetings in ninety days, and about following the twelve steps.

A summary of the **goals** of each member included: open admission to anyone expressing an interest in learning about alcohol/drugs; being helpful to one another; improve communication and overcome inhibitions; learn about the experiences of others; explore one's own issues; and membership and participation in a group.

The second meeting opened with a review of the statement of purpose and goals. These ideas were explored and agreed upon by twelve consumers in attendance, including seven new participants. The group proceeded with discussing one **goal or activity** they personally would like to achieve. Their responses included: improve sobriety, quit smoking, improve mental health, gain clearer insight into drug cravings, learn coping mechanisms for illnesses, transition into the community, deal with stigma, improve self-confidence, and gain more independence.

The members outlined the tasks necessary to achieve their goals. It was agreed that **tasks would be shared and rotated.** An initial list of tasks was developed, and jobs were delegated for the next meeting.

In the third meeting members pared down **the tasks** to nine. The general job categories included: facilitating the meetings; shopping; setting up; cleaning; clerical work, and acquiring materials. Members also voted that two meetings would be the length of time for each position to be held. Leaders would choose the next person to perform the job from the next volunteer who had signed on to that particular job list. If a member did not feel comfortable performing a particular job alone, a "buddy" could accompany that member. A volunteer could sign her/his name to several job lists.

At the fourth meeting members established dues of one dollar per month from each participant for refreshments. They established the job of a treasurer to collect and account for dues. This job was to last for three months, and an assistant treasurer would replace him or her at the end of the appointment.

Item five on the agenda, **ground rules for group participation** was discussed. These included: participate in turn; stay on the topic; maintain touch with reality; exhibit self-control; share in job responsibilities; and refrain from physical violence. If anyone was to become violent for any reason, he or she would no longer be allowed to attend the group.

This was followed by establishing **rules for membership**. It was agreed that if a member missed three meetings, his or her membership would be evaluated for continued participation. Members were required to call if they were unable to attend. Members who did not pay their dues (unless they were in a financial crisis) were not to share in the refreshments.

The last item on the agenda, giving the **group a name**, was also accomplished at this meeting. The suggestion to combine ideas resulted in "Helpful People in Touch (Two Way Street)." As a result of all of the consumers' decisions, "Basic Guidelines for Facilitators" were developed to complement the purposes, goals, content and format of the meetings. Leaders relied upon these guidelines when conducting groups. The role of the leader included structuring participation of all members in discussions and decision making, and ensuring assignments and completion of each member's tasks. Near the close of each meeting, the members would decide the format and content of the next meeting. They would select from the use of reading materials, videos, a discussion topic, an invited speaker, or an open discussion. The decision to adopt "a nice way to end meetings" from the A.A. tradition (the serenity prayer), resulted in ending each meeting by reading aloud from *The Promise of a New Day: A Book of Daily Meditations* (Casey, 1983). The specific passage read was sent to all of the members with the minutes.

At the fifth meeting, co-facilitators were assigned for the next two meetings. The sixth meeting was consumer-led without a professional in attendance.

As agreed upon by both the consumers and training site staff, a staff member was on the premises during meetings (but did not attend the meetings). Staff were available to assist members with requests for materials, mailings, and to handle situations such as occasional attendance by an intoxicated individual.

Some of the ground rules emerged out of the concerns various members had about their ability to handle potential situations. These included behaviors deemed out of control or threatening such as intoxication or violence. Another concern was that of leading a group with a member or members who may be experiencing acute symptoms of their mental illness such as loss of touch with reality. For these and other reasons, the decision to have a staff member on the premises was mutually acceptable. Other ground rules such as speaking in turn, and staying on the topic, were addressed in the Guidelines for Facilitators. Group facilitators were responsible for assuring that each person has a turn to speak about topics, decisions, materials, or other group content. The guidelines also suggest that leaders keep participants on the topic, and bring them back when they have strayed from it.

Consumers took the responsibility of formulating this program very seriously. Each item on the agenda was carefully explored, and decision making included everyone in attendance. This responsibility carried over to the leadership and participation in the consumer led meetings. Consumers were concerned and supportive of one another. They participated in a candid manner and shared their own experiences generously. This led to trust and caring. For example, if a member was absent it was a matter of concern. They also concerned themselves with outreach to new members, and assuring that others in need of their support group would find their way to it. Members encouraged one another to continue to work on their issues, and lent their insight to the matters presented by their peers. Members who led the meetings worked through their personal issues of shyness, self confidence, etc., and focused on the responsibilities of leadership.

Content of Meetings. The format and content of each meeting was agreed upon by members at the previous meeting. An educational meeting might include a video about alcoholism, drug addiction, mental illness, interaction effects of medications with various substances, treatment approaches, or a relevant movie. In dual disorder programs, learning about these topics always goes beyond the information presented to the exploration of the interactions between symptoms of substance disorders and symptoms of mental illness; and interactions between prescribed medications and illicit substances. Written materials might include fact sheets or articles about topics such as depression, cocaine addiction, stress, genetic/family diseases, etc. Members select and highlight the important areas, and may take turns reading the passages, and then discussing them. Some examples of a planned discussion topic include themes such as developing new substance-free social networks; interactions between mental health symptoms and substance abuse relapse; dealing with the stigma of a mental illness and a substance disorder, and so on. In contrast, planning an open discussion meeting does not include a topic; these meetings are open to discussing each individual's issues or concerns without a particular common focus. Meetings that include an invited outside speaker usually need to be planned more than one week ahead and involve scheduling a speaker around a particular topic.

Benefits to Participants

This program demonstrates that MICAA consumers are enthusiastic about taking responsibility for their own self-help program and motivated to assist others. They are eager and competent to provide leadership, support and opportunity to their peers. In effect, they can provide a positive working model of support and education and make improvements in the system's gaps in services for the dually diagnosed. Benefits from participating in this program included personal development inherent in new roles and responsibilities, and an increase in support and stabilization. The benefits from each participant's exploration of his or her dual disorders varied in degree from gaining insight to attaining or maintaining abstinence. Each participant experienced some benefit, regardless of length of participation. Participants gained insight into their addictive disorders and the interactions of their dual disorders through their ability to be candid among their peers; through the support and insight they provided for one another; through the educational materials and topics they selected and explored; and through the peer identity formed among the members. In particular, peer identity is not found in programs that do not address all of the symptoms and experiences of the MICAA consumer. This is not to be underestimated. One of the healing factors of self help programs is peer identification with others who understand each others' symptoms and plights. In "Helpful People in Touch," all symptoms were accepted and explored in a non-judgemental, non-threatening manner, and were understood by everyone. Consumers were not ostracized or stigmatized and therefore could openly identify with their mutual experiences. These opportunities allowed consumers to assist one another in their movement along the continuum to sobriety, stable mental health, and community living.

The initial planning meetings constituted hard work and a lot of thought and decision making. Some members expected to talk about their own situation instead. Others found planning difficult or stressful, but each member met the challange. The majority of the members agreed that it was the planning and decision making that made "Helpful People in Touch" truly their own program. At the end of the planning phase, members exuded personal satisfaction and a sense of ownership of their program.

The presence of a professional in the planning phase appears to benefit this process by freeing up participants to focus exclusively on the decision making process. It also provides a model of leadership and group process that may be adopted or changed by participants. An outside leader at the onset may also foster equality in the "shared" consumer leadership that follows. If a participant were to organize and lead the planning phase, it would be important that he or she not be perceived as the leader of the program, since that may deem the group leaders that follow as subserviant to a primary leader. In this process, the exit of the professional leader removes what may be perceived as a level of leadership. It does not appear to be essential to the development of these programs that a professional leader be included. It does take the initiative of individuals to begin the organization of this process, and to acquire the space, equipment and materials that may be needed.

Some members were enthusiastic about the leadership role and volunteered to co-facilitate meetings early in the process. Group leading and other job responsibilities involved members in new ways. The importance of these responsibilities was unanimously heralded as essential to the program's stability by the members. In effect, the empowerment of developing, running, and sustaining their own program was met by responsibility, personal resources, and caring.

Considerations for Implementing Consumer-Led Self-Help Programs for MICAA

It is recommended that each consumer be referred by a provider. Since the program took place in a non-treatment setting, it was important to have a contact person in the event of an emergency or a crisis. The consumer is not required to be in a treatment program. For example, case management referrals were acceptable.

Strategic announcements for the program and upcoming meetings are important. Announcements sent to the Alliance for the Mentally Ill (AMI) local chapters facilitated consistent notices of upcoming meetings to a broad community of mental health advocates. Listings in self-help clearinghouse newsletters, local newspapers, and mailings to providers and institutions were important and ongoing.

This program was developed in a community where formal MICAA treatment programs had been implemented, and some members were recruited from these programs. This helped facilitate the development of this program in several ways. Those members who had received some formal MICAA treatment had begun to address some of their dual diagnosis issues and had some familiarity with them. The members who had previous MICAA treatment had experienced a non-confrontational, educational model of intervention, this led to the decision to include education in the self help program. Previous knowledge held by some of the members was useful in assisting others who had not addressed their dual disorders. It also facilitated acceptance of other members regardless of where they were along the continuum of readiness or motivation. For example, this group also attracted participants who had a history of adversity to formal treatment, and therefore had not previously attended any kind of programs at all. Such referrals often come from case managers or hospital discharge planners. However, from the beginning, leadership was rotated among members who had prior knowledge of MICAA issues and members who did not.

For participants with some prior MICAA treatment, the format provides new and advanced ways to address dual diagnosis issues, and opportunities for new roles in group participation. Consumers who receive formal treatment elsewhere continue to do so. This program is intended to provide additional support and networking as part of each individual's over-all plan of recovery. The program is an example of a consumer-led adjunct to treatment or to traditional self-help programs, depending upon the situation of the individual. For some members, it is their only involvement in programming. "Helpful People in Touch" provides a positive working program model for support, peer identity, growth and change, for people who have not had this opportunity, and who prefer this program to others available.

Consumer Experiences and Comments

In February 1991, more than two years into this program, four of the core members spoke about their experiences in this program. The members were told that their interviews may become part of a verbal presentation and/or a written article with the use of pseudonyms. Each member gave written consent and the group session was audio taped (Sciacca, 1992). Their comments addressed diverse areas of this process. Some excerpts include:

Don: "I think being a facilitator or co-facilitator or even being called on as a member of the group can help more inhibited types perhaps even function at a higher level. I found the group helped me along because I had a lot of trouble with public speaking, but at one point I was leading the group with maybe eight or nine members. I found it was helpful the way it was structured and it got me over some of my shyness. I didn't feel at ease to talk to large groups. I led it for two or three months I think, and I found that the subjects we'd talk about and the films we saw—it was a good group to go to. I wish that it was run more often and with more people and more films. "

Joe: "I came in when the planning was going on, I felt there were too many rules, too much business. I know most people liked that. After a while, I dropped out because it wasn't fun. I came back for something to do. I liked meeting new people. I find it difficult to lead the group when the people don't know me. I really like staff-run groups; I don't know why I'm that way. I like shopping; I did shopping for at least two or three months. As long as this group is here, I'll still come."

Bob: "When I was facilitator and went to buy cookies it gave me something to look forward to. These people are depending on me for cookies, leading. If I'm not here the group ain't going to go. I got something out of the group. I've seen what I'm doing to myself in the long run, but I'm still doing it. I was brought here for a D.W.I. (driving while intoxicated) referred by a case manager; I came here by myself. I also have a mental problem where I'm taking medication. I'm still drinking; I haven't changed my way. I didn't know I was an alcoholic; now I know I'm an alcoholic. I was very relaxed with the group, even though I was drinking. I was comfortable because they understood my problem. I like leading—not for self-esteem or anything like that. I wanted to try to conduct...if I could help somebody out, I would help somebody out."

Mark: "There were a lot of people when I first came in. Then I left and went into the hospital. I realized that when you're on medication and you drink, it's a lot more serious. I take a drink, it exaggerates everything, alcohol exaggerates everything. Before this group I didn't have any treatment. I got medication from the pharmacy. This is the only place I come to; it's fun. Before I came here I didn't realize it was that much of a problem. Because I have this group, I have something to think about during the week."

Some of the previous members of this "Helpful People in Touch" group have moved on to more traditional self-help programs. Others have moved out of the community, or dropped out of the group for other reasons. This particular group sustained itself for more than three years. A core group of seven members was the stable force, with other members remaining for various lengths of time. New participants were accepted as space allowed.

Challenges Met by This Group

Some of the deterrents to the growth and stability of this program were discussed by the members in 1991. These included change of program space and loss of mailing funds. When the Training Site was closed (due to budgetary cuts), the group was relocated to a clinical setting. Members stated that the clinical setting did not provide the privacy or exclusive use of the kitchen for preparing refreshments, and it was not as pleasing visually as the previous meeting place. This change interfered with job responsibilities (refreshments) which as a result were frequently taken on by the professional monitor to avoid conflicts. Members unanimously expressed their agreement that the structure for job responsibilities should not deteriorate. They experienced these responsibilities as a factor that further involved them in the process.

The notices of each meeting which were mailed to numerous professionals, family groups, consumers and members, were discontinued due to loss of funds for postage costs. This was replaced by a limited telephone chain that only included members in attendance, and therefore did not usually generate new members.

The members were clear about the areas they believed required rejuvenation and support. They considered changing the location to a church room or other non-treatment oriented milieu. New ideas included doing personal outreach at existing MICAA treatment programs by visiting and discussing the program. This regrouping (1991a) gave members the opportunity to address the changes that took place. The commitment expressed by the core members to continue their group was clearly evident. The meeting gave them an opportunity to explore the reasons why they were invested in the survival of this program, and to consider solutions to the changes that disrupted the original structure.

Other challenges for members included overcoming internal conflicts among themselves, including personality conflicts. The challenges of new roles and responsibilities did not appear to be as stressful. They were met with enthusiasm for the most part, even though some members needed to overcome personal obstacles. Flexibility is important in sustaining the program. Changes in meeting times such as day of week, time of day, and frequency of meetings may need to be revised to accommodate members or to sustain the continuation of the group. Each of these challenges was met by the members of this group.

Subsequent Groups and Materials

This program has been implemented in other communities and as a part of other program models where MICAA treatment programs have preceded them. In one subsequent program implemented in the clubhouse model of service, additional materials were developed at the request of the members. This included a structured interview to be conducted by two members with each new applicant prior to attendance. These members requested group leadership training that was provided after the planning sessions were completed. This group had the goal of presenting their program to community groups and other programs for purposes of recruitment and education. Guidelines for their presentation were developed along with a video tape of excerpts of the planning sessions and the group leadership training.

Resources Needed for Program Development

The supports necessary to develop a new group include temporary leadership, clerical services, meeting space, and availability of equipment and educational materials. The sustenance of a group requires some motivation and commitment from the original members and continued outreach for new members and group building. Long term sustenance requires motivation of the members, continued outreach, and stable supports. Ideally, if there is an initial provider leader, turned monitor, he or she could remain available to support the efforts necessary for long term sustenance. The meetings, on the other hand, are sustained by the leadership and participation of the members. The resources such as space, funds, and in this group, eventually the monitor, were not in the control of the members. A cohesive group may be able to replace these resources if called upon to do so, but would still need to rely upon the affluence of the community.

In sum, in each of the programs developed thus far, "Helpful People in Touch" has provided a positive example of a consumer-led self-help program for people with dual disorders of severe mental illness, drug addiction and/or alcoholism. Consumers demonstrate both a willingness to take responsibility for developing these groups and the ability to maintain them. They also demonstrate an enthusiasm in their efforts to help others who have dual disorders, and to have their own needs met. As a result, the symptoms of their dual disorders may be greatly improved and stabilized. For some, this program may be the only place to reap these benefits, particularly in communities that lack services and program models for persons with dual diagnosis, and/or rely upon traditional self-help programs.

Consumers and providers are clearly in a position to foster the development of new and similar groups, and thereby provide opportunities for growth and support to many people who may benefit.

References

Alcoholics Anonymous (1976). New York, NY: A.A. World Services.

Casey, K., and Vanceburg, M. (1983). *The promise of a new day.* Harper Hazelden,1983.

DSM III R, *Diagnostic and statistical manual of mental disorders* (1987 rev. 3rd ed.) Washington, DC: American Psychiatric Association.

Rogers, J.A. (n.d.). How to start a self-help/advocacy group. Unpublished paper.

Sciacca, K. (1987, July). New initiatives in the treatment of the chronic patient with alcohol/substance abuse problems. *The Information Exchange TIE Lines,* Vol. IV, No.3., pp. 5-6.

Sciacca, K (1987a). Alcohol/aubstance abuse programs at New York State Psychiatric Centers develop and expand. *This Month in Mental Health,* New York State Office of Mental Health Publication, Vol.10, No.2., pp. 6.

Sciacca, K. (1990) *The MIDAA service manual: A step by step guide to program development and services for persons who have dual/multiple disorders.* New York, NY: Sciacca Comprehensive Service Development for MIDAA.

Sciacca, K. (1991). *An integrated treatment approach for severely mentally ill individuals with substance disorders.* New directions in mental health, series #50, Minkoff and Drake (ed.). San Francisco, CA: Jossey-Bass.

Sciacca, K. (1992). Unpublished conference address, *The person with mental illness and substance abuse.* Philadelphia, PA: University Medical College of Pennsylvania,

Sciacca, K., Hatfield,A.B.,(1995) *The family and the dually diagnosed patient double jeopardy: Chronic mental illness and substance use disorders,* ed. Lehman & Dixon, Gordon and Breach Publishers, pp.193-209.

Sciacca,K., Thompson, C.M., (1996) Program development and integrated treatment for dual diagnosis: mental illness, drug addiction and alcoholism, MIDAA In press, *The Journal of Mental Health Administration.*

Solomon, J. (1982). Alcoholism and affective disorders. In J. Solomon (Ed.), *Alcoholism and clinical psychiatry.* New York, NY: Plenum Medical Books. pp.81-85.

Kathleen Sciacca, M.A., is the executive director of Sciacca Comprehensive Service Development for MIDAA in N.Y.C. She is former director of the MICAA Training Site for the New York State Office of Mental Health.

Chapter 7
Schizophrenics Anonymous and Psychiatric Rehabilitation
John P.

Self-help groups have been in existence since the founding of Alcoholics Anonymous in 1935 and Recovery, Inc., a few years later. There are now self-help groups for almost every major ailment or life predicament. Although Recovery, Inc. exists for people with mental illness in general, to date there has been no self-help group specifically for people with schizophrenia that has reached national proportions, that is, with meetings in all major cities and in all fifty states.

The question has arisen as to whether people with schizophrenia are capable of managing or benefiting from their own self-help group meetings. Perhaps schizophrenics are too disruptive and unruly to have their own meetings; or too disorganized; or too irresponsible; or can't sit still; or don't care enough about their own recovery; or don't care about the recovery of others enough to apply the concept of mutual support. However, when one analyzes the ten years' experience of Schizophrenics Anonymous, it becomes clear that these questions and claims are off target. Schizophrenics Anonymous (S.A.), founded in the Detroit area in 1985, has demonstrated that people with schizophrenia can manage their own self-help group meetings and that members can grow during the period that they attend these meetings. To a large degree, there is an element of psychiatric rehabilitation involved in this process, although S.A. does not act as an organization providing professional services. Rather, it relies on self-help support within the group in conjunction with outside professional help.

Background of Schizophrenics Anonymous

Schizophrenics Anonymous is a self-help support group resembling Alcoholics Anonymous in that there are weekly meetings for members, steps for recovery, a program philosophy, and mutual support between meetings. According to its mission statement, S.A. strives:

> "...to add the element of self-help support to the recovery process of people suffering from schizophrenia. We hope that this will contribute to the sense of well-being of S.A. members and help them cope with the difficulties imposed by their illness."

Although S.A. can make no guarantees regarding any uplifting of members' well-being (as hoped for in its mission statement), most members who attend meetings regularly and try to apply the ideas in the program seem to do better and feel better over time. This may partially be the result of three key features that the program offers: fellowship, good information, and a recommended pathway for recovery.

Fellowship is key in that many members have limited opportunities to make friendships. S.A. encourages bonding between its members. Relationships often follow. The role of good information about schizophrenia is handled by various publications of S.A.: a one page Schizophrenia Fact Sheet; the monthly *Schizophrenia Update*, providing the latest information about the illness; and items found in the national newsletter, *The S.A. Forum*. Also, one can discover a lot about schizophrenia by just listening to members describe their experiences with the illness.

What we call our pathway for recovery is the guts of the S.A. program. It includes our group philosophy, six steps for recovery, and a variety of guiding principles regarding recovery from schizophrenia. These aspects of recovery are summarized in written form in the S.A. Blue Booklet, a 32-page publication officially titled *Schizophrenics Anonymous — A Self-Help Support Group*. The ideas expressed in the Blue Booklet are intended as a pathway to recovery, a sort of down-to-earth compendium of insights into the S.A. program. In fact, a university professor who reviewed the booklet said that it was full of practical wisdom. (The Blue Booklet has been translated into Japanese and Portuguese and has been required reading in a social work course at the University of Michigan.)

Organization of S.A.

Schizophrenics Anonymous is not an incorporated organization and there is no intent on the part of central S.A. leaders to incorporate, because organizational matters could become too cumbersome and take attention away from recovery activities. The organizational function of central S.A. is administered through the Mental Health Association in Michigan, which has enabled Schizophrenics Anonymous to develop to its present level. Regarding group autonomy, it could be said that S.A. members govern the S.A. program, while the Mental Health Association governs its administration. (For a more detailed description of these issues see John P., 1995.)

There are dozens of S.A. groups in existence in Michigan and many more across the United States. These groups operate with little centralized supervision, although central S.A. does keep contact with local groups by way of the monthly *Group Leaders Circular* newsletter. Some personal contact is also made between central S.A. and various group leaders.

S.A. Groups

The S.A. meetings are a function of the individual S.A. group, which meets at a set time and place, usually each week. The group is headed by an S.A. group leader, a member with the illness who chairs the meeting and performs organizational tasks for the group. (Some S.A. meetings are chaired by facilitators, who are mental health professionals willing to carry on the meeting until a group leader with the illness can be found.)

Much of the essential types of information a group leader would need to know is found in the *S.A. Group Leader's Manual.* These include how to form an S.A. group and how to conduct an S.A. meeting. The Mental Health Association in Michigan serves as the doorway to persons wishing to form a group, providing them with a beginners packet of reading material and telephone liaison help as well. (I am currently employed, part-time and by contract, with the Mental Health Association, to write S.A. literature and to do some organizational work for S.A.)

S.A. and the Mental Health System

As discussed previously, S.A. is integrally related to the Mental Health Association in Michigan. S.A. has also maintained close relationships and has received warm endorsements from the Alliance for the Mentally Ill of Michigan, the Michigan Psychiatric Society, the director of the Michigan Department of Mental Health, and Thomas Powell, Ph.D., a professor at the University of Michigan who specializes in the study of self-help groups. Endorsements have also been received from Dr. E. Fuller Torrey and the director of the Center for Mental Health Services in the federal government's Department of Health and Human Services.

In recent years, S.A. has worked closely with numerous community mental health agencies in establishing S.A. meetings in their geographic areas. These CMH agencies tend to be supportive of Schizophrenics Anonymous and fledgling S.A. groups.

Our experience in Michigan is that governmental agencies and organizations representing families and professionals are willing to work closely with Schizophrenics Anonymous when discussing the topic of self-help recovery for people with schizophrenia. It is not unusual for S.A. group leaders to be called on to represent persons with mental illness in policy oriented committees, although not specifically as representatives of S.A.

Observations of Three S.A. Groups

There is much variation between individual S.A. groups. Over the years, I have been active in three different ones: (1) the Southfield home group meeting; (2) the state hospital group in Pontiac, MI; and (3) Pontiac's first community-based group.

Below is a summary of some of the observations of how group members moved toward growth in these three groups. Emphasis will be placed on the growth that I witnessed while members attended the meetings, as well as what members stated about their perceptions of doing better and feeling better. This will deal with the matter of psychiatric rehabilitation — loosely defined.

References to individuals will be made along with generalities about groups of people within the meetings.

Southfield Home Group Meeting

The first S.A. group was founded in Southfield in 1985 by Joanne Verbanic. Joanne led this group for nine years and it has given us some idea of how effectively an S.A. group can work under given circumstances. The following generalities can be made about the Southfield group over the span of its existence:

- Approximately 15-20 people attended these meetings, which lasted about two hours.
- Members of this original meeting went on to form six other groups throughout the metro Detroit area and the core of central S.A. leadership was formed from members of this group.
- The meetings were characterized by congenial behavior; rarely did disagreements turn into arguments, and expressions of hostility were rare.
- Regulars tended to be proactive and interested in forming friendships and engaging in recovery-oriented behaviors, such as work (paid or volunteer), school, church activities, avocations and the like. Many graduated to more independent living situations. Although hospitalizations were not stigmatized, most regular members stayed out of the hospital for long periods of time.
- As in most self-help groups, most people who attended the group for the first time did not return to become regulars.
- Shy members were well accepted and many became more vocal and expressive as they became more familiar.

The Southfield group had numerous social activities, and although the group does not now meet, its core of members are still friends and keep in contact.

Pontiac's Community-Based Group

Pontiac's community group, founded in 1988, met at a local church for roughly five years. It was slow in attracting membership, but eventually had eight regulars, with five or six attending each meeting.

Although all of the members of this group lived on psychiatric disabilities checks, the value of work was affirmed. As a result, virtually all of its members were engaged in volunteer work.

Paula, a co-founder, house-sat and cared for an elderly woman with Alzheimer's disease, which enabled the woman's daughter to maintain employment and earn an income to keep the household afloat. Janet, 62, lived in a group home and had worked many years in a sheltered workshop. Although she did not own a car, she got on a bus twice a week to reach the public library, where she volunteered with various tasks in circulation. Paul's family owned a small tractor. During the winter he shoveled snow for over ten homes in his neighborhood and cut lawns in the summer, usually for no fee. Gary volunteered at a drop-in center serving persons with mental illness and won a volunteer-of-the-month award there. Joanne volunteered at a local hospital. Nancy offered her services at a clothes closet for the disadvantaged, and Linda helped out at her church.

With only a few exceptions, members of this group stayed out of the psychiatric hospital during their involvement with S.A. Ironically, it was me — the group leader — who reported psychiatric symptoms most often, during my psychotic depressions in 1992.

Although lasting friendships external to the group did not develop, during the period that the group met, members developed fondness for each other, and reported that they missed members who could not attend on given weeks.

Pontiac's State Hospital Group

The S.A. group in Pontiac's state psychiatric hospital was founded in 1987 and continued for five years. Whereas in the beginning years it was open to all patients in the hospital who had passes (between 15 and 20 attended), in its last years it focused on approximately 15 patients from a back ward of the hospital, most of whom had been patients there for a very long time. Pontiac's state hospital group could be characterized by the following general statements:

When the meetings were first established they were chaotic, unlike any of our meetings in the community. Within a year, the meetings became orderly enough to be called working S.A. meetings. Confidentiality held firm. Members could talk about the most personal things and there were no repercussions.

Although for back ward patients, attendance was required for the opening of the meeting, patients were allowed to go to the cafeteria as they desired. However, after short rest periods, most of them returned to the S.A. meeting to participate in some capacity.

It became clear that for these patient-members, discharge from the hospital or acquisition of hospital privileges were of paramount concern. The S.A. meeting became a place for discussing strategies to reduce behaviors that would lead to cancellation of privileges or delay of hospital release. It also became a place where patient-members could express the fear and anger content of their symptoms and the frustrations of their situation. Patients reported fewer and fewer instances of restraint and seclusion practices over the course of the group's existence.

Although the back ward patients were long-term patients, most of them had gained release by the end of the group's existence. We like to believe that S.A. was a contributing factor in this, although we realize that we were not the deciding factor.

Sometimes S.A. is characterized as a group designed only for "high-functioning" people with schizophrenia. The experience of this state hospital group showed that the program can be adapted for some of the people at lesser functioning levels.

My Personal Experience with S.A — John's Story

How does S.A. impact on the lives of its individual members? There is a lot of variation, of course. This section of the article is about my own experiences with S.A. and is an attempt to personalize some of the benefits of S.A.

Self-help groups often publish this sort of testimonial to their programs in their literature. S.A. has published over fifteen of these stories so far. In general, these S.A. stories lavish less praise on the S.A. program than, for instance, the corresponding stories in Alcoholics Anonymous. The S.A. stories nevertheless affirm Schizophrenics Anonymous as an endearing program in the members' lives. For example, my story simply serves as an example of how the program can work.

My name is John and I feel that S.A. has been very helpful to me. It has, in fact, been crucial in my journey toward recovery. I tell friends in the program that S.A. has saved my life twice. That is, I gained a circle of valuable friends and have found life worth living during two different periods when I was immobilized by psychotic depressions. S.A. has made the struggle more meaningful in that the program has channeled emotional pain into opportunities to grow and gain insight. S.A. is a program where insights won through hardships and adversity are highly valued. (I know I still have much growing to do.)

My first saving period within S.A. was about eight years ago when I first went on disability payments — after previously earning several college degrees and holding jobs for more than twenty years. I was quite devastated at being blown out of the job market by a brain disorder that I really did not understand. Also, by that time, most of my old gang of friends from pre-illness days had exited from my life, leaving me practically friendless. My life resembled a meandering river seeming to go nowhere.

I joined Schizophrenics Anonymous in 1987. Within a year, I had plenty of work to do, made many buddies and friends, and regained a sense of purpose in my life. Of course, there were other factors involved in this swift turnaround: family support, a beneficial day hospital stay, involvement in Twelve Step groups, and others. But the strongest movement toward recovery began through attending my first S.A. meeting in February of 1987.

In S.A. jargon, we distinguish between internal functioning and external functioning when discerning whether any one of us is doing better. My internal functioning, within S.A., was helped a lot by Joanne Verbanic, founder of S.A. and leader of the first S.A. group in Southfield, Michigan. She remembered my name after my first S.A. meeting. This meeting was characterized by feelings of comfort that twenty people with schizophrenia could sit around a large table, conduct themselves politely, and share their experiences, feelings, and hopes meaningfully. I left those early meetings with the feeling that people with schizophrenia could survive and function in the world, even those who were living on disability checks as I was. Joanne served as an example of an individual with schizophrenia who was making it.

Joanne helped me by providing the opportunity to become involved in volunteer work for the program. My first tasks were making coffee during meetings and clean-up afterward. After applying myself to these tasks, an opportunity to co-lead an S.A. group at a local state psychiatric hospital arose and I took it. When the staff at the state hospital affirmed that these hospital meetings were working quite well, the other co-leader and I formed a group in the community with the help of our community mental health program. I felt better over time as I saw other people seem to grow at our meetings. I felt good about myself by contributing something to the community and to others. Also, I began working on S.A. literature, particularly the Blue Booklet.

My external functioning, outside of S.A., improved at a similar pace through volunteer work. I did computer input work for a religious retreat center (where I learned not to fear the computer); I joined the staff of a weekly newspaper in my home town (where I learned I could publish articles every week for five years and still stay out of trouble); and I began working on a patient resource booklet at my local community mental health agency (where I learned that it was still possible for me to work in a white collar environment under flexible conditions). This kind of work was encouraged by Schizophrenics Anonymous, where growth is always applauded.

Also, through my S.A.-related activities I began building the circle of friends that I now have. S.A. folks — like Joanne, Larry, David, and Paula — are precious in my life, and help me feel better. After being plagued with frequent psychiatric hospitalizations in previous years, I stayed out of the hospital for four straight years, largely due to S.A. I was seeing positive results.

However, for reasons I'm not sure of, I broke down again in 1992. I was hit by severe psychotic depressions and had three hospitalizations during that year. This depressed period lingered on for almost two years. Often during this period I felt that the support network within S.A. was not developed well enough to give me the help I wanted or needed. Perhaps I expected too much. (People close to me tell me that I can be demanding, testy, and judgmental.)

But S.A. did come through and saved me once again. I began working on a Choose Life Project, under the auspices of Schizophrenics Anonymous, which I hoped would help me to experience more inner peace, joy, and fortitude. For whatever reason, working on this project has given me a lot of relief from depression.

In conclusion, I'm grateful to S.A. for saving my life twice, giving me meaningful work to do, and giving me a loving circle of friends.

Evaluation Research on S.A.

As with most self-help group programs, Schizophrenics Anonymous does not have a body of social science research to prove its effectiveness. Nevertheless, people with schizophrenia continue to come to S.A. meetings, requests for leaders to lead new S.A. groups continue to grow, and S.A. members continue to report doing better and feeling better at S.A. meetings. Fortunately, a research study (although limited) has been done on S.A.; one conducted by the University of Michigan's Center for Self-Help Research and Knowledge Dissemination.

Deborah Salem, Ph.D., Larry Gant, Ph.D., and their colleagues from the University of Michigan conducted a qualitative/quantitative case study on Schizophrenics Anonymous in the early 1990's. The study involved experienced S.A. leaders conducting a series of meetings in four different group homes in the Detroit area. Among the purposes of the study were to see if S.A. groups would work in group homes and to identify why some of the groups might work and others might not.

After S.A. leaders ran six introductory meetings in each of the four group homes, the researchers determined by their own criteria that two of the group homes had had a working series of meetings, one was non-working, and one was mixed, having the characteristics of both working and non-working meetings.

The residents at the two working groups seemed to see a lot of value in the introductory meetings. In fact, nearly 80 percent of these residents expressed an interest in continued participation with S.A. once the introductory meeting series was over. In evaluating the meetings, the residents of the working groups expressed positive attitudes toward the S.A. meetings, as evidenced in the following items.

- S.A. meetings were helpful (100% and 88% agreed)
- Meetings will help them cope better with illness (80% and 75% agreed)
- Was helpful to talk in group (100% and 88% agreed)

- Was helpful to hear others (100% and 100% agreed)
- Learned about schizophrenia (80% and 75% agreed)
- Better understanding of the problems of the illness (80% and 63% agreed)
- Learned about the purpose of medications (60% and 75% agreed)

Although the sample size of the two groups was small (combined n = 13) and it is not possible to make global generalizations based on the above responses, these data resemble what regular members of S.A. groups in the community say about their experiences in Schizophrenics Anonymous.

The University of Michigan's study goes to great length in discussing why two of the four experimental groups worked and two did not. For a discussion of this topic see Salem, et al, (1995) or John P. (1995).

Replicating S.A. in Other Places

As stated at the beginning of this article, there is no national self-help group specifically for people with schizophrenia. Those of us at the center of Schizophrenics Anonymous hope that our model for such a group would be considered for establishment in the fifty states.

We know that S.A. can grow quickly under the proper conditions. To some extent, S.A. has already been replicated. Between 1985 and 1987 there was one S.A. group in existence — the Southfield home group. By 1991, this number had grown to 12 groups in the metro Detroit area. Now in 1995, after three additional years of organizing, there are 12 more S.A. groups in Michigan outside of the Detroit area. In all, there are 24 S.A. groups in Michigan and 36 groups in other states. Also, there is one group in Canada and two groups about to begin in Brazil.

Schizophrenics Anonymous could reach all fifty states and most major cities by working closely with existing organizations. For instance, appropriate efforts could be made to establish S.A. groups with the help of the over 400 affiliates of the National Mental Health Association across the country. Similar efforts could be made at Fountainhouse-model clubhouses in each state.

In the coming years, we need to further explore appropriate means of establishing S.A. groups independently in the community, in state psychiatric hospitals, and in drop-in centers. The above tasks should give S.A. leaders enough to do well into the next century.

Basically, there are five requisites to set up an S.A. group. These are: (1) a capable and caring group leader; (2) a place for the S.A. group to meet; (3) a modest dollar amount to cover the cost of S.A. literature; (4) means for publicizing meetings; and (5) staff support (i.e., if working with a hospital, day program, or a community mental health program).

The role of the leader is perhaps the pivotal role in a successful S.A. group. Successful groups usually have a leader who is strong enough to survive the difficulties in getting the group firmly established. This often involves persistence during the period of attracting regular members to the meetings. Later, personal strength is needed to ease leader burnout that often comes from the demands of leading a weekly group.

The Mental Health Association in Michigan may be contacted in order to secure literature and videos, as well as technical assistance for those who wish to form an S.A. group. This agency has had much experience in helping to establish S.A. groups and may be able to put a prospective S.A. group leader in touch with experienced S.A. group leaders for advisory purposes.

To summarize, S.A. groups can sprout up wherever there are people with schizophrenia and the five requisite conditions are met. It seems that if the need is there, S.A. will become more available to people with schizophrenia. The need for S.A. will probably exist wherever people with schizophrenia want fellowship, good information about their illness, and a pathway toward recovery.

Conclusions

The work of Schizophrenics Anonymous over the past ten years has established that people with schizophrenia can manage their own self-help group meetings and that they can benefit from them. We hope that this puts to rest any claim that people with schizophrenia are too unruly to have their own self-help meetings. We know that people with schizophrenia can become regular attendees of S.A. meetings and can grow under their influence. We know that group leaders report seeing members make strides toward recovery while coming to meetings. Simply put: regular members seem to do better and feel better.

While regular members of S.A. do benefit in personal growth, most people with the illness don't become regular members of S.A. — even those who are aware of the program's existence and have transportation. The program readily admits that S.A. isn't for everybody, but one can't help but wonder why some people stay away and what might be done to reach them. In the future, it will be a challenge to address this situation.

We in S.A. leadership have identified three weaknesses and have framed them into statements of what we need to do differently in the coming years. They represent activities that we hope to pursue.

1. **We need to put more energy into leadership development.** Numerous long-standing S.A. groups have folded because they did not develop leadership of members to take over once the original leader stepped down. Also, we need to integrate more members into central S.A. leadership. Our group in Dayton, Ohio, is already experimenting with an S.A. leadership seminar and has six members attending.

2. **We need to encourage more mutual support between meetings.** Members often feel isolated between the weekly meetings. Methods of encouraging members to support each other at such times need to be explored. To a large extent, mutual support turned into friendships in the Southfield meeting. Can this be replicated elsewhere?

3. **We need to integrate support between group leaders.** We need to develop the means by which group leaders can be of more support to each other. Many report feeling isolated. Perhaps this can be done through increased personal contact between group leaders, by phone and letters. This has worked well in formal group liaison efforts in the past few years. Can it work in a more expanded version?

The three action steps above would make for stronger groups and happier S.A. members. The leaders of S.A. and the Mental Health Association in Michigan are committed to making S.A. more available to the many people with schizophrenia who want it and who can be helped by it.

References

John P. (1992). *Schizophrenics Anonymous. Schizophrenia—Handbook for clinical care.* Judy A. Malone (ed.) Thorofare, NJ: SLACK Inc.

John P. (1995). *Adapting self-help group concepts for schizophrenia: Ten years experience of Schizophrenics Anonymous.* Southfield, MI: Schizophrenics Anonymous.

Salem, D.A. (1991) *Self-help in group homes: A collaborative case study.* Paper presented at the third biennial conference on Community Research and Action, Tempe, AZ.

Salem, D.A. & Gant, L.M. (1990). *Developing and implementing a self-help intervention: The collaborative process.* Paper presented at the annual convention of the American Psychological Association, Boston, MA.

Salem, D.A., Gant, L.M., & Campbell, R. (1995). *The introduction of mutual help groups in group homes for the mentally ill: Barriers to participation* (submitted for publication).

Schizophrenics Anonymous (1989). *Schizophrenics Anonymous: A self-help support group.* Southfield, MI: Author.

Schizophrenics Anonymous (1990). *Group leader's manual.* Southfield, MI: Schizophrenics Anonymous.

NOTE: Some of the ideas in this paper appeared originally in S.A. newsletters: *The S.A. Forum* and the *Group Leaders Circular.*

John P. Is a member of Schizophrenics Anonymous and is under contract with the Mental Health Association in Michigan to work on matters related to S.A.

Lawrence P. Ackerman

DISCLAIMER: I am not a Recovery scholar or expert or teacher but rather, I am an average group leader, doing what the other hundreds of group leaders in the U.S., Canada, Puerto Rico, Israel, and the British Isles do every week.

As we say in Recovery, Inc., I am an average nervous person who found that being a Recovery member and group leader is a very necessary part of my ongoing recovery. To many who come to Recovery meetings, this distinction between nervous personhood and (for example) paranoid schizophrenic (my own diagnosis) seems silly. But in our scheme of things, we see that a diagnosis is not a prognosis and averageness is less stigmatizing than words and phrases which emphasize danger, hopelessness, and exceptionality. This distinction inspires us to reach out toward our averageness, learn what is each person's average, and eliminate the dangerous stigma that still pervades the vocabulary of mental illness.

Abraham A. Low, M.D., Recovery Inc.'s founder, was a Vienna-trained psychiatrist who began the Recovery project in November of 1937 after thirty ex-patients of the Psychiatric Institute of the University of Illinois medical school asked for his help in avoiding the setbacks which seemed an unavoidable part of their mental illnesses. Already a critic of the accepted psychiatric schools of Freud, Jung and Adler, Dr. Low started a program of intense aftercare so revolutionary that he was forced to leave his position at the medical school and was denied access to its facilities and patients.

Dr. Low called his many patients his "dear ones" and became convinced that their suffering was not due to the conflicts of id, ego and superego; stages of sexual development in infants; inferiority complexes; or hidden unconscious drives and collective discomforts. Dr. Low developed a new philosophy of aftercare for mental disease. This philosophy had a definite vocabulary (the Recovery language) for life with mental challenges. He emphasized the central position of the Will as guiding behavior, especially behavior in groups wherein impulses and symptoms could be controlled with sustained effort. He also advocated rigorous training and the importance of positive feedback of the patients to themselves and from the groups in Recovery meetings. Success bred success and post-psychotic individuals improved.

Dr. Low held that nobody must be held responsible for the kind of disease (they have) contracted and he involved his patients' families in his aftercare efforts. For these families he wrote a book called *Peace vs. Power in the Family,* and enlisted their aid in helping him help his patients. He did not blame his patients' families for illness and held lectures for these families and involved them in parties, picnics and many Recovery social events. He did not stigmatize his patients and fought hard against the mass media and popular psychologies of his day. He believed that mental illnesses were biological in origin but not beyond repair. Now in the 1990's, the Decade of the Brain, we are learning that chronic behavioral disorders are linked to neurotransmitters, brain structural and receptor abnormalities and as-of-yet-not-understood metabolism of oxygen, glucose and proteins. And the pop psychologies are as vicious as ever. But Dr. Low's Recovery Method is helpful to us today because we are not slaves to our sex instincts, unconscious drives or our upbringing; we are not even slaves to our brains! Dr. Low taught us that we can choose to bear the discomfort of our sensations, thoughts, feelings and impulses, that we can learn to stop the suggestions of our symptoms and conduct ourselves with dignity as if these features of our mental illness were gone or going. Panics, fears, phobias, angers and apathy, discouragement and fatigue all are subject to control. Delusions, hallucinations and feelings of unreality give in when we stop sabotaging our mental health and follow the prescriptions and directions of our mental health professionals and the practice of our dear Recovery Method to the best of our abilities, acknowledging that the Method is simple, but not easy, and that the science of medicine is still young. We gain self-respect and self-esteem in the knowledge of the Recovery Language, a basic grammar of hope.

Dr. Low set up Recovery, Inc. to be totally self-help before his death in 1954. He wrote the basic texts for his patients to read and study and recorded seventy lectures to be played in future meetings. The Recovery Method is learned not just by reading and study. It is taught by the many examples given at meetings by veteran members and leaders, who share their experiences, their hard won victories over nervous symptoms.

In these examples of Recovery practice, members share, in a structured and disciplined way, how they dealt with a specific life event, which must be about trivialities of everyday life. We do not discuss issues of right and wrong, morals or laws or religious beliefs. These are not trivialities. But our symptoms are trivialities when seen as part of our everyday lives as nervous persons. Trivialities are situations wherein no set rule of life is broken but average people and average nervous people get irritated or upset. A dropped cup of hot coffee may be the occasion for an expletive or an expression of pain but it is nothing to get worked up about. Getting cut off in traffic may be due to a poor driver or a simple mistake made by someone answering their car phone. It is, again, nothing to get worked up about, even though many average drivers do work themselves up. We in Recovery know that for the sake of our mental health we must not work ourselves up into panics and despair. These simple phrases, like "trivialities" and "averageness" are still worth knowing today because in the language of an earlier generation, they express universal truths of behavior management and good mental health.

My involvement in Recovery began in the winter of 1979. I had spent sixteen months as an inpatient at a private Midwestern psychiatric hospital and five months in the day treatment program there. I had put a lot of effort into building a support base away from the hospital and wanted a support group to join. Then one Monday my doctor mentioned Recovery and said they had some interesting ideas for good mental health. I called that afternoon and discovered that there was a group just down the street from the hospital! I went to that evening's meeting and my life was changed.

At the meeting were about a dozen folks led by a middle-aged woman who struck me as very well adjusted and compassionate. She said she was an average nervous person. I asked her whether she thought Recovery could help someone with schizophrenia and she was not put off by my nervousness. She gave me a sense of hope. I had two major impressions from that first meeting: here was the support group I had desired and here was an opportunity for me to grow into leadership and help others with mental illnesses.

My initial impressions were both correct. My use of the Recovery Method in my own personal coping and eventual group leadership so impressed my psychiatrist that he began sending most of his patients to Recovery meetings and at one point had three of his patients as Recovery group leaders. He even prescribed a set number of weeks in Recovery meetings before his patients could stop going. Eventually I got a job at a local research firm and really began to put my Recovery training to the test.

My time on the lab job was very stressful and not just because I was working with wild monkeys. I had three teenaged co-workers who were more interested in smoking marijuana (as I later found out) than in working. They would leave the job and I was left with most of the work, not knowing why. I became very depressed. Finally I gave this problem as an example at Recovery and I received the help I needed.

Now an example has four steps, but these steps are nothing like A.A. steps. The first step is a summary of the situation wherein we have symptoms; in my case the situation was the job. The second step is a summary of the symptoms themselves; for me these were feelings of despair, apathy, and not wanting to go to work. The third step is the labeling of the situation and symptoms using the Recovery language tools, called spotting, in such ideas as averageness, triviality, etc.. "My average is high standards for myself and others." "The extra work is a triviality compared to my peace of mind and mental health." "The teens are sabotaging their job not mine." When they were fired, I looked good to my boss. I was given more responsibility and more money in the long run. The group spotted my symptoms as distressing but not dangerous and average for anyone in my situation and above all they spotted my great need to give myself credit for my own bearing of discomfort and, finally they told me I was to endorse myself over and over again at work. Endorsing myself, giving myself a pat on the back for my efforts on the job, gave me a whole new way of seeing my work. I began to look forward to work and my depression gradually lifted because I made a business of my mental health. My psychiatrist liked the idea so well that he wrote me a prescription with two words on it: ENDORSE YOURSELF! He gave that same prescription to many other patients. The same advice helped me stop smoking and I have not been back to tobacco since 1979!

The fourth step in the example is a brief sharing of what the person would have done in former days. In my pre-Recovery days, I was always wishing or trying to change the situations around me instead of adjusting to them myself. I lost lots of relationships because I was always trying to control my outer environment instead of my inner environment. I had attempted suicide and was very lucky to be alive. Now I live a disciplined life; I have been married for 14 years, and although I still have schizophrenia, I am not discouraged. The Recovery concept works!

As a group leader for nearly 16 years my self esteem is level and continuous. As a group leader I have seen the Recovery concepts work on people with a wide variety of mental health problems. To illustrate, I share two examples from my experiences.

Angie came to Recovery after reading about the group in Ann Landers' column. Angie had been shopping when all of a sudden she felt she couldn't breathe and like she was all closed in so she panicked and hurried from the store. She feared shopping and could not force herself to go.

The group and I suggested that her sensations were distressing but not dangerous. We told her that she could learn not to be afraid by following Recovery ideas like using muscle control whenever her brain preached danger to her. She needed to control her breathing muscles and let the air flow into her lungs. She needed to stand still when she was scared and watch the people around her move in the store, taking the secure thought that she was building up her Will to Bear Discomfort. We encouraged her over the weeks and months that followed to go to downtown stores and turn her disability into an opportunity to develop her Will. She made a recovery and has not been back in years.

Gina came to Recovery because her psychiatrist ordered her to and she was not happy about it. During the thirty-odd years of her bipolar affective illness, she had been hospitalized many times against her will and once again she was itching for a fight.

I told Gina that I was there for my own mental health, too. I told Gina that if I had free choice in the matter, I would not be at a Recovery meeting on a beautiful Saturday afternoon. She started to cry and eventually settled into becoming an average member of the group. As the years went by, Gina became a staunch advocate of Recovery and later started her own group. Her favorite Recovery practice was controlling her speech muscles instead of letting loose with a mouthful of angry words every time she was irritated. She learned that there was value in silence. She kept her university job in spite of her hot temper and eventually retired with a pension.

Probably the best that Recovery has to offer is a sense of belonging and being acceptable to others in spite of our mental diseases. In the calm of a Recovery meeting, tears can be shed freely and we learn that no feeling is a wrong feeling. We treasure each other and share some of that deep dark stuff that in most places goes unshared. Gina and Angie and I were accepted as equals in Recovery and the measure we gave was the measure we got. Recovery is like an ideal family, the ideal that in most life, is never found. We are grateful to Recovery!

For more about Recovery, Inc. and about the newest project, The Recovery Families Project, write to:

> Recovery, Inc.
> 802 North Dearborn Street
> Chicago, Illinois 60610

There are Recovery groups all around the country and the world; ask for a listing of the meetings near you.

Larry Ackerman, diagnosed with paranoid schizophrenia, has been a leader and assistant leader of Recovery groups since 1979.

Chapter 9
Self-Help: A Never-Ending Resource in Enabling Self and Others

Karen K. Tracy

When I was completing my course work for a Ph.D. in experimental psychology, a man I encountered at a university cocktail party asked me, "Most people who go into psychology are a little crazy: what's wrong with you?" I was initially annoyed; however, instead of launching into my usual intellectual, technical response, I had a sudden idea. I replied, "Being crazy is not an absolute requirement for the profession, but it certainly helps." The man hastily carried his double Scotch to the opposite end of the room.

Although that man knew nothing of it, I had actually been hospitalized with two manic episodes in college with a six month disabling episode of clinical depression in between. At that time, many people who had episodes such as mine were labeled as schizophrenic; one psychiatrist told me that I would never have good enough health to graduate from college or hold a job and advised me to marry a nice young man quickly so that I would be provided for for the rest of my life. Fortunately, I was given lithium during my second and last episode; it had just been approved by the FDA for experimental use, and my psychiatrist had a hunch it might work on me. It proved to be a wonder drug at that time; I came out of my psychosis twice as fast and was able to go straight back to college after leaving the hospital. After three years on a maintenance dose, I was advised to stop taking it and during fifteen years of not requiring psychoactive drugs, I obtained a Master's degree, had two children, and completed my Ph.D. After three years of part-time teaching, I obtained a tenure-track position as a psychology professor in a liberal arts college while struggling through a difficult divorce.

A custody battle nearly ensued over our children, then aged 3 and 5. It could have been argued in court that my previous mental illness and my depressed mood at that point in time made me an unfit mother. Rather than risk losing custody, I suggested private mediation, which culminated in agreement to joint physical custody — rare at that time in Michigan. I was shunned by the community; one man I had just met asked me, "What did you do to only have your kids half the week? Were you engaging in prostitution?" This was the worst period of my life, but by going to psychotherapy, continuing to function despite my emotional anguish, and retaining my hope, I was able to stick to my primary goal of settling the divorce with the primary consideration placed on the welfare of our children.

Getting Involved with Recovery, Inc.

The way I got involved in Recovery, Inc., was serendipitous. After my fourth year of teaching, a recent graduate, Alice, went into a suicidal psychotic state. Since she had no family or medical insurance, she called me, and I helped her through seven weeks of hospitalization and her subsequent readjustment to the community. This experience brought back many unpleasant memories for me, yet gave me the opportunity to give back some of the help I had received when I was ill. I visited her several times a week, spoke with her social worker regularly, called her daily, took her out on passes, and attempted to advocate for her with her psychiatrist, whose foreign accent she had trouble understanding. My own therapist advised me to leave the situation alone. She was afraid that I would become psychotic by helping Alice and believed that the public mental health system could be relied on exclusively to restore Alice to health and give her appropriate follow-up care. As a non-professional advocate for her in that very beleaguered system, I had no such faith, so I persisted in my advocacy and connection with Alice.

Not only did I keep my own health throughout this crisis, but I also found out about Recovery, which was to improve my mental health in a way that no professional had been able to do. Since Alice couldn't drive, she asked me to take her to some meetings. Intending merely to observe, I found myself actively participating. Even after Alice decided to quit after several weeks, I kept on attending and heightened my commitment to the group. At first I told myself that I was going purely out of academic interest to find out about a group which could be of help to some of my troubled students who could not afford therapy. However, as I continued to attend meetings, I found that many other individuals in the group had very similar symptoms to my own, and that the method prescribed for calming down those symptoms worked very effectively for me. It also helped me lose some of the feelings of guilt and shame from having been hospitalized for a mental illness and still having nervous symptoms despite years of psychotherapy. A key tenet to Recovery philosophy is that nervous disorders are not self-imposed, reflecting a weakness of character, but rather involve a weakness in the nervous system, which is a major part of the body's functioning. Having such a disorder is no more the fault of the afflicted individual than inheriting or acquiring a weakness in any other bodily system such as the cardiac or pulmonary systems.

What I immediately liked about this group is that it is totally self-supporting and all the leaders, who have extensive experience and training, are recovering nervous patients themselves. Therefore, except for the leader's extra training, we are all peers, unlike a typical therapist-patient relationship in which you as the patient are automatically relegated to a secondary role, which you will never be able to transcend. Regardless of what specific symptoms each of us have had, whatever our walk in life, whatever our current state of functioning, we share a common history and a common malady: We are peers following the common goal of improving our own mental health through self-help and peer support. Fortunately, those of us with emotional illnesses can have some control over our illnesses by learning and practicing skills to maintain and improve our functioning.

Brief Description of Recovery, Inc.

Recovery, Inc. was begun in 1937 by a Chicago area psychiatrist, Dr. Abraham Low, who wished to develop an aftercare program for mental patients which would prevent relapses and help people regain their self-confidence and position in the outside community. After many years of careful study, he wrote a book on basic self-help for former mental patients and nervous patients, which is still used as the central focus of the group's method today. He developed a less emotionally volatile vocabulary for describing nervous symptoms which members use in meetings and in dealing with their own daily frustrations. Members are reminded that the group does not provide diagnoses, offer medication recommendations, or do therapy. For these services, participants are actively encouraged to follow the professional advice of their self-chosen therapist or physician. It is also stressed that just as there is no hopeless case, there is no dishonor involved in being on medication, relapsing on occasion, or having to be re-hospitalized in some cases.

Discovery and Acceptance of Major Mental Illness

After attending Recovery for a year, I began falling into another depressive episode. One of Recovery's sayings is that without solid mental health, a person cannot be effective in work and family life so that working toward that state of health must be a primary value. Thus, I realized that I needed to see a psychiatrist, whom I had shunned before due to fear of stigma and the belief that only the very ill had to resort to psychiatrists and psychoactive drugs. After several bad experiences with psychiatric services covered by my health insurance, I persevered, supported by the group, and found a psychiatrist in private practice who was willing to work with me conjointly in finding the right combination of drugs and psychotherapy. I also worked hard on the Recovery method, which essentially is focused on dropping behavior patterns which are dysfunctional and on acquiring and maintaining new habits which encourage good mental health practices. Cognitive understanding came quickly; however, practicing healthier ways of coping with people and situations until they became habitual took a great deal longer.

With these supports, I was able to keep my employment and take care of my family, despite enduring several months of clinical depression. It was not until this point that I was able to accept having an illness with genetic as well as environmental features which would require monitoring and possibly medication for the rest of my life. Without Recovery, I don't think that I could have lived with this situation, and my depressions would have continued to come with more frequency and severity.

After I had attended the group for several months, the leader encouraged me to become an assistant leader, sharing some of the responsibility of leading meetings and ultimately taking over for her when she could not be present. At first I declined, feeling inadequate to the task. She kept on urging me, however, and I began to assume more responsibility in meetings. Members were very supportive in my efforts to lead the group in her absence. Initially, I was extremely anxious, but leading gradually became easier for me and I found that I could perform that role even when my own mood was low.

My performance improved at work, and I found that I could write more easily, travel alone, and speak at conferences with confidence. I remarried and received tenure and promotion at my college. Two years ago, I began to participate in a few carefully chosen professional and community activities, which I had ceased to do some years before, feeling inadequate to the tasks. Although I think it probably takes me more effort to get through my week than the average wife, mother, and college professor, I have been able to reduce my medication and avoid another clinical depression for the past five years.

After the structured part of Recovery meetings, we have fifteen minutes for informal mutual sharing, and some of us continue our discussions over coffee at a nearby restaurant. This aspect of the program has been very important to me although I live in a different community and have only gone out socially, apart from post-meeting coffees, with one woman from the group. There is an empathy, appreciation, and respect which we share with each other that we cannot find other places; at times we have all had to fight tenaciously to keep our minds on track and our emotions from overwhelming us in a quantitatively and qualitatively different way from average people. Unlike victims of less stigmatized diseases such as heart problems and cancer, we can't tell acquaintances and friends that we are fighting a battle with a serious and unpredictable illness, all the more frustrating for its alternating remissions and relapses despite our own best efforts and good mental health care. Our families and friends, even if we learn not to complain very often, cannot usually fully understand the nature of our illness and often get frustrated with us. Some more distant relatives and friends may be ashamed of us, avoid us, or treat us like children decades after we have returned from a hospitalization.

Recently, after learning of a serious illness of a much beloved relative, I began to feel my mood dipping enough to cause me to function with great difficulty. I went to a Recovery meeting, somewhat ashamed because I'd not attended meetings for several months and because I felt that I should be able to handle my low mood better than I was doing. Members whom I knew smiled immediately when I entered the room and did not chastise me for my period of absence. After the meeting, I walked out into the parking lot and two of the members casually invited me to join them for coffee. We chatted about inconsequential topics for several minutes. I tried to put on a cheerful face and did not talk about my state of mind; I felt helpless and useless, a burden to my family and a nuisance to my doctor. Suddenly, one of the pair sincerely and spontaneously said, "You take good care of yourself. I have had feelings like you're having now, but they passed with time. When you're feeling bad, re-member that we love you and don't want to lose you!" I was astonished; apart from our participation in the group, we were no more than acquaintances, yet the emotion expressed was sincere, reflecting a kind of intuitive empathy I've frequently felt among us which transcends words and carefully composed faces. I repeated those words to myself on subsequent days during particularly try-ing moments, and they helped me to emerge again believing in my intrinsic value even when my symptoms kept me from performing and relating as well as I would have liked.

In my work, I have taught Introductory Psychology more times than I care to count. In the past, before Recovery, I would skip the chapter on Abnor-mal Behavior, cover it cursorily, or even make light of people suffering from various mental disorders. It was a difficult chapter for me to teach although I felt that my problems were purely situational; that I had fully recovered from the brief bouts of mania and depression which I had experienced in college. Now I take great care in teaching that chapter, and it does not make me uncom-fortable. I show a PBS videotape which depicts people suffering from a variety of affective disorders. Some are shown while they are ill and hospitalized and later when they are in a normal state. Individuals present their own stories and talk about the enormous effort it has taken them just to stay alive for the sake of friends and family. One segment portrays a self-help meeting and shows a subgroup of that organization at an informal picnic. One member who has little or no support from family and friends describes how he curbs his occa-sional impulses to commit suicide by thinking how his death would adversely affect other members of the group.

In the next class period, I briefly lecture on the complex nature of mental illness, highlighting both its physical and psychosocial dimensions before ini-tiating class discussion. Students who initially had often joked about crazies or expressed disdain for people who were weak enough to let themselves fall into mental illness now ask serious questions and the class seems to develop some respect for the individuals depicted in the videotape, seeing them as people who suffer from an emotional illness, not as hopeless mental cases. Frequently they later refer friends with questions about emotional symptoms or mental illness to me. I make it perfectly clear that I have no training in the clinical side of psychology, but invite them into my office to chat. Sometimes they just want someone to listen to them attentively and non-judgmentally. If the prob-lem is serious enough to warrant mental health services, often I can refer them to an appropriate professional or service thereby averting more serious prob-lems. Often they are aware of services available, but want to be reassured that they will be treated respectfully and effectively before they seek assistance.

When I was in graduate school, I was funded for three years by the United States Public Health Service. Since I was in experimental rather than clinical or counseling psychology, I always felt it was strange that this agency would fund my education. However, I believe that I am effective in the prevention aspect of mental illness through my teaching, my participation in self-help groups, my research assistance to clinical colleagues, and my ability to accept people in emotional crisis, seeing their underlying strengths. Part of this I owe to my Recovery peers, who have shared painful personal experiences as well as practical, daily coping techniques and who have so clearly supported and respected me as a person through good times, average times, and emotionally challenging times. I have also seen them struggle and emerge functional again and again over the years. Above my office door hangs a poster distributed by the National Alliance for the Mentally Ill with names of famous politicians, writers, actors, artists, and musicians who suffered from a major mental illness. Silently I add the names of scores of others whom I have met, not so famous, but suffering with similar afflictions, who not only endure themselves, but help others on the road to recovery.

How Self-Help and Psychiatry Complement Each Other

Because Recovery, Inc. is based on the premise that members will follow the advice of their self-chosen physicians, including taking medication as prescribed, I do not feel a basic conflict in seeing a psychiatrist and using self-help methods. My carefully self-selected psychiatrist endorses self-help groups and sometimes asks me specifically how my self-help group helps me to cope. She listens with interest and has never suggested that any method used is incompatible with her beliefs. Without Recovery, Inc., I believe that I would have to be on more medication with attendant increased annoying side effects and that I would make more urgent calls to my psychiatrist than I currently do.

Because Recovery attaches no stigma about taking psychiatric medications, I am more willing to comply with the pharmacologic part of my treatment. Initially, I was very resistant to being on medication since some relatives, friends and society in general urged me to discontinue psychiatric medications, judging me to be more severely ill if I needed medicine. I felt also it was a failure on my part to be dependent on medication as part of coping with my illness.

As a result of Recovery's emphasis on trusting your own judgment, I have been able to establish a collaborative relationship with my doctor and participate in the selection, modification, and supervised experimentation with psychoactive medication. Also due to my Recovery training, I attach less danger to taking drugs, persist in phases of drug treatment that may introduce days or weeks of discomfort, and call my doctor if I feel that a drug may be producing more harmful than beneficial effects.

Effects of My Illness on Relationships at Work

When I began my position at my college, I was going through the anguish of divorce and fears that my late adolescent history of mental illness might result in my losing custody of my children. Having lived in Michigan only a short time and lacking a social support network, I tried to get emotional support from members of my Division at the college. I therefore told everyone in my Division of my acute illness while a college student. I was also open about being in psychotherapy. At the time, some individuals supported me and others remained silent. However, due to comments that were made to me several years later when I was being reviewed for tenure, I think that both my revelation of prior illness and my behavior reflecting high anxiety and low mood states that first year permanently damaged my credibility and reputation with many of my peers. Those who seemed most distrustful and who had been discussing me negatively behind my back were often those involved in mental health fields, something I had not expected. Recent polls indicate that the majority of the American population believe that mental illness is mainly due to weakness of will; I don't think that college professors are much different from the majority.

Outside my Division, I have only told a few peers whom I felt I could trust after several years association; they have been supportive. Cautiously, I have begun to be more spontaneous and genuine with them. Inside my Division, I am more careful.

I have no illusions of ever attaining any administrative power in my institution; I focus on teaching and research, which are my strengths anyway. While I try to be pleasant to all colleagues on an individual basis, I realize that a few peers have disliked me for years. I no longer blame myself for this or try to win them around, seeking to be liked by all. I am polite to them, but have learned to limit my interactions and make it difficult for them to make disparaging comments, which can bring on symptoms in me as I realize I am more emotionally vulnerable than average. I have learned not to discuss my emotional illness with my peers. If I am in a low mood and someone notices, I say my allergies are bothering me or that I have head aches, or that I'm tired. If I wake up feeling especially low on a work day, I dress in my best clothes, smile a lot in public, and reduce my expectations of myself when alone in my office. On better days, I seek out interactions with peers.

The most difficult situation for me at work is attending large, emotionally charged faculty meetings. Although I have done everything short of taping my mouth shut to keep down my intermittent excessive verbiage in large meetings, I realize that sometimes I talk too impulsively and with too much emotion. However, I try to remember to think before talking and have often been told that my comment or question was cogent, creative, or courageous. I thus am still working to achieve a balance so that I neither talk too much or totally detach myself from important issues by sitting in silence, which has been a temptation.

Early on, before I realized that I still had a major mental illness, I would tell some of my classes about my breakdowns in college. However, after I had accepted that I do have a major mental illness, all I have said is that I know more than most social psychologists about mood and anxiety disorders because a few relatives have had some difficulties. However, if students come to me on an individual basis and tell me that they or people close to them have emotional problems or a mental illness, I first listen and make suggestions to them. If I know someone fairly well, I tell them briefly that I suffer from a mood disorder and give them suggestions on coping from my own experience. Although no one has ever taken my advice to go to a Recovery group, sometimes my revelation has given them the courage to seek individual counseling for themselves or relatives and has helped give them hope about their own situation. Other non-troubled students whom I know well know of my illness. Some have sincerely told me how much they admire me for undertaking my career and carrying on credibly, even when I am experiencing a low or anxious mood. I feel that in general, I have had more success with students accepting me both as emotionally challenged but as personally and professionally valuable than I have had with my colleagues. I no longer agonize over this and dwell on my weaknesses; I focus on my strengths.

Factors Contributing to Prevention of Illness

My guiding principle in living my day to day life is that without my mental health, I cannot be useful to anyone else. Since my physical health impacts on my mental health, I try to follow good health habits and contact the appropriate doctor if I am having difficulty with any aspect of my health. I work to establish a collaborative mode of treatment, even if the doctor resists, and if we can't negotiate, I keep looking until I find a doctor who is respectful of me. I read about how to deal with different health problems that come up and ask about treatment options and risks. Sharing in this decision-making makes me feel less hopeless and more able to control what I can. My psychiatrist has helped me learn to assess when my brain is not functioning optimally and to slow down when I need to. We have tried to systematically study my mood variations and have discovered that I have a seasonal pattern of mood changes which I can anticipate and plan adjustments for. We have discovered that if I take a vacation in the South during the winter months, I will start feeling a little too high after several days of sun; knowing this, I can prevent riding the high and thus getting depressed when I come back home. We have also discovered which psychosocial situations and family situations are difficult for me and have discussed ways of coping with those situations. Optional stressful situations I skip.

My doctor believes that my illness is partly heredity but has also been worsened by life experiences beyond my control. Thus, I require both psychotherapy and medication and also seem to profit more from psychotherapy than many others with my disorder. She is careful with my medications since I have an unusual sensitivity to drugs of all sorts and we are both cognizant of my need to be alert to side effects if they worsen after a reasonable amount of time. Incidentally, I do not smoke, drink, or use any drugs other than those prescribed to me by doctors.

My psychiatrist encourages my self-initiated use of art and poetry writing, which I sometimes bring to therapy. I listen to music of many kinds and have many creative pursuits which help me to maintain my mental balance. I also read light fiction, watch T.V. and videos for pleasure, and practice utter sloth at times.

Although I have had trouble all my life being comfortable as an actively involved participant in conventional religion, I have discovered that my love of beauty in music, art, plants, animals, and a sense of oneness with nature is spiritual. Having religious and spiritual beliefs and practices are vital to my mental health, but I no longer chastise myself for failing to find regular church attendance personally meaningful.

There are certain rules that I have developed for myself over the years for maintaining my mental health. I keep essential commitments regardless of how I am feeling emotionally, get up and dressed each day, and make it a point of never being socially isolated for more than one day. I have discovered that being very social is tiring for me. However, allowing myself regular periods of solitary, quiet time is essential.

It is still sometimes hard to sort out who I basically am and I have to be careful not to allow myself to lose perspective when in low moods or to over-commit myself when I am feeling well. Extreme highs and lows are easy for me to spot and take seriously; however, milder mood states are harder to identify. Some days, especially in the early fall and spring, I have sudden highs and lows all day long, which are extremely disconcerting, however, I know that these fluctuating states will not last long and have a logical cause in the changes of light in these seasons. I know that my personality is confusing to others; when I am low, I tend to be quiet and shy; when mildly high, extroverted and energetic. I have developed friendships with people who can tolerate the ambiguity that exists in my personality, many of whom also have a mood disorder. I no longer feel scared or guilty when I cannot enjoy much or be emotionally available to others or get much accomplished; I know that my low mood will lift and I will regain my normal ability to enjoy life, nurture family and friends, and participate fully in work and leisure activities.

Rather than dwell on the negative features of having a bipolar disorder, I try to accentuate the positive aspects. No more do I pour over self-help books dictating how I can overcome my depression or anxiety forever by following the author's strictly outlined method. Instead, I seek out books on people who were or are creative or influential despite intense personal suffering from mood disorders from time to time in their lives. I keep up with the most recent findings relevant to mood disorders, but not compulsively so. Finally, I do not feel guilty about paying someone or asking someone to do chores when I am low; I am not being lazy, I am staving off a major depression by not exhausting myself. When feeling especially good, I no longer fill my days with frantic activities. Rather, I take quiet pleasure in watching a full moon bubble up through the branches of a wild cherry tree or delight in playing tag with the waves on a fresh blue sunlit day with my family.

Karen Tracy is an associate professor of psychology at Marygrove College in Detroit, MI. She is active in teaching and in professional and self-help organizations. Her research deals with psychosocial aspects of male-female relationships, multiculturalism, and mood disorders.

Section 3

Consumer-Controlled Alternatives

Introduction to Section 3: Consumer-Controlled Alternatives

As in the previous section, the chapters in this section place an emphasis on the benefits provided to individuals involved with a service option provided by consumers for consumers — this time, consumer-controlled alternatives. The benefits described are diverse and include social and personal achievements. Two major themes predominate. The first concerns an increased sense of competence, productivity and personal agency which participants experience. This is symbolized by the designation of participants as members, not consumers or clients. These positive feelings come from individuals having ownership of the consumer-controlled alternative, knowing that they are solely responsible for operating the service, that members have done this on their own, and that the service can be anything that members want it to be. In many cases, members also increase their self-worth because the consumer-controlled alternative is providing them with jobs, supplying the symbol of productivity recognized by outsiders, as well as increasing members' well-being and economic stability. Obtaining employment and/or running the consumer-controlled service also produces related tangible benefits to members through receiving training and education, acquiring concrete skills in business practices, advocacy and/or service delivery, and having opportunities to solve problems, exercise decision-making, and make choices.

The second theme concerning benefits which permeates these model programs involves providing members with a sense of physical and emotional safety — a genuine sense of community and camaraderie. The consumer-controlled alternative creates an environment where members can come and feel welcomed. Establishing trust is important and most programs maintain an open door, no eligibility, and no appointment policy. However, to ensure members' feelings of safety, doors to the outside may be locked and non-members (which might include mental health providers) are kept out. The safe and secure environment is designed to address members' fears and isolation, as well as their needs for social support and for knowing that they are not alone.

Similar to the self-help group models described in Section 2, these models of consumer-controlled alternatives began with consumers coming together out of a desire to address needs not being met by formal mental health services; "...in many ways the mental health system is not really a system of recovery, but rather a system of illness" (Paynter). Usually gaps identified by groups of consumers concerned the ready availability and acceptability of services that are needed. Thus, Silverman describes how the individuals who started "on our own..." were those who didn't meet eligibility requirements of the clubhouse, were isolated, had dropped out of traditional services, were without shelter, etc. However, although all the consumer-controlled alternatives started with the focus of meeting prospective members' needs, they all evolved in different ways. This, of course, is to be expected, since we know that individuals with psychiatric disabilities are extremely heterogeneous and that these differences expand over time and across locations. Thus, the models described started with small numbers of consumers and peer support groups and evolved into other service and business entities. For example, "on our own..." (Silverman) evolved from a drop-in center to providing service information and referrals, supportive housing, and consumer care management. OASIS Drop-In Center (LeDoux) has expanded the number of drop-ins it operates and its consulting activities to other localities and states. The Shining Reflections Tea Room has expanded from provision of a few vocational opportunities to operating vocational training and offerings in the arts to promote members' development (Paynter). The evolution of these programs has been in response both to opportunities presented and to member needs expressed. It seems unlikely that consumers could have predicted these directions when their groups were initiated.

Despite their evolution in multiple and diverse directions, however, all programs described have had a vision which guided them. This vision is described in the chapters in terms of a set of goals, an articulated mission, or shared values. Some of the groups have invested considerable energy in formulating their vision through a process of reviewing and combining values from other practice and epistemological frameworks into their own eclectic model (Silverman). For others, their mission seemed to evolve naturally over time (Paynter). Interestingly, although services provided by these models vary tremendously, their vision statements and the values behind them are quite similar, promoting a personal empowerment philosophy. They articulate the importance of consumers having a choice, providing consumer-members with personalized support and assistance as needed, but always encouraging individuals to do for themselves as much as possible.

Operationalizing their visions has been a challenge for many of these programs. Often the only program operations that consumers knew were "ones which had dis-empowered them" (Silverman). Most of the consumer-controlled alternatives started with a premise of no formalized policies or procedures, i.e., no intake, no timeframe (Silverman). However, the programs soon found that they needed rules in order to successfully operate and ensure that individual behaviors (smoking, verbal abuse, sexual harrassment, unauthorized "borrowing") were not driving the majority away. Rules have usually remained simple and reasonable, and have been developed on an as-needed basis.

To promote efficiency and to meet the accountability demands of funders, programs also had to formalize their operations with organizational structures and documentation: a board of directors, formal offices, incorporation, job descriptions, bylaws, etc. Again, however, these structures and procedures have evolved to meet the needs and style of the consumer-controlled alternative. Adapting the organizational and operational models of traditional mental health programs did not prove successful (LeDoux). The need for formalization in order to function successfully on a long-term basis versus the desire for fluidity and limited rules in order to meet the immediate and ever-changing needs of members may be a constant strain for consumer-controlled alternatives and a dynamic that must be continually reviewed and assessed.

Descriptions of the model programs in the chapters that follow make it clear, however, that effective business, organizational, and administrative practices are absolutely essential in order to obtain funding and maintain operations. Funding sources are multiple, fluctuating, and offer limited stability. They have included grants from state and local mental health authorities, corporate and foundation funding, cash and in-kind donations from individuals, advocacy groups, community organizations, students and universities. In order for consumer-controlled programs to compete effectively for these resources, they must provide evidence of effective management to skeptical reviewers. In order to maintain their operations, they need to utilize their usually very limited funding efficiently. Perhaps more so than others, nontraditional programs need well-developed business plans and/or plans for programming to meet the resource levels available. Many of the programs described in these chapters offer advice for other consumer groups concerning the business practices they have found most helpful to their survival and/or expansion.

Finally, as in the previous section, relationships between these model consumer-controlled alternative programs and mental health services and professionals are quite diverse. Some programs have experienced considerable help from individual mental health providers (Paynter, Prout, Silverman). Others have experienced skepticism or backlash. Most commonly, however, the mental health system appears to be in a business-like relationship with these programs. That is, mental health authorities are frequently sources of funding support. Their relationship with the consumer-controlled alternative is neutral as long as performance and accountability demands are met. One does not sense efforts at outreach, assistance, or support. In funding and advocacy, these consumer-controlled alternative programs, like their members, are "on their own." This reality has been recognized and accepted. In fact, too much support from the traditional mental health system may be eyed warily with the envisioned possibility of cooptation (Paynter, Silverman). Perhaps in recognition of the need to establish themselves independently, many of these programs have voluntarily sought out evaluation systems to document their benefits and enhance their credibility and operating effectiveness.

Thus, these successful consumer-controlled alternatives offer substantial benefits even more directly related to rehabilitation objectives than appears to be the case with self-help. However, to be promoted as a major rehabilitative strategy, considerable challenges will need to be overcome. Starting up a small business is a difficult activity in any field; most small businesses fail. In today's highly competitive, down-sizing, managed-care oriented system of mental health services, successfully initiating consumer-controlled alternative services is likely to be risky at best. Allen and Granger suggest that consumer-controlled businesses need a sponsoring organization. As an example, the Shining Reflections Tea Room found that support from local business establishments, the Chamber of Commerce, and key business people was invaluable to the program's commercial and organizational development (Paynter). These consumer initiatives also need to find consumer leaders who have the requisite skills, recognizing that these skills need to change over the life of the business. They need to find ways to identify and develop new leaders, as well as avoid the burnout that comes when performance cannot meet expectations (Paynter). Such consumer-controlled businesses need to negotiate a balance between formalization for business survival and funding accountability with the mandate for supportive, individualized, and flexible services which truly meet the needs of their members.

Chapter 10

Recovery Through Partnership: "on our own, charlottesville, virginia"
Shela Silverman

The mission of "on our own, charlottesville, virginia" is to provide mutual support, self-help, advocacy, education, information and referral services to individuals who have experienced significant problems in their lives due to mental illness — and who acknowledge it, and to advocate for positive changes within the traditional mental health system.

History and Development of the Consumer Alternative

In 1989, over a period of several months, a group of mental health consumers, many of whom were members of the clubhouse in Charlottesville, held several meetings to discuss the unmet needs of other consumers within the area. No one in the group wanted to replicate the existing system; rather they wanted to create one which empowered consumers, one which truly helped, not hindered. They wanted a system that reflected the best in society and within the individual — rather than one which controls consumers. (Allen, 1974; Beaurline, 1993; Chamberlin, 1979; Harp et al., 1994; Zinman et al., 1987) The only day program available at that time was a clubhouse which offered services to approximately 120 persons diagnosed with serious mental illness. Clubhouse membership could only be offered to consumers who were referred by a psychiatrist. Other consumers who were also diagnosed (numbering over 300) had no program to attend and spent much of their time isolated and at great risk for hospitalization. Additionally, there were consumers who were receiving services through the private sector, and others who had dropped out from the service system entirely and often were without shelter. The final group whose needs were not being met were consumers within the corrections system for behaviors which the community felt were dangerous. This core group of consumers made a commitment to address these needs, submitted a grant to the Virginia Department of Housing and Community Development, and was awarded their first grant of $15,115 to open a day shelter in July of 1990.

The name chosen for the program was "on our own..." after the book by the same name, written by Judi Chamberlin, a consumer advocate from Boston. This book explored the concept of providing an alternative to the traditional mental health system, based on the values of ex-patients who had been incarcerated involuntarily in mental hospitals. At that time, this represented a radical position which was met with little acceptance by the bureaucracies which administered mental health treatment based on a medical model (Chamberlin,

1979). Since consumers are often without community, living isolated lives, alone, often ostracized and stigmatized by their illness (Chamberlin, 1979; Harp et al., 1994; Zinman et al., 1984), the "on our own..." project was established as a community for persons in recovery. A major focus of the program was to provide an environment where consumers would come, feel welcome and safe, and be supported by other consumers. More importantly, the support which consumers could give each other within the community could help in recovery. Mental health is a continuum; there are periods when consumers are desperately ill and other times when they are free of symptoms. There are also times when consumers can, and do, support other consumers who are experiencing similar difficulties. This peer support model of recovery is the one which the founders favored for the program. There were no criteria for entrance into the program — all were welcome — and there were no intakes, no diagnosis, no treatment records of any sort. There was no time frame; consumers could come and stay for one hour, one day, two years or for however long they chose to remain. They could also come whenever they wanted to: evenings, weekends, holidays — we decided to remain open at these hours because the members said these were the most difficult hours for them.

During its first year, "on our own..." operated as a project of the Commonwealth Clubhouse Association (CCA), a 501(c)3 program, which began during the mid-1980's as an area-wide advocacy organization for clubhouse members. When additional funds were sought for the drop-in center, one of the potential grantees attempted to validate the 501(c)3 status of the CCA, and they found that the organization was not in compliance with the Internal Revenue Service. A meeting was quickly held with an attorney and the recommendation was for "on our own..." to become an independent entity — a private, non-profit organization. Fortunately, after considerable effort, and many telephone calls to the 800 number of the Internal Revenue Service, the application was approved. By having this determination, "on our own....." now had the opportunity to access additional funds to enlarge the scope of the program.

Along with the highs there were many lows. No one had anticipated the need for rules; however, they became essential when food purchased for the group was taken by one or two; or when smoking, verbal abuse, and harassment occurred. These incidents became topics for discussion and the process evolved whereby rules were developed. Each new member was given the opportunity to sign a Statement of Attitude which provided some structure for persons unfamiliar with expectations. Contrary to the way traditional programs operated, rules were developed only when a need became evident. With the exception of rules prohibiting alcohol and drug use, no rule was pre-set until group consensus agreed there was a need for one. Gradually policies were developed to address these rules and the By-Laws and Articles of Incorporation were added. Incorporation was a simple task. A Board of Directors, consisting of mostly consumers, was appointed and meetings were held. A framework was being created by consumers, for consumers, and not to consumers.

Bookkeeping, supervision of volunteers, directors, a secretary, a treasurer — all of these roles and responsibilities were added to the framework. Job descriptions were developed. Most were done by consensus — some by the newly appointed Executive Committee which was made up of all consumers. Meetings were held constantly, sometimes daily, generally weekly. Some of the enthusiasm of the original group had begun to wane, but fortunately there were people who picked up when others dropped out. It became clear that due to the nature of our illnesses, there would be times when some of us could not participate at the same level, or might even desire not to be involved. Roles were intentionally fuzzy; members were volunteers, staff were members. Members who were used to being recipients of services often had difficulty in being service providers; some members had difficulty with the idea of another consumer being a provider. Often the only models available were the ones which had dis-empowered them: traditional models in which decisions were made for them by professionals. The trick was not to be co-opted by these ideas nor by the system which had taught them that they were sick and would never recover.

Clearly we had no precedence for making any decision which would be accepted by all parties. We realized that in spite of staff feeling as though they were not any different than any other member, the membership did not think of us in the same way. Philosophically we had to make a decision which was based on reality; but whose reality? Members looked toward staff to make decisions which reflected the values of a consumer-run agency. And what exactly were those values? We attempted to articulate these values along with our mission and spent months writing down values which we agreed upon. Many of the values which we included were compromises. We found that there were consumers who did not want to be called consumers; some saw themselves as clients, or survivors, or even ex-patients. These labels became an object of discussion. Several of the more radicalized wanted only to be thought of as people, but all agreed that there had to be consensus on a set of values, which would offer direction as the group became ever larger.

Several of the original group of consumers dropped out of the project once it got underway because they were uncomfortable with the lack of structure at the center, the lack of direction from staff, and the stress of making decisions which might not be correct. All of these consumers were long-time members of the clubhouse, used to receiving directions rather than giving them, more inclined to expect others to provide answers, and very comfortable with it. Once new members came to the drop-in center who were not clubhouse members, many of them left and returned to the clubhouse. Several of these same members, uncomfortable with consumer staff, believed that professionals were more trustworthy and more knowledgeable about their problems. These issues were often discussed among members but were not resolved. Consequently, the majority of the clubhouse member/consumers returned to the safety of the clubhouse.

Principles and Philosophy of Services

During the first years, we shared personal experiences about how mental illness had impacted our lives. Those of us who had been fortunate and had attended consumer conferences, or who had read the consumer literature, began to develop an eclectic model which we believed would help us provide the structure for members, staff and volunteers. Consumers meeting during the 1980's articulated their beliefs and values at conferences which one of our founders attended; the context of the material was radicalized by the participants at these meetings. The bible of the consumer movement, Judith Chamberlin's *On Our Own: Patient Controlled Alternatives to the Mental Health System*, (1979) was read and reread by the founders of our agency. Ideas which Judi presented in this book became the basis for many consumer-run programs.

We took an approach which included many of the ideals of feminist thought: each person's experience is validated; members are part of an empowering society within the drop-in center; members do not need to internalize negative stereotypes about mental illness, a process which belittles them into subordinate positions within society, and poses formidable obstacles to empowerment (Sands, 1991). We also adopted a modified strengths perspective which looks at the ways that consumers have been able to achieve success, rather than looking at their problems (Sands, 1991). Finally, in our eclectic blend, we have determined that we are partners in our journey to, and through, recovery (Kanter, 1989). All of us, in this eclectic model, bring strengths, valid perspectives of where we have been, plus the knowledge that, as staff, we are in partnership with members, traveling together. In the past the partnership model was used within the traditional system as a bridge toward consumer control but clearly most perpetuated the old notions of inequality between client and provider (Harp et al., 1989). In the traditional model of partnership, staff continued documenting clients, made important decisions, and continued to know what the client needed. Within the partnership model which we utilize, we are true partners since we all have had similar experiences, and are all consumers and value these experiences. Consumer members are involved in all aspects of the program, and are considered competent to make decisions. They are involved in policy, administrative and budget decisions, as well as daily responsibility for the functioning of the center.

Incorporated into all of the services which are provided in partnership with members are the values and philosophy of a true consumer-run alternative. What follows is a series of heavily discussed statements which are undeniably critical for any consumer group that provides services which go beyond socialization, for without a framework which is value laden, services can go awry and turn out to be carbon copies of those offered by traditional systems.

- The value of *choice*, the recognition that all services should be designed and implemented to demonstrate respect, to enhance individual dignity and values, and to be available whenever, wherever, and for as long as the consumer requests them. In short, we are there for the duration, and wherever the consumer is: streets, jail, hospital. We make no decisions for anyone. We teach consumers problem solving so that they can enhance their own choices.

• Services are provided within the community, utilizing natural supports: friends, family, community institutions. There are consumers who want their families to be an integral part of their lives, and request that we assist them in mediating differences. Others may wish to develop friendships with neighbors. We often attend social gatherings with persons who are from the community and bring members with us for the experience of being part of the greater community. In the past these members often remained isolated, their only social contacts were with other consumers or family. We encourage consumers to join clubs, attend concerts, and become active members of any and all groups and churches. We link them with other community members and frequently they bond quite well.

• Any services which are provided are comprehensive: housing, supports, employment, training, education, advocacy and assistance with accessing entitlements and/or financial resources, all the while teaching the consumer both the means and processes of self empowerment. The goal is for the consumer to become self reliant, and if possible, to help other consumers.

• Services are organized around consumers, not places. There are no service plans, no documentation. Outreach is essential as it helps to connect people with the services. We do not wait at the drop-in center; there are no appointments. Consumers are met in a variety of places: restaurants, the mall, houses, the park.

From the very beginning, there was significant impetus for this program to be a part of the greater community — both in location and involvement. The origin of many misconceptions regarding mental illness can be, and is, caused through misunderstanding and misrepresentation of consumers. Most people do not have the opportunity to knowingly experience consumers first hand, and thus realize that consumers are very much like themselves. In order to reduce the stigma of mental illness, as well as to "...advocate for positive changes within the traditional mental health system" (mission statement, "on our own..."), it made good sense to involve the community in our program.

Many volunteers, particularly students from the University of Virginia, arrive with trepidation, but after spending time at the center, leave with a much different attitude about persons with mental illness. We are a visible community, participating in community sponsored projects and events. This places us in an enviable and reciprocal position by providing the community with our resources, and receiving theirs as equals. Our agency is located within the downtown area, one block from a large mall. We have always been involved with our community, and they have been extremely supportive of us. Folks drop-in, bring food, clothing, furniture, cash — and often volunteer to be here. We are part of the community and assist at city functions. For example, for New Year's Eve/First Night, held annually on the downtown mall, we provide an open house with refreshments so that we can return something to the community that provides so generously for us. We are good neighbors, offering assistance to others during inclement weather, by shoveling snow, if necessary. We are part of the landscape, and find that the more our neighbors get to know us, the more we are accepted as people, not mental patients! We made a conscious decision to be in the downtown, knowing that real estate is costlier there, but that is where consumers congregate — and so we are highly visible, providing services 365 days per year!

Operations

For the first year and a half, due to a shortage of funds, the all volunteer staff at the drop-in center, witnessed an ever increasing number of visits. At the beginning there were six to eight persons per six hour day, then 20, or even 30 per day, within this first year. Card playing, socializing, use of the telephone, reading, assisting with the daily clean-up, shopping for the coffee, these were the activities which represented the very beginning of the center. Gradually information and referral to other service providers were requested by the members. Staff had to become "generalists", actively seeking out information which could be disseminated to the membership. An intentional decision was made by the staff that members would be assisted with accessing information but they should do as much as they could by themselves. This is empowering. We never do anything for consumers that consumers can do for themselves, rather we either do it together, or the consumer does it alone — with support from the consumer staff.

During the second year, there was an influx of members whose needs were quite different from those of the clubhouse members. Some of these people had no shelter, slept in abandoned buildings, or went from friend to friend. Rather than being consumers who had a difficult time managing on their Social Security and food stamps, these people frequently had no resources at all. They also often had major physical and emotional problems which were not being addressed. They were not as interested in the socialization which was being practiced at the drop-in center; these people had more immediate needs. Socialization was, and is, the most important function of the center, but there were new and different challenges which we now had to deal with as members, staff, and community. The level of understanding among the core group of consumers, volunteers, and staff was tested, and was found lacking. A major issue was building trust with consumers alienated from traditional services and professionals who had disempowered them and whom they often felt had no understanding of their problems. Building supportive relationships was essential prior to doing anything else. We are all consumers, walking the same path. In fact, we often are walking in each others' footsteps. We are friends, and because of this we are far more compassionate and less judgmental than others who might view homeless persons with mental illness as being non-compliant with treatment or living in the streets by choice. Instead of having preconceived notions, we as staff and community assist each consumer as an individual.

Issues around confidentiality, values of choice — whether or not to take medication, all required a great deal of discussion. We found that if we retained our articulated values then most of these questions were resolved. Choice is assuredly our most basic and most important value. We realized during this period that in spite of our antagonism toward control and authority as it is practiced within the traditional mental health system, there was some benefit in providing some structure for the membership. The ancient Israelis, after achieving the freedom celebrated during the Passover, also celebrated the holiday of Shevoueth, the festival of the law. If we can continue the corollary, opening the center was our freedom from a system which we found oppressive; but we also found that we needed some law by which to achieve the work of which we knew we were capable. Thus we began to put together guidelines which we could live by.

Consumers who provide services are often caught up in a never never land of not having a model of service delivery to follow — except for the one which has served them — often quite poorly. Once our agency clearly articulated a model of service delivery and a philosophy and values which are consumer driven then the rest was fairly easy. Identifying these values was more difficult. The literature provides models but obviously most are medical models. Our needs were met in utilizing an eclectic model due to the experience and knowledge of our founders.

The majority of positions on the Board of Directors, including officers, are consumers. They are responsible for all policy decisions, hiring, and are the final arbiters for all grievances which cannot be satisfied. All members are encouraged to participate in Board meetings, which are held alternate months, as well as weekly house meetings where issues pertaining to day-to-day operations are discussed and decisions made regarding activities, fund raising and other group functions.

Another aspect of our services is problem solving which is taught by staff to consumers. Throughout the five years that we provided services, we found that consumers request assistance with problem solving, often not having the skills to perform nor having been given the opportunity of doing this while being in the role of client within the traditional mental health system. Too often, they say, decision making and problem solving were done by staff members. In order to be successful, consumers believed staff had to make their decisions. This obviously created a conundrum for consumers who had little or no practice in making decisions — good or bad, and who were frightened of failure! The teaching of problem-solving skills is one of the most essential tools for these consumers.

Another service which consumers requested was medication education. There is essentially a lack of knowledge of medication, side effects, symptoms — and even what mental illness is, among a large number of consumers. It is shocking that consumers who have schizophrenia are uninformed about their illness, and cannot discuss symptoms, let alone side effects. Staff at our agency have made an intentional decision to read as many first person accounts of the illness as they can. They also talk with consumers and family members about the illness and its effects upon their lives. We provided a support group for persons taking Clozaril when members requested it. The clinic which provided the medication did not offer any such support groups. During the course of these weekly sessions, members began to speak of their anger about losses in their personal lives due to the illness. Each of the group members provided support to the others, as they all felt the same!

During the latter part of 1994, we began to offer care management to our members. They requested that staff assist them in locating housing, accessing entitlements, securing training or employment, and being with them — wherever they might be. The funding for this project, Project Together, came from a special grant from Virginia Housing and Community Development. It targeted homeless consumers, the majority of which were receiving no services from any other agency. Many of the consumers were still in the hospital, in jail, or living on the streets. This project has been a real challenge and has tested our values, mission, and abilities as no other project has. This particular project was one in which we intentionally utilized the partnership model of providing services. In this way we recognize the strengths and limitations of both parties in the partnership: consumers all, we share skills and knowledge which we utilize in coming together. In contrast to any professional model, we share personal experiences and often rely on them to assist others. The boundaries which professionals talk about do not exist for us. We hug, cry and laugh together, and are there for each other. Thus far we have had both successes and failures. It has also given us validation in the eyes of other service agencies who provide services to persons who are homeless. The focus of these services was to develop a relationship and build trust with the consumers who contracted for our services. Services were offered, explained, and if both parties agreed, then a verbal or written contract was made. The contract could be terminated by either party — if either felt that it was not in their best interest to continue the contract. This has a very empowering effect on all parties, particularly consumers who had never been given such choices prior to this.

Housing

Consumers from our agency developed a model of supported housing within the community as the need was defined by consumers leaving the state hospital. The model for housing was a direct offshoot of the peer support model from the drop-in center. The house, chosen with staff assistance by the residents from available real estate within the community, is a three bedroom house in the city. Two of the residents are from the hospital; the other person living in the house is a peer, hired by "on our own..." to be there during evenings, weekends and holidays. The men live in the house, just as any group of men would live: shopping, cooking, dating, working. Meetings are held regularly with case managers from the community mental health center and staff from "on our own..." The house is a home; major emphasis is placed on choice (of roommates and staff), as well as assisting with issues of living as each resident requests. For example, one of the men, hospitalized for nearly five years prior to discharge into the house, has major problems with substance abuse. The peer support person spends enormous amounts of time going to meetings with him as well as talking to him when the desire to use drugs is very strong. The house and the consumers living in it represent what is possible when normalization and choice are actually realized. Costs of the house are divided between the two ex-patients; the peer support person does not pay for anything except telephone and cable. At this writing, the lease for the house will revert to the men living in it. Prior to this year the mental health center signed the lease and provided some of the funds, but this year there has been a dramatic decline in financial support and thus the center stated that they could no longer subsidize the men in their home. After much discussion, the men decided to remain in the house, and all three, including the peer support person, agreed to divide the costs equally.

Funding

During our second year we began to access additional funds from the Commonwealth of Virginia Department of Mental Health, Mental Retardation and Substance Abuse Services as the only consumer-run program in the state. A great deal of time was spent discussing whether accepting funds from this source was a form of co-optation. We were all agreed that we needed to remain aware of this problem. If any pressure was placed on us to compromise our values or mission, then we would not accept these funds. Thus far we do not feel as if there has been any influence by the Department of Mental Health to do anything contrary to these values. We are, however, always on guard and will continue to be so in the future in case anything changes in this regard.

We continue to receive funds from both the Department of Mental Health and Virginia Housing and Community Development. In this, our fifth year, we were awarded a $100,000 grant from the United Parcel Service which we will use toward the purchase of a permanent home for our agency. This grant, a highly competitive one, was awarded to us after many months of intense and very difficult work convincing a rather skeptical group that our organization was indeed worthy of such a sum. The concept of consumer values and our dedication to providing an environment where consumers could recover within a community of support, was very appealing to this group of business people.

A small Charlottesville based foundation, the Charlottesville-Albemarle Foundation, has supported us on three occasions, providing us with funds to purchase furnishings, a washer and a dryer, a television, videocassette recorder, and a camcorder. We have received considerable support, financial as well as volunteer, throughout our tenure. Students from the University of Virginia assist us in many ways, coming to the center, cooking meals, donating time and money. One student group, SAHAH (Students Against Homelessness and Hunger), held a fund-raiser for our organization and donated $800. Students also donate clothing, warm blankets, sleeping bags and coats. This past winter our agency began an outreach project in collaboration with these students. We took hot food, blankets, and coats to scheduled places around the city. During the warmer weather we began a picnic in the park, taking a picnic lunch to many of the homeless people who congregate downtown. These projects were funded through the Federal Emergency Management Agency (FEMA).

We have been recipients of many private donations. Just prior to Christmas, 1993, a gentleman came to the drop-in center, asked if we were a private agency, unaffiliated with the City of Charlottesville. When he learned that we were not, he asked if we accepted donations, and wrote a check for $1000. We often receive donations from the Alliance chapter in Charlottesville. These donations are used for attending conferences and training. Nearly all of the furniture at the drop-in center has been donated, and much of it is quite good. Donations of food and clothing are quite common, and during the past winter we received over 300 blankets.

Outcomes

The consumers who began the drop-in have benefited from the process and the program. None of us actually believed that what we talked about for months and months would become a reality. All of the hard work, the discussions, the approval of the grant, the sense of power gained by the consumers was unbelievable. Consumers learned that they were capable people who could succeed, even though they did not believe it at first. Interestingly, one of the consumers spoke of his psychiatrist's concern that the ideas he was espousing were symptoms of his grandiosity.

Many of the consumers who were service recipients had not received services anywhere prior to coming to the center, or had dropped out from the traditional mental health system years ago. Each consumer had a different reason; each reason was respected. The project and its safe, open environment attracted many consumers who realized that they could come, utilize whatever service they wanted — or none at all, and after a time in which they began to trust, then they could come and request additional services. The open door policy plus the no appointment policy was an attraction. Consumers do not have to wait days to see someone when their needs are crucial. Weekends, evenings, holidays are often times when consumers face problems, and traditionally when there is nothing available except crisis services. Being available at these times has been a great help to consumers and prevented several consumers from having to be hospitalized. An example of this approach was illustrated by Ruth, age 38, who came to the drop-in center nearly three years ago. She was homeless, had been hospitalized for many years in a state institution, had spent several years in prison, and was dropped off in Charlottesville by a friend. She knew no one, had no personal effects except the clothing on her back and a small bag which held her seizure medication and a tooth brush. She had been coming to the center for several weeks, arriving first and leaving last. She gradually began to speak of her immediate problems: shelter, clothing, medication, and eventually allowed us to help her. But she had her own goals and she did the majority of the work, contacting agencies, securing resources. Our role was to assist her in this process, helping her connect with the right people, accompanying her whenever she requested, but always being cognizant that she was a capable person who could make her own decisions, even her own mistakes. We offered her a place to be, a telephone to make and receive calls, an address to receive mail — plus we advocated for her to be admitted into a shelter. She is now living in the first apartment she has ever had and is beginning to attend adult education so she will be able to earn her GED. Upon coming to the center, Ruth became part of a partnership; all of us walking the path together.

Another example which illustrates how we provide for consumers who are quite symptomatic and in acute distress is the story of a very agitated gentleman who arrived at the center without any personal effects, saying that he had walked from another state. He had been picked up by the State Police, walking on the interstate, and taken to the Salvation Army Shelter in town. There he went to sleep for several days without eating or bathing. On the third day, staff woke him up and told him to leave because he had not done his chores. He arrived at the drop-in in the middle of the day, quite confused about what had happened and in apparent distress, both physically and mentally. Staff spent a great deal of time with him, offering him food, clothing and talking to him. After several hours he requested that someone accompany him to the emergency room at the university hospital so that he could be admitted to the psychiatric unit. This man had left a psychiatric hospital in Maine nearly one year prior to his arriving in Charlottesville. He had been wandering all over the country, was in a serious automobile accident in Louisiana (hit and run), which left him with a badly damaged foot after surgery. In addition, he was hearing voices and seeing people long dead. He told us that in all the time he had been traveling, no one had spent as much time with him as we had. He also said he trusted us to help him make the decision which he knew he needed to make.

One of the benefits of providing services for consumers by consumers is the empowering feeling that each of us receives for having helped one another. It is difficult to know who feels better, the provider or the recipient. We administer surveys to members about the environment and services which they receive. From 150 surveys, we have found that there is little discrepancy between the ideal environment and the real environment at the center. This evaluation was done for a number of reasons, but the primary purpose was to determine if the center was performing services to the satisfaction of the membership. We used Moos' Community-Oriented Programs Environment Scale (1988). Although the surveys were extraordinarily lengthy, we decided to use this particular instrument because of its wide use and validity. Several graduate students in social work, including one of the co-directors from the center, and a retired nurse administered the surveys over a ten month period. The Community Oriented Program Environment Scale measures relationships, personal growth or goal orientation and system maintenance.[1] All of the results were discussed with members. There was also a good amount of discussion regarding the necessity of providing some outcome measures to our funding agents.

A doctoral student from Virginia Commonwealth University completed a pilot of three drop-in centers within Virginia. The particular instrument which she used is similar to the one used by Mowbray and Tan (1993) in their process evaluation of six drop-in centers in Michigan. The results of the pilot study in Virginia were similar. Members interviewed in both studies were satisfied with the drop-in centers and felt that the centers had a positive impact upon their lives (Mowbray & Tan, 1993; Boyd, 1995).

We have never presumed to know what consumers need or want, rather we assist them with what they request. We do perform a Quality of Life Interview (Lehman, 1988) with interested consumers to aid them in seeing, concretely, what their needs are. This survey also assists staff members to conceptualize problems which consumers want assistance in solving.

Consumer-Run Programs: The Future

During the first years of "on our own...," there was a very distinct coolness from the more clinically or medically oriented staff who worked in the clinic at the community mental health center. Clearly there was some anxiety on the part of clubhouse staff that consumers would attend the drop-in center and not the clubhouse. There was a great deal of concern about this since clubhouse funding was based on attendance. Our position was quite different. Since we value choice, then clearly having alternatives from which consumers can choose is valuable. Obviously there are consumers who favor the structure at the clubhouse as opposed to the relatively unstructured program at the drop-in center. However, there are also consumers who prefer the drop-in center — and some consumers who attend both. Psychiatrists are rather skeptical it seems — how can a person with mental illness be a provider? Their solution has been to say that we are not real consumers. According to them consumers are persons who are schizophrenic. All staff at the drop-in center are mindful of this criticism — and we resent the implication. None of us feel the need to debate this issue; rather we understand the reasons the medical model and clinical staff members say this.

[1] Copy of evaluation will be sent upon request.

In September, 1995, a project which we proposed, in collaboration with the local mental health center, "peer helper," was funded. This idea of hiring consumers who are clients of the local mental health center was discussed at length approximately three years ago. The notion was abandoned because of irreconcilable differences about the value of hiring consumers — rather than having them volunteer. Our position was to hire consumers, train them ourselves, and give them the same job description as any case manager hired by the mental health center, but use the title peer helpers, as the title of case manager is offensive to many consumers. Their idea was to train consumers to act as para-professionals on a volunteer basis, denying them access to any medical records. Since that time, we have proven ourselves to decision-making people within the mental health center in many ways. When new block grant funding for the state was announced, we were approached to write a grant collaboratively for consumer case management. This was great validation for us. We had worked very hard to establish ourselves as an agency that is doing the job that needs to be done — and doing it well.

All of the training of peer helpers is being done by our agency, and the case manager hired by the mental health center will be working together with the peer helpers to provide services in the manner in which our agency provides them—not in the clinical setting, and not during hours which are generally based on the convenience of the clinical staff. All meetings between staff and consumers are open meetings; no longer will there be treatment team meetings where decisions are made for clients without their input. The partnership between any peer staff and consumer will be the vehicle for any decisions. Now that we will be initiating the consumer peer helper project with the mental health center, there will be more opportunity for their staff to observe, firsthand, the quality of consumer help. This will be, for many, the first time that acknowledged consumers will work side by side with other staff members. There are bound to be changes once this occurs.

There are presently five or six consumer-run programs in Virginia — ours was the first. Each program is quite different. Some are consumer-run, meaning that consumers are employed at the programs, but the local mental health center has provided all of the training, is responsible for keeping all of the money, and makes policy. But only two of them are *completely* consumer-run and managed; we are one. The others are more or less independent, but are still closely allied with the mental health system. The Department of Mental Health published a manual on December 1, 1994 entitled *Primary Consumer Involvement in the Mental Health Service System in Virginia*. There have been several meetings held throughout the state to discuss this manual, and it is interesting to note that in the introduction it states that the Department:

> has a long-standing commitment to increase opportunities for mental health consumers and family members to participate in various ways in the planning, development and operation of Virginia's mental health system. One aspect of this goal has been to strengthen consumer and family representation on policy-making bodies such as the State Board and the community services boards..." (p.1)

The appearance of this manual, after the appointment of the new Commissioner of Mental Health, seems to suggest that there are many consumer-run programs within the State, but when one reads what they are, they are not consistent. Many are tokens, meaning that they are groups of consumers who are functioning as part of the mental health system, and not within their own system. Clearly this is a step, but since there are always staff people around who lead or who make decisions and thereby control the group, then the question is: are these consumer-run programs? I think not! Several of the mental health centers (called Community Services Boards in Virginia), thought that placing suggestion boxes in clubhouses meant having consumer involvement in evaluation activities (p.7). Consumers are, by their reckoning, least involved in staff training (p.8), and staff meetings (p.8). Consumer membership on policy making boards was also quite low (p.8). When we come to the area of consumer employees, once again the numbers are relatively low, but there is a huge discrepancy between the types of employment: support positions, 47%, and those employing consumers as managers 12.5% (p.9).

The idea of hiring consumers to work with other consumers is finally being examined — in light of shrinking funds. It is often stated that consumer-run programs are more attractive these days because we can do the job for fewer dollars. But this is certainly not the only reason for their attractiveness. Managed care companies have courted consumer programs in other states (Texas and Minnesota to name two) for the same reasons: cost effectiveness and increased quality of life. Persons in recovery from substance abuse have long been acknowledged to work well with other substance abusers — because they have been there themselves. It is finally coming to be our time, for many reasons. What is taking longer, however, is the recognition from mental health professionals that consumers can, and do, work effectively with other consumers. This is due in part to the socialization which takes place for most professionals: social workers, nurses, physicians — especially psychiatrists. They do not value the knowledge of persons with mental illness, rather they follow the medical model, label and project illness on consumers, thereby finding what consumers say to be of little value. The way to change that is to do what professors such as Dr. Bentley, Professor of Social Work in Richmond, do: have consumers be part of the class process and value what they say. That is the only way that the traditional system will change. Expecting consumers to change the system from within is not possible. Giving consumers their voice is perhaps the only real way to change this system.

The mental health system is not entirely culpable as there is an additional issue as to whether consumers are willing/trusting to invite other consumers to help educate them on values rather than relying on professionals and their models. This is not to say that they, the consumers, should be blamed for this. Consumers have been at the mercy of professionals for so long that many have taken on the aura of the professional as role model. Consumers can be co-opted so easily when professionals train them to do counseling, behavior management or the like. These consumers become more like the professionals than the professionals, using their language, imitating their ways, laughing at consumers. Consumers must be educated on the real value of consumer alternatives to a system which has controlled them and has kept them disempowered. Consumers, as a valuable resource, can be taught to administer, direct and advocate for others. They can make mistakes, but they can also correct them. But they must believe it is possible!

References

Allen, P. (1974). A consumer's view of California's mental health care system. *Psychiatric Quarterly*, 48, 1-13.

Beaurline, E. (1993). My name is Erica. *The Observer, Health Quarterly*, 1-7, Charlottesville, Virginia.

Bentley, K.J. (1993). The right of psychiatric patients to refuse medication: Where should social workers stand? *Social Work*, 38 (1) 101-106.

Bond, G.R. (1994). The role of drop-in centers in mental health services. *Innovations & Research* 3 (1) 46-47.

Boyd, A.S. (1995). *Piloting the drop-in center interview form for relevance in Virginia.* Unpublished manuscript.

Harp, H.T., and Zinman, S. (1994). *Reaching across II: Maintaining our roots/the challenge of growth.* Sacramento, CA: California Network of Mental Health Clients.

Johnson, D.L. (1994). Drop-in centers are a great idea, but do they work? *Innovations and Research* 3 (1) 41-42.

Kanter, J.S., (1989). Clinical case management: Definition, principles, components. *Hospital and Community Psychiatry* 40 361-367.

Kanter, J.S., Harris, M. and L.L. Harris (eds.). (1988). *Clinical issues in the case management relationship in clinical case management: New directions for mental health services, no. 40.* San Francisco, CA: Jossey-Bass.

Lehman, A.F. (1988). A quality of life interview for the chronically mentally ill. *Evaluation and Program Planning* Vol 11 51-62.

Meek, C.M. Consumer-run drop-in centers as alternatives to mental health system services. *Innovations & Research* 3 (1) 49-51.

Moos, R.H. (1988). *Community-oriented programs environment scale manual, second edition.* Palo Alto, CA: Consulting Psychologists Press.

Mowbray, C.T., and Tan, C. (1992). Evaluation of an innovative consumer-run service model: The drop-in center. *Innovations & Research* 1(2) 19-24.

Sands, R.G., *Clinical social work practice in community mental health.* New York, NY: Macmillan.

Silverman, S.H., Taylor, L., & Blank, M. (1995, working paper). *On our own, preliminary findings from a consumer-run service model.*

Tan, C.B., Mowbray, C.T. & Foster, J.(1990). *Consumer-run drop-in center study technical report.*

White, M. (1994). The evolution of a drop-in center. *Innovations & Research* 3 (1) 44-46.

Zinman, S., Harp T. H., and Budd, S. (1987). *Reaching across: Mental health clients helping each other.* Sacramento, CA: California Network of Mental Health Clients.

Justice in Mental Health Organization, Inc. (1993). *Project doors development manual Draft.*

Shela Silverman is co-founder and co-director of "on our own, charlottesville, va., inc." She is a board member of the Virginia Mental Health Consumers' Association, a member of the Advisory Council of the PAIMI (Protection and Advocacy for Individuals with Mental Illness), and devotes a great deal of her time to providing technical and hands-on assistance to consumers throughout the Commonwealth of Virginia who are interested in starting consumer-run projects.

Chapter 11

Revitalizing a Consumer-Controlled Alternative
Ed LeDoux

Background

After many years of involvement as a consumer in the mental health system I decided to get involved and do something about it. I joined the Coalition of Consumer Self Advocates in Cranston, Rhode Island, worked my way up the organizational ladder and one day was asked by both consumers and the state to take over and revitalize the dying OASIS Drop-In Center. I accepted this challenge, and was able to use my education in political science and public administration to turn OASIS around, just by educating members so they could see their own great value and ability to participate in the operation of this 100% consumer-run enterprise.

The OASIS Drop-In Center serves mental health consumers. It is consumer run and directed and, in part, serves as an alternative to structured programs. OASIS is, and can be, whatever consumers want it to be. People can come in simply to talk or they can join a group or start their own group or activity. Peer support is difficult to duplicate in appropriateness and effectiveness yet OASIS is the place to go for the best! If computers are your thing, we have a 386 machine and laser printer. There are games, FREE meals, snacks, drinks, and coffee.

Consumers are employed to greet and sign in members and to perform all the daily tasks. We are the largest employer of consumers in Rhode Island. As executive director, I have full management authority and responsibility, aided by an assistant executive director. Both of us are consumers. Together, we all prove every day that although people have disabilities, they also have abilities. The increase in self-esteem at OASIS is remarkable. People believe that they can do things and help others, too, and OASIS has been doing that for the last seven years.

My Early Struggle

As I think about today's OASIS, I can't help remembering the earlier days when nobody thought the OASIS Drop-In Center would survive. OASIS was first incorporated in 1988 and was located in an old tenement house in Providence, Rhode Island. It was a project of the Coalition of Consumer Self-Advocates, the local consumer advocacy organization, itself in its incipiency. I wasn't involved in the consumer movement at that time.

I was hospitalized in 1989 and released in January, 1990. At my local mental health center I went through the usual bureaucratic nonsense that was making me worse instead of better. Convinced that the hospitalization was inappropriate, I was attempting to correct the situation but was getting nowhere—a familiar scenario for consumers.

Being unemployed and too "high-functioning" to be on SSI or SSDI, I concluded that I needed to get a job. But, I needed help. I asked the mental health center. I experienced a nightmare. The center assigned me to their vocational program where I was tested and tested while I worked at the center's "affirmative business," a picture-framing operation that dealt directly with the public. Interestingly, my therapist didn't feel that I would want to work in a frame shop; the fact that I worked for nine years as a freelance photographer apparently escaped his memory.

For over a year, I worked and tested. After six months or so, I got an appointment with the placement person who informed me that I, "...needed a job." I knew that before walking through the door. He wanted to know, as did all the other staff, what I was doing to get employed. I wanted to know what they were doing to get me employed. We battled, and still do. But the difference is that I, that is, consumers are now winning.

In March, 1991 I saw a flier that read, "Change the world! Join the Coalition of Consumer Self-Advocates (CCSA)." It went on to tell how community organization techniques were powerful tools and that the following Saturday there would be an all-day training. I went; I joined CCSA and that May I attended Midwest Academy in Chicago to learn more about community organizing techniques.

I grew in CCSA and was elected to the Board of Directors and ultimately co-chair. This training was very useful, as I began to take on the mental health center over my unemployment problems. Using the power of CCSA, I had a meeting with all the people involved in my case. The center's operation, compliance, and funding being closely scrutinized by the state provided a little leverage, too. They wanted to know what I wanted. It was the same: a life, starting with a job, appropriate medical and psychiatric care and continuous support, all of this being in a service plan with shared commitment. They were horrified that I wanted them to get me a job. I was willing to do my part, but they just weren't hearing that. Finally, I was again asked—what I was going to do to get a job! That was it! I used a very crude sexual analogy to make the point that you don't have consumers get their own jobs when there are paid vocational professionals around.[1] The shocking remark had its effect. There was a hush. It was agreed that there would be a plan with commitments to the components I wanted and a six-month deadline for me to be employed at a minimum of $25,000 per year.

The plan was drawn up and cosigned by the other CCSA co-chair. We got copies, a marketing specialist/job coach was assigned, and off we went. In

[1] Th editors have requested that Mr. LeDoux not use a direct quote, because it was expected that some readers would find it offensive.

five months I was employed by the OASIS Drop-In Center and scared to death. What a job lay before me. But I'll get back to that later. Interestingly, I turned this job down many times, not really understanding what the whole drop-in center concept was all about. At that time, I had many board and committee memberships which took a lot of my time and effort. To earn a few dollars, I did work as a freelance photographer.

My reputation and influence as a mental health advocate was steadily growing. Getting things done helped. One major accomplishment was compelling my mental health agency to open access to consumers' mental health records and give them copies, if the consumers wanted them. The law, our mental health advocate (an attorney), and the state agreed. That year I was elected to my local agency's Board of Directors.

Meanwhile the OASIS Drop-In Center was crashing fast. Budget deficits, bad management, the total lack of an effective management system, hostile relations between consumers and the funding source, and other problems brought OASIS to the brink of closing forever. The state official managing the grant and his superior asked me to look into the matter. I did and reported to them the nightmare described above. What a mess. They agreed that drastic measures were necessary and they would get back to me.

The job of manager of OASIS Drop-In Center was advertised, as the person on board was in a transitional position. On several occasions friends and associates suggested that I apply for the job. I wondered what I ever did to them! The two state officials then asked me to take the job if they could convince the OASIS Board to bypass the ongoing job search and hire me to turn the place around. The bottom line was that if OASIS couldn't soon become viable, the grant would be terminated. Finally, considering the stakes, I agreed that if they could do it, I'd take the job. The Board agreed and on June 26, 1992, I became manager of the OASIS Drop-In Center.

OASIS Grows

The budget deficit had been "handled" by the state, and the remaining line items in the budget left a balance of over $5,000 that had to be spent before July 1, 1992 or we'd lose it and our budget would be reduced by that amount the following year. Four days to spend $5,000! An easy task for one of the "bi-polar" persuasion! We made a list and off my assistant and I went. Two computers, laser printers, dishware, appliances, office supplies and on and on. But we did it and inventoried the whole lot. Quite an undertaking.

The next major task was designing a whole new system that saw to the needs of consumers, advanced the consumer movement and was sound fiscally and operationally: a major task when you consider that historically the drop-in center had no real system or direction but was loosely overseen by a state worker miles away. Consumers hung around, some getting paid, some drop-ins, with little, if any, functional distinction.

The design of the management system was to have the Board of Directions (in this case, the "Steering Committee") on top with the manager serving as the delegated administrative agent of the Board. There was a part-time assistant manager, several stipend workers (now there are 14 of them, with more to come) and volunteers. All consumers!

Financial management at OASIS escaped description. What a disaster! Fortunately, this was the start of the fiscal year, and we had the opportunity to start fresh. And so we did. In the past years, all requests for funds had to be countersigned by a state official. It was agreed that this was not very empowering, so from that point on only my signature was needed to secure funds or pay bills. The Mental Health Association of Rhode Island remained our fiscal conduit through all of these changes and their people have been very insightful, progressive, helpful, and not paternalistic. They should be commended.

Policies and procedures were set up to govern the day-to-day operation of OASIS, such as signing in people as they entered, making them comfortable, offering them free food and drink, mostly from the food bank, and keeping the doors locked. The last item was quite a point of contention at more than one board meeting. One time we had a protection and advocacy lawyer present who objected to the locked doors and believed, for that reason, that OASIS was not a "true" drop-in center. I managed to make the point, in concert with all the board members, that the doors were locked for security reasons, that is, to keep non-members out and not to lock members in. It's important for us all to feel safe in our own place. Other drop-in centers have since adopted this policy.

By wisely managing the budget, using large quantities of very inexpensive items from the local food bank and donations from a local bakery, OASIS is able to offer free food and drink to all its members. Several meals plus continuous snacks are the norm.

Every organization has to have rules to function in a fair and orderly manner. The Board and I developed a set of rules with progressive discipline and appeals. They're simple and reasonable, for example: "No Violence or Threat of Violence — Directly or Indirectly," "No Stealing," "No Alcoholic Beverages or Illegal Drugs," and "You Must Be Clean and Sober."

I maintained my connections with the system and the consumer movement and gradually expanded involvement at all levels, including the state planning council, several boards, committees and consulting, although the Board often protested and twice had me report in detail what I was doing on OASIS time and why. Good for them. I have no problem with accountability and I am clearly accountable to them, as I should be.

The state also had problems with my activities. It took some time before I could convince them that this was part of my duties. They were concerned that if I was out of the building, it would cost more to pay part-time workers to run the place. True. But more part-time workers were employed as a result and OASIS grew more powerful as I used my other positions to promote and protect our organization. The state ultimately agreed when the board officially approved of my activities. Larger budgets and greater credibility followed.

Credibility and Power

Throughout all this ongoing development, some people in the state system, advocates, consumers and various others wondered if we could "do it" without supervision of some kind. After all, we were mental patients, who, like little children, needed knowledgeable adults to watch over us. We've proven that idea wrong. There hasn't been a situation that we haven't been able to handle, and handle well. We are all believers in the concept of recovery. As chair of our Rhode Island Consumer/Family Monitoring Committee, I've helped develop our definition of recovery:

The maximization of consumers' lives and the minimization of their illness (es) with appropriate, relevant and continuously flexible services and supports collaboratively developed and chosen.

Other principles of the Monitoring Committee that form our fundamental values are:

Consumer Focus. The consumer/service recipient is the center and focus of the system, with all other components being subordinate.

High Expectations. The "best" a consumer can be, not the "least," "easiest" and/or "cheapest."

Normal Goals. Goals appropriate to the consumer and the same as "normal" people, while consistent with those for progressive and sustained recovery.

Independence. The consumer being able to manage his/her life with others supplying varying degrees of help, but not control.

Respect. The consumer is treated like an equal and valued member of society, instead of a "bad" and "stupid" child and/or criminal.

Hope. Belief in a consumer's dream of recovery and ability to achieve and sustain it.

Partnership/Collaboration. The consumer working with the system to develop and implement a flexible plan for recovery.

Service Plan. Comprehensive, integrated, balanced and flexible service plan and contract between the system/center, the consumer and others stating the rights, responsibilities, tasks, deadlines and expected outcomes for all parties necessary to achieve and sustain recovery, manage crisis, and restore the consumer to the recovering state.

These principles have guided us through some very difficult times to get to where we are today at the OASIS Drop-In Center. But principles are only as good as the people and we have a great group of people at OASIS. We often look back and are amazed, but not surprised, that "mental patients" have done so well.

A Bright Future

Less than three years ago we were threatened with the end of the OASIS Drop-In Center. Now we're a division of the Coalition of Consumer Self-Advocates (CCSA), which also has advocacy and education divisions. We now have a combined budget of nearly half a million dollars and growing as we expand drop-in centers through a Dartmouth College grant.

We'll be hiring new people, both full and part-time, co-locating our central offices with the Alliance for the Mentally Ill of Rhode Island, and entering into various collaborative enterprises. We are also doing consulting, as our once-failed enterprise is now considered a model around the country.

And personally, I've gone from unemployment, poverty, and near homelessness to a position where I could not only help myself but help others to build a great place where consumers can all belong. We're more than a simple drop-in center. We're now, as our brochure says, "an exclusive private club run by and for consumers of mental health services." I've gone from manager to executive director to director of social services and programs for CCSA. And this isn't the end of this story. This is only the beginning of a better, more empowered, more recovered life for consumers.

Some Free Advice

I've often been asked about the ingredients or the secrets of success. The answers are simple. First, know what you want. Have a dream. Build a dream. Dreams are realized by breaking them up into goals and smaller pieces, such as objectives. You can't succeed, or fail, at anything unless you know what the dream is. Keep refining your dream. Be flexible, move forward, never backward.

Listen to all people who are negative and say they can't. But, don't follow them! Follow your dream. Never give up! Never back off! If a way of doing things is the norm or the way it's done, target it and move to change it, as it's probably an enemy of your dream.

Seek out friends of your dream. They're everywhere, and often where you least expect them. They want your dream as badly or worse than you do. They're essential and valuable. Look hard for them and bring them into your dream.

Finally, do it! Or your adversaries will, and at your expense. But if you follow your dream and do it, it will come true, as my dreams have and continue to come true. Anyone can do it. And the saga continues...

Ed LeDoux is director of social services and programs for the Coalition of Consumer Self-Advocates in Rhode Island and is also executive director of the OASIS Drop-In Center in Providence, RI, a private club for consumers of mental health services.

Chapter 12

Offering Sanctuary and Safety: Rainbow House, A Peer Support Facility

Nancy Prout

Putting Support First for Persons with Mental Illness

Persons with mental illness have found themselves caught in an uncompromising paradox of mental health modernism. In the past fifteen years, increased awareness about mental illness has helped more people to get earlier and correct diagnoses, but at the same time, mental health care has become increasingly snarled in rigid, economically based systems. This has made it more difficult for persons to get the ongoing support for treatment that is necessary for recovery. Many have reported that they feel buffeted between the demands of an amoral health care market and their own need for continuity of care.

Already burdened by stigma, many persons with mental illness have had to face the added stress of being viewed as overly demanding by insurance providers or community mental health programs. Indeed, many have been dismissed by provider systems for not meeting some arbitrary standard. To make matters worse, just finding services can be frustrating. And once a person has gained entry into care, they have the pressure of the clock ticking — they are not given a choice about how long services will last. Others have found that just getting in the door does not solve problems. They find themselves in programs which demand complete compliance or threaten a quick trip back out the door.

Therapists often report that they do not have enough time to provide the constant support that their clients need. They are frustrated when their clients are in and out of hospitals and day programs that offer little or no appropriate aftercare support. There have been almost no programs available to help clients stabilize and manage their day to day living. Consumers report that although their illnesses are 24 hours a day and do not keep schedules with traditional clinical hours, they are being asked to respond to treatment under those conditions. There needs to be a bridge between Monday to Friday program type models and after-hours crisis type help. The pressing desire for a buffer — a refuge, a place for friendships, 24-hour support, easy access, and non-stringent criteria for entry are recurrent wishes being expressed by consumers.

In response to such frustrations, persons with mental illnesses and care providers have begun seeking alternatives. The need for friendly, supportive and consumer-driven services has led to the development of unique programs and facilities. One such program is Michigan's successful Rainbow House —

A Nonprofit Center for Persons with Dissociative Disorders. Rainbow House was incepted by and is run for and by persons with Dissociative Identity Disorders (DID)[1]. By allowing easy access, involvement at will, and placement of peer support over bureaucracy, Rainbow House has established an environment in which persons with DID can relax, build friendships, and work on their own goals. Rather than enormous amounts of time being used in making paper trails, members spend their time doing what they feel is in their best interest. Members share in all aspects of running the center, doing everything from cleaning to finance. There is a real sense of ownership. Once a member — always a member, unless an individual decides otherwise. No authority figure holds the keys. Members hire professionals who they feel will be useful to the Rainbow House community. Members use the center as they need or want to use it. By relating their past suffering and sharing their problems and strengths, members have been able to find support and fortitude. The isolation and shame that have so often accompanied DID is eliminated. Advocacy skills are exchanged and members are able to then use these skills to get their needs and wants fulfilled. Real work skills are developed as members initiate and run all programs and business activities themselves. But first, and foremost, is the opportunity to have a sense of ownership and be able to make use of the house at will and at any time. This has allowed these consumers to maintain themselves in the community while having the peer support they yearned for as they meet the challenges of living with their illnesses.

Starting A Peer-Run Facility

Step One

The inception for Rainbow House began innocuously enough when one client in an outpatient psychotherapy session told Detroit's Harper Hospital chaplain/clinician, Fr. Joseph Mahoney, that she would just like to meet one

---

[1] Dissociative Disorders are a group of psychiatric conditions which share certain common features and which are not due to an organic mental disorder or any other disorder:

   a) Psychogenic Amnesia — the sudden inability to recall important personal information too extensive to be explained by ordinary forgetfulness

   b) Psychogenic Fugue — sudden unexpected travel away from one's home or place of work, with the assumption of a new identity and the inability to remember one's past

   c) Depersonalization Disorder — persistent or recurrent episodes of depersonalization in which a sense of one's own reality is lost or changed sufficiently to cause marked distress

   d) Dissociative Identity Disorder (formerly labeled Multiple Personality Disorder) — the existence of two or more distinct personalities, each of which is dominant at a given time. The dominant personality determines the individual's behavior. Each personality has a consistent pattern of perceiving the environment and self.

   e) Dissociative Disorder Not Otherwise Specified — A category of disorders which predominantly features dissociative symptoms, but which does not meet the criteria for the specific Dissociative Disorders stated above

See Diagnostic & Statistical Manual of Mental Disorders, DSM-III-R.

other person with MPD (Multiple Personality Disorder). The chaplain soon after started a trial support group to see if interaction between persons recovering from MPD might be beneficial. The focus of the group was on peer support, not therapy. The group members quickly formed a bond and were soon expressing their wish to be able to meet for more than the twice monthly sessions. The chaplain, always an avid advocate for self empowerment, encouraged the group to identify what they wanted and needed. The group expressed their desire for a 24-hour support facility that offered a relaxed atmosphere where they could drop in and socialize or unwind after a tough therapy session or hard day. They then identified their wishes for a place that did not hinge on insurances or ability to pay. A mission statement was developed to help keep the focus on primary objectives: "Rainbow House is a nonprofit center, run for and by persons with Dissociative Disorders whose aim is to provide a relaxed, supportive, recovery-oriented atmosphere for them and others of like diagnoses." Many also expressed their desire for adjunct therapies such as art, writing, and psychodrama. Many had found therapeutic arts helpful to them in inpatient settings but nonexistent or cost prohibitive in their communities. The group knew what they wanted — how to achieve it came next.

> **Conclusion:** Define your group goals. This works best if members personally list their own visions for the facility. The group members then join together to identify the points that they have in common. These common issues then serve as a springboard for a mission statement.

Step Two

Several members contacted the Small Business Administration for information on starting a business and began researching articles on business plan development. Although the facility was to be nonprofit, the group knew that there would be a definite business aspect to running a 24-hour drop-in house. Many of the members had been out of the workforce for many years. The challenges of developing a business plan and the desire to see it implemented spurred major growth in the self-confidence of those involved. A comradery developed and there was an almost humorous aspect to proving it was possible to defy tradition and institute a consumer run model that would be workable, logical and serve as a springboard for consciousness raising in the mental health community.

> **Conclusion:** Develop a business plan. This will be helpful in focusing on what your group wants to do and how they plan to achieve their goals. This will be conducive to securing funding and community support. Contact your local Small Business Administration Office for literature on developing a business plan.

Step Three

Rainbow House's founding members were very lucky to have the financial support of one member and her husband for initial capital to secure a lease. Many in the mental health community were well-wishing, but the underlying skepticism was evident when the request for start-up funding was met with avoidance and misgiving. One major break occurred when social worker, Ben Helmke, became enthused about our cause and was willing to negotiate for less than fair market value on a lease for a site which he owned. Members helped with deposits on utilities, local licenses, fire inspection fees, etc. The local Alliance for the Mentally Ill donated $200. Members solicited donations of furniture, household and business items. One member persuaded an attorney to volunteer his services to help with obtaining a nonprofit 501(c)3 status and filing the necessary Articles of Incorporation. Timidity and fear of social settings were diminishing as Rainbow House consumers used the impetus of their goals to network and advocate for their dream.

Conclusion: Taking care of business matters is important from the onset. Draw from the resources closest to you including members, business persons, family, and friends. Again, the local Small Business Administration has a plethora of information on the steps involved in starting out. Your initial financial footing must be sound. Future funders will want to know that your members have invested in the project. Some grantors and contributors hinge their commitment on match monies from member contributions.

Step Four

With the foundations set, we proudly opened our doors in October 1992. We negotiated with art and music therapists to conduct weekly group sessions and to work with individuals on a sliding fee scale. Our chaplain friend from the Harper Hospital support group willingly moved the facilitated support meeting to the newly opened Rainbow House. Another therapist volunteered her services to facilitate a twice monthly support group for friends and adult family of Rainbow House members. A psychodrama group was formed under the direction of an experienced social worker. Many members used their own personal skills to offer classes in areas such as ceramics, crafts, sign language, and computer literacy. Rainbow House was becoming increasingly well known, but at the same time we began to experience the problems of rapid growth. More persons were joining, but the ideas of self-empowerment and volunteerism were not necessarily associated with their desire for membership. Some members were not paying the very modest fees for groups, and community chores such as housework, bookkeeping, and answering the phones were falling on the shoulders of only a few members. A group of professionals was selected to serve as an advisory board. This volunteer board meets monthly and is available by phone to members at any time there is need for help with intergroup conflict or with business advice. Bimonthly community meetings were instituted so that members would be kept up to date on business matters and workload distribution could be more evenly divided. As each member began contributing to the work of maintaining the house and working more collaboratively with other members, there was a noted increase in the maturation of work proficiency and interpersonal relationship skills.

Conclusion: Make certain your programming wants are equally matched with realistic volunteer and professional backing. Be certain that membership expectations are evenly matched with membership enthusiasm for sharing responsibilities.

Step Five

Also with growth came the necessity for securing outside funding. Several members worked diligently at networking. One member had some grant writing experience and began preparing project proposals. When Michigan Department of Mental Health Director, James Haveman, was in town for a speaking engagement, members invited him to tour Rainbow House. Haveman, a well-known proponent of consumer involvement, was very enthused with the project and his alliance proved extremely beneficial when the Department of Mental Health was requesting innovative project proposals from consumer-run organizations. Rainbow House was able to secure its first substantive grant. Members began attending the local community mental health board meetings. Networking has become instrumental in obtaining funding to sustain day-to-day operations. One member applied for a position on a state advisory council on rehabilitation issues and received an appointment from the Governor. This proved to be another powerful opportunity to network and advocate for the needs of persons with mental illnesses. The local chapter of the International Society for the Study of Dissociation is kept updated on the activities of Rainbow House and many of the society's members have been helpful in forwarding information, speaking at Rainbow House and referring their clients. Rainbow House is also actively involved in outreach and has given technical support and information to many other groups throughout the world on starting their own consumer-run facility. The pride that has come from being considered the experts has helped many Rainbow House consumers to venture into areas they once had thought beyond their realm. Many consumers have entered college and the work force. The confidence that has been built through involvement in the positive experience of being instrumental in breaking ground in a model that has caught nationwide attention has helped many consumers venture into endeavors that they formerly would not have even considered.

Conclusion: Network, research, and learn to write grants. "A Country unto itself is not known," applies here. It can be difficult to sit through meetings, attend public events and call on politicians, but without the support of others, it is almost impossible to keep your group afloat. Many colleges offer grant writing classes and it can well be worth the investment of time and money if no one in your group has previous grant writing experience. Your local library also can be invaluable in researching foundations and organizations that can help you financially. A group of consumers attending a community mental health board meeting or government policy making session can feel make a more powerful impact than going it alone. After a while, an understanding that persons with authority are there to serve consumers rather than consumers being there to please those in power positions, begins to predominate. Consumers learn that they have a voice that can be used to institute change and advocate for their needs.

Challenges, Effects, and Future Implications

The major concern that therapists have in recommending a client for membership at Rainbow House has been a fear that their client will be triggered or overwhelmed by being with other persons with multiple personalities. For that reason, we keep the focus on peer support and not on primary therapy issues. Most members report that it is comforting to be accepted as they are. The building of friendships with others who understand the challenges of living with a dissociative disorder has been described as instrumental to recovery. The idea of having a truly safe place to go at any time of day or night has helped many members reduce their feelings of fear and isolation. Rainbow House does not replace primary therapy but is a wonderful adjunctive aid for those striving to recover from dissociative disorders. The personal growth that comes from being involved in a model that is truly self-empowerment focused has proven highly beneficial to consumers. "If it is to be, it's up to me!" replaces time worn patterns of subservience and complacency.

There has been some backlash among traditionally oriented mental health professionals. The concerns that consumers need only professional care and will not get well or be able to function responsibly without supervision has been raised by some who have worked in medical-based systems. Rainbow House was viewed as thumbing its nose at all traditionally based programs. Rainbow House members are quick to point out that the sanctuary that they have designed for themselves works as an adjunct to traditional models and was implemented to supplement what was available as well as to provide support on a day-to-day basis for members living with chronic mental illness.

Certainly this approach has been cost effective. Membership has grown from an initial group of seven in 1992 to 76 consumers in July, 1995. Total Rainbow House expenditures for 1994 were just over $17,600 which meant that for only $282 per consumer (61 consumers were members at the end of 1994), or only $5.45 per week, members had found a way to provide the support they desired at costs certainly unprecedented in any of the traditional models.

The need for hospitalizations among members has been low. Five out of 61 consumers were hospitalized in 1994, utilizing a combined total of 64 hospital days (one consumer was hospitalized for 28 days, the other four consumers averaged nine days inpatient each). One consumer also utilized 25 days of day hospital treatment. In a self-report survey, 38 Rainbow House consumers responded that they had been hospitalized much more frequently prior to membership at Rainbow House with an average of two inpatient hospitalizations per year at 14 days per stay.

Rainbow House has been successful primarily because it was designed to fulfill an unmet need expressed by mental health consumers with dissociative identity disorders to have ongoing support and a place of refuge they could call their own. The movement away from the medical model and toward the use of peer support to build and sustain programs which embrace rather than regulate consumers has been paramount to the ongoing favorable growth. By working in conjunction with community mental health and other program providers, Rainbow House has been able to help with the extended needs of consumers so that managed care limits and nine-to-five-then-out-the-door scheduling problems are circumvented. The high value placed on member initiative and member work contributions to sustain Rainbow House has helped consumers grow in self-esteem and contributed to the high sense of pride in, and ownership of, Rainbow House. By placing self-reliance above compliance, and allowing consumers to individually and collaboratively find their way to their personal and joint goals rather than meeting expectations circumscribed for them, Rainbow House has fostered new approaches that have caught the eye of consumers, therapists, and others nationwide.

Rainbow House has proven that consumers can be the most viable advocates for getting their needs met. The success of the program has been contingent on the initiative and advocacy of its members. Rainbow House members have learned that their needs can be met by looking at the mental health system from a new perspective — that of peer providership in partnership with existing systems. This model has an ever increasing appeal as the dollar-driven, managed care models become more pervasive. Consumer choices in the traditional models seem to be narrowing. Consumer run programs such as Rainbow House are likely to become more a necessity than an oddity in the future. The challenges that will continue to be created as providers and consumers learn to "play the cards we are dealt" as the managed care debate and public funding cut realities continue may well be met by Rainbow House-type models.

Almost any mental health group can successfully implement a peer support group or facility. By identifying your goals, building financial and professional support, and sharing the responsibilities, a supportive and empowering environment can be built.

References

American Psychiatric Association (1987). *Diagnostic and statistical manual of mental disorders, DSM-III-R, third edition revised.* Washington DC: American Psychiatric Association.

Nancy Prout is a founding member of Rainbow House and served for two years as the administrative director. She is currently in her senior year of study in Pastoral Ministry at Madonna University in Livonia, Michigan.

Chapter 13
Shining Reflections: Alive, Growing, and Building Recovery—Who We Are

Nila Paynter

Shining Reflections is located in the rural community of East Liverpool, about as far east as you can go in Ohio. Our organization was begun nearly ten years ago by a group of dedicated, visionary people with mental illness. It was initially founded to offer a place for people to come together in the community, in part for fellowship, in part for support, and in part to undertake something of our own. We began as the Shining Reflections Tea Room, but we have since expanded. If you visit us, you will find a group of remarkable people engaged in the arts, community service, higher education, mutual support, and personal development.

The idea of the Tea Room was a natural one. Providing good food in a pleasant atmosphere was important and remains important. People can come into the Tea Room for breakfast and lunch. We serve good food and our people are well trained in all of the responsibilities needed to run a top notch eatery. People from all walks of life eat at the Tea Room since we are very much part of our community. The full service restaurant provides management and employment opportunities for people with psychiatric disabilities as well as people with physical disabilities.

The Tea Room is now only one element of our group. Shining Reflections offers a support group and vocational training. And, in the past few years, we have expanded our offerings to include the arts which serve as a vehicle for the expression of our members' creativity. The vocational program's overall goal is to enhance and develop linkages between the support group, local vocational rehabilitation programs, and local mental health providers.

Shining Reflections is really a consumer-operated service. We are responsible for developing our own programs and businesses, and we are responsible for making sure that our vision becomes a reality. We do all of this on our own, without the involvement of mental health professionals, not because they are not welcome as allies or partners, but because Shining Reflections is a peer support alternative, run for and by consumers. This is a fundamental characteristic of our organization — one we share with many other facilities and support groups emerging across the state of Ohio and the United States.

Shining Reflections was founded because something was missing in our community—something the mental health system was not offering. People wanted to be involved in productive activity. People wanted to share their talents while learning new skills. Why? Because in many ways the mental health system is not really a system of recovery, but rather a system of illness. Shining Reflections represents recovery in action: people joining together in fellowship and in support of one another to learn new skills and to share their talents with their peers.

Consumer-operated services are valuable because in developing and implementing our own programs and businesses, we are able to gain a sense of who we are, and what we can be beyond the limitations often defined for us by mental health systems. Consumer-operated services—those run for and by consumers—are devoted to personal development and to personal support. And, as a consumer-operated service, Shining Reflections must confront and challenge the stereotypes surrounding mental illness. Like mirrors in a fun house, the misperceptions and stigma attached to mental illness often result in a distorted view of people who are labeled. People too often see only these distortions, and fail to recognize the living, breathing person behind the illness who thinks, laughs, cries, loves, and hurts as all people do. Shining Reflections is working to eliminate these distortions. It helps people labeled as mentally ill to move along the road to recovery, recognizing that it is as important to address how people in our communities contribute to stigma as it is to help people with mental illness gain more support and develop personally.

We are not a small organization. For a rural community, our membership has overcome many barriers to grow and develop. Since our inception about 10 years ago, we have grown to 40 members. Our budget is well over $180,000. And we employ at least eight staff members. Our volunteer ranks are strong and involve well over 100 people. In 1993, the Tea Room was presented with the Employment Program Award from the National Association of State Mental Health Program Directors, an accomplishment that underscores the relevance of our services and the supports we offer.

A History of Challenges and Success

A small group of consumers established a peer support group in early 1985. The group was very beneficial and members decided to incorporate so they could raise funds through the operation of a business to support activities and reach more consumers in the area. In 1986, the Shining Reflections Support Group applied for funds from the Ohio Department of Mental Health and with the successful receipt of a $30,000 grant, opened the Tea Room in downtown East Liverpool.

The local mental health board and the city of East Liverpool encouraged our development. They provided Community Development Block Grant funds for assistance and for needed renovations to our facility. There were numerous problems encountered during the renovation and start up process, but in February of 1987 the doors opened for business.

Opening this restaurant took guts. We were entrepreneurs. The East Liverpool central business district was severely depressed and contained many empty storefronts. The newly formed support group organized a benefit luncheon for "May is Mental Health Month" during 1987. The invitations stated that people's presence would do two things: It would help the recently formed support group raise the funds needed for the start up of its activities and it would demonstrate their commitment to understanding the plight of individuals who are mentally ill, and to supporting people to regain a place in community life. With the support of the Ohio Department of Mental Health, the local mental health board, the city of East Liverpool, and committed citizens, we were able to make a go of our dream: to have an active support group (and eventually a support network) for people who want to define their own recovery, and to achieve their own aspirations.

The Tea Room offered a lovely environment for everyone in the community. On the outside, it looked like a restaurant with a quaint but inviting facade. On the inside, it looked like a restaurant with real home cooked meals at breakfast and lunch. And it smelled like a restaurant—with the fresh odors produced by soups, pastries, and sandwiches. We put in place a menu that appealed to the community. And we committed ourselves to offering delicious food at a reasonable price.

But we were not satisfied with a restaurant per se. We wanted Shining Reflections to offer training and vocational development to our members. When Shining Reflections opened, its organizers proposed the development and implementation of an "on the job training program" to mental health consumers, and to other underserved people in Columbiana County. It was our belief at the start (and still is our belief) that our training approach could offer a unique vocational alternative in helping prepare people for work and employment. After all, we were a business. But we were a business operated for and by consumers.

Our sensitivity to the situations people with mental illness experienced could only elevate the relevance and effectiveness of our training. We were unfamiliar with traditional rehabilitation methods—perhaps an asset when we found out that many of our members were very dissatisfied with the low expectations and regimented services offered by traditional rehabilitation providers. These programs were time limited, and often failed to be sensitive to the personal issues created by serious mental illness and psychiatric disability.

Early on in our history, we linked the Tea Room with a consumer-driven program that created a very supportive training situation in the context of a real life restaurant—but a real life setting in which consumers could readily get support from other consumers, and give it in return. Participants in the program would not be pushed through the training, but would receive supports to work and learn at their own pace in an environment that brought them into contact with the community. In October 1993, Shining Reflections was one of six programs across the country to receive a three-year federal grant for a vocational training program to expand upon its existing services. Successful funding of this project enabled Shining Reflections to formalize its training program, to develop its management, and to increase secretarial and clerical support.

In the third year, the Tea Room began experiencing problems that are common to many businesses. A full 85% of small businesses can fail within the first five years. While business had improved, economic conditions in East Liverpool remained poor (and they remain poor to this day) and this made a negative impact on our revenues. What kept us going? It was the idea of support! The camaraderie and support of the group was strong enough to enable us to get the Tea Room operating and keep it going. But it did not stop there. The community's support and encouragement was an unexpected pleasure. Most pleasing was the support offered by other merchants and commercial establishments in the downtown business district. Most of our initial customers were professional people or customers of other businesses who had been referred to the Tea Room by merchants. After all, we were first and foremost an eatery. And what better way to create connections with people than through food, especially through the serving of good food?

The Tea Room was one of the first consumer-operated businesses in the state of Ohio. The success we have enjoyed is somewhat remarkable because the business was opened by people with no experience in operating a business, by people who faced major barriers to employment in the private sector, and by people who generally lacked any long-term employment history or skills that would make them job competitive.

Expansion of Our Mission

The Tea Room has prospered, and it developed our courage to expand the mission of Shining Reflections. By the early 1990s we accomplished one of our principal program goals: "To operate a nonprofit restaurant business that employs and trains adult persons who have or have previously had a mental illness." We were ready to move on to our second principal goal: "To build a long-term community support group for adult persons who have or have previously had a mental illness in order to encourage personal and/or group resource development and access to resources."

Several projects have been introduced successfully to expand the range of supports available to our members, especially ones that promote their creative, personal, or social development. These projects include "Rain Voices," "Words from the Heart," and "Families Understanding Naturally."

Rain Voices

The membership of Shining Reflections has come to realize that many people in recovery suffer from severe depression, and fear that the pressure of a full time job may cause a reoccurrence of their illness. The support group offers a medium in which such individuals can address their foremost concern, mental illness, but take it outside of themselves and bring a better understanding to others of its social and personal consequences. The support group is able to offer these members a format for active and creative responsibility with others in a relaxed atmosphere which serves as a valuable transition from total dependence to full time employment. To provide this format, Phoenix Studios of East Liverpool is working in association with Shining Reflections to establish Rain Voices, a sound and video production studio. The purpose of this studio will be to document the pioneering supports offered by Shining Reflections, to produce public service announcements, and to produce educational programs about mental illness, its causes, treatments, and effects.

People suffering from mental illness, and those struggling in recovery, suffer from prejudices—often extending from some mistaken belief that they are violent, that they have diminished intelligence, or that they are undesirable as neighbors or employees. In response, people with mental illness often hide their afflictions to escape these prejudices. As a result, feelings of profound isolation can be experienced.

Rain Voices offers an opportunity for the members of Shining Reflections to escape isolation. For those members who have a serious interest in video and media projects, we believe that by writing, acting, and directing, people will experience many positive effects found in self-expression, in team work, and in collaboration. Several members have already found Rain Voices production to be an outlet for their creativity, and have discovered the many positive talents they possess. They become alive with enthusiasm and cast off mannerisms that characterize their illnesses.

Whenever possible members are encouraged to be performers and technical assistants. We envision Rain Voices as a forum for the intimate expression of ourselves, and for collective support of the artist that is alive in many of us. Rain Voices is a forum in which those people who are most intimately involved with mental illness can have their voices heard, dispelling common misconceptions while offering people an opportunity to express their own perspectives, feelings, and innermost thoughts.

Words from the Heart

Words from the heart, soul, and mind are coaxed from their hidden recesses to take shape as poems and essays that convey feelings and memories for participants in the Shining Reflections writing workshop. Shining Reflections created a partnership with Pig Iron Press in Youngstown, Ohio to help members express their creativity through words. With the technical assistance and mentoring of the editor of the press, Mr. Jim Villani, the "Words from the Heart" workshop was offered in February, 1995 for mental health consumers from Ohio, West Virginia, and Pennsylvania. The 90-minute, hands-on, writing workshops are funded through a grant from the Ohio River Border Initiative and are designed to help participants strengthen their creative writing skills, with a focus on self-discovery, the incorporation of living history, and the infusion of regional identification.

As part of the workshop, participants are introduced to all writing formats including poetry, fiction, literary nonfiction, journalism, personal narrative, biography, autobiography, and journal writing. Participants are very receptive to this opportunity and they express an interest in working with somebody on their writing. The group is very productive. According to one participant, "It's been a personally rewarding experience. Because it's not structured like traditional teaching, people aren't being thrown at me who really do not want to be there. It's been fulfilling."

Writing is a release of deep emotions which often cloud the insight to identify and solve problems. Writing offers multiple opportunities. First, by sharing hidden feelings and thoughts, participants can move beyond the confining hold of mental illness. Second, participants can share with others those events and experiences that have shaped their lives. Writing is a means to identify oneself in society, and to master oneself.

Thus, the project with Pig Iron Press is another outlet by which Shining Reflections serves its members. It has been very successful. Presently, Shining Reflections is celebrating the publication of the book which is a product of the creative endeavors of the participants in Words from the Heart.

"Families Understanding Naturally"

The acronym of "Families Understanding Naturally" is F.U.N. and it is the purpose of this project to provide positive social interaction, education, increased understanding, and constructive activities that bring kids and parents together. The goals of the project include the building of supports between parents and children, the offering of affordable and accessible recreational and enrichment alternatives, and the provision of opportunities to alleviate family stress and improve family stability.

Many people feel captive in a frozen state of helplessness, fear, apprehension, and mistrust. Stress on families is enormous. F.U.N. recognizes the importance of offering families opportunities to enjoy themselves and to experience positive interactions. We organize events that bring a family together, and that bring families together collectively. Emphasis is placed on exploring the community and on experiencing recreational activities often for the first time. A cook-out, a trip to an amusement park, or an outing to a museum are some of the activities undertaken within F.U.N. Reaching out to families in this way often results in very positive interactions—for example, the willingness of children and adults to get along and to cooperate. F.U.N. reflects another opportunity for sparking the process of recovery. And, it is this kind of spark, often achieved through small group activities, which helps people to be people first, that Shining Reflections seeks to put in place.

What Supports Our Success

Shining Reflections is consumer-developed and incorporates a self-help model that offers opportunities for successful employment and training through the operation of a business and a network of peer support services. If Shining

Reflections was not offering these kinds of activities within our local community, it is unlikely that another organization would undertake this work. Thus, fundamental to our success is a commitment to peer support and to relating to people as human beings rather than as people with mental illness.

Shining Reflections has enjoyed the support of its community. The community at large has invested in us and there is a positive upswing in attitudes concerning mental health issues and serious mental illness, in particular. Our marketing analysis indicates that we are viewed as a viable and desirable downtown restaurant business. The general public supports us because our service and food are great and the atmosphere we create in the Tea Room is both pleasant and welcoming. Shining Reflections is part of the fabric of the community, and our members are not isolated from the life of the community.

Community support has been encouraged, in part, through the development and sustenance of an active advisory board composed of key business people, representatives from the Chamber of Commerce, special education teachers, an accountant, restaurant professionals, and an attorney, among others. The advisory board has assisted the Tea Room staff in numerous activities and tasks aimed at improving the overall operation of the business.

An Employer Advisory Board is sustained by Shining Reflections to offer practical assistance in solving problems related to the employment of people with severe disabilities and to create a network of employment resources that can help members make formal and informal job-related contacts. In our relentless, continued search for quality, appropriate and innovative employment opportunities that significantly engage the abilities, interests, desires, and strengths of Shining Reflections participants, we actively seek new membership on the advisory board and we expand interactions with our current advisors. We collaborate with our advisors in a multitude of ways and we successfully enlist their involvement in situational assessments, training, employment, and in work adjustment, job skills, and job search programs. The advisory board is an important structure in linking Shining Reflections to its community. It serves as a principal way the organization broadens the base of work experience opportunities that help our members to bring together community support and employment.

Overcoming Challenges

Our success at Shining Reflections does not mean that we have been without challenges — now and in the past. Some of the challenges emerged internally while others came from the outside. All of them, however, tested our commitment, and tested the stability of our organization. The fact that we are able to present what we have learned about peer support in this book means that we were able to overcome these challenges and to prosper as a result of our work.

Internal Challenges

One of the most crucial challenges that we faced emerged several times during the course of our development. We can identify this as the "leadership challenge." Shining Reflections was founded by very innovative and committed individuals—people who possessed a specific vision concerning what Shining Reflections was and what it was to be in the future. The membership become very dependent on the leadership of these remarkable people, but unfortunately this prevented us—the membership of Shining Reflections as a whole—from developing different leaders and grooming as leaders people who were new to the organization. Thus, as the life situations of our founders changed, and they began to make decisions about their personal lives that took them in new directions, we found that Shining Reflections did not have the leadership it needed to move ahead. Fortunately, we soon found out that we did have this leadership, and that there were a number of people who were available to our organization to lead us in new directions. Leadership development needs to be a purposeful aspect of any self-help organization, and we found at Shining Reflections that the purposeful expansion and grooming of leadership is important to our vitality as a consumer-run entity. It is simply unfair to the organization to become too dependent on a small group of leaders.

Related to the leadership development issue is another challenge. This one involves board development. The evolution of Shining Reflections as a consumer-run organization required us to undertake the purposeful development of a board. Although having consumers on this board is a defining characteristic of any consumer-run organization, we have been mindful of the need to expand board membership so that key community members and community organizations are represented within this critical structure of the agency. The board as a pool of skills, talents, commitments, and connections soon became apparent to us as our needs expanded and as demands for advocacy within the community grew. At this juncture, the development of our board has become more and more important, and our board president along with other key members of the board, have become very important as advocates of our organization.

A third internal challenge involves maintaining our momentum. People can get worn down through involvement in self-help and consumer run activities. We have found that people can get too involved, and that they can get drained by the day to day activities and the hard work demanded by peer support. Maintaining our momentum means that people have to be very conscious of the commitments they make and the pace they take. We have found that people may increase their involvement during one period of their lives and then reduce it as the fulfillment of other life tasks competes for energy. This is fine. In fact, it should be expected. At Shining Reflections, people need to be able to set their own pace and to be supported for whatever choices they make about their commitments to the work and to the organization. Addressing this challenge requires us to be conscious about what we mean about membership and the expectations attached to membership. People are not to be exploited just because they are members. Rather, we must help people to make conscious choices about the form and extent of their involvement in consumer self help.

External Challenges

The principal challenge coming from the outside involves our identity as a mental health program. Are we part of the mental health system? Well, yes and no. We are a part of the mental health system when you look at what we do. Shining Reflections offers a number of good, practical community supports that no other agency within the locale offers. As noted above, we offer support and cultural enrichment. Advocacy and socialization. Vocational development and employment. Our identity is based on consumer support and self-help—a distinctive aspect of the local service scene.

But we do not see ourselves as a "professional" mental health organization. We welcome collaboration with these other organizations, and we see the importance of mental health services when they are proactive, meaningful, and driven by the hopes and wishes of consumers. But we do not share the ideology of the mental health system. Nor are we professional caregivers.

The formation of this identity within our local community has not been without conflict. We have had some "bumps" with the local mental health system, and there has been some competition. But this conflict has been productive. It has offered both parties an opportunity to reflect on what they do best, and on how best to respond to the many needs experienced by people who are labeled as seriously mentally ill. The conflict and its resolution also offers consumers a louder voice in the system.

The formal mental health system does not have to do everything. Shining Reflections—like many of its peer organizations across the country—demonstrates that consumer-run organizations can fill important niches within the community, and can emerge as a peer and equal of "professional" mental health organizations. Shining Reflections is necessary to an effective mental health system. Why? Because consumer self-help is an intregal part of any strategy of recovery.

Conclusion: What Others Can Learn from Shining Reflections

Shining Reflections "reflects" what is integral to consumers as providers of psychiatric rehabilitation. The organization is consumer-operated. This means that Shining Reflections is operated by consumers for consumers. Its business and training programs depend on many members to make them successful: members working with members often as volunteer peer supporters adds to the distinctiveness of Shining Reflections as a consumer-operated program.

Shining Reflections also possesses another integral quality: many of its services and supports simply would not be offered by other mental health organizations. Many consumer needs were not being met prior to its existence. Shining Reflections, like many other consumer-operated programs, emerged specifically to address these needs. Employment, training, support, recreation, peer assistance, and opportunities for self-expression and self-exploration are some of the needs that have been addressed creatively by Shining Reflections. "Rain Voices," "Words from the Heart," and "Families Understanding Naturally" are concrete examples of this creativity in action.

A third integral quality of Shining Reflections is found in its demonstration of the power of consumers supporting one another. Locally, we demonstrate that consumers can be self-directed and independent without constant intervention and support from the system. We have redirected attention away from pathology and diagnosis to rehabilitation, improvement, and healing. And we have shown how to tailor services to the specific needs of consumers because consumers are the driving force of our program.

Consumers must make a go of all of our programs—their presence is necessary for successful operation, and their energy is absolutely essential to maintaining open doors, supportive hearts, and freshly prepared meals. Unlike formal mental health programs, like day treatment, our members cannot wait around for direction. They must do something! They have to get involved! At Shining Reflections, people are given "the green light" to make decisions, and make mistakes. We have discovered a simple but long forgotten truth: People are more comfortable when they are in charge of their own recovery.

The value of the programs offered by Shining Reflections are found in their innovativeness, their individualization, and their focus on basic human needs. Like a church, people come together as a group, and gain strength and support as they benefit from one another. Consumers also gain strength and support when they can come together as a group to learn, grow, and help one another. It hasn't been easy to achieve this end. But Shining Reflections is still going, going, going.

Nila Allison Paynter is currently project coordinator for Shining Reflections Vocational Training Program. She has been involved in various capacities with the Shining Reflections program since its beginning, 10 years ago.

Consumer-Run Entrepreneurial Businesses: Issues and Opportunities

John B. Allen, Jr.
Barbara Granger

The past two decades have seen the rise of psychiatric survivor organizations reflecting the values inherent in the right to self-determination (Campbell, 1991; Furlong-Norman, Warner & Polak, 1993, 1988; Yaskin, 1992; Zinman, Harp & Budd, 1987). Major challenges have been launched critiquing the system of services that do not necessarily meet the needs of people in recovery from varied experiences of mental illness. Consumer-run alternative service and advocacy organizations have emerged throughout the country; some of these have developed alternative vocational services, such as helping people find jobs or creating jobs by running their own entrepreneurial business (Engels, 1994; Friesen & Viti, 1994).

Getting back to work is important for people with psychiatric disabilities, as unemployment continues to be quite high (Anthony, Howell & Danley, 1984). Surveys of consumer/survivors continue to support their interest in getting back to work (Rogers, et al, 1984). Supportive services developed to help people find employment have most often been provided through supported employment programs, offering individual placement with job coaches or transitional employment with short-term employment experiences. Recently, agency-sponsored businesses have emerged as a way to help people return to work; however, very few consumer-run businesses were found in a national survey of entrepreneurial businesses employing people with psychiatric disabilities (Granger & Baron, 1993). Despite this, a consumer-run business appears to be a promising way to provide alternative employment services and career development opportunities.

What is a Consumer-Run Business?

Consumer-run entrepreneurial businesses are those which: (1) produce a product or service for sale to people or organizations in the community; (2) provide employment opportunities for consumers; and (3) are owned and/or managed by consumers. A few examples of current consumer-run entrepreneurial businesses include On Our Own Computer Center, Wyman Way Co-op, The Network, White Light Communications and INCube.

On Our Own Computer Center (The Center), founded in 1990 and located in Silver Spring, Maryland, is a member organization which both trains members in learning or upgrading computer skills and completes varied outside contract work using its extensive computer hardware and software resources. Contract services include design, typesetting, and preparation of printed materials, such as forms, calendars or newsletters; maintenance of mailing lists; and customized mailing services and development of a series of databases for social service agencies. The Center involves consumers in a business that is technologically current and highly valued in the community at large. The Center is run according to principles of a cooperative, with monthly member meetings and weekly staff meetings open to all members. The Center is managed by 20 volunteer members who work with the executive director.

Wyman Way Co-op, initiated in 1984, is a non-profit small business, which provides supportive vocational opportunities to consumer/survivors. Wyman Way Co-op has 40-45 employees who work part-time or full-time. The business is run as a cooperative and is sponsored by a community mental health center in New Hampshire; it receives less than 20% of its funds from government, generating the majority of its operating budget from business activities. The business includes groundskeeping, cleaning, building maintenance and repair, sale of organic produce and woodworking. The co-op recently expanded its woodworking capability by building and marketing a line of outdoor furniture from their new woodworking shop in Keene, New Hampshire. Wyman Way Co-op has received state and national recognition for its efforts in assisting people in their recovery.

The Network grew out of the successful O.J. Sarah's, a breakfast and lunch restaurant in Santa Fe, New Mexico. The Network is a nonprofit enterprise that serves as the corporate and fund-raising umbrella and management locus for a set of employment projects. The Network is managed and staffed by people recovering from mental illness. The Network businesses have included O.J. Sarah's restaurant, Resource Recovery (a nonprofit recycling business), "El Refugio" (a solar adobe house in the mountains built by consumers as a rural work retreat), desktop publishing, and contract community organizing. The Network businesses include supportive consumer-run services such as peer support groups, peer counselors, peer job coaches, and job developers.

White Light Communications, started by Paul Engels, in Vermont, in 1989, is a nonprofit television production and telecommunications company owned and operated by consumers. The initial capital to start the business was provided through a five-year grant from the National Institute of Mental Health. White Light has produced numerous video tapes providing educational information on the issues and personalities of the consumer/survivor/ex-patient movement. It received an award from the Naples Florida Film & Video Festival for the video "Together Tearing Down the Walls," based on the Sixth Annual Alternatives Conference in 1990. In addition, White Light has produced a set of video tapes based on the Self Help Live Series, a direct link via interactive satellite television among consumer organizations (Engels, 1994).

INCube, Inc., located in New York City, was founded in 1988 by a partnership of consumers and concerned professionals. Their mission has been bridging the gap in consumer access to mainstream business development resources. INCube is a technical assistance agency supplying marketplace resources, legal and accounting services and management consultation services to consumer/survivors who wish to start up their own businesses. These services also include linking people with state vocational rehabilitation systems and assisting them with Social Security Administration work incentive programs. INCube has facilitated the start up of more than 20 businesses and service projects in the areas of maintenance, food service, retail, film and video, graphic design and photography. Not-for-profit projects have involved advocacy, housing, substance abuse, family and client support, and drug education.

Each of these consumer-run businesses has created jobs and careers, while at the same providing a supportive workplace. Their values include customer satisfaction, employee supports and a management approach which are accountable to both the customers and employees. Like other psychiatric survivor organizations, participation in a consumer-run business can be an empowering experience.

Empowerment in Consumer-Run Businesses

Consumer-run businesses can provide empowerment to consumers through:
* participation in the research and decision-making at the initial planning and design stages of the business;
* participation in the everyday decisions concerning business practices and business growth decisions;
* increased skills in peer supports;
* employment and/or advancement from production into supervisory and management positions;
* sufficient income from employment to increase personal choices (i.e., housing options, transportation, health care providers, education or leisure opportunities, etc.);
* development of specific technical skills to increase employability in the broader community; and
* sufficient business development and management skills to increase the potential to start one's own business.

However, there are challenges for developers and managers of consumer-run businesses beyond those faced in employment in a traditional business; added supports are needed for individual employees and there is a need to develop a management style that reflects both the peer support and mutual support expected of a consumer/psychiatric survivor organization.

Individual Supports

Individual employees in consumer-run businesses may need added support to build self esteem, self confidence and specific skills enhancing their ability to contribute to ongoing business activities. An entrepreneurial business flourishes when each person brings his or her individual perspective and skills assertively to the business agenda. Furthermore, employees often need assistance in managing their SSI/SSDI and public health benefits in ways that do not put them at risk, regarding needed treatments or medications, hospitalizations and other health care needs. It may take a number of years before a small business such as a consumer-run business can generate the capability to offer private health benefits that could replace public benefits. The primary challenge in providing support is to do it in a way that meets both the mission of support and the needs of a healthy business providing a quality product or service to customers.

Management Style

Consumer-run businesses need to address their management style—that is, their approach to leadership and decision making given the potential for power differences in any organization. Howie the Harp (1994) refers to this issue as maintaining a "delicate balance," given the nature of hierarchies. A cooperative approach to business management complements the management style of other consumer/psychiatric survivor organizations (Chamberlin, 1994; Zinman et al, 1987; Yaskin, 1992). Individuals coming into the business as employees may have little or no experience in cooperative decision making. The National Cooperative Business Association in Washington, D.C., which represents over 47,000 cooperative businesses, provides training and technical assistance for those who would like to start a cooperative business. Participating in a consumer-run business is not just a job, but a full participant responsibility in the business as a whole organization. A cooperative management approach is successful when there is clarity in, and consensus about, all the procedures related to participation and decision-making in the business: personnel issues such as procedures for hiring and firing of production or management employees, and financial issues such as setting wages and benefits, bidding for contracts, investment policies, and use of outside technical or management assistance. The primary challenge to management decision-making is the dual mission of the business in being a profit making entrepreneurial venture, as well as a place for compassionate peer support.

General Electric has long been considered the birthplace of modern management practices and theory; in 1988 they began a company-wide plan to involve employees in major decision-making. As General Electric chairman John Welch says, "We've got to take out the boss element." In planning for a consumer-run business, one needs to keep in mind that all businesses are looking at management styles that change managers from planners, organizers, implementers and measurers; to people who counsel groups, provide resources for them, and help them think for themselves. "We're going to win on our ideas," says Welch, "not by whips and chains" (Stewart, 1991).

Starting up your business, developing employees, generating teamwork throughout the business activities, and planning for business life cycle changes are key points for discussion for anyone planning a new, or evaluating an existing, consumer-run entrepreneurial business. These topics need to address both the entrepreneurial and peer support objectives inherent in consumer-run businesses.

Starting Up a Consumer-Run Business

Business planning is crucial to a successful consumer-run business, which like any other, includes product/service selection, financial planning and management planning. Product/service selection includes choosing a type of product or service based on interest, skills, and resources of the business participants; and on marketing, testing, and developing a viable product or service to respond to customer demand. Financial planning involves development of an accurately projected investment and cash flow needs assessment, balanced against realistic estimates of sales and public support revenues over time. Management planning involves the selection of an appropriate corporate structure which formalizes the business leadership and participation options. There is considerable technical assistance available locally where new businesses are usually a welcome contribution to the community (Warner & Polak, 1993, Friesen & Viti, 1994). Technical assistance is often available from the following business planning resources:

- SCORE—The Service Corps of Retired Executives;
- the Small Business Development Center Programs of the U.S. Small Business Administration;
- national associations of the product or service you plan to develop (see local library for Gale's *Directory of Associations*);
- local public and private business development organizations such as the Chamber of Commerce, managers of Enterprise Zones and Community Block Grants; or
- local banks (try the one you use first) may have a technical assistance service for new business development.

Don't overlook the business experience of the members of your board, their families, and those of the consumers who will be involved in the venture. However, before you seek outside help, it is important to clarify your own mission and the values supporting your mission. This will serve as a base for assessing decision-making choices throughout the planning process.

Mission Clarification

The business planning process requires a clarification of the business mission. As previously mentioned, a consumer-run entrepreneurial business by definition is both an entrepreneurial venture and a consumer-run venture. The entrepreneurial venture reflects a mission committing the business to providing a competitive product or service for public consumption and managing business finances efficiently to make a profit. A consumer-run venture reflects a mission committing the business to providing real job opportunities for consumers with career potential and consumer participation and/or ownership of the business. The two missions can be both complementary and conflicting. The missions are complementary when increased contract opportunities or higher sales cause the business to grow, providing more job opportunities and potential careers for consumers. The two missions could cause conflicts if personnel policies do not assure an adequate workforce available to keep up with contract deadlines and customer satisfaction. However, commitment to continuous reflection on, and resolution of, issues as they relate to the dual missions of a consumer-run/entrepreneurial business can facilitate and promote successful business planning.

Selecting a Product or Service

Selecting the product or service for your business needs should include a discussion that balances both a full assessment of the resources available among the consumers who wish to start a business, and an assessment of the potential customers who would buy your product or service. Consumer resources include everyone's interests, skills, and connections. Before the group selects any specific product or service, there should be tests and small starts focused on the potential product or service selection. For example, if you plan to open a bakery or restaurant, try catering some events to a friendly organization. The marketplace for prospective customers must also be included in your selection process. A marketing plan is part of the development of a business plan. National associations concerned with the product or service you are considering should be able to assist you with some marketing information. Furthermore, there is a national association to assist catalog sales business — The National Association of Direct Marketers. Part of market planning is to gauge the pricing of the products or services you select. Pricing estimates need to include a realistic estimate of production costs, balanced against the competition. Technical assistance should be available from the resources listed above. Your market plan will provide important information for your overall financial plan.

Financial Planning

Based on a recent national survey of agency-run and consumer-run businesses, current business managers reported that one of the most important planning tasks is to develop a business plan which includes, for the most part, a substantial effort at financial planning (Granger & Baron, 1993). Financial planning involves the development of a feasibility study to project the flow of capital needed, expected income and anticipated expenses given the type of business selected and any market planning that supports your figures. Technical assistance is available through the resources listed above to assist small business planners with financial planning. Local banks, and anyone else you turn to for financial investment in your business, will need to use your financial plan as the major criterion for their decisions about whether or not to invest in your business.

Support for Individual Employees in Consumer-Run Businesses

The employees of any business are one of its major assets. In today's business environment, managers of every kind of business, including those that are consumer-run, are concerned about hiring and keeping the best personnel. Owners and managers are always looking for motivated employees. As in many small businesses, employees in a consumer-run business often view their relationships as extended family, providing much more than merely paychecks.

In numerous studies on consumer preference, work is usually the number one item that consumer/survivors desire most after housing. Typical fears related to working are often accompanied by lots of other issues that are disability-related. Housing, financial stability, medical insurance, accommodations for the disability, cycling symptoms, assertiveness, self-confidence, problem solving skills, and education are typical issues that need to be addressed in order to create a sound employment opportunity for individuals with more severe psychiatric disabilities. Creating an environment in which people with psychiatric disabilities work productively can be time consuming, but can also produce rewards in terms of workers who are loyal and motivated, thereby reducing operating costs associated with employee turnover. This is one of the primary reasons consumer-run businesses are created. For businesses in general, *In Search of Excellence* authors said it best: we need to "instruct our leaders in the rock-bottom importance of making the average Joe a hero and consistent winner" to achieve employee excellence (Peters & Waterman, 1982).

Our systems of providing support for individuals with psychiatric disabilities are one of the largest barriers to creating consumer-run businesses and employment opportunities. There are few consumers who have not heard about some of their peers' losing financial support, medical insurance, housing or food stamps due to returning or beginning to work. There is significant anxiety produced by complicated rules which can make it difficult, if not impossible, to regain entitlement/supports, after beginning to work. However, an employer's knowledge of the various work incentives within entitlement programs can establish the safety net to regain entitlements if it becomes necessary; both On Our Own Computer Center and Matrix Research Institute have developed manuals for support personnel and consumer/survivors (Allen, 1994; Matrix Research Institute, 1995). Recent research findings focus on access to support (job coaches), use of positive feedback, and options for part-time work as job accommodations used most frequently by employees with psychiatric disabilities (Granger and Baron, 1995). Furthermore, fostering the extended family notion that occurs in many small businesses can create opportunities to provide informal supports and accommodations, without the organization being the primary support agent.

Effective interpersonal communication skills are essential to any and all businesses. For individuals with psychiatric disabilities who have spent time in hospitals and community-based institutions, these skills may be diminished or severely lacking. As their manager or employer, these employees may continually seek the assistance of managers as they have been trained in various institutions to solve their basic problems through other people. Helping individuals develop the ability to be assertive and communicate effectively can easily be considered a task for rehabilitation providers and not employers. However, most seasoned managers know that helping employees with personal issues means removing obstacles to performance on the job. Typical training on assertiveness or communication does not often work to accomplish this task since the environment in which it operates is artificial. Managers who take the time to teach assertiveness as a part of dealing with employee interpersonal issues should find it extremely productive over time. One method of accomplishing this is to be clear about whose issue is being addressed. If it is the employee's issue with a co-worker, then providing training and support while the employee attempts to address the issue is preferable to your simply solving the problem. Working with individuals by asking what they can do to solve the problem reinforces the fact that it is their problem and not yours. Although it is simpler and faster in the short term to solve these issues as a manager, employees will repeatedly use you as their only resource in dealing with these issues unless you can provide them with the skills to deal with issues directly.

Basic problem solving skills are ones that seem to confound many individuals as they approach work. In teaching job skills many individuals can "parrot back" answers in the classroom; however they may have difficulty performing these basic tasks when the environment or problem is slightly different. To solve this problem, members at On Our Own Computer Center created a style of teaching and supervision they call "Guided Discovery." Guided Discovery is a method of teaching skills and supervising by modeling problem solving, rather than memorization of tasks involved. The benefit is that no matter how the environment or problem might change, the learner has better abilities to respond and solve the task. Guided Discovery is based on the learning theory principle that individuals retain the most from an experience when they perform the actual tasks. Guided Discovery helps build the kind of self-confidence that an employer desires in every worker. To the manager, individuals who are able to solve problems that arise effectively without intervention are highly valued.

Guided Discovery Defined

Guided Discovery consists of six steps: (1) identifying the problem; (2) identifying resources to solve the problem; (3) evaluating potential solutions; (4) implementing a potential solution; (5) evaluating outcomes (and obtaining feedback when necessary); and lastly, (6) using resources again, if necessary, to find another potential solution and continuing the process. It is really a problem solving process that has been converted to a teaching process. The strength of this methodology is that changes in the environment or the problem do not materially affect an individual's ability to deal with it. In a classroom or training setting, the instructor using this approach would typically set up a real life situation, then guide individuals as they go through the steps in solving the problem. The guidance may be teaching some element of the task, but usually it is broadening the individual's horizons by asking questions that guide them to find solutions.

Step 1

The initial step of identifying a problem sounds simplistic, but many individuals tend to focus on the outcome and not on the steps involved. Most individuals can tell you what they want to accomplish, but have trouble identifying the tasks to be completed and in what order to accomplish the tasks. The initial phase of Guided Discovery is to break an outcome into basic steps, then identify keywords associated with each step. If, for instance, an individual needs to prepare a price quotation, he/she can tell you what the outcome is, but never having seen a price quote, he/she may have no idea what the tasks are to accomplish this objective. The initial problem, then, would be to identify a price quote. Although an employee would not usually be hired to perform a task like this (one that they do not understand), many tasks include elements that would require tremendous amounts of initial assistance or training for them to be accomplished.

Step 2

Identifying resources that will solve a problem is very easy for most employees: the manager will solve the problem. If we want to be productive as managers of a consumer-run business, we need individuals to use other resources to solve problems that arise. Problem solving resources are virtually limitless, but are typically limited to a person's successful experience in using them. Helping to broaden the resources a person has available for problem solving pays handsomely to managers in increased productivity.

Step 3

Evaluating potential solutions is a taught skill where an individual looks at the resources that they have available, including time, manpower, machinery, skills, and money and then selects a potential solution. Most common is to limit the solution to the skills that the individual currently has, and yet that may be the most time consuming in the long run. As a supervision technique,

Guided Discovery focuses the employee on defining problems, proposing potential solutions and identifying the pros and cons for each solution. The supervisor's main role is to help the individual with the process of selecting the solution to be implemented and giving authority, or providing resources for its implementation.

Step 4

Implementing the solution is usually the easiest part of Guided Discovery. Although it may be time consuming, once the potential solution to a circumstance is identified, implementation is usually a matter of performing the necessary tasks. While following the proposed solution, it is critical for the employee to make notes of areas to be considered for the next implementation.

Step 5

Obtaining and using feedback, like interpersonal skills, is probably one of the hardest areas for employees of any business, particularly a consumer-run business. Evaluating the outcome and learning from it are critical to growth and success as an individual and as an organization.

Step 6

The failure of an attempted solution can cause many individuals with or without psychiatric disabilities to give up. When an individual becomes stuck in one phase of Guided Discovery, the guide or supervisor facilitates the process by asking questions which are designed to lead the individual to identifying resources needed to solve the problem. Each question asked should lead the individual to think about solutions, resources or methods of moving the process forward. By having the employee constantly identify his or her own resources, over time, the number of interventions needed by an instructor or supervisor can diminish greatly.

Teamwork in Consumer-Run Businesses

The last two decades have generated extensive discussion of the value of teamwork in managing a successful business (Peters & Waterman, 1982; Brown, 1992). Teamwork is also an important tool for a consumer-run business in the following activities: monitoring quality control for the business product or service, assessing business financing and budgeting, providing mutual support among employees and making business management decisions concerning expansion or other basic changes to the business.

Teamwork provides opportunities for creativity to emerge in problem solving. That is, individuals with ideas about ways to improve the business have a place to work out their ideas through a teamwork approach. Effective businesses are "close to the customer" and need to have a fluidity about them, with lots of small groups addressing the ongoing issues of business decisions (Peters & Waterman, 1992).

Howie the Harp (1994) and Brown (1992) caution those who seek effective teamwork, noting that they must address issues of resistance and/or power differences among team members. That is, it should not be assumed that consumer-run businesses automatically function with perceptions of equality and total participation. Awareness of resistance to participation or perceptions of unequal power in the relationships among participants is the first step in a dialogue that should continue throughout the life of the business.

Effective teamwork must be based on a common understanding among the employees as to the complete picture of the business, which includes an understanding of business outcomes (satisfied customers and profits to the business) and an understanding of the roles and relationships of people throughout the business experience (managers, co-workers, supervisors). Effective teamwork is dependent upon clarity about the business mission among all the employees, and the need for mutual supports as part of the team process. Mutual respect begins with the development of policies and procedures by all those participating in the business.

Personnel Policies

Consumer-run businesses need to develop personnel policies at the outset. Even as the group is planning and testing the product or service of the prospective business, it will begin to experience the need for these policies. Personnel policies should reflect agreement among the founding business employees that the policies are a fair representation of the work and of the business experience. This will mean many meetings for everyone and draft policies before the final ones are acceptable to all concerned. Ownership of these policies by all involved in the business is crucial to the process of the evaluation and changes that will come through day-to-day experiences with the business.

Personnel policies, as would be expected in any business, should include the basic descriptive information for paid employees such as job descriptions and qualifications, hiring procedures, supervisory relationships, benefits, and paid sick and vacation leave arrangements. Further, there is a need for policies to deal directly with difficult issues such as sexual harassment or substance abuse. There should be careful attention to the development of policies concerning volunteer work, job accommodations, sick leave, dismissal, and grievances. Policies should be designed for flexibility to meet individual needs, while at the same time providing procedures, such as job sharing or use of temporary workers, to assure an adequate workforce to get the job done on a day-to-day basis.

Business Management Policies

The most important aspect of managing a consumer-run business is to eliminate secrecy with regard to business finances and to schedule regular meetings with a commitment to address business problems directly and fairly.

There should be clear policies and procedures where people handle and/or manage money for the business. Reports on business finances in a consumer-run business should be available to any of the workers. The wages and benefits of the workers will need to be part of the overall business decisions. Open financial books provide support for decisions about investments in the business or suggestions on how to deal with losses or needs for changes in salaries or contract bidding. However, there should be an understanding and trust among the employees about the privacy of business affairs in relation to people and organizations outside the business.

Regular meetings, weekly or monthly, as appropriate to the business management agenda, are necessary to provide an opportunity to assess and evaluate the various business experiences from both a customer satisfaction and an employee satisfaction perspective. Smaller standing committees or special task forces may be useful to provide research or draft materials for decision making at the larger meetings. Again, meetings need to be open to all employees and participants need to agree on the best way to come to agreement on their decisions. Since cooperative decision making may not be a process people understand, consumer-run businesses may wish to bring in outside expertise in consensus or cooperative decision making techniques. Not all problems can be solved in the group; where there are individuals who cannot seem to resolve their concerns and where these concerns are interfering with business activities, mediation may be an alternative problem solving tool.

There are both formal policies and informal approaches to teamwork. Formal teamwork is reflected in the written policies and procedures which need to be developed by the business employees and managers themselves. These policies define roles and relationships within the business. The more informal approaches to teamwork involve the experience of the everyday activities of working together on the business product or service. Informal teamwork is also reflected in the peer support individual employees provide to each other, given the stresses that may affect working together on the job. The discussion of the policies described above reflects the formal approach for a consumer-run business. These formal policies set the standards for defining people's relationships within the business — entering and exiting, participation in decision-making and responsibilities to each other as co-workers. Both the formal policies and the informal relationships developed through the business' day-to-day activities support a process of trust that participants will need to participate in the team activities. With teamwork in place co-workers can apply themselves to quality control.

Quality Control

A consumer-run business, as any business, needs to be customer-driven in order to be successful. Teamwork needs to be nurtured in all aspects of customer satisfaction. Open communications to address any problems in production, distribution, contracting, complaint handling and any other areas of customer relations provide the substance for ongoing teamwork to assure quality control. *In Search of Excellence* authors note that, "self-generated quality control is much more effective than inspector-generated quality control"; thus, in planning consumer-run businesses, it is preferable to think in terms of how the group process includes quality control (Peters & Waterman, 1982).

Working With a Sponsoring Organization

Based on information from a 1990 national survey, agency-sponsored entrepreneurial businesses were usually started to provide employment opportunities for consumer/survivors (Granger & Baron, 1993). They expected that, with some employment experience, consumers would then move on to other competitive jobs in the community. These businesses also experienced the dual mission tensions outlined above where business objectives and program support objectives influenced ongoing business decisions. Agency-sponsored businesses did not view their business ventures as consumer-run entities. However, a few consumer-run businesses have indicated that sponsor relationships may be useful, if there is clarity in the relationship. Sponsors can facilitate funding supports, share space or equipment, provide supportive services or participate as technical advisors.

What is most crucial is that participants in the business planning process work out the organizational relationships between a consumer-run business and sponsor including the need to address the variety of missions that complicate the dialogue — consumer and agency organizational missions and the business mission. For the purposes of a consumer-run business, it will be especially important to assure sufficient independence from sponsor influence to maintain the integrity of a consumer-run organization. Furthermore, prospective sponsoring organizations who wish to facilitate the development of a consumer-run business need to understand the value of the consumer-driven planning processes — that is, anything that the sponsor staff needs to research or consider in the development process are the same questions that consumers must consider. That is, the higher the degree of consumer control in the planning stages, the more likely the outcome of a genuine consumer-run business.

Business Life Cycles and Consumer-Run Businesses

In planning any business, and particularly consumer-run businesses, the need to plan for change is imperative. Building a business around a single individual or group of individuals can become a death knell of the business should something happen to that core. Also businesses and their products or services, like people, have a life cycle which includes creation, growth, maintenance, and decline phases. In each phase of the business and product service life cycle, a different focus of management is needed.

Planning for change can take many different routes. In many organizations it takes the form of cross education of workers, but often leaves out management. In consumer-run businesses, the ability to involve members in all decision making provides an ideal method of planning for and supporting change. Members can be exposed to all aspects of running the business and be trained in decision-making processes, which can prepare members to assume new roles as people leave the organization. Key individuals often do not include their functions in this process though, which leaves the organization vulnerable when they leave or something happens to them. For the organization to survive longer, planning for this change as a part of overall change is imperative.

In thinking about top management changes, one needs to remember the business life cycle. Starting an organization takes great entrepreneurial skill. The growth phase relies heavily on marketing. The maintenance phase extensively uses skills in administration and finance. The decline phase requires someone with knowledge of consolidation or of rebirth through planning new products and processes. Each phase requires a concentration on a particular style of leadership and ability. Planning to bring the right type of leader in at the right time is critical to long-term survival. In large businesses, the opportunities for an individual company to maintain all leadership types is a given, but in a small business, the founders may not be the ideal people or have the skills to successfully guide the organization through subsequent phases.

Each phase of business development typically requires different strategies in the payment of wages and investment as well. At the start of a new business, members and founders might be willing to take a share in the potential future earnings since the business may not initially support them. During the maintenance phase, most organizations begin investing heavily in research and development activities to find new opportunities or products. At this phase, investors typically want to see a return on their investments. For consumer-run businesses, financial decisions over time may concern sensitive issues— for example, pay rates, benefit packages, or business cutbacks or expansion. These need to be addressed openly, with clear consensus about these decisions to avoid unnecessary conflicts.

Summary

Starting your own consumer-run business is challenging and can be very rewarding for the individuals involved. Joining the entrepreneurial business community is yet another approach to genuine community integration — the focus is on creating a productive business and jobs in the community. Planning is the key to success. Planning needs to include clarification of the business mission, financial planning, product/service marketing, management style and employee development and support policies. A consumer-run business, like any consumer-run organization, needs to be concerned with issues of power, authority and responsibility in the organization and the relationships between individuals and the group as a whole. And lastly, a consumer-run business, like any business, needs to consider the possibilities of its own life cycle and plan for it.

References

Allen, John B., Jr. (1994). *Disability, entitlement and employment: A reference guide for individuals on disability entitlements desiring to work.* Silver Spring, MD: On Our Own Computer Center Inc.

Anthony, W.A., Howell, J. & Danley, K. (1984). The vocational rehabilitation of psychiatrically disabled. In Mirabi M (Ed) *The chronically mentally ill: Research and services.* Jamaica, NH: SP Medical and Scientific Books.

Brown, S.A. (1992). *Total quality service: How organizations use it to create a competitive advantage.* Englewood Cliffs, NJ: Prentice Hall.

Campbell, Joseph F. (1991). The consumer movement and implications for vocational rehabilitation services. *Journal of Vocational Rehabilitation,* 1(3), 67-75.

Chamberlin, Judi (1994). Direct democracy as a form of program governance. In Howie the Harp and Sally Zinman (Eds.) *Reaching across II: Maintaining our roots/the challenge of growth.* Sacramento, CA: California Network of Mental Health Clients.

Engels, Paul (1994). Starting and running your own business. In Howie the Harp and Sally Zinman (Eds.) *Reaching across II: Maintaining our roots/the challenge of growth.* Sacramento, CA: California Network of Mental Health Clients.

Furlong-Norman, Kathy (Ed.) (1988). Consumer/ex-patient initiatives. (special issue) *Community Support Network News,* Boston University, Center for Psychiatric Rehabilitation.

Friesen, Marianne & Viti, Franco (1994). *Group hallucinations—Overcoming disbelief: yes you can start a community business.* Toronto, Ontario, Consumer Survivor Business Council of Ontario, National Network for Mental Health.

Granger, B. & Baron, R. (1993). *A national survey of agency-sponsored entrepreneurial businesses employing individuals with long-term mental illness: Final report.* Philadelphia, PA: Matrix Research Institute.

Granger, B. & Baron, R. (1995). *A national survey on job accommodations for people with psychiatric disabilities: Findings from a mailed survey to practitioners.* Philadelphia, PA: Matrix Research Institute.

Howie the Harp (1994). A crazy folks' guide to reasonable accommodation. In Howie the Harp and Sally Zinman (Eds.) *Reaching across II: Maintaining our roots/the challenge of growth.* Sacramento, CA, California Network of Mental Health Clients.

Howie the Harp and Zinman, S. (Eds.) (1994). *Reaching across II: Maintaining our roots/the challenge of growth.* Sacramento, CA: California Network of Mental Health Clients.

Matrix Research Institute. (1995). *Questions and answers about the social security work incentives.* Philadelphia, PA: Matrix Research Institute.

Peters, T. J. and Waterman, R.H. (1982). *In search of excellence: Lessons from America's best-run companies.* New York, NY: Harper & Row.

Rogers S., Danley, K. & Anthony, W.A. (1992). *Survey of client preferences for vocational and educational services.* Boston, MA, Center for Psychiatric Rehabilitation, Boston University.

Stewart, Thomas (1991). *Fortune*, August 12, 124(4), p. 40(8).

Warner, Richard and Polak, Paul (1993). An economic development approach to the mentally ill in the community. Boulder, CO: Mental Health Center of Boulder County.

Yaskin, Joseph C. (Ed.) (1992). Nuts and bolts: A technical assistance guide for mental health consumer/survivor self-help groups. Philadelphia, PA: National Mental Health Consumer Self-Help Clearinghouse/Project SHARE.

Zinman, Sally, Howie the Harp and Su Budd (Eds.) (1987. *Reaching across: Mental health clients helping each other.* Sacramento, CA: California Network of Mental Health Clients.

Zinman, Sally. (1987). Issues of power. In Zinman, Sally, Howie the Harp and Sue Budd (Eds.) *Reaching across: Mental health clients helping each other.* California Network of Mental Health Clients, Sacramento, CA: 1987.

John B. Allen, Jr. is currently the director of the Office of Consumer Affairs for the Maryland Mental Hygiene Administration. He is best known for his work as a mental health consumer advocate after founding and managing On Our Own Computer Center in Silver Spring, MD. He has an extensive background in private industry managing large corporations and providing consultation to small businesses on formation, management, and public relations.

Barbara Granger has been a senior staffer at Matrix Research Institute for the past eight years directing a number of research and training projects focused primarily on vocational rehabilitation programming for people with psychiatric disabilities. Prior experience includes teaching, research and community organizing/development concerning health and housing for older people and people with physical disabilities.

SECTION 4

Consumer Initiatives

Introduction to Section 4: Consumer Initiatives

Chapters in this section describe initiatives developed by consumers within mental health or psychiatric rehabilitation programs. These chapters reiterate themes from previous sections: that consumer-initiated programs originated to fill gaps in existing mental health and/or PSR services; that benefits result for both consumer-recipients and consumer-providers; and that diverse relationships exist with mental health service providers. However, the chapters in this section offer additional perspectives on challenges to be confronted, especially involving leadership and the development of leadership skills for consumers who are service providers. Collectively, the chapters underscore the important role consumers can play in service innovation and responsiveness to emergent needs.

The chapters in this section are quite diverse in terms of the roles consumers play in the initiatives described: leading a support group (Hanna), co-leading a more formal educational group (Hopkins); outreach and peer counseling in a Clubhouse (Colon and colleagues); skill development and education (Chapman); and leadership training (Jasper). However, each initiative evolves in response to specific gaps in the existing system; e.g., the fact that sharing of perspectives and provision of support among peers for school and work is missing in the mental health system (Hanna); or a vocational program which is experiencing too high an attrition rate before peer-based preparation and support is initiated (Hopkins); a clubhouse needing to expand avenues for member involvement to better meet needs of those with substance abuse problems (Colon et al.); the reality that mental health services seldom provide consumers with strategies and models for recovery from psychotic, disabling syndromes (Chapman); and the need for consumers to gain leadership skills and experiences (Jasper).

As in the other sections, consumer-recipients can gain markedly from consumer-provided services, which have unique advantages compared with those provided by professionals. The advantages include their flexibility and individually-tailored nature (Hanna); the ability of consumers to help each other gain skills and support (Hanna); the inspiration and hope provided through the sharing of personal experiences (Hopkins); the fact that consumers are better able to "break through" to their peers than professionals (Chapman, Hanna, Colon et al.); and their ability to meet needs for emotional support (Hanna). In these initiatives, perhaps more so than with self-help groups and consumer-controlled alternative services, the help and assistance provided has a strongly rehabilitative focus. Thus, there is an even greater emphasis on consumers supplying resource information, providing role models, and facilitating empowerment through the shared knowledge that persons with psychiatric disability can and do succeed (Hanna, Hopkins).

Personal benefits to the consumer-providers are described, as in other sections. Noted by many programs are the increases in confidence and the growth-producing experiences which involvement in leading these initiatives offers (Hopkins, Colon et al., Jasper). Some articles recount specific opportunities these experiences provide, in terms of visibility or public speaking (Hanna, Chapman, Jasper). Many of the authors express satisfaction based on their interactions with others, respect they receive from them, and pride in demonstrating new abilities.

The consumer initiatives presented in this section have quite diverse relationships with mental health systems and professionals. Several of the programs describe supportive and collaborative relationships: a consumer training initiative which is supported by federal, state, and local mental health funding (Jasper); an educational group where the consumer and professional co-leader have complementary and supportive roles (Hopkins); or consumer outreach and counseling in a clubhouse that is integrated into overall service provision, enhancing peer and staff relationships (Colon et al.). Other authors report little if any contact with mental health care providers (Hanna, Chapman).

In a number of chapters, authors talk about less than full involvement and participation from consumers who could be potential recipients. Whether consumers believe they can receive help from another consumer may reflect the stigma of mental illness (Chapman). Deferral to professionals (Hopkins) might also reflect stigma, or, alternatively, the disempowered status of many recipients (Jasper). Experiences described in these chapters, however, suggest that these barriers can be overcome, often with the help of non-consumer professionals (Hopkins).

The major theme of this section is leadership. Many of these initiatives arise from the leadership of individuals who step forward in the belief that they have something to offer the group (Hanna, Hopkins). Often, despite anxieties of varying magnitude (Hopkins, Jasper), they are willing to take on leadership, educate others, and disclose their personal experiences. Some individuals appear able to do this naturally (Hanna); others have background skills and experiences they can muster (Chapman); still others respond to requests for involvement (Colon et al., Hopkins). Jasper reminds us, however, that for the most part, consumer leaders need to be developed. Even more so than in the majority population, these are individuals who have been hindered by experiences produced by their illness and/or by the treatment system. Consequently, we might expect that unless psychiatric rehabilitation or mental health providers focus resources specifically on leadership development, initiatives such as those described in the chapters that follow may be rare, dependent on the few "natural" consumer leaders out there, or those with leadership experiences pre-dating the onset of their psychiatric illness. While these programs may be valuable pearls and helpful to those who participate in their services, they are still scarce in the sea of service needs of those with psychiatric disabilities.

Chapter 15
A Consumer as a Provider in a Work/School Support Group

Barbara Hanna

Jenny is a 28-year-old woman with an anxiety disorder. Determined to one day hold a job, as her father did, she is now working to get her GED. Scott is 33 and carries the diagnosis of schizophrenia. He took classes at a local technical college. He recently quit and works nights as a janitor at a restaurant. Pat has severe depression. She is a 55-year-old grandma working to get her associates degree in Human Services. These three people have two things in common: (1) they all have a mental illness and (2) they have issues surrounding school and/or employment.

As a student at the University of Minnesota with a psychiatric disability, I became frustrated and concerned about people like myself and people like Jenny, Scott, and Pat. I knew that we could be successful in our endeavors. But something was missing. We needed support from our peers around issues of school and work. In 1991, in Minneapolis, at the Riverside Club (a community support program for people with mental illness)[1], I started a work/school support group completely facilitated by consumers. Now it was possible for consumers to gather strength from each other concerning employment or school.

The work/school support group met twice a month for one to one- and one-half hours at the Riverside Club in a group room. Just before group was to meet, I would gather people taking part in the drop-in at the Riverside Club to join in our session. Our group size ranged from two people to up to ten people. I would say that just about every member of the Riverside Club attended the group at least once.

The group session centered around everyone being allowed to check in and talk about their own school and work issues. When Jenny came to tell us she needed to take a break from GED classes, we all supported her. When Mary informed us she was registering for a class at the University of Minnesota, she received lots of encouragement.

There were times when a member attending would require more time for check-in and we would try to allow for it. Debbie was trying to decide whether or not she wanted to attend college. She was experiencing symptoms of her mental illness that interfered with her volunteer job. She needed help with problem solving. We gave her extra time to assist her in sorting things out. As a result, she decided to just concentrate on her volunteer job for the time being.

The group was not always faithful to check-in. Many times our conversations would get off track. Sometimes, it was due to someone's behavior

---

[1] A program of Mental Health Resources, St. Paul, Minnesota

becoming intrusive. More often it was because we got on some hot topics such as: "Can people with mental illness really work?" or "Just how much do I have to disclose about my disability?" Each of us had our own unique perspective on these topics. By sharing these perspectives a great deal was gained, something not provided by the mental health system. I shared my experience of meeting a lawyer with bipolar disorder. Yes, people with mental illness do work in respectable positions. Another member shared how he disclosed his disability on a job and from that point on experienced discrimination. This led to quite a discussion in group; everyone had something to contribute.

If time permitted at the end of group, we would do a little exercise or I would bring something inspiring to share. I remember once doing an exercise entitled "My Special Family." This involved each member picking a group of people they would want to have support them in their work and discussing why they chose this group of people. Another time, I brought in an inspiring poem on self-esteem. We all read it together. Afterwards, each member kept a copy.

At one point, Paul, a consumer/staff member of the Riverside Club joined me in facilitating the group. He was a nice addition to the group, and this addition gave us both the female and male perspectives in facilitating. I learned a great deal from him sharing his experiences. He continued facilitating the group when it came time for me to move on to other things.

What I think we gave each other most in the group was hope concerning school and employment. Many people were inspired by the group to start classes and to become employed. We never wanted to give up the hope that was stirred up inside of us.

What role did I play? First, as I saw it, I was a role model. I had been struggling with a mental illness just like they were, with some good periods as well as down times. However, I didn't let the illness totally define me. I was also a mom, a student at the University of Minnesota maintaining a 3.6 GPA, a women's advocate at a battered women's shelter, and a facilitator of this work/school support group. What I wanted to give was encouragement to everyone in the group, but above all I wanted to support people. We've all experienced setbacks, but I wanted to instill in people the belief that they can overcome and recover. Second, I played the role of a resource person. I had a bulletin board where I displayed different jobs, as well as volunteer opportunities. This was helpful to members of the Riverside Club. The bulletin board was headed by such catchy phrases as, "We all have our talents" and "Re-define success." These phrases got a great deal of attention. Third, I had the role of facilitator of the group. I led the group and made sure that it centered around issues concerning work or school. I also encouraged everyone to participate. Furthermore, I tried to prevent anyone from monopolizing the conversation and gave feedback when appropriate.

What about the consumer's role? The consumer's role was to be there to not only get support in group but also to be a provider of support. We are there not only to receive but to give as well. Sue got encouragement in finding a job after she finished nursing school. She also gave support to Jane as she was preparing for law school. In the group, I had played a role and the consumers had played their roles. The group had also brought some personal meaning to me.

I was not the same person after being involved in the work/school support group. I changed my career path to rehabilitation counseling and became eager to help those with psychiatric disabilities to reach their greatest potential. It is my belief that we underestimate what those with a mental illness can do. For themselves and for peers, people with mental health issues do not want to give up hope that one day they will hold down a job and become productive citizens.

Opportunities opened up for me and brought with them added personal meaning. I was invited to several conferences on mental health issues. I also was asked to give educational presentations at the university and in the community. At the present time, I am doing an internship at a community college providing accommodations to students with disabilities.

The work/school support group also revealed to me what a sense of community those with a mental illness really have. This was meaningful to me, as there was a place I could go and be among people who were struggling with the same issues I was. We can really gather strength by supporting each other. Not only did the group have personal meaning, it also provided benefits to other consumers and to the mental health system.

How did the work/school support group benefit other consumers? By proving that consumers can help other consumers. When Pat shared her experiences of getting accommodations at a community college, those interested in school were better informed as to what they were entitled to. Through a discussion of how John was discriminated against on the job, a great deal was gained by consumers. Many people shared their stories. The knowledge that others had experienced similar circumstances and that something could be done to remedy the situation brought power back to the consumers in the group.

The work/school support group also benefited the mental health system by filling a gap that the system couldn't fill. I always found the system distant, impersonal, and not helpful in my own rehabilitation needs. That's what led me to start the work/school support group. It was evident that many consumers who joined the group felt the same.

Another way in which the work/school support group benefited the mental health system is the special role the consumers took on as providers. Consumers relate to other consumers in a way that cannot be compared. When Scott shared his decision to quit school and work as a janitor, I supported him in my provider role. I supported him in a way that showed that I understood him and the ups and downs of his illness. Possibly, because of my own mental health history, I was better able to reach him. Having a sensitive consumer in the provider role benefits the mental health system. Perhaps the consumer/provider could move out of the system. That would be a goal worth attaining.

What about people like Jenny, Scott, and Pat mentioned in the introduction? Will they find the support they need to be successful in work and school?

I'd like to think that the work/school support group made a difference. It made a difference to me as I faced the new challenges in my life. No experience could be as rewarding as the work/school support group was to me, for it meant being a consumer in a provider role. I am confident that this positive experience as a consumer/provider will stay with me in whatever direction my future career path takes me.

Barbara Hanna recently graduated with distinction from the University of Minnesota with a bachelor of science degree in family social science. She is pursuing employment in rehabilitation counseling.

Chapter 16
Collaborating With a Professional in Leading a Pre-Employment Support Group

L. Michael Hopkins with Joyce Tryssenaar

Sharing a group leadership experience between a consumer and a professional was a challenging, but inspiring experience for Joyce and I. Challenging because it was an unfamiliar experience for both of us and I had to take on a different role as a group leader. Inspiring because, looking back, we would not have been able to do as good a job any other way. We were able to combine our skills and experience and therefore offer a broader perspective to the group. Together, we had a good picture of what lay before us and the students.

I work part time and have a social life with rewarding hobbies. I love to write, listen to music, and socialize. I love to speak my thoughts, inspirations or teachings to others to explain my understandings, beliefs and ideas, so when I was asked to be the co-leader of a group I decided to take the offer. I was asked to prepare new students for a college program that trains the students for work placements in society. I felt I had something to offer the group as I had graduated from the program that summer. I wanted to join the group and be supportive as one of the group co-leaders. The group sat around a large table in an office room where the therapist, Joyce, and I explained what was to be expected of the students at college. This included learning about lifestyles, assertiveness, problem solving, self and job expectations, and job placements. I believe education and work experience are a part of our well-being and success or peace of mind.

Setting

The local community college offered a vocational rehabilitation through education program, called Employment Strategies for Success (ESS), for young adults with schizophrenia. It was a two-year, school/work program of life skills and job readiness training in the classroom combined with a cooperative work phase. The majority of work experiences were in the private sector. The objectives of the program are:

1. Create a program of life skills and job readiness training focused on job competencies to prepare students for the work co-op placement;

2. Prepare students through work co-op placements for integration into the work force in a competitive work environment;

3. Create a successful program that could be transferrable to other municipalities and localities.

The program had funding for a three year period. In the first two years, ESS experienced a 50% attrition rate within its first 36 week classroom component. This had a significant effect on ongoing funding and the viability of the project. There were many reasons for this, but one of the most important was that students found the transition into the school and job environment highly stressful. This, in turn, produced increased symptoms and withdrawal from the program. Students left due to discomfort and problems and misunderstandings between students and teachers.

I was accepted in the ESS class and wanted to do well at school as this was a priority for me. I was nervous at first, but the classroom and students reminded me of a good, clean family-like atmosphere. The teachers made us aware that there were no immediate pressures or concerns to worry about. They wanted group involvement and taking turns. We had our choice to leave the classroom if we felt uncomfortable at anytime. We could discuss our feelings, thoughts and concerns freely. This is what I stressed to the new students in the pre-group.

Over 50% of all referrals for ESS came from the Hamilton Program for Schizophrenia (HPS), a community based psychosocial rehabilitation program which provides long-term care for young adults with schizophrenia. The program's philosophy and design have been described elsewhere (Dermer & Landeen, 1991). HPS is for persons with schizophrenia and assists them to survive at a good level of independence and interdependence within society. HPS helps people cope with schizophrenia while living a rewarding and meaningful life.

Development of the Group

The staff at HPS decided to develop a preliminary orientation and education group for clients who were accepted for fall entry into ESS. The group was seen as a method of assisting the clients in the transition to the student role and teaching the skills required for success in the school environment. New students would be prepared for what was to come. The goals of the group were to:
1. decrease attrition and increase success;
2. provide group support;
3. teach and/or program skills;
4. demystify the process;
5. provide access to a successful role model;
6. initiate structure.

The leadership for the group was provided by a consumer and a therapist. I was asked to co-lead the group because I was a successful graduate of the ESS program. I was working for six hours a week in a community college library during the school year (September to May). My success and satisfaction with my employment continued in spite of ongoing positive symptoms. I also enjoyed talking with others and felt I could be helpful to people who were just starting ESS. I had been involved in two community presentations with ESS as well as being interviewed by the newspaper about the program and was therefore pretty comfortable talking about my experiences—my illness and the ESS program. I wished to help others learn the skills I learned at ESS since I felt that the life skills portion of the college course was both worthwhile and rewarding to me. I benefited from the skills and information about expectations and surviving at school and at work. I remember telling the students ESS was flexible and enjoyable, helpful to me, and taught at my level of communication and understanding. The job placement portion was more difficult, but I did complete it successfully.

I was paid at a competitive hourly rate equal to the amount I was earning at the library. The pay included preparation time, actual group leadership, and post group discussion time. It seemed fair to be paid for my contributions to the group, as I was expert at being an ESS student. I also have a need for money and a love for what money can buy. The funds helped me with a little extra.

The therapist leader was an occupational therapist and vocational coordinator at HPS. She referred all clients to the ESS program. She consulted with the ESS staff to increase their awareness of illness and medication and the impact of these on work and classroom performance. She also assisted staff and clients to develop strategies to promote work skills and successful placement.

I met with Joyce to discuss my role as a group leader. We felt we would have a partnership in leading the group. She shared the objectives of the group, and we developed a tentative schedule to meet the group's needs. The group was held for four weeks, two hours per week, in the month prior to the ESS classes starting. The leaders met and developed a group protocol for the four week period. The protocol provided some structure, but also allowed for individual issues to be brought forth. The first session covered educational material about the ESS program. It included pragmatic information about hours of class, tasks required, a description of a typical day, and explicit and implicit requirements of the learning environment. The second session focused on concerns and questions of the group members, and clarifying their expectations. The group was structured around the following questions: what are you worried about, what are you looking forward to, and what further information do you need? The third session was based on strategy building. Strategies for success in the program were developed by the group and covered issues related to time and stress, working in groups, and using supports in and outside the program. The final week included problem solving around barriers to attendance and participation, wrap up, and good luck for the future.

At the first meeting, we talked about the group purpose and what we hoped to do. I understood the basic idea of the group but some of Joyce's terminology was a little unclear. I picked up from the clients in the group what they were concerned about, especially their discomfort about a new experience, financial concerns, and well-being. I liked the group and liked to voice my opinion to help guide them to success or completion of the ESS program. They were mostly worried about how difficult it would be for them. I tried to help them understand that it wasn't too demanding and in fact was enjoyable, rewarding and beneficial. The group members who were unsure or worried about going back to school seemed to need encouragement or reassurance that it would be okay. I told them how helpful ESS had been to me and that they would probably feel the same way.

The leaders met prior to each group to review the previous week, discuss possible changes to protocol, and prepare for the session. Although we did not identify how we would split responsibility for group leadership, a natural evolution occurred. Process and feeling issues were, for the most part, dealt with by the consumer leader. I shared my experience with entry into the program including times when I felt like quitting and how I felt upon graduation. Group members could identify with my experiences and feel hopeful about a change in their lives. This role modeling including both positive experiences and struggles gave group members a realistic picture of the experience. I also could show group members that success was attainable in spite of symptoms. To our advantage, I was also a smoker so at break all smokers had to go to another part of the building where members could continue to ask for more information. They wanted to know what to expect at school and what it was like for me. I told them the teachers were nice, the program was flexible, and that the life skills component was worthwhile. I also emphasized that at times it was fun and good experiences were found at both the school and work components. This allowed group members to feel positive and motivated about their future in the ESS program.

The therapist leader received questions which were more content based, such as, "What about my disability pension?" and "What kinds of jobs are available?" She was also available for individual contact during the break. She had the "big picture" of the program and its goals in the health care system. I had the in-depth personal picture, the lived experience of the program. At first, I wasn't sure how being a group leader would go, or if I could help or not. I wanted to be a good leader on this occasion because the ESS program was good for me and I thought it would help others too. The group was understanding and eager to hear more. Joyce was helpful, encouraging and fair, to me and to the group. The shared experience for both leaders was an inspiring one. It was apparent throughout the process how valuable each perspective was to the whole experience.

There was a good, working relationship between the two leaders and a recognition of the unique contributions each could make built on a history of partnership in the vocational rehabilitation process. We had known each other for two years, primarily through meetings at the ESS program and in some of the social groups run by HPS. We both have a good sense of humor and are pretty relaxed, so that was helpful. Joyce was always fair, open, and honest. We shared our concerns maturely while still having fun. She could communicate with me, although she does have some unique terminology that I did not always understand. If I asked her to clarify, she would.

The therapist leader noticed that initially most questions and comments were directed to her, but she redirected many of them to me. The members soon began to ask questions of both of us. She also took responsibility for the structure of the group, while I shared my experiences and opinions.

The group members indicated participation in the group was particularly helpful for sharing feelings, problem solving, and receiving and retaining information about the program. The number of students successfully entering the work placement component of the program increased to seven (of nine) compared to four (of 11) the previous year.

From my perspective, I gained confidence and experience. We had fun and the group went well. I answered the group members' questions and I felt respect for them. I wanted them to know ESS was a good program. I learned to be an equal as co-leader and that we each could make contributions to the group. I did my share of advising and disclosing pertinent information.

From my own experience of being a service provider as a group leader, I learned people can make a difference. I thought the preparation group for ESS that I co-led went well. I was happy to be of service to other people with schizophrenia. At times I felt some pressure, stress, and restlessness until the topic was changed or we tried something new. Since this group, I've been a little more responsible to others and more confident in my self, my abilities and assets. ESS taught me how to focus my concerns on needs and goals through the life skills component. I understood better how people are and the expectations of individuals in society. Particularly with job readiness and assertiveness training, I became wiser, more alert, gained mastery and responsibility so that I could be a co-leader of the group. I discovered that I could help others get ready for a useful experience at school. I believed in what I said to them and feel good about it.

I continue to work at the community college library throughout the school year, but it might be time for me to make a change. I write new age poetry, lyrics, and philosophy and share my writings with others who like them. I base my life on harmony, love, and peace and discuss this with everyone who is willing to listen.

In summary, the combined perspectives of consumer and therapist provided a unique and valuable learning experience for group members and leaders. The involvement of a consumer in collaboration with a professional in running the support group was of benefit to the group members since it reduced the attrition rate for students entering the employment program. It also broadened the knowledge and skills of the consumer and the therapist. I reached inside to help others and felt rewarded. The wheel was in motion.

References

Dermer, S.W. and Landeen, J.L. (1991). Establishing a model for care in schizophrenia: One program's experience. *Canadian Journal of Psychiatry* 36: 588-593.

L. Michael Hopkins is a writer and a consumer who has schizophrenia. He works part-time and strives for health, well-being, and happiness in his life.

Joyce Tryssenaar is an occupational therapist. She is an assistant professor, School of Occupational Therapy and Physiotherapy, McMaster University, in the Northern Studies Stream, Thunder Bay, Ontario.

Chapter 17

Evolution of a Member Assistance Program in a Clubhouse/Partial Care Program

Louis Colon
Joanne Healion
Diane Ritchie
Michael Thomas
Robert Ward

The Member Assistance Program (MAP) is based on the Employee/Student Assistance Program (EAP/SAP) concept. EAP/SAP programs provide referral and support services to workers/students who are in need of guidance in managing personal, family, and chemical dependency issues. MAP is a work unit in the STEP program, a clubhouse/partial care program. It combines the elements of EAPs in business and SAPs in the schools, peer counseling, 12-step recovery, and circles of support in a collaborative effort by members and staff, as well as the larger community, to empower consumers by providing outreach to members in their own homes. It also promotes personal responsibility, educates the community regarding mental illness, and has members available for peers in time of need.

Overview of the Organization

Greater Trenton Community Mental Health Center, Inc. is a private, nonprofit corporation that provides a continuum of mental health and substance abuse services. These include clinical case management; outpatient, adolescent and adult partial care; intensive outpatient addictions services; training; and management information services to other agencies in the Trenton Mental Health Network. Greater Trenton Community Mental Health Center, Inc. operates three projects targeted to persons who are homeless and mentally ill; one of these is STEP. The majority of consumers served reside in Trenton.

The target population are individuals with severe mental illness who experience difficulty in keeping scheduled appointments but require less structure than traditional partial care programs and outpatient settings. Consumers receiving services from STEP come from a disadvantaged urban environment. There is a wide variety of psychiatric diagnoses, many with a secondary diagnosis of substance abuse. Many have a history of frequent psychiatric hospitalizations and limited connections to aftercare programs, and are at high risk of homelessness.

Development of STEP as a Clubhouse/Partial Care Program

STEP was initially developed as a half day drop-in program. The program operated off-site from the main office building, thus providing a separate identity, yet not being an independent clubhouse as recommended by Fountain House. As a half day drop-in program, the focus was on consumer engagement through social/recreational activities that strengthened staff-member relationships. The goal was to expedite consumer linkage with after care services or, at the very least, monitor stability in the community to prevent rehospitalization. We began to refer to consumers as members, a term that originated in the Fountain House Clubhouse model of rehabilitation. Member connotes a sense of belonging, acceptance and empowerment.

In 1990, STEP converted into a half day partial care program providing a traditional array of services. As services and member need continued to grow, STEP transitioned into a full-day clubhouse/partial care program in the fall of 1992. Emphasis was placed on engagement and staff-member relationships. Groups were offered and members encouraged to attend, although this was not mandatory. Focusing on the psychosocial philosophy, members were encouraged to participate in all aspects of the Club. Developing relationships based on trust and acceptance was crucial in connecting members to STEP.

Although STEP continued to provide partial care services, we were committed to the philosophy and principles of the clubhouse model and incorporated program components into the design which included clerical, food service, operations, and horticulture units. We became committed to the Fountain House philosophy of guaranteeing members the right to a place to come; the right to meaningful work and relationships; and a place to return. We saw the clubhouse's empowerment of members as being the successful method of engaging and rehabilitating consumers who had experienced very little success in their lives, who had difficulty being accepted because of their illness, and who were isolated from the community.

Therapeutic groups are offered simultaneously with the work units. Members are given the option of choosing to participate in a work unit or attending group but, as noted, they are not mandated to do so. Members who display no interest in participating in activities receive encouragement from staff and other members. Staff meet with members on their assigned caseload to review the weekly schedule and discuss the benefits of group participation as it relates to individual needs.

As the prevalence of substance use increased among patients, groups were expanded to provide substance abuse services to a greater population ranging from members who continue to use to those in recovery. As the availability of mentally ill chemical abusers (MICA) groups increased, substance abuse decreased and more members began working a program of 12-step recovery.

One of the unique aspects of STEP is the outreach component. When designing the program, our focus continued to be providing services to individuals reluctant to participate in services. For this reason, a case management component was added to assist members with housing, medical, and financial needs. Staff also perform outreach to member residences when they are absent for two days or more without notice. The purpose of this intervention is to re-engage members and to assess whether clinical intervention is needed.

Our Transitional Employment Program (TEP) is in the developmental stages. Therefore, we have extracted components from the TEP model to begin offering work opportunities for members. STEP has five part-time and one full-time TEP positions. We also have two part-time jobs for van aides, who accompany the van driver to pick up members for the program. Members refusing to come to program are encouraged by the van aide to do so.

MAP Developmental Process

As STEP continued to grow, we explored new ideas to expand member roles in the clubhouse. Our goal was to enhance member empowerment by developing a plan that involved members helping other members. As noted, approximately 80% of the membership were substance abusers, and a growing number of these were in recovery. Thus, some consideration was given to the idea of sponsorship similar to that found in 12 Step programs of recovery.

Simultaneously, members were visiting other clubhouses and were returning feeling frustrated that many of these other clubhouses did not fully meet the needs of those with addiction and substance abuse problems. Members in recovery and MICA staff were interested in developing a method to address addiction that would be consistent with clubhouse philosophy and the concept of the work-ordered day. When we asked the question, "How could the work place handle a substance abuse problem?", we replied, "With their EAP!" From that, we developed the idea of a Member Assistance Program (MAP) as a work unit that would not only meet the members' concerns for addressing substance abuse and other addictions in a clubhouse, but also the concept of member helping member. In the Fall of 1993, the concept of a MAP unit took hold and ideas were borrowed from what we knew or learned about EAPs in industry and SAPs in schools. MAP unit participation is open to all members. Currently there are twelve members who participate in MAP on a regular basis.

Member Orientation

MAP members greet newcomers, introduce them to members and staff and orient them to the clubhouse. The work units are explained and visited, groups and meetings are reviewed, the on-call system is explained, and a tour of STEP is provided. They also give new members buddies to help them acclimate to the program. In addition, MAP members give them a temporary schedule to follow until a counselor has been assigned. During the first few days that newcomers are at STEP, MAP will answer questions and help them adjust. MAP also compiled, in conjunction with the Clerical unit, an Orientation and Welcome Packet for new members.

Outreach Activities

One of the first activities members initiated was outreach to members who were not attending STEP. Previously, this had been a staff responsibility. MAP now does 90% of all outreach to engage members in the program. The staff continues to outreach members in situations in which clinical intervention may be necessary or where there is a potential for danger.

The role of member outreaching member is twofold: (1) encourage members to come to program; (2) determine if the member needs assistance with other problems or just wishes to talk with someone. The outreach is of a supportive nature. Our experience suggests that members are more likely to respond to their peers than they are to respond to staff who have an inherent authoritative role. If the member needs help, MAP offers assistance. Staff is alerted should the problem require clinical intervention. Prospective members who have been referred to STEP, but who are fearful about coming in, are also outreached so that a relationship with members can begin. When MAP began doing outreach to bring in members who stopped coming, they were seeing an average of five members per day. That number has dropped to less than two members a day. We feel the drop in the number of members being outreached is significant in that it demonstrates MAP's success in connecting with members who had not been attending the program.

An outreach letter is left at the home in situations where MAP is not successful in making contact with the member. This letter states that a visit was made and that another contact will be attempted; a telephone number is provided for the member to call. When a phone number is available for the member, phone outreach will be made as a follow-up to the home visit.

Upon return to the program, MAP members complete an outreach memo for staff. This information helps the assigned counselor to record contacts made and plan clinical intervention when necessary. It is also used for agency data collection purposes. When MAP outreach began in the Spring of 1994, members encountered resistance from landlords who questioned why a consumer was visiting in lieu of staff. Once members demonstrated responsibility and gained the landlord's trust, they were accepted and viewed as welcome supports.

Another form of outreach is to visit ill members in hospitals. This helps hospitalized members remain connected to the program and demonstrates our concern for them. MAP members have visited the homes of members who have experienced a death in the family and attended funerals to offer assistance and support.

Peer Counseling

To enhance their skills, several MAP members were trained in peer counseling. Peer counselors are selected based on the following criteria: (1) If in recovery, they must have at least one year of sobriety; (2) they must have an ability to understand and honor confidentiality and anonymity; (3) they must have emotional maturity and the ability to articulate clearly; (4) they must be able to act as a role model in the general club community and; (5) they must actively participate in other aspects of MAP, e.g., outreach, office duties, etc. Serving as role models and establishing trust with other members are critical functions of being a peer counselor.

Peer counselors were in training for five months. Three months had been the goal for a peer counselor trainer, however, additional time was needed to build member confidence to the point where they felt comfortable with counseling. The trainer met with the intended counselors twice-weekly. The training process included use of a manual, other resource materials, and role playing with emphasis on listening skills. Role playing scenarios were developed by members. A major difficulty experienced by the trainer was that members too often relied on her to help them through the counselor role. The trainer noted that it was the confidence building aspect of the training that she found most difficult.

Currently STEP has four peer counselors who approach members currently undergoing difficulties, and offer help. Peer counselors remain in constant communication with staff for feedback and support in their work. Since many members go to a peer counselor with a problem instead of going to staff, peer counselors are trained to know when the problem needs to be addressed by staff and how to help the person seek staff's help while maintaining trust and honoring confidentiality. As with EAPs and SAPs, peer counselors assist with many member problems, ranging from addictions to family problems. Members have reported to their counselors and the public how peer counselors have helped them learn to relax, handle stress, write a letter, fill out an application, negotiate a Social Security appointment, find their way to a medical appointment, or decide what to say at a funeral. One peer counselor, Rob, assisted a member after program hours who was feeling suicidal and had turned to him for help. Rob stayed with the member and talked with him while another peer counselor called the after hours number for help. Both stayed with the member until assistance arrived. On another occasion, peer counselors assisted a person who became an AA sponsor for the first time and was unsure of himself in that role.

A new skill that peer counselors are learning is to offer support to staff should a conflict occur among members. Louis's experience as a peer counselor has helped confirm the desire to pursue a career in counseling. Two MAP members have indicated a goal of working toward becoming professional counselors as a result of their role in MAP.

Peer counselors are also trained to support each other in their work. This includes asking another peer counselor to assist them when an especially difficult or emotional situation arises with a member.

A staff counselor works closely with peer counselors for support and feedback to allow them to process their own feelings and difficulties about their work. As with work units in general, daily morning meetings are held with MAP members to discuss the day's activities and review concerns from the previous day. The current peer counselors will take part in the training of new counselors.

Peer Counselors' Achievements

In November 1994, we presented a workshop on the development and implementation of MAP at the New Jersey Psychiatric Rehabilitation Association (NJPRA) conference. MAP has also received requests to give a presentation of their work to other partial care programs in the area.

We have seen an increased confidence in the peer counselors through their interactions with other members, and they have demonstrated the ability to handle difficult situations. MAP members are dedicated role models and we have yet to experience a problem with a member in this role. An example of the increased trust and confidence in the peer counselors can be seen in an incident where two members had a serious and ongoing personal conflict with each other. Subsequently, one of them became a peer counselor. She was able to put her personal feelings aside and act objectively to help another member in crisis. Not only was the other member able to accept her assistance and support, but he was able to thank her publicly in a community meeting. This member felt able to return to her again for more help in the future.

In regard to addictions, recovering MAP members have been contacted on numerous occasions after program hours to help a fellow member who was struggling with issues of sobriety. MAP members have accompanied others to 12 Step meetings. They have taken a lead in speaking to our Intensive Outpatient Program for addictions and have been role models for this population.

Members have expressed appreciation for the warm, friendly manner in which they are greeted and welcomed by MAP when they first arrive. They also appreciate the encouragement that MAP provides whenever times are difficult. Members who have been hospitalized have indicated that the visits by MAP have not only improved morale, but have helped them feel they are still connected to STEP. The CEO of the agency feels that the efforts of MAP, particularly the outreach component, have been one of the main factors in a markedly decreased recidivism rate for STEP.

Confidentiality

A guiding principle for MAP has been honoring the tradition of EAP's strict confidentiality of all assistance provided to the consumer. Since there have been no breeches of confidentiality, trust of MAP members, and especially peer counselors, is high. When a member is being assisted by a peer counselor and there is need for staff to be involved, the peer counselor helps the member go to staff by emphasizing the need to do so, makes suggestions on how to approach staff, and offers to accompany the member. If the member is still unable to do so, the peer counselor explains why they will need to go on the member's behalf. The peer counselor offers the member the choice of going to their assigned counselor or to the trainer who supervises the peer counselors. At no time does a peer counselor reveal to the clubhouse community who he has helped and how, without the consent of the member.

Next Steps

Since the STEP Clubhouse has been successful in the areas of secondary (intervention and treatment) and tertiary prevention (relapse prevention) for addiction, members (particularly those in recovery) expressed a desire to expand their activities into primary prevention. Primary prevention is averting a problem before it starts. MAP members felt they wanted to reach out to the youth in the community and try to prevent them from experiencing what the members had with their addiction, and also to inform them on how to seek help for emotional problems before they escalate.

In conjunction with Greater Trenton Community Mental Health Center, Inc.'s Adolescent Day Services program, a grant has been received to develop an educational presentation to youth in schools, religious organizations and other city youth programs. This project has helped MAP members feel that they have come full circle in their recovery from both mental illness and addiction.

The use of MAP members to assist clinical case managers with outreach, to visit members in the state hospital, and to participate in mental health awareness days has been well received by agency staff. Exposure to members on an informal basis has been instrumental in breaking down societal stereotypes of individuals with mental illness. The agency has begun to integrate members into the overall decision-making process by means of the Future Search Conference and continuous quality improvement focus.

The success of MAP has demonstrated the impact that members can have on members. We have begun using this model for our addictions component and plan to develop a separate MAP unit for this population.

Conclusion

A number of agencies have expressed interest in replicating the MAP program in response to conference presentations. Based on our experience, we feel the MAP concept is relatively simple to replicate. Member empowerment, enhancement of peer and staff relationships, and a reduction in relapse and recidivism rates are just a few of the benefits.

Future goals of MAP include organizing Circles of Support for members in need of additional support in the community. Circles of Support is an organized group of people who consumers personally invite to assist them in reaching their individual goals. Circles of Support had their beginnings in the developmental disabilities field and in religious communities, but are relatively new in the mental health field. This approach increases public involvement by advocating for consumer acceptance and decreases the stigma attached to mental illness. The development of MAP has been an ongoing evolutionary process. MAP will continue to grow in order to address the ever changing needs of the clubhouse membership.

Joanne Healion, MSW, LCSW, is the STEP program director.
Diane Ritchie, BA, CIAC, is an addictions specialist.
Louis Colon is a STEP member.
Michael Thomas is a part time STEP van driver and member.
Robert Ward is also a STEP member.

Chapter 18

Eliminating Paranoid Delusions and Telepathy-Like Ideas in Schizophrenia: A Personal Account[1]

Robert K. Chapman

After a few years of suffering from schizophrenia, I became angry at the illness. It wasn't myself with whom I was angry. I was not to blame for having this disease. I plowed through the necessary steps to restore my sanity. Yet I did this at the pace of a passive snail—too afraid to get out there and live life. There ought not be a race in trying to recover. Even though it was made known to me verbally that I would remain ill indefinitely, it did not strike me as an unchangeable situation. My delusions of persecution impressed upon me that I was targeted to be doomed. Despite this, learning that I might always be ill with schizophrenia was something that I thought could not be true.

I can remember saying to myself convincingly as I paced the floor with determination, "I'm going to conquer this mental illness." I reasoned that if some of my thoughts were disturbed, I could use my unaffected mind to think myself well again. To the general public, this might sound unbelievable. But I was confronting an unbelievable illness!

Through a period of years, I came to realize that there was a method to my madness. By this I mean that every time I compared reality to a delusion, I found reality to be the very opposite of what the delusional idea was making me believe. It began to seem obvious to me that reality was something to be considered. This "opposite principle" later became what I referred to as reciprocal thought affect which I explain in my book. It was a relief for me to discover that the opposite of what I thought was real, was in fact real and I became aware of the falsehood of my belief. The nature of these beliefs had caused me to become antisocial and suspicious of people, especially the people who had the knowledge to help me. I had looked upon life as though it were a trap.

Recovery Strategies

My first insight into my delusions was that they were opposite to reality, truth and rationality. It became apparent to me that in order to undo my delusions, I had to develop an awareness of reality and exercise objective thinking. I was much too subjective in my perception of the behaviors of others—the presence of police cruisers, a group of people laughing on the bus. I misinterpreted what was going on around me. This lasted five years. Then a counsellor told me that my hallucinations and delusions were not external to me, but

[1] Condensed from *On Second Thought—Eliminating Paranoid Delusions in Schizophrenia*

were products of my own mind. This piece of information helped me tremendously. It took me about six months to believe this was true. This began my three-step strategy.

The first step was to recognize the delusional scenarios. Evidence for delusive ideas were found to contain doubt. Second, I developed counter-arguments and explored alternative interpretations. The third step was to replace the delusion with reality, truth and rationality.

Believing that people frequently knew my thoughts or made me think things I did not want to think, I eventually was backed into a psychological corner. I thought if I'm going to die at any moment from this antagonistic source, I may as well investigate who it is and face my tormentor. Over a period of time, I repeatedly found nothing that would substantiate the convictions of my delusions. The presence of doubt became a welcomed discovery. As I looked in the ceiling fan ducts, the cracks in the wall, and other orifices in my apartment, I could find no one or no recording equipment. On the way to a friend's house I had to stop at a donut shop to use the washroom. I still had the same feeling that I was being watched. I began to wonder how "they" could be so fast in setting up their spying equipment when I didn't even know beforehand that I was to stop off at this washroom. Over a three year period, I began to doubt the various delusional scenarios, one at a time, until they were gone. I worked on each one until the delusions were not just diminished, but totally eliminated.

I believed that I was being persecuted by way of mental telepathic intrusions, having thoughts inserted into my mind that I did not believe to be mine, having my thoughts known by others. I believed someone knew what I was doing and thinking. When you educate yourself rationally on how this could be done, you realize that no mind can read the thoughts of another. Even if you imagine being able to know the thoughts of others, it is nevertheless an imagined acquired skill. I learned that "why?" questions were answered with delusional answers. "How?" questions became dynamic and resourceful.

Attaching ill judgement to a simple situation can produce suspicion, therefore blanketing suspiciousness over every and all activities. You think you know a part of a whole, but the whole situation of which you are paranoid is never made fully known to you. The circumstances around which you feel persecuted are those that must be viewed objectively. My principle is based on the premise that whatever the mind can believe, it can also reverse or eliminate. The following are the steps I use.

1. Recognize the Delusion

Despite the profound conviction of my beliefs of being a victim of some parapsychic mind tormentor, how is it that I am never confronted by those involved in my demise? How is it that I am not killed in a cover-up manner? I believed for years that I would die at any moment at the hands of my unseen antagonist. One learns that false beliefs can have no veritable, substantiating, truth to them when measured against reality testing and a rational gauge of thinking. I realized that they can have the appearance of truth and provision for believability. Discovering this, I have come to recognize the delusion.

Delusions, I came to realize, were forced on me. They were not a chosen belief. Delusions are unwanted beliefs. I did not choose to believe that bad people were pursuing me in such a disturbing way. Another difference is intentionality. Most of what we choose to believe contains a purpose or an intention. Although all beliefs (whether ordinarily accepted or delusive) have meaning, intention stems from choice. In delusions there is no choice with regard to their theme, content, or intensity.

Reality is something that is neither derivative nor dependent. It exists necessarily, independently of the mind. On the other hand, delusive ideas exist only as much, and as long, as they are believed by a person. Because false psychotic beliefs can be proved to be misbeliefs, they can, therefore, be cancelled. Delusions, I believe, are modifiable.

One's recognition of his delusions to be resembling the activity of telepathy can be explained by his knowing about telepathy, a commonly known subject. A delusion is an experience that is imaginable. In order for one to be "followed" by someone to the extent he believes, that person would have to be as close to him as he is to himself!

I had to learn that people were not reading my mind. It was paradoxical for me to realize that in order for me to have the notion that somebody was reading my thoughts, I would have to be telepathically inclined! Space will not permit me to share what has become an exhaustive research of arguments against the concept of mental telepathy. Constructive doubting prompted a reevaluation of my delusion. Doubt established a foundation of certainty.

2. Counter Argue and Deny

At my own pace, my approach was to investigate my delusions and develop an ability to assess fantasy from reality. Reality checking, I looked in wall vents, etc., in which for me there posed a large degree of fear and apprehension where I believed there might be a hidden camera, or a tape recorder. In the whole scheme of ideas, what sense which may be perfect by itself may be grossly imperfect while compared to the rest of the whole. Many professionals don't go into delusions. A belief, in and of itself, can't kill a person, neither can a misbelief. How can confronting a belief be any worse than what he believes it is doing to him already? G.W.F. Hegel (1770-1831) in *Truth and Rationality* wrote "Reality is a synthesis of all truth." With trepidation, I began to read scores of books on ESP to see if I was really a victim of a telepath's torment. I am now comfortable in knowing that mental telepathy cannot work. I came to accept that the source of my delusions was opposite to that from which I believed they came, namely myself. When a delusion is stacked up against a conscious awareness of reality and rationality, the delusion begins to fall apart. While the delusive ideas disintegrate, the pretense is revealed. The question "How?" is important when employing a sense of reasoning to a delusion of reference.

3. Replace the Delusions

Replacement is truth, that the delusion is a false belief. Mental telepathy does not work. The counter-arguments I have as to why ESP cannot work are greater than the span of this article.

Informing Others

I decided to go public with my illness because the stigma is unnecessary. For ten years, I have appeared on TV, in newspapers, and at conferences and have had only pleasant responses for what I am doing. The audience usually consists of consumers, family members, and mental health-care professionals. Much of the guts to do this came from years of being a stand-up comedian during which time the onset of my illness began. What I am doing works. After my talks, some consumers have shared their delusions for the first time unbeknownst to their care-givers. Without being able to do any follow-up, I have on occasion learned that some consumers have taken from my talks details applicable to reducing the impact of their delusions. That's precisely what I intend to happen.

As I began writing a book on how I eliminated my delusions, it became evident to me in my research that there were no other accounts such as mine. Except for a few, there were no articles written on successful delusion reduction efforts. I have not found writings showing how contradictory evidence can be used to disprove telepathy-like delusions of reference. There are only a few texts solely on debunking the concepts of mental telepathy and other pseudosciences.

Consumers, I have been told, feel encouraged by my recovery but I am quick to extinguish any false hope. We are all individuals and so, too, is the symptom make-up. I believe that delusions which are telepathy-oriented, and which are commonly featured in schizophrenia, are cancellable. Yet, I have not come across anyone who has done what I have done. I cannot help but think that if a consumer was to successfully eliminate his delusions, his feelings of paranoia would also disappear. The benefit of this would decrease negative symptoms (cognitive deficits) and better prepare his readiness for vocational rehabilitation. He would become more successful in his social, learning, and working environments.

Benefits and Challenges

Educating people in this vein is exciting for me though there are obstacles. I remember one consumer thought I was a doctor who was just saying that I used to have this illness. This kind of response did not throw me off; this was a unique situation for a patient education group. I am familiar with suspicious thinking; I may have thought the same if I was an in-patient faced with such a guest. Other obstacles are people who suggest that maybe I really didn't have schizophrenia; how could I have had this illness if I recovered? I have looked at my medical records and the DSM manuals and I fit the criteria. It may seem a bit odd for me to be verifying my diagnosis when so many others in the throes of their psychosis are, instead, denying theirs! Dealing with these barriers has better prepared me to answer the quite legitimate questions people have.

I feel a little ahead of my time in being a past-consumer endeavoring to assist other presently ill consumers. Many aren't ready for this. Without traditional academic credentials for working in the mental health field, as a professional speaker, I am using experiential knowledge. Aside from this I am a graphic designer. There is another unique barrier. For the most part, the people I am trying to assist (the consumers) do not want me to assist them. Most believe that they aren't affected by delusions and do not see a need to gain insight. It's like trying to trade real gold for pyrite; they believe they have the real stuff already! And I do not expect their therapists to refer them to me, but I am not disheartened, for there is so much to gain from this vision. Years ago when I began my speaking engagements, I was very cognizant of the fact that others might view what I am doing as being grandiose. Having had grandiose ideas and pursuits during my illness, I became especially keen on legitimizing my workshop presentations in which I talk about my full and "un-superficial" recovery.

Having been invited to speak at Canadian Mental Health Association branches, International Association of Psychosocial Rehabilitation Services conferences, Self-Help/Mutual-Aid conferences, psychiatric hospital conferences, etc., I have received many letters of appreciation. But there has not been one mental health professional who has shown an interest in what I am doing beyond the close of my workshop/symposium. People, in whatever discipline they are in, focus on the security of their own jobs. Still I feel that someone should have taken more interest in the heuristic and comprehensible cognitive therapy I managed to apply.

I have received permission from Mikhal Cohen, (*Psychiatric Rehabilitation Training Technology*, 1992, Center for Psychiatric Rehabilitation, Boston University) to adapt the center's "Rehabilitation Readiness" for assessing readiness to recognize persecutory-type delusions in schizophrenia. The clinical practice objectives chosen integrate knowledge I have learned in previous modules of my Psychosocial Rehabilitation program. By adapting the use of the "rehabilitation readiness" assessment, I wish to explore the viability of assessing patients' readiness and/or need to recognize existing delusions. Many PSR principles and values are related to doing this; for example, persons with psychiatric disabilities benefit from having control over decisions which affect their lives, have needs that are unique and multi-dimensional, have the potential for growth, have the ability to make choices regarding learning environments, and have the capacity to improve their level of functioning.

Having done oral presentations on cognitive deficits, my interest is to study whether identified impairments such as difficulties with attention, concentration, problem-solving, information processing, and inability to show good social judgement are negative symptoms underlying those with schizophrenia, or are produced by positive symptoms, namely delusions and/or hallucinations.

Is one a negative symptom patient or a preoccupied patient? Are some cogni-tive deficits separate positive symptoms among a group of symptoms indig-enous to schizophrenia; or are they a result of being preoccupied with disturb-ing ideas about being the victim of a hex, spell, thought withdrawal, ESP intru-sions, etc? Does one beget the other?

I believe that to some degree assessing readiness to learn about delusions is practical on an in-patient basis and certainly more so for out-patient popula-tions. I believe that the popular one-third fraction of those who recover from schizophrenia can shift. With a properly administered and accessible delusion approach in place, I believe that those who are in the middle third, who are not recovered, can move toward those in the one-third recovery population. My experience (H.P.H. G-1 ward, Patient Education Group) as a monthly guest speaker for three years, has been that patients feel more comfortable in sharing their delusional experiences with someone they know has had the illness (Hope principle). Staff who have sat in on this patient education hour have told me on several occasions that patients had shared delusional experiences for the first time, and that they believed my approach facilitated this.

Summary

During my illness, I thought circumstances were contrived and were de-signed as a ploy to get me or try to make me go crazy. I had become highly suspicious of what might be lurking between the last delusion and the next day. In my recovery, I objectively viewed each delusional experience from a reality standpoint. This new understanding proved to be credible enough and the verification I needed to acquire peace of mind. For me to understand my-self objectively required an effort on my part to learn the truth. If there is a tendency to re-believe a delusion, then a person hasn't investigated enough (Counter-Argue Step). Although the delusion may be described in different ways, the main theme is persecution. It took time to get over the thought that a delusion might still contain some realness. If I began to think this way, then I would counter-argue and investigate some more at my scared crawling pace. Then there were two or more years of getting over the trauma of having had the illness. I think that psychiatrists ought to do more field work and be a partner with the consumer in this transitional phase. Resource opportunities such as I present to diminish/eliminate delusions are not accessible to con-sumers. I was successful in learning that my sense of the functions of mind-reading were those I had imagined. The activity of mind-reading was not some-thing of which I was victim, but rather a concept I had falsely believed to be occurring.

The following is a lighthearted job description I created to describe what it is that I do. It is a part of my P.R. folio.

Job Title: Speaker/Presenter (On contract basis, as well as invited guest speaker for occasional annual general meetings and conferences).

Job Description: Oral presentation of speaker's own experience with schizophrenia and how he managed to recover from it.

Skill/Competency Level: The prerequisite strengths required to deliver this service are as follows:

• must be recovered fully from paranoid-type schizophrenia, being symptom-free for over five years while not requiring medication.

• candidate must have suffered typical symptoms such as hallucinations, delusions, grandiose-type thinking, extreme paranoia, detachment from reality, emotional blandness. May have experienced a psychotic breakdown and an anxiety attack as well as negative symptoms which required hospitalization.

• must have a desire to educate others and to share his personal experience. He must possess a boldness and a courageous spirit to go public with his experience wherein there lies an enormous stigma. This person must fulfill a leadership role in order to be a forerunner in the progress of psychosocial rehabilitation.

• must have public speaking ability, share his personal experiences clearly and coherently in an organized manner, and be comfortable with presenting this to consumers of psychiatric services, relatives, and mental health care workers. Television, radio, and newspaper appearances are necessary.

• candidate must have a knowledge of useful cognitive strategies (the dynamics by which he managed to eliminate delusions) that are pertinent, proven effective, and instructive and comprehensible to others. He ought to have a good understanding of psychosocial rehabilitation principles and see himself as being an important extension of psychiatry.

Mission Statement And Philosophy

Because of my direct experience with paranoid-type schizophrenia and my commonality with consumers, having been there, I can breakdown barriers that sometimes professionals can not. My unique position creates a certain believability in assuring consumers of their diagnosis and their need for medication. I treat consumers as though they can, and will, recover. I do not try to represent the whole population of those who have schizophrenia but share cognitive strategies that have worked for me. I give hope for the potential of recovering, but not false hope, considering that the illness differs for each individual. I share thoughts and beliefs management skills that have proven successful for:

• Eliminating and overcoming specific paranoid delusions.
• Gaining a realistic and feasible approach to grandiose-type beliefs.
• Gaining realistic and achievable vocational goals.
• Understanding the truth regarding the origin of hallucinations.

I believe that not all of consumers' thought-processes are faulty, and that they can recognize some reality and learn to exercise an awareness of reality and objective thinking with my instructive and comprehensible coping skills.

I believe that consumers can adopt strategies (that have worked for me) specific to their delusion descriptions. Working on these at one's own pace is best. I stress that recovery takes time and that relapses may occur. I emphasize the importance of medication which allows the consumer to better understand his illness and to learn coping strategies when ready. Also weaning off medication must be done very gradually, with discipline, and a doctor's medical assessment.

I believe (on the basis that one-third fully recover, a middle third are maintained by meds and function in the community, and the latter one-third may require on-going hospitalization) that some of the middle one-third can learn and adopt cognitive skills and join those who fully recover.

Robert Chapman is a past consumer, psychosocial rehabilitation certificate course graduate, speaker/presenter on delusion reduction/elimination skills. He has appeared on TV, in newspapers, and magazines educating about, and destigmatizing schizophrenia. He is the author of the book On Second Thought—Eliminating Paranoid Delusions in Schizophrenia.

Chapter 19
Moving Forward: Consumer Initiatives Through Leadership Development

Colleen A. Jasper

The consumer movement emerged in the late '60s with the focus on advocating for the rights of mental health consumers. The oppressiveness and abuses of the institutional years created a climate that demanded involvement of consumers in rectifying the many problems plaguing mental health service systems. This movement continued to grow as deinstitutionalization became a reality for many consumers, bringing with it a whole new set of injustices. As recognition of these injustices were acknowledged, and as the demand for change grew, the pressure for leadership in the movement correspondingly grew. New leadership emerged, comprised of people willing to recognize, speak out, organize, and push for justice, equality, and quality of life for all consumers.

As leaders emerged in the early consumer movement, mental health consumers spoke about what they perceived was wrong with the system and voiced their opinions. However, this quickly changed. With a sense of responsibility to others with emotional and mental health problems, consumer leadership became more democratic. The focus went beyond the personal needs of the individual, and consumer leaders began taking on issues that affected many others: freedom of speech, rights, inadequate services, medication abuses, alternative services, empowerment needs, funding for programs, equal representation, consumer employment, and other changes needed in mental health systems.

Consumer leadership fostered supportive networking with other consumers based on experiential knowledge and connectedness through identification with their peers. The ability to bring this experiential knowledge to the foreground is an essential element in creating quality mental health services. Consumer perspectives are often substantively different from those of mental health workers and providers. The ability to use this experiential knowledge as an instrument of change is one goal of effective consumer leadership.

The need for consumer leadership is ongoing and continually requires more consumer leaders who are innovators in the struggle for empowerment and the advancement of rights. As the consumer movement in the mental health field grows, so does the need for the development of consumers' leadership skills. Although there are many active consumer leaders for whom leadership comes naturally, others need to develop and enhance their own leadership with guidance, support, and skills development. Many consumers are hindered by the experiences of their illnesses: the symptoms, negative treatments, stigma in the community, and a society that is not ready to alter the negative and limiting expectations it holds regarding consumers' abilities. Some consumers, living in the shadows created by a lack of community support, are inexperienced in the skills of leadership:public speaking, organizing, assertiveness, personal confidence, empowerment, and problem solving. Their experiential knowledge and expertise in issues affecting consumers' lives can be an essential element to successful advocacy for change. But with a range of educational levels, diverse mental health experiences, and varying amounts of personal and professional supports, consumers are in need of concrete tools to take on leadership roles.

As the movement expands, and consumer leaders evolve, consumers are looking to other avenues for change — including service provider roles to create and promote change from within the system itself. Although the need for systemic change is often reluctantly acknowledged by professionals involved in mental health systems, consumers recognize the importance of service provider roles in bringing perspectives instrumental to change to the foreground. Leadership development is an avenue for the acquisition of skills needed in these service provider roles. In turn, as consumers develop their leadership skills, they begin to see service provider roles as a means to utilize their skills. Consumers recognize that change can be generated through service provision, thereby having a greater impact on the mental health system.

Leadership development provides much needed preparation for involvement of consumers in role innovation. Overcoming internalized stigma and developing leadership skills creates confidence, generates empowerment, renews self-esteem and embraces assertiveness. These are the same struggles facing many consumers who wish to take on any employment, including service provider positions within the system. In turn, these positions demand leadership skills in relating to consumer issues, problem solving, and maximal utilization of their experiential knowledge as a principal asset.

Leadership development contributes to greater expansion and demand for consumers in service provider roles. As consumers voice their ideas and expertise, recognition of their abilities and skills can become known, creating a push for more places within the system to utilize their talents. The connection between consumer leadership and service innovation is vital since both utilize the skills of consumers as positive forces of change within the system.

Recovery and Leadership

Leadership development is linked to recovery. Recovery is an outcome of the consumer empowerment movement of the '70s and '80s. Consumers asked for more than a survival, maintenance, stay-out-of-the-hospital way of life. The recovery movement is founded on the belief that individuals with emotional and mental health problems can move into wellness and enjoy quality lives. It is not definitive as an end in itself, but rather an ongoing, life-long process. Consumers in recovery ask for hope — that their quality of lives be productive and based on equality.

When we talk about recovery, a question arises: What are we recovering from? The most obvious answer is from mental illness, of course. But it is much more than that. We are recovering from the symptoms, the consequences of the symptoms, negative treatment, institutionalization, stigma — both external and internal, discrimination in the community, personal shame, and the limiting expectations held by many for individuals with diagnostic labels.

Recovery is not generic but instead is individualized and unique to one's personality, skills, needs, and desires. There are no broad generalizations as to the correctness of recovery, no stereotypes of individuals in recovery. It is not easily defined, classified, diagnosed, analyzed, or catalogued. Furthermore, recovery operates outside the constraints of mental health systems; involving a multitude of individuals in a supportive network of consumers, professionals, friends, family, and the community—who work together. The emphasis of recovery is on personal freedom, focusing on possibilities rather than limitations. Recovery is going beyond the expectations and limitations of a diagnosis, and its resulting defined reality. It is the holistic approach to health and life involving all aspects of one's personhood. It is not just the medical model.

In the process of recovery, one's ownership of the illness and factors of responsibility are critical aspects. The focus is NOT on others to take care of us, to fix us, to heal us, or to cure us: recovery concentrates instead on developing an internal locus of control rather than externalization of responsibility. At the basic level, recovery includes a positive emphasis, a wellness focus rather than a constant concentration on the illness. Most of all, recovery embodies hope. With hope and willingness to change, individuals are able to achieve health and wellness in life.

Consumer leadership can be an outcome of recovery, or it can be a factor producing recovery. Initially, leadership development involves advocacy for oneself, but it can quickly grow to include a sense of responsibility to others who suffer with emotional and mental health problems. Self-advocacy has more than one reward. In learning to think and stand up for oneself, consumers can replace shame with pride in their independence. From the recovery perspective, leadership is a form of personal growth and an expansion of that growth as one advocates for the needs and concerns of other consumers. In turn, consumer leadership contributes directly to recovery by generating confidence, pride, and compassion for self and others. From the recovery perspective, leadership is fulfilling to the self as one takes on roles that voice the unheard needs and concerns of other consumers. Another aspect of both recovery and leadership is a proactive rather than reactive approach to one's life; independence is sought while dependence on others is relinquished.

In the development of skills essential to becoming leaders, consumers have to overcome many personal struggles. Consumers whose lives were dominated by the struggle of controlling symptoms and combating stigma are in need of solid supports and the renewal of their self-esteem. Increased self-esteem as part of recovery is an important underlying aspect to leadership development. In addition, the need for support from other consumers in the development of leadership skills is also important in creating an environment of safety where consumers can share, identify, and learn from one another — the focus of recovery.

Recovery intertwines with leadership development. Both emphasize growth, change, learning, and process. Leadership, like recovery, is more than a single event. Both leadership and recovery roles are commitments to continuous enhancement of self. Recovery is the vital and critical linkage between voice and empowerment: both traits of leadership. It is no wonder that leadership fosters and grows in an environment emphasizing empowerment and recovery. This intertwining of leadership and recovery occurs both at personal and the professional levels. Realistically, in order to participate as a leader, one must have a sense of self-esteem, self-empowerment and voice. However, that voice is more likely to grow and speak if generated from the safety, security and support of a recovery-focused environment.

Modeling is another important factor in both recovery and leadership. Because there is so much negativism connected with disorders, one can easily become enmeshed in the hopelessness and helplessness that too frequently accompany the diagnosis of mental illness. However, seeing and hearing from other mental health consumers who have grown into health are fundamental in creating hope and change. In leadership development, modeling is an instrument in teaching skills to others. As consumers learn from other consumers who are leaders, they become empowered in the belief that they too are capable of health and leadership.

A Program to Develop Consumer Leadership and Recovery

In recognition of the need for leadership training and in support of the recovery initiative, the Michigan Department of Mental Health sought external funding from the Center for Mental Health Services (CMHS). CMHS had funding available to states for grants to demonstrate and evaluate service system improvement strategies through its Community Support Program (CSP). The goal was to integrate consumers and family members at local and state levels in the planning and provision of mental health and support services.

Through a grant-writing collaborative application involving the Justice in Mental Health Organization (JIMHO), a nonprofit organization well-known in Michigan for its role in consumer leadership, and other consumer and family groups, the Michigan Department of Mental Health[1] was awarded a three-year grant from CMHS starting in January, 1991. Through grant support, JIMHO created a state-wide Leadership Training Project for mental health consumers. This author, a mental health consumer, was hired to develop and implement that project.

The project initially proposed to create, develop, and implement a promotional presentation with mental health consumers about individual needs,

[1] now the Michigan Department of Community Health

empowerment, and consumerism. This first presentation was designed to reach mental health consumers in clubhouses, drop-ins, assertive community treatment teams, and day programs. From this group of consumers, individuals interested in further leadership training were identified.

The goal of the Leadership Development Project was to teach skills to generate more involvement opportunities for consumers in the public mental health system. The presentation strategy initially used traditional teaching, but we quickly realized the benefit of asking consumers questions and involving individuals in exercises. Anecdotes about personal experiences with hospitalizations, medications, and treatments created the vital connectedness and identification essential for a productive adult learning environment. After the training, consumers were given the opportunity to utilize their skills by giving presentations on related consumer issues to other consumers, professionals, and the members of the general community.

As the project evolved, further changes were made in order to accommodate the needs of participants. With technical expertise and support from JIMHO, the project changed to include an additional promotional presentation focusing completely on building self-esteem. In this presentation, the development of self-esteem was from a mental health consumer perspective. It addressed experiences with institutionalization, deinstitutionalization, the label of mental illness, pros and cons of medication, self-help, and internalized shame and stigma, offered within a recovery orientation and focus. Throughout the presentation, realistic and practical examples were given to help participants view themselves positively.

At the end of the first presentation, information about the second promotional presentation was shared with the participants. Information about a four day training workshop which was open to all interested consumers was also available. In many sites the second promotional presentation on self-esteem building was included to encourage consumers to participate in further training. Out of an average group of 25, approximately five consumers would come forward for further training. (We estimated this as about the same number of leaders that would come forward in an average high school class of 25.)

Further training in the Leadership Development Project included four days of workshops each lasting five hours. The content of the workshops was determined with assistance from JIMHO, defining the needed skills of consumer leadership. Training initially focused on developing listening/observing skills, increasing motivation, leadership styles, meeting protocol, increasing self-confidence, and techniques for conflict management. After reviewing the expectations of the original grant, the activities were expanded to include assertiveness, responsibility, wellness, advocacy, person-first language, issues of consumerism, public speaking skills, and recovery. These modifications helped participants become involved in individual activities and group exercises. These collaborative and cooperative efforts were found to be essential in creating a positive environment of acceptance, trust, and bonding which was critical for a recovery-focus.

Each workshop utilized an adult learning perspective. Strategies to access individuals' experiential knowledge involved problem-solving and active participation. Another strategy used in the workshops was experiential learning. This was achieved through practicing public speaking skills. Trainees developed speeches on mental health issues and video-taped themselves in action. The tapes were then evaluated and reviewed. Not only was content, nonverbal behavior, and tone examined, but also the positive aspects of the individual's speech were emphasized to encourage mastery and skill-building. We reinforced the individual's success through repetitive practice of the speeches. Developing public speaking abilities was chosen because it utilized many aspects of leadership development. From a recovery perspective, learning public speaking was also a tool for enhancing self-esteem and self-advocacy.

Implementation Issues

Reaching Consumers

During the outreach process and throughout the project, many challenges had to be addressed in order to successfully complete the project. These barriers were also problematic for consumers in their own development of leadership skills and interfered with their moving into recovery. The challenge of reaching consumers was integral to the project. The targeted audience was individuals labeled with serious mental illness who were participants in the public mental health system. It was estimated that one-third of the presentation sites were initiated by professionals, another third initiated by consumers, and the final third initiated through connection with JIMHO. This three-team dynamic worked very well. The flow of presentation sites was generated naturally by word-of-mouth and was on-going throughout the three-year life of the project. Presentations were held at clubhouses, drop-ins, partial-day programs, and assertive community treatment groups. This outreach work made the barrier of reaching consumers quickly disappear.

Multicultural and Rural Outreach

As stated in the grant, outreach to minorities was a desired outcome. Consumers are very diverse so diversity needed to be a major focus. With assistance from individuals with multi-cultural backgrounds, sites were selected. Outreach to urban Michigan cities was a priority: Detroit, Kalamazoo, Benton Harbor, and Grand Rapids were targeted.

Reaching consumers in rural areas was also important, and site locations were chosen in the upper peninsula and northern Michigan. Networking with community mental health centers in these rural localities was a strategy that helped identify and recruit interested consumers.

Transportation

Transportation was a serious barrier as consumers expressed interest in further training. Some consumers said they did not have a car or did not drive.

To resolve this dilemma, project staff encouraged them to take the initiative and seek out their friends or staff at the clubhouse or community mental health center about providing transportation. How resourceful many consumers became once they had a sincere interest in participating. Encouraging the participants to recruit their own transportation was an aspect of empowerment. Finding transportation to and from their own presentations was also an important endeavor. Consumers were willing to take the responsibility for finding alternative transportation.

The Illness Itself and Side Effects

Two of the greatest barriers many consumers experienced were the symptoms of the disorder itself and the side effects of the medication. I believe that for many consumers, their disorders and resulting side-effects were too strong and overwhelming for them to participate beyond the initial promotional presentations. For example, some consumers' hands trembled too much to write. Others had trouble sitting still for long periods of time. Some others had trouble making clear statements and yet others had trouble with their ability to concentrate. However, even attending only the promotional presentations, they were able to hear ideas about self-esteem building, consumer empowerment, consumerism, and meeting individual needs.

Anxiety

Anxiety was another barrier for consumers as they risked attempting something new. This anxiety was apparent as they shared their fears about the workshop, about learning public speaking, and about doing presentations. For some individuals, this performance anxiety was overwhelming and kept them from doing presentations after the training. It was acknowledged that the fear of public speaking is strong among many individuals whether or not they have mental health problems. Participants were encouraged to participate as much as possible within the training environment and to work through their anxiety.

One of the best ways to reduce anxiety is doing whatever it is that produces the anxiety. The emphasis on preparation for doing presentations reflects a popular saying — practice, practice, and practice. Practicing the speech in a repetitive fashion in front of other participants was an effective method for reducing the anxiety. Breaking down the steps of risk-taking was also effective in reducing anxiety. Keeping the training atmosphere a safe environment, without critical judgments and analysis, was most advantageous for learning to cope with anxiety.

Institutionalization

Connected to the aforementioned barriers were the effects of institutionalization on consumers. Some consumers would ask permission to talk, to get a cup of coffee, to leave the room, to stand up. A sense of self-empowerment was absent for many who had a long history of hospitalizations or recent inpatient episodes. Everyone was encouraged to participate in further training, whatever their stage of empowerment. In fact, the training directly challenged

the effects of institutionalization by encouraging individuals to speak up, practice public speaking, and take risks for self development. However, I do believe that the lingering aftereffects of institutionalization held many consumers from further participation in the project.

Educational Issues

For some consumers, illness had interrupted their life at an early age and
they were not able to complete their formal education. For others, education
may include some college, a college degree, or graduate work. This variance in
educational levels created a challenge in the training. In order to resolve this
variance, the workshop was geared to reach all consumers by active questioning, participation, and sharing of ideas in a safe environment of respect and
encouragement at any level.

Disclosure

Another barrier that came up in the training sessions was disclosure.
Although it was a safe environment where consumers willingly talked about
their history, disclosure was a stumbling block in doing presentations to the
community. I encouraged consumers to share information about their past to
the extent they were comfortable. Although personal disclosure is a very shame-
reducing and stigma-fighting act, I do realize that sometimes the result is negativism from others that is extremely painful. However, the majority of consumers who went on to do presentations with others also shared their mental
health experiences.

Stigma and Low Self-Esteem

One major block which was difficult to overcome was the stigma of mental illness. Rather than having many audience opportunities for presentations,
some consumers simply had no opportunities. No one was eager to listen to a
person who had a serious mental illness. The stigma and fear about mental
illness could not be eased. However, in some areas, consumers spoke out in
the community and acknowledged stigma — its damage to the well-being of
consumers — and fought to overcome it. Being a model who was willing to
speak openly about their mental health experiences was one effective step in
combating stigma.

Most consumers internalize stigma, producing low self-esteem which acts
as a major barrier to their active participation in leadership roles. Consumers
voiced questions as to their own capabilities. However, sensitizing individuals in the community to what mental illness is about can most effectively be
done by individuals who have experienced emotional and mental health problems themselves. Although anyone can find disclosure and public speaking
anxiety-producing, many consumers found it also growth-producing, actually
alleviating some of the internalized stigma.

Outcomes

Approximately 2,045 individuals participated in the promotional presentations over the three year period of the project. Sixty individuals completed a four day workshop on leadership skills. Approximately one third of these participants (20) were involved or became involved in employment situations — seven of which were within the mental health system (ranging from drop-in center directors, peer specialists, to leaders of self-help groups.) Others became more active in clubhouse responsibilities. Still others continued to do speaking engagements about consumerism with professionals in the community after the project ended.

Participants were given the opportunity to give feedback about their experiences through an evaluation process conducted in conjunction with JIMHO and the University of Michigan. Overall the results were extremely positive. The most important element in the success of the Leadership Development Project was that it was consumer-run and recovery-oriented. The effectiveness of the training workshops was dependent on the close identification between the facilitator — a consumer — and the individual participants — also consumers. The courage demonstrated in the sharing between consumers could only take place in a close, safe, and recovery-oriented environment, among individuals who were comfortable with each other, and protected from stigma and inequality. The consumer participants could share their mental health experiences in a safe environment, thereby breaking the secrecy of shame associated with stigmatized disorders. The recovery orientation to the workshops was also vital in generating hope, inspiration, and willingness to change.

The realization that consumers themselves can advocate for changes in the treatment of individuals with emotional and mental health problems will be empowering to the consumer movement. Consumers can stand up and say, "That's wrong, that's stigmatizing, that's not effective, and we need to change it." This was a strong focus throughout the Consumer Leadership Development Project.

Summary

Consumer leadership is effective because of its experiential knowledge base. Someone who has experienced mental health problems will view life differently than someone who has never suffered from such problems. Often, however, in our society the consumer perspective is viewed as weak, sick, and inferior. Consumers taking on leadership and service provider roles directly confront stereotypical and stigma-oriented beliefs. Yet, these beliefs are most damaging to consumer leadership and employment. Attitudes are difficult to change, and many individuals continue to believe the negative stereotypes of individuals with emotional and mental health problems rather than listen to their experiences with empathy and compassion.

A limitation for consumer leadership is that some in the mental health system are hesitant and reluctant to listen and become involved with consumers from a perspective of equality. The result of this exclusion is often tokenism or complete exclusion. Although attitudes are changing, people are still slow in recognizing the equal value of consumers.

For many of the consumers who participated in the promotional presentations but did not go on for further training, internalized stigma is a barrier which is difficult to resolve. Some consumers are afraid to become involved and have great anxiety in asserting their voices. It is easier not to become involved. The damaging effects of negative stereotypes and stigmatizing perspectives are taken personally and to heart — and may hinder the healing process.

The Leadership Training Project teaches us that consumers are not often given opportunities to work on positive mental health. Rather mental health services, staff, and programs are geared to focus on problems, symptoms, and limitations. As a result, quality of life means something very different for an individual labeled with schizophrenia than someone with an MBA. Consumers need safe opportunities to take on safe risks, to learn and grow in positive directions with knowledge of mental wellness and an internalized image of their own recovery. The Leadership Development Project offered consumers this opportunity, and this opportunity is the road-map to wellness for many.

In closing, consumer involvement in the mental health system will continue through both leadership development and service provider positions. The greatest barriers will be the slowness in recognizing the great need for consumers in these roles and the importance and value of having consumers participate for their own empowerment and for the benefit of others. The consumer movement will look forward to the future when input and involvement from consumers will be inherent at all levels of the mental health system.

Colleen Jasper is the director of the Office of Consumer Relations for the Michigan Department of Community Health.

SECTION 5

Employment Roles for Consumers in Mental Health and Psychiatric Rehabilitation Services

Introduction to Section 5: Employment Roles for Consumers in Mental Health and Psychiatric Rehabilitation Services

This section features programmatic descriptions and personal accounts of employment roles created for, or filled by, consumers. Most of the positions described in these chapters are currently identified as exclusively for consumers. This designation creates complexities beyond those described in previous sections, as it produces increased interaction (and sometimes competition) with non-consumer agency staff, requires disclosure and accompanying effects of stigma and discrimination, produces unique benefits to recipients, but also increased costs to consumer providers.

The designated positions occupied by consumers employed as providers in mental health programs are diverse, just as in previous sections. Chapters include descriptions of consumers being employed as peer counselors in inpatient, vocational and community support programs; respite work; housing support; patient advocacy; and case management. Many of these positions share functions such as advocacy, resource acquisition on behalf of clients, socialization with clients, group work, and information dissemination (writing newsletters, media and public presentations). All are prominent in emphasizing role modeling as an important aspect of the positions.

The chapters identify unique and positive benefits which accrue to service recipients who are provided assistance by a peer. Rapport and trust are more easily established and empathy received. Recipients are more willing to disclose information to a peer who is seen as "having been there" and is less anxious about negative reactions. Having common knowledge and experience enables the consumer-employee to discover information that professionals wouldn't know and to alert professionals to emerging problems before they reach crisis states (Allen). Peers may also be more helpful in that they have more accurate and complete knowledge to share and perhaps more time to provide support, to problem-solve and discuss strategies. In their role modeling function, consumer employees can also share information and experiences not known to professionals concerning the recovery process. But perhaps their greatest contribution lies in offering continued hope for the recipient's own rehabilitation and recovery and inspiration for overcoming barriers and setbacks.

There are also numerous benefits enumerated by the consumers who occupy these employee roles. As in previous chapters, the opportunities to develop work habits and specific skills (e.g., empathic listening — Brown) are described. Several authors mention positive effects of increased responsibility, the satisfaction of giving to others and seeing them benefit, the value of these work experiences for career decision-making and for increasing aspirations for the future. Chapter authors emphasize the increase in self-esteem that results from employment experiences, as well as from pride associated with being able to work and being a productive part of society.

While service recipients reportedly see only benefits from disclosure of consumer-providers' experiences with mental illness, this is not true for the consumer-providers themselves. Occupying provider roles can create costs. Negative feelings may be experienced: self-doubt, fears about over-working or job performance, fear of the unknown, as well as fears of losing disability benefits. Consumer employees may experience symptomatic flare-ups and consequently be unable to consistently perform expected duties. Boundary issues are reported, such as being too supportive or too disappointed concerning a recipient's outcomes, over-identifying with recipient issues, difficulties differentiating friend versus worker roles, switching from fluid and unbounded relationships to ones that adhere to professional limitations. When consumers act as spokespersons, they must put "painful private aspects [of their lives] on stage" (Brady). Being in a restrictive psychiatric setting may also trigger old feelings of discomfort or trauma (Oursler).

Aspects of the jobs themselves may create problems. Some of these jobs, such as respite worker, are very stressful and demanding, even for individuals without mental or emotional problems. Some jobs contribute to stress because of low rates of pay, inconsistent work hours, lack of benefits (Allen, Brown). Many of the jobs lack role clarity and so contribute to increased stress, i.e., What is this position supposed to do? What are the responsibilities? What are the limitations?

Problems also emerge from negative staff reactions which include: questions concerning consumer-employees' abilities to maintain confidentiality (Oursler), being distrustful of self-advocacy (Brady), and treating workers like patients and looking for symptoms (Oursler). However, most chapter authors report overall positive effects on staff working with a consumer-provider: staff see consumers in new roles, negative myths about consumers are dispelled, and new understandings of consumer perspectives on services and positive outlooks on recovery are gained. These attitude changes can promote an increase in meaningful dialogue between recipients and staff, resulting in more sensitive and responsive support systems.

Positive benefits are reported for the mental health system overall. Consumers have become increasingly involved in planning, evaluation, and agency operations (Oursler, Brady). In one program (Sharac and colleagues), the community gained positive evidence of consumers' abilities. "Yet much remains to be done" (Brady). Gaps can easily be identified: programs described in the chapters, while positively received, do not appear to be experiencing widespread expansion. Only one program reported establishing career ladders for consumers occupying targeted positions (Bichsel). Without such considerations, where is the vertical or even lateral movement for consumers in these provider roles?

Thus, many challenges exist to successfully employing consumers in created roles. Some of these challenges are inherent in the innovativeness of these employment initiatives. There is "no road map" to guide our progress. There are no standard protocols (Sharac et al.). As stated in one chapter, "...we would prefer more preparation and less 'training as we go'" (Gregory et al.). Flexibility is needed, but also efforts to establish consistency, fairness and equity.

As uncharted as this course may be, many of the chapters have attempted to identify some actions that seem to produce more positive outcomes. Consumer employees should be given full employee status, vis-a-vis privileges they are accorded and conditions of employment (e.g., receiving ward keys, attending treatment meetings, being provided fringe benefits, and being paid a living wage that would allow them to leave disability if appropriate and desired). This will often require top-level administrative support to effectuate (Oursler).

Secondly, a substantial amount of time and resources from established agency personnel may be necessary for training and supervision. Communication between all staff is integral. Consumers should be seen as part of the service team (Bichsel, Gregory et al.). Appropriate supervision includes the ability to individualize job assignments (Oursler). The chapters do not agree, however, on the extent to which agency support differs for consumer versus non-consumer employees.

Finally, some of the chapters suggest that employing consumers in specially created roles may be more appropriate in some settings than in others—for example, in settings where work focuses on rehabilitation rather than treatment (Oursler) and where it is characterized by less formality in service provision (Bichsel).

Perhaps the greatest challenges facing *employment* of consumers as providers emerge from its greatest strengths. That is, the success consumers have in establishing rapport and building trust with recipients also puts them at risk of stress due to lessened abilities to protect their personal boundaries. Similarly, working closely with nonconsumer providers increases the likelihood of existing staff experiencing significant cognitive shifts towards consumer involvement, but also can foster staff feelings of being threatened and of resistance. Finally, consumer-employees disclosing their psychiatric status appears to increase their ability to work closely with and get the support of service recipients; however, it also increases the likelihood of their personally experiencing stigma and discrimination.

Some might conclude that consumers should only be hired competitively, into non-designated jobs. Others in this section would disagree, citing the benefits directly received by recipients from the role-model of recovery presented by employees identified as consumers. Some might conclude that consumer provision of services only works in consumer-controlled programs; that otherwise consumers will inevitably face discriminatory and unequal treatment by nonconsumer employees. One consumer in this section disagrees with this conclusion as well; she reports experiencing greater expectations to be stable when employed in an integrated program, versus one that is consumer-operated (see Bichsel).

Such varying perspectives suggest that there is no uniform answer to the complexities which consumer employment presents. This variability that offers opportunities to consumers, nonconsumer providers, and administrators to reflect on the benefits to be provided by a particular option. Thus, attempts at pattern matching may be more appropriate. As we read the chapters in this section that follow, we might ask: Is this like my situation? Would this work in our setting? Why or why not? Answering these questions will result in a configuration of consumer employment that makes the most sense for a given situation.

Chapter 20
Consumers as Providers: A Peer Counseling Program
Janice Oursler

Overview

Recovery from major mental illness in a public psychiatric facility has traditionally been a staff-led process. Deegan (1988) presents an alternative viewpoint, stressing that psychiatrically disabled people need not be passive recipients of rehabilitation services who "get recovered" but rather, become active and responsible participants in their own rehabilitation plans. Manhattan Psychiatric Center (MPC), a public psychiatric facility, developed a peer counselor program which employs consumers who provide services for other consumers to promote the process of recovery. As peer counselors joined the treatment team, there were changes in roles for both staff and consumers. Although there were some difficulties to overcome from these changing roles, the program as a whole demonstrated substantial benefits in expanding consumer participation in service planning and delivery at MPC.

MPC, serving residents of the Borough of Manhattan, is the largest inpatient facility operated by the New York State Office of Mental Health (OMH), with an inpatient census of over 900. MPC also operates comprehensive outpatient services including licensed Clinic Treatment, Continuing Day Treatment (CDT), and Intensive Psychiatric Rehabilitation Treatment (IPRT) programs as well as an Intensive Case Management (ICM) program. IPRT is based on the psychiatric rehabilitation model developed by the Boston University Center for Psychiatric Rehabilitation to help consumers choose, and keep goals for their future. MPC's outpatient services are community-based in Harlem.

MPC primarily serves individuals with severe and persistent mental illness. By agreement between the city and New York state, New York City hospitals have as their mission acute psychiatric treatment while state psychiatric centers assume responsibility for intermediate and long-term care. Thus, individuals are typically admitted to MPC after several weeks of inpatient treatment at a New York City hospital. MPC's inpatient facility is located on Ward's Island, across the East River from Manhattan in a country-like setting (at least compared with Manhattan). Many patients have had extended lengths of stay at MPC, and some have come to consider it home. Preparing such long-term patients for discharge is difficult. In many instances, patients have been reluctant to leave the facility for residence in the community. The peer counselor program was supported by a grant from the New York State Office of Mental Health. This grant was from funds for MICA (mentally ill chemical abusers) training and emphasized services for consumers with this dual diagnosis. The grant was available for the purpose of paying peer counselors only, and pay was at the rate of $6 per hour. Grant monies have been renewed annually, and the program is in its third year of operation.

Planning and Implementing the Program

The two staff who planned and implemented the program were myself and Steve Rabinowitz, the ICM Coordinator, who handled administrative aspects. I was responsible for day-to-day operations, including clinical supervision of the peer counselors and coordination with their on-site job supervisors.

Program Principles

Two major principles guided program development. One was consistency with MPC's mission, defined as assisting seriously mentally ill and psychiatrically disabled persons to reduce their distress and increase their capacity for self-mastery, self-care, and social integration so that they could function successfully in the least restrictive environment ("Our Mission," 1992). This mission statement had its roots in the principles of psychiatric rehabilitation with an emphasis on hope and consumer choice as key values (Anthony, Cohen & Farkas, 1990).

Drawing from the principle, it was decided to develop a project to address one or more of the four environments identified for rehabilitation goal setting. These environments are living, learning, working and socializing (Cohen, Farkas, Cohen & Unger, 1990). Additionally, we wanted to develop a program that would both address areas important to inpatient services and incorporate special knowledge peer counselors have about the recovery process. Thus, it was decided to focus the peer counselor service on two intermediate treatment units. These units contained many extended-stay patients who could benefit from interaction with other consumers. Peer counselors provided a service around the process of recovery, drawing from their own personal experiences. They also used concepts of psychiatric rehabilitation with a focus on living environments and the transition from hospital to community. The principal benefit of the program was expected to be an increase in rehabilitation readiness (Cohen, Farkas, Cohen & Unger, 1989) for service recipients through interaction with peer counselors, who provided learning experiences in the process of recovery.

The second principle was that peer counselors would be considered employees of the facility with the rights and responsibilities accorded to all MPC staff. This principle was articulated by Dr. Michael Ford, the Executive Director, who made clear his support for the program. This proved to be critical philosophically and practically for implementing the program and for resolving issues during operations. Being an employee meant peer counselors would have ward keys, employee ID cards, lockers and could use employee bathrooms. They could attend staff treatment planning meetings and have access to patient records.

Selecting Peer Counselors

A major element in the selection process was the consumer's interest in being a peer counselor. Additional selection criteria included an extended period in recovery in the community, a history of substance abuse in addition to mental illness, and demonstrated consumer activism, such as being a member of the local mental health planning committee. Consumers had to be willing to talk about their own recovery. There was no education or experience requirement, nor did peer counselors have to be recipients of service at MPC.

Peer counselor candidates were recruited in several ways. Flyers were posted in the outpatient programs, announcements were made at mental health planning committee meetings, and staff were asked to discuss the job openings with their patients. Candidates completed a brief application expressing their interest and all applicants were individually interviewed. This proved particularly useful in assessing candidates' willingness to discuss their recovery process.

The four individuals selected to be peer counselors formed a diverse group. Their common element was long experience with mental illness and all had experienced psychiatric hospitalization but not necessarily at MPC. There were two men and two women in the group whose education ranged from some high school to some college. Three of the four had MICA (mentally ill chemical abusers) histories. All had extended periods of recovery in the community. Three resided in community residences; the fourth had maintained an apartment for many years.

Program Beginnings

From start-up, the peer counselor program would require coordination of many areas of the hospital. To initiate this process, visits were made to the designated inpatient units and the CDT Program to discuss the concept of peer counseling, introduce peer counselors to staff, make staff aware that peer counselors were employees, and gain staff input about how peer counselors could contribute to their particular program. There were also contacts with other key staff, such as the safety department where employees obtained IDs, to let them know about the program.

While the program had originally been conceptualized as occurring only at the inpatient site, one peer counselor indicated unwillingness to travel to the facility and a strong preference to work in the community. This was one of the first examples of a major dilemma the program faced. It concerned defining the appropriate authority relationship between staff and consumers in a program based on the premises of self-help and consumer initiative, yet dependent on staff expertise for negotiating the system and learning the skills of peer counseling. While a staff-led consumer program is obviously an oxymoron, it was evident that this program could not take place without substantial staff input—given the facility's limited experience with consumer initiatives—as well as the scarcity of outside consumer resources who might serve as advisors. Knight

(1994) has warned about the limits of professional involvement in consumer self-help endeavors, suggesting that an appropriate role for professionals is to foster self-help groups and then let them go. In keeping with psychiatric rehabilitation principles which underlie the program and emphasize choice and the active involvement of consumers in the rehabilitation process (Anthony, Cohen & Farkas, 1990), it was decided to honor the peer counselor's request and conduct the program both inpatient and at the CDT Program, a program in which this peer counselor was not enrolled.

The basic structure of the program was set from these discussions with peer counselors and staff and in consideration of budget parameters. The work week consisted of 20 hours divided into two full days at the work site plus a half day for clinical supervision at the outpatient location. Peer counselors were paid monthly under terms of the grant and were responsible for their own transportation and lunch expenses. If needed, arrangements could be made to advance bus tokens against pay. Peer counselors were advised to discuss their situation with the Social Security Administration regarding how their earnings would affect benefits and to plan ahead both with their own budgets and their community residences. A Social Security representative was invited to give an on-site seminar to reinforce this. The peer counseling program was planned to last three to four months until grant funds were exhausted.

Job Assignments

The work of the peer counselors was structured so they had an administrative or task supervisor and a clinical supervisor. This arrangement was based on the facility's matrix supervision model in which all staff receive both clinical and administrative supervision. The task supervisor on the job site provided day-to-day work supervision and was readily available to answer questions or help address any difficulties peer counselors might encounter. Clinical supervision was used to teach counseling techniques and to process on-the-job experiences. The clinical supervisor contacted task supervisors regularly to monitor the program.

Job assignments differed between job sites, but had in common working with consumers to choose living environments, in part through discussion of peer counselors' experiences in recovery. The CDT Program (community-based) peer counselor had the following job assignments:

- Co-leading with a staff member, a group for individuals coping with situational housing crises. This group, based on psychiatric rehabilitation technology, was designed to assist consumers to set an overall rehabilitation goal for a new living environment.

- Leading an informal socialization group. This group provided an opportunity for the peer counselor to talk with small groups of consumers about their futures. It offered a chance for the peer counselor to discuss personal experiences associated with recovery.

• Accompanying consumers to appointments in the community, for example, to get a physical examination or to go to the Social Security Administration.

• Assuming a major role in planning consumer led activities. This included leadership in starting up a committee of consumers and staff to plan a family day for community services, as well as organizing a consumer conference which involved the short-term hiring of 20 consumers under the grant to work on various aspects.

Inpatient peer counselors generally worked as a group in providing services, although in certain circumstances they decided to divide services. For example, some peer counselors would go with a group to play basketball in the gym while another peer counselor accompanied patients to dance therapy. The major inpatient job assignments included the following:

• Co-leading with each other, a group to discuss planning for the future. This was the main setting for peer counselors to talk about their own experiences and to address the perceptions of group members about living in the community. This group culminated in a visit to the community residence where the peer counselors lived.

• Participating in recreational and socialization activities. These activities served an important purpose in enabling peer counselors to connect with other consumers. They also promoted informal conversation about social life in the community including socializing without substance abuse.

• Attending Therapeutic Community meetings and Treatment Team meetings. These meetings often were the forum for peer counselors to offer their own perspectives on service delivery. Staff reported that hearing these perspectives broadened their awareness of the recovery process, especially regarding what was helpful and what was not.

Training and Supervision

This occurred both on the job and in the weekly clinical supervision group. The group lasted about three hours and was broken into two parts; one part focused on teaching skills needed for the job, while the other addressed the experiences peer counselors were having at work.

Counseling skills and techniques taught in the group were based on psychiatric rehabilitation philosophy and service delivery. Three topics were emphasized. The first topic was confidentiality. The second was the concept of choice especially relating to recovery as a highly personal experience. Related to this, peer counselors were taught listening skills as well as how to present their personal experience as one method, but not the only method of recovery. The third topic involved teaching techniques used in identifying personal criteria and describing alternative environments.

Outcomes

Outcomes were evaluated from follow-up interviews with peer counselors and staff from the initial program as well as from my observations and notes during the program. Interviews were conducted with three of the four peer counselors and also with clinical and administrative staff from both inpatient and community services. Follow-up interviews took place about two years after the conclusion of the first peer counselor effort at MPC. This interval made possible an assessment of some of the long-term program effects. The peer counseling program appears to have had an effect on the peer counselors, other consumers, staff, and the system as a whole, but the outcome was not always as expected. When the program was started, it was expected that the major impact would be on consumers receiving services. However, it appears that the major influence has been on the peer counselors themselves.

Effects on Peer-Counselors

The peer counselors were pioneers in a new service. This proved to be a mixed blessing. On the one hand, peer counselors reported positive reinforcement of their level of self-esteem from being role models for their peers. They were pleased to have the opportunity to work and to learn new skills. They agreed that the level of pay was high enough to recognize the importance of their work, in that the $6 exceeded the level attainable in MPC patient work programs where maximum pay is the minimum wage.

Despite these benefits, all peer counselors experienced substantially increased levels of stress during the program. For peer counselors working inpatient, stress was related to the experience of working on locked wards. Peer counselors found that this work setting triggered recall of experiences they had had as inpatients and restimulated many old feelings about those experiences. This was true even if they had not been hospitalized at MPC itself, and, as they commented, was not alleviated by their status as employees having keys. Processing these recollections and the effects of mental illness on their lives became an important topic for discussion during weekly clinical supervision meetings. Also discussed in the group was the stigma attached to mental illness and how this had influenced their own process of recovery. Despite efforts made to reduce the stress through clinical supervision and the clinical supervisor's ongoing interactions with task supervisors, one peer counselor experienced a significant return of symptoms requiring an increase in medication. When this occurred, the peer counselor was given a vacation from work until symptoms abated and work was able to be resumed.

The peer counselor in the CDT also experienced increased stress which she attributed to her new role and, in particular, to her disclosure of her diagnosis. In her opinion, this disclosure contributed to staff reacting to her as a patient rather than as a worker. The situation creating the most stress took place when she took on different group assignments as she became a college student as well as a peer counselor. Her clinic psychiatrist told me about the problem upon my return to outpatient services after several days off. He said CDT staff contacted him to express concern that the peer counselor was experiencing relapse, but he found no symptoms in his interview with her. My meeting with CDT staff and the peer counselor revealed everyone's unhappiness about her job assignments which, in my analysis, could be attributed to lack of role clarity. The peer counselor was experiencing stress from her new assignments because she was not sure what she was supposed to do in each group— that is, be an observer, a consumer participant, or a leader. Staff saw her efforts to negotiate this as emerging symptoms of her illness. After several meetings with CDT staff and the peer counselor to clarify her purpose and role in each group, no further difficulty was noted. It appears staff interpreted her behavior through the lens of illness when the lens of new worker would have been a better fit.

In the follow-up interview two years later, the peer counselor still had strong feelings about this experience and described long-term effects from it. Currently a full time college student planning a career in human services, she no longer chooses to disclose her mental illness as she once did and no longer wants to work as a consumer advocate. She said, "I originally wanted to be a mental health advocate when I went back to college, but not now. It was a mistake to ever tell staff my diagnosis in the first place. Now people know me as a college student, not a person with a mental illness. I like that."

This experience highlights another major dilemma in peer counseling, that is, the need to disclose the illness and talk about the process of recovery as a part of employment. While this can be an aid in recovery and certainly can assist others in understanding the illness, it also can open the way for discrimination (Fisher, 1994). Some consumers have concluded that work in a recipient slot is a dead end situation without chance for promotion and requiring continuing, painful disclosure for other people's benefit ("Regrets," 1994).

Another peer counselor, now employed full time as a unit leader in a mental health program, also expressed ambivalence about peer counseling work and its requirement to disclose. This peer counselor said that disclosing has been worthwhile so far in advancing opportunities for work but had concerns about its possible impact on future jobs. She added, "I want to be the one to decide when to disclose rather than being on the spot to talk about my illness."

Effects on Staff

The major impact of the program on staff was to see consumers in a new role, as workers who are peers rather than as patients. Peer counselors gave staff a new outlook on consumers' perceptions of service delivery and the process of recovery. Generally, the impact on staff was positive in expanding their awareness of the recovery process and how consumers could assist staff as well as other consumers in promoting an environment for recovery.

Effects of peer counselors on inpatient staff were immediately apparent. A number expressed amazement to meet consumers who had experienced a process of recovery. It became obvious that many staff still subscribed to the view of mental illness, in general, and schizophrenia, in particular, as inevitably following a chronic course. Staff apparently were not aware of the findings of long-term follow-up studies of schizophrenia. Harding, Zubin, and Strauss (1987) in their review of such studies, found a much more heterogeneous picture of long-term outcome, with marginal or deteriorated states as the exception rather than the rule. This outlook was not surprising, however, as inpatient staff rarely see consumers who are successful and satisfied in their recovery. Instead, they repeatedly see patients who either make little progress or return for rehospitalization. This one-sided picture affects staff by limiting, if not eliminating, hope for recovery. Peer counselors personified the concept that recovery is possible.

Staff interest in learning about these consumers in recovery helped pave the way for their acceptance at the inpatient work sites. In follow-up interviews, both inpatient and CDT program staff reported peer counselors were helpful to them personally in giving them another point of view about how services may be perceived by consumers. They thought peer counselors promoted dialogue between consumers and staff about service delivery. They found that having peer counselors encouraged consumers to be more receptive to services they might initially have rejected as the peer counselors explained how the services helped them, and might help this consumer, too. Finally, staff thought the peer counselor program had a benefit in making them more open to roles consumers could play both in their own programs and in the mental health system.

Staff were always supportive of the general program concept. However, one staff member commented that personal reactions to events in the program sometimes led to reexamining one's inner beliefs about what consumers could do. One example of this was the reluctance of some staff to have peer counselors in treatment planning meetings as questions were raised about their ability to maintain confidentiality, especially since they socialized with other consumers. There was lengthy discussion among staff including the clinical supervisor about this issue which was resolved in the short run through application of the principle that peer counselors were employees and would do what employees do. This included attending treatment planning meetings. As time passed, staff who initially expressed reservations became more comfortable about this. It appears the peer counselors' training on confidentiality and their ability to maintain it were important factors in resolving staff concern, but successful staff experience with peer counselors was particularly critical. As the program has progressed since initial implementation, this type of issue has become infrequent as staff have become more accustomed to working with consumers in new roles.

Effects on Consumers

The effects on consumers who received services is difficult to evaluate since the peer counselors interacted with many consumers during the period of the project, and no formal follow-up was possible. On the inpatient service, the major outcomes identified by peer counselors and staff were consumers' expanded interest in learning about life in the community, increased hope for their own recovery and eventual discharge, and, in some instances, steps toward discharge.

Peer counselors recounted that the visit to their community residence had an especially powerful influence on consumers. After using the clinical supervision group to assess the pros and cons, the peer counselors took a group of inpatient consumers to see their own apartments at the community residence. This helped make real the peer counselors' lives in the community and promoted motivation toward discharge. In the follow-up interview, one peer counselor reported that a patient had been discharged to that community residence, in part, due to peer counseling.

The influence of the peer counseling program appeared to be similar but more diffuse in the CDT Program. In fact, both the peer counselor and CDT staff remembered some resentment by a few consumers who viewed the peer counselor as "uppity." The majority of CDT consumers, however, were receptive to peer counseling, and it appears the program stimulated consumer interest in assuming new roles especially as activists in the consumer movement. Several CDT consumers have become peer counselors themselves. Additionally, others have become active in consumer activities such as chairing the MPC Consumer Council (which advises MPC administration on service delivery including satisfaction with services), maintaining liaison with the MPC Patient Council (which is the inpatient equivalent), participating in planning consumer conferences, and becoming members of local mental health planning committees.

System Effects

There appears to have been an impact on the mental health system as well, although this is hard to assess. The assessment is made especially difficult since the program occurred in a time of expansion for the consumer movement in general. However, the work of the peer counselor program has clearly had a continuing legacy at MPC. It provided a blueprint for consumer work in subsequent grant renewals including modifications of the peer counseling program based on knowledge gained in this initial experience. While at one time it seemed unusual to include consumers in what were then considered staff functions such as program planning, assessment of consumer satisfaction with services received, and participation in local planning efforts, it now seems strange to think of these activities without consumers.

Besides continuing the peer counselor program, MPC took a number of other steps to support the peer counseling concept. One of these steps was making application for full time, civil service positions as peer specialists, a title recently instituted by OMH on a state-wide level. When approved, peer specialists will specialize in MICA services. In the interim, a half-time consumer ombudsperson was hired with funds from other grant sources to address consumer complaints and enhance consumer representation and participation in the functioning of the inpatient service. Another step was to make the presentation by a consumer about peer counseling and other consumer initiatives at MPC a routine part of the orientation program for both new employees and new volunteers at the facility. Participation of MPC consumers has continued at a high level in local planning efforts, and the area of Manhattan served by our outpatient services has gained a reputation for the high percentage of consumers serving on these committees. We have also received numerous inquiries as well as visits from other providers interested in learning how to promote consumer initiatives.

Peer Counselors Two Years Later

Follow-up interviews indicated major long-term benefits of this experience for the peer counselors themselves. The program had a definite impact on the way peer counselors think of themselves and on their level of aspiration for the future as they became providers to others. Of the original group of peer counselors, one has been employed full time for more than a year as a unit leader in a clubhouse program based on the Fountain House model; one has completed an associate's degree and is in her last semester of full time study for a bachelor's degree; one is working in a transitional employment program, and one is preparing to take the high school equivalency exam. All three who lived in community residences at the time of the program are now living in their own apartments.

Recommendations

The original peer counselor program provided many opportunities to learn about the elements promoting the growth of such programs as well as the factors impeding their development. In retrospect, both peer counselors and staff declared the program an overall success despite some difficulties encountered during its course. In considering their recommendations from follow-up interviews and my own observations, three major factors were identified as key contributors to success. These are as follows:

- Top level administrative support. The facility executive director as well as top administration of inpatient and outpatient services were supportive of peer counselors as employees and offered enormous support for the program. This resolved many issues about how peer counselors were to be treated. They were to be treated as employees. This guideline was applied in a number of situations to clarify what peer counselors would be doing and how they would be doing it.

• The clinical supervision group. All peer counselors recognized the support the group provided as the key to its usefulness, and each was able to recall specific topics discussed in the support segment. The main topics they recollected were talking about their reactions to the job, ways to deal with job situations, and discussions of stigma. Only one peer counselor was able to recall the content portion of the group, and named specific topics covered like listening skills as being helpful in gaining current employment. In follow-up interviews, peer counselors also identified the outlook of the clinical supervisor as an important element in the group's effectiveness. One peer counselor said, "It's so important for the clinical supervisor to believe consumers can do the job and to be flexible in planning. Some workers have preconceived notions about what consumers can do, and this holds you back." The group also served as a springboard for my ongoing consultation with staff who were task supervisors. This, too, was critical to success as processing staff concerns about the program helped them to think about consumer roles in new ways.

• The level of pay. Two aspects of the pay level were seen as critical. One was it distinguished the work from other jobs at the facility; for example, the patient worker program which employs patients in a variety of job training situations but is capped at minimum wage. The second was it recognized the importance of the work. However, everyone was unanimous in calling for pay to be received more frequently than monthly as this created hardships for consumers in budgeting and paying work expenses. Ideally, pay would be every two weeks.

Areas for Improvement

Both peer counselors and staff recommended increased job structure and more clarity about what the job entailed. From my vantage point, this would have been difficult in a new program where there was no experience in what peer counselors could do either on the part of the peer counselors, the program staff, or the clinical supervisor. This lack of experience necessitated a certain amount of flexibility to sculpt job responsibilities to the situation as the program developed. However, with the growth of the consumer movement, there are greatly expanded opportunities for consumer input into such programs from groups within MPC as well as other groups in the community. Some of these groups specialize in providing peer counseling services, and it would be helpful to have their advice on program development as well as taking the lead in training consumers as providers.

In replicating the program, a major change would be to make the locus of inpatient service in an area other than the ward. In selecting the ward as the job base, we overlooked the critical distinction between treatment services and psychiatric rehabilitation services (Anthony, Cohen & Farkas, 1990). Treatment services are directed toward decreasing emotional distress and symptoms of mental illness while psychiatric rehabilitation services have as their mission working with patients to make choices about life roles and environments so that they will be successful and satisfied in the environment of their choice. Many patients on the wards are still heavily in the treatment phase or even nonresponders to treatment so that they have limited readiness for rehabilitation. A better place to establish the program might be in central rehabilitation programs where patients are more likely to have benefited from treatment services and have more interest, as well as more readiness for peer counselor services. Locating services at this site might also reduce the stress peer counselors experienced on locked wards.

We also learned in this first phase the value of time-limited work assignments. Initially, time limits were forced on the program by gaps in funding due to the termination of the grant at the end of each state fiscal year and the wait for new funding. However, these gaps pointed up the benefits of time-limited assignments in permitting evaluation on a regular basis of the impact and outcome of services for both service recipients and peer counselors. Peer counselors are advised as they start work that this is a time-limited assignment with the possibility of either renewal or a change in job assignment depending on the quality of their work and their personal reaction to the work. Generally, assignments are longer than in the initial program, typically lasting six to nine months.

The Next Phase

What was learned from the original peer counseling program has been implemented in subsequent grant funding periods, and each succeeding program continues to be modified in the light of experience with both consumer and staff input. We have learned to individualize job assignments in terms of specific job duties, that outpatient location is often more practical, to limit the number of hours worked per week, and how to provide the needed training and on-site supervision. Job assignments initially concentrated on the inpatient service have become primarily outpatient based since this has proved to be less stressful for peer counselors. The number of hours worked per week is generally less than 20 hours, as the requirement for this number also created stress. The maximum hours worked per week is usually 16 with work hours more flexible and individualized.

The variety of peer counselor jobs has expanded to meet the individual needs and preferences of both peer counselors and consumers receiving services. As the program has developed, consumers have been more involved in defining peer counselor jobs. This is in contrast to the initial effort where staff took the lead. Assignments are geared more to individual consumer talents and aspirations as well as to supporting the consumer movement at MPC. Examples of jobs peer counselors have done as the program has developed include leading Double Trouble MICA groups, operating a consumer food co-op, conducting consumer satisfaction surveys for both outpatient and inpatient central rehabilitation programs, working one-to-one with other consumers to teach the use of leisure time without substance abuse, participating in planning and running consumer conferences, maintaining liaison between the outpatient Consumer Council and the inpatient Patient Council, conducting voter registration drives, and teaching personal computer skills to consumers and staff.

While initial program development concentrated on the benefits to be gained by service recipients, our experience has pointed out benefits are as likely, if not more likely, to be experienced by the peer counselors themselves. Currently, the program is viewed as one point of entry for consumers into the consumer movement, as well as an opportunity to identify whether working with other consumers is an area peer counselors wish to pursue as a personal goal. To assist them in preparing for their own futures, all peer counselors are offered intensive psychiatric rehabilitation treatment services either in conjunction with their peer counseling work or after assignments have ended. Also, peer counselors interested in pursuing this line of work are encouraged to investigate enrolling in training offered by community consumer groups.

The peer counselor program continues to work with the dilemma of defining the role of staff and consumers in a program where the consumer movement adjoins treatment and rehabilitation services offered by staff. There is more consumer input than initially, but given the substantial role of staff in training and supervising peer counselors, it is clear this is not (nor was it intended to be) a pure self-help program. It is also clear that over its course the program has had a positive outcome for the peer counselors, for consumers they have worked with, and for staff who have increased their understanding of the recovery process and learned to see consumers in new roles. There has been positive outcome for the mental health system itself, both at MPC and in the community, where consumers routinely occupy larger roles in service planning and delivery. Finally, there is no question that a major contribution from the peer counselor program has been providing a forum for consumers and staff to talk to each other about how they can work together to promote the process of recovery.

References

Anthony, W., Cohen, M., & Farkas, M. (1990). *Psychiatric rehabilitation.* Boston, MA: Center for Psychiatric Rehabilitation.

Cohen, M., Farkas, M., Cohen. B., & Unger, K. (1989). *Assessing readiness.* Boston, MA: Center for Psychiatric Rehabilitation.

Cohen, M., Farkas, M., Cohen. B., & Unger, K. (1990). *Identifying personal criteria*. Boston, MA: Center for Psychiatric Rehabilitation.

Deegan, P. (1988). Recovery: The lived experience of rehabilitation. *Psychosocial Rehabilitation Journal, 11*(4), 11-19.

Fisher, D. (1994). A psychiatrist's gradual disclosure. *OMH News, 11,* 16.

Harding, C., Zubin, J., & Strauss, J. (1987). Chronicity in schizophrenia: Fact, partial fact or artifact. *Hospital and Community Psychiatry, 38,* 477-486.

Knight, E. (1994). Guarding against pseudo-self-help. *OMH News, 9, 7.*

Our Mission (1992). *MPC Update '92.* (Available from Manhattan Psychiatric Center, Ward's Island, NY 10035).

Regrets (1994). *OMH News, 11, 7.*

Dr. Janice Oursler is the former director of rehabilitation services at Manhattan Psychiatric Center, Ward's Island, New York.

Chapter 21

Project WINS: A Consumer's Perspective

Charles R. Allen

Introduction

I have been a consumer of mental health services since September, 1981. In June of 1982 I became a member of an assertive community treatment team at Harbinger of Grand Rapids, Michigan. In April, 1991, I secured employment as a peer support specialist with Project WINS. The Project was funded by a grant from the National Institute of Mental Health. It was administered by Harbinger. Project WINS provided vocational services to consumers in two mental health agencies in Grand Rapids. The funding for the project ended in September, 1993.

My activities were under the direct supervision of a vocational specialist. Training for the position was conducted in a group setting over four, four-hour sessions. As a peer support specialist, I was employed to support my peers in the attainment of their vocational goals. The project used the Choose-Get-Keep model in determining the appropriate action to be taken with a given peer. Clients were referred to the project for services by their treatment teams. In keeping with the goal of client self-determination, peer support services were at the client's option. I was asked to be a role-model in the delivery of peer support services in the mental health community. As a consumer, I carried with me the perspective of a person who has also been affected by mental illness. Though this was a vocational grant project, my experience touched all areas of my peers' lives. I was asked to perform a wide array of assignments. Some of these came easy and others tested my abilities and forced me to overcome my shortcomings.

An Important Lesson

In the beginning I learned a lesson about boundaries. One of my friends was also a client of the project. He was having a bad day so I took him to a local mall. I billed the project for my time. My billing was denied. I was also informed that though he was a client of the project, he had not been assigned to me for peer support services. Additionally, it was decided that because of our prior relationship, it would be inappropriate for me to work with him. At first I resented the decision. As time went on, he would call at all times of the day and night. It seemed because I told him I couldn't work with him, he wanted to talk to me more. I felt like he needed peer support services and yet I could not give them to him. However, the project director kept firm on the decision that I should not work with him. Today I see that the decision was correct. I should note that the phone calls became annoying to the point that police intervention was required and I changed to an unlisted phone number after the project ended.

Challenges of the Position

As a peer support specialist, I considered myself a para-professional. One of my duties was to schedule a contact and evaluate my peers on their work readiness and report back with my evaluation to the vocational specialist. On one such appointment, I had scheduled to meet Joe at a local restaurant. I arrived ten minutes early. After sitting for twenty-five minutes, I called Joe to see why he had not kept his appointment. He answered the phone and said he would be right over. I was a little perturbed and intended to let him know when he arrived that I expected him to be punctual. When he arrived, it appeared he had just gotten out of bed. I told him that I had been waiting and that I would expect him to be on time in the future. This was the first time I had met Joe and I didn't want to be too harsh in my comments. Yet I needed to try to help him in his attempt to get ready for employment.

In our meeting, it was necessary to have Joe fill out a few forms. I noticed him fumbling through the forms without writing anything. When I questioned him, I found out he could not read the forms. Joe was illiterate. When I reported this information back to the vocational specialists, they were surprised. They were not aware that Joe could not read or write. With my help, Joe was linked to a local organization that teaches adult literacy. Joe was assigned a tutor and began to make progress in his reading skills. With Joe it was also necessary to improve his personal hygiene and appearance. I coached him in these areas.

Joe eventually gained employment in a rehabilitation setting. I was assigned to help him learn the bus route to and from the workplace. After he started working, I was used as a job coach to help him do the work better. Side effects from his medication required him to make frequent trips to the restroom and this affected his productivity. This was a problem for a number of the peers I worked with.

In another instance, I found myself in the role of mediator. A local firm employed a peer to whom I was providing support services. There was a problem at the workplace between the supervisor and my peer. I was asked to visit the job site and try to resolve the problem. I arrived at the site and asked to speak with the supervisor. He told me that John had left the work floor and went to the rest room and smoked a cigarette. When I asked John about the situation, he said he had intestinal problems the night before and had used the bathroom and smoked while there. John also suggested that everyone else smoked in the bathroom and the complaint might be racially motivated. In the interest of good relationships, I told John that I would explain the intestinal problem to the supervisor and made the decision to overlook the race issue at the time. I explained John's intestinal problems to the supervisor and John continued employment. I should note the supervisor was terminated for making a racial slur at a later date.

One of the things I was required to do in my role as peer support specialist was to facilitate a support group. We formed two such groups which ran the length of the project. The make-up of the two groups was different. One met at a local restaurant and consisted of consumers who were employed. This group was comprised of about six individuals who regularly attended. The second group was originally held in the project office. It was comprised mainly of people looking for work. The attendance at this group was very irregular. After a few months, a decision was made to move the meeting place to a downtown cafe. Attendance increased, but the group was still transient in nature. As facilitator, it was my role to keep the group focused on vocational-related issues. At times the group would get divided into side conversations or stray from the topic. I did not want to deny my peers the right to expression, but my position required me to maintain certain guidelines. At times it was difficult to determine if we were on a coffee break or we were in fact a support group. I felt conflict because I wanted to be loyal to my peers and yet I was being paid to do a job.

I was also challenged to be a role-model within the organization. I was one of twelve initially hired for the position. After ten months, I was the only one of the original twelve remaining. During those months, I had helped to start the peer support groups and facilitated them on a twice weekly basis. I wrote articles and edited a newsletter entitled, "THE WINS WINNER." I had provided one-to-one counseling to my peers and served as a link to the case management team, when needed, concerning behavioral problems. This included problems of substance abuse and medication compliance.

Conflict Created by Two Roles

At the end of the first year of employment I was asked to give a presentation at a conference in California about my position as a peer support specialist. About a month before I was to give the presentation, I became manic and required hospitalization. I was put on a medical leave of absence. I was not sure if I would be allowed to return to work in time to represent the project at the conference. I felt like I was recovered before the team felt I was. It seemed like they were being overly cautious and were trying to sabotage my plans. The situation seemed complicated by the fact that I was a client of an agency team and also an employee of the project which was administered by the same agency. The hospital psychologist and psychiatrist felt I was ready for discharge after four days, and yet the team kept me in the hospital for ten days. After discharge from the hospital, I was forced to go into supervised housing for a week. If I did not comply, I would forfeit my trip to California. I complied, but I didn't like it. I felt like my rights were being violated because employment and treatment were so intertwined. I made the trip to California but I was a bit frenzied while there because my financial situation had been eroded by three weeks out of work prior to the trip. I made the most of it and gave a good presentation and enjoyed myself as best I could.

Personal Issues

Probably one of the hardest parts of this position for me was dealing with my own illness. I faced fear on many levels. I had been hospitalized and required intervention on over a dozen occasions prior to my employment at Project WINS. When I took the position, I didn't know if I would be able to handle the stress of working. I had led a very sedentary lifestyle for the three years prior to taking the peer support position and was not sure if I could adhere to a work routine. Except for the hospitalization mentioned above, I did well for the first year. Then I began to miss meetings and was put on disciplinary probation for a 90 day period. At first I felt I was being picked on. But I made the decision I would try to do my best for the disciplinary period. At the end of the 90 days, I had improved substantially in all areas and was given an excellent rating in all categories on my employee evaluation. I was also given a pay increase at that time. When I received these, I was elated and felt a true sense of accomplishment for the first time in years.

When I came up with the idea for a newsletter, I was faced with feelings of self-doubt. I wasn't sure if I could write an article, how it would be accepted, or if it would be beneficial. I solicited literary contributions from other peer support specialists and edited them. I also set up a format on my word processor. I even gave it a name. I believe I benefited most from seeing it through. The "WINS WINNER" not only contained stories about clients, but also served as a tool for inspiration for myself and the other peer support specialists. Though the newsletter was mainly for distribution to peers, it was also sent to the Director of the State Department of Mental Health. On a number of occasions at various conferences he thanked me for sending it to him.

When I was hired for the position of peer support specialist, I was told I could work up to thirty hours per week. As time went on, it became evident that this was possible but highly unlikely. In fact, I averaged under fifteen hours per week during the two and a half years I was employed. I was limited by the number of peers I supported and seldom worked for more than two hours at any one time. The position paid a straight hourly wage with no benefits. The low hours combined with the lack of benefits made it unlikely that I could keep the job without staying on Social Security Disability assistance and maintaining Medicare hospitalization benefits. At one time, I approached the Project Director and asked for health club membership as a benefit and was denied. I felt as if we were sub-standard employees because we were denied the benefits of the other employees of the project and were also limited in our earnings.

When the project ended in September, 1993, there was one other peer support specialist who had been there for longer than eighteen months. All of the others on staff at the time had been with Project WINS for less than one year. Most of the attrition that I saw was due to the onset of psychiatric problems. This problem plagued me twice during my tenure at WINS and yet I was able to persevere. I learned in my position how the team concept works. I was able to alert the psychiatric treatment team on a number of occasions to potential problems with my peers. These ranged from my peers exhibiting manic signs to substance abuse problems and problems with side effects from medication. Many times peer trust had to be balanced with job responsibility. On one occasion, a peer support specialist drank with a client and was suspended.

In my position I noticed that the rehabilitation agencies were at a loss much of the time in dealing with my peers. I think the revolving door syndrome that occurs in the hospitalization of psychiatric patients like myself is part of the reason for this. My peers tended to be set apart in how they were handled almost as if they were a different class of people. This tends to perpetuate the stigma in the community and in the peer.

I must also note that the mental health community is not far ahead in this matter. As noted earlier, by denying benefits and limiting hours I was kept from truly becoming part of the agency. When it was evident the funding for the project would not continue, I was offered a position running peer support groups. Though my services were considered valuable, the position was to be unpaid. I was also told that my services were needed to help in the training of a group of peer support specialists in another part of the state. I was called and scheduled dates on several occasions to complete this task. Each date was cancelled and the meeting never took place. The project director also called and told me I would be interviewed for a peer support position at a local rehabilitation agency. I followed up the call with an inquiry and was told I would be contacted by the rehabilitation agency. The call never came.

Conclusion

In my position I learned a lot about myself, my peers, and the way the mental health system works. I am thankful I had the opportunity. My position with Project WINS ended almost two years ago. I have been employed in the private sector since that time in an unrelated position.

Charles R. Allen is a former peer support specialist with PROJECT WINS/Harbinger of Grand Rapids, Inc.

Chapter 22

The Benefits and Stresses for Consumers Providing Respite to Their Peers

Lauri Brown

Respite can mean time away. For me, respite meant an occupation. While I was a respite worker, I lent my ears and gained much in return. I found a vocation in life of which I could be proud. Respite work both healed me and brought me hope. Years ago, a doctor said that I would never work in the mental health field. He said that I would take my problems to work and go home with three times my own load. I believed him and worked toward a degree in business. Yet, I decided to add to that business degree and graduated also with a social work minor.

During my last semester of college, I began to work for my mental health center as a respite worker. As a respite worker I dealt with every kind of problem. I learned quickly that I was not there to solve problems for my clients; I was there to listen. How did I learn to listen? Listening to brutal rage and character shredding as I grew up, my life was mostly me hearing people. I spoke infrequently. Consequently, I had little practice in empathetic listening. Added to this, I became ill and hid inwardly. When I did begin to speak, I felt something was missing. I wondered why people did not talk to me or want me as a friend. As I learned empathetic listening skills in respite worker training, I learned that people like to be listened to.

The mental health center where I received services offered a job as a respite worker. I did not realize then that I would gain a lifesaving ability to listen. Respite presented individuals with an alternative to a lengthy hospitalization or repeat trips to the hospital. The services included meeting with a crisis counselor for evaluation at a mental health center or the local hospital emergency room. In the respite program, trained consumers sat with the consumer who was having difficulty. Once an individual decided to go to respite, the respite workers' team leader would call around to see who could take the first shift.

When the possibility of respite work was first introduced to me at a consumer network meeting, I questioned whether or not I could handle the work. I really had no idea what I would be doing. Nevertheless, I agreed to try it. I first had an interview with the director of the Impact Crisis Team at my mental health center. I was unaware of the workings of the program, and in a sense remained blinded to the demands of this job.

To become a respite worker, I had to have six months of health and no current hospitalizations. This indicated that I had gained coping skills and an ability to cope with stress. I was accepted to be a respite worker and trained for twenty hours. I realized that the greatest hurdle to doing this job would be that I would be called at any time of day or night. Clients who might be in crisis did not walk in for help at 9:00 a.m. and leave at 5:00 p.m.

As a respite worker I learned to accept that I was on call twenty-four hours a day, every day. As I worked more frequently, a call from the team leader might come in at 11:15 p.m., when I had laid down at 11:00 p.m. In this case I might arrive at the location at 12:00 a.m. and work until 12:00 noon the next day. So for three days, respite workers juggled usual schedules so that at least one respite worker could be staying with the client.

I believe it takes a learning mind to cope with the stressful scheduling and to detach from the problems encountered on the job. A learning mind, in my opinion, has to be cultivated and nurtured. In my life, school helped, the mental health system helped, and association with people who know how to detach helped. In respite work I see a learning mind as the ability to know when to respond and when not to get entangled.

To simply take in all of the client's information and write notes accordingly, then go home saying "I can forget it," led me to hold tightly to what was said. Team meetings for respite workers encouraged me to vent frustrations, exchange experiences and touch base with the director of the program. Yet it took a resolve from within to realize that my job was simply to listen, not to cure. Apparently, listening touched people's hearts. Respite clients stayed either at the respite apartment or at a local hospital. I enjoyed the apartment setting because, when I worked a twelve hour overnight shift, I could doze on the apartment couch. I could then rest and keep an eye out for my client. The clients were always free to come and go at either location. The hospital was convenient for me because I could talk to the nurses on the night shift or watch movies. Yet, unlike the apartment, at the hospital I could not doze off on the couch and sometimes I spent hours sitting next to the bed on a hard chair. I thought that bringing reading material could help pass the hours until my shift ended. Reading was difficult when my body thought it should be sleeping. Daytime hours also could be difficult when the client slept. A good book and a relaxed attitude made these daytime shifts pass more quickly.

I felt tremendous fear of overworking. I was lucky that I could work less for the first few months. After I graduated from college, I worked any shift. I learned to function with little sleep. It was hard to know when to take my medication. I took it on schedule and sometimes felt sleepy and forced myself to keep awake and remain alert when on the job and while traveling to or from work.

I felt the intensity of my work most prominently after long shifts, back to back. One week I worked 59 hours in six days. Fortunately, we had no work for over a week after that. I am not sure how I would have reacted to a continuous interruption of sleep. Somehow, though, for short periods of time, I could live with sleep deprivation. It took either utter stupidity or a sincere need for money; or maybe I loved my work. Maybe the lack of sleep was bearable because I felt accomplished and significant to others after work.

The positive feelings intermingled with feelings that were sometimes scary. One scary feeling was fear of the unknown. Fear of the unknown crept into my being and mixed with excitement each time I sat with a new client. This occurred because each new client presented new difficulties and opportunities. After learning more about each person, sometimes I felt that I was correct in my fears. Most of the time, my fears lessened greatly once I listened and saw things from other viewpoints. This led to the opportunity to offer understanding. For me it was easy to commiserate and more difficult to listen carefully and attentively. Altogether I felt resolved and separate from each client's problems once I moved past fear and moved toward skillful listening.

Skillful listening, as I learned both during training classes and experiences, required some discipline. Most of us talk back and forth in a competitive way. With discipline, I learned that what I had to say was less important than what the client needed to say. In order to accept this fully, I had to maintain friendships where I could be rude and competitive in my conversations. By contrast, on the job, I mainly listened and utilized my listening skills. One listening skill was silence—or more accurately, allowing moments of silence. At first, I had to count thirty seconds. Eventually, after noticing positive results, I decided when silence was necessary and when to speak. Clients reacted positively.

This work has given and continues to give me hope — hope that is contagious. After a client and I spoke for a while, I might tell him or her that I also was a consumer. Then without sharing personal information about myself, the conversation became more personal. I felt that I had rapport when the client and I conversed freely. I think that even a nod of my head, without any personal disclosure, created rapport. Listening and reflecting what the client told me gave the client a feeling of trust.

Positive regard for all clients was the norm of the team. Consumers who are ill often feel left out and concerned that people can just look at them to see their illness. I first learned to look at everyone with positive regard at the state hospital. My dad and I were walking through one of the facilities and, as we walked through this building, the smell and dirt on the floor (where people were laying) overwhelmed me. I bumped into some people as I walked through. My dad told me to never do that. He said I was rude. That taught me that I needed to respect all people. In terms of respite work, I found myself accepting each person's life, even if I would not choose their lifestyle. My social work classes contributed knowledge that people who live this way have a history. For instance, for a consumer involved in an abusive living arrangement, listening rather than calculating how to make their life better, showed that I cared enough to let them make their own decisions.

Empathy is different than sympathy. I had the choice to commiserate with the clients or to listen and show that I wanted to understand them more. I learned to place myself in the client's shoes. Asking relevant questions gave me more information. I felt that I could feel what the client felt.

I do not believe that my respite worker experience will ever leave me. Social work classes allowed me to experience the value of listening skills in two different contexts: as student and as provider. The best aspect of respite is that there exists no concrete definition. Respite could be described as the difference between life and death. Some days I was more ill or more down than my client. The only difference between me being a provider and the client being the consumer was that I had developed coping skills. Yet, admittedly, I learned from the consumers/clients. This gave me an opportunity to care about and think about someone besides myself.

As a human resource management graduate, I feel that more pay or more benefits would increase the success of consumers helping consumers in respite work. In my case, for instance, I could have used a more steady income. Nevertheless, many people can benefit from being a respite worker as the job carries consumers beyond personal problems to be there for fellow consumers.

The consumers who went to respite gained because they did not have to go to the hospital in most cases. Many consumers partaking of respite were amazed that the people sitting with them were also consumers. We had a bond with our clients and we had a bond to each other.

Nothing can ever take away the respite experience for the consumers involved. Just knowing that someone cares and wants to listen, provides an opportunity for increased health for workers and clients alike. Furthermore, I will always remember my respite experience. There will always be that longing to move back to Tennessee to work, to see how I have truly helped people. Living in Arkansas, I may have a long wait for a similar opportunity.

Whatever occupation I choose, I have learned how to listen. I know how to meet life's challenges. Years ago, someone told me to take the cotton out of my ears and put it in my mouth. Of course, talking is necessary for communication. I believe that when consumers meet the needs of consumers, we see each other differently. Crisis intervention itself creates bonding. An extra bond comes from a level of trust, where I could say "I really understand." Respite gave me the hope that I could be useful and the faith that the consumer/client expressed through sharing. I believe that in respite consumers meet the needs of consumers like a circle of trust.

Lauri Brown received her college degree from East Tennessee State University. Her current focus includes writing, her supportive family, and friends at a drop-in center. Her plans for the future are to learn to accept life on life's terms.

Chapter 23
Consumers as Supported Education Mentors

Jo-Anne S. Sharac
Bernice Yoder
Anne P. Sullivan

Utilizing students as aides to other students has had a long and respected history both at the secondary level (Fazio, 1995) and at the post-secondary level (Holly, 1987; Russel & Skinkle, 1990; Winston & Enmder, 1988). Peer aides have held a variety of titles, including peer tutor, counselor, educator, and mentor, and in varying settings have fulfilled diverse duties (Jones, 1984; Pliner, 1994).

Peer programs have existed long enough for comprehensive training and support materials to be developed. For example, with an emphasis on individual support models, D'Andrea & Salovey's (1983) training program addresses issues and concerns most pertinent to general peer counseling programs. In a complementary vein, the program by Gimblett (1992) outlines activities for a ten-session peer mentoring support group for students with disabilities.

Simultaneous with the development of peer programs has been the development on college campuses of support services for students with disabilities. Initially focusing primarily on students with physical or learning disabilities, college service providers more recently have added services for students with psychiatric disabilities (Sullivan, 1994; Unger, 1993).

Program Organization

Initiated in 1989, the Supported Education Program (SEP) at Quinsigamond Community College was one of the first efforts to address the needs of college students with major mental illness (Walsh et al, 1991). The program receives approximately half of its funding from the College while the remainder is disbursed from a Massachusetts Department of Mental Health grant awarded to the Center for Psychiatric Rehabilitation at Boston University with QCC serving as a subcontractor.

Currently the program provides on-campus support to 50-60 individuals per semester, including enrolled students and new applicants. Support services are individually adjusted and range from emotional support and arranging academic accommodations to advocacy and academic crisis intervention.

The SEP is identified administratively as a component of Disability Services, Student Affairs, but is physically located next door in the Counseling Center. Since supported education programs are a hybrid of counseling center and disability services, this arrangement is both efficient and practical. The program is staffed by one full-time supported education specialist/coordinator and a quarter-time program assistant.

As the number of students requesting services increased, the need for additional staff became critical. In keeping with the program philosophy of maximizing consumer involvement and responsibility, the decision was made to employ student-consumers as mentors. Mentors are paid $8/hour (the same rate as that for other QCC peer tutors), initially funded through a federal grant from the Office of Special Education and Rehabilitation Services and now through a Department of Mental Health grant. Many, however, prefer to volunteer in order to avoid jeopardizing Social Security, housing, or other benefits.

The mentors are students who have received Supported Education services, maintained a minimum 2.3 GPA, and have been enrolled at QCC for at least two semesters. Most are considering human services careers and have described their interest in being a mentor as a way of expressing appreciation for the benefits they have derived from the assistance received.

After an initial training, four to eight mentors per semester are each assigned up to six students based on common interests such as similar major or being an older student. Where possible, matching on common psychiatric diagnosis is avoided since the program emphasis is placed on being a student rather than on having an emotional disability. Depending on the needs of their assignees, mentors are assigned tasks that can include tutoring, assisting with the use of campus facilities (math lab, library, gym, etc.), encouraging participation in, and accompanying students to, social events, and in general providing friendly support. The overall mentor goals are to assist student recipients in overcoming academic hurdles and in becoming participants in the social life of the college community.

Mentors' Perspectives: Benefits and Difficulties

Mentors are almost unanimous in reporting that being a mentor is a positive experience. Mentors describe themselves as being more self confident, more patient, sensitive, and understanding with others (not just with those they mentor), having grown as a person, and also having gained much satisfaction from sharing personal techniques for coping with the impact of anxiety, medication side-effects, and psychiatric symptoms on their academic performance. Others credit the mentor experience as helping with career decision-making, the development of work habits and social skills (especially when this is a first job), and the enhancement of one's ability to work with individuals who have psychiatric disabilities while having a mental illness oneself.

On the other hand, mentor difficulties or frustrations are more likely to develop around issues of mentored individuals missing or being late for meetings without notice, feelings of inadequacy when they withdraw from school or do not perform well, flare-ups of one's own symptoms, and over committing to the number of hours serving as a mentor. Initially, a few students become too supportive of those they mentor in that they complete a portion of a student's work or they venture across the academic and social boundaries into therapeutic issues.

Another encountered difficulty is the mentor forgetting, even after training, that mentoring occurs within an organizational context of established policies and procedures. On occasion, without consulting the coordinator, mentors have escorted those they mentor to the president or a vice-president when a difficulty could and should have been resolved at a different level. Similarly, some mentors have protested strongly when certain policies or sanctions were applied to their proteges. Typically mentors meet at least once a week with the program coordinator to address such issues and make adjustments.

Recipients' Perspectives

As reported by student recipients, the benefits of having a mentor include having someone who can listen, understand, and lessen the hardships involved in being a student, or who can serve as a sounding board, a tutor, or a compatriot who can "get me through the tough times, proving there is hope for me after all and that I can do the work." Recipients are also grateful for the mentors' support in getting the student involved in campus activities. Many state that they would not have dared to participate on their own. Further, the mentor is often viewed as a personal role model demonstrating that academic success is possible with an emotional disability.

From the recipient's perspective, difficulties occur when the mentor appears to be impatient with having to re-explain concepts, is too intense or inflexible, or expects the recipient to progress at a pace faster than the recipient feels comfortable. Such frustrations have been resolved by the mentor and student themselves, through mediation of the program coordinator, or as a last resort, reassignment of the mentor.

Mentors' Impact on the Program

The Program has also benefitted in a number of ways by employing consumer mentors. First, without mentors, fewer student-recipients could be served. Second, mentors provide a service or assistance that professional staff cannot. For example, fellow students can share information about course content and faculty teaching style from the student's perspective, introduce the individual to other students informally, study together, and attend extra curricula activities together as students.

Knowing that the mentor also has an emotional disability has provided the student recipient with increased opportunity to discuss and compare strategies for managing the disability as well as its impact on daily living issues. For example, whether, when and how to explain to a date or to a study group that one has an emotional disability have been topics for comparative discussion. Similarly, the recipient can feel less anxious about the mentor's reactions and be less hyper, vigilant and tense about maintaining symptom-free behavior.

Employing mentors has also changed the duties of the specialist/coordinator. Previously, this individual's duties were primarily direct service. Now more time is devoted to training, coaching, assigning and synchronizing activities, monitoring, and mediating. This year some of these duties were also transferred to an experienced mentor who is now working with the program as an intern. In addition, some mentors are now involved in training new mentors.

Mentors' Impact on College and Community

The employment of consumer mentors also benefits the Massachusetts mental health system, which has repeatedly and publicly emphasized consumer preferences, consumer employment, and community integration, not just community placement. Employing consumer-mentors and encouraging their participation (along with that of their consumer-recipients) in college and community activities are examples highlighting the Department of Mental Health's commitment to these goals.

Other consumers anticipating future college enrollment at QCC or living in the local community also receive residual benefits. For instance, observing mentors responsibly and successfully serving as tutors and guides significantly reduces stigma and worry on the part of administrators and staff when other consumers enroll. Similarly, students without emotional disability who have experienced working and studying together productively with students who do have an emotional disability can help to decrease future anxiety when individuals with mental illness become neighbors or colleagues at work.

Success Factors and Recommendations

Without question, the major factors in the success of the mentor program are the mentors—their enthusiasm and energy. Many contribute more hours than they are paid because they enjoy the work. Equally important is the establishment of a connection—a personal relationship—with the recipient, because that relationship is often the base from which the recipient's willingness to try new activities is launched.

Also important is an inclination on the part of all staff, including the mentors, to be flexible, interested in trying new directions, and capable of creating and conveying a welcoming, informal and caring atmosphere. For example, the overall program is for the most part run on an open door, drop-in basis. Next in importance, careful matching of mentors and recipients is also vital. Selecting mentors from a diversity of backgrounds, ages, majors and life experiences allows the greatest flexibility and most effective matching. Finally, mentors being able to risk being open about having a mental illness, but not placing undue emphasis on it, is a key component.

Recommendations to those replicating such a program would include incorporating senior mentors responsible for some training, coaching, and monitoring of other mentors. Also, review carefully the college's student-related policies and establish new ones as needed, especially where liability issues may exist and incorporate discussion of these repeatedly in mentor training. Sample issues include the student code of conduct, procedures to follow in emergencies on campus or at off-campus college events, transporting fellow students in personal vehicles, and setting boundaries on topics for discussion and type/style/frequency of interaction with student recipients.

The overriding recommendations from QCC mentors are to enjoy interacting and having fun with those they mentor. Both mentor and non-mentor staff have found being involved with a mentor program and supported education to be one of the most energizing, hopeful, and positive experiences of mental health services and systems.

References

D'Andrea, V.J. & Salovey, P. (1983). *Peer counseling: Skills and perspectives.* Palo Alto, CA: Science and Behavior Books.

Fazio, T.J. & Ural, K.K. (1995). The Princeton peer leadership program: Training seniors to help first year students. *NASSP Bulletin, 79,* 57-60.

Gimblett, R.J. (1992). *Peer mentoring: A support group model for college students with disabilities.* Columbus, OH: Association on Higher Education and Disability (AHEAD).

Holly, K.A. (1987). Development of a college peer counselor program. *Journal of College Student Development, 28,* 285-286.

Jones, G.P. (1984). The tutor as counselor. *Journal of Developmental Education, 8,* 12-13, 25-26.

Pliner, S. (1994). *Peer mentor network: Resource guide 1994/95.* Amherst, MA: University of Massachusetts.

Russel, J.H. & Skinkle, R.R. (1990). Evaluation of peer-advisor effectiveness. *Journal of College Student Development, 31,* 388-394.

Sullivan, A.P. (1994). Supported education: Past, present, and future. *Community Support Network News, 10,* 1, 5, 9.

Unger, K. (1993). Creating supported education programs utilizing existing community resources. *Psychosocial Rehabilitation Journal, 17,* 11-23.

Walsh, D., Sharac, J., Danley, K.S., & Unger, K. (1991). The campus support project: An innovative supported education program model. *Innovations and Research, 1,* 18-21.

Winston, R.B. & Enmder, S.C. (1988). Use of student paraprofessionals in divisions of college student affairs. *Journal of Counseling and Development, 66,* 466, 469.

Jo-Anne Sharac, M.A., L.R.C., is coordinator of supported education services at Quinsigamond Community College, Worcester, MA.

Bernice Yoder, A.A., currently a student at Framingham State College, Framingham, MA, served several years as a mentor and as a master mentor assisting other mentors in Quinsigamond Community College's Supported Education Program.

Anne Sullivan, M.S., C.R.C., is concurrently project director, Supported Learning Program at Boston University's Center for Psychiatric Rehabilitation and an instructor in Boston University's Sargent College.

Chapter 24
Housing Support Providers: Expanding Community Supports Through New Roles for Consumers

Harold H. Gregory
Kevin S. Machon
Mike Askew
James Moody

Park Center is a psychosocial clubhouse in Nashville, Tennessee. Originating in 1983, Park Center grew quickly. In 1987, it merged with The House of Friendship, an older day program. This more than doubled the membership to about 100.

In 1988, a decision was made to take advantage of available funds and purchase two duplexes and two homes. This decision was the beginning of the Park Center housing program. These sites provided long-term housing for 14 consumers. A new staff position, housing coordinator, was created to manage the program. Later, a part-time case manager was added to provide after-hour supports. These supports included shopping trips, social activities, and case management. Within two years, the case manager position was discontinued and another full-time housing coordinator was added. Services were expanded and offered to all adult consumers in Nashville. The housing program was separate from the clubhouse program. Those being served by the housing program were not necessarily members of Park Center.

The coordinators developed housing resources, received referrals, interviewed consumers and matched them with appropriate housing and, if necessary, roommates. Housing program members could accept or decline any housing or any roommate. Social supports were still provided. Because case management was now available from other sources in the city, the housing program was able to significantly expand its membership.

In 1992, The Resource Foundation, a nonprofit organization which provides affordable housing to low-income families, had recently purchased and refurbished a 10-unit apartment complex, Germantown Apartments. It was planned that another agency would screen and place applicants in the building. When that agency could not complete its obligations, Park Center stepped in. It was agreed that The Resource Foundation would receive the rents, maintain the apartments and employ a resident manager. Park Center would place consumers in the apartments, provide supports, and supervise the resident manager. Since the manager was to be a resident, he or she would be a member of the housing program. It would be a part-time position involving record keeping, rent collection, maintenance inspections and reports, planning social activities, planning and facilitating monthly meetings, and resolving tenant issues. Compensation for the position would be waiver of all rent by The Resource Foundation and payment of phone service by Park Center.

The executive directors of Park Center and The Resource Foundation interviewed the applicants and selected James Moody to be the resident manager. The relationship between Park Center, The Resource Foundation, James, and the tenants of Germantown proved of benefit to all. Here is what James had to say about the experience:

> "When I first became mentally ill, I felt like I would never be able to work ever again. I have now been working for three years. The people I work for are great because they are there when needed. I am the first in Tennessee, a resident manager of housing for mental health consumers, who is also a consumer. A key point of this program is that the manager is someone that the tenants know can understand where they are coming from."

Because he was the first, the development of the position actually took place after the position was instituted. A job description had been developed and the role of each party defined, but many changes were made as the position developed. The housing coordinators met on a regular basis with the resident manager and discussed issues in the complex or supports that were needed. The resident manager's case manager was very involved in the development of his position. Her suggestions about his work led him to find his own ways of doing things and to try new things. She also provided constant encouragement and emphasized his progress and successes.

In 1994, Park Center deepened its commitment to developing housing for consumers. Park Center formed a relationship with the Council of Community Services (CCS) similar to that held with The Resource Foundation. The Park Center housing program would manage one 12-unit apartment complex and one supported living facility and would supervise the management of the complex. Both of these facilities would be owned and maintained by CCS housing.

The apartment complex would house 16 consumers in 11 one and two bedroom units including two which were designated for single parents. The arrangements also included a resident manager position which was patterned after the position at Germantown Apartments. The supported living facility would provide housing and independent living skills training for eight consumers. The tenants would live in four separate apartments in the building. Each apartment has an outside entrance. Tenants are encouraged to live as independently as possible. The staff would maintain the common area, ensure the security of the facility, work with the tenants on living skills, such as housekeeping and medicine compliance, and would keep a log of these activities. This meant that a staff of overnight and weekend workers and skills trainers would be hired. They would have to be motivated workers desiring entry-level positions which could lead to a social service career. Both non-consumers and consumers were interviewed and selected.

About one-half of the number hired were members of Park Center. This involved much discussion of whether this was a violation of accepted clubhouse standards which prohibit a clubhouse from employing members in "segregated clubhouse enterprises, or sheltered workshops" (Propst, 1992). It was decided that because the program was physically separate from the clubhouse — the purpose of the program is not to provide jobs for members, the staff consists of non-consumers and consumers, some of whom are members — that this was independent employment.

Since it was necessary to open the house as soon as possible, training for the positions happened, and still happens, mostly in monthly staff meetings. The entire staff discusses possible problems and appropriate solutions. We review log entries and criteria for decision-making. The focus of these meetings is communication and learning from each other. With the assistance of a consultant, we have now nearly completed a training program and manual.

The exchange of ideas has been very important. Because most of the tasks of the staff involve decision-making, the discussion of options and the probable outcome of actions led to the development of guidelines for the staff. Staff members know that they can call the housing coordinators at anytime, and page them on beepers if necessary. The guidelines for action and the availability of the coordinators allow the staff members to act with increased confidence. As the staff's understanding of philosophical issues increased, the staff became very adept at handling difficult situations while providing tenants support and offering options.

For those staff members who are also members of Park Center, this is a natural extension of the philosophy of the clubhouse. They take pride in being service providers who respect those they serve. These staff members are encouraged to involve Park Center employment supports and to discuss their work with their case managers. Another standard of clubhouses is the stipulation that working members are entitled to have available all clubhouse supports (Propst, 1992).

Read what Mike Askew, a resident advisor of the supported living facility, has to say about his job and it becomes evident that offering support and encouragement to tenants without infringing on their rights, has positive effects on him.

"I try to treat the residents the way that I would want to be treated. I can share my experiences, strengths and hope with them. By working with them, I never forget where I came from. Watching the residents grow and get better is very encouraging. The work helps me.

Before I started at Park Center Housing, I had been out of work for about two years. I had a hard time at first, but the staff helped me to adjust and encouraged me. I have held this job for a year now; this is the longest that I have ever held a job.

Going back to work has made me feel good about myself. I am a productive part of society. I used to be disgusted with myself. I could not even look in the mirror; I could not imagine holding a job or being a part of society. Now, I can look in the mirror and smile. I can say that I accept myself. I honestly believe that I will get better and better every day.

I plan to go back to school so I can get a better job. I want people to see that they too can be successful. All that people like me need is love and a chance."

Certainly the biggest factor in Mike's success is his own efforts, but he needed a place to try, a place to realize that success. James Moody expresses similar ideas about how opportunity combined with respect for consumers brings rewards. "You would not believe the difference it makes to us to have a place of our own and not have to scrape," he writes. "The quality of the housing makes us glad to call it home. A key to the program is that the manager is someone who they know can understand where they are coming from."

Of course, this is also a unique working situation for the nonconsumer staff members. From their first day, they see consumers as service recipients, service providers, and peers. They depend upon consumers as part of their team, socialize with consumer members and staff, and often, seek advice from consumer staff members. Such interaction forces a breakdown of their generalizations about consumers. Some consider it invaluable preparation for their social service or medical career.

Several things have been integral to the success of our program. Foremost is the communication between the staff members. Resident managers, resident advisors, and housing coordinators share ideas, methods, and discuss philosophy. This increases confidence, provides a frame of reference for decision-making, and provides continuity in the facility. Ensuring that the work is independent employment means that clubhouse standards are not violated and consumers are allowed to develop confidence. These jobs were advertised and all applicants were interviewed. No one was hired because they were consumers or Park Center members. They were hired because they were qualified. Our performance standards are no different for those staff members who are consumers or members. Of course, none of this would have been possible without dedicated, motivated staff members. These managers and advisors were successful and of great benefit to the residents because they wanted to be successful and believed that they could be.

If we could do it all again, we would prefer more preparation and less "training as we go." While developing the jobs this way provided many learning experiences, more preparation would have resulted in a better definition of the jobs sooner and reduced wasted effort. This type of program could be reproduced in many types of housing programs. Being sure that the jobs are truly independent employment, maintaining lines of communication, focusing on solutions instead of problems, and having adequate and accessible supports are requisite for success. These characteristics are not dependent on the type of program, but rather on the way it is operated.

We have learned just what we have been telling other employers for years. Consumers are just like the rest of us. If we have the necessary skills for a job, receive support when it is appropriate, and have some motivation, we can be good employees. Any employer should appraise the skills, motivation, and work habits of a potential employee in the hiring process. Designing a program that will employ consumers is about ensuring adequate supports. We recommend a three step approach. First, identify the supports that any employee would need. These may include training, scheduled communication with supervisors and co-workers, and access to information. Then, identify supports that will be needed by all or most consumer staff members. Examples of these supports include the involvement of case management, employment supports from the clubhouse, or information about how wages affect SSI or SSDI income. Finally, identify the supports needed by individual staff members. Each employee, consumer or not, is different and some will need supports that others do not. Individual supports needed by employees in this program have included flexible schedules, literacy training, and bus training. Note that not all of these supports have to be provided by the program. Identify the supports needed and draw on all available resources.

It is our hope that many more programs will hire consumers as housing support providers. Their experiences provide unique qualifications for the jobs. These same experiences often provide ample motivation for superior performance. Maybe in the future more of us will see what James Moody now sees: "Where once there were clients going in and out of mental clinics, there are now tax payers."

References

Propst, R. (1992). Standards for clubhouse programs: Why and how they were developed. *Psychosocial Rehabilitation Journal*, 16, 28.

Harold H. Gregory is a housing coordinator for Park Center's housing program. He has been with Park Center since March 1989.

Kevin S. Machon is housing coordinator for Park Center's housing program. He has been with Park Center since October 1989.

Mike Askew is a resident advisor for Woodland Street Apartments. He has been with Park Center Housing since 1992.

James Moody had been with Park Center since 1990. He was resident manager for Germantown Apartments for three years, until his sudden death on September 15, 1995. He is greatly missed.

Chapter 25
Ex-Patient Advocacy in an Inpatient Setting[1]
Will Brady

I began working at Connecticut Valley Hospital (CVH), the state's largest psychiatric hospital, in June, 1993, as a consumer to help develop a training seminar for hospital and community agency staff. This was to help the Connecticut Department of Mental Health (CT-DMH) meet its tandem goals of reducing the inpatient population and providing skills training for state hospital employees who would follow the patients into the community. But within three months, the focus of my role changed to that of Patients' Advocate.

Although I wasn't looking for the job, it seemed a natural progression. Prior to coming on board at CVH, I had worked at Connecticut Self Advocates for Mental Health, Inc. (CSAMH), an independent statewide self-help and advocacy agency. Before that, since 1986, I had both advocated for others and participated in the review of community based mental health services.

When I was named Patients' Advocate at CVH, I was asked to say a few words during a hospital-wide employee Open Forum about my role at the hospital. Before I had a chance to speak, a clinician stood up, to declare: "Everyone should know that he is an ex-patient."

The comment caught me off guard, although it shouldn't have. From my own experience, I knew that many in the audience were hostile to the very concept of self-advocacy. I found myself thinking, "This person has denied me the right to say this myself," and I suspected it was said in order to discredit whatever I might have to say.

At the time, many staff members had a very negative impression of patient advocacy. Their most recent experiences had come from dealing with another, self-styled, advocate who, while effective at drawing attention to injustices, seemed to prefer combativeness to problem solving.

Many of the staff felt confrontation and hostility were the principal tools of anyone who advocated on behalf of mental patients. Furthermore, some of the staff about whom patients complained most frequently (for abuses of dignity, for being overly controlling, or skeptical about recovery) truly believed they were the only real advocates for their patients. Yet legitimate complaints often went unaddressed or uncorrected by these same individuals. Fortunately, not everyone in the mental health system holds such attitudes.

---

[1]Since writing this chapter in 1994, several changes have occurred at the hospital. First, the hospital described is now the General Psychiatry Division of a newly consolidated and larger facility. The other divisions are Forensics and Addictions Services. Additionally, in 1995 the Department of Mental Health was merged with Addictions Services. Finally, the concept of advocacy, itself, has gained a greater acceptance.

Why Ex-Patient Advocates, and Why "Inside?"

Many people working in professional capacities do not have any direct experience of what it is like to be on the receiving end of mental health services. This spotlights the need for the empathy of ex-patient advocates. Also, outside defenders, while available, aren't actually on-site, which makes patient contact with an advocate more difficult.

The benefits of on-site advocacy are many. When patients feel they have to go it alone to get a grievance resolved, it is sometimes impossibly difficult. Even if I am unable to get someone's complaint resolved to their satisfaction, the fact that there is someone who will lend a sympathetic, understanding ear can ease tension. I can certainly understand how the patient feels when complaining about a staff member who is sarcastic or treats him or her in a demeaning manner. Finally, just being a constant, visible presence can make staff more aware of their own actions and comments directed toward the patients.

Initially, I expected complaint resolution would be my primary function. This turned out not to be the case. The patients' rights officer remained the primary investigator of complaints at CVH. Clinical staff have recently begun to recognize my role in this kind of problem-solving. There have been other changes as well. Before clarifying these changes, it will help to outline how complaints are dealt with.

How the Complaints Process Works

If a patient makes a phone call to register a complaint with an outside advocate, he or she may be dialing an agency's office on the other side of the state. The caller is likely to be placed on a waiting list to speak with someone who may be busy or out of the office. The patient then must wait for a call back.

The grievance process can be complicated. "Within ten business days," is standard policy language used to indicate there will be a wait. This follows in EVERY STEP of the process.

The more difficult the grievance, the less likely it will be that a patient actually sees the complaint to the point of resolution. A complainant may believe staff will not bear true witness to a patient-initiated complaint. Or he or she may feel intimidated and walk away believing nothing will get resolved.

As an on-site advocate, I am free to help a patient file a complaint; I can help them more clearly articulate their grievance and ascertain whether or not there has been a violation of hospital policy.

Being on-site, I am more aware of day-to-day operational problems at the facility than an outside advocate would be. Some new administrative policy, for example, might be a current hot spot for both patients and staff. An outside defender would not know about these local tensions when a complaint is called in. Or, as another example, a newly admitted patient might be upset because second shift staff doesn't know where first shift staff put her clothing. These are concerns that I can address immediately — an outside advocate can not.

In the past, for a variety of reasons, patients rarely learned of the outcome of an investigation. Now I participate more directly, conducting follow-up on the status of a complaint and report directly to the patient. As a result, patients will know that their specific complaint is being addressed and may actually be corrected. Not incidentally, other hospital personnel now are more attentive to addressing problems—even those that are not specifically technical policy violations.

Outside Advocacy Resources?

Considering the complexity of issues they must address and the caseloads with which they are confronted, the advocacy resources available are inadequate in number. Using Connecticut as an example (a state whose mental health support services rank among the best in the nation by the National Alliance of the Mentally Ill), only a handful of career advocates are available to help address the complaints and larger concerns of people with psychiatric disabilities.

Five advocates work for the state's Office of Protection and Advocacy (P&A) investigating complaints generated from state and private residential facilities and from discrimination charges against Rehabilitation Services. P&A received between 500 and 600 original complaints last year. Less than 200 reached the investigative stage. Even fewer were resolved.

The Connecticut Legal Rights Project (CLRP) employs about 20 other people (including administrative, paralegal and clerical support staff) to provide legal assistance in abuse and neglect cases. CLRP was the outgrowth of litigation that forced CT-DMH to assure that such representation was available. CLRP serves clients in eight different CT-DMH facilities and is also mandated to be on hand to assist when clients from contracted community based agencies file grievances.

DMH facilities also have Patients' Rights Officers (who serve a dual role as Affirmative Action Officers representing employees). They work within narrowly defined areas, addressing only complaints that are clearly statutory or work rule/ethical violations. At one facility, in 1993-94, of 137 complaints filed, only 39 involved formal violations. In that facility's annual report, all other complaints (including respect and dignity complaints) were declared to be unfounded.

Facets of CVH's Patient Advocate Position

Developing effective tools as Patient Advocate has been critical. I have re-activated defunct activities and developed initiatives from scratch. The main components include the following:

Patient Self-Governance
Disbanded prior to my arrival at CVH because of lack of interest according to hospital reports, the Patient Advisory Council was re-established. Once

the group resumed meetings, I found staff opposition to be a major problem. Some staff refused to allow me to monitor elections of ward representatives or selected patient representatives who were disruptive, argumentative, tangential, or who refused to participate in discussion at all during the meetings.

On one ward, staff made it difficult for patients to leave the wards to participate unless I personally escorted them to the meetings, even when those patients had privilege levels that allowed them to move about freely to other activities on hospital grounds.

In spite of these difficulties, meetings have ranged in size from 5 to 30 participants, and they have been successfully held twice monthly on a regular basis since January 1994. Our discussions have been animated and productive on many subjects.

We have discussed patients' perceptions of how safe they felt at the hospital, debated ward smoking policies, and, in one example of getting policies changed, convinced the hospital's superintendent to lift a ban on the use of peanut butter (initiated at the insistence of medical and psychiatric staff after a single former patient choked to death while eating a sandwich). The Patient Council has held discussions on patients' rights, the use of leisure time, and the vocational rehab department's "pay for patients" employment program, to name but a few of many issues we've covered.

The CVH hospital superintendent has included regular meeting attendance as part of her schedule. Other participants in these meetings have regularly included the patients' rights officer, representatives from Connecticut Legal Rights Project, the hospital's chief financial officer (who walked away from his first meeting a bit awestruck — and impressed), as well as outside speakers and presenters.

I have been proud to watch how some who initially came to the meetings as disruptive individuals, saw what we were trying to accomplish, and became active, productive participants themselves.

Resource Room

I developed the Resource Room materials from scratch, sought after and obtained staffing for the Resource Room, and developed training plans for Resource Room staff. The Resource Room now employs three patients and makes use of one to seven volunteers, depending on specific projects or availability of volunteers. The Resource Room is now open 22 hours a week with at least one person using this service each hour it is open.

Said by one reviewer to resemble a prison inmate legal library, the Resource Room materials include books, pamphlets, clippings, article reprints, as well as video and audiotapes. Over 140 different subjects are represented in the materials collected in our files and library with special emphasis on self-help and advocacy, patients' rights, communications skills development, diagnostics/medications/treatment information, voter education/awareness, legislative links, governmental/departmental/organizational statutes, policies and procedures, alternative treatment modalities, forensics, social services and first person life accounts. The Resource Room also has two computers and other communications equipment available for patient use.

Interestingly, the Resource Room is much used by hospital staff for reference materials (especially when preparing for meds education groups with patients). While it has been difficult to get hospital staff to review what resources we have for everyone's use, it's been a revelation to me that once they've seen the diversity and quality of the materials we have compiled, their response to this facet of my efforts has been quite positive.

Networking

As a service of the Resource Room, we are able to link patients and staff to information about support groups, disabilities rights organizations, other advocates throughout the state, and have begun locating grants/funding sources for consumer self-help, advocacy or empowerment initiatives. Patients have participated in regional and state-wide conferences and workshops, and twice we have been able to participate in National Consumer Teleconferences. We have also sent representatives to Alternatives 94 and NARPA conferences and maintain links with other patient advisory councils, some as far away as Broadmoor Hospital in England.

Quality Assurance

Planned before my arrival at CVH, a Patient Satisfaction Survey has been conducted monthly since June 1993. I participate in the continued development, implementation, data collection and information dissemination of these surveys. This entails interviewing patients about perceptions of services they receive, data entry and retrieval on the statewide DMH data network, preparing reports and narrative report writing.

As part of the hospital's Human Resource Development Committee, I also work on developing training and education programs on a variety of subjects. My responsibilities include lecturing at in-service classes and workshops as well as finding and contracting with patient and family presenters for training of patients and staff both in and out of the hospital.

How Do Other Consumer-Survivors Benefit?

In addition to services provided above, a more visible benefit to mental health consumers has come from my begrudging acceptance of the role of "poster boy." I have appeared in videos about recovery which have been televised on Connecticut broadcast stations. While I personally feel that tokenism and role modeling can be and often is exploitative, and I find my placement in a modest celebrity role uncomfortable, I find my public speaking efforts as a spokesperson demonstrate that we can and do speak up on behalf of ourselves, and that we can do this effectively.

I do not relish having more painful, private aspects of my life on stage before strangers, and that, regrettably, is exactly what mental health practitioners demand of people when they constantly ask them to talk of their experiences. On the other hand, I have to admit that the recognition has made me feel aware that I have accomplished a lot of productive things in my lifetime, something that I had long ago learned to disbelieve.

I have worked hard to dispel the myths all of us may buy into. For instance, practitioners (who agree former patients belong in the workplace) sometimes dismiss idiosyncratic behaviors as symptomatic. This patronizes people and does not hold them responsible for their actions.

The mental health consumer movement is not a plea to "please help us poor mental patients." It is a human rights movement. The rights of people with psychiatric labels have been, and continue to be, violated long after the so-called acute phase of an illness has disappeared. Other, very real problems that people with psychiatric diagnoses face have yet to be addressed. Stigma (prejudice against citizens with mental illnesses) can be as devastating as the illnesses themselves and care givers (albeit inadvertent) often aid and abet in its perpetuation.

As a class, those of us who are working in one capacity or another as providers in human services and who also have a psychiatric history or disability, give life to the belief that the mentally ill do recover.

We provide very concrete benchmarks. We prove that people who have been categorized as helpless can assume control of their own lives. Also, it has not been surprising to us who are disclosed to find others working in mental health who will privately confess to being on medications, or to having been incarcerated for some lengthy segment of their lives before going on to work with others in distress.

We also furnish hope for family members — all too often paralyzed with embarrassment or distress about their loved ones — that recovery from a prolonged period of disability is not only a possibility, but can be a reality.

What Got Me Started as an Advocate

It is important to note that more than a decade and a half elapsed between my own periods of incarceration and when I finally went to work as a patients' advocate at CVH.

I spent many of those years avoiding direct contact with the psychiatric system, feeling that the services at the time were not in keeping with my needs or interests. What assistance I received—with regard to returning to life in the community and in the workplace— came not from formal community mental health services (only beginning to be developed in the late 1970's and early 1980's) but from acquaintances who were willing to help steer a soul in distress through a very confusing period of life.

The time lag gave me the opportunity to reflect on my own experiences. I was able to meet others and learn that I was not alone in having tangible, legitimate and serious criticisms about the quality of care in the mental health system. I was able to learn more about self-help efforts, how advisory and oversight boards were organized, and how to make an impact with these boards. I also became educated about community organizing efforts.

In addition, while I had been given varying diagnoses during treatment, I was able to discern that my difficulties were more in line with what many recognize as a situational mental illness brought on by several overwhelming life stressors all hitting me at the same time.

Regrettably, the reality of a series of severe psychic traumas hitting someone simultaneously, and subsequently crippling them, is still ignored by some clinical professionals who prefer to make a diagnosis that relegates the patient as "chronically mentally ill." As a result, the diagnosis, once ascribed, becomes the individual's disability and label. It creates the groundwork for other barriers to be placed before the newly diagnosed person and this can impede recovery.

When I finally started working as an advocate, I did so on behalf of another whom I saw as receiving inadequate, irrelevant, punitive, and contradictory services. The system, I concluded, was at times far more dysfunctional than many of its patients. To get help from the working parts of that system required having some assistance from outside.

When I began this effort, I wasn't even aware that it had a name. I was just trying to help someone else I cared about. And, initially at least, I did not disclose to mental health service practitioners that I, too, had been a patient.

Where Do We Go From Here?

In the past decade, a great deal has been accomplished as a result of mental health consumer/survivors standing up and speaking out for themselves and their peers. We are represented on policy making bodies, advisory boards, and task forces. In increasing numbers, and a wide range of areas, we impact how mental health services are conceptualized, designed, and delivered.

Yet much remains to be done. Environmental, social and economic stressors in people's lives are often causative factors in their going into psychiatric hospitals. Quick fix solutions, which rely primarily on prescribing medications, are not enough. Ex-patients know this very well. Other treatment directions need to be examined and explored and fiscal decision makers in the system need to learn this.

We also must look very closely at the ways in which punitive and stigmatizing prejudices impact on our ability to provide appropriate services for people in severe distress. People need a system that gives them a chance to recover and productively participate in society.

We need to be ever vigilant against those who would come up with some new "final solution." We live in a terrifying world at the end of the twentieth century. Mental health providers, as former patients or dedicated careerists, must always remain cognizant of this and bring it, constantly, to the forefront when talking with those who decide how mental health funding resources are allocated. Thus, we all need to be advocates for a healthier society and assist when folks who are fragile ask for help in their time of need.

Will Brady has been an advocate for citizens with psychiatric disabilities for several years. He currently works at Connecticut Valley Hospital. He is also an accomplished painter and illustrator.

Chapter 26

Consumers as Case Management Assistants: Making Consumer Employment a Viable Part of Psychiatric and Support Services

Susan L. Bichsel

The Pass Program

The Setting

Jewish Family Service Association, a nonsectarian contract agency of the Cuyahoga County Community Mental Health Board in Cleveland, Ohio, provides community-based support services to mental health consumers and their families. The agency provides a wide range of services as a family agency and is accredited by the Ohio Department of Mental Health as a community mental health facility. The PASS (Psychiatric and Support Services) Program within the agency specializes in community-based support and mental health services for approximately 150 people with severe mental illness. Started in 1989, the program is still young, but has evolved to meet the special needs of this particular population.

Our PASS program offers intensive case management, daily activity and socialization groups, psychiatric assessments and medication monitoring, adult protective services for individuals over 60, counseling, peer support, and one community residence, with two more approved by HUD. The average caseload size is approximately 22 to 28 clients. Our program is governed by the PASS Advisory Board, which is comprised of consumers, family members, several of the agency's Board of Trustees, and other community advocates. The program itself has a director, six case managers, a clinical supervisor, a psychiatrist, one group specialist, our community residence staff, and five to seven case manager assistants (CMAs).

The Case Manager Assistant Model[1]

The CMA program was developed in 1989 with the help of a Cuyahoga County Mental Health Board grant for consumer and peer support initiatives. CMAs are individuals who have themselves experienced a major mental illness, most typically some form of schizophrenia. The CMAs provide services to our consumers that are an extension to case management services such as: cofacilitating socialization groups, transporting individuals to medical appointments,

[1] See appendix to this paper for the position description.

helping individuals through employment/entitlement interviews, monitoring clients during crisis, and educating consumers, staff and family members about medication and the mental health system. They are often a bridge between the agency and consumers in need, bringing isolated individuals to us who would otherwise feel intimidated by the system. The CMAs perform about 4000 hours of work each year in addition to the work of our case managers. As part of the case management team, they report directly to the PASS Director. CMAs receive an hourly rate of pay, as well as mileage reimbursement. CMAs who work half time or more receive medical health insurance, sick leave, and vacation benefits.

Our CMAs have heightened awareness and understanding about mental illness within the agency, and have educated the community through newsletters, speeches, and various media exposure. They have spoken at high schools, universities, congregations, police academies, the Alliance for the Mentally Ill, support groups, public television programs, and with families in need. Our primary goal has been to reduce the prevalence of stigma and discrimination while increasing knowledge and awareness about mental illness. The CMAs have most recently finished making a training video for the Cleveland Heights Police Department, and have published three editions of our PASS newsletter targeting a wide audience that includes universities, families, other mental health agencies, and consumers. Each of the CMAs works flexible hours and provides rehabilitative services including crisis intervention, peer support, outreach, socialization, group services, education, and transportation to consumers in need.

Used in conjunction with traditional forms of case management, our peer support model denotes a pivotal change from a medical illness/outpatient based model of treating mental illness, to a model which is markedly more client centered. In the past, services to people with mental illness were provided by "highly trained individuals engaged primarily in therapeutic activities" (Rapp & Chamberlain, 1985, p. 417). This fact highlights some problematic features of traditional approaches. First, as Rapp and Chamberlain explain, "Many chronically ill people return to state hospitals not because they lack the relevant therapeutic programs but because they have breakdowns in their performance of the tasks of every day life" (p. 417). In order for consumers to succeed in the environment, they need daily living skills, environmental resources, and community supports—services central to the CMA model. As one of the CMAs states:

> CMAs at JFSA are, as peers, especially suited to help others who suffer because of mental illness with self-esteem, identity, and role model issues. CMAs work closely with clients, their case managers, and the director of the program. We work as a team. The position is largely peer support, which does enhance recovery and mutual empowerment as well as increase choice. Consumer choice and peer support have become buzz words within the mental health system. At JFSA they are a reality because CMAs are or have been consumers, so they are sensitive to issues of choice and have a voice in how things are run (Hinds, 1994).

Our CMAs vary in education and in their knowledge of social work models and theory. We have had a total of 13 consumers work as CMAs over the last six years. Four of these individuals have gone on to find other full-time work. Our present program has three members who have worked in the program for more than three years. Only two of the thirteen have become too ill to stay or work elsewhere. We have had two CMAs in the last five years who had Ph.D.s, one in Psychology and one in Social Work. The first has gone on to become a therapist within our agency and the second to employment elsewhere. Others have had no prior experience in the mental health system except as clients. As an integral part of our case management team, the CMAs receive weekly group supervision with the rest of the case management staff and participate in continuing education programs offered by the agency.

By integrating the CMA component into our existing models of supervision, there is less of an opportunity for professionals to make distinctions between themselves and the others whom they serve. Group supervision helps to promote a sense of shared responsibility and interdependence among the team. Through communication, we become closer to those we serve. We are educated on the feelings and experiences of the individuals for whom we create life goals and treatment plans. In a subtle but distinct way, rigidly defined roles of case manager, consumer, client, psychiatrist, etc., are blended in an attempt to best treat the client at hand. One senior CMA explains:

> The case managers treat us as equals, and listen to our opinions at weekly meetings, advising us on difficult situations when necessary and vice versa. We all believe it is extremely important to minimize the difference between service recipient and service provider, knowing that we all have weaknesses and needs, and that we all have something to give and the ability to be helpers (Hinds, 1995).

Benefits to Consumer Providers

The CMAs have stated that working in the mental health field has provided them with an opportunity to give support to other consumers in ways that they had done all along without pay. Many of our CMAs have a long history of advocacy for consumers in the local mental health system, and were known by other consumers to be available for support and guidance. By switching their role from friend to professional, our CMAs almost unanimously say they have learned how to construct useful limits with our clients (many of whom were personal friends) that help to preserve their own health and energy more effectively. Many of our CMAs came from consumer operated organizations, where they felt there was not enough guidance, support, or protection from burnout as a result of helping peers.

Our CMAs almost universally claim that working in integrated teams of consumers and non-consumers has helped them to emulate well behaviors rather than feeling protected by the disabled or sick label. This by no means denies what many of these consumers gained by participation in consumer operated services. Many still volunteer for such organizations and participate with them on other levels. What they did say was that while there existed a period of time when this type of protection in the workplace was necessary and useful, working in an integrated workplace provides them with the additional push to continue their growth and development after the onset of their illness. One CMA explains:

> Since working at JFSA my self-worth, confidence and self-esteem have returned abundantly. I have been accepted as part of the staff and that has made me feel as if I belong there. I have respect for my fellow workers and it has been returned to me. I take great pride in my being able to do this type of work, which has a wide range of duties. I now have a steady source of income and my ability to do more has increased greatly. I also have a deep sense of accomplishment. I am grateful for this opportunity and chance to give something back to the community that I received from when I was down and out and not doing well (Barnhouse, 1995).

Another states:

> My life has been changed by the opportunity to work at JFSA as part of a team of other professionals. I feel more self-respect, more responsible, I have more self-esteem, and feel more worthwhile. I have felt no stigma directed toward me by co-workers at the agency. The recipients of our services are a delight and are very appreciative of us. Having meaningful employment, and knowing that others depend on me has helped me stay out of the hospital longer than ever before, and I feel a peace and joy within myself that I can't remember ever having felt before (Hinds, 1995).

The Role of Self and Identity in the Healing Process

Self concept and identity are central to individual development and achievement throughout the life span. Terms such as self-esteem, self-efficacy, identity, and self-worth are attempts to define how we come to regard ourselves as valued and valuable individuals in the world around us. The formation of identity and self-concept, involves an interplay between individuals. Identity and self-worth do not simply develop within the individual, but are developed in synchronicity with the world around.

Sue Estroff (1989) writes that schizophrenia is an "I am" illness, one that can take over and redefine the identity of the person involved. As a cultural anthropologist, Estroff believes that the relationship between the self and sickness has not been adequately researched with reference to its influence on prognosis. She asks such questions as who and what existed before the illness, and who or what endures during and after. Is there an identity after mental illness? Strauss (1989) suggests that individuals have a relationship with their disorders that influences course and outcome. If this is so, it seems to some degree that the ways in which consumers and their helpers respond to the above questions will influence course and outcome considerably, an important issue when addressing the long-term vocational needs of individuals with mental illness.

Because, as Ogbu (1988) writes, one's adult status is largely measured in terms of the "ability to compete for and obtain a desirable job, to earn a reasonably good income, to manage one's affairs, and to participate in the social and political life of one's community" (p. 172), our CMAs are often evaluated by others and come to conceptualize themselves in terms of their success and ability to meet these standards. As a result, employment opportunities and meaningful life activity emerge as a key issue for those recovering from debilitating illnesses.

Much of the work of Estroff and Strauss follows the inquiries and research of Goffman (1961) on the effects of stigma, the total institution, and what he describes as the mortification process. Once stigmatized, an individual is often subjected to experiences that come in direct conflict with the concept of self. Goffman suggests that this results in a disidentifying role, due to a marked loss of self-determination and autonomy with regard to the client's freedom of action (Goffman, 1961, p. 23). It is unlikely that individuals experience the stigma and discrimination that are directed toward people with mental illness without some assault to their psychological health and functioning. Indeed, Frosh (1989) suggests that oppressive and stigmatizing processes "achieve power by being inscribed deeply in individual psychology" (p. 210), in his attempt to show how social opinions and prejudices are ultimately internalized within the individual. Recovering consumers are thus forced to struggle with their perception of who they were, who they are now perceived to be, and who they can possibly become.

One outcome of these dynamic processes between the ill person and society is clarified by labeling theorists who maintain that stigmatized individuals come to define themselves from the perspective of those in power (Goffman, 1963). Goffman claims that we are taught to believe that the stigmatized person is inferior to us and on this assumption we "exercise varieties of discrimination, through which we effectively, if often unthinkably reduce his life chances" (p. 5). The result is that what people think of us and expect from us is bound to influence what we are and what we can possibly be, in a material but also psychological sense. This has direct implications for consumers who work in an integrated agency. One CMA frames this idea in terms of working in the mental health center as more valuable to her personally than working in a consumer-run alternative. She states:

> It has been my experience that services that are entirely consumer operated have tended to allow me to feel more free to be sick when I was anxious or unsure about my ability and desire to work. In a more integrated environment, expectations to be stable and dependable are higher and there is more of a push knowing that others believe in you and are counting on you to stick with it if you are at all able. Consumer operated services also often have too few truly valuable positions available (Hinds, 1995).

Estroff (1989) suggests that the degree to which one's identity is eroded by schizophrenia may rest on how individuals locate or situate their illnesses and symptoms in relation to themselves. Learning to have control over how much of a role one's illness will have in one's life is central to some individual's struggle for an identity post-illness. A former case manager assistant left her job at the agency stating that while for some time she had needed the nurturing of colleagues knowing she was ill, she was "tired of having my identity and employment based solely on this status; I am ready to move on." Still others have found that it "takes too much energy to hide the realities I face having a mental illness. It is a relief to work in an environment where it is understood."

Funding

Our program received limited funding for the first year through our county mental health board. For the next four years we did not receive any financial support from our local Board for our CMA model, despite the growing mandate for client-based/client-driven services. During the past year, we received support that covers the full cost of our CMA services through a grant from the mental health board entitled Self-Help and Peer Empowerment (SHAPE). It is unclear at this time whether this grant will be renewed due to budget constraints at the local Board.

Funding for our services continues to be a frustrating obstacle. While CMAs do much of the same work as other mental health professionals, sometimes more, their work has never been reimbursable through our local Medicaid system, the primary reimbursement source for our case management services. Reimbursement has been made difficult because of state requirements that case managers work full-time, and due to education requirements that have existed. In addition, much of the work they do such as transportation, shopping, and residential care, is not reimbursable according to current standards and regulations.

Programmatic Lessons

While for some, part-time work within our program seems to meet individual needs, others find that a fourteen hour week is not enough to keep up with their own personal growth and development. We soon discovered that stable consumers wanted more responsibility and opportunity for growth from their employment. At the same time, we were discovering that newly hired consumers, sometimes just back to work after many years, were not being supported in the way that they needed to be. In response to this need, a career ladder was formed within the CMA program. Consumers initially train at five to seven hours each week with other consumers and professionals, doing simple and routine transportation for clients, and accompanying other providers during their interventions and contacts.

Some individuals are content to remain at this level of participation. For others, we have developed alternatives and a wider range of employment opportunities at the agency and within our program. We now have two senior CMA positions within the program which provide medical, sick leave and vacation benefits. These positions require a commitment of between 30-40 hours a week, based on what the individual wants and is able to handle. These positions engage in more crisis intervention activities, peer counseling, and the management of our community residence. One of our senior assistants will become coordinator of our new community residence which is scheduled to open in January, 1996. In addition to work within the program, as an employee of the Agency, consumers have an opportunity to become involved in other unrelated activities such as United Way campaigns, in-service training programs, staff luncheons, retreats, and outings.

Taking on this level of work commitment does come at a cost for our CMAs. For those who work full-time hours and receive benefits, government benefits and entitlements are put at risk. For those individuals who have suffered long-term illnesses with many setbacks, as most of our CMAs have, this choice is a difficult one and requires a level of confidence that our CMAs may not have initially.

The CMAs also identified role change as a significant challenge in the beginning of their work. Particularly for those workers who have an extensive history of informal client advocacy, switching their role to one of a professional with boundaries and limits is difficult at times. Many of our CMAs have been at odds with professionals in the mental health field, assuming an assertive positive stance with those who are seen to have power. While such a posture has strengths, such as allowing for the development of a consumer movement and united identity, it can be difficult for those who wish to expand their individual identity and role in the community. One CMA elaborates:

> Having prior friendships with consumers at JFSA can cause a great deal of conflict for the CMA, particularly in terms of our responsibility to employer vs. our responsibility to friend. Prior friendships with clients can be a plus or a minus depending on the attitude of the client about the fact that you are now being paid to socialize with him or her. This must also be balanced in a careful way with the case manager's feelings and opinions about the individual client (Hinds, 1994).

Other challenges cited by the CMAs include a tendency to over-identify with client issues, as well as a tendency to take on client issues as their own. In addition, one CMA states that on evenings and weekends it becomes difficult when the phone rings to know if it is a friend calling for support, or if the call is more work related. Learning to discern these shades of gray becomes a central part of group supervision with CMAs, as well as for case managers who struggle with many of the same issues themselves.

Programmatic Challenges and Opportunities

One of the dominant themes during the preparation of this chapter was that of identity (re)development and growth after the experience of mental illness. The difficulties experienced by those attempting to find meaningful work after a period of illness are profound. For some, full-time work is not the goal, but rather a meaningful connection with one's community is sought. Flexibility on the job and at least reasonable (though not excessive) accommodation and understanding on the part of the employer about mental illness were felt to be the most essential components of a successful experience.

CMAs are often able to work from their home and have regularly scheduled weekly appointments and meetings which offer an important degree of structure. Shared caseloads and flexible work hours have blended well with our consumers' lifestyles. As one CMA put it, "this is the perfect job for people with short bursts of energy and for those who need some time for rest between duties." The job can also be tailored to the CMA based on their particular strengths and a desire to work and relate closely to others. While transporting clients and shopping for the elderly and disabled satisfies some, others are more willing and skilled at supportive counseling and sharing their personal histories with clients who feel alienated and ashamed of their own illness.

An additional benefit of the CMA program is the opportunity to gather important data on the efficacy of consumer case management models. By employing consumers as part of the case management team, consumers are involved in the planning, development, implementation, and evaluation of mental health services for others. Because we recognize consumer involvement as critical to the successful implementation of mental health services, we have been careful to monitor, evaluate and track the services provided by CMAs. Goals and individualized service plans for clients include CMA contact, education and support. CMAs also write progress notes for each service they provide, and these become part of the client record. As we develop and refine our outcome evaluation instruments for case management, CMA work will be easily tracked.

Conclusion

CMAs, like other mental health professionals, feel valued because of the important work they do. Without a doubt, they have enabled us to provide services that are more consumer-driven, consumer-focused, and client-centered. In addition to simply performing the work task, they are teaching other people with mental illness about what Markus, et. al. (1990) refer to as "possible selves." In their work, possible selves are beliefs or representations of one's self in future states, more specifically notions of what and who one can possibly become. The authors claim that possible selves are "essential for putting the self into action and are the selves we could become, would become, or are afraid to become" (p. 207). When first working with individuals whose lives have been devastated by mental illness, trying to help clients imagine themselves as successful can be daunting. Possible selves, while only images, are likely to be images of what one has already witnessed about what is possible, making the role modeling of the CMA critical to how consumers perceive and imagine themselves.

References

Barnhouse, B. (1995). *Working as a consumer in the mental health field.* Speech given to a class at Cleveland State University, Cleveland, OH.

Estroff, S. (1989). Self, identity, and subjective experiences of schizophrenia: In search of the subject. *Schizophrenia Bulletin*, 15, 189-196.

Frosh, S. (1989). *Psychoanalysis and psychology: Minding the gap.* London: MacMillan.

Goffman, E. (1963). *Stigma: Notes on the Management of a Spoiled Identity.* NJ: Prentice-Hall.

Hinds, K. (1994). *Case manager assistant program: A personal account.* JFSA speech given to the Board of Trustees, Cleveland, OH.

Hinds, K. (1995). Interview with senior case management assistant, Cleveland, OH.

Markus, H., Cross, S., & Wulf, E. (1990). The role of self-esteem in competence. In: R.J. Sternberg & Kolligan (Eds.) *Competence considered.* 205-225. New Haven, CT: Yale.

Ogbu, J.U. (1988). Class stratification, race stratification and schooling. In: L. Weis (Ed.) *Class race and gender in American education.* 163-179. Albany, NY; State University of New York Press.

Rapp, C. and Chamberlain, R. (1985). Case management services for the chronically mentally ill. *Social Work*, 30, 417-422.

Strauss, J. (1989). Subjective experiences of schizophrenia: Towards a new dynamic psychiatry. *Schizophrenia Bulletin*, 15,179-187.

Susan Bichsel is the director of the PASS (Psychiatric and Support Services) Program in Cleveland, Ohio, and is currently pursuing her Ph.D. in urban education and counseling at Cleveland State University.

Appendix 1
Job Description for
Mental Health Case Management Assistant
Jewish Family Service Association's
Psychiatric Support Services

Reports to the director of the Psychiatric and Support Services (PASS) program. Provides some case management services to adults and elder adults with severe mental disabilities via assigned specific tasks.

The assigned tasks are part of the case management team, comprised of professional case managers and paraprofessional case management assistants. Responsibilities involve outreach to people already receiving services and to people who could benefit from case management/case management assistant services. Outreach work involves establishing a relationship with individuals who have been unable to use needed community resources and services. Case management assistants work educationally with agency clients and potential clients regarding the nature of severe mental illness and the potential usefulness of medication, case management, counseling, activity groups, and other services. Assistants instruct people receiving services in activities of daily living, such as accessing services, shopping, budgeting, cooking, banking, traveling, etc. Case management assistants provide transportation to services and resources, and assist in monitoring clients' mental status and general functioning. Changes in these areas are reported to the client's case manager or the director of the program. Case management assistants are responsible for recording basic information regarding each contact with persons served. This and other assistant services take place in the natural environment of the person receiving services.

Qualifications for this position are personal experience with a severe mental illness, good communication skills, and a strong commitment to help people with severe mental disabilities to enjoy lives rich in meaning and dignity.

SECTION 6

The Struggle for Identity as a Professional

Introduction to Section 6: The Struggle for Identity as a Professional

The authors of the five papers of this section recognize that serious mental illness does not prevent someone from contributing as a professional to mental health and rehabilitation systems. All of the contributors in this section reflect on their own experiences as consumers, and illustrate how a bridge can be erected connecting personal experiences and professional identity. They personally and courageously outline the issues and barriers that must be overcome in order to become effective and committed practitioners. Thus, this section highlights a different perspective on consumers as providers since it examines the process of becoming a mental health professional, focusing on the personal, social, and organizational contexts in which this occurs.

These chapters are built on wisdom garnered by the authors through their own personal encounters with mental illness. Several of these authors graphically present personal experiences. We do not seek to generalize from these experiences, but to reflect on them as stories of systems that are still struggling with their own enlightenment concerning serious mental illness, and with their own acceptance of this issue. Unfortunately, there is also a common discouraging thread interweaving these chapters; all speak to negative reactions the authors have experienced from mental health and rehabilitation providers, and in some cases, how the attitudes of these providers became barriers to progress and personal development. Several of the authors identify the stigma fostered and reinforced by colleagues. These reactions damage consumer providers — people who are very committed to addressing serious mental illness through sensitivity, understanding, and deep empathy — the qualities of practice they achieved by personally navigating a psychotic illness.

Many of these chapters indicate that mental health systems may not be the most enlightened places for professionals who have personally struggled with serious mental illness to find acceptance. It is not surprising to find as salient the theme of whether or not to disclose one's background to colleagues, supervisors, or administrators. Disclosure may be a vital service to consumers who see first hand recovery in action, and who can benefit directly from role models who understand both sides of treatment, support, and rehabilitation. Disclosure can be inspirational in that it may help some people to heal. It can also suggest to people who are struggling with serious mental illness that employment and a career in mental health or rehabilitation systems is a possibility.

Yet disclosure for the mental health professional can have serious repercussions. Barbara's account of her situation suggests that the professional in recovery should be wary of sharing one's personal history and background. Disclosure can lead to personal setbacks, and to the exacerbation of symptoms. Dr. Carol North's story of her early medical training suggests that physicians can be abusive when they know a colleague has a personal background of mental illness. The authors illustrate the costs involved in disclosure: loss of status within an organization, discrimination by colleagues, ostracism, lowered expectations for performance held by supervisors, and disbelief that one can actually perform well in a mental health role.

What may be most disturbing is the possibility that disclosure poorly received by colleagues can backfire and so contribute to a vicious self-fulfilling prophecy. The professional who discloses can experience a setback in response to the negative social reaction and the ensuing stress, and this setback can be used as a justification to conclude that the person really is not qualified to work in mental health settings. This conclusion on the part of colleagues may further reinforce an attitudinal set that labels all consumer providers as incapable.

Perhaps the costs are too high, even though patients, clients, or consumers may benefit from the revelation that their social worker, psychologist, nurse, counselor, physician, or minister has an illness or disability. We, however, must offer a qualification here. These high costs may prevail when the system or organization is simply not ready, not enlightened, or too limited to see its own prejudices. In these situations, to paraphrase Cavanagh-Daley, the world may be unwilling, and understanding and acceptance may be elusive. But what about those systems or organizations seeking enlightenment, and that are seeking ways of becoming more responsive and supportive of the people they serve and those they employ? Perhaps disclosure will make sense for those professionals who trust that their systems, organizations, and colleagues have the insight and maturity to make the best and most proactive use of their gifts of self-revelation.

A theme that stands out in many of the papers in this section involves the notion of mentorship and personal support as crucial to success for developing professionals in the field of mental health and rehabilitation. Whether these supports were offered by university faculty, colleagues, fellow students, friends, or family members, several authors point out the importance of the faith other people have in them, and in the contribution such faith can make to personal recovery. In several papers, authors point out that these supports came just in time — just as they were about to give up on themselves and their dreams.

The presence of these supports is a tribute to these authors possessing the wisdom and openness to make use of them in the pursuit of their dreams. The availability of these supports is also a tribute to the willingness of others to give and to offer assistance. And, these supports underscore a fundamental principle of psychiatric rehabilitation: that people can extend their reach when others in their immediate situation are helping them to stretch and grasp.

There is another theme operating in these papers that is quite provocative. Why does providing supports and committing oneself to a career of helping people with serious mental illness produce progress towards one's own recovery? The answer is not so clear in these papers, but there are a number of insights:

- A feeling that one is an advocate, and is unwilling to see people disenfranchised or abused helps to strengthen one's resolve and sense of personal power (Cavanagh-Daley);

- A sense that one's own recovery contributes to seeing oneself as a healer and to one's competence and efficacy in responding to the needs of people (North);
- A sense that one's own struggle with depression offers insight into the challenges faced by others, and results in a better understanding of what one needs to maintain personal health (Barbara);
- A desire to improve the "system" for others so they will not also experience the profound deficiencies caused by mental health treatment that loses sight of the individual, and only responds to the diagnosis or behavior, gives one an understanding of what is required for effective mental health service delivery (Gallagher); and
- A willingness to offer support to others while actively managing one's health and well-being (Sweeney).

Despite the self-disclosure risks but congruent with themes evident in chapters in this volume, there is a feeling of spirit, positive energy, and hope in these personal accounts. Each author tells us in subtle or in detailed ways the constituent elements of recovery, at least for them. Each author also describes, often in graphic terms, the forces that run counter to their recovery, forces that can become the object of change by people who have personal understanding and who commit themselves to a career of offering support.

Unfortunately, many of these forces are operating in our own mental health and rehabilitation systems today. But perhaps we are being too critical. Perhaps we are fortunate in having these authors point to counter-recovery forces. To illuminate these forces is to begin to demystify them. To enlighten ourselves is to begin a discourse on how these forces can operate in our own practice and in our own organizations — to show how these forces can keep us from truly understanding and accepting one another. And, to show how we can conquer them and thus begin the process of our own systemic and collective recovery.

These authors are not destructive. Rather, they are proactive. They point out what is wrong without indicting. They do not engage in hyperbole but rather tell stories about their own treatment in contemporary mental health and rehabilitation systems. They underscore that the job of recovery is not merely an individual responsibility or requirement, but that it also involves systemic reform and revisioning of organizational purpose.

Chapter 27
From Patient to Provider: The Quest for Equity in an Unwilling World

Lois Cavanagh-Daley

Self-Determination

My quest for equity as a consumer provider began eleven years ago, as I found myself on a psychiatric unit in a general hospital after attempting suicide with a drug overdose. I voluntarily committed myself to the unit, but that did not make my situation any less excruciating. The motivation to become a mental health services provider stemmed from this, my very first hospitalization, when I did not understand what had happened or what was happening to me. My most vivid memory is of staff members walking through the unit carrying large, neon lime green paperback books with the letters *DSM III* written on the cover. I did not know what information the book contained, but I did know the staff had the books and the patients did not. It was at this point I consciously decided to persevere against the injustice I felt regarding my mental illness.

First, I decided I would have to find out what was so important in those lime green books. My opportunity to discover the answer came about after I had begun my own home services company. Desperate to have a substantial cash flow to meet the costs of medication and psychotherapy and being unable to work, I turned to an idea I had since college. It was tough going, but it did pay for my treatment. One of my customers was a resident at a local hospital and he had a *DSM III*, so I looked up my diagnosis and, then, I started reading everything I could get my hands on about psychiatry and psychotherapy. As my recovery began in earnest, I began to realize it would not be months before I was symptom free, but years!

Soon, I was to learn that recovery from mental illness is not common. Often treatment is not framed as recovery, but known as baseline stabilization. Mental health care providers do not think or feel it is possible to recover from mental illness. Over and over again, I was told I was a good candidate for psychotherapy. To this day, I still do not know of anyone with mental illness who could not benefit from someone caring and compassionate, willing to listen and empathize with them, yet this is relatively rare for most individuals with serious mental illness.

As my knowledge base began to grow and expand, my relationships with my mental health providers also changed. My tenacity was recognized and I used it to my benefit. One summer early in my recovery, my therapist wanted me to attend day treatment. I refused. I knew what I needed and it was not day treatment, but more psychotherapy. We argued about this decision for several sessions until we both relented. I came to see him three times a week instead of two. Also, at one point, I decided not to take antidepressants because of a very bad reaction after a cutback. For sixteen months, I took no medication. As I look back, I would not have made the same choices, but I now have the medical knowledge I did not have then. Nevertheless, the important aspect is that the choices I made were mine, and my mental health care providers supported them.

Empowerment

With my changing relationships, I became less afraid of mental illness and wanted to know more. I most wanted to know why recovery rates are so low. In my experience, the patients with caring mental health services providers are the ones who heal. Why do some providers care and others do not? The situation is not nearly so black and white as I once thought. Mental health services providers must have clinical training and clinical supervision which makes sense to them. Providers cannot help someone to become empowered if they do not feel empowered. Nor can they make choices available if they have no choice or power in their own lives. I realized early in my recovery that I wanted to be a mental health services provider. It scared me too much to think of being a therapist and helping others through their emotional traumas, as I could hardly handle my own. However, I could not move away from working in psychiatry. For a while, I did fantasize about becoming a psychiatrist. I consider it essential for anyone working with individuals with mental illness to have adequate knowledge. Without knowledge, it is virtually impossible to counsel anyone in psychiatric distress.

Choices

My main reasons for not pursuing psychiatry in a formal manner were economics and time. As of this writing, I have been in treatment for eleven years. When I was in the hospital for the very first time, my therapist told me I would probably be in treatment for about a year. I do not think he actually believed that, but what is a therapist to say? If I had been told I would need treatment for a very long time, I probably would have created more denial. Treatment is expensive and I would not settle for just any therapist or psychiatrist. During the course of my treatment, I have separated from both therapists and psychiatrists. In all instances, the separation was extremely painful, but I knew it was the right choice for me. This is the price of empowerment: not always making safe choices, spending money on treatment rather than vacations, new clothes, what have you. My husband and I are still paying off the debt for my treatment.

I would not change any of my treatment choices because it is from striving for excellence that I derive my own standard of commitment, determination, and caring which I bring to the mental health service consumers I work with side by side everyday. Intuitively, I knew this was my calling. I had at long last found the purpose and meaning of my life through the many doors and corridors of my own pain.

Self-Responsibility

In the summer of 1987, I decided I had had enough of the home services business. Not only was I weary of meeting the many needs of my customers, but I never felt truly satisfied or fulfilled. I listened to my anger. At my very next therapy session I told my therapist I was giving up the business and going to look for a full-time job. I will always remember him saying to me to wait just a minute! I had a successful business, I was stable psychiatrically, and now I was going to look for full-time work. In previous years, I had had several part-time jobs but was unable to keep them due to recurrence of symptoms. Nonetheless, I felt the time was right and I started job hunting. Within a period of eight weeks, I had an interview at Sunshine Projects, a Fairweather Lodge Model psychiatric rehabilitation program. They were looking for someone organized, who understood customer service and knew the janitorial business. I was so excited I could hardly contain myself. In a matter of two weeks I had had three interviews. My first interview was with the executive director of the agency. She asked me to return to meet the residential coordinator. The job I was applying for was that of work services coordinator. I attended the second interview with the executive director and the residential coordinator. We all hit it off right away. I could not believe there was a residential/vocational program designed for individuals with psychiatric disabilities which focused on empowerment, personal choice, self-determination, and self-responsibility!

My third interview was with the Lodge members at their work site. I was very nervous about the interview. In fact, between interviews, I was becoming symptomatic and experienced long crying spells. I will always remember my dear friend who is a medical anthropologist, my therapist, and my husband encouraging and reassuring me that I did have the necessary skills and abilities to not only work full-time, but to be successful with consumers in psychiatric rehabilitation. It was a scary time for me, but I knew if I were ever to get my life off the ground again, I would have to push forward and take the risk. I jumped off my safe plateau and started the climb to the next level. Immediately after the third interview, the executive director offered me the position and I said yes!

Wellness

My first week on the job is still very vivid in my mind. Mostly, I read the writings of George Fairweather. I could not believe how fortunate I was to be employed where I was so philosophically aligned. I was taking large dosages of tricyclic antidepressants and benzodiazepams, attending therapy twice weekly for forty-five minutes, and did not have a driver's license. What I did have was dedication, tenacity, determination, commitment, and loyalty to the agency and to all of the Lodge members. I walked, took the bus, hitched rides, rode in cabs and generally did what I needed to do to meet the responsibilities of my job. I could not let my fellow consumers down, no matter what!

Whenever I have worked in a psychiatric setting, I continually worry about my fellow workers knowing my status as a consumer. I feel consumers take a considerable risk when they reveal their status or the information is disclosed in some other way. Although many professionals claim not to be biased against consumers as providers, experience tells me differently. While I would not say to a fellow consumer not to ever disclose your status, I would advise providing for yourself first, especially clinically. I feel advocates need to be as articulate clinically as they are legally. The true battles for dignity of risk and the right to autonomy occur in clinical contexts and can be much tougher to negotiate a consensus or compromise. I remember several months after I had started working for the agency, the executive director told me she had never seen anyone mesh into the group of Lodge members as I had. I laughed to myself instead of crying, for I knew some of the pain and devastation they felt. I had felt it many times myself.

Stigma

One day my two Lodge staff and I went to the local mental health center to meet with the Lodge members' therapists. I clearly remember the therapists stating it was their opinion that the members were some of the sickest living in the community. Shortly afterward, the meeting was over and we got back into our car for the ride back to the office. We all looked at each other and said, "The folks don't seem to be the sickest in the community. They are just the folks." This was my introduction to stigma—a word I had heard a great deal about, but was unsure of what it truly meant. Now, I knew.

In March of 1987, my husband was offered a permanent sales territory in North Carolina. This came as a bittersweet reality for me. After a lot of soul searching, we finally decided he would move the first of June, and I would move at the end of December. We were very much in agreement on this decision, but it was very difficult.

Sometime that summer, one of the Lodge members and I were talking about the business, the Twelve Steps, and medication. He asked me if I had ever taken Trilifon and what effect it had on me. I was somewhat taken aback and briefly hesitated before replying that yes I had. I still have mixed feelings about telling him the truth, yet it is not clear to me who or what I was trying to protect.

When I announced my resignation to members, everyone was quiet. I encouraged the member I had spoken to so candidly to please speak with me about his feelings about my leaving. I also asked him about his feelings, but he always assured me he was ok. Just before I was to leave for North Carolina, he began to have a very difficult time psychiatrically. It wasn't until after I had moved that I learned he was greatly distressed. Would the next coordinator treat him with the same respect, treat him as an equal, acknowledge his presence? It wasn't until then that I realized what a profound effect providers of psychiatric rehabilitation can have on the consumers that they interact with daily. We like to think that only psychotherapists, psychiatrists, psychiatric nurses, and psychologists evoke such a strong reaction from their clients. However, anyone who shows compassion and true caring can and does have an effect.

If consumers are to be providers of psychiatric rehabilitation, they need to be acknowledged for their experience. If a consumer chooses to participate in psychiatric rehabilitation in an employment context, they need to be validated. The immediate empathy and sense of urgency consumers/providers have cannot be underestimated. A consumer/provider can be the conscience of the organization, providing an advocate who will speak for their clients. Remember, all other providers can go home and get away from it all. On the other hand, mental illness and health are never far from a consumer/provider's thoughts.

Moving On

A major concern before leaving for North Carolina was finding a new psychotherapist/psychiatrist who would meet my particular needs, someone to be available 24 hours a day. I was willing to pay the price for that security. My psychiatrist in Hartford gave me several names and I started calling. All these calls kept leading me back to one particular practice and one particular psychiatrist. I spoke with him on the telephone and set up an appointment to meet with him upon my arrival in Raleigh. What I remember most about TJB was his desire to work with me and make a long-term commitment, so I could achieve wellness. One of the most memorable therapeutic interventions was that for ten weeks we had therapy in my car. This enabled me to finally conquer my fear of driving and get my driver's license. This is a concrete example of how a truly caring and therapeutic alliance can produce outstanding and life-changing results!!!

Advocacy as a Provider

Before leaving Sunshine Projects, I started to make inquiries in Raleigh about possible jobs in mental health. At the time, I was not aware that this particular area of North Carolina was heavily populated with degreed individuals and was an employers' market; especially in mental health. I did not realize the lack of a B.S.W. or M.S.W. would be such a barrier to employment. Again because of the fear of stigma, I could not list my consumer experience on my resume or job application. Eventually, I was hired by the local mental health authority in a pilot program to provide complete community support services for individuals with both mental illness and mental retardation. The job as a rehabilitation specialist was very challenging, but extremely rewarding. I became friends with one client in particular. Unfortunately, the funding for the pilot program was recalled and the clients were returned to a state psychiatric facility.

I was struck by the lack of compassion of the area mental health authority for these clients. The clients had done what they had been asked to do. They proved they could live safely in the community; nonetheless funding was withdrawn. I was heartsick and knew there was nothing I could do except monitor the situation. I distinctly remember my fellow team members warning me not to give one of my clients my telephone number because they would surely abuse it. I did not doubt my ability to maintain my boundaries, so I gave this person my number. It was through this connection that I was eventually able to advocate successfully for this former client.

Another deficiency of this pilot program was the pervasive attitude that direct care providers do not need extensive clinical knowledge or continuing staff development. It was a very sad situation, to recognize several of my team members as having the potential to become excellent mental health service providers rather than mediocre ones. I remember taking a horrendous required class for employment known as Preventative Intervention Certification. During this training, I believe my fellow team members did not truly understand intervention with words; rather, they understood intervention only as therapeutic holds! I strongly challenged the clinical team, but it was a losing battle. I could not convince them that clients were due choice, self-determination, and opportunities. For some reason, I was relieved when the pilot program came to an end. The professional clinical attitude was dismal at best. The only hope for the clients hinged upon a pending lawsuit which was technically settled, but not fulfilled.

Advocacy as a Consumer-Provider

After leaving the local mental health authority, I ran into one road block after another for employment. I wanted a position as case manager, but none was available without a M.S.W. Being unable to find a mental health position, I applied for whatever positions I felt I had the qualifications to do. For the next three years I had many jobs. I worked for a national hotline. I taught remedial basic skills, both in a community college and in a learning center. I worked in customer service. Finally a big break came for me. I was hired by the local ARC chapter (formerly the Association of Retarded Citizens) as a part-time volunteer coordinator. At the same time, I was volunteering at a local historical society and as training coordinator. During this time, I met a fellow advocate who was also trying to find his way to full-time employment.

It was during my tenure at the ARC that I was able to establish myself as an advocate in North Carolina. ARC/NC needed someone to fill their seat on the human rights committee of the local state psychiatric facility. I jumped at the chance. This experience gave me the knowledge of the system I desperately needed. It also exposed me to other advocates and gave me encouragement. When I first joined the committee, I did not disclose my status; I was again, too afraid.

Mentorship

In December of 1992, my friend and fellow advocate told me that the local mental health authority had hired a new and progressive deputy executive director. I was doubtful. My friend assured me that this administrator was different and that I needed to meet her. We arranged to meet for lunch. MBK was extremely quiet, but the few stories she told me really stayed with me. She told me that one summer she had been a recreation assistant and she had been helping a nurse give an injection of Thorazine to a woman who was out of control. During the struggle, the nurse accidentally injected her. She was out cold and slept for three days. We wonder why individuals with serious mental illness like to drink large quantities of caffeinated coffee and smoke endless cigarettes! MBK told me about supervising a psychiatric facility in another state. She told the staff they had one day to get rid of all of their restraints. When she arrived, she started looking for them. She didn't see any. Finally, a nurse very sheepishly stepped forward and said the basement was filled with bags and bags of restraints. She left them one pair in case they needed them!!! I thought, "Maybe she is progressive."

In the next months, my fellow mental health advocates and I endeavored to form our own advocacy group and it was tough going. We have never disbanded officially, but we no longer meet. After that, I joined The Alliance for the Mentally Ill (AMI)—not so much because I agreed with their positions, but AMI always had information consumers never had, and without information advocates cannot advocate!

Nothing was happening with the class action lawsuit to get my friend and others out of the psychiatric facility. We communicated on a regular basis; however, it was not reassuring to me. These conversations frequently described physical abuse. I was beginning to think my friend might never leave the facility or leave the facility alive. Alarmed, I called MBK and asked her if she was willing to meet my friend. I did not want my friend's psychiatric record to be the only consideration. She agreed to meet us and I was thrilled. Now, perhaps my friend had a chance to survive and to experience a quality life.

Several months after visiting the psychiatric facility, the local mental health authority invited me to become an incorporating member of a newly organized 501(c)3 nonprofit agency. This agency was designed to build and purchase housing for mental health services consumers, developmental disabilities consumers, and individuals suffering from substance abuse, including the homeless population and persons who were diagnosed HIV positive. I was chosen to be the consumer representative on the board. I knew a little about housing, Housing and Urban Development (HUD), grant writing, and block grants, but was in no way an expert. MBK was very involved in getting this board off the ground. One of our first tasks was to hire an executive director. I volunteered to participate in this process, as I wanted to be truly involved in making a difference in people's lives. We all worked hard, but it was the staff who wrote the grants and did the really hard work. We received several grant awards and felt we were truly sitting on top of the world.

Later that year, I wrote a job description to become a consumer liaison and community support resource specialist. At the same time, MBK was working on upgrading the client advocate position, and she encouraged me to apply. This turned into a very difficult task to accomplish. The personnel office adamantly refused to list me as a viable candidate. MBK advocated repeatedly for me. Finally, personnel relented and agreed to allow me to be interviewed if I could somehow document my knowledge base. When I asked what exactly this format was to be, I was told I would have to make it up on my own. Also included in this compromise was the stipulation that I could not use all my years experience as a consumer, just some of them! In the end, I finally had two interviews both lasting over an hour. I must say the questions I answered in these interviews were the hardest I have ever been asked. Personnel wanted to be sure that the questions were not skewed in my favor. The only thing the interview committee did not ask me was if I spoke Russian!

This was a very low point for me. The person who was given the job held not only an M.S.W., but a law degree as well. Now, as I look back over the situation, I realize that to have had me on their executive management team would have been too much! I would have been there every day pricking their consciences and upholding MBK's progressive views.

In the next several months, the situation became better. I had been elected second vice president of the local AMI affiliate and I had been nominated to serve on the NC Protection and Advocacy for Individuals with Mental Illness Committee. By this time, I had three or four part-time jobs and numerous meetings to attend. I had a great deal to occupy my mind, but was not satisfied. My yearnings were for situations in which I could employ my advocacy skills, such as guiding, teaching, training, facilitating, and directing. Furthermore, I longed to be in an environment where I felt at ease philosophically. I wanted to work with mental health services consumers to demonstrate that recovery is a journey, not a destination. I felt I had what it would take to make a difference in other people's lives who had not been as fortunate as I had in my treatment options.

Throughout this time, MBK continued to encourage me to follow through on my beliefs. As time went by, I was buying into her attempt to make a public mental health services system more client-driven and responsive to the needs of consumers. In April 1993, I was asked to speak very briefly before the NC/AMI Spring Conference to describe what consumers really wanted from providers and the system. I spoke of opportunities for education, employment, recognition, and quality of life. I have never known consumers who wanted more than this. To be like everyone else in a world where stigma and prejudice abound would be truly miraculous!

One night I received a call from a civil rights lawyer from a state mental disability law project. She got my name through the grapevine and thought I could be a good resource for a video she was producing on the Americans with Disabilities Act and how the judicial system could be made more user friendly. When DG asked me if I was interested, I immediately said yes! I quit several of my jobs to pursue my new career as a temporary video consultant. As we neared the end of production, DG asked me to appear in the video. In the video I discussed the lack of opportunity and the subtle but very real nature of stigma. I mentioned specifically that when status as a consumer is revealed, there is a slight shift in individuals' viewpoints. Without being insulting, implicit questions abound. Can I trust this person to be competent? Will this person become symptomatic without warning? Can this person do the job? If I had been asked when I had first been diagnosed with a mental illness, I would have said I was skeptical of stigma; however, the more I disclose, the more I feel stigma. It may be elusive, but it's real!

Welcome to Clubhouse

In May 1993, I applied for a part-time psychiatric consultant position. I had recently updated my resume with the help of a friend who is a career counselor. We decided that since I was involved in so many advocacy activities and I considered myself to be an advocate that I needed to list advocacy skills on my resume. I had applied for so many jobs that this particular application did not strike me as outstanding. Prior to sending the resume, my friends from ARC encouraged me to apply for the position of family resources coordinator. I knew I was qualified, but I also knew if I did not hold out for some kind of mental health position I would never get one.

I went to the interview as scheduled. I met with the executive director and learned the program was a Clubhouse Model Rehabilitation Program. I had heard of clubhouses, but I was not entirely clear on what it was or how it functioned. I thought the interview was very clinical for a part-time job coach position. At some point during the interview the executive director asked me if I was interested in full-time employment and I said yes!!! He said, "You have had the interview for the full-time position." I still do not ever remember seeing the advertisement for a full-time position. The executive director gave me a tour of the club, and it really did seem like a neat place. We made arrangements that day for me to return the following week to just hang out in the club. I was also to be interviewed by members and staff. I left the club somewhat in a haze. I wanted full-time mental health employment, yet I was unsure of my ability to carry out full-time direct care.

The next week I went in for my second interview. I had coffee in the snack bar, browsed through the Thrift Store, and wandered down to the kitchen where they were making stir-fry chicken and eggrolls. The staff member in the kitchen asked me if I had ever had any experience with this population and I said yes, while laughing to myself. I told her of my experience both with the pilot program and with the Fairweather Lodge. Then I was to be interviewed by members and staff. The questions were again hard, but I sensed I did very well with them. The executive director walked me out the door and said he would be in touch. I still had mixed feelings and some anxiety, but decided to take the job if it were offered to me. If for no other reason, I wanted full-time employment to pay on our debt from all the years of my treatment. JB called back and I took the job. My starting date was July 19, 1993.

I was anxious and a little overwhelmed during the first days. My first morning I was scheduled to make lunch for twenty-five people using the snack bar, as the kitchen was being remodeled. We would work out of the snack bar for sometime. This was truly trial by fire. How to expedite twenty-five meals in a small space was a continual challenge, but it also gave me many opportunities to work side by side with members and to learn the work of the club. Before I knew it, I had given my heart and soul to the clubhouse. As it worked out, my fellow unit mate and I were of like mind, and we began in earnest to build a strong and viable unit with members.

My relationship with the executive director was very positive. I felt more and more at ease with him. I was scheduled to attend many advocacy meetings, however; six months into the job I gave up most of my activities except the housing board and my seat on the PAIMI Committee. I wanted to be at the club working, helping members, talking with members and enjoying a supportive psychosocial rehabilitation program which is its own private, nonprofit organization.

As JB and I developed our working relationship and friendship, I began to feel confident enough to tell him my status as a mental health services consumer. I felt I wanted to tell him rather than have him guess because I was involved in so many advocacy issues and I knew so many people, some at the state level. This turned out to be a great relief to me as he did not make me feel stigmatized. JB and I would often discuss the issue of urgency in the lives of individuals with mental illness. We have already lost so much to mental illness; we do not have time to waste waiting for opportunities for our lives to be ours again. Working for the Clubhouse was, in many ways, a big disappointment. MBK had given me so much support, validation, and understanding. Yet, the established system was impenetrable for a consumer without a human services undergraduate or graduate degree. In many ways, I became a much better advocate and provider because now I was so much closer to consumers and their needs on a daily basis. As for establishing credibility, I must have known what I was talking about because I had suddenly become a professional. Fortunately for me, I work in one county and I am involved with advocacy in another. So there are still many individuals who either know me as a consumer or as a provider, but not as both. However, as I become more confident in my abilities, I am less concerned about revealing my status.

My true struggle is revealing my status to members and staff of the club who do not know. I am still unsure how they will respond. Will they still trust me to be there for them? Will they still trust my judgment, especially in a crisis? If I have a recurrence of symptoms, will they have confidence in me to know whether I can do the job and fulfill my responsibilities?

At the local mental health center, I often see individuals who know me from various state level meetings where I was a consumer representative, yet they walk by me as though I were not there. One very positive outcome, however, is that at one of these state level meetings, I had a chance to have lunch with a top level psychiatrist from the Division of Mental Health. Out of that conversation, he has come to speak at the clubhouse about medication and now is on a steering committee with me to develop, organize, and present an ethics conference concerning treatment of individuals with mental illness.

One Step Forward, Two Steps Back

During early 1994, I also decided to submit a presentation outline to be delivered at Alternatives, a consumer conference in Anaheim, California. I did a lot of advocating on my own behalf to raise the necessary money or vouchers to cover my trip. I was elated when my presentation was accepted. I had never traveled that far by myself before, so it was very challenging for me to make the trip. Unfortunately, my presentation was not as well received as I had hoped it would be. I spoke on self-determination, empowerment, and advocacy in recovery from mental illness. I cannot say my audience was openly hostile, but I felt a great deal of resentment because I had become a provider. It was a disappointing experience. I cannot say I have not felt that bias before because I have. Now that I am a provider, I can no longer be a consumer advocate or I'm not sick enough to be an advocate. Individual consumers have been very effective in creating positive change in their own lives, yet coming together as a larger group has been difficult to affect systems change where it is so desperately needed.

In early December, I had an automobile accident which was quite traumatic for me emotionally and soon afterward I began to have symptoms. This was an especially frightening time for me because I had thought I would never again have symptoms. I was faced with many hard decisions; one of which was to go back into treatment on a more regular basis. Up until then I had been seeing my psychiatrist once every six months. Another very difficult decision was taking JB into my confidence and telling him the situation as to why I stopped driving. In many ways, my decision had already been made for me in that the club had become my life. I needed the club, the members, and the staff as much as they needed me. JB was very supportive, adjusting my job duties and allowing me to take time off.

During the writing of this chapter, I had my 18-month evaluation which was very satisfactory. I now have on paper the qualifications I need to be a Qualified Mental Health Professional (QMHP). I think this is quite ironic because I've considered myself to be a QMHP for a long time. Also, during the writing of this chapter, a member of the club passed on. In some ways I felt as though I had walked over my own grave, as the member was the same age as I am. The sensation reminded me of the saying "there but by the grace of God go I."

Vision for the Future

To conclude, I will comment on what the public mental health system needs, based on my experience. First and foremost, only individuals who truly wish to work in community mental health should do so. I am weary of hearing providers complain there is too much work to be done and not enough time to do it. I am very aware how difficult and draining community mental health work can be. My belief is every dissatisfied mental health provider needs to look for other employment or seek to improve the system. Further, mental health providers, no matter what type or kind of care they provide, need clinical training and clinical supervision. One of the primary reasons I have been so successful in my work is that I have had both. I, also, intend to continue to improve my clinical knowledge and seek guidance from individuals who have sound clinical knowledge.

Next, to truly reform the public mental health system, the system needs consumers to buy into a vision of public mental health. The mentality of us versus them cannot continue. The framework of the system must be recovery, not symptom management. The opinions and impressions of consumers need to be sought out. Somehow, this seems to be the most threatening aspect of reform. So many providers seem frightened of their clients, have no relationships with them, and in general, do not particularly like people with mental illness. This is very sad.

Finally, consumers will need to be given professional credit for their experience if they choose to become providers. The consumer movement is not as strong as it could be because many consumers get well and never want to be involved again. The stench of stigma is ever present. Others feel no purpose for becoming involved in advocacy. Periodically, my fellow advocates and I feel like running away from it all. Nevertheless, we always come back. The understanding, empathy, and compassion consumers can bring to clients as providers is immeasurable. The knowledge that it is possible to conquer mental illness is a powerful motivation and testament to what can be and is being done daily.

Lastly, as I conclude, I am reminded of a somewhat schmaltzy series for children developed about twenty years ago by Marlo Thomas. The name of the series is FREE TO BE YOU AND ME, and this is the most forthright way I can explain what consumers want. We want the freedom to make our own choices and decisions, including the right to refuse treatment. Some will be appalled by this statement. In my own experience, mental illness is like being locked in a black box with no way out. Help us to be free; what we can give in return is still only a dream.

Acknowledgment

This article is dedicated to my dear and wonderful husband, Thomas B. Daley, who has stood by me for better or worse and in sickness and in health. Special thanks to JRB and MBK for their support, their opportunities, and their validation.

"Trust your heart....Never deny it a hearing. It is a kind of house oracle that often foretells the most important."

Balthasar Garcia'n (1601-58)

Lois Cavanagh-Daley is a consumer provider currently employed as a program specialist and social/recreational and educational coordinator at Threshold. Threshold is a clubhouse model rehabilitation program, serving adults with serious mental illness in Durham, NC. Threshold's executive director is Jonathan Beard, son of the late John Beard, one of the founders of the clubhouse model at Fountain House in New York City.

Chapter 28
"From Schiz to Shrink": A Personal Description of Transition from Psychiatric Patient to Psychiatrist

Carol S. North

Barriers

My journey to becoming a physician, and now a psychiatrist, suffered significant delays from my own psychiatric illness, fortunately a thing of the distant past. My illness, diagnosed as schizophrenia and resulting in serious psychiatric impairment for about eight years, generated overwhelming barriers to accomplishment of my dream of becoming a physician. I recovered from this illness in 1978 with the help of an esoteric, experimental treatment that unfortunately has not subsequently proven to be of general usefulness (due to problems of the research methodology as well as to the heroic, difficult nature of the treatment). Therefore, I regard my recovery as nothing short of a miracle (specifically, a medical miracle). I believe my personal experience with serious mental illness has been invaluable to my unique development as a psychiatrist and has enhanced my work in helping others with serious mental illness. I have written a book-length description of my illness[1] to help people understand what it is like to experience this illness from the inside, from the vantage point of one who not only has lived it first-hand, but who can also describe it with technical psychiatric clarity.

My transition from "mental health consumer" to mental health professional was of little consequence to me aside from externally generated obstacles to pursuing my medical education. My primary life goal was to become a physician, and once I re-established myself as a viable medical student, the topic of my past illness played only a small role in this transition. My biggest difficulty occurred during my second year of medical school when I became too psychiatrically ill to continue with my studies and had to take a year's leave of absence from school. During the year of my leave, I experienced my remarkable recovery and subsequently requested reinstatement as a student in medical school. Due to what I perceive as stigma and discrimination on the part of administration of the medical school I attended, I was unable to negotiate a fair agreement for my return to class. I was devastated.

---

[1] Carol S. North. *Welcome Silence: My Triumph Over Schizophrenia.* New York: Simon & Schuster, 1987 and Avon, 1989.

A New Start

Not to be daunted, however, I applied for transfer to another medical school. This effort was made more difficult by the fact that I am inclined to act with total honesty, and felt it necessary to bare my soul about my psychiatric history to the prospective school. I did not want to have to live the next three years of my life under the typical massive stresses of medical school plagued by constant fear that someone might find out about my secret past. My new school, Washington University in St. Louis, turned out to have an enlightened attitude about psychiatric illness. Washington University's department of psychiatry had effectively educated the admissions committee that a history of serious psychiatric illness with apparent total recovery might not put them at risk of admitting a student who would pose a danger of violence to patients or bad judgment that would endanger lives. Therefore, in spite of my psychiatric history, I was admitted as a transfer student with no restrictions. (When individuals contact me about dilemmas regarding honesty in reporting their history as part of matriculation in school or applying for jobs, I usually recommend that because this information is not appropriate material for such decisions, they may be justified in keeping it quiet. I also recognize, however, that some individuals, such as myself, are not comfortable concealing this information and feel compelled by a need for complete honesty, and in that case I cannot recommend lying.)

On admission to this enlightened medical school, I felt I had a "new lease on life." I did not feel I had to hide my history of psychiatric illness from my peers, as I was not ashamed of it. In line with the "medical model" of psychiatric practice at this school, I was not made to feel any more embarrassed by my past psychiatric illness than if I had recovered from diabetes or kidney disease.

An amusing anecdote of my medical school experience, with a sad note, merits recounting here. When I was a student on my third year medical rotation on psychiatry at Washington University, St. Louis experienced a record-setting snowstorm, with two feet of snow falling overnight. Being a resourceful person from colder climes, I responded to my assigned on-call duties that day with my usual northern resourcefulness. I strapped on my cross-country skis and packed a backpack with my white coat, medical instruments (stethoscope, oto-ophthalmoscope, reflex hammer, etc.), and reference books, and charted a six-mile course through the St. Louis ghetto (with which I was totally unfamiliar). I began this journey at six o'clock in the morning, and after being chased through the snow by threatening residents of the area, arrived at the acute state psychiatric hospital on time for duty two hours later.

I was scheduled to be on call that day with a supervising psychiatrist, and because of the record snowstorm, the two of us were obliged to cover all physician duties at the hospital for the next 36 hours until other psychiatrists could get there. My supervising psychiatrist was an odd young man who, it was discovered later, was in the early stages of developing schizophrenia; he subsequently went on to develop bizarre delusions and hallucinations of the full-blown disorder. Our experience in this emergency snowstorm must be the only time in past and probably future history in which two individuals with schizophrenia were placed in charge of running a mental institution! Fortunately, we managed the situation with no untoward incidents.

The task of completing medical school at Washington University was routine for me, in that I was no longer psychiatrically ill and functioned as any other medical student. I was awed by being able to attend one of the best medical schools in the country after previously having had difficulties with my studies (due to psychiatric illness) at an ordinary state school. In spite of any concerns I had, I graduated in the top one-third of my class and received two honors, one of which was awarded to only two students out of every graduating class of 120. I decided during the course of my medical studies that my past experience as a mental patient was a unique qualification that could allow me to make special contributions to the field of psychiatry, and this convinced me to make psychiatry my specialty.

Transition to Psychiatrist

I opted to stay at Washington University for my residency training as I considered this to be the world's best institution for the study of psychiatry. Upon completion of residency, I again chose to stay at Washington University and pursue additional fellowship training through the National Institute of Mental Health in the study of psychiatric epidemiology (which is the study of psychiatric illness and diagnosis in populations), the area in which Washington University psychiatry specializes. I was invited to join the full time academic faculty at Washington University—a position that involves conducting scientific research, teaching, and treating patients in clinical practice. In this position, I have conducted epidemiologic studies on mental health issues of homeless populations and disaster victims (with post-traumatic stress disorder), work for which I have become nationally and internationally recognized. Recently I was invited to return to the medical school that had rejected me to deliver Grand Rounds in psychiatry on an area of my recognized psychiatric expertise. While I was there, the new department chairman, who knew nothing of my history, offered me a job! (I didn't take it.)

I currently spend approximately twenty hours a week in clinical care of patients. This work offers me a chance to repay to members of society some of the goodness that was bestowed upon me by my excellent caretakers when I was ill. This clinical work is also vital to the quality of my academic research, because it grounds my research in the reality of live patients in the real world. Pursuit of academic research is my main activity, which reflects my firm belief that scientific research is the most important part of medical activity because it generates the treatments that are the basis of all clinical practice. I also spend a good deal of my professional time educating medical students, residents in psychiatry, other physicians, and graduate students of psychosocial disciplines. In my teaching activities, I convey my understanding of patients' experience of psychiatric illness and my empathy for patients' concerns as an integral part of clinical education.

I do not use the word "client" in my work. Psychiatrists and psychiatric nurses treat psychiatric disorders of patients in medical settings; therefore, I promote use of the terminology of medical work in my own professional activity. I accept the use of the word "client" for social workers and therapists who work with different aspects of the problems of persons with mental illness. The term "consumer" seems to belittle the professional mental health relationship, minimizing it to a business activity that does not fit with my own model of clinical work.

Perspectives on Psychiatry from Personal Experience as a Patient

I am not a radical "ex-consumer" who is angry with the mental health system. To a degree, I sympathize, however, with the "ex-consumer" movement that criticizes all of psychiatry and the mental health system as failing to meet the needs of its members. From my exposure to these individuals, it seems that the mental health system has not served them well. It appears that many have been misdiagnosed and provided somatic treatments, such as medications and electroconvulsive therapy, that may not have been appropriate for their particular disorders. While they appear to have been badly served by poorly representative members of the system, it is clear to me that skillful and well-trained members of the system might still have been helpful by diagnosing and managing their psychiatric problems appropriately.

The denouncement of the total field of psychiatry and the entire notion of major mental illness by radical ex-consumers clearly constitutes the proverbial throwing-the-baby-out-with-the-bath-water. While I do concede to their claims that while psychiatric diagnosis can indeed be used inappropriately to label people and control them for political reasons (well documented in Communist bloc countries in previous decades), I don't think such influence occupies a significant chunk of activity in the American mental health treatment sector today. Having personally suffered a serious psychiatric illness and received appropriate treatment for it, I know that mental illness can be a severe condition causing tremendous suffering and disability, and that people can also greatly benefit from appropriate treatment that is well crafted. My experience as a mental health professional strongly underscores my own personal history. I have repeatedly observed individuals with psychiatric disease receive medical help that has made an important and meaningful difference in their lives. Too many patients and family members have expressed deep gratitude for my efforts to allow me to believe that appropriate psychiatric treatment is anything other than humane and helpful.

There are a number of things I have learned from having been a psychiatric patient that I can pass on to colleagues and students, things that I did not encounter in my own medical and psychiatric training. I learned first-hand from the good examples of the professionals who treated my own illness about what to do as well as about what not to do, leading me to articulate some principles regarding the clinical practice of psychiatry. These principles include regarding patients as team members, working with their family supports as a part of a larger team, and considering oneself merely as a consultant who works for the patient and his or her family support system to provide medical services that improve the patient's functioning and comfort. Past tradition in the mental health field has focused on treating symptoms of disease without adequately considering the day-to-day life of the patient and his or her household, and without including the family as a valuable potential asset. The mental health field formerly blamed the family for the patient's problems and ostracized them. When I was ill, my own family was one of my greatest strengths. It disturbs me that some of the mental health professionals treating me blamed my mother for causing my illness and tried to alienate me from my parents— which is the opposite of what my family needed.

Medications: Weighing Side Effects and Symptom Level

My personal experience has taught me that eradication of all psychiatric symptoms at the expense of reducing quality of life is not the ultimate goal of treatment. Eradication of all psychiatric symptoms with no consideration of the individual can result — at the extreme — in eradication of life, and at a lesser extreme, eradication of quality of life. In my own experience, I discovered that the medications to reduce my psychotic symptoms had unfortunate side effects that interfered with the pursuit of my life's activities. In college, I was a dance major. In dance class, I could not tolerate the drop in blood pressure to 60/20 due to the Mellaril I was prescribed. Dizziness from the medication prevented me from spinning off my usual series of pirouettes. Some days, low blood pressure prevented me from getting out of bed to attend class at all. With this medication, I could not succeed in dance class, and in fact I could not succeed in any class because I could not stay awake to hear the lecture or study the course material.

Other side effects also bothered me. The side effect of lactation produced embarrassing wet spots on the front of my blouses. I developed involuntary movements such as curling toes and alien finger movements that made it difficult to walk and impossible to write (diagnosed as a side effect called dystonia). My doctors responded to this unpleasant side effect by changing my medication to one with a different side effect profile. Unfortunately, this other medication caused blurred vision, which prevented me from seeing well enough to study and take exams. The blurred vision was the side effect that ultimately led me to drop out of school—a devastating experience for a person for whom education and future career were of central importance. Reasoning that I would have a better chance of succeeding in school under conditions of hearing voices and thinking people were trying to harm me than I could without being able to read, I stopped taking the medication. The medication had also caused me to gain twenty pounds, which also was not acceptable for a ballerina. After I quit the medication, I was able to salvage my college years, but not without a heroic effort on my part to devise new and innovative ways to cope with psychosis.

Once in medical school, I was fortunate in finally obtaining a psychiatrist who was sensitive to my difficulties with the medication and who was committed to helping me achieve the goals I identified as most important to me (i.e., school). His capacity to listen to me helped him understand the importance of my goals and the perspective of my illness in relationship to them. To the extent that the symptoms of my illness interfered with my goals, he prescribed antipsychotic medication, and to the extent that the medication side effects interfered, he adjusted my doses and tried other medications with different pharmacologic profiles, as well as prescribing medication to combat side effects. This helped for awhile, but eventually my illness became so severe that I failed to bathe or change clothes for more than a month, and my behavior became so bizarre and disorganized (e.g., posturing and staring for hours) that I simply could not continue my medical career.

The philosophy practiced by my last psychiatrist made an indelible impression on me. In my own practice, I share most physicians' desire to eradicate every psychiatric symptom of every patient encountered, but I now realize that this goal is not only unobtainable but it can be obstructionistic to effective treatment. If the medication I prescribe to reduce psychiatric symptoms has side effects that effectively inhibit the person's ability to function or make the patient uncomfortable, then that regimen is of no value. Effective treatment always weighs therapeutic effects against unwanted side effects in arriving at clinical decisions.

Non-Pharmacologic Assistance

Another aspect of my last doctor's help was his willingness to devise nonpharmacologic measures along with the medications to help me survive the psychosis. He worked with me to devise psychosocial techniques to deal with psychotic symptoms. He helped me plan a feedback strategy, so that when I heard voices I could do a "reality check" by leaning on people I trusted to ask them if I should believe these voices. When I was not in the company of one of my trusted social supports, I could check it out by looking around to see if other people seemed to be hearing the voices or responding to them. If they weren't, then I would know that the voices I heard were those "special" voices that I must not respond to in public, and that I must not rely on these voices for information or advice. This strategy helped me resist the voices, and the beauty of it was that it was very practical and common-sense.

This psychiatrist also took advantage of the pattern of the usual ebb and flow of psychotic illness. At the times when I was doing better, he would work with me to improve my insight into my illness and get to know my pattern of relapse. When I started to relapse, he was able to build on the work he had pursued while I was less ill and more able to reason. He would remind me of the patterns we had observed, e.g., that when I was becoming more ill I typically heard more voices and the sounds of helicopters, and that was a signal to me that I should take more medication for awhile. He helped me realize that if I took more medication for awhile, it might prevent me from being hospitalized, which I abhorred.

In the therapeutic relationship, trust is vital to the outcome of treatment. Once I had developed trust in my psychiatrist, I was willing to let him guide the treatment, especially when I was too ill to provide organized input. Reciprocally, he developed an important trust in my ability to alert him to my signs of relapse so that he could therefore reduce my medication at times that I was less ill knowing that if I started to relapse I could signal him to action (i.e., adjusting the medication) and hence avert relapse. My trust in him allowed me to believe that as soon as the crisis was averted, I might not have to take so much medication, and he would decrease it as soon as I was able.

Most important of all, this psychiatrist really believed in me. He did not see me as a pathetic, wretched mental patient without human value. He sensed my frustration and my desire to succeed, and he believed in my potential as a human being. He did not discourage me from trying to succeed in medical school, even when his colleagues told him he was crazy to keep trying to help me stay well enough to stay in school. Too many psychiatrists just assume the individual with schizophrenia is a sick person without potential, and this assumption blocks the patient from having an opportunity to succeed. When my patients want to try to go to school, work at a job, or attend a day program, I encourage their motivation to do so. Occasionally the severity of illness turns these activities into overstimulating or overwhelming ventures, and then I try to help the patient moderate at least temporarily by working less hours or taking a leave of absence. In schizophrenia, where the frontal lobes of the brain that would normally generate motivation are damaged, any sign of a glimmer of motivation is something to be cultivated and nurtured.

I believe in the worth of my patients as people, and I try to find out what is important to them and help them work toward reaching their goals. If their goals are unrealistic due to origins in psychosis, I try to help them work to obtain more realistic goals through taking small steps toward those loftier goals. That way, they are less frustrated by the seeming distance they are from the big goal and they obtain satisfaction from meeting smaller goals along the way. Occasionally patients manage to achieve the big goals as I myself did, but regardless of their degree of success, with this strategy the person is allowed to reach the outer limits of his or her own abilities.

Going Public: Decision and Response

Once I had recovered from my illness long enough to rebuild my life, I was presented with a compelling yet frightening decision. I considered the possibility of going public with my story in a book about it. I wanted to help people understand this illness, and help people suffering from it to realize that they are not alone. I knew the best way to fight the stigma and discrimination of society that unnecessarily adds to the suffering of people with psychiatric illness was to address people's ignorance of mental illness. Going public with my story meant risking everything I had worked for: my career as a psychiatrist, my newly realized life goal! After extensive soul-searching, I decided that it was right to go forth with this effort, and that doing the right thing cannot, by definition, be wrong. I knew that I was well, and that this act would be yet another affirmation of my security in my wellness.

Going public wasn't easy. People have said silly things, such as that I couldn't have had schizophrenia because schizophrenics don't ever recover (which isn't true). Others maintain that I couldn't possibly be well now because I was so ill! My response is that when I was ill, I demonstrated all the diagnostic criteria of my diagnosis and not of any others; and now that I am well I have proven my health by completing medical school and residency training and post-doctoral work and another graduate degree in the most rigorous of surroundings under the watchful eyes of some of the top psychiatrists in the country, with no concerns that I have relapsed back into psychosis. Going public has allowed me to educate people and to reduce human suffering through eradication of ignorance. These experiences have confirmed my original decision that this was the right thing to do.

Going public with my story has created some awkward moments in my psychiatric practice. Right after my book was published, I was called to provide psychiatric consultation on a medical inpatient floor for a woman with schizophrenia. A few days previously, I had provided an interview with the local paper, and to my chagrin, the newspaper with the printed story about me (photo and all) was sitting right on her bed; the front-page section in which I appeared was lying right on top. It turned out that the patient was so disorganized and psychotic that she did not make the connection, and I was relieved.

It took me some time to decide how to handle my notoriety with patients. When they ask, I tell them very briefly of my past illness and answer any specific questions they have. I understand that my patients come to me for attention to their illness, not to mine. Only once or twice have I ever volunteered my personal psychiatric history to patients; on these occasions it was to help these individuals come to grips with having an illness they were having trouble accepting. In these rare situations, my openness did seem to help their acceptance. Otherwise, I do not spontaneously offer my personal psychiatric history to patients.

I follow a policy in keeping my personal psychiatric history separate from my academic and clinical activities. Although I speak openly about my illness on national television and radio and to national audiences, when I attend scientific meetings I put on my other "hat" and put away my personal illness "hat." I find this boundary in my professional life immensely helpful. When I speak to scientific colleagues I want to be known for my scientific work, not my psychiatric illness which is really irrelevant in that context. Occasionally I am invited to speak about my own personal illness at scientific conferences (where I would prefer to be presenting my scientific work instead), and I decline these offers. This separation of public education efforts relating to my personal history and my academic activity has helped advance my scientific career in an appropriate manner. It's not that I keep my psychiatric history a secret, I just compartmentalize it into what I view to be the relevant contexts.

I'm sad to report that not all of my colleagues have been entirely professional about their comments (usually made behind my back) regarding my history. Happily, most of my colleagues have responded with very mature and respectful if not overtly supportive behaviors. I recognize that the few unfortunate, unattractive responses of my unconstructive colleagues are part of the territory of opening up one's personal psychiatric history, and they do hurt (I wouldn't be human if they didn't). I am not devastated by them, however. The value of my work to educate the public with dignity despite my history of devastating mental illness provides the meaning that carries me past these slights which are insignificant in the greater perspective.

It's been an uncharted road that I have travelled upon deciding to reveal the details of my personal psychiatric history for public consumption. There was no one to guide me, no mentor who had been there before. I was warned that the media would be mean, hurtful, dishonest, and hateful, and such reports scared me. Fortunately, for the most part, I have been pleasantly surprised by the professional nature of media representatives with whom I have come in contact. I have learned that the media is an important vehicle for public education which mental health professionals can learn to utilize effectively to help the world better understand mental illness.

A Healthy Balance

What I have learned most about in my journey is the continuing desperation of patients and families struggling with the cruelest diseases that afflict mankind. Their stories tear at my heart because I've been there, I've felt some of what they've felt (and some that they haven't), and I will not forget the pain. Granted, time has smoothed some of the jagged edges of my memory, but I shall not forget the experience of being mentally ill. Regardless, I like to believe that I have developed a healthy and professional balance in providing the best of psychiatric and professional care with the unique understanding that only someone who has been there can have.

And I continue to believe in miracles.

Carol S. North, M.D., M.P.E., is assistant professor of psychiatry at Washington University in St. Louis, Missouri, director of the psychiatry consultation liaison service, and author of Welcome, Silence *(Simon & Schuster, 1987).*

Chapter 29
Some Negative Consequences of Self-Disclosure
Barbara

I moved to the southeast of the United States in 1984 as a result of my husband's military transfer. I am 37 years old and my native country is Germany. I received my first degree in social work from a Catholic college in Mainz, Germany in 1982. During my studies I focused on early childhood development and special education. I received my second degree in social work from a state college (B.S.W.) in 1992. The second degree became necessary because I experienced problems with the academic acknowledgment of a German degree in the United States.

Among many areas of social work, I have always been very much attracted to the mental health field. Part of my interest in mental health stems from my own vulnerabilities. Since my very early childhood I have been suffering from depression. This resulted from a history of abuse and frequent hospitalizations related to a medical condition. However, it wasn't until 1989 that I was first diagnosed with major depression. Since that time I have had several recurrences that have made a normal and active life difficult. Helpful in the treatment of my depression have been an understanding psychiatrist and medication (the new selective serotonin reuptake inhibitors).

Nearing the end of my senior year working on my second social work degree, I considered myself very fortunate to be able to do my six month internship in a local state mental hospital. I worked with two other social workers on an admissions unit where I had contact with people who had various mental illnesses and who came from different walks of life. I enjoyed the process of learning the social work trade in the setting of a psychiatric hospital and built a good relationship with the patients. At that time I felt that the staff was responding adequately to their needs, although I was a little disturbed by comments of the psychologists who would negate patients' feelings and portray them as basically incorrigibles.

After my graduation, I continued to work at the state mental hospital, this time on a long-term care unit. Patients on this unit had been there for years and were less functional than those on the admissions unit. I was the only social worker on this unit and had about 40 patients. My primary duties consisted of finding placements for them once they were well enough to be discharged into the community. I was also a multidisciplinary team member and linked patients and families to outside agencies and other resources. In addition, I provided crisis intervention, education, and counseling.

Soon after I began to work on this unit I noticed that these long-term patients were not being equally treated by the staff. In fact, a lot of the statements that they made were discounted. They were often accused of faking their symptoms, always wanting attention, and wanting to stay at the hospital. One patient experienced daily catatonic, seizure-like states in which her eyes rolled up in her head. Nevertheless, she was accused by the nursing staff of giving an academy performance and faking her severe seizures. After much insistence on my part, a neurologist saw her and changed her medication, after which her condition improved considerably. Occasionally some of our female patients—diagnosed as mentally retarded—were taken advantage of in a sexual manner by other patients. Most often, however, incidents like these were not taken very seriously by the staff. On the contrary, these victims of sexual aggression were portrayed as being promiscuous and to have liked it anyway. They did not receive the emotional support that they needed and were left to cope with these events alone.

While I was working on this unit, I was battling severe bouts of depression that occurred about 3 to 4 times per year. Depression for me means intense feelings of mental pain, the need to isolate, low energy, and bouts of crying. Being in such a state I often prayed that no one would ask me any questions and I spent many hours lying on the floor in my office. However, I had to maintain a facade, to act in a professional and socially acceptable manner. The need to be normal often put me in a difficult position because I was afraid that someone would find out how worried I was that I would not be able to do my job anymore. I reached an especially low point in June 1994, when I realized that I could not handle another day of work. I consulted my psychiatrist who prescribed two weeks of sick leave. When I told my superior about the urgent necessity for me to go on sick leave, she had to let me go, but she did convey to me (nonverbally) that she felt depression was not a valid reason to abandon work.

I decided to take the risk and to disclose my struggle with depression after I returned to work. For one thing, it would explain my sudden and mysterious absence and for another, I was now feeling better and stronger. Although I had been aware for some time that patients with mental illnesses were not regarded as equal partners in treatment at this hospital, I felt that as a staff member I could set a good example and function as a role model for them. As a matter of fact, I expected support and encouragement from the staff. What better place to get it than by working in a psychiatric hospital?

However, my decision to disclose my illness to some of my co-workers proved to be irreversible and a major mistake. Instead of being considered as a team member with valuable insight, I began to be regarded with suspicion and as a bothersome cog in the wheel of daily hospital administration — especially because I had been and still am a strong advocate of patients' rights. My own status as a patient made it easier to empathize with the needs of the patients on a daily basis.

When I made my decision to disclose, I had not anticipated the material for gossip that I would provide. Often when I stated an unpopular opinion or made a legitimate complaint, I was accused of being delusional and even of hearing voices, although this has never been a part of my condition. Needless to say, none of these accusations were openly addressed and discussed with me. Not even by my supervisor.

Without doubt, this stressful environment was not very conducive to my mental health and I was transferred in October 1994 to another unit, this time a rehabilitation unit where I would have about 24 patients. The transfer was intended to be a fresh beginning and I was looking forward to a normal work environment. Indeed, during the first few weeks everything went well. The patients functioned on a higher level and most of them were able to ask for what they needed. I developed a good relationship with them. Very subtly, however, the old suspicious feelings toward me by the nursing staff returned. I began to overhear remarks regarding my mental condition, and once again I was being observed for signs of delusion or psychosis. In the meantime, I functioned as well as any other social worker at the hospital, without incidents.

On the unit I had some support from some of the male attendants who defended me against allegations. This, however, only made things worse. More gossip regarding my true intentions developed. My clothes were criticized and my friendliness toward the attendants became the subject of severe scrutiny. With regard to my mental disorder, an almost mass hysteria developed: staff pretended that they were afraid of me, locking doors in front of me and locking me out of community meetings. They also approached the nursing supervisor with complaints about my alleged behavior and mental condition. At no point did anybody at any managerial level discuss with me the freely circulating allegations and rumors. I approached my supervisor with reports about the treatment that I had received on the unit; she talked with the nursing supervisor but little changed. In fact my supervisor did not seem to be quite comfortable with the subject, especially as it related to my own depression. Things became so oppressive that I asked my psychiatrist to write a statement about my condition, including that I never heard voices or suffered from delusions. I then forwarded this statement to my supervisor, but I don't think that it achieved the desired effect. Eventually I felt that I had no other choice but to file an EEOC complaint.

This complaint is still on file. Since this official complaint, things have gotten better, but I am still trying to recover from my ordeal. One of the questions that I ask myself is why in a psychiatric hospital an employee with a mental disorder has to experience so many difficulties and so much suffering? One explanation that I have come up with is that people with mental illnesses are still considered as people of a different class and not as equals. I now regret that I have disclosed my struggle with depression to my co-workers and in retrospect I would not do it again. However, in my work with the psychiatric patients, I have found that my personal experience with mental illness has made me more sensitive and open to their needs. Despite their own illness, they in turn show understanding and empathy when I have a difficult day.

Barbara is a 37-year-old German social worker. She has lived in the southeast since 1984 and has worked since 1992 as a social worker in a state psychiatric hospital.

Chapter 30
Life in Time: A Personal Odyssey
David Gallagher

This is my story — a true account of my trials and tribulations. I am a consumer of mental health services who was diagnosed as manic depressive in 1978, and I am a professional social worker. I have never concealed this fact, nor do I wish to. There are some who say I walk around with a target on my back so that others may shoot arrows at me. Today I can say that's okay. By wearing a target, I know that I can help someone else and I am happy to do that. But it has not always been this way.

Background

I have a family history and, I believe, a predisposition to mental illness. My parents dealt with the suicide of my maternal grandfather when I was an infant. They were raised with a strong work ethic; they were a byproduct of an agrarian life style and then were thrust into an industrial revolution. My father raised us as practicing Roman Catholic. As a child I saw God as punitive and going to church as fire insurance to keep me from going to Hell. My parents' struggle to give their three boys the best material things in life robbed them of their serenity and ultimately produced a family of overachievers. Throughout their heartache and pain, they have tried to understand and cope to the best of their ability. And I love them for that.

My first experience with mental health professionals was when I was referred to a psychologist when I was ten years old, because I was incorrigible at school. Dr. H. was an interesting guy; we had fun with ink blot tests and other games. His words of wisdom still stick with me today. "If someone hits you, hit them back twice as hard and they'll never hit you again." Practicing this technique revealed that he had lied to me. That is one of the reasons that I am a social worker today, instead of a clinical psychologist. I have learned that conflict resolution is better; hence, "a soft tone breaks a bone." Loving your enemies and turning the other cheek produces better results in the long run.

By the age of fourteen I was trying to fulfill my internal need for love. Or as some would say, my co-dependent needs. I was quite active, my mind had racing thoughts, my body had uncontrollable urges. To control these emotions I turned to tobacco, alcohol, drugs, sex, and science fiction fantasies. It appeared to me that no one at school or at home seemed to notice or care. My grade point average was high, I was involved in school activities, I was working part-time, and I sang in the Christian minstrels. So to the outside world, I was a productive fourteen-year old who managed to conform to societal norms. Looking back at that lonely part of life, I remember a man who cared for me.

He was both my English and History instructor for two years. Mr. D. knew me well. He knew I smoked before class; he knew I was actively abusing drugs and alcohol, yet he did not condemn me. He befriended me. He nurtured me and told me about his college experiences and life in general. He and his wife took me to two operas. He tried to give me hope; he reached out to me, right where I was. For the first time in my life, I felt assurance on the inside. I had always presented confidence on the outside, but I could not control my emotions. Sadly though, he moved on and out of education altogether when I was about sixteen. By the time I graduated from high school, I was searching and seeking hope. I became more involved with science fiction fantasies, substance abuse, and paralogical thinking. My life had no plan. I was envious, materialistic and fearful of the future. At the age of eighteen, I wanted to marry my first love, but I was being prompted to "go to college and make something of myself." So off I went to Michigan State University with absolutely no idea what the college experience was all about. I had a three-hour orientation, and I was left to figure out the rest. Being alone with complete freedom, sometimes one makes bad choices. At the end of the year, I was on social probation, academic probation, and was asked to leave the University. I left Michigan State University with a 1.9 grade point average.

That summer I worked for Ford Motor Company, a lifestyle I did not enjoy, so I enrolled in Eastern Michigan University. Again, I had a three-hour orientation and was off to school. I knew that I liked money so I thought I'd take business administration. It was in my first introduction to business administration that I met my second mentor, an associate professor and Ph.D. candidate. I became his disciple. He helped me become involved with the Administration Management Society, the Dean's Board of the School of Business, and other prestigious positions and events. Concurrently, I joined a social fraternity. Soon I was active in everything. I was hypermanic, enjoying the attention, the power, the prestige. I was out of balance. "Power corrupts and absolute power corrupts absolutely." Ultimately, I was a runaway locomotive. My grade point average at Eastern dropped to a 2.39. My need to be important and accepted by others drove a wedge between my girlfriend and I. I could feel that I was losing her respect. Other people close to me were fearful of me. On November 15, 1977, my girlfriend was strong enough emotionally to identify my insanity, and stated that she could not take my power playing, manic behavior anymore.

The Role of the Psychiatric Patient

There were many precipitating psychosocial stressors leading to my first hospitalization, in February 1978. My substance abuse increased, I lost my part-time job, my funding sources dried up, my finals went poorly, and my parents decided that this would be an opportune time to practice tough love, which is a good concept when alternate supports are in place. I went to unemployment; I was turned down. I went to social services; I was turned down. I was physically, emotionally, socially, and spiritually bankrupt. And, in psychosis, I collapsed emotionally. I learned that when we cannot cross a threshold, we take that hurt and we hurt ourselves more.

From 1978 to 1980, I worked part-time at Kroger's and then I worked in the field of collections at a bank. I struggled to get back to school. I was fortunate that in 1980, Vocational Rehabilitations offered to sponsor me to go back to school. If I could complete two semesters at Schoolcraft Community College, then they would reevaluate the possibility of me finishing up my Bachelor's in Business Administration Degree. I was doing well; I had a good support system. I felt so good that I decided, against medical advice, that I did not need my Lithium or other neuroleptics. Within three months of discontinuation of my medication, I was hospitalized in a state institution for one of my longest periods ever. The years 1980 through 1985 involved a rapid succession of hospitalizations. I was put on Social Security Disability for approximately three years. I worked part-time at a Clark gas station. When I felt strong enough, I worked in a flower delivery business full-time. Then I went off Social Security Disability.

In 1985, a life-long friend, and now spiritual mentor, shared with me the good news that God was not a punitive dictator, but that he gives us a free will to choose between his world or negativity. I felt a peace that I never felt before. It was during that period that I made a decision to accept Jesus Christ's love for me and I started to play guitar at a mission in Detroit. Working with individuals who were homeless, I decided to be an advocate by becoming a social worker. The people I met that year had touched my heart.

Entry Into the Role of Professional

I formulated a plan, and started the process of getting admitted to a school of social work. I filed for financial aid and applied for guaranteed student loans. In my personal statement to the school of social work, I stated the reason for my desire to become a social worker was that I am a consumer and I wanted to help other consumers. I had two entrance interviews for admission to the Bachelor of Social Work program. I felt discriminated against in the verbal questions asked of me. I really wanted to be a social worker, so I accepted the situation and the decision made. I was to go through the College of Life Long Learning to seek admission, and take the Introduction to Social Work class as well as getting a recommendation from the professor. I took the class and received a 4.0 grade point average and the instructor sponsored my entrance into the program.

The university experience can be frustrating to the average person, let alone to a person who is perceived as different. I found in my personal situation that when I was open about my emotional recovery, many persons in academia were guarded, apprehensive, and at times obtrusive when it came to evaluating my ability to function as a student. It may be noted that during 1985 to 1990, when I attended Wayne State University, I was completely medically stabilized; I was not hospitalized during that period. I did find some supportive faculty at Wayne. One professor taught me the prevention model of social work. His visualization of society's need to "just quit taking the dead fish out of the end of the polluted stream and instead clean up the stream," sticks with me today. His teachings were in part responsible for the substance abuse prevention program I designed and implemented at William Dickerson Detention Facility through People's Community Services of Metropolitan Detroit. Another professor, who had sponsored my entrance into the Masters of Social Work Program, taught me the importance of trying to put on another person's moccasins to understand where a person has been before judging them. This is a good concept. I wish that all mental health professionals would practice this. I graduated from Wayne State University in 1989 with a Bachelors Degree in Social Work, and a grade point average of 3.18. Although I had significant support from the faculty, I felt that my ability to complete the Masters in Social Work program, due to my diagnosis, was in question when I was interviewed at the entrance conference to the program. The acceptance letter to the program actually meant more to me than the diploma I received for the Bachelor's program. I knew that all along, without a Masters Degree in Social Work, I could not be what I wanted to be. I felt that I would not be respected enough in the field to be heard on issues of advocacy.

The next year in the advanced standing program was like being in boot camp. I did not work; I lived off guaranteed student loans. I was totally immersed in social work, day in and day out. I knew that a failure at this level would devastate me. I also knew I could do all things through him who strengthens me (Phillipians 4:13.) That's when I met associate professor DPM. I could tell that he truly understood the pain of mental and physical disabilities. I saw that he devoted his life to helping people help themselves. Dr. M. taught me the importance of being eclectic; he taught me that if your only tool is a hammer, then every problem you encounter you'll probably beat to death. His visualization has spurred me on to this day to continue to weigh alternatives in the helping process. Professor H. was also instrumental during that year. I was having a difficult time in the psychodynamic course accepting Sigmund Freud's philosophies. As my field advisor, Dr. H. prompted me to research and explore Freud's work under the direction of a psychodynamic field instructor at Sinai Hospital. It was intense, to say the least. The little I did learn of psychodynamic therapy has taught me that it does not work in crisis intervention, or in short-term treatment, nor is it effective on a homeless, hungry individual who wants to work and needs to be stabilized medically.

It is important that we learn from the past, then let go of the past and allow healing. When a wound is infected, a doctor may cut it open and clean it out, put antiseptic on it, and then bandage it up. With the right environment and a little love, the wound should not have to be cut open again and again. If we do not learn from the past, we repeat the same mistakes in the future. Insanity is repeating the same mistakes and expecting a different result.

Graduating from the Masters Program in 1990 was one of the highlights of my life. I graduated with a 3.54 grade point average. I had a new girlfriend. My family showed complete acceptance for the first time in my life. I was interviewing all around the state for jobs. I was doing consultant work. I lacked humility. Once again, I tried being captain of my own ship. In my personal life, I was into the power play mode; I was of course, David E. Gallagher, M.S.W. I started to psychoanalyze my girlfriend; she was healthy enough to exit from my life for her own sanity. I was becoming hypermanic. I concealed my feelings from my psychiatrist, because I truly enjoyed having the illusion of complete control.

I was hired as coordinator of an assertive community treatment team at a community mental health agency. They were looking for someone who had organizational capabilities. In the interview process, I told the director I was being treated for manic depressive disorder when he asked me, " Is there anything you want to share about your personal life?" He hired me anyway. Life was great; I had a good job, a company car, good benefits. Boom, I started not sleeping! I did not tell my doctor. Eight business days after starting to work, I totaled the company car. I broke my collarbone and was in full-blown mania.

While I was in the psychiatric hospital, I received notice that I was fired. After recovering from the broken collarbone and thirty days in the hospital, I was hired by another community mental health agency. The clinical supervisor was truly happy to have me on staff because of my psychodynamic background at Sinai, which was also her orientation towards therapy. Soon after being hired, I confided in one of my coworkers that I was being treated for a bipolar condition. It got back to my clinical supervisor. She called me into her office and told me that she had heard that I was a consumer of mental health service and asked me if it was true. I said yes. She told me that due to the nature of my illness, it would be important that all the staff in our department know. She asked me to announce this at the next staff meeting. I told her no problem. So at the next staff meting, I explained the nature of my illness to approximately ten people, all professionals. Soon there were rumors that I was not doing my job. I had to sign a memo that I would not use scripture or give hugs to my clients. I still have that memo. I had found that this technique seemed to give some people hope. Soon, I was called into the clinical supervisor's office and told that someone had been listening in on my sessions and documenting my verbal confrontations. I was not using scriptures, I was not giving hugs, I was never late for work, I never took time off from work, all my paperwork was up to date. Six weeks after being hired, I was fired without cause.

I was hospitalized for depression. When I got out of the hospital, I was broke, depressed, and socially isolated. No one wanted to hire me, so I went to the Clark gas station, handed the manager my resume, told him that I could learn his computer cash register system and he hired me that day. It was a very humbling experience, but it paid some of the bills, brought up my self esteem and got me out of the apartment. I sent out over 200 resumes. Finally, I was hired part-time contractually at a private practice doing individual and family counseling. I continued to work at the Clark gas station. With both jobs, I was able to pay the rent, but I was having a difficult time paying my health insurance and medical bills. This continued for eight months.

I was hired at People's Community Services of metropolitan Detroit in 1991, to be a social group worker. Soon after, I became the supervisor for the Hamtramck programs. I was able to develop a social adjustment group at the consumer-run Northeast Drop-In Organization Center (NEDO). It was my pride and joy. Using the concepts of self-help, affirmation and empowerment from NEDO, I then developed the program and directed it at the detention facility.

A Consumer-Oriented Service Philosophy

My goal one day is to be an advocate for all consumers of mental health services. I enjoy counseling individuals and in some cases, individual therapy is very much needed. But I believe self-help alternatives are more productive. I was taught this by one professor: "Where do warriors go to cry?" The fact is they go to other warriors because no one else understands the pain. I am a member of a 12 step self-help group. I work the twelve steps on a daily basis. I have always recommended 12 step support groups both at NEDO and at the county jail, where I work. I have found the wisdom of shared experiences, fellowship, and spirituality helpful. I see members who work the program living happier, healthier lives. I believe accountability is needed and this can be found in having a home group to go to. There is equality in self-help support groups. Through the group process, you learn that if you're not in balance, recommendations may be offered. More importantly, I have found people who care about me and do understand where I have been.

When seeking a support group, you cannot just go once and form an opinion. Attend a support group a minimum of four times. If you do not like that one, go to another one. Most important is that we must not box ourselves in. As consumers, we isolate. Isolation is one of our biggest enemies. Today, I do not isolate. I belong to a gymnasium, a support group, an Al-Anon Club, and a church. I have found the importance of taking care of my physical needs, my health, my emotional needs; also the importance of 12-step programs, social needs, new friends, and spiritual needs. It is my opinion that without balance and accountability, we may lead a productive life for a while, but sooner or later, we will collapse.

Self-help alternatives are important, but they do not negate the need for medical compliance. The majority of my hospitalizations were due to the fact that either I did not communicate how I was feeling to my psychiatrist, or I did not take my medication as directed, or I just decided to discontinue it. Usually, when I discontinued my medications, it was because I felt healthy and I was in denial that I had a genetic predisposition to my medical condition, or I just felt that I did not trust the doctor.

I recognize that it is hard to tell every doctor your life history. I know that many times in the system one may get a new doctor every three months. I have found that I have had to take some responsibility for informing each new doctor what medications have or have not worked. For those of us who have a hard time expressing ourselves, it is important that we have an advocate or a family member that is very familiar with our medical history, to orient each doctor to what has or has not worked. I have found that many psychiatrists have their own orientation toward medication. Based only on a brief initial consultation, they give a prescription. This usually reflects the symptomology present in the client during the session and the last few progress notes on file. With a new doctor you may be anxious or nervous and not communicating what your feelings are and what is really going on in your life. You may get overmedicated with psychotropics, or if you're withdrawn and scared, you may get a prescription for anti-depressants. The concept of having an interdisciplinary team to identify pathological history, formulate a treatment plan, and review past medication history is important. However, the cost factors have limited its plausibility. Thus, in many places, the doctor alone reviews the chart, formulates an opinion, and writes a script. So, if a prescription is not agreeing with you, be assertive and communicate to your advocate or therapist. Some of us become passive-avoidant and allow discomfort until the next appointment which may be four to six weeks. With current medical technology, we have the capability of reaching most all of those who are diagnosed with a long-term mental illness. Sadly though, it is a matter of cost today.

It is my opinion that we have relied too heavily on the use of psychotropics and have not allowed consumers to work through the feelings associated with their symptomotology, which is often related to the basic need to be loved and to give love. All of us have the need to bond. All little children give love; unfortunately there may be a cycle of abuse which perpetuates a child's emotional hurt. In the awkwardness of searching to be somebody, sometimes bad choices are made. What is needed is acceptance. Love, affirmation, and attention heal. Rejection, negativity and hostility destroy. If our clinical services would adopt this simple model, recidivism would decrease. Instead, what I have seen in the profession is either newly graduated, high-tech, or know-it-all professionals who have no real knowledge base concerning those with severe mental illness besides what they have learned from the DSM or have read. On the other hand, we have the long-time, burned out professional who barely makes it through the day. In both cases, the focus is on the importance of paperwork, deadlines, and productivity. Unfortunately, the client suffers from issues of abandonment in the very system from which he or she is seeking help.

Consumer-controlled alternatives such as drop-in centers are important and need to be given more attention. It is unfortunate that we spend thousands of dollars on institutionalization and we neglect, understaff, and underpay workers at consumer-run drop-in centers. I have observed a fine drop-in center, Northeast Drop-In Center in Hamtramck, Michigan, for four years. The excellent staff of indigenous workers have devoted their lives to helping other consumers. It is shameful that they are forced to rent, at an extravagant rate, a dilapidated building, when all over the community there is property which could be developed into a quality operation. Just as the nonprofit organization which employs me did, right across the street from them, at minimal cost.

I was on medical leave in the fall of 1994 and as a consumer, I decided to visit other drop-in centers. No one knew me other than as a consumer. What I observed was understaffing, burn-out and apathy. It appeared to me that these centers were a congregation place for the homeless who utilized the facilities for warmth, coffee and in some cases peanut butter sandwiches. It also appeared to me that the consumers with chronic illnesses sat in the corners, isolated, as they do in the state institutions. I did see some volunteers from the community, but the outreach was limited. With proper support and staffing, increased emphasis on socialization and empowerment through social adjustment groups, every one of these drop-in centers could reduce recidivism rates. Another need in consumer-run drop-in centers is a quicker response time to crisis intervention by the sponsoring community mental health agency (CMH). When a client who is in crisis needs to be seen immediately, the CMH needs to recognize the recommendation of the consumer paraprofessional; either that, or put an MSW (preferably indigenous) at all locations. Or better yet, like more progressive community mental health agencies, provide complete services in locations readily available to the consumer, if need be in a satellite capacity.

Consumers, when given a chance, make excellent employees. The puritan work ethic is important to self esteem. SSI and SSDI are meant to be safety nets and are needed for individuals who suffer chronic disabilities. However, the limits set and enforced on the earnings under Social Security have made many consumers give up hope and lose their desire to work. Stigma experienced at any level of employment limits the applicant's ability to gain future work. While some of these stigmatizations are self-imposed by the way we present ourselves to prospective employers at the time of the interview, much of it comes from the employer's fear of the unknown. Prejudice hurts. We who are consumers are all geniuses who have been injured emotionally along the way. Responsibility, forgiveness and constant self-improvement are the answers. Anger can be a good motivator as long as one is not consumed by it.

I was taught the need to have goals and objectives, recognize barriers, and utilize resources. Keeping that perspective, I have experienced hope at every level. In 1987, I was very happy to work in a group home with individuals with developmental disabilities. Sure, it was only a part-time job at $4.65 an hour, but I knew that if I did the best I could, in 90 days I would get a ten cent raise, and I did. I also always had the hope of a full-time position with benefits. In 1988 and 1989, I truly enjoyed being a chore worker at $5.25 an hour. Quite frankly, that meant I cleaned toilets for the homebound senior citizens. But for me, it was an opportunity to learn about people. College may not be for everyone. The quest for knowledge, in whatever capacity, can be a stimulus for success. In my two years in private practice in the northern suburbs of Detroit,

I have worked with many successful individuals. Most of them have very limited scholastic credentials, but they all had one thing in common: they all failed, many times, they all kept on trying, and they all learned from their mistakes.

Today I continue to grow. I have taken an insight course on personal balance through life accountability, by Dr. Terry A. Lyles. I have found in my own life, that in the past, there usually have been two modes of operation: hyperspeed or immobilization. With medical compliance, and the proper support systems, I can achieve balance. I also know that as a consumer, I cannot use or abuse alcohol and drugs without repercussions. I am leading a successful life. I am learning that I am accountable; I am responsible and ultimately my security comes from a higher power, which is God. In my travels, which have included sixteen psychiatric hospitalizations, I have found a lot of pain. I have been abused physically and emotionally by attendants at two different state institutions; I have had my fingers and ribs broken by staff; I have had teeth busted out by patients, I have been sexually attacked by patients. I am happy to say that state institutions are now more closely monitored and recipient rights are being honored. I remember a period when if you filed a recipient rights complaint you were singled out or harassed by the staff. So no one filed recipient rights claims. Today we have advocacy groups to address these problems.

I no longer look at my illness as a debilitating situation, but rather as a medical condition. It has become the motivation and catalyst for my desire to help others to understand themselves. I have found that by helping others, I help myself. This journey can be lonely and sometimes just giving another person a smile may be what keeps them from giving up all hope. When we are smiling, we cannot be frowning. I tend to look up more now. When we're looking down all the time, we tend to miss the beauty in life. I am learning to view problems as opportunities. Today I have learned that we cannot depend on people, places or things for happiness. I have learned to quit hurting people, including myself. It is only by grace that I make it through the day, one day at a time.

Acknowledgments

I would like to give special acknowledgment to the medical doctors and the mental health professionals who have contributed to the stabilization of my condition. These professionals went beyond the call of duty and I am truly grateful to them for their compassion for myself and others. There is Dr. Elaine Meyendorf, M.D., whose pioneer work with Tegretol has helped many. Dr. Meyendorf's empathy and patience with me shined in a system where abuse was prevalent. There is Dr. Julie Elgas, M.D., who has been my internal medicine physician since 1980. Her coordination of efforts with all my psychiatrists through the years has been important to me. There is nurse Mary Roy, R.N., who spent many hours encouraging me from the year 1980, until she retired in 1988. There is Curt Vanderwall , MSW, CSW, Ph.D. candidate. He is the first clinician to understand my spirituality and relate to me using scriptural-based confrontation methods. He is also the first therapist to give love by sharing a hug. After many years of therapy, it was through his short-term treatment that I was able to work through and fully grieve earlier abandonment issues. There is Dr. Cecilla Farina, M.D. who has been my psychiatrist since 1989. Her diagnostic abilities and expertise in the latest technologies in medicine have been instrumental in giving me a new lease on life after experiencing neuroleptic malignant syndrome in 1994. There have been numerous paraprofessionals who have given me dignity and respect, sharing themselves during periods when I could not love myself.

I would like to give special thanks to both my brothers. My brother, Greg, has dedicated the last twenty years to being a mental health professional. He has reached countless thousands, directly and indirectly. His insight into the human psyche as well as his understanding of the need for advocacy has influenced the availability of least restrictive environments for consumers of mental health services. What I admire most in him is that he always knew the direction he was going. From the age of 14, he was reading *Psychology Today* magazine. He always kept focus on the fact that he wanted to help others through psychology. His faith in me gave me hope when I lacked all faith in myself. I love him for that; I love him for his strength and his courage. My younger brother, Leonard, has also been an encouragement to me. His past role as a consumer advocate combined with his doctoral training in neuropsychology has given him a unique perspective on recovery issues. I love him and I am encouraged to see him work through the trials and tribulations of his own life. Above everyone else, I would like to thank God, who has allowed me choices in life; He does not make junk. I have learned that He loves us all.

David Gallagher is a graduate social worker who practices as a mental health advocate involved in the promotion of consumer self-help options. His professional background includes substance abuse prevention, counseling and psychotherapy, and psychiatric rehabilitation.

Chapter 31

Four Perspectives on Mental Illness
Maggie Sweeney

Over the years, I have seen mental illness from four different perspectives. First, as a family member, later as a psychology student, then as a provider, and finally as a consumer. Up to now I have not met anyone with all four views. I believe this makes my experience unique.

Forewarnings

My first experience with mental illness occurred when I was quite young. My mother suffered from major depression. Although we never really talked about it, I was very aware of her condition. At times I was more tuned into her than anything else. My moods paralleled hers. If she was feeling well, I could relax. When she was moody, I was uptight. Somehow I felt I had to keep her together.

Looking back, my family believes that my older brother had Attention Deficit Disorder (ADD). He has never been formally diagnosed, but he was a difficult child and had a lot of characteristics that match ADD. Although he was very bright, he had a lot of problems in school.

Between my mother's illness and my brother's problems, our family was generally in trouble. My father, for reasons of his own, was unable to help with the family problems. In fact, he could not see that there were problems. My mother insisted that we go through family therapy, but she had to drag us the whole way.

During high school, I started having problems, but kept them to myself. I became "pre-suicidal." I wasn't about to act on my self-destructive thoughts, but the feelings were constant. While walking to school, I thought of being run over by a bus. I didn't think I would live past my teen-age years, although I didn't know what would do me in. I was doing well in my classes, so no one ever suspected that anything was wrong. I guess that's how I wanted it.

I hated my school, though. We had moved to a small town in central New York when I started 8th grade, and I never really adjusted. Family life was still difficult; my father lost his job teaching at a local college and my mother had to work, which she wasn't up to at the time. I knew that I was unhappy, but I thought things would get better if I could get away from the stress of my family and school. When I was in the 11th grade, I learned of a small liberal arts college that accepted students as freshmen after 10th and 11th grades. I was interested; it would get me away from both my high school and my family. This was my way out.

The Problems Deepen During College

I started at Simon's Rock College after 11th grade; my parents moved to Taiwan the year that I started college. In some ways I felt happy for the first time in a long time. Although enjoying my independence, I was still moody and had suicidal thoughts. I was in therapy off and on, and found it addictive, but not too helpful.

During this time, I also became interested in psychology and illicit drugs. Looking back I think I was "self-medicating" or trying to control my feelings with the drugs. I have heard some say that they are afraid of using drugs because they don't want to lose control. For me they had the opposite effect. My moods were normally out of control; with drugs I knew what to expect. It wasn't a healthy control, but most of the time it seemed better than nothing.

After two years at Simon's Rock, I earned an Associates Degree and transferred to Earlham College in Indiana. I continued to study and use drugs. I also made my first suicide attempt, and was told to start therapy at the local mental health clinic. My therapist focused primarily on my drug use, but I wasn't interested in quitting. She found this frustrating, and finally I told her my reason for doing drugs. I was becoming more actively suicidal; instead of thinking I would die, but not knowing how, I began to believe that I could kill myself if only I could "go crazy." The thought that drugs would make me crazy was my main motivation for doing them. My therapist found this to be an unusual reason (out of her league) and referred me to another psychologist. I did not make much progress with him either.

My studies continued, although it wasn't easy. I was terribly shy and unable to participate in class discussions. Having been this way my whole life, I accepted both the shyness and its consequences — discomfort in class due to pressure from professors and other students to speak, and, consequently, lower grades. I now believe that this debilitating shyness, which I inherited from my mother and may be perpetuated by others down the line, was my first symptom of mental illness. In 1987, I graduated from Earlham with a Bachelors of Arts Degree in Psychology. I then moved to Providence, RI and began working in the mental health field.

Entering the Workforce

My first job was in a school for people with severe behavior problems including autism. Many were very violent, both to themselves and to others; it was a rough job. The school used controversial behavior modification techniques and required staff to go through extensive training. It was very educational. At first the job was overwhelming, but also exciting. I decided early on that I would stay at this job until I learned it inside out. During the next three months, the job consumed my life. Because of its intensity, I could not stop thinking or even dreaming about it. I was tired of being beaten up everyday, and felt that I had mastered the job and therefore achieved my goal. I began looking for a new job.

Shortly afterward, I found a wonderful job at a group home for people with mental illness who had been institutionalized for 40 years and longer. A team of us opened the home and helped the six consumer-residents adjust to community life. I loved working with the staff and consumers, and continued to learn.

Officially Mentally Ill

Still suffering from extreme mood swings, I worked at the group home four days on and three days off. I had a lot of difficulty structuring my time off. Very often I got into trouble during the weekends. During one of my days off, I was drinking and took an overdose of medication. I must have become frightened because I called my psychotherapist. She was out of town, but her answering service was able to contact her. She made arrangements for me to be taken to an emergency room by a friend. I remember a woman at the emergency room becoming angry by what I had done. This was my first experience with this kind of stigma. Most medical staff don't understand what drives some people to self-destruction. Because they don't understand, they may react emotionally. Sometimes they perform unnecessary medical procedures in order to punish people, believing that this will prevent them from doing it again. I have been told, by a psychiatrist, that I have had my stomach pumped unnecessarily at least once.

After spending the night on suicide watch, I was transferred to the local pychiatric hospital. This was the first of 18 hospitalizations. Although I hated being locked up, I tried to look at my time in the hospital as an empathy lesson, the people I worked with in the group home had been locked up for most of their lives! What was one week out of my life? Now, like my clients, I was officially mentally ill. I probably had been given a label or two, but I didn't know which ones. I didn't tell people at work what had happened. When I returned to work, I had lost weight and was pale. My co-workers assumed I had been physically ill and I let them believe that.

After working for a year at the group home, I was interested in moving up, and took a job at a city mental health center as a case manager. I worked intensively with mental health consumers who lived in their own homes. My job was to help them live as independently as possible, and to advocate for the rights of the consumers I served. It was interesting, but stressful.

I also started taking graduate social work classes at a local college. The classes were enjoyable, but I was still finding it impossible to participate in class discussions. I knew that in order to advance in the mental health field I would have to continue my education. My application to the Boston University of Social Work was accepted and I was thrilled. My recommendations from supervisors were excellent, which meant a lot to me.

Unfortunately, I was still quite ill. I had many short hospitalizations. This was especially hard on me because the clients of the center where I worked were treated at the same hospital when they became acutely ill. I would run into them and the center's psychiatrists who treated them and worked with me. I was constantly hiding from them. One day another patient approached me and told me that she had worked at the same center. She told me that I had as much right to be in the hospital as anyone else and not to be ashamed. I stopped hiding.

Encountering Stigma

After many prolonged absences, my employers wanted to know the nature of my illness. I told them that I suffered from mental illness. From that time on they treated me differently. They had taught me not to discriminate against people with mental illness, and to advocate for their rights. But I was learning from these very people that the same attitudes didn't apply to me. Fear that mental illness could affect one of them seemed to poison their feelings toward me. It became more and more difficult for me to work in this environment. My school work suffered, I found it difficult to concentrate, and I became unable to read. After what seemed like the millionth hospitalization, I quit working and started collecting temporary disability. I tried to continue with school, but found it impossible. My professors were very understanding. They encouraged me to keep at it, despite my illness and offered me additional support, but by then I was too sick to continue. I went from reading professional journal articles to children's books; I had always been a reader and couldn't give it up all together.

Retreat Back to Family

My struggle continued. I tried many psychotropic medications — anti-depressants, anti-psychotics, anti-anxiety drugs—receiving only brief relief. I was hospitalized frequently. My family, now living in Pennsylvania, was very concerned and pressured me to move back with them. Unwilling to lose my independence, I fought this idea. I didn't want to live with my family the way I remembered them from high school. Finally the money ran out, and I had little choice but to return home.

A New Viewpoint

Things at home weren't as difficult as I expected. My parents had grown over the years — we had all changed. I started receiving Social Security Disability. My biggest problem was finding things to do. I slept a lot and played games with my parents. The highlight of my week was seeing my psychologist. This was no kind of life and I knew it. Although living at home was okay, life in general was not, and again I was hospitalized.

In the hospital, I was visited by my minister who told me to look at my illness in a different way. He said I should not say "I am mentally ill," but rather "I have a mental illness." Being mentally ill was not all that I was, I was a person first. No one says "I am cancer," they say "I have cancer." He also told me about a mental health consumer-run drop-in center called Involved Consumer Action Network (ICAN) in Lancaster. The first time I went, he was there to meet me. The atmosphere was casual so I didn't worry about trying to impress people. It was nice to have a place to go, to spend time with people my own age who understood mental illness. In the beginning I just hung out, which was plenty. I made some friends. I had somewhere to go. Gradually I became more involved. After about 6 months, I was elected to the Board of Directors and became the Executive Secretary. I also began writing ICAN's monthly newsletter and was grateful for the added responsibility. I didn't always feel well, but the flexibility of the job enabled me to work when I could and take time off when I needed to. I think this was critical to my success at work. After a year of being an ICAN member and six months of being on the Board, I learned that ICAN was in need of a director. After not working for so long, I was frightened to enter the work force. However, ICAN was offering me a chance to work in my chosen field, and have the support and flexibility I needed to be successful. I was also free of the discrimination I experienced in the work force previously. In the past, employers were not sympathetic to my mental health issues and, in fact, they added so much stress that I could not continue. I was told by a previous employer and those treating me, that I should get out of the mental health field. They felt that such work made my condition worse. No one seemed to understand that I loved working with people with mental illness. It wasn't just any career choice; I felt I had a calling of sorts. The offer from ICAN was an opportunity I could not pass up. I applied for the position and was hired.

Turnabout

Working at ICAN has been a wonderful growth experience. For three years I had been able to find jobs, but unable to keep them. Employment at ICAN has been one of the most important aspects of my recovery. I have structure to my days. It is a very positive place for me to be. I am very independent, yet I am never alone. I still get sick at times, but the job is flexible, and I can ask someone else to work if I need time off. I am able to be open about my illness, instead of keeping it hidden as I had to in the past. Sometimes I wonder what it would have been like if I had been able to acknowledge my illness to the consumers I serviced previously. I think it would have been very positive for them to see that even providers get sick. I think it would have been good for me as well, I wouldn't have had to make such an effort to hide my feelings. This effort only made things more difficult. All of this has been vital to my recovery.

I feel that ICAN offers a positive and unique way for people with mental illness to recover and grow. At ICAN, members are not subject to the stigma that they may feel in the community in general, or even within the mental health system. They get support from others going through the experience of mental illness and dealing with the mental health system.

At ICAN, members are invited to participate at whatever level they are able. Some just rest or smoke cigarettes; others come to particular groups. As our members have said, ICAN is a place to make friends and socialize, it prevents isolation, and provides a stepping stone for people on the road of social and vocational rehabilitation. It has certainly been a stepping stone for me and for others who have become active volunteers, board members, and employees.

Between ICAN, therapy, and a new medication that really works (Clozaril), I have stayed out of the hospital for two years; this is a record for me. I have also lost all interest in illegal drugs, including alcohol. During this time, I have become stronger in ways I never dreamed possible. Because of Clozaril I am able to communicate better, and I am not so trapped within myself. After a lifetime of self-imposed seclusion, I can meet the world half-way. I now speak about my experience with mental illness and the mental health system to large groups of people. For me this is nothing short of a miracle. I have been able to find benefits in having a disability: benefits that I can put to use at ICAN and elsewhere in the community. I am more able to help others with mental illness here in an atmosphere where I can be open about my experience. It is no longer something I have to hide. I have come out to people in other areas of my life. This helps reduce stigma. People see that I don't look mentally ill (whatever that means). They start to see that persons with mental illness are not frightening, although they may be different in some ways. Frequently people will tell me of emotional problems that they or their loved ones have had. I know that it is my openness that has made them able to talk; they seem relieved to have this outlet.

Living with Mental Illness

When people ask how I manage to live with mental illness, I tell them you first need to figure out what your limitations are. You must learn to accept your limitations and live within them. A lot of people with a mental illness are ashamed that they can't do everything that they perceive others as being able to do. I tell them that everyone has limitations. No one expects someone who is blind to get a job driving a taxi. There is no shame in that. It may be harder to figure out limitations with a psychiatric disability because it is not so visible, but it can be done. Personally I need independence and flexibility. I also don't like to be alone. At ICAN these needs are met. Being able to work successfully is helping me to grow as well. I see every crisis or difficult person or issue as something that will help me grow; during the past few years I have grown a lot. Every step up the ladder of recovery makes me more able to keep climbing, but nobody starts at the top. Now, after a year and a half as director at ICAN, I am ready to continue my education where I left off. Success in that area will strengthen me more, making me more able to climb.

Conclusion

ICAN offers benefits to the general community, as well. We provide referrals to people new to the system; relief time for family and significant others at home; and help to eliminate stigma, reduce hospitalizations, and save tax dollars.

Being the director of ICAN has enabled me to do more about mental illness than I could as a case manager. I am now out of the closet about my mental health issues; the members know this and I am their equal. As a case manager, this would not be possible; I would have to keep my mental health issues a secret. Being open engenders a trust which is hard to build across a desk separating case manager and client.

The journey from family member, to student, to provider, and finally consumer has been long and arduous. However, these issues make me uniquely qualified to work with those suffering from mental illness. ICAN members know I have been through their hell, they know that I have a perspective on their work that non-consumer providers will never have.

Maggie Sweeney is the director of the Involved Consumer Action Network (ICAN), a mental health consumer-run drop-in center in Lancaster, PA.

SECTION 7

**Organizational
Issues**

Introduction to Section 7: Organizational Issues

The chapters composing this section examine organizational and programmatic issues pertaining to the success of consumers as providers. Together the chapters underscore the changing relationships among and between consumers and professionals in the quest to expand service delivery options available to people with serious mental illness. The chapters demonstrate that a serious commitment to making consumer service provision occur successfully and effectively is not easy. Choosing this pathway for expanding service options presents numerous challenges: trying different alternatives when one programmatic approach does not succeed (Hilderbrand and colleagues), working through role relationships within interdisciplinary teams that expand to include consumers as providers (Miya and colleagues), positioning a consumer-run alternative to be financially viable (Solomon and colleagues), and transitioning an organization from one form of consumer service provision (i.e., self help) to another (i.e., consumer controlled service).

What is remarkable about this section is the hope offered to others who are venturing down this path, and to those who are actively involved in fostering the development and/or transition of such programs. These authors illustrate the critical decisions they have made to strengthen or foster the success of their programs, and the challenges they met to implement the required changes to achieve success. These chapters constitute an "evolutionary" agenda for consumer service provision. They demonstrate that success of these programmatic alternatives evolves over time, and in different contexts, and that the contexts themselves are important to promoting success.

The first two papers in this section share a similar focus on the importance of defining consumer and professional roles within consumer service provision. They underscore the need to invest considerable effort in packaging these roles in a manner that works for consumer service providers. An important theme in these two papers is that roles should not be construed as "us versus them," to quote Hilderbrand and colleague. Professionals working with consumer providers cannot see themselves as separate and radically different from their new colleagues. Likewise, consumer providers working with professionals or with their peers cannot separate themselves into distinct reference groups that follow their own priorities, or that shape their own sense of reality. For Miya et al., role perception becomes very important, and perhaps these authors get to the crux of the organizational issue: how can individuals who hold different perspectives (formed by different organizational positions, roles, and "realities") shift paradigms and create a new collective reality?

Indeed, Miya et al. assert that for consumer service provision to be successful within the context of established mental health treatment or clinical systems, new roles and new realities must be created. This, from our perspective, is the essence of interdisciplinary or transdisciplinary practice. Participants within these new structures must abandon old conceptions of role. For professionals, this means interaction with consumers as empowered individuals with valuable knowledge to share about treatment and rehabilitation. This means that professionals legitimize the important perspective consumers hold about treatment and rehabilitation systems. It requires professionals to move beyond relating to their new colleagues as former patients.

For some consumers, it may mean giving up the sick role, or the view that the system is evil. It requires consumer providers to respect the skills and abilities of their new colleagues. For both stakeholder groups, the "organizational or systems change" demanded by successful consumer service provision lies in the ability to define and blend new roles into new ways of delivering mental health services.

These two chapters also highlight the promise and pitfalls of blending roles. On the negative side, roles for consumer providers can become ambiguous, and characterized by strain and conflict. New roles held by consumers as providers do not fit well with roles still held by their peers (Hilderbrand et al.), and consumers may be very confused as to how to act, and how to help. Alternatively, consumers need to blend their ways of knowing and helping with professionals who are struggling with relating to them in new positions, as providers rather than as recipients (Miya et al.). This successful blending is fundamental to team development and to good team performance. Fortunately, we receive some excellent guidance from the authors of both chapters. What is significant to note here is that these authors identify the importance of role modeling. All of us must be conscious of the fact that we are demonstrating new ways of relating to one another, and these behaviors serve as models for others seeking to negotiate the role changes demanded by consumer service provision.

Organizational transitions are the substantive focus of the next two chapters. Both of these chapters remind us that consumer service alternatives are not static entities, but like other mental health and relationship alternatives they must evolve in order to remain viable. The chapter by Solomon et al. identifies the importance of resource viability for a program, and underscores just how fraught with issues this area can be for consumer providers. The chapter by Levin also addresses viability, and describes the transition Project Return needed to negotiate in order to sustain itself as an on-going community support system with its own mission and identity.

Both of these chapters describe and analyze many changes that are needed organizationally, programmatically, and technically in order to remain viable. For the initiative described by Solomon et al., this meant gaining support for financial independence from other agencies, making adjustments in service provision to comply with Medicaid regulations, shifting qualifications of key positions, and upgrading information technology to support documentation and billing. For the initiative described by Levin, this meant making the decision to become consumer controlled, staffing as a consumer controlled organization, creating an internal organizational structure, reinvigorating membership, and developing committed staff leaders.

These chapters also suggest that the human resource development system in which consumer service provision unfolds cannot be ignored, and must receive attention from program developers and administrators, during program design and implementation. It is imperative to remember that a mental health or rehabilitation system is not merely recruiting consumer providers to serve people with serious mental illness in more innovative or cost effective ways. Involvement in these new roles produces major implications for the consumers filling them — implications for self image, self concept, career, and employment. Failing to consider the nature of these positions and, most importantly, the match between consumers and the jobs to be done will likely derail the initiative, a possibility Hilderbrand et al., and Levin identify in their chapters. Of course other human resource development issues will emerge, including issues pertaining to career advancement, professional development, skill acquisition, comparable pay, and status. All of these human resource development issues must be considered by the progressive organization committed not only to making consumer service provision work but also to fostering consumer leadership within an expanding matrix of innovative supports and opportunities for people with serious mental illness.

These four chapters all share a common focus on change. Consumer service provision highlights important issues any organization committed to fostering involvement of consumers in new structures and in new roles must negotiate and ultimately resolve in a productive manner. The content of these papers reflects the complexity of the challenge. Change, however, can be brought about in effective and meaningful ways, provided that the organization is committed to succeed in its change efforts, and provided that consumers are meaningfully involved and taken seriously.

Chapter 32

Try Another Way: Transitioning Peer Support Specialists to Roles as Social and Recreational Support Providers

Kim Hilderbrand
Lisa Jardine
Pam McVay
Sandra O'Dell
Pat Zurek

"Progress is impossible without change; and those who cannot change their minds cannot change anything."

—George Bernard Shaw

Adaptation to change has been the essence of our success in utilizing consumers as peer support specialists. We recount our experiences with the programs: the ways in which we identified obstacles, responded to the challenges that resulted, and made the necessary changes to turn the obstacles into positive experiences.

Background

Child and Family Services of Southwestern Michigan, Inc. (CFS) is a private, nonprofit agency providing contractual services to Riverwood Community Mental Health, located in Berrien County, Michigan. One contractual service that Child and Family Services provides is the Supported Independence Program (SIP) which provides individually tailored training in living skills and housing support services to mental health consumers. The supported independence program employs life skills consultants (LSCs) to assist consumers in locating housing and to provide life skills training. Life skills training consists of any activity that will assist consumers in becoming independent. For example, a life skills consultant might help a consumer learn to prepare a simple meal, budget funds, shop, clean and perform other general home maintenance tasks. The program provides a bridge for consumers from more restrictive living situations to independent living.

In 1991, Child and Family Services received a grant from the Michigan Department of Mental Health to supply the necessary funds for security deposits and the first month's rent to any homeless mentally ill person in Berrien County. In 1992, the contract coordinator of the Special Populations Unit visited the Supported Independence Program and observed a life skills consultant (LSC) with a consumer. She was struck by the rapport that was apparent between the LSC and the consumer and could not identify which was the professional and which was the consumer. From that, the contracts coordinator decided to provide funding to begin a pilot project that would employ consumers as life skills consultant aides, also identified as peer support specialists (PSS).

Program Initiation

Child and Family Services decided to approach an already existing prevocational and vocational training program, Crossroads, a psychosocial rehabilitation/clubhouse, which is operated by the community mental health center. Collaboration between the two agencies occurred as Crossroads was enlisted to assist with the recruitment, hiring, and training of consumers to be employed as peer support specialists.

Crossroads began providing potential applicants to begin the interview process. The peer support specialist positions were posted at Crossroads and members of the Crossroads program applied. Applicants were pre-screened by Crossroads based on their performance at the Crossroads program, ability to interact well with fellow members, and their general interest in working in this type of position. As soon as Child and Family Services received applications, interviewing began, involving the supervisor of the SIP and the life skills consultants.

The peer support specialist position was designed to provide assistance to life skills consultants. Peer support specialists were paired with life skills consultants whose consumers would most likely respond to their peers. PSSs were to assist consumers to develop skills in household maintenance as well as other household organizational tasks, such as grocery shopping. Additionally, peer support specialists could provide social outlets for some consumers who were too shy to attend social events or were isolated or withdrawn. Thus, a peer support specialist might take a consumer out for coffee and just chit-chat. The peer support specialist's duties were identified on an individual basis depending upon the goals of the respective consumer. Other duties included completing paperwork which outlined what goals were being addressed and any activities that related to these goals.

Peer support specialists received $4.25 per hour for face to face contact with consumers, phone contacts, and scheduled meetings/activities within the agency. As part of the fringe benefit package, the peer support specialist received pro-rated vacation, sick and holiday time as well as mileage reimbursement.

Initially, Child and Family Services hired two persons. One job requirement of the peer support specialist was to attend an employability skills training course that was tailored specifically for the PSS positions. Crossroads provided job coaching too and was available to the peer support specialists directly before or after an activity (somewhat different from traditional use of job coaches because of the nature of the client contact, confidentiality, etc.). Life skills consultants assigned various duties to the peer support specialists and provided training with regard to paperwork, activity selection and goal completion.

Within the first year of this pilot project, an additional consumer was hired as a peer support specialist, totaling two males and one female. Each PSS presented different skills which contributed diverse and unique input to this program. For example, one peer support specialist was very skilled at developing rapport with consumers, while another was more skilled at providing direction regarding household maintenance activities.

Challenges

As the program progressed, problems emerged. Peer support specialists began challenging and testing authority. It seemed that they felt because of their own personal experiences with mental illness, they had a better understanding of the issues involved and began giving advice to their clients. The LSCs felt that the peer support specialists were overstepping their boundaries. A feeling of "us vs. them" began to permeate the team, where peer support specialists and life skills consultants were each bringing complaints to the supervisor regarding each other's activities. Peer support specialists were sharing negative feedback with Crossroads regarding Child and Family Services, stating that Child and Family Services was being unfair to them.

The entire pilot program seemed out of control because of these conflicts. One peer support specialist advised one of her clients to stop taking medication and acted as if she were a case manager, doctor, and therapist. As the minor problems grew, evaluation of the pilot project became necessary. A decision regarding future direction was needed. Due to these problems, the entire group (Child and Family Services, Crossroads and Peer Support Specialists) met to brainstorm regarding the source and nature of the difficulties. After several meetings and discussions, systemic issues were identified. The difficulties that surfaced were not necessarily because of individual peer support specialists, but more because of the challenges all were facing with this new and unchartered territory "consumers working with consumers." The following systemic issues were identified.

Lack of Communication

Brainstorming sessions revealed communication problems between the PSSs and the supervisors. The first question that the peer support specialists had was: "Who is my supervisor?" Indeed, PSS's were responding to Crossroads staff, Child and Family Services staff, consumers and life skills consultants. Also, Crossroads and Child and Family Services were taking information at face value and not exploring with each other some of the difficulties. To remedy this problem, we decided to have a supervisory team, which included the Crossroads manager, Crossroads vocational coordinator and the supervisor of the Supported Independence Program. We were to meet weekly with the peer support specialists.

Another communication barrier was the indirect pressure we placed on the peer support specialists to be successful. Because this program was funded by the Department of Mental Health, constant evaluation and scrutiny occurred. Subtle messages were sent to the peer support specialists that success was imperative. Peer support specialists subsequently felt uncomfortable communicating their stresses, difficulties, and fears. At a time when we were all experiencing something new, there should have been constant communication regarding problems. Additionally, the PSSs were being evaluated by supervisors as well as by the consumers with whom they worked. They did not have a forum to share their perspectives or to evaluate their own experiences.

One PSS was evaluated after six months and received a positive evaluation. He left town immediately thereafter. When we talked to him about this recently, he stated that he felt too much pressure to succeed and felt that there was only one way to go — "down." He also said that he was no longer interested in this type of employment — he wanted to work in a restaurant but could find no easy way out. Thus, he felt his only avenue was to escape to another state.

Finally, there was the lack of clarity regarding the peer support specialist's job description and guidelines. We developed policies and guidelines when things went wrong instead of being more proactive and preventive. This caused a great deal of confusion and anger among the peer support specialists as they did not know what was acceptable or unacceptable. Without specific guidelines in place and due to lack of unity among the supervisory team, peer support specialists received contradictory information. Decisions were made in response to crises that often seemed dogmatic and punitive to the peer support specialists. This occurred more often than not as the team attempted to get more control over problems that had escalated, in turn causing the peer support specialists to feel isolated. This in turn contributed to another major systemic problem — lack of consumer involvement.

Lack of Consumer Involvement

When the pilot project was first proposed to this county, many professionals became involved in the initial planning. In retrospect, it seems that the first step might have been to include consumers in the planning process. This may have eliminated some of the problems that occurred throughout the course of the first year. Because of the lack of consumer involvement, a message was sent that the input of consumers was not valuable. Consequently, we developed a program to hire consumers but did not include them in the process — a contradictory message at the very least. Even more than that, we did not utilize peer support specialists to provide input to problems that were occurring.

This type of program must have consumers involved from the beginning, otherwise it will simply be a token effort to employ consumers. We need to "walk the talk." Upon reflection, it is doubtful that consumers felt empowered. A participatory style of management would have led to involvement of personnel and recipients of services at all levels and increased ownership of the program — both its successes and its failures.

Lack of Collaboration

Initially, interagency collaboration consisted of Child and Family Services providing supervision of the PSSs and Crossroads providing the applicants. This left Child and Family Services' staff alone in all areas of guidance and left Crossroads out of the loop once a consumer was hired. The success of Crossroads' employment program has been based on the provision of job coaching, follow-along support services, and participation in clubhouse activities. These services were not utilized in PSS employment, creating a gap. We realized that only limited supervision was being provided. It was not surprising that the peer support specialists began to experience problems with boundary issues. Upon examination, we determined that these issues might have been prevented if there had been more intensive and collaborative supervision. Engaging in collaborative efforts would also have been beneficial to avoid the next major challenge.

Lack of Boundary Determination

Boundary issues materialized as the lack of clear guidelines gave way to confusion. First, the peer support specialist position was too closely aligned with that of the life skills consultant. The peer support specialists were essentially providing the same services as the LSCs, but were in a position where they were directed by them. The positions, although similar in duties, differed in levels of pay, responsibility, authority, and status. The blurred boundaries between them caused a lot of dissension among the group.

As previously discussed, the peer support specialists were frustrated and an "us vs. them" attitude became apparent. While it is true that the PSSs did have a better understanding of the difficulties that consumers faced, this identification with their peers sometimes led to lack of objectivity. That is, some of the peer support specialists so resonated with the issues that their peers were facing that they began to take these problems on as their own crusade. For example, one peer support specialist was about to terminate employment and encouraged the consumer he was working with to quit his own job.

Furthermore, the rapport between PSS and a consumer at times became problematic when the PSSs were not sure whether to befriend their clients or provide services. At one point, a PSS did both and it became difficult to separate friendly vs. professional advice, e.g. when a PSS told a consumer they could stop their medication. The strength of the project, "consumer working with consumer," became its weakness. The peer support specialist position did not have much structure to begin with and lacked a clear definition of job duties.

If these areas are addressed prior to hiring PSSs, it is conceivable that they could be counselors or life skills consultants. However, the PSSs would require the same education/training as those who are currently providing this service. They should also have the same job description as a counselor and be bound by the same code of ethics and agency policy. The difficulties appear to lie in the PSSs providing a similar service without role definition but with similar expectations.

Making Positive Changes After Identifying Problem Areas

A consumer satisfaction survey was given to those who received services previously from PSSs. The results of the survey provided clues regarding what worked and what did not work for the consumers receiving services. Overwhelmingly, consumers appreciated the support of the PSS in decreasing isolation by providing social/recreational activities. They seemed less comfortable with intensive, one-on-one interaction.

PSSs also communicated similar feedback. First, peer support specialists seem to do their best work when with a group of consumers focusing on social interactions, i.e., going to the mall, having picnics or dinners at apartments, or attending concerts. One PSS stated that the social activities "drew people out, they really laughed and had a good time and they looked forward to seeing us. The group decided what you were going to do when you got there. Consumers said things like, 'If it wasn't for you I would have never got to do this.'"

Peer support specialists were not only providing a needed activity, they were also reaching a larger group of people. At the same time, the life skills consultants were concerned with the lack of recreational/social activity in the lives of the consumers who were now living in apartments. At Crossroads, there was a need to have more evening and weekend recreational/social activities, but the program was hard-pressed to provide them because the staff was unionized and would not be able to work such hours.

After a series of meetings with all involved parties and the distribution of the consumer satisfaction survey, we realized that there needed to be changes and shifts in the peer support specialist positions. After careful consideration, the team decided to draw on the strengths of the previous peer support specialist position and meet a crucial need among the consumers in the mental health system. At the time, there was one PSS who was still working. We involved her in the redirection of services. At first, she was very hesitant but as she embraced the idea, she became excited and made contributions. We contacted consumers and obtained feedback regarding their desires and needs.

We needed to clearly identify what type of program this would be, who we would serve, and develop a job description. The title "peer support specialist" remained the same but the job changed drastically. To avoid pitfalls experienced in the first PSS position, the team needed to ensure that job duties, job descriptions, program design, etc. would be clear and concise. Guidelines for transportation, planning activities, number of activities needed per month and other issues were all discussed and included in a procedures manual. This has given the peer support specialists and the supervisory team a sense of direction, structure and solidarity.

Implementation

Upon developing the guidelines and structure, we decided that it was time to implement the program. The first order of business was marketing. Fliers were developed and mailed to all recipients of the Child and Family Services Supported Independence Program as well as to all Crossroads members. Announcements and posters were distributed throughout the Crossroads Clubhouse; case managers and other agency staff were notified. Next, the peer support specialists decided to have a contest to name the new program. "Ventures" was the name chosen. Some of the activities offered were: picnics, informal women's and men's groups, outings, beach activities, video evenings, bingo nights, etc. The variety was welcomed by consumers who participated in Ventures. Comments by the participants included: "I look forward to weekends," "I used to be all alone but now I have friends," "I have more self-confidence."

Initially, there was a great deal of concern regarding transportation for participants in this program, especially since the services would be offered during evening and weekend hours. Berrien County is somewhat rural and transportation is minimal. We decided to transport consumers the same way they are transported to Crossroads during the day — by agency vehicle. Riverwood agreed to provide the van and Child and Family Services was to hire and pay the driver. An additional consumer was hired as a peer support specialist whose primary duty was to transport consumers to and from events.

The Ventures program was implemented and it seemed as if things were running smoothly. However, the team was concerned that the activities being planned were not necessarily activities that consumers were interested in. The other concern was that the peer support specialist who organized the activities was not enjoying her new job responsibilities. She did not feel that she could plan activities that were cost effective or that consumers would attend. The team began to provide feedback that would assist the PSS in planning and organizing events. This helped, but it was clear that she was not enthused. At this time, an additional peer support specialist was hired to assist in planning and organizing activities. The driver and the two peer support specialists were to work together as a team. The new PSS had several ideas and was very excited about being employed with the Ventures program. He became frustrated as he was trying to get the program moving forward and the other PSS was saying "yes, but" to the new ideas.

We then had a difficult decision to make. After several attempts had been made to assist this PSS in correcting her work performance, we mutually agreed to her resignation. She appeared to be relieved and stated that she preferred working one-on-one with persons in their apartments and had difficulty adjusting to the changes that had occurred. Crossroads offered their assistance in helping her find alternate employment. She then began another PSS-type position —assisting elderly consumers in a structured day program.

This situation demonstrates that constant changes in a job can create stress for anyone. For someone who is reentering the work force, all of this change and ambiguity can create more upheaval than is necessary. That is why it is important to establish clear guidelines and job duties from the onset. When the original PSS moved on, two additional consumers were hired. There was an immediate difference in the way the PSSs felt and responded to their jobs. Because everyone was clear about job duties and responsibilities, there was open communication and all decisions were made with the PSSs; they never experienced many of the problems that occurred with the pilot project.

We then had three PSSs with one driver on staff. As Ventures continued to grow, the need for additional peer support specialists became evident in order to cover absences related to medical leaves, illnesses, and vacations. Staff was increased, so PSSs feel comfortable taking time off, knowing the program would continue to run smoothly. Turnover has occurred, but it has been minimal.

The Ventures team is now diverse and staff members bring their own special talents. One PSS is very knowledgeable regarding the computer and has developed a monthly social calendar, newsletter, and flyer. Another PSS has been involved in public relations and marketing.

PSSs have a suggestion box and regularly ask feedback from other consumers regarding activities. They are in the process of updating the consumer satisfaction survey to obtain feedback regarding Ventures on a quarterly basis. Much of their feedback occurs by "word of mouth" and the consumers who utilize this program have developed a trusting relationship with the PSSs.

The peer support specialists have a positive working relationship with the rest of the staff. They are now treated as staff and are equal members with a vital service to contribute. They work with limited supervision. We all meet weekly and review any issues, upcoming activities, changes, etc.

Implications

Ventures has doubled in size since its inception and is constantly growing and changing to better meet the needs of the recipients of services as well as to provide a positive experience where consumers work with consumers. The program has to be flexible. Without flexibility to change after evaluating what works and what does not work, we would all still be "spinning our wheels."

PSSs are receiving much more support than previously from co-workers and supervisors through the structure that we developed together on an ongoing basis. Also, the Ventures staff has worked with case managers to educate them regarding their jobs and have subsequently received their support.

The Ventures program has been successful for a variety of reasons. The peer support specialists state they feel more comfortable working in a social group as opposed to one-on-one, intensive interaction. Problematic boundary issues that were so prevalent in the initial position have all but been eliminated. Not only is there a clear job description, there is a new sense of commitment on the part of professionals to collaborate and communicate with the peer support specialists. A greater number of consumers are being served than ever before — over 70 consumers per month. Because Ventures is consumer-driven, there is camaraderie between the peer support specialists and consumers that is not present in other programs. The program has also been successful in providing normal social outlets for people which have increased their ability to remain in semi-independent or independent housing as well as creating an outlet for consumers who are working in the community during the day. The social outlet has increased job stability in that consumers are leading more balanced, full lives. In fact, the program has been so positive in the aforementioned areas, the community mental health center provided line item funds to maintain the program once the grant dollars ran out. Additionally, the local mental health employment task force is reviewing this concept and requesting expansion of this program to more consumers, including those with developmental disabilities.

Berrien County's history with the peer support specialist has provided many lessons for those who are endeavoring to implement such a program. First, there has been constant evaluation and reevaluation to restructure the approach to improve services. This restructuring has enabled us to develop clear guidelines while providing the Ventures team enough autonomy to be a consumer-driven program, designed and implemented based on the needs expressed by consumers. Second, it is at times difficult to work with more than one agency. However, Child and Family Services and Crossroads have pooled resources to work together and developed a relationship that works. Third, this program is distinct in that the design provides a social program run by consumers for other consumers. This has created employment opportunities for consumers as well as making a peer support service available. Due to the increased social supports, participants are now leading more stable, fulfilling lives.

Kim Hilderbrand, CSW, has a masters degree in social work and is the manager of Crossroads Clubhouse.

Lisa Jardine has a bachelors degree in psychology and was formerly the vocational coordinator of Crossroads Clubhouse.

Pam McVay has a bachelors degree in psychology/sociology and is the vocational coordinator of Crossroads Clubhouse.

Sandra O'Dell has a bachelors degree in education and is the coordinator of the Supported Independence Program of Child and Family Services of Southwestern Michigan, Inc.

Pat Zurek has an associates degree in secretarial science and is the administrative assistant of the Supported Independence Program of Child and Family Services of Southwestern Michigan, Inc.

Chapter 33
Addressing and Resolving Role Issues Between Professionals and Consumer Employees

Kenneth Miya
Suzane Wilbur
Benjamin Crocker
Frank Compton

The experience of hiring consumers as staff in programs which are charged with providing services to the highest utilizers of psychiatric hospitals and emergency rooms care has proven to be an interesting and productive journey for consumers, staff, and management. These programs serve individuals who have serious and persistent neurobiological disorders, primarily of a psychotic nature, and apply psychosocial rehabilitation theory in integrated models of care.

Most of the clients served by these programs have not been able to effectively use the traditional system. They have tended to view the public mental health system with negativity and suspicion. They see it as the agency that is reactive, forces them to be hospitalized against their wills, does not meet their needs, and is not user friendly. Frequently, professionals are perceived as distant, coolly clinical, unempathic, and stigmatizing. Inviting consumers to team with mental health professionals can help change this system to better meet consumer needs. That is, consumers can contribute to the treatment of peers in a way that professionals cannot (Felton et al., 1995) by facilitating engagement, hope, trust, and cooperation. Professionals and consumer employees can learn a great deal from one another, leading to an enriched and enhanced system of care.

Little has been written which describes the experiences of professionals and consumers who collaborate on the same treatment team (Dixon, Krauss, & Lehman, 1994). Role issues that emerge when this collaboration occurs are the focus of this chapter. Personal accounts from the perspective of the clinic manager, a member of the professional staff, and a consumer, who together implemented consumer employment, will be shared to illustrate these diverse experiences.

Paradigms and Perceptions

Among the greatest barriers to consumer employment today are stigma and prejudice which shape our perceptions and influence behavior. A useful tool for understanding these issues is the concept of the paradigm. "Paradigm" has been defined as a pattern, example, or model in *Webster's New World Dictionary*, (1986). Used here, it is a model which has the effect of a perceptual lens or filter through which we view, understand, and interpret stimuli. Thus, paradigms inflect values and priorities which can lead to actions. Paradigms can guide us in the right direction or cause us to stray off course.

Bill O'Brian from Boston University provided a great example during a talk he gave in Los Angeles. He spoke of the now archaic schizophrenogenic mother paradigm which led legions of clinicians to "understand" an important aspect of schizophrenia. This "understanding" provided impetus in the interpretation and treatment of "the schizophrenic" psychotherapeutically, even though it didn't seem to work very well. This paradigm invoked blame from clinicians and guilt in parents. It implied a faulty etiology and wreaked havoc with important support systems. It paralyzed and confused.

The human mind relies on stereotypes which are functionally necessary for important, fast decision making. Quick decisions based on minimal information are frequently essential for survival. Discriminating between friend or foe, immediate danger or relative safety on a daily basis is crucial. These processes save us from danger and destruction on the one hand, but can lead us astray, on the other.

Perception is an active process wherein people color the world with their expectations. We see what we believe. A paradigm may be seen as an example of "belief perseverance" which is a perceptual process of seeing the world in familiar ways. People tend to discount evidence that does not fit their paradigm. If they believe that people with schizophrenia are hopeless, strange, and unable to work like "normal people," but meet someone who differs from that perception, they don't revise their paradigms; they say, "that's the exception" (Nisbett & Ross, 1980).

Studies on perception have steadily demonstrated that biases operate unconsciously, influencing judgments so that the fact of subjectively wanting to be fair does not enable fairness. How then, can we impact this seemingly unchangeable phenomenon of the brain? One key in dealing with this problem is to understand that it is a problem in the first place. "If you can understand that your car tends to drive to the left because your wheels are out of line, you can correct it" (Cole, 1995).

Role Transitions

While not new to the notion that work is an important factor in the recovery of people with serious and persistent neurobiological disorders such as schizophrenia, the authors were relatively new to the act of actually hiring consumers in their own clinics, in particular, hiring people who had previously been served as clients in these very clinics.

Robert was one such consumer. He was hired to provide clerical support (typing, filing, faxing, answering phones, and running errands) to a program from which he had been receiving mental health services for two years. Everyone on the staff had encouraged Robert through the process of becoming a worker — after eight years of unemployment. Everyone was happy when

Robert was hired into the half-time clerical position. Robert came to work daily, on time, and without missing a single day for six months. Robert had been very productive on the job, but had occasions when hearing derogatory voices caused him to slump over his desk and cry.

One day, the manager walked into Robert's work area and found staff hovering over him, talking softly to him, and trying to help him through a "psychotic moment." Nothing seemed to relieve the voices or his resultant certainty that "nobody likes me." The manager showed Robert a thick packet of papers and said, "Robert, does this mean that you can't do this typing project for me? I need to have it done right away." Robert immediately took the packet from the manager and began typing. He said, "Oh no; I can do it." He completed the entire project over the next two hours. Later, Robert told the manager that working helped him to "put the voices and paranoia aside," even though the symptoms did not disappear. This illustrates the fact that work can be therapeutic and can change the way everyone views the person with a disability. The more important point to keep in mind, however, is that the manager has a very good employee who has never failed to complete his assignments, and who is reliable and punctual in spite of his symptoms.

The staff in this program still perceived Robert more as a client than as a co-worker. It is likely that, in a cohesive team, staff would attempt to assist any co-worker who became ill on the job. It is doubtful, however, that they would continue to make allowances for work undone due to illness on the job. Robert saw himself in the sick role every time staff rushed to "help" him through his symptoms. The manager gave everyone the message, through modeling, that Robert was a worker and, as such, was expected to meet his job responsibilities.

A Consumer's Perspective

Frank Compton was another person hired to provide mental health services on the very team on which he had previously been a consumer. His own very personal story further illustrates the process of role transition as a person moves out of the patient role and into the worker role:

I won't hesitate in expressing my elation at being a working consumer. Employment is arguably the most meaningful part of my identity. I feel very much a part of the status quo again.

My condition was so morbid that at one time I was certainly destined for the streets. For four years, I spent most of my days and nights sitting alone in a room listening to voices, entertaining them, and being entertained by them. I had little use for the outside world.

My mother suffered from a chronic mental illness and had to be hospitalized. I have two older brothers and an older sister who have been diagnosed with emotional disorders. One of the brothers has been gravely ill and has been in and out of hospitals for 20 years.

I should have known a lot of things over those four years when I was very ill. I should have known not to walk outside with no clothes on. I should have known not to take all of my prescribed medicine at once. I should have known not to walk out on four good paying jobs, or not to forget my friends. I should have known not to lie to my doctor and family in the process.

In going from client to caregiver, I've familiarized myself with many roles. I've kept wellness as the top priority for myself and for how I service clients and present myself to others. I'm happy to be in remission and eager to share my good fortune with others, whether to reinforce family pride or encourage other consumers in their efforts to recover. I try to stress the importance of self motivation and self esteem, two principles which helped guide my recovery.

I received services from the agency in which I am now working. This has aided in my progress because a trust had been established and I already believed in the services. My former case manager took the lead in accepting me in my role as co-worker. She helped train me, gave me invaluable advice, and answered my questions. Moreover, she gave me highly responsible assignments and allowed me to work independently. This boosted my confidence and made me feel a part of the team.

It is really an advantage to have obtained services from a program and then work in the same program, because it puts you in a position of legitimacy. I know the value of the services and I know they work. I like my job. I believe in what I'm doing because it worked for me and I get to deliver these same valuable services to others.

I serve as a role model for other clients. I'm also a teacher, giving presentations and sharing my experiences. My success has been welcomed by my peers, and I am often asked for advice as to how my successes can be spread to others. My peers have also been cooperative with me as I offer services. I work with persons who have not experienced significant gains from prior exposure to the system. I have assisted successfully in helping those clients benefit from our services.

A rewarding outcome from turning it all around is that I have gotten to visit some of the facilities where I was once an inpatient. Their response has been supportive and encouraging. I've been asked to come back and give a talk on my successes to the patients and the staff. Everyone is so glad to see my progress and a feeling of hope is shared by all.

By being a consumer and participating in consumer oriented programs, I gain insight into other client's needs. At staff meetings I welcome the opportunity to present the client's perspective. I ask a lot of questions of my fellow consumers at meetings and functions. There is a lot of room to learn. I believe that, in representing clients, it is essential to be honest and clear, to encourage active participation, and to ensure that the client's dignity is maintained.

In going from a person needing assistance to a service provider, I've learned some valuable lessons. I was once uncooperative and my ultimate success came at a point when I finally became responsible for my own recovery. What the client wants is a fundamental issue. I was in denial for years and all the services offered in the world wouldn't get me to cooperate. It took my own internal acceptance and cooperation to finally make a change and turn things around. When that happened, things changed swiftly. I think that is how it works for many other clients; the road to recovery is basically in their hands. That's pretty much how we want it.

A Manager's Perspective

Assisting Mr. Compton through this process was Dr. Ken Miya, who discusses hiring a former consumer to become a team member:

> Over the years, I had slowly become exposed to the notion of the great value of work in the recovery of consumers with neurobiological disorders. I had even helped conceive and implement a very successful program which enabled the hiring of consumers who others thought could never work. In fact, many of the consumers themselves held the same belief.
> In the planning document for that project, I wrote:
> ...the system...often encouraged the goal of benign passivity, where success was measured in terms of ease of maintenance and compliance on the part of the client. The objective was to bring the client to a point of not being a management problem, an embarrassment or a trouble maker in the community. The "good client" was one who took his/her medications, stayed quiet and did what he/she was told. The client with a serious mental illness deserves more. Like everyone else, this person should have the opportunity to grow and pursue valued objectives which bring a sense of accomplishment, self esteem and respect from others. Work is one such objective which is accepted and esteemed by society. Those who work receive the benefits of a positive feedback loop naturally reinforced by societal norms.

So when Frank's case manager, Vickie, charted his steady progress over the months at our team meetings, everyone came to know him well while he was emerging from the depths of psychosis. The steady and intense work from the time of our initial contact with him during his last hospitalization and his own hard work was beginning to pay off. As the months went by, Frank was doing so well that he was linked to vocational rehabilitation services but no one would hire Frank due to his history of serious mental illness. Months went by.

One day, Vickie came and asked if we could hire Frank in our own clinic. I could see her frustration at having worked with someone to a point where he was ready for the next step but being unable to remove a critical barrier. I told her I would look into the possibility but the probability was low. Our budget wouldn't allow it.

The very thought of beginning to seriously consider hiring Frank to be an employee triggered a long list of concerns. In retrospect, it demonstrates where I was coming from at the time. I was not looking at this prospect as an opportunity. I came to understand that my list of questions and concerns were highly diagnostic of my own paradigm at the time.

I was very much an advocate for mental health consumers being hired by others—but not by me. Truly, my facility for seeing the many barriers was the manifestation of my defensiveness and resistance to change and potential problems. My focus on barriers prevented me from addressing solutions. Fortunately, I was far enough along the road that I was conflicted and uncomfortable with myself and my thinking. I think it was Samuel Clemens who said something like: "It ain't what you don't know that's the problem. It's what you know for sure...but ain't so." I had not been conscious of my own resistance, thinking I had none.

I recall talking with Dr. Areta Crowell who is the director of our department. Our conversation took the form of my saying that I would like to hire a consumer, but all the while, focusing on the many barriers to so doing. Dr. Crowell gave me one of her warm, knowing smiles. She said that she thought I should hire a consumer and that she was confident that I would find a way. This was a critical point of transition for me. My thoughts changed from why I couldn't to how I could make it happen.

Suddenly, my list of barriers became identifiable targets for which I was challenged to provide solutions. Many of my concerns simply faded away. Since I had gone through the experience myself, I became acutely aware of the pervasive barriers which were erected, making the employment of mental health consumers difficult. The Department of Rehabilitation, prospective employers, the Department of Health Services, and our own personnel bureau all evidenced subtle and not so subtle barriers in one form or another. The subtleties probably were proportionate to the levels of sophistication regarding political correctness and familiarity with current law — greater levels often leading to the construction of more sophisticated barriers — not their removal.

Now I was in a problem-solving mode and could be a true advocate. It reminded me of my own background of experiencing stigma and prejudice as an ethnic minority person. I was flooded with memories from the past, experiencing the pain of being "on the outs." This fueled an even greater sense of empathy, energy and purpose. The most important factor was my success in making an essential internal change, which resulted in a clearer view and goal directed behavior congruent with the change. My behavior was now "ego syntonic." I felt good.

We hired Frank and he has been an absolute joy. I remember a very simple but memorable conversation soon after Frank reported for work at our clinic. I said, "How are you doing, Frank?" He said, "Great!! I couldn't wait to get to work this morning!!" "Great, Frank. You're great." This small interchange reminded me of how his attitude was so refreshing. Those of us who have been continuously employed, who have been so blessed as to have been relatively free of the serious and chronic illnesses that tend to rob us of dignity and self esteem, often take our jobs for granted and too frequently, we complain of minutia which become part of our office culture.

Gradually, Frank became a real presence on the team. Not only was he a nice guy but his attitude, energy, excitement, and cooperative spirit were felt by everyone. Clearly, he wanted to do whatever he could to help. Almost immediately, other team members began reporting that certain clients were more responsive and were relating to Frank in positive ways, which had not been in evidence before. This was not altogether because he was known to them as a consumer. He shared his personal experiences as a consumer of the system with care and selectivity.

He became a sought-after personality in numerous mental health organizations, consumer support and advocacy groups. Still another new role was that of teacher and presenter at local, state and national conferences and classrooms. His latest accomplishment is that of co-author of this chapter. I see him grow almost every day and I feel I'm growing along with him.

A Physician's Perspective

Dr. Benjamin Crocker, who works with Mr. Compton in the Intensive Case Management Program, and who interfaces daily with Dr. Miya, discusses a psychiatrist's view in the following personal account:

Among mental health service workers, psychiatrists are perhaps the best insulated against identifying with patients. The ritual training traditions of medical school are in part designed to desensitize physicians to disease and suffering so that they can be dispassionate in their prescriptions and not be emotionally overwhelmed by the distress of those who seek their advice. Physicians maintain special privileges and high status, which tends to support their denial that they too can become ill. Physicians' special status and trained capacity to use denial can make them vulnerable to depression and substance abuse.

Compared with other physicians, psychiatrists have been offered more opportunities to explore their own vulnerabilities. Until recently it was fashionable for psychiatrists to take on the role of patient in psychotherapy as part of training. This experience rarely extends to the point of identifying with the role of sickness or disability. While receiving psychotherapy is tolerated by physicians as one of the prerogatives of the upper-middle class in which most physicians can be found, taking psychotropic medications is highly stigmatized, even among psychiatrists, and generally kept as secret as possible. Most physicians find the idea that they might have or develop a neurobehavioral disorder intolerable, and assume that they would be considered impaired if they did and lose their livelihood. These fears may not have a significant factual basis, but nonetheless tend to lead physicians to overgeneralize and unwittingly support the stigma borne by all who are diagnosed with a neurobehavioral disorder.

The "consumer" I have known best in my life was my father, who was, like me, a psychiatrist, and who, probably like several members of his family, had some kind of bipolar mood disorder. He was significantly disabled at times by this disorder, and felt potentially stigmatized by it. I am sure that my decision to go into psychiatry was at least partially determined by my frustration at the persistence of his illness and my desire to guard myself against a not unlikely inheritance of something similar. While it may have been somewhat adaptive for me to learn as much as I could about psychiatry, my medical training conveniently offered me plenty of reinforcement that it couldn't happen to me, even though I had seen it happen to my father. Consciously, I have struggled against denial and the tendency to stigmatize both personally and professionally with some success. The opportunity to work with identified consumers has helped me to appreciate less conscious denial mechanisms within myself.

The temptation to closet the fact of psychiatric illness in the face of stigma is significant. It is likely that we all have colleagues who are in recovery from psychiatric illness and disability, but we usually don't know who they are. I have several physicians, some psychiatrists, in my private practice who are quite closeted about their psychiatric treatment, and who travel inconvenient distances to ensure that it is not known to their community. Many states require physicians to disclose a history of mental health treatment as a condition of licensure, a stipulation which is being contested in light of the Americans with Disabilities Act.

Recently, increasing numbers of mental health practitioners who have been treated for psychiatric disorders are disclosing in order to educate their colleagues about stigma and disability. Interestingly, one of the most common reactions among mental health clinicians when hearing a story of how a person in recovery has achieved high professional and personal goals is to discount the severity of the illness, question the accuracy of the diagnosis, and identify the person as a rare exception. Some clinicians even go so far as to opine, usually in private, that to publicize successfully recovered people with major psychiatric diagnoses is a cruel hoax on the masses of people with persistent neurobehavioral disorders, who will be made to feel like unlucky failures if they do not fully recover. My experiences in learning how to work in an intensive case management team have helped me to overcome these attitudes, and to recognize how I myself have used this kind of black and white thinking, which seeks to maintain denial mechanisms, to segregate the well from the sick, the competent from the incompetent. As long as we maintain the imaginary line of segregation, we can locate ourselves on the safe side.

It is challenging to clinicians who have mostly worked in clinics to adapt to the demand for role flexibility, because even though issues of professional boundaries have to be re-drawn in the field, they must still be there to protect everyone and allow us to maintain clinical roles. This ongoing challenge to fine-tune roles within a range of appropriate possibilities can bring out the best in clinicians. An intensive case management team, having a broad clinical range of responsibilities for a group of clients whose needs are not entirely predictable, must develop intra-team role flexibility so that all team members can significantly cross-cover each other. Relating to clients as a team offers them a more balanced and consistent set of clinical contacts over time, and it requires that the team members act in concert to present the team's organization to the client. An agreed-upon tension between role definition and flexibility among team members is ideal, and requires maintenance through regular group process.

In welcoming consumers into a clinical case management team, we need to be sensitive to the fact that it is usually harder to model and learn highly flexible roles than more static ones; but that on the other hand, we need to be as clear as we can and in general agreement about how much role flexibility is appropriate for people with less formal training or experience.

Jerome Frank (1991), in his landmark book, *Persuasion and Healing*, has widely popularized the idea that in some instances, trained lay people put in the role of psychotherapist may produce outcomes as good as trained therapists. In recruiting consumers who are not formally trained to work in mental health service teams, we seem to be acknowledging the equivocal advantage that certified practitioners have in providing effective services in some areas. While there is evidence that the execution of specific psychotherapies which are effective in treating symptoms of depression and anxiety requires technical training and probably a certain professionalization of attitude, there is considerably less clear evidence in the application of other kinds of psychosocial interventions. The issue of professionalism and training is a dynamite labor issue, but one which cannot be avoided in the process of recruiting consumers who may have varying educational backgrounds. Consumers do potentially have knowledge and experiences that uniquely suit them to help plan and deliver services to other consumers — knowledge and experience that professional training imparts only indirectly. And yet, if professional providers endeavor to reduce the denial mechanisms that keep the experiences of the ill at arm's length, they can learn a lot from their new consumer colleagues.

What strikes me the most about the consumers who are my working colleagues is their openness about the facts of their illness. It seems reasonable that this openness is a way of de-stigmatization by explicitly avoiding the closet. As with other demeaned identifications, like being gay, openness confronts the conflict between the distortions of the stigmatizing constructs and the perceivable reality. Yet this openness runs so counter to general social norms, particularly the social norms of health professionals, that it continues to be bracing to me on a daily basis, and reminds me of the persistent residues of denial and stigmatization that are within me, not just about mental illness, but about many other aspects of life. The confidence and positive self-regard that the particular consumers I work with exhibit almost always impresses me personally and challenges me to clarify the ongoing sources of my own self-regard.

Working with people who are open about the fact of their neurobehavioral illness and at the same time are doing a good job at their work is a great help to clinicians' gradually accepting the modern rehabilitation concepts that differentiate severity of psychiatric diagnosis or symptoms from the capacity to work. It is helpful to work together with a person who has experienced psychosis when trying to evaluate psychosis. How often I have strained at length to make sense of psychotic word-salad, hoping that if I could discern some pattern or symbolic communication, I could help more. What a relief to hear my consumer partner's opinion that the patient's speech and behavior are simply not understandable.

This is not to say that professionals do not have their own communication problems, most professional teams invariably externalize their feelings of fear and rivalry. Teams may make jokes about people, identify them by their diagnoses, and in various ways tend to make hostile or condescending generalizations about people and systems outside the team, be they clients or other providers. Consumer-providers as representatives of the "Theys" we externalize about, help us "non-consumers" be more conscious about scapegoating and distancing.

Discussion and Recommendations

Stigma, Bias, Prejudice

As is the case in current society, many mental health professionals harbor biases and prejudices which can contribute to the stigmatization of those with neurobiological disorders. Frequently, this is an unconscious process. Anything that can be done to promote their conscious recognition is desirable as the first step towards correction. Programs methodically developed to foster a group culture with folkways and mores which promote personal vigilance and advocacy for consumers are crucial. Ongoing group process should include the regular reinforcement of values and philosophical ideals which are intended to combat stigma, bias, and prejudice against inclusion of consumers as bona fide staff.

To combat stigma, advocates need to gain clear support from top administration and work to create a culture in the employment setting that values diversity, past experience, equality, personal honesty, and outcomes. Everyone should be included in planning processes. The agency should promote team work, valuing each individual and the knowledge they have gained through personal life experiences, role flexibility, and the expectation that everyone can learn from one another.

Role Perception

The script is clear and well delineated for the "patient" and the mental health "professional." When the roles change because the "patient" becomes a colleague, paradigm shifts become necessary to account for a "new reality" and to promote and nurture positive outcomes. Stigma, prejudice, jealousy, envy, power, fear, and defensiveness can prevent effective interactions with consumer colleagues.

Search for and own your biases as initial steps towards corrective action. Ask staff to examine their perceptions in anticipation of problems. Acknowledge the fact that the changing of unconscious, stereotypic perceptions is a slow process and that one's verbalizations do not necessarily mean that more accurate views are internalized.

Role Transitions

The transition from one role to another can be difficult, even though it may appear on the surface to be quite clear and simple. Again, old paradigms and unconscious perceptions can shunt us along old, archaic pathways to impede progress. Clearly, the personal experiences of the authors demonstrate that this is an evolutionary process which takes place across time. To optimize role transitions, staff and consumer/workers should be knowledgeable, in advance, about potential problems which can arise when workers are treated with undue deference to their illnesses. The expectation should be on getting the job done and the focus on a person's abilities, not their disabilities. Hire for abilities. The temptation for consumer employees and professionals to maintain static roles serves to retard effective transition.

Modeling is a powerful way of helping mental health program staff to change their perceptions, confront their conflicts, and transition between roles. Leaders should be the first to walk the talk. Treat people with respect. Our greatest, most critical strength lies in our human resources. Nurture them, strengthen them, support them. View change as an opportunity for creativity and learning.

The concept of the paradigm and studies on brain functioning which shape perception reveal the extensive difficulty peoople have with change. Our perceptual apparatus continuously militates against seeing the world in a different way, even when our conscious minds may so desire. This phenomenon is a double-edged sword with positive and negative consequences. The paradigm enables a sense of order, predictability, and quick decision-making capabilities which at times may be critical to preserving our very lives. On the other hand, it explains why individuals, organizations and systems are highly resistant to change and tend to perpetuate inaccurate, stereotypic views of people, constituting perhaps the greatest barrier and challenge to the hiring of mental health consumers in mainstream work settings. With support, consumers can be powerful role models as workers, teachers and advocates for social change, not just for other consumers but for the system at large.

Role Conflict and Flexibility

Consumers working as providers stimulate non-consumer providers to examine their tendencies to stigmatize. The consumer as provider breaks through the boundary separating the "ill" from the "healthy," the "able" vs. the "disabled." By confronting such a strong and almost universal set of stigmatizing boundaries, the hiring of identified consumers as providers challenges various status relationships, and at the same time, can make providers more conscious of their own need for role flexibility. This is especially important in models of service such as intensive case management, where all members of a team share clinical responsibility and represent one another.

The social distance between mental health professionals and clients is great. By adopting highly defined roles, professionals work hard to institutionalize and maintain boundaries through clinic walls, the symbolism of the white coat, etc. Most have little or no experience in working with identified consumers as colleagues. The stigma associated with a serious mental illness can be perpetuated due to this increased social distance.

Professionals being more flexible is critical in enabling consumers to utilize their strengths and potential in the mental health system as therapeutic agents. Learning and supporting just how and under what conditions they may best intervene is relatively uncharted territory. Accepting the tension between role definition and flexibility enables the dialogue necessary to come to grips with these emerging issues.

Concluding Remarks

As the months have gone by, we have all come to realize that we are experiencing many serendipitous events. Our consumer colleagues have become symbols of hope and success (without their even knowing) for other consumers and staff. They remind us daily of what and who we are working for. They are the living representation of our collaborative success. They are the hope that people with serious neurobiological disorders can recover. They help us to remember not to make people diagnoses and categories which rob us of relating to their humanity with empathy and understanding, and they enable us to appreciate the special joy which frequently comes from working together, working better, knowing that we can make a difference. Our experiences with our consumer colleagues have touched and changed our lives in many ways, personally and professionally. Great programs are the result of great staff. Old paradigms could have caused us to miss this opportunity. That would have been tragic. Unless we act and hire consumers, we may never be challenged to break through deeply held, unconscious perceptions which are a detriment to ourselves and the very people we serve.

Consumers have personal knowledge of the system and many of its resources since they have used them. As they are given the opportunity to be part of the system, they become important agents of change. As they work with other consumers as service providers, role models, advocates, and symbols of hope, they are being active participants in their own rehabilitation.

Clearly, we do not say that you will have the same or similar results from hiring consumers. But, we believe that you may be missing out if you do not, solely for the reason that your paradigm tells you that people with schizophrenia can't do the job, that "they" are not like "us." Our experience demonstrated to us that when "they" were invited to truly become one of "us," we were all awakened to some wondrous changes.

References

Brooks, E. (1995). The politics of diagnostic identity. *Psychiatric Services, 46,* 1013-1014.

Dixon, L., Krauss, N., & Lehman, A. (1994). Consumers as service providers: The promise and challenge. *Community Mental Health Journal, 30,* 615-625.

Felton, C., Stastny, P., Shern, D., Blanch, A., Donahue, S., Knight, E., & Brown, C. (1995). Consumers as peer specialists on intensive case management teams: Impact on client outcomes. *Psychiatric Services, 46,* 1037-1044.

Frank, J. (1991). *Persuasion and healing* (3rd ed.). Baltimore, MD: Johns Hopkins Press.

Kaufmann, C., Ward-Colasante, C., & Farmer, J. (1993). Development and evaluation of drop-in centers operated by mental health consumers. *Hospital and Community Psychiatry, 44,* 675-678.

Mowbray, C., & Tan, C. (1993). Consumer-operated drop-in centers: Evaluation of operations and impact. *Journal of Mental Health Administration, 20,* 8-18.

Nisbett, R., & Ross, L. (1980). *Human inference: Strategies and shortcomings of social judgment.* NJ: Prentice-Hall, Inc.

Nikkel, R., Smith, G., & Edwards, D. (1992). A consumer-operated case management project. *Hospital and Community Psychiatry, 43,* 577-579.

Quinlivan, R., Hough, R., Crowell, A., Beach, C., Hofstetter, R., & Kenworthy, K. (1995). Service utilization and costs of care for severely mentally ill clients in an intensive case management program. *Psychiatric Services, 46,* 365-371.

Solomon, P., & Draine, J. (1994). Family perceptions of consumers as case managers. *Community Mental Health Journal, 30,* 165-176.

Stephens, C., & Belisle, K. (1993). The 'consumer-as-provider' initiative. *Journal of Mental Health Administration, 20,* 178-182.

Stocks, M.L. (1995). Perspectives on chronicity. *Psychiatric Services, 46,* 13-14.

Webster's New World Dictionary (1986). New York, NY: Prentice Hall Press.

Kenneth Miya, Ph.D., is Los Angeles regional director of development, Telecare Corporation, and former director of intensive case management program, Los Angeles County Department of Mental Health.

Suzane Wilbur, M.S., R.N., is director of the AMI/ABLE Program, assistant professor, UCLA School of Nursing, adjunct clinical professor, Mount Saint Mary's College.

Benjamin Crocker, M.D., is psychiatrist, Holy Innocents ACT Team, Portland, Maine, and staff at the Maine Medical Center. He formerly practiced in Los Angeles.

Frank Compton, B.S., is community worker, Intensive Case Management Program, Los Angeles County Department of Mental Health.

Chapter 34
A Consumer Case Management Research Demonstration Project Achieves Independence[1]

Phyllis Solomon
Jeffrey Draine
Warner Rodgers
Samuel Edwards
Ernestine Ross

For over a decade, the federal Community Support Program, currently housed in the Substance Abuse Mental Health Services Administration, has been funding service demonstrations, including consumer-operated or delivered services. Similarly, other governmental agencies and private foundations have funded innovative services. One of the concerns for consumer-operated services, as well as other mental health agencies and organizations, has been that at termination of grant funding, services also terminate due to a lack of resources for continuation. In a few instances, innovative programs that are effective in fulfilling a need may receive operating funds from a state or local governmental funding source. But, generally these demonstration programs need to obtain continued operating funds from a reliable funding stream or cease to exist. This chapter will discuss the strategies employed by a consumer delivered service, specifically a consumer case management research demonstration project[2], to obtain operating funds and become financially self sufficient after termination of a federal grant.

The Program Model

The consumer case management research demonstration project was a three year collaborative effort among a consumer-run organization, a city/state funded mental health agency, and an academic institution. The consumer case management service portion of the project was administered by Project SHARE (Self-Help and Advocacy Resource Exchange), a consumer-run program, under the auspice of the Mental Health Association of Southeastern Pennsylvania.

---

[1] The research which initiated this project was funded by NIMH/SAMHSA grant #R18MH46082.
[2] A research demonstration project is a new or innovative service which is evaluated with a rigorous research design.

The consumer case management program was designed to be staffed by four case managers and a project director. One of the case managers was to be a nonconsumer. This was intentionally done to make it more palatable to the funders and reviewers who may have been skeptical of an all-consumer team at the time the proposal was submitted for funding in 1989. However, the nonconsumer case manager left the position and was replaced with a consumer after about one year. Thus, the consumer team eventually became composed entirely of consumers. In the second year of the program, a full-time clinical director and a part-time psychiatrist were hired.

The team provided services in an assertive community treatment model (Stein & Test, 1980; Bond, Miller, Krumweid, & Ward, 1988). In this model, case managers saw clients[3] in vivo, the environments where the clients lived, attended programs, received treatments, and socialized. Rarely did the team see clients in their offices. Each case manager had their own caseload. In crisis situations and sometimes for social activities for their clients, team members worked together; otherwise case managers functioned relatively independently in serving their own clients. Case management activities included an array of housing, rehabilitation, and social activities that were necessary or desired for the community life of clients. Case managers performed brokering, assistance, and support functions as opposed to clinical management and treatment.

The program was designed as a research demonstration project to assess the efficacy of consumer delivered case management service as compared to the same service delivered by a team of nonconsumers. Through the use of a rigorous experimental design, 96 clients from the caseload of a community mental health agency were randomly assigned to either the consumer or nonconsumer team of case managers. At the end of two years of service, there were no differences in outcomes for the clients served by the two teams. In other words, both teams were equally effective (Solomon & Draine, 1995b). It was also found that although both teams provided the same amount of service, consumer case managers delivered more services face-to-face with the clients and fewer services in the office and in interaction with family members or other mental health service providers (Solomon & Draine, 1996).

Achieving Financial Independence

Continued funding for the consumer case management team (independent of the research demonstration grant) was desirable for at least three reasons. First and most importantly, the consumer case managers had established working relationships with their clients and they wanted to continue those relationships, thus enhancing continuity of care. Second, the feasibility and relative efficacy of their services had been established through a rigorous evaluation. Third, the services delivered were unique compared to usual case management services in that they focused more personally on the lives of clients (Solomon & Draine, 1996).

[3] The term "client" is used to refer to a consumer in the service recipient role. This prevents confusion in the use of the term "consumer" as well as "consumer case manager."

Achieving financial independence involved a number of key changes in the way the project operated. When the project director post was vacant in the final year of grant funds, the third author was hired with the specific charge to achieve financial independence by acquiring Medicaid (MA) reimbursement for case management services. The project, including a director, a team leader, four case managers, a billing clerk, an administrative assistant and a part time psychiatrist, is now totally funded by MA reimbursement. In this chapter, we outline the tasks that needed to be accomplished to achieve financial independence, the barriers that needed to be overcome, and the future plans for expansion of the project.

Agency Cooperation

From the beginning, this effort required the support of both the agency that provided an organizational home to the project, Project SHARE, and its umbrella agency, the Mental Health Association of Southeastern Pennsylvania (MHA), with the local mental health agencies, the city's Office of Mental Health (OMH) and the mental health planning authority, the Philadelphia Mental Health Care Corporation (PMHCC). The MHA provided a willingness to support project staff in their goal to achieve financial independence and also to continue providing a home to the project. On occasions when the project has sought to expand its services, some reflection on the role of the agency was required since the agency characterizes itself as an advocacy organization rather than as a service provider. However, it has consistently supported the project's need to expand its treatment and service resources. If anything, it is now using the project's success as a role model for the rest of the agency.

City OMH provided concrete support in two ways. First, it was willing to add a new MA provider to its system. Second, it was willing to provide clients to the case management team. Many seriously mentally ill clients were not being served with intensive case management because their local community mental health centers (CMHC) had long waiting lists for this service. A number of these clients were able to receive case management services through the consumer case management project, which serves the entire city and not just designated catchment areas. Among its functions, PMHCC provides information systems support for case management services in the Philadelphia mental health system. PMHCC staff were committed to providing the technical assistance project staff needed to implement and operate an MA billing system.

Consumer case managers won the support of OMH and the mental health system in several ways. They took many cases which were among the most difficult and worked with them. In this process, they sought resources from OMH for their clients. Through this interaction between OMH staff and the case managers, relationships were developed and enhanced over time. OMH maintains an organizational philosophy that values consumer empowerment. Promoting and supporting a consumer-delivered service was both consistent with this philosophy and politically astute.

Adjustments in Service Provision

One of the important changes that had to be made in order for the service to be self-sufficient, was for case managers to produce more service units on a regular basis to enhance the funding potential. The initial step was assessing the service units provided in past years. In the year prior to the certification effort, about 2500 contact units of service were provided. The team now averages 1200 to 1500 contact units of service per month. The increase in service units was achieved partly by setting daily, weekly, and monthly goals for service units per case manager with the minimum number of face-to-face contacts required by the regulations. Case managers were encouraged to be more diligent in completing service documentation than they had been in the past. This was accomplished over a two year period without any consumer case manager attrition that could be attributed to additional work stress.

Service plans also had to be reassessed and made more comprehensive. The new plans included more breadth in the areas of community living, such as benefits, housing, medical treatment, and activities of daily living. Objectives were more explicitly linked to overall goals and stated in measurable terms. Activities were more clearly linked to these objectives. Thus documentation of service units was more easily linked to work toward goals established for each client. These goals were established in collaboration between client and consumer case manager.

Case managers experienced a shorter average length of time per service contact. However, the only client response to the change was that some clients missed the small gifts that were distributed during the holiday season in previous years. The switch to MA funding decreased the discretionary funds available for use with clients. It is important to note that many of these case manager-client relationships are five years old (since the inception of the project). There is an element of continuity that was only minimally impacted by the program change to MA billing.

Staff Training and Preparation

The initial staff was largely qualified to provide MA billable case management services. One case manager, however, barely missed qualification because she was not hired at a time when a grandfather clause would allow her to be certified with only a high school equivalency certificate. Basic qualifications of case managers have been raised gradually through hiring goals. With each hire of a new or replacement case manager, the director's goal is to hire an individual with incrementally higher educational credentials. Thus, over time, the educational qualifications of the case managers have improved.

The shift in case manager qualifications could be attributed to the salaries and benefits enjoyed by project case managers relative to their peers at CMHCs. Some experienced CMHC case managers have applied for vacancies on the consumer case management team. In addition to pay and benefits, case managers are afforded a professional status within MHA which is a position of strength from which case managers can more effectively advocate for their clients. In contrast, case management positions in many CMHCs are treated as low-status entry level positions. Many case managers see their positions as temporary and seek to quickly move on to higher status jobs in their agency. There appears to be much less turnover and much longer tenure among SHARE case managers than among their CMHC peers.

Case managers participate in the OMH sponsored training provided to all case managers in the system (which they had done when they were a demonstration project as well). This training includes an orientation to serious mental illness, its treatment, and case management practice. Training also includes periodic continuing education sessions. Within the project, inservice training is planned to discuss relevant topics and increase case managers' clinical skills. Recent inservice session topics have included borderline personality disorder, psychopharmacology, HIV disease, and effective symptom monitoring.

Upgrading of Infrastructure

Infrastructure upgrading included acquiring equipment and establishing procedures necessary to operate an MA billing operation. A billing clerk had to be added to the staff to facilitate this process. Computers had to be upgraded and loaded with software with which to enter billing data. Staff had to be trained in the proper use of the service documentation forms and in data entry. Eventually, the project was directly on-line with PMHCC, OMH, and the state office of mental health. The billing process is under constant review as the procedures change because of modifications in regulations, state or city requirements, or project growth. For example, the project wants to use a psychiatrist for treatment of clients as well as consultation. This will enable the project to provide the necessary medication prescribing and monitoring of clients so that they are not required to go to local CMHCs, which some clients want to avoid. This will require new private practice billing procedures which need to be instituted.

Barriers

The first barrier to overcome was a certain amount of skepticism among project case managers. They were afraid that MA billing would change the way they worked with their clients. This was addressed by an approach which emphasized an overall improvement in the project's work. The director's motto was "quality generates quantity." While the case managers were quite familiar with the social aspects of their work, they were less confident in their clinical expertise. Routines were established which provided more structure in the work environment and provided opportunities for case managers to have high quality clinical feedback on their work with clients. This included a decision to replace the clinical director with an overall team leader.

Case managers have noted, however, that under MA billing, there is less time for more casual interactions with clients. These interactions, while not clearly treatment oriented, did serve an important function for some clients. For example, when a client appeared to be withdrawing or going through an anxious time, a case manager may have simply spent the day with that individual to diffuse a potential decompensation. With MA billing, such attention becomes more difficult to justify and clients in these situations may only come to the attention of their case managers when decompensation is imminent. One case manager observed that some of her clients seem more "needy," with more undesirable outcomes, such as homelessness or unplanned pregnancies. This is attributed in part to the change in service delivery patterns.

The resistance of staff was also addressed through a more pragmatic approach. They were told directly that their survival as a project, and thus the survival of their jobs, depended on the success of independent funding through MA billing.

Future Plans

Future plans are built around being prepared to be competitive providers of MA-funded case management and rehabilitation services, as the administration of mental health care shifts to managed care organizations. The project currently operates with an informal agreement for client referrals from OMH. The staff are working under this arrangement until they are sure that they are proficient enough to compete for a formal letter of agreement with the city. The project's competitiveness is enhanced by the lower overhead costs incurred, given the nature of the MHA organization relative to CMHCs.

The project staff is eager to show that they can carry their own weight in this environment. The project now maintains a minimum caseload policy of 14 cases. Eventually, they hope to move to a minimum caseload policy of 17 cases, which is the city OMH minimum for intensive case managers. The project is also moving to provide rehabilitation option services, and to act as a source for psychiatric treatment as well. This rehabilitation option will be made possible by the consumer drop-in centers and clubhouse program recently initiated by Project SHARE and the MHA. It is hoped that a full-time psychiatrist can eventually be supported through MA billing and other mixed sources of funding. In this way, clients who dislike receiving services from CMHCs can have an option for receipt of treatment and rehabilitation services though the consumer case management project.

Conclusion

Resources for community mental health services are dwindling. Federal, state, and local governments are under pressure to reduce spending. Private charitable funds, such as the United Way, are struggling to meet a growing demand for their resources. The consumer case management research demonstration project was able to become financially viable and independent in this environment. By doing so, it becomes an example for other research demonstrations and consumer delivered service projects.

Several elements of the transition are key indicators of success. Principally, continuity of care is enhanced both by the continuation of the project and the stability of project staff. The staff have matured considerably in their jobs through both training and experience. New leadership is a positive force, which maintains the infrastructure needed to continue current funding through MA, and to obtain future funding as managed care becomes more of a factor in public mental health services. Lastly, through the process of seeking MA funding, the project's self-help philosophy has been enhanced through requirements to operationalize goals for client treatment.

Many of the barriers faced by the SHARE case managers are the same problems faced by all case management programs. Few can be exclusively attributed to the fact that the team is dominated by consumers. For example, among these barriers are "bureaucratic blinders," the tendency of some system administrators to have a narrow vision of mental health services and their potential. To overcome this, case managers are often put in the position of advocating for clients who don't fit neatly into pre-determined client roles and the services designed for them. Consumer case managers feel they have an extra advantage in this advocacy role because they have their own experiences to draw upon for motivation. But consumer case managers feel that little credence is given to the input of intensive case managers in general, not just those who are consumers.

The service demonstration phase of this project served to season the team and give them experience. It is not known whether such a project could have succeeded with MA funding without the transition period afforded by its research demonstration status. In this time period, individuals who were novices as service providers gained confidence, learned the mental health system from a different perspective, learned how to advocate, and demonstrated their effectiveness. This learning period would have probably not been tenable while also seeking MA funding.

For demonstration services or projects that are considering an MA funding strategy, there needs to be advance consideration of key issues. This should reduce the need for future adjustments in program staffing and operations. First, it is important to understand the staff qualifications that are required for MA certification. Hiring initial staff who can meet the qualifications before MA certification is sought reduces the need for staff changes in the future. Second, it is important that data collection and service documentation procedures be established and maintained. This is particularly useful as it is vitally important that project leaders be able to estimate service projections for planning. A reliable service data system helps the director of the program in planning and budgeting for program growth by providing a basis for revenue projections. A third requirement for MA eligibility which can be planned for in advance is the need for clinical record keeping in terms of setting comprehensive goals and objectives in measurable terms. Fourth, it is important to generate data tracking for the provision of service units. These data are useful in planning, budgeting, and evaluation. Goals for increasing service units may be gradually instituted with specific time frames at the beginning of the project.

Lastly, prior experience is most useful. This can be sought in two ways: similar projects which have sought MA certification can be contacted and used as a technical support resource. Or prior experience with MA billing certification and procedures can be considered a required qualification for hiring a director at the initiation of the project.

It is recognized that these recommendations are related to medicaid billing, which is a likely source for funding of case management and rehabilitation services. Similar steps must be followed if another funding source is anticipated. It is likely that other funding mechanisms, such as managed care companies, will require comparable types of considerations.

Given the nature of demonstration projects where the clients have to meet specific eligibility criteria, a cautionary note is in order. Caseloads in these projects are generally capped and the initial referral of clients is often slow. It is not unusual to have lower levels of service units than other agency staff who are required to meet billable service unit standards. In the current project, both teams had comparable service units for the first year of the project (Solomon & Draine, 1996). But these realities do not preclude the institution of these recommendations, as they do not require meeting specified standards in terms of units of services delivered. Certainly, monitoring service units will set expectations for when such demonstrations are converted to billable services. These types of data will provide needed information to negotiate with funding sources, be they governmental entities or managed care companies, to reimburse consumer-delivered services. In this financially conservative environment, consumer-operated services that do not have to support large infrastructures as do community mental health agencies may have a good competitive edge.

References

Bond, G. R., Miller, L. D., Krumweid, R. D., & Ward, R. S. (1988). Assertive case management in three CMHCs: A controlled study. *Hospital and Community Psychiatry, 39,* 411-418.

Solomon, P., & Draine, J. (1994). Satisfaction with mental health treatment in a randomized trial of consumer case management. *Journal of Nervous and Mental Disease, 182,* 179-184.

Solomon, P., & Draine, J. (1994). Family perceptions of consumers as case managers. *Community Mental Health Journal, 30,* 165-176.

Solomon, P., & Draine, J. (1995a). One-year outcomes of a randomized trial of consumer case management. *Evaluation and Program Planning, 18,* 117-127.

Solomon, P., & Draine, J. (1995b). The efficacy of a consumer case management team: Two year outcomes of a randomized trial. *Journal of Mental Health Administration, 22,* 135-146.

Solomon, P., & Draine, J. (1996). Service delivery differences between consumer and non-consumer case managers in mental health. *Research on Social Work Practice, 6,* 193-207.

Stein, L., & Test, M. A. (1980). Alternative to mental hospital treatment, I. Conceptual model: Treatment program and clinical evaluation. *Archives of General Psychiatry, 37,* 392-397.

Phyllis Solomon, Ph.D., is professor of social work and social work in psychiatry at the University of Pennsylvania School of Social Work and has extensively conducted mental health services research for over 20 years.

Jeffrey Draine, Ph.D., is research assistant and professor, Center for Mental Health Policy and Services Research, Department of Psychiatry, University of Pennsylvania.

Warner Rodgers, M.Ed., is director of the Share ICM Program since 1992. He has worked in the mental health field for over 17 years.

Sam Edwards, A.S., has been working as an intensive case manager with Share ICM since 1991. He also sits on the Board of Directors of the 1260 Housing Corporation, which provides subsidized housing for individuals with mental illness at below market cost.

Ernestine Ross is one of the original intensive case managers associated with Share ICM. She has been employed in the mental health system since 1988.

Chapter 35
Project Return: The Next Step— Transition from a Self-Help to a Consumer-Controlled Agency
Shelley Levin

Project Return: The Early History

In 1980, ten people living in a graduate house of a board and care home met to find a way to relieve the isolation and loneliness in their lives. They were looking for a way to add friendships, a sense of meaning, and a feeling of belonging to a community. This group became the first Project Return club. Building on this club and the potential for others like them, two mental health professionals, John Siegal and Rhoda Zussman, wrote a proposal to the California State Department of Mental Health for $60,000 to sponsor and staff Project Return, a county-wide network of self-help clubs.

The primary responsibility for running Project Return fell to the Mental Health Association in Los Angeles County, a private, nonprofit agency whose mission is to educate citizens and the community about mental illness, and to advocate for and serve people with mental illness. The Mental Health Association provided technical support and assistance in a variety of ways to Project Return. The grants which funded Project Return were applied for and administered by the Mental Health Association. Founded with a grant from the California State Department of Mental Health, the Los Angeles County Department of Mental Health later took over responsibility for funding the program. Employees of the Mental Health Association, one of whom was a mental health consumer, served as regional directors, charged with keeping existing Project Return clubs up and running, and helping to form new ones. Additionally, Mental Health Association staff members provided assistance and support to Project Return on issues ranging from governance to budgeting.

With the motto "People helping people to help themselves," Project Return clubs began as self-help and peer advocacy groups. Trained facilitators, professionals, or non-consumer volunteers from the community, were to act as partners with mental health consumers in organizing clubs to provide social activities, with the goal of improving the consumers' quality of life. While conceived as an equal partnership, Project Return quickly reverted to a more traditional model where club members assumed a passive role, and professional staff facilitators took over the responsibility for leading the groups.

Project Return gave consumers the opportunity to play leadership roles within the organization. Governance of the clubs was made up entirely of members. Some clubs, however, had great difficulty recruiting consumers to serve in leadership roles. Ideally, each club was to elect its own set of officers and two delegates to the Project Return Federation. The Federation elected officers from the club delegates and was responsible for organizing group-wide events as well as producing the monthly newsletter.

During the early 1980's, Project Return's four regional directors started 50 new clubs at a variety of venues including county mental health clinics, board and care homes, churches, parks and community centers. The development of clubs was based on the needs and interests of the consumers. Some clubs adopted a special focus, such as employment or the arts. Other clubs were developed to serve monolingual clients in the multicultural Los Angeles community. At its height, Project Return had over 1,000 members.

Originally, the Los Angeles County Department of Mental Health offered their mental health staff the opportunity to make a long-term commitment to serving as club facilitators on county time. Many professionals jumped at the chance to have unique, non-therapy relationships with mental health consumers. Under their direction, the clubs grew and prospered. Cutbacks to the County Department of Mental Health in the mid-1980s, however, eliminated the availability of county staff as facilitators.

The greatest barrier to establishing and maintaining clubs at this time was finding enough volunteer facilitators. Project Return staff looked to college intern programs for facilitators, but this created turn-over each semester. For a short time, several community volunteer groups, such as the Junior League, provided facilitators, but these groups were unable to make a long-term commitment to Project Return. The underlying and unspoken assumption during this period was that consumers could perhaps "co-facilitate" a club, but the clubs required a non-consumer facilitator to be successful. As fewer new clubs were established, and more and more facilitators dropped out, membership, energy and enthusiasm in Project Return began to decline.

It was at this time that the Mental Health Association established three Social Centers. Each Social Center had its own building and staff. The Social Centers hosted some of the Project Return clubs, while other clubs continued to meet in different community locations. The Social Centers were able to reach additional consumers with a wider variety of services than the Project Return clubs.

With the development of the Social Centers, however, the energy of the Mental Health Association staff shifted from Project Return clubs to building and maintaining the Social Centers. While participation in the Social Centers grew, membership in Project Return clubs declined. It soon became clear that in order to stay alive, Project Return would have to undergo a radical transformation.

Beginning the Transition

The transformation of Project Return to a consumer-controlled program was brought about by three converging forces: the drain of Mental Health Association administrative and direct-service staff time and energy by the Social

Centers; the continuing decline in interest and participation in the Project Return clubs; and the strong and rapid growth of the consumer empowerment movement in the 1980s.

The decision to transform Project Return into a consumer-controlled program came from the Mental Health Association, rather than from the membership. A loyal core of Project Return members continued to be satisfied with the usual way of doing things. In fact, if the Federation, the governing board of Project Return, had been allowed to vote, they would not have agreed to become a consumer-run organization. The leadership of the Mental Health Association, however, recognized that continuing along the same path would lead to the ultimate demise of Project Return. An executive decision was made to transform Project Return in order to insure its survival.

This decision was met with much fear and trepidation by the club members. Many felt abandoned, as if the Mental Health Association had asked for a divorce. Others were afraid they might lose the comfort and status of the positions they had obtained in the existing organizations. Finally, many members resented the imposition of something they weren't asking for. While not ignoring or dismissing the validity of these concerns, the decision to go ahead was ultimately made by the Mental Health Association's Board of Directors.

In 1992, Project Return: The Next Step was formed. Its mission is to "offer social opportunities, promote self esteem and community involvement while encouraging leadership." The initial plan called for the Mental Health Association to continue to serve for one year in an advisory role in the transition to a completely consumer-run organization. The Mental Health Association was also to continue to manage the funding and bookkeeping of the new organization.

The search for staff members for the new Project Return: The Next Step began immediately. A hiring committee was formed with members from the Mental Health Association, members of Project Return, and other interested mental health consumers. Announcements were circulated to all Project Return clubs, and throughout the Los Angeles mental health community. There were 45 applications and seven individuals were hired: a coordinator, an administrator, and five regional aides who were responsible for organizing and overseeing clubs within their region. All the employees were mental health consumers.

The Transition Takes a Detour

Project Return: The Next Step began with much optimism on the part of the Mental Health Association staff and many Project Return members. Quickly, however, the optimism began to fade as problems became apparent both at the administrative and regional levels.

The hiring committee had decided to split the top position in the organization between a coordinator and an administrator. It was hoped that this would avoid concentrating power in one individual. Unfortunately, the division in authority turned into an ongoing power struggle between the two individuals. Job assignments were unclear, and there was much infighting and jockeying for control, taking time and energy away from rebuilding the organization. Additionally, Mental Health Association staff were called upon to mediate the problems, reinforcing the idea that consumers were unable to run their own organization.

After a year, both the original coordinator and the administrator left. Based in part on the administrator's work experience with Project Return: The Next Step, the Los Angeles County Department of Mental Health offered her a full-time job, and she accepted. In taking a job with the County, the administrator became a role model for other consumers involved in the program, demonstrating that additional job opportunities were available. Unfortunately, this rapid turn-over left Project Return: The Next Step without top consumer leadership.

Obstacles were also apparent at the regional level. The pool of experienced consumers to fill the regional aide positions was limited. Keeping with its commitment, Project Return: The Next Step insisted on hiring only mental health consumers, many of whom lacked the necessary expertise to perform the regional aide job. Many regional aides had not worked for a long period of time, nor had they been taught the planning, promoting, and coordination skills necessary to perform the job. The Mental Health Association tried offering workshops on leadership skills, and making Department of Mental Health inservice training available to the regional aides, but few regional aides completed all the training.

Regional aides often lacked the transportation necessary to attend all the different club meetings. Los Angeles is a geographically large county, about the size of the state of Rhode Island, and lacks adequate public transportation. Few regional aides were able to afford their own cars, leaving many club meetings uncovered, and the regional aides very frustrated.

These problems led to rapid turn-over in the regional aide positions. The jobs went unfilled for long periods of time or were hastily filled with consumers who did not have a history with the organization. The clubs, which were accustomed to being staff run, didn't meet on their own if there was no regional aide in attendance. Thus, the number and activity level of clubs continued to decline.

The deterioration in club membership had two serious consequences. First, participation in the Advisory Council dwindled, further weakening the leadership core. Second, the decline in club membership meant Project Return: The Next Step was not delivering the units of service required by its contract with the Los Angeles County Department of Mental Health, and thus was in danger of losing its funding.

By the end of 1993, it had become clear to all involved that Project Return: The Next Step was not ready to become an independent organization. Club members, the leadership of the project, and the leadership of the Mental Health Association all agreed that the time table had been overly optimistic and could not be met. All the key players met to re-map the journey. It was decided that changes needed to be made at all levels of the organization.

A New Route

Several changes were implemented almost immediately. First, it was decided that there should be only one top administrative position, the program director, and an administrative assistant to support him/her. A very charismatic director and an unusually capable administrative assistant were hired, and they brought stability, enthusiasm and technical expertise to the organization.

The new Director, Bill Compton, had been a Project Return member for only a few years but had become an active participant. Prior to joining Project Return, Bill had been in and out of psychiatric hospitals, on the streets, and on legal conservatorship. After his conservator placed him in a board and care home, he joined the home's Project Return club and quickly became its vice-president. Bill credits Project Return with helping to keep him out of the hospital and on the road to recovery.

Bill has a Masters degree in Theater Arts and acted in, directed, and produced numerous plays in New York City. In Los Angeles, he worked as the assistant manager for a large theater. The management expertise he brought to Project Return: The Next Step was invaluable. As a result of his new position, Bill has been able to move to independent housing, buy a van, and take a trip to New Zealand to celebrate his 50th birthday.

Sandi Craddick, the administrative assistant, has been a member of Project Return since its inception. She began working for the Mental Health Association as a volunteer, moved up to a supported employment clerical position working four days per week, and eventually became the editor of the Project Return Newsletter. Sandi has always viewed Project Return as her support network, stepping in when her family was absent.

Sandi was initially quite hesitant to apply for the new administrative position with Project Return: The Next Step. She had a secure, comfortable, enjoyable job with the Mental Health Association, and at first asked if she could return to that job if the new job didn't work out. In keeping with the agency philosophy of "high-risk-high support," she was told no, and Mental Health Association staff actively encouraged her to take the risk, which she did. Initially, Sandi found the job quite difficult. She had been used to a job that was very structured and routine, and was thrown into a job where the job duties are constantly changing. Sandi has learned to like this variety and feels it has increased her independence and self-esteem.

One immediate decision was to re-appropriate those funds budgeted to pay for the regional aides. The money was split between six service area aides and a club aide for each club. Regional aides were re-named service area aides because the Los Angeles County Department of Mental Health divides the county into "service areas." The service area aides' territory was defined to mirror the service areas of the Los Angeles County Department of Mental Health.

Service area aides work 10 to 20 hours per week and are paid between $5.50 and $6.50 per hour, depending upon their experience. They are required to attend a meeting of each club in their area twice a month, hold a meeting when a club aide is absent, and meet with all the club aides in their area once per month. Additionally, they may plan and carry out large social events. In 1995, Margaret Keller, a service area aide, organized a Fourth of July picnic for several hundred people, including 28 mental health professionals from Japan who were visiting to study the Mental Health Association's programs.

The primary role for service area aides is to create communication links. By meeting with all the club aides collectively, they are able to facilitate the flow of information and ideas between clubs. They also serve as the link between the administration of Project Return: The Next Step and the local clubs.

Each Project Return: The Next Step Club is designed to have a club aide assigned to it. Club aides are drawn from the existing club members, and are required to attend weekly club meetings, facilitate rather than lead the meetings, and complete all the paperwork required by the funding agency. Club aides also attend a monthly meeting with their service area aide. Club aides receive a $50 per month stipend check and are given $10 per month to purchase club supplies. Some club aides were recently invited to participate on a panel organized by the Los Angeles County Department of Mental Health designed to educate their professional staff about the competencies of consumers.

The club aide position was formed with several ideas in mind. First, club aide candidates were drawn from current club members, and thus they had a vested interest in keeping the club going. Second, having multiple club aide positions gives more individuals the opportunity to earn money and gain job experience. Club aide positions provide consumers with work experience which allows them to develop leadership skills, thus strengthening the pool of consumer employees for the organization. Successful club aides provide a trained labor pool for the service area aide positions, which in turn frees up additional employment opportunities for new consumers to be club aides. Additionally, the Los Angeles County Department of Mental Health has a staff position requiring one year of working experience with persons with mental illness, and it is planned that the club aides will become eligible for these positions.

All these changes appear to be paying off. The turnover in the service area aides positions has slowed, due to their increased satisfaction with the job. Club aides are heavily invested in building their clubs and as a result, attendance is increasing. Several club aides have moved on to other employment opportunities, opening additional opportunities for consumers. Finally, the governing core of Project Return: The Next Step has been strengthened.

Issues to Consider When Making a Transition

There are three categories of issues to consider when attempting to make the conversion from a self-help to a consumer-controlled organization: (1) how the changes will affect current members; (2) how the changes will affect existing staff; and (3) organizational issues.

Issues Affecting Current Members

Abandonment Fears

Many Project Return members expressed fears that the Mental Health Association was abandoning them, and that the new organization would sink, leaving them with no social outlets. This is certainly a legitimate fear. Many of the members had lived through deep and painful budget cuts to the Los Angeles County Department of Mental Health, and had seen programs disappear overnight. Additionally, many members had experienced abandonment by their family and friends when they first became ill.

The Mental Health Association repeatedly reassured the members that they would not abandon Project Return: The Next Step. In fact, when the organization initially floundered, it moved in to be a more active participant. The fears of many members were eased, although some members did leave the organization, perhaps abandoning Project Return before it could abandon them.

Internalized Oppression

There is a well known phenomena that exists in many minority communities. After hearing criticism over and over from the dominant group, minority group members begin to accept this criticism as truth. Consumers have been taught for years by mental health professionals that they are incapable: incapable of holding jobs, incapable of making decisions for themselves, incapable of building close relationships with others. All this, of course, is untrue. However, some consumers have internalized this view.

When the Mental Health Association announced that they were turning Project Return into a fully consumer-controlled organization, the first reaction of some members was, "We can't handle it." These consumers had "learned" they were helpless, unable to do things for themselves. They were not only sure that Project Return: The Next Step would fail; they also believed many members would become irrevocably ill in the process.

Ironically, the professional staff of the Mental Health Association had more faith in the consumers than they had in themselves. The Mental Health Association had always held the view that mental health consumers were competent, knowledgeable, able adults, but now it was time to more forcefully advocate this view. Mental Health Association staff repeatedly and confidently voiced their opinion that mental health consumers are indeed capable of running their own organization. As a few brave consumers stepped forward to test this, and succeeded, they became role models for the others.

New Relationships

Related to the previous issue of internalized oppression, is the issue of negotiating new relationships with non-consumer staff. Consumer employees of Project Return: The Next Step were now on equal footing with non-consumer employees of the Mental Health Association, the Los Angeles County Department of Mental Health, and other agencies. This was the first time many consumers viewed themselves as having equal power, and were viewed by others as their equals.

Any role change can be difficult, and both groups felt uncomfortable in the beginning. Initially, Project Return: The Next Step staff members looked to the staff of the Mental Health Association for permission to make certain decisions or act in certain ways. Gradually, due to the commitment on both sides, Project Return: The Next Step staff began to make more independent decisions and see themselves as truly equal.

Lack of Skills

Despite the initial optimism of the Mental Health Association staff, locating consumers who had managerial skills proved to be more difficult than initially expected. Many mental health consumers become ill in early adulthood, and either are unable to enter the employment arena or have participated only a short time. Administrative skills are usually not learned on the first job, but rather after a series of promotions to the management level. Many mental health consumers never get this opportunity.

Project Return: The Next Step felt fortunate to locate Bill Compton, and his previous administrative experience has contributed much to the organization. With Bill's guidance, Project Return: The Next Step has taken on the role of educator. Club aides are taught the administrative, budgeting and interpersonal skills necessary to run a club. Thus the organization has expanded its role from the social arena to include employment training.

Issues Affecting Current Staff

Loss of Jobs

Once The Mental Health Association and Project Return: The Next Step affirmed their commitment to hiring only consumer staff, it was clear that most regional directors would lose their positions precisely because they were not mental health consumers. These regional directors were angry, and many club members were upset that their relationships with their regional director would be severed for what seemed like an arbitrary reason.

The Mental Health Association worked hard to find alternative jobs for employees who lost their positions. Fortunately, the Association operates other programs which employ non-consumer staff. The issue of what to do with existing non-consumer staff is one that needs to be carefully thought through when a transition is made.

New Relationships

Just as consumer staff had to adapt to their new roles, so did the staff of the Mental Health Association. Despite having worked in a progressive, innovative agency which held the philosophy of consumer empowerment, some staff discovered they still stigmatized mental health consumers as incapable. Initially, some Mental Health Association staff members treated Project Return:

The Next Step staff as "junior staff" rather than as equals. With gradual, gentle confrontation on both sides, this ceased to be an issue. It had become clear, however, that when roles change old prejudices emerge and must be confronted.

Organizational Issues

Funding

One concern that must be addressed before assisting a self-help organization to become truly consumer-run is the issue of funding. The Mental Health Association with its long and established track record of providing excellent service to mental health consumers is an attractive agency to funders. New organizations, particularly nontraditional ones, are often on shaky ground when seeking funding.

Fortunately, Project Return had a long and supportive history with the Los Angeles County Department of Mental Health, its primary funder. The Department of Mental Health remains strongly committed to consumer empowerment, and was a willing partner in the transition.

Training

It was obvious early on that the pool of consumers who had the job experience and skills necessary to run an organization was small. This came as a surprise to the Mental Health Association staff, particularly given its location in a large, urban area. In retrospect, it may have been wiser to delay the transition until selected employees could be fully trained. Certainly, Project Return: The Next Step needed to take on employment training as one of its missions.

The Present

As of June 1995 Project Return: The Next Step had 47 clubs and a budget of $169,000 (up from $100,000 at its inception). Twelve clubs meet in county-operated mental health clinics; 14 in board and care homes; six in community mental health agencies; four in homeless service sites; four at medical centers/ hospitals; and seven at diverse community sites, such as a United Way Office, parks, and senior centers.

Project Return: The Next Step publishes bimonthly issues of the *Next Step News*. Over 2,000 copies are mailed to club members and other interested readers. Each issue offers announcements of coming events, reports on current activities, and features a variety of articles authored by members.

Project Return: The Next Step offers its members opportunities to attend cultural, sporting and other recreational events throughout Los Angeles, often at a discounted cost. Eighty-five members recently enjoyed a low cost, four-day vacation in the mountains near Los Angeles. While under the auspices of Project Return, nonconsumer staff had been responsible for planning and carrying out this popular trip. This year, only consumers were present and many vacationers reported it was the best trip they had attended.

Twenty-eight members recently spent four days in a houseboat on Lake Mojave, which included a casino trip to Laughlin, Nevada. Renting three houseboats, members piloted themselves around the lake, docking at beaches during the day, and cooking meals on the boats at night. As is often the case at events sponsored by Project Return: The Next Step, one member turned out to have an invaluable skill: he had previously worked as a river boat captain and was able to help train others in how to pilot the houseboats.

The Future

If funding can be secured, Project Return: The Next Step plans to grow to 60 clubs by the end of fiscal year 1995-1996. Priorities include starting clubs for Asian-Pacific Islanders, for Veterans at a V.A. facility, and for consumer/college students in cooperation with the University of Southern California School of Social Work.

Project Return: The Next Step is requesting a budget of $228,000 for fiscal year 1995-1996 from the Los Angeles Department of Mental Health. At this funding level, they could serve 600 members at a cost of $380 per member per year, making it the most cost effective county-run mental health program. The program would employ two consumers full-time, five at half time, two at a quarter time, and offer 60 stipend positions to club aides.

Project Return: The Next Step's goal is to have a strong network of 100 clubs (and 100 club aide positions) with 1,000 members by June 30, 1997. By that target date, the organization will have built its infrastructure so that it will have a broad pool of consumer staff members and advisory board members to enable it to be a successful, independent, nonprofit consumer-run organization. By June 1997, Project Return: The Next Step will need an operating budget of $260,000 to meet the demands of its growing membership. The Department of Mental Health remains committed to funding the program, in part because it will offer one of the lowest per-member-served costs of any program within Los Angeles County.

The Final Uncertainty

The issue of defining the ongoing relationship between the Mental Health Association and Project Return: The Next Step remains to be negotiated. It is unclear whether Project Return: The Next Step will truly sever its relationship with the Mental Health Association, or whether it will continue in a modified form. Currently Project Return: The Next Step operates under the Mental Health Association's powers of incorporation. Plans to draw up the papers for Project Return: The Next Step to incorporate separately were put on hold in 1993 when the decision was made for it to become a separate agency.

The political climate for mental health services has changed rapidly since Project Return: The Next Step's inception. With the advent of managed care and managed competition, more and more small, nonprofit agencies are joining with larger ones for protection. The Mental Health Association is able to provide such services as bookkeeping, payroll, management information systems, and benefits administration to Project Return: The Next Step — services that would be difficult for Project Return to render on its own as a small agency.

Additionally, Project Return: The Next Step is dependent upon a single source, the L.A. County Department of Mental Health, for its funding. While enjoying strong support from the department, the state of California remains in a recession, and budget cuts are expected to be widespread and severe. A relationship with the Mental Health Association, an agency founded over 70 years ago with a strong reputation in the community and diverse funding resources, may help Project Return: The Next Step to obtain alternative funding not otherwise available to a new, small agency.

Before the decision for or against complete independence can be made, several issues remain to be examined. First, is having a consumer-run program enough, or does it have to be a completely independent agency? While the Mental Health Association can offer Project Return: The Next Step some services they would have difficulty providing for themselves, does the connection with Mental Health Associations dilute the strength of Project Return: The Next Step? This is a version of the difficult question, "Does every single employee of a consumer-controlled agency have to be a mental health consumer?"

Another issue is whether Project Return: The Next Step can remain a part of the Mental Health Association and still retain its consumer-controlled organization enough to truly empower those that it serves. By maintaining the relationship, would Project Return: The Next Step always be in a subordinate role, even unintentionally? Would its members and the outside community truly look upon it as a consumer triumph?

These are certainly difficult issues to resolve, and are dependent on factors outside both organizations such as funding availability. While the resolution of these issues is currently unclear, Project Return: The Next Step members, staff, and board of directors are now strong and cohesive enough to insure the program's future in whatever form that might take.

Conclusions and Recommendations

Several points have emerged from the Mental Health Association's experiences with Project Return: The Next Step that can serve as a guide to other agencies wishing to build a similar consumer-run organization. The first is that it doesn't matter whether clubs are initially staff-lead or consumer-lead. We have, however, found that true "co-leadership" is almost impossible. Both professional staff and consumers almost unconsciously look to the non-consumer to take the lead, with the consumer playing the role of "second in command." Thus, it is better to be honest and direct about the leadership structure.

Of more initial importance than the leadership structure, we have found, is building club membership. It has been our experience that clubs are very difficult to start from scratch. The first step, therefore, must be to find an existing group of consumers interested in participating in a self-help club. These groups may be formal or informal. Many of our initial members come from Project Return clubs where there was already a group structure in place. We have also, however, formed groups from consumers living together in the same board and care home, consumers who have banded together to live communally on the streets, members of outpatient psychotherapy groups, and informal "coffee klatches." Building on some sort of existing group structure is vital, and takes precedence over leadership issues in the beginning.

Another point we have discovered is that we must allow consumer leadership to emerge. This is a delicate stratagem. As discussed earlier, it is important to teach consumers the leadership skills necessary to run a club. It is equally important, however, not to "choose" who those interested and able consumers will be. Rather, the process is one of waiting and watching, and at times encouraging natural leaders to emerge, and then offering skills training to those individuals. Some of our most successful club aides are individuals known to the Association for a long time whom the staff never would have guessed had the emotional or intellectual capacity to assume leadership positions. Thus, you must be willing to give all interested consumers a try.

Above all, when building a self-help organization it is important to think of the process as an evolution. It is important to build a structure which allows clubs to evolve, natural leaders to grow, and a fully consumer-run organization to develop. For Project Return: The Next Step, this evolution continues to unfold.

Acknowledgement

The author wishes to thank Bill Compton, Sandi Craddock, John Siegel, Ann Stone and Richard Van Horn for their valuable contributions to this chapter.

Dr. Levin is the director of research for the Mental Health Association in Los Angeles County and assistant professor of social work at the University of Southern California.

SECTION 8

Proactive Supports for Consumer Service Provision

Introduction to Section 8: Proactive Supports for Consumer Service Provision

The collection of chapters that compose this section addresses the supports needed to put consumer service provision into practice and to sustain it as a viable aspect of psychiatric rehabilitation. Although the authors do not totally agree, or may not emphasize the same types of supports, together the chapters underscore the commitment and intentional action needed by organizations and systems interested in introducing and sustaining consumer service provision. There are numerous themes identified in these chapters — some are salient and others are more subtle.

An important theme that runs through at least four of the chapters concerns the establishment of organizational intent and the translation of this intent into an administrative and organizational commitment that legitimizes consumer service provision. Kerouac emphasizes this idea when he identifies the sheer number of tasks, procedures, and decisions that have to be in place in order to foster a support group for prosumers — that is, for staff who see themselves as both consumers and professionals. Inspection of these actions suggests that few of these will be sustained unless administration (especially, as suggested by Kerouac, top management) identifies the importance of creating and implementing these support systems: whether for staff who are consumers and later adopt the role of professional, or for professionals who also have backgrounds as mental health consumers.

Zipple and his colleagues also emphasize the need for explicit organizational intent. These authors, like Davidson and his co-authors, see a need for grand concepts at the highest organizational and programmatic levels that call for the fostering, protection, and support of consumer service provision. The papers authored by Zipple et al. as well as by Davidson et al. identify the need to adopt an affirmative employment perspective and set of policies. This perspective and the accompanying policies underscore the importance of valuing previous personal experience as a mental health consumer, the importance of relating to consumers in service provision roles as colleagues, the establishment of priorities for respecting the unique knowledge brought by consumers to service provision, and the commitment of organizational resources (often in the form of agency-wide training) to make these new policies happen in practice.

The notion of organizational intent is seen in the chapter authored by Jonikas and her colleagues who link the effectiveness of internal training and the work of a peer provider internal change team to administrative commitment. Indeed, these authors point out that consumer service provision will only be possible and/or effective when there is an agency context that is receptive to and supportive of consumer involvement in service provision. Jonikas et al. point to the importance of creating intention through an overall organizational strategy and system for making consumer service provision a successful and permanent aspect of the agency's service delivery model. According to these authors, the restructuring of agency culture and climate, mission, values, and goals is an essential feature of an overall strategy of support for this kind of role innovation.

The two chapters by Kerouac and Davidson et al. suggest that informal support systems will also be most effective when there are strong organizational intent and commitment. Informal support systems that have organizational sanction can be used to help people to successfully negotiate a "dual role" which is reflected by the concept of prosumer. Membership in these informal support systems, like self-study groups, support groups, and mentoring systems, and the great effort needed to keep them organized and operational, will be most successful when senior administrative leadership says that such support is needed in order to sustain innovation in the area of consumer service provision. In other words, legitimization of support is a support.

Role modeling is identified in at least two chapters as a potential proactive support. Bledsoe-Boykin offers a personal account of her own involvement as a role model within the context of a drop-in center. She identifies the personal benefits of filling this role, and also identifies how she helped others to understand what people struggling with serious mental illness can offer to one another and how this mutual support can contribute to recovery. She notes how consumer service providers can model recovery and personal success and overcome "hospitalization, loss, depression, stigmatization." She emphasizes the benefits of showing first hand that people can grow in their work, their education, and in their professional development.

Davidson et al. also discuss the benefits of role modeling. But they point out that role modeling may be fraught with ethical concerns since it can require people to reveal themselves as consumers, and possibly open up their psychiatric history to public knowledge. Some people, according to these authors, may not wish to engage in such self-disclosure. They may want to become involved in the provision of services but to do so in a manner that protects their privacy. Davidson et al. suggest that the preservation of choice concerning self-disclosure is itself a support, and indicative of good practice that follows a framework of affirmative employment. According to these authors, disclosure itself may not be as important as the "enhanced sensitivity to, and comfort with, a client's situation that a prosumer may have based on his or her first person experiences and familiarity."

Another theme operating in this section is that of the "good match." Davidson et al. emphasize the need to reflect on the match between prosumers and the program within which they will work and practice. The match between consumer and job in terms of achieving a correspondence between someone's preferences, skills, and career direction is important but the idea of match must be seen within a broader framework. Prosumers, according to Davidson et al., may operate best in those programs to which they can make contributions to the programmatic mission, in which the culture supports active consumer involvement, and in those that value consumerism. They note that prosumers may not operate as effectively in acute care settings that value traditional interactional patterns among disciplines and between professionals and consumers, while prosumers may be most effective and potent in innovative settings that value outreach, advocacy, and consumer empowerment. These authors offer an interesting caveat: Understand the programmatic culture and seek a good match between consumer involvement in service provision and the nature and purpose of the actual program.

Supervision and internal coaching cannot be overlooked as principal supports, and it is not surprising that several authors capture these in their chapters. The chapter authored by Weklar identifies the supportive qualities of the coach who assists the consumer to master her role as a case manager. In her chapter, Weklar identifies herself as a support person rather than a treatment professional. She is someone who assists the consumer to focus on issues created by the job, and is a colleague who is prepared to serve as a sounding board, problem solver, and front line supporter. As a coach, Weklar focused on work success and was flexible enough to adjust support to the situation by becoming an advocate, when needed, or by simply staying in the background. This form of coaching becomes vital to professional development, especially when people have not worked for some time. The provision of this kind of direct support within an agency may be an important accommodation. Zipple et al. underscore the importance of putting into place accommodations that will help people to be successful as prosumers and that these accommodations often involve the creation of new internal work arrangements, such as coaching and internal support.

Coaching may or may not be offered through supervisory arrangements. Weklar points to the importance of making available to consumer service providers relationships that are nonhierarchal and colleagial, ones that are often less threatening than supervisory ones. Nonetheless, Zipple et al., as well as Jonikas et al., identify the importance of preparing supervisors to be supportive of consumers as providers, to be interested in and committed to their professional development, and to help them master their roles and their work environments. Davidson et al. add that supervisiors will need to support people with little or no work experience. And, they may need to be prepared to help consumer service providers handle distress that can arise from overly identifying with other consumers.

These chapters tell us a great deal about proactive supports. At least two authors point to the need to be concerned about tokenism. But this tokenism can be reduced or eliminated by helping people to make good matches, offering choice in the range of roles that are available, and involving people in the identification of supports they need to help them be successful in new work roles. According to Zipple et al, tokenism is prevented by focusing on the provision of support. This support is put into practice through recruitment, training, reduction of role conflict, career and job mobility, skilled supervisory staff, good supervision, and respect for confidentiality and privacy. Zipple et al.

argue that support for consumer service provision will unfold naturally when the overall agency is committed to making an organizational policy of diversity happen in day to day practice.

Support for consumer service provision will occur, according to Davidson et al., when organizational leaders make work environments supportive and flexible for all employees. Perhaps the principal lesson in this section is that all of us involved in psychiatric rehabilitation need to make our work settings and organizations more supportive of diversity. As we achieve this, our agencies will become increasingly more hospitable to consumers as service providers.

Chapter 36

The Consumer Provider as Role Model

Cherie D. Bledsoe Boykin

After numerous bouts in and out of hospitals, I felt my life consisted of one revolving door, going nowhere. On one occasion, I was released from the hospital on a Friday around 3:30 p.m. A case manager picked me up and dropped me off at my home. Minutes later, we honked the car horn and my three children excitedly greeted me. I could feel the anxiety and pressure shooting through my body as I tried to pick up all the pieces of home life and readjust to a community environment that seemed very distant and terrifying. By Monday morning, I was on the brink of an emotional breakdown. My case manager thought I had been released from the hospital too soon and recommended re-hospitalization. At that point, sparks popped within me and I screamed out. Had I not been dropped off on Friday without any help, maybe I would not be like this now. She agreed. The subject of hospitalization was terminated. But for me, I was left wondering why the system had not done anything to prevent this or if they even saw the void. Afterall, I thought, that was their job and I was their responsibility.

Introduction

That was to be my last hospital stay. I was enrolled in our mental health center's partial hospital program — highly structured by design, with minimal consumer input. In 1990, the Kansas Mental Health Reform Act (HB2586) became law. Due to this law and the subsequent changes, whisperings of consumer-run programs found their way to our mental health center. We heard terms such as independence, empowerment, networking, and advocacy. These ideas were foreign as well as frightening. But they set off a curiosity inside me to find out what this "consumer movement" was all about. Cautiously, consumers, with the support of staff, began to talk over the possibilities of designing and developing their own place to govern, to provide jobs, and to call their own. As I became involved in this venture, I sensed a change happening within me. I felt compelled in the mornings to get to our mental health center and present to my peers all the wonderful ideas and thoughts that were streaming through my head about the proposed new drop-in center. The skills of writing and planning that I once thought were lost or buried were now uncovered as I wrote the first grant for funding our program.

The Spectrum Drop-In Center, Inc. opened in June 1992. I was hired as one of six part-time aides. The mission of our center is to provide individuals with severe and persistent mental illness a safe place to relax, socialize, build friendships, increase personal growth, awareness, and self-esteem, improve social skills, and enhance one's ability to live independently in the community. My initial role as a drop-in center aide was to keep the center running as smoothly and efficiently as possible. My responsibilities included opening and closing the center, coordinating program activities, light housekeeping, and clerical duties (answering phones, maintaining daily attendance records and logs).

Additionally, I was hired as a peer support counselor to support consumers who were experiencing difficulty with loneliness and daily living stresses, especially those transitioning from the hospital to home life. This support came in the form of home visits or through telephone contact. I would identify myself as a mental health consumer and offer my friendship, similar experiences, and knowledge as a link to assist my peers in learning to re-integrate in the community and connect with social supports through our drop-in center. Peer support services were generally offered during evenings and weekends when traditional mental health services were not readily available.

Personal Benefits

My new role as drop-in center aide and peer support counselor was like a rebirth. I was awakened from my narrow focus of only seeing the label of mental illness. My perception had sealed me inside a tomb. Since being diagnosed, I had no reason to do anything. My mother took on a lot of the responsibilities for raising my children (I felt undeserved to call myself their mother). The majority of my day I could be found lying in bed. I really didn't care about or like myself at all.

The new responsibilities with Spectrum gave my life a focus. I was able to look beyond my illness and see me. It gave me responsibilities and expectations for myself. I was responsible for writing quarterly reports on which our grant funds were dependent. I conducted consumer interest surveys. We planned special events and activities that were both fun and educational. I was asked to be a presenter at various consumer forums and conferences on topics of peer counseling, crisis intervention, and the development of our drop-in center. I was able to see and utilize the skills and talents which I thought were gone.

I looked at myself in the mirror each day and saw that I did have a smile, a laugh, and a personality that was not that bad. It made me want to get out of bed, go to work, and do a good job. It felt good knowing that someone was counting on me to be there in the morning to open the center, to greet them. The feelings of being needed, expected, and responsible — that without me it would not happen — made a difference in me. I gained power and self-worth from making decisions that not only affected me but others. I began to see myself as a person that had something to offer and to contribute to society. My mental illness was not the end of everything but just a stumbling block or a different turn to which I had to adjust and build around. My brain was still intact; I was a talking, thinking, functioning human being that people enjoyed being around. The drop-in center gave me the desire to break the stigmas of mental illness to which I had fallen prey.

My work provided an avenue that made my life feel more normal. My illness became secondary. Once again, I had the self-confidence to be a mother to my children and accept their respect. It gave them the security of a normal, stable home life. I remember one day my youngest daughter ran into the house and observed me watching television and commented, "I'm so proud of you, Mommy. It's good to see you coming home from work and watching Oprah like all the other mommies." Working as a consumer provider brought stability, direction, and a sense of accomplishment to my life. I was an agent of change. This experience was empowerment in action. When working in the drop-in center, I felt personally driven to be patient and empathetic, to listen actively, and to give the unconditional support that I myself desired from others. These qualities allowed me to give my peers the respect and dignity they were so deserving of, but often lacked. The additional income also helped me by providing a better home life for my family. But most importantly, my work started the beginning of inner healing. I realized God had not forsaken me. Instead, God had taken my life on a different road and had given me something else to do. I regained love for myself where for so many years hate had festered. A friend remarked to me, "You were really weird when you first came to the mental health center. I mean, really sick. Now you're OK."

Consumer Benefits

As the drop-in center evolved, it became more and more the place where consumers came together to converse about hospital experiences; illness and medications; relationships with significant others, families, and case managers; challenges with the various social agencies; and daily living situations. More importantly, it became a place where consumers sought support, comfort, and acceptance from the loneliness that seems to go hand-in-hand with mental illness. People were more open to sharing their personal experiences and situations. Because of the limited involvement of "professional" staff (they are required to knock before entering the drop-in center), consumers started to seek advice and support from peer counselors and aides to problems and situations they felt were too threatening to present to their case manager or other professional staff.

My role as an aide became the vehicle for many consumers to help fill their needs. I saw my job shift from being one of mainly overseeing the operations of the drop-in center to one of being a provider of support, an advocate, a leader, and a role model. I think my peers saw me first as a friend who they could talk to without feeling they were at risk of losing anything. I was able to relate to that fear. Often I was approached for my opinion on a situation or for advice about how to solve a particular problem. I recall one time when a consumer I had formed a close bond with was extremely upset. Upon exploring why, she stated that I hadn't said hello to her and given her a hug. I realized then how important my role was in the eyes of many of my peers. My opinion and perception of them seemed to play a vital part in how they saw themselves.

The body language or manner in which I initially greeted my peers seemed to make a difference in how their day went. I had become an important support to them. We were able to share concerns and anxieties such as homelessness, or finding resources to purchase medications, food, and clothing. I was also looked upon to assist them in obtaining these needs. Peer providers would direct consumers to food kitchens, clothing banks, and thrift stores, or assist with housing needs (such as making roommate matches), usually through first-hand information passed on to us by other consumers.

Most of the time, I tried to reassure my peers that their problems were the same ones I constantly faced or was concerned with, and I supported them in sharing these problems with their case managers or other staff. Many times, discussions would center around feelings of suicide, medication issues, mental illness stigma, substance abuse, sexual abuse, personal and family relationships, or personality conflicts. The aides or peer counselors often were called upon to be the facilitators of such discussions. Aides were looked upon as important sources of information and their opinions were highly valued. Also, I believe feedback was more readily accepted from peer providers because of their common bonds and first-hand experiences rather than from case managers who had not had the same experiences. It seemed we had our own consumer movement which pooled our collective knowledge and awareness.

Advocacy

At times, we would use this shared awareness to question the policies and procedures of our mental health center, to point out areas in which we had concerns, and to present projects and ideas of interest. These ideas included advocacy for a Saturday drop-in center day, consumer van drivers, and additional work and vocational opportunities. Most of the time, consumer providers were the leaders in these negotiations and empowered their peers to become involved in what they wanted.

Our drop-in center's open door policy allowed the consumers to feel free, supported, and at ease, allowing conversations to flow naturally. A pattern developed in which consumers used peer counselors and aides as sounding boards before sharing their ideas with professional staff. As peer providers, we did not carry any rigid professional boundaries, titles or language. I was a friend who simply wanted to help. My son often stated, "Mom, I didn't realize you had so many best friends." Since we had already developed bonds, established trust, and retained the title "consumer" provider, we were viewed as people on their side. On occasion, consumers wanted me to advocate for them to their case managers. Sometimes, this simply involved a phone call describing the situation and/or escorting consumers to their case manager's offices. At other times, peer providers were asked to relate the problem directly to the case manager in the consumer's presence. This made the consumer feel safer about sharing information because the ground was already broken. Receiving initial feedback from the professional along with a consumer provider created a less threatening and more inviting climate, open for sharing. Other consumers liked having peer providers assist them because they felt their case managers would not understand what they were trying to communicate (unlike peer providers who spoke their "language"). A common request from a peer desiring advocacy was "You know what I mean, tell them."

Consumer-Staff Partnership

The staff and administrators from the mental health center provided the foundation and framework for my position as a consumer provider. From the beginning, they have been supportive of our efforts. First of all, they gave us encouragement when we asked ourselves, "How will we ever do that?" They provided in-kind support in the form of building space, furniture, supplies, and phone service. They made valuable connections to people who had experience in consumer-run programming. Training came in the form of resources and ideas during planning meetings and informally in the hallways. Staff helped us brainstorm options allowing us to make plans pro-actively. When we did have needs, they were open to helping us find solutions either within the center or the community. Throughout it all, consumers were the ones who had control over the final outcomes — and the consequences.

Because we perceived the staff as having more expertise, we often did not challenge their ideas or decisions. But gradually, I began to notice a shift in power taking place. We began to ask questions and make our own decisions. We started problem-solving ourselves and finding viable options and solutions. As our confidence increased, the involvement of staff decreased. Their role became one of consultant. When staff were not available, we had to find ways to deal with the problems ourselves. We learned to test our own limits and when it was necessary to seek staff involvement.

Now when staff are aware of a consumer who is having a problem, they alert us to the situation. But more often, it is the consumer providers who are the first to notice and report concerns to staff. Although this relationship has not always been ideal — or the most comfortable — we have learned to work together in partnership.

Positive Outcomes

Consumers constantly struggle with self-esteem. I felt it was important for consumers to see themselves as lovable, capable people, deserving of respect and having their own personal goals and dreams. For me, I discovered that treating myself to a beauty regimen — pampering myself — helped me feel better about how I saw myself on the inside. One project that was started in the Spectrum Drop-in Center was our "beauty salon." Initially, the center purchased combs, brushes, nail polish, nail files, make-up and other beauty supply products. At first, consumers appeared bashful to use our supplies so I offered to give fun, amateur "make-overs" to anyone interested.

The results were amazing. I felt as if we should have done before and after "TV commercials." The difference in the way women involved carried themselves was remarkable. They walked and sat straighter, smiled and talked more, and generally just seemed to radiate a stronger image and confidence. I remember one consumer who used a cane to assist her walking. She informed me that her mother wanted her to have her hair styled for church. After finishing my creation with her hair and applying her makeup, I saw a different personality emerge. She was like Cinderella. As she was exiting the drop-in center, I reminded her she was leaving her cane. She told me that she didn't need it. As I observed her holding her head up and walking without the use of the cane, I could sense something magical was happening to her inside. Later, she purchased her own supplies and, with a little practice, began to do her own makeup. It reminded me how the little things we do for people can be so empowering — a start to independence, self-reliance, and building competencies.

Our consumer providers had basically started on the same life course as their peers: hospitalization, loss, depression, stigmatization. However, their successes with employment, education, and independent living, modeled the reality that recovery is possible — and this recovery comes from within ourselves. As I became more competent and set higher goals for myself, I felt it encouraged others who desired to work or go to school take the first step. Consumers could observe the growth and incentives of consumer providers, especially in such tangible terms as a consistent monthly paycheck. Questions and comments like, "Do you think I could work in the drop-in center?" and "You are really doing well now. I remember when you weren't," emphasized the empowerment resulting from consumer providers. Many participants used their consumer providers as references on resumes or asked their assistance in completing employment applications. The connection of consumers helping consumers led to our collective understanding of how empowering it is to make our own decisions and choices, allowing the natural consequences to follow.

One story I would tell is about a middle-aged man I will call Ray. When he first came to our drop-in center, he would sit in a corner having little verbal or visual contact with anyone. Ray's eyes were generally lowered and his face was expressionless. On occasions when we did make eye contact, I would smile at him. I sensed a connection was forming between us. Another peer aide and myself looked forward to seeing Ray each day. We would greet him with a smile and wave. In return, he would smile and wave back. We all burst into laughter. Later, our special greeting to each other included a smile, a wave, and a blown kiss of friendship. This established greeting of rapport with Ray touched other consumers who soon began to greet Ray, too. I remember the first time he verbally greeted me. Not only did he say "Hello," but "Hello,

Cherie." The other aide shared similar experiences. Ray went from being a man of no words to one who expressed himself in sentences and brief conversations. For me, his changes were astounding. Ray now comes in smiling and greeting people and generates conversation. I believe that nobody had given much thought or attention to Ray's conversation to the point that he did not talk anymore. In time, I discovered Ray's love for music and dancing. To everyone's surprise and delight, he danced at a consumer talent show. When given the opportunity, Ray showed everyone the person he really was — his talents, his remarkable sense of humor, and his contagious smile and laugh.

Challenges

As a consumer provider, one of the challenges I face is setting clear expectations for myself as well as my peers. Sometimes it is hard for me to say "no" to added responsibilities or requests because I don't want to hurt anyone's feelings or disappoint them. Trying to maintain personal friendships and doing the job that I am paid for sometimes causes conflict. I was told by one consumer, "I don't like you anymore because you never have time to spend with me." The truth of the matter is, as I set priorities, my evening and weekend peer support activities cut into my social time.

One reason consumers utilize peer support is a fear of hospitalization, particularly when feelings of suicide or harm to others are shared with a staff professional. As a peer provider, I feel I have to brainstorm options in which the peer I am supporting is safe while keeping their trust in me intact. What works is to provide reassurance that that person is important and would be missed. In many instances, by listening and sharing, the problem will resolve itself or seem less life threatening. At other times, I inform the person up front that I will have to share any information of self-harm or harm to others with someone who has more expertise as that is my responsibility as a peer supporter. More importantly, I let them know I care about them. I always try to lay a foundation of unconditional support and to let them know that even if their path toward recovery took them to the hospital, I would be there with them.

Presently, I consider myself a professional in my own right in the role of peer counselor. Initially, I directed all my energy into becoming the perfect peer role model. This caused me to become overwhelmed as I began to overstep my limits and boundaries by taking on too many jobs and responsibilities. As I have been able to receive specialized training and experience, I am now able to set limits more effectively.

I realized as a peer provider the importance of taking care of myself first, finding and taking the time to relax and do something enjoyable. A major accomplishment for me has been gaining the ability to say "no" to consumers as well as staff without feeling guilty. I have also learned skills to handle situations of stress in my life so the stressor does not turn my whole world upside down anymore. I am able to call on my own network of support and to research options where I once would have taken them to bed with me. I am calmer and more patient in dealing with crisis situations and interventions in the lives of my peers.

Multiple Roles

With the multiple roles in which I find myself involved (i.e., family member, community participant, consumer, worker, etc.), transitioning from one role to another has sometimes been very clear and smooth, while at other times it has been a major undertaking. Being a mother, wife, or church member are clear-cut and distinct. However, my role as a consumer includes many gray areas.

As a consumer, my roles are often blurred, going from consumer to consumer-provider to staff member. There are three areas that I have found to be particularly challenging. Having the label "consumer" can lead to a double standard of treatment. Others may see me as consumer first, not as an equal. If I make a mistake, is it due to my illness or my lack of training? I'm moving out of my consumer role but I'm not quite staff. My life experiences (which includes a bachelors degree in special education and psychology) may be just as important as those with advanced degrees. It is difficult to be consumer-friend and paid peer counselor at the same time. And although I realize the disadvantages of having the label, there can be advantages. (consumers go first in the lunch line at the center!)

The second area has to do with confidentiality and the ethical issues regarding consumer provider roles. When I am involved in a conversation with a peer, topics may arise that require further intervention (e.g., the consumer decides to quit taking or alters his/her medication). I must decide if that consumer's rights will be violated by sharing confidential information with staff.

Finally, taking risks and knowing my limits is a recurring challenge. I may be unwilling to speak up for myself for fear of making waves or pointing out obvious problems ("Is what I'm feeling normal or is it related to my illness?"). Or I find myself trying to be the best or overextending myself (in which case I may be denying my illness and its limitations). Being a consumer provider means never being on vacation (everyone knows your phone number and where you live). You have to be able to set boundaries.

Professional Development

My role as consumer provider has given me the opportunity to be involved in numerous educational experiences to enhance my professional development. These trainings, offered through our mental health center and in the community, have given me the confidence and ability to provide the best assistance possible to my peers.

The most important training in which I have participated is a two-day workshop on the strengths model of case management. This model was developed by the University of Kansas, School of Social Welfare, and the training was offered through Wyandot Mental Health Center (WMHC). This model focuses on working with the strengths in people to increase their personal growth and independence. The key pieces of the strengths perspective are:

- assisting a human being vs. treating a patient
- valued consumer vs. compliant client
- collaboration in the community vs. office-based brokering
- sustaining activities vs. palliative care
- focus on daily living circumstances vs. focus on intrapsychic factors
- concrete goals vs. abstract goals
- interdependence of people vs. independence of people
- community options and alternatives vs. state hospital as social welfare responses

This model allows a partnership with the case manager, it gives consumers control, and allows them to be the directors of their own treatment (Kisthardt & Rapp, 1992).

Training in conflict and crisis case management as well as stress management was provided by the crisis case management team at our mental health center. The conflict and crisis training focused on the importance of verbal/nonverbal cues and instructed us how to use the lowest level of intervention possible. I have also found that a clear understanding of rules and expectations is important in preventing conflict. We have guidelines posted in the drop-in center which consumers and staff can refer to when problems arise.

The stress management course provided clues to recognizing burnout. These include irritability, feelings of being overwhelmed, clouded thinking, self neglect, depression, and low energy. Again, setting boundaries and knowing your limits is important, especially in the struggle with multiple roles. We also received helpful hints on how to take time for yourself (e.g., relaxation techniques, finding quiet time, working on a hobby).

"The Mandt System: Managing People" (Mandt, 1994) is a two-day program required for all consumers in provider roles as well as mental health center staff. This system of nonphysical interaction is based on the principle that all people have the right to be treated with dignity and respect. Through Mandt, I was reminded to "see all individuals as people first, to avoid unnecessary reference to disabilities, and to know your own limits" (Mandt, 1994). The benefits of working as a team member were also stressed.

The most recent course I have participated in is "Developing Capable People" (Glenn & Nelsen, 1989). This nine-week course taught foundations for success in communication based on the principles of dignity and respect. It focused specifically on the awareness of barriers vs. builders in communication. When these barriers (assuming, rescuing, directing, expecting, and adultisms) are eliminated and replaced by the builders (checking it out, exploring, encouraging, celebrating, and respecting), our relationships are greatly improved. I found that these trainings have added to my knowledge and capabilities in developing and carrying out consumer-run programs.

Empowerment

I believe that one of the most powerful elements about being a role model for other consumers is to encourage the consumers in their own empowerment. As an advocate pushing for educational awareness about mental illness in my community, I have received the following benefits:

- a power base of mutual support from people who understand what I've been through
- the return of my sense of responsibility and natural consequences
- an awareness of the capabilities of every individual, regardless of illness or handicap
- the ability to set and reach my own personal goals, to see my potential and assist others in seeing theirs
- becoming a contributing member of my community again
- hope and determination for a more normalized life
- the knowledge that I am somebody to be respected and deserving of the best.

Being an advocate for myself and others has given me back my own sense of power, with all the rights as well as responsibilities. The Americans with Disabilities (ADA) law gave legal rights and provided accessible means through which persons with mental illness could obtain gainful employment within their communities. The consumer movement gave it the push and has served notice across our country that people with mental illness are a rich resource that is ready—and willing—to be tapped.

Networking

Staying in touch with what is going on within the consumer movement is one of my top priorities. I have accomplished this through attendance at local and state conferences and meetings, and by keeping in contact with other consumers throughout the country involved in the consumer movement.

I have been involved with the Kansas Mental Illness Awareness Council (KMIAC) which consists of consumer representatives from various catchment areas across the state. KMIAC serves as our power base to the consumer movement. This council is in the forefront of lobbying our state legislature for funding of services and educational programs. These services consist of consumer-run programs, decent, affordable housing, and vocational opportunities. Educational programs strive to raise awareness, fight prejudice and discrimination, and eliminate stigma. Annual state conferences and site visits to consumer-run programs help build across the state a kinship of support, friendship, and fellowship. Our work is accomplished through a speaker's bureau, workshops, consumer forums, teleconferences, publications, and conferences.

Our Consumer Leadership Council (CLC) brings together consumer and staff representatives from consumer-run programs and mental health centers in the Kansas City metropolitan area. In a show of mutual support, the council provides an informational network and communication channel for sharing, discussing, and brainstorming issues of concern by having monthly networking meetings where participants introduce themselves and share successes and problems within their programs. We then offer feedback and have discussions. We have come together to present joint avenues and projects for mutual funding opportunities and educational awareness. CLC keeps everyone generally updated on " what's happening" within our own metropolitan area and legislative dealings across the bi-state area of Kansas and Missouri. Another avenue of networking which has been useful is subscribing to publications from other consumer organizations and groups across the country and maintaining contact with local and state groups for the Alliance for the Mentally Ill.

I have gained personally from connecting with other consumers I view as leaders and role models in their particular programs. They add to my own support circle and serve as a bridge for me to listen, share, and exchange information. More importantly, networking experiences give me a gauge of comparison for my own expectations, challenges, and responsibilities from others doing similar work.

Disclosure

One personal battle that challenges me is disclosing my illness within my community. Because of the mental health center's philosophy of providing a safe and confidential environment (little or no perceived risk), I have always felt free to share my personal story openly with professionals. But when first asked to do an educational awareness presentation within my community — to step out and claim my mental illness — it was a major undertaking. I felt at the time the risks of disclosure were far greater than the perceived positive outcomes (breaking stereotypes, prejudices, and stigmas). The perception of how people (my neighbors, church members, school associates, and other friends) would now see me was very frightening. It seems that all the stereotypes and stigmas about mental illness that I had carried with me before becoming ill, came blaring back at me. It was so overwhelming.

My first presentation about mental illness was to a class of occupational therapy students at a major teaching hospital in my community. This speaking engagement was also very significant to me because I had worked eight years as a secretary at this same hospital until the onset of my illness forced me to quit. It was like facing all my ghosts and pulling my past and present together. With butterflies in my stomach, I agreed to present.

As I began to address the students, I simply said, "Hello, I'm Cherie and I have a mental illness." I felt like I was in an AA group or something. I felt a sensation of release and freedom. So, I said it again. I looked around the room and at the students. I noticed that the walls did not come tumbling down and no one walked out. At that moment, it just felt good — really good — for once in my life to declare I had a mental illness but that I am about much, much more. It felt good to present the facts about the people who were dealing with an illness about which the majority of our society is ignorant. I was able to tell them that I am mother, sister, daughter, church member, peer counselor, aide, and neighbor. I once sat in the classroom where they were sitting. I once worked and did an outstanding job for this hospital. I was able to tell them that people with mental illness come from the college classrooms, from urban, suburban, and rural communities, and from all races, religions, and economic backgrounds. I was able to share with them that this illness is not the fault of the person. It is something life takes us through, curves and tunnels and all.

This first disclosure gave me the encouragement and power to face my illness for myself and see that my own fears were " just all in the name." This is me and I was there to set the record straight for all people with mental illness.

As a role model, I have found that the closer a person is in relationship to me (family member, neighbor, or close friend), the greater the risks to me in disclosing my illness. For instance, one of our day program activities was to get hair cuts at the school of hair design at our local area vocational technical school (AVTS). Some problems of acceptance arose with the students assisting our consumers. After some brainstorming with the director of AVTS and our professional staff, it was agreed that a presentation to the students might help offset their fears and break some stigmas. I eagerly accepted this invitation, but as I stepped into the classroom, I observed many familiar faces (former schoolmates, neighbors, and friends). My heart sank for a moment. Through-out my presentation, I could feel a connection with the very faces I feared. Many responded to me by revealing their own battle with a particular mental illness or by sharing about a friend or family member. Many continued to talk after our presentation about their own experiences. Some just wanted to catch up with me about my family and my life since our last contact. We were asked to come back and get our hair styled and my children were even invited.

Many who were there for the presentation saw me as someone they knew quite well — whose children play and go to school with my children, who work with me in church and associate with me socially. They realized that the majority of their fears were based on ignorance and misunderstanding. As I listened to their feedback and comments, I saw many of their fears were rooted in how the media portrays people with mental illness and with their insecurity about their own mental and emotional problems.

With 40 million Americans (Project Awareness, 1991) suffering from some form of major mental illness, it shouldn't have been such a surprise to me to see familiar faces. I came to the conclusion, which I freely share with other consumers who have the fear of being labeled by the mental health system, that "everybody goes somewhere for something." I tell them that with every-thing going on in the world, I'm more afraid of those they call "normal" folks. It is my belief that we can all benefit from some type of supportive mental health network.

Summary

I know how the diagnosis of mental illness can leave a person in a fragile, hopeless state. Being a role model to my peers has shown me another side. From listening and sharing with my peers, I have been able to draw from them a handbook of knowledge filled with hope and faith. Knowing that somehow together, we were making life a little easier for those coming into the mental health system. I saw how a smile and a hug from someone who has been there takes away the sting of the all alone feeling. Since I began working, I have enjoyed being in the company of wonderful human beings, full of personality, humor and loaded with a wealth of talent, skill, common sense, and wisdom. I see each person for who they are and not for the label that I once feared.

Acknowledgments

The author thanks Millie Crossland, M.S., and Lori Davidson, for their technical assistance in the writing of this paper, and the consumers and staff of Wyandot Mental Health Center for their support and encouragement.

References

Glenn, H.S. & Nelsen, J. (1989). *Developing capable people.* Fair Oaks, CA: Sunrise.
Kisthardt, W.E., & Rapp, C.A. (1992). *The purpose of case management in the strengths model.* Lawrence, KS: University of Kansas, School of Social Welfare.
Mandt, D. & Associates. (1994). *The Mandt system: Managing people, revised* (Available from David Mandt & Associates, P.O. Box 831790, Richardson, TX 75083.)
Project Awareness for Major Mental Illness. (1991). *The faces and facts of mental illness: A mental health handbook for the 1990s.* (Available from Project Awareness for Major Mental Illness, P.O. Box 3584, Wichita, KS 67201.)

Cherie Bledsoe Boykin is a consumer advocate and the supervisor of the Spectrum Drop-In Center, Inc. at Wyandot Mental Health Center in Kansas City, KS.

Chapter 37
Supporting a Consumer-Employee Inside the Agency

Eileen Conti Weklar
Karen Wands Parker

Supporting a Consumer Inside the Agency

The Social Center for Psychiatric Rehabilitation (The Social Center) is a community-based comprehensive psychosocial rehabilitation program that has served persons with serious mental illness since 1963. The Center is headquartered in Fairfax County, Virginia, and operates three clubhouse programs in Merrifield, Alexandria, and Reston. Individuals who traditionally may have been excluded from competitive employment have the opportunity to participate in the vocational program at the Social Center. The goal of the vocational program is to provide members with the skills necessary to move into community-based employment and then to offer the supports needed for members to remain competitively employed. The offering of a safety net is a distinguishing advantage of the vocational program at the Center and helps members and employers in a smooth transition into the workplace. This support consists of on-site training, follow-up visits to liaison with members and employers, employer education and assistance in designing job accommodations, crisis intervention, individual supportive counseling, and linking our members to community resources.

Karen Wands Parker, a member at the Social Center, secured employment as a mental health assistant counselor at a local private, nonprofit agency that has been a leader in developing and providing permanent affordable housing to citizens of Fairfax County who have serious and persistent mental illness. For over two years, I worked with Karen as her vocational counselor and job coach. Ours is a story of two mental health providers who took on the challenges of a unique working relationship in an innovative community-based residential agency. The story was constantly changing and had elements of adventure, drama, comedy and crisis. The best part of the story is that it has no ending — Karen continues in her position in the mental health field as a mental health assistant counselor. I have moved on to a new role at the Social Center as supervisor of vocational services, but I still see Karen when she comes by for her meetings with her current job coach. We fondly remember the early days of providing her job support.

Background

Karen developed her interest in mental health consumer issues soon after becoming a member of the Merrifield Social Center in 1987. On several occasions, she participated in conferences to discuss consumer issues, particularly housing needs and employment opportunities for consumers to provide mental health services.

In the spring of 1991, the Commissioner of the Virginia Department of Mental Health, Mental Retardation and Substance Abuse Services convened a housing forum in Richmond, Virginia. Karen attended with the local consumer group and participated in the work sessions along with other consumers, families, public and private service providers, and administrators. Karen reported her work in an article for the consumer's newsletter, highlighting one of the goals set by the 1991 Housing Forum: the development of a consumer-friendly housing program that offered choice of services and location and that hired consumers as service providers. One year later, Karen was about to realize her dream of working in such a program.

In 1992, a program was developed to serve as a model and demonstration of the value and effectiveness of utilizing consumer empowerment, involvement, and choice in all levels of program development and implementation. This was an exciting new development for Karen, who was determined to be a part of this ground-breaking new program. The goal of the residential program is to assist consumers into housing of their choice and to use program resources to serve as a bridge for transition into permanent housing options that are decent, safe, affordable, and independently leased. For the first time, consumers were involved in all areas of program development and implementation, from the initial development of the program to ongoing participation on steering and program development committees. Consumers were encouraged to apply for the assistant counseling positions and Karen was able to move closer to her goal.

The residential program is operated by the Fairfax County Community Services Board in cooperation with the three county mental health centers. Karen works at the community mental health center in Reston, Virginia and receives her direct supervision from the community residence program staff at the mental health center. As a mental health assistant counselor, Karen offers the support services that program participants desire and need to live independently in the community, to assume increasing responsibility and control over their own lives, and to continue on the transitional bridge to other permanent housing options. She assists her clients with a wide variety of independent living skills: budgeting, menu planning, shopping, cooking, and travel training. Karen also helps her clients identify and access additional community resources they might need to increase their independence, such as furniture, clothing, support, and advocacy groups.

New Challenges in Job Coaching

Karen began her job in April 1992, feeling nervous yet excited about her new responsibilities, her dual role as consumer and provider, and the increased demands on her time. From the beginning I tried to be a potent job coach for

Karen so she could feel her own power, feel accepted, and be encouraged to go on and use her own potential. I often acted as a mirror or a sounding board for Karen to process frustrations or pent up feelings which often blocked clear thinking. Mostly, I served as Karen's truth detector—supporting and challenging — because one without the other is insufficient for real growth. As Karen became more comfortable with my humorous yet confrontational style, we were able to develop a high level of trust to deal with negative feelings and perceptions.

Because of the unique nature of Karen's position, I did not perform traditional on-site job coaching activities at the workplace. Since she provides direct services for clients in the mental health system, it would have been a breach of confidentiality for her clients if I were to directly observe and provide job coaching support during scheduled work hours. Instead, she met with me on a weekly basis for vocational and emotional support. This weekly two-hour session enabled me to monitor Karen's psychiatric stability and job performance and problem solve around any impinging issues. This provided me with the opportunity to help Karen stay focused on job behaviors as she built a successful work history.

Initially, I assisted Karen in adjusting to her new environment, understanding her job responsibilities, communicating effectively with her supervisor and co-workers, and organizing her work day. As Karen grew more comfortable in her position, I provided guidelines for feedback on problem areas and developed strategies to anticipate and deal with problems before they arose. During her first year of employment, I made weekly site visits to act as liaison with Karen's supervisors. I was also available on an as-needed basis to discuss issues with Karen via telephone. On many occasions, Karen needed additional support in order to perform work duties, and she felt comfortable in seeking additional assistance from me.

As a consumer-provider, Karen faced an ongoing struggle as she tried to separate the professional skills needed for the job versus philosophical views as a consumer. She was very hard on herself and needed constant encouragement to view her job performance in more balanced ways. She was often overwhelmed by the stress of her dual role but continued to utilize on- and off-site supports to assist in reframing perceptions of difficult situations on the job. At my weekly liaison meetings with Karen's supervisors, I was updated on Karen's job performance to date, offered my vocational support and expertise to her supervisors, assisted in developing and implementing job accommodations, and did some education when needed.

At the three month mark, it became apparent to Karen's supervisors that she was having difficulty performing the primary tasks of her job, and she received a written evaluation. Karen did not accept this for her own evaluation. She had a hard time hearing feedback without personalizing and generalizing failure overall. Karen placed considerable pressure on herself to succeed in the job. These unrealistic expectations of self-performance contributed to her difficulty in completing tasks. She had serious difficulty in taking risks and completing tasks for fear of making mistakes. She was encouraged to do the job one day at a time, and was told she would get feedback when she made errors. Karen also experienced some problems with judgment in problem solving. Her limited experience in case management was a barrier to her ability to distinguish between urgent versus routine requests for assistance from her clients. She was directed to seek guidance before making independent decisions. Supervision was increased, instructions were reviewed, guidelines and deadlines were clarified, and within two weeks some improvement was noted.

Our Monday work sessions back at the center became an odd mix of supportive counseling, role playing, practicing, reality testing, hand-holding, and gentle pushing. I was very concerned about how Karen was coping with the stress and we focused on strategies to maintain her stability. Her stress increased as she battled the negative thinking that jeopardized her stability. Karen was experiencing some angry feelings toward one of her supervisors, thinking he had already formed a negative opinion of her based on past history. Karen had first met her supervisor when she had been discharged from the hospital, at a time when her level of functioning was poor. Once again, she was struggling with feeling afraid and unsure, wondering whether she should give up. I encouraged her to continue with the process and be open-minded as we prepared for her six-month evaluation. One thing was clear — Karen wanted to stay on the job.

Karen and I focused on the following areas to help improve her job performance: narrowing her focus to one task at a time when working with her clients; setting time limits for herself and requiring herself to stick to them; paying attention to her communication and increasing reflective listening; and writing briefer, more concise clinical progress notes and increasing the speed at which she completed tasks.

Karen's evaluation meeting was held in October 1992 to exchange information on her job performance to date. The director of the residential agency facilitated the meeting which was attended by Karen's supervisors at the mental health center and their immediate supervisor, the residential program director, Karen, and myself. Once again, her supervisors noted her strengths (attendance, punctuality, improvement in paperwork) and also some areas of concern. The program director at the mental health center praised Karen for her continued interest in learning and eagerness for feedback, but expressed concern regarding the high degree of supervision Karen was requiring on the job.

Karen was given the opportunity for input and did an excellent job of conveying her desire to keep the job and do whatever it took to stay in the position. As a result of this meeting, Karen was granted 60-day continued employee status. December 20, 1992 was set as the deadline with the condition that the group would meet again in early December to review her job performance. In the meantime, Karen agreed to work on reflective listening skills, staying present and focused, and using supervision to practice these skills. Her supervisors agreed to be as specific as possible with Karen and provide concrete parcels of time to practice .

Off-site support at the Social Center was maintained at two hours per week. Karen and I practiced her counseling skills through intensive role-playing situations. She utilized my time completely and occasionally had difficulty when I set time limits with her. As the time drew closer for the December deadline, Karen reported increased forgetfulness, anxiety, and depression and started feeling overwhelmed by the many other activities in her life. She was not able to see the benefits of limiting some of her activities, could not bring herself to just say "no," and often became rageful when she recounted the events of the preceding months.

I sometimes felt like I was spinning my wheels in my attempts to assist Karen in reframing her black and white thinking. Serving as a job coach for Karen was very different than serving the other consumers with whom I have worked. Because I was not physically present to support Karen on the job, I often felt ineffective in helping her determine her needs, brainstorm potential options, and evaluate her job performance. I felt pressured to be readily accessible and responsive to the needs of Karen and her supervisors. It occurred to me to follow my own advice and seek some natural support. I enlisted my supervisor and co-workers for suggestions on how to get unstuck. I got relief by sharing my concerns and frustrations proactively. Karen's relief came when her supervisors agreed that she had shown sufficient improvement in the targeted content areas to warrant a permanent appointment.

Karen started the new year on an upbeat note. Her supervisors were pleased with her many gains on the job. While she was able to manage her stress well on the job, struggles with finances and disorganization played a major role in increasing her anxiety. She continued to utilize the vocational supports at the center wisely, attending and actively participating in weekly scheduled meetings with me. Despite positive vocational feedback from her supervisors, Karen still felt an enormous lack of confidence in her ability. I began to lay the groundwork for her upcoming yearly evaluation in order to prepare for possible negative reactions on her part in response to areas needing improvement.

My instincts were correct when it came time to process Karen's one-year job evaluation. At first she was very angry at the evaluation, feeling she would never be able to please her supervisors. After lengthy discussion, she was able to focus on all the positive feedback in the evaluation and use the section on areas needing improvement as a guide for growth and change. She also agreed to follow up with questions to her supervisors and for the first time expressed some feelings of confidence regarding her job performance.

In addition to our regular vocational work, Karen and I were in the process of preparing our presentation for the conference of the International Association of Psychosocial Rehabilitation Services (IAPSRS) which was being held in New Orleans at the end of July. Karen felt able to continue the work on our presentation topic: "Hiring Consumers: An Idea Whose Time Has Come." We couldn't wait to get to the conference to share our experiences, both positive and negative, and to encourage other consumers to seek out the rewards and challenges of working in the mental health field.

Late one evening, one week before the conference in New Orleans, Karen called the Social Center in crisis, feeling suicidal and trapped by her job issues. I had left for the day but luckily our center director was working late and was able to take the call. She helped Karen stabilize and accepted Karen's promise to see me the next day. Karen came in and announced she had faxed her resignation to the director of the residential agency and also notified her supervisors at the mental health center, citing inability to work due to a variety of stressors. Initially, Karen felt relieved to be free of her job responsibilities, but as time wore on, she sought continued support from me because she felt she had acted impulsively. She remained undecided, reacted negatively to my feedback, and was at times on the verge of tears. Her mood remained negative for most of the day. Late in the day we spoke with the residential director, and he offered her one week in which to reconsider her decision. Karen was surprised and suspicious of the offer. He told her it was an option he would offer any staff member who resigned due to stress. She agreed to notify him of her decision on Monday morning.

Karen decided to return to work. We had a planning meeting with her supervisors to clarify ongoing issues and remove any barriers to her successful return. Her best interests were the focus of this meeting. Karen disclosed some clinical information to help explain her mental status during the events leading up to her job resignation. All in attendance were supportive of her struggle with black and white thinking, negative thoughts, stress, and physical complaints. Also, her supervisors agreed to her request to be more aware of her confidentiality issues at the mental health center and examine sensitive issues during staff meetings, especially her perception that staff joked about mental illness. I encouraged Karen to use her supervision time more effectively and capitalize on informal opportunities to exchange information with her supervisor to avoid build up of potential crisis issues. Everyone left this meeting with a sense of relief.

Several days later Karen and I flew to New Orleans to share our experiences. We were careful to include our most recent crisis in our presentation to our colleagues. Our work was very positively received, and we spent the remainder of the week listening to and learning from some of the leaders in the psychosocial rehabilitation field on topics focusing on clinical, programmatic, and administrative innovations across the United States, Canada, and the world. With a variety of training and workshops to choose from, it was hard to catch up with Karen during the conference, though I did spot her at the Mardi Gras Mambo. It was a good feeling to share fun times with her and not always to be engaged in work.

Karen returned to work without incident, and as fall approached, reported no major problems on the job. She occasionally called, however, to report that she was really messing up. She felt disorganized, had trouble locating things, and felt she wasn't following her supervisors' directions and that her job was in jeopardy. Karen was also distressed by her perception that her supervisors were not readily available. After some reality checking, though, she was able to find ways to access them and have her needs met. I often reminded her of their commitment to supporting her on the job.

In December 1993, one year after a near job disaster, Karen proudly presented a plaque to her supervisors and the director of the residential agency who was named the Employer of the Year at the center's annual holiday party.

By spring, Karen was back on track and feeling less emotional about her work. She was more realistic with her expectations of her job performance but still lacked self-confidence on occasion. Reports from her supervisors continued to be positive and as we approached the two-year mark, we knew her evaluation would be excellent. Karen tried not to focus too much on her upcoming evaluation and instead concentrated on her upcoming marriage. Karen received her two-year job performance evaluation in May, and was able to discuss it with her supervisors and agreed with its accuracy. She received a pay raise for her positive performance. The next week, Karen attended and presented at the IAPSRS conference in Albuquerque, New Mexico. In July, Karen was married, and it seemed that at last we were on solid ground.

No one could have prepared Karen and me for the events of the next few months. Karen called me in early October to report her father's death. She appeared to be holding up well and was grateful for my support and assistance in negotiating some time off for the funeral. Within a few days, another personal tragedy occurred. It seemed impossible to believe when Karen called me to report the death of her mother-in-law. This second tragedy necessitated more time off from work, but her supervisors were supportive and even assisted in her paperwork backlog. Despite my reassurances, Karen continued to worry about her excessive leave.

Karen returned to find many personnel changes at the mental health center. One of her direct supervisors was moving into a new role and there were several new members of the residential program staff. She worried that these changes would necessitate her taking on increased job responsibilities at a time when she was already struggling with recent tragic events. Karen was reassured by her supervisors that her job duties would remain the same. They encouraged her to continue to utilize supervision as a vehicle to discuss ongoing concerns on the job.

Work was always a positive force in Karen's life and now it actually became a place to focus after many weeks of unsettling personal events. Karen disclosed feelings of intense sadness at being abandoned by many significant people in her life. Her sense of loss was so strong that I dreaded telling her of my upcoming new role on our vocational staff. Karen was supportive of my new professional opportunity but left our meeting feeling more stressed and abandoned.

After much reassurance that her transition to working with a new job coach would be gradual, Karen had an improved sense of self-esteem. She was relieved that her new vocational partner would be a more experienced vocational staff member. Karen and I used the month of December to give her new job coach a better understanding of Karen's role as a mental health provider who did not want to lose sight of her consumer orientation and sensitivity.

On the last day of the year, I officially transferred Karen over to her new job coach and vocational counselor. For over two years I had worked intensely and intimately with Karen. I had many mixed feelings on this day but was proud of our work. The new year would present new challenges and opportunities for both of us.

Special Issues and Their Resolution

From the beginning, Karen and I had special issues to work on which went beyond my inability to work on-site with her. Karen struggled with self-disclosure as a service provider at the same mental health center where she received mental health services. Karen worked hard on using discretion when disclosing information, often resisting the urge to self-disclose just to fill a need or vent. She was confused, hurt and angered by what she perceived as staff insensitivity and joking at the expense of consumers during her weekly staff meetings at the mental health center. Karen had a difficult time accepting that humor could be a coping tool that some people used to lighten stressful and painful situations. This became an area of intense work for the both of us, but eventually Karen was able to see that appropriate humor did not dismiss the importance of people's pain but made it easier to bear. Her supervisor was instrumental in helping Karen's co-workers to examine their professional sensitivity and to be responsive to a consumer point of view. Staff at the mental health center struggled with not knowing which hat Karen was wearing—consumer or provider—especially when she brought a consumer point of view to a traditional mental health center. Change has a way of making everyone uncomfortable.

Another challenge we faced during our working relationship was building and maintaining good communication with Karen's supervisors. As a job coach, I have learned never to underestimate the degree of misunderstanding and stigma surrounding mental illness and long-term community-based supported employment. This was particularly important for me to keep in mind as I developed my working relationship with Karen's supervisors. Because mental health professionals are trained and oriented to provide treatment, it was necessary for me to find a sensitive, supportive way to validate their diagnostic input while keeping our focus on issues relating to job performance. Utilizing my sense of humor and diplomatic skills was the key. I always tried to bring laughter to our working relationship. This was difficult and challenging work and I knew it would be crucial to use our meetings to acknowledge, validate, recognize, and appreciate her supervisors' efforts .

It became clear early on that her direct supervisors needed some additional support along the way. The concept of mental health consumers as providers was new and this newness presented problems in the early days of our relationship. Because consumer employment was an evolving process, there were few guidelines on how to proceed. Her supervisors struggled with where to draw the line on accommodations and knowing when to hold Karen accountable to existing performance standards. They left the decision to disclose information on her disability up to Karen, but they had trouble maintaining the boundaries as her supervisors and avoiding becoming her therapists when she did disclose. It was a challenge for her supervisors to keep a balance and work with Karen on not being adversarial. Karen also needed guidance on what information to trade, when, and how often.

A great deal of work went into examining our group experiences more objectively, seeing strengths and weaknesses as they related to job performance rather than clinical issues. Her supervisors were genuinely committed to going the extra mile and not acting precipitously but rather staying tuned in and working through whatever came up. Our communications were not always successful, but when they were, we all grew. Few things can compare to the joy of being heard and understood, for nothing is more essential to job success than the ability to communicate well.

Lastly, it was vital to find ways to take care of myself professionally, personally, and spiritually during my work with Karen. It was very easy to find myself in the trap of giving too much, trying too hard to keep everyone stable, happy and motivated. Supporting a consumer within an agency is challenging and creative work, but it was often stressful and draining as well. My sense of humor kept me healthy and centered, and I used it often to lighten stressful situations and create a path to creativity and insight. I was also careful to pay attention to the warning signals of stress so that I could discuss it in supervision. My supervisor was instrumental in helping me deal with boundary issues that often drained my energy. I also had the luxury of an amazingly supportive staff who never failed to energize me when I felt personally or professionally disenchanted. Ours is a staff that understood and acknowledged my intense involvement in supporting Karen's vocational goal. It was easy for me to develop healthy stress reduction techniques in such a supportive organization.

Conclusion

I think the challenges and problems on the job were inevitable. The idea of consumers as providers was new and innovative. There were no clearly defined guidelines or rules on how to proceed, how to offer support. This was new territory for everyone involved. Pioneers usually mark the way themselves and make up rules as they go along. Pioneering is about risk-taking and is essentially what supported employment is all about.

I think mine was a positive presence within Karen's workplace. Would I have done anything differently? Probably not. The essential ingredients were good communication, responsiveness, empathy, and commitment. It took me over two years to get Karen to laugh about the imperfect nature of human services delivery. My self-disclosure regarding my own job duties at the Social Center was effective when I needed to reassure Karen and help her make sense of her job. Karen seemed to enjoy the fact that I shared many of her frustrations in the role of helper. We often talked about effective use of supervision, being at odds with supervisors because of differing philosophical views, feeling angry and ineffective, feeling drained by not having enough hours in the day to complete job tasks, and being overwhelmed by the never ending mountain of paperwork.

Karen's growth has been remarkable. She has developed the skills of reflective listening and giving feedback. She has adapted some skills for solving communication problems instead of being immobilized by fear, anger, and hurt feelings. Karen is much improved in her ability to assert herself and set limits with others. She has finally learned to trust herself and rely on her inner voice. Fear has been a major barrier for Karen and often prevented her from being herself and relating comfortably with others. As her self-confidence has grown, she has developed a better understanding of how to care for others while caring for herself. Karen possesses unique insights into the mental health system because she wears the hats of consumer and service provider.

Working with Karen has given me the unique chance to examine the therapeutic qualities that I consider vital in a successful counseling and working relationship. As we talked about empathy, genuineness, respect, self-disclosure, warmth, and honesty, it occurred to me how very little I really knew about the struggles faced by consumers who worked as mental health providers. As Karen grew into her position, I grew into mine. She has been a demanding, formidable teacher, but she has taught me well about how to improve the quality of life of consumers in our mental health system. I began our working relationship trying to strengthen her abilities and ended up strengthening my own. I am proud to have Karen as my colleague in human services.

Acknowledgment

The author wishes to gratefully acknowledge the contributions of Karen Wands Parker who shared her memories and insight for this chapter. She was instrumental in helping me recount our story.

Eileen Conti Weklar, M.A., is supervisor of vocational services at The Social Center for Psychiatric Rehabilitation in Fairfax, VA.

Karen Wands Parker is a mental health assistant counselor in a residential program. She has presented several workshops, and serves on committees and the Clubhouse Advisory Board.

Chapter 38

Developing a Support Group for Staff with Mental Illness

Joseph W. Kerouac

I first realized that I was ill in the fall of 1986. My father had died, my marriage was ending, I was going to lose custody of my children, I was "coming out," I had some physical problems that needed surgery, and I had taken a new job that I hated. By 1987 and through 1988, I was nearly dysfunctional. I could not be in crowds. I did not want to see anybody that I knew. I became suicidal and was hospitalized six times. I attempted suicide twice. I received 24 treatments of electro-shock therapy. My life was over. I had lost my father, my wife, my children, my career, and my self-esteem. I just wanted to roll up in a ball and die.

A Personal Account of Recovery

There were two events that helped me in my recovery process. The last time I was hospitalized was in January 1989. My new psychiatrist came in and told me that he was going to put me away for good, so I would never attempt to harm myself again. (I believe he even diagnosed me as having borderline personality disorder.) For one of the first times in my life I was assertive. I said, "Try it buddy, my family and lawyer will be here in the morning." It must have worked as I was released the next day. I have not been hospitalized since that incident.

The other event that had tremendous impact on my recovery was my mother's heart condition. Over the past 30 years, my mother had suffered several heart attacks and strokes. Finally, in 1988 she was scheduled for open heart surgery. We were told it would be very risky because of her poor health. In fact, on the morning of her scheduled surgery, her heart did stop and she was "paddled" back to life and rushed to surgery at Northwestern Hospital in Chicago. By the time the family got there, she was in surgery. In the early evening hours, her surgeon finally approached the family and told us that she had made it.

We were then escorted into the recovery room. There lay this frail, old woman who had been fighting death for several years. She was hooked up to a number of tubes. She was unconscious. What I noticed most was that she was shivering as if she were cold. I don't remember much else because I collapsed. I thought to myself later, Why? Why has this woman struggled for so long and now is fighting with every ounce of life left in her. And here I am, purposely attempting to end my own life.

After my last hospitalization, during which I had major hip surgery, I went to live with my semi-invalid mother. "The blind leading the blind." I began to become frustrated as I was an intelligent man with three college degrees, living on disability at home with his aging mother. That spring of 1989, my thoughts became more clear. I had no intention of living this way for the rest of my life. I began to exercise, pray, socialize, and live each day. In the late spring, I worked up a resumé and started my job search. In June, I was contacted by Thresholds Psychiatric Center in Chicago to interview for a teaching position. It was a unique position, working with people with mental illness who wanted to further their education.

Wait! I grew up in Manteno, Illinois. At one time Manteno State Hospital was the largest in the country. I had been there several times with our high school chorus and marching band. I knew what went on out there. Why was I applying for a job with an agency that works with people with mental illness? I thought, "Oh well, here goes." I sent in my resume, got called for an interview, and was hired. I knew this opportunity might be the last I had to prove to myself that I could do something. I came to Thresholds in July 1989. I became the Education Coordinator for the agency-wide college preparatory program known as the Community Scholar Program.

It was a natural. It was a blessing from above. I had found my niche. As my ex-wife, Sue, said, "Maybe God put you through all of your problems so that you could learn and help others." Though not as spiritual as she, I think she may have been right. I love what I am doing. I taught elementary school for fifteen years and hated it. As time progressed, the Community Scholar Program (CSP) became an inner healing process for me. I actually enjoyed working with the members; teaching and counseling. But... there was no way I was going to let anyone at the agency know about my past hospitalizations or mental health history. I guess I had to prove to myself that I could do it before I could share that part of my life. And was there really a need to share that? Sometimes such openness can be destructive.

The Need for a Support System for Staff Coping with Mental Illness

After being at Thresholds for about two years, a staff member who I knew, but not very well, took a leave. Everything was hush-hush at the agency. Since I am located off-site, often I don't get the whole story. The staff member made an attempt to come back but it was fruitless. He was too ill. Members were coming to me and telling me that he had AIDS. I guess I was not surprised because I had seen him out in our gay community. But the truth finally came forth. He was mentally ill. It had nothing to do with the person being HIV positive. I was sickened that I had not reached out to him, a coworker who needed support.

Out of the anger brewing inside, I felt the need to do something so this would never happen again. Why is it that we can deal with our members on a daily basis but we could not deal with one of our own staff becoming ill? I gathered up my strength, my courage, my determination, and set out to solve this problem. I could conquer anything. I was just going to have to expose my own history of mental illness. I had a wonderful supervisor at that time. Virginia Selleck is a compassionate, caring individual. When she came to my office one day, I summoned up the courage to tell her my story. We wept together. She embraced me and I knew I had done the right thing. Next, I needed to approach our executive director, Jerry Dincin, and explain to him that I had been doing some reading on support for staff with mental illness. I told him I would like to poll the entire staff and see what kind of response I got.

I began by writing an article for the Thresholds in-house newsletter, *In Touch*. This would introduce the staff to the concept of what a prosumer is. I followed this article a few weeks later with an informal letter and detachable form asking other staff if they had a mental illness and would they be interested in some kind of support group. The response was overwhelming. I received 40 replies. That is about 10% of our total staff. Some of the staff put their names on the return form. Many chose to send it back anonymously. I kept all of the forms locked away in my office for reasons of confidentiality. I did tell our executive director the number of responses I got. At first he was surprised. Later he stated that there are probably even more.

So what should I do with the information that I had just gathered? Little did I know I would be creating a job for myself that would take a great deal of time. I sent out another letter to those who had responded by name. We set a date, time, and an off-site place to meet. A small group of six showed up at my house for our first meeting. Several issues were discussed. What is our purpose? What should we try to achieve? Is there a need for this kind of support? I am not sure we have answered any of these questions yet.

The group now meets monthly. We are a confidential support network for any Thresholds staff member who has a diagnosed mental illness. We do have some staff members in the group who do not have a diagnosed mental illness but who do see a therapist.

Out of this first meeting came an incredible feeling of alienation. If we dared to expose ourselves as being staff with a mental illness, we would probably be victimized by other staff. Fear! That was the number one obstacle to overcome. And in the beginning I was the only consumer who saw the need for all of us to step forward. My God, we are working in the field of mental health and we are scared to death of the reaction of our co-workers. As time went on, some members dropped out of the group, but new people entered with the same fears.

What was it that made me feel compelled to come out about my mental illness and my sexuality? No, it was not courage. It was anger. This is who I am. I have proven myself at Thresholds. My education program is one of the best known in the country. I will no longer be judged by others for being white, gay, mentally ill, a recovering Catholic, a gay parent, or French Canadian. I am a person first. Accept me for who I am or get out of my way because I will run right over you. Thank God for the Americans with Disabilities Act (ADA). The two most important people in the world, my son Kyle and my daughter Colleen, have accepted who I am. I am their dad ! I don't need anyone else's

approval. Yes, I am fortunate. My ex-wife and family have been very supportive. I know I put all of them through hell with my depression and panic/
anxiety disorder. I am sure that my "coming out" about being gay was not too
easy to deal with either.

The Operation of a Support Group

The Thresholds Prosumers Support Group is open to any staff member
who needs mental health support. The idea of prosumer groups or peer support groups as a support mechanism for staff with histories of mental illness
has been addressed (Fishbein, Manos & Rotteveel, 1993). We will be changing
the name of our group to the Thresholds Consumers as Colleagues Group.
The reason for this is that Thresholds itself has grown in its agency policy. We
are now openly hiring members and others with mental illness. This was not
done five years ago. When I first came to Thresholds, the stance was pretty
rigid about hiring a member (consumer). Oh, how I hate that term: consumer.
It makes me feel like I went out shopping and bought my mental illness. But I
am not going to play a game of semantics. I realize we have to have a term to
identify people as long as we put the person first and the descriptor after. I am
a person first: then go ahead and label me anything you want to because I am
finally confident of who I am.

Most of us in the staff support group see a therapist or psychiatrist. My
psychiatrist is also my therapist. I am on Xanax and Prozac. I am doing quite
well. Not only do I direct the Thresholds Community Scholar Program but I
am the liaison for the Prosumers Support Group. I also lead a support group
for gay/lesbian members of our agency. I am an instructor at National-Louis
University in Evanston, Illinois, and a consultant on hiring people with mental
illness for the Matrix Research Center in Philadelphia. My life is full.

Steps to the Development of a Support System

I want to caution those of you who may want to start a support group
within your own agency for staff with mental illness. What follows are steps
which I suggest are workable.

1. Send out an information flyer explaining what you are attempting to
do. It should explain in detail that the goal of the support group is to serve as
a confidential network for staff members who suffer from mental illness. It
should also announce that the agenda of the meetings will be to form the support group, set goals, set a purpose, and check interest in the group.

2. Make sure that people know this will be confidential and only one staff
member will know who returns the form.

3. Send out a confirmation letter about your first meeting. The confirmation letter should include time, date, and place. Make sure this letter restates
the confidentiality clause.

4. At your first off-site meeting, set some common confidentiality rules

and any other rules that need to be incorporated to keep the group running smoothly. This should then be put in written form to give to new members who enter the support group.

5. Keep the group informal. Let people designate what they need and want to talk about as opposed to having a set agenda every meeting.

6. Appoint a liaison from the group who can go back to the executive director with suggestions on what the agency can do to better support all staff but especially those who are also consumers. Examples: flex-time, nonmandatory attendance at certain workshops, better mental health insurance coverage, sensitivity training workshops and seminars for non-consumer staff.

7. It is important to establish a telephone network among prosumers. The telephone network will give all group members a listing of home and office phone numbers of the other group members. Members can then use this list to call anyone in the group they feel comfortable speaking with if an issue arises or they need additional support. This will be a valuable resource for staff who start to feel symptomatic. It will also spread out the duties so that no one consumer staff becomes the contact person for everyone in the group. Initially, this is what happened in our group. Everyone called the group liaison person and he could not deal with handling everyone's crises.

8. Another item that we have found useful is the joint consent contract. This is a contract written up by a consumer staff and another staff member with whom the consumer staff feels most comfortable. The contract should be notarized. The contract basically gives the other staff member the right to call the consumer staff member's therapist/psychiatrist if the staff member starts to become symptomatic. The chosen staff member can be a consumer staff or a nonconsumer staff. That decision is left entirely up to the consumer staff at the time the contract is written. For example: John is a former Thresholds member who is now working full-time at Thresholds. He chose Emma, a nonconsumer staff, to be his contractual partner. Anytime Emma feels or sees that John is becoming symptomatic she will first talk to John and then make a decision as to whether or not to contact his therapist or psychiatrist. At one point, Emma used the contract to hospitalize John.

Fair Warning! You are probably going to make a number of mistakes in setting up a support group. Hey, use your mental illness as an excuse. (Just kidding!)

Our biggest mistake was the assumption that I was in charge of the group and everything had to be done by me. I accepted the challenge at first, but incidents occurred that made my role far too time consuming.

Case Vignettes

I would like to tell you of some incidents that happened and how you may be able to avoid them in your agency. I have changed the names for obvious reasons.

Case Study #1

Judy was a day program staff member. She was becoming symptomatic. It became so bad one day that the program director asked her to leave the building. Judy immediately called me. I told her to go home and I would see her after work. An hour later, her supervisor called and consulted with me on what to do about Judy. After much deliberation and a short leave of absence, Judy was allowed to return to her position on a contract agreed upon by the supervisor, Judy, and me. All seemed to go well until Judy once more became symptomatic. Unfortunately I was on vacation. Judy was hospitalized in an unsuitable facility. When I returned, the support group had Judy transferred to a better facility. It was mandated by Judy's psychiatrist that I was the only staff member from Thresholds who was to have contact with her. This was done because Judy was interrupting the flow of things back at the agency. She was calling staff and members. She was not working on her own issues. It became clear that maybe Thresholds was not the best place for her to work. The plan was for Judy to return to the agency for two weeks to complete closure with her members. She had a difficult time abiding by this new contract but she did complete her requirements and has successfully moved on into another field of social work, working with children.

Case Study #2

Gerald is a staff member who is both mentally ill and HIV positive. He had a great deal of difficulty getting going in the morning because he was frequently nauseous. He then became paranoid that he would lose his job. He lost trust in all coworkers and supervisors at the day program facility. Here is where a support group can play a vital role. He knew of us and felt somewhat comfortable calling for support. As his illness progressed, he became more symptomatic. It was hard for him to be rational. The support group spent a lot of time with Gerald. How could we abandon a wonderful case manager who was both HIV positive and mentally ill? We couldn't, and we didn't. The group and the staff responded well as Gerald told his coworkers in a staff meeting of his condition. He then surprised us with his resignation. He wanted to live his last few healthy days doing what he wanted to do. The regimen of coming into work every day was entirely too taxing on him. On his own, he decided to resign and seek disability. He is now living downstate and doing well. He made the right choice and I am glad the support group was there to help him.

Case Study #3

Betsy, a staff member in another day program, announced her resignation. Since she had been one of the best case managers we had ever had, I asked her to explain her decision. In a confidential exit interview, Betsy shared that she was all right, but that she did not find Thresholds to be a healthy environment for her. The staff couldn't believe that she would quit her job without having another job offer. They didn't understand. Self-preservation is more important than a paycheck. If your job is making you symptomatic, then get the hell out. If you can't change it, retreat. You may feel like you have lost the battle, but in fact you will have won the war. What angered me most about the situation with Betsy was the insensitivity of the staff toward her. They thought they knew what was best for her, though they didn't have her complete story. Betsy made a choice. She will have to live with that choice. I am positive it was the right choice for her. I am glad she had the support group to turn to in helping her with her decision.

How many more case studies do you want to read? I have a dozen more. In my opinion, I think the solution is sensitivity training for all staff members. They need to know that they may be working next to a consumer staff. They need to be careful about their unprofessional jokes about people with mental illness. They need to be educated that staff with a mental illness history are only looking for fair and reasonable accommodations. We are not looking for an easy way out or to make it more difficult on nonconsumer staff. Where is people's sensitivity?

Self-Disclosure

Did I come out about my mental illness to my students in my college preparatory program? Not at first. I saw no point to it and I was not strong enough yet to let my guard down. But now I openly let my students know some of the details of my illness. I do tell them I was hospitalized several times, take medication, and see a psychiatrist. And I am doing very well. So now you get on with your life. You take control of your life and responsibility for your illness and you can improve the quality of your life. I stand before them as a role model. I do not stand in front of my members to boast, brag, or give false hope. But some of them will and do get better. And many of them do go on for post-secondary education.

There is a wonderful woman in Philadelphia named Kathleen Wilson. She works for the Matrix Research Institute. I met Kathleen a few years ago in New Orleans. She and I now go around the country promoting the hiring of "Consumers as Colleagues." Kathleen also suffers from mental illness. Our purpose is to help other agencies begin the practice of hiring consumers. If we won't hire the people we serve, then aren't we hypocritical ? Let me state clearly at this point that I do not believe that every person with a mental illness should or can work in the field of mental health. I believe that all staff need training and stability. I do know that many consumers can work in the field and should be given the opportunity. If I had not come to work at Thresholds, I do not know where I would be right now. Maybe still on disability. I do know that through support and my own motivation and determination I began the road to recovery by rebuilding my self-esteem. I think the loss of my self-esteem was the most crippling aspect of my battle with mental illness. And I do believe that a staff member who has or is recovering from mental illness has an inner dimension of understanding. All of the textbooks in the world will never teach you how it feels to be so depressed that you want to take your life.

No book can explain what a panic/anxiety attack feels like. I certainly can relate to those issues and offer suggestions. But in the same vein, I can only be sympathetic to someone with schizophrenia as I have never suffered from it. Experience is the best teacher.

In my lifetime, I doubt if we will see the bigotry against people with mental illness go away. We do have to start somewhere. I think suggestions such as developing a support group within your agency is a beginning. Sensitivity training is another area to tackle. Having people like Kathleen Wilson speak to the issue of hiring consumers will help to break down some barriers.

Where do we go from here ? I don't have the answer. I am not an expert in the field of mental health. I have yet to meet someone who is. It is such an inexact science that all we can do is keep trying and looking for more breakthroughs. For more information look at the manual *Positive Partnerships: How Consumers and Nonconsumers Can Work Together as Service Providers* (Solomon, Cook, Jonikas, & Kerouac, 1994).

Conclusion

I am beginning to overcome my anger towards the mental health care system. It has taken several years. Let me relate two stories.

I was an inpatient in a private psychiatric hospital in downstate Illinois. I was complaining that my right knee was killing me. I could hardly walk. The orthopedic surgeon they sent to examine me stated that it was all in my head. Test results had shown nothing wrong with my knee. But my right hip was dead ! I had avascular necrosis caused by taking massive doses of legal steroids in college for a hemorrhaging retina. Further testing proved the pain in my knee was radiated from the diseased hip. I underwent surgery which proved successful. But, I also faced this fine doctor at a later time and told him that I knew he didn't believe me because I was on a psychiatric ward. He blushed. I was right.

I was hospitalized at Riverside Medical Center in Kankakee, Illinois. I had been transferred there from another hospital where I had been admitted for overdosing. My psychiatrist was on vacation. The psychiatrist who was covering for him decided to put me on a new medication. This new drug gave me such a case of constipation that I thought I would explode. I told him of the side effects. He said this drug doesn't produce that kind of side effect. Well, guess what, it did for me! When I was discharged, I flushed the rest of the medication down the toilet and amazingly the symptoms stopped.

OK! So maybe I am still a little bitter. But I have learned how to use the system as an educated consumer and will never let the mental health system use me. As negative as this sounds, I truly am positive about what is going on in most of the field of mental health today. But we must still advocate for change and equality. We are a misunderstood population that must now begin to fight for our rights.

And yes, I am Jack's cousin!

References

Fishbein, S.M., Manos, E., & Rotteveel, J. (1993). *A unique collegial support system: Supporting mental health professionals who may also be consumers or psychiatric survivors.* Presented at the 1993 Tampa Conference: Rehabilitation of Children, Youth, and Adults with Psychiatric Disabilities, Tampa, Florida, January 29, 1993.

Solomon, M.L., Cook, J., Jonikas, J., & Kerouac, J. (1994). *Positive partnerships: How consumers and nonconsumers can work together as service providers.* Chicago, IL: Thresholds.

Joseph W. Kerouac, M.S.Ed., is the education coordinator for Thresholds Psychosocial Rehabilitation Agency in Chicago. He is also an instructor at National-Louis University in Evanston, Ill., and a consultant for the Matrix Research Institute of Philadelphia. Kerouac has co-authored a manual entitled Positive Partnerships: Consumer and Nonconsumer Staff Working Together. *He has also published four college preparatory curricula for students with mental illness. Mr. Kerouac is a consumer and a well-known advocate for the rights of people with mental illness.*

Chapter 39

Consumers as Colleagues: Moving Beyond ADA Compliance

Anthony M. Zipple
Maureen Drouin
Moe Armstrong
Melissa Brooks
Joan Flynn
Will Buckley

During the last twenty years there has been a dramatic increase in the number of employees with disabilities in the human services workforce. With the advent of Section 504 of the 1973 Rehabilitation Act, most human service organizations were obligated to provide reasonable accommodations for individuals with disabilities. Passage of the Americans with Disabilities Act in 1990 reinforced this obligation to provide reasonable accommodations and extended it to the general workforce. Consumer advocacy in a variety of disability areas has reinforced this legislative action and raised the consciousness of service providers about the value of hiring individuals with disabilities as staff. As a result, in many areas of human services, such as those serving individuals who are deaf, with spinal cord injuries, drug and alcohol disorders, HIV disease and so on, it is commonplace to see staff with these same disabilities providing formal rehabilitation services to their peers.

Willingness to hire individuals with psychiatric disabilities to work as providers in mental health organizations has been much slower to develop. Several factors appear to account for this reluctance. Traditional mental health clinical models which emphasize strong boundaries between patient and provider may discourage the dual roles of consumer and provider. Issues such as confidentiality and objectivity often are raised as concerns, particularly when a consumer seeks employment from an agency or program in which he or she receives, or has received services. In addition, many mental health organizations have relatively paternalistic cultures which reflect a belief in the need to protect individuals with psychiatric disabilities from work that is "too stressful." This appears to include jobs as mental health professionals. Finally, mental health organizations are not immune to the stigma in American culture regarding serious mental illness.

The same kinds of negative stereotypes that pose obstacles to the employment of individuals with mental illness in the general workforce appear to exist in mental health organizations as well. For too many of us, mental illness still connotes traits such as instability, explosiveness, irrationality, impulsiveness or worse — characteristics often considered to be incompatible with employment. Clearly, such erroneous generalizations should be challenged through education and example; however, citizens with disabilities should not have to wait until stigma in the workplace has been eradicated to be given the chance to work. While the landmark legislation cited above has opened the door to employment, it is up to employers, particularly those in mental health organizations, to put out the "welcome mat" to all applicants, including mental health consumers.

Although the last decade has seen a growing interest from some mental health organizations in hiring consumers as employees, most of the activity in this area has taken the form of hiring individuals with psychiatric disabilities into specialized jobs such as case management aide or advocacy positions which are designated specifically for individuals with disabilities. There has been far less interest in recruiting, mentoring, and supporting consumers with psychiatric disabilities to work as providers in a broad range of positions at all levels of mental health organizations.

This chapter will describe the experiences of Vinfen Corporation as a mental health and mental retardation services provider in this area. Our experiences recruiting and supporting employees with psychiatric disabilities will be outlined. In addition, we will discuss several key learnings based on our experience which we think have value for the field generally.

Vinfen Overview

Vinfen Corporation is a Massachusetts-based 501(c)3 (tax exempt) organization providing clinical and rehabilitation services to individuals with special needs. Groups which Vinfen currently serves include individuals with disabling mental illness, mental retardation, HIV disease, and the elderly. Approximately 65% of Vinfen's annual budget of $43 million is focused on meeting the needs of individuals with severe and long-term mental illness.

Vinfen's mental health services include a wide range of residential, clubhouse, clinical, and children's services. Vinfen's Mental Health Division serves individuals with special needs beyond those directly connected to their mental illness, including individuals who are deaf, drug- or alcohol-involved, HIV positive or who have special cultural or linguistic needs. All of Vinfen's mental health services have a strong emphasis on consumer empowerment and rehabilitation.

It is worth noting that Vinfen has a strong corporate-wide commitment to diversity in its workforce. Nearly 40% of Vinfen's employees are members of federally identified cultural, racial or linguistic minority groups. The organization has a significant number of gay and lesbian employees who are able to be very open about their sexual orientation. Our work with individuals who are deaf or HIV positive has led us to hire many staff with these conditions. In addition, Vinfen sponsors many activities to support and celebrate diversity in its workforce. These include a large annual multicultural festival and a recent cultural diversity audit.

Vinfen's commitment to hiring individuals with psychiatric disabilities is seen as an extension of its broad commitment to meet the complex needs of its multiply disabled consumers and support its diverse workforce. Vinfen's belief in the value of diversity and emphasis on rehabilitation and consumer empowerment have provided a supportive framework for operationalizing our commitment to hiring individuals with psychiatric disabilities. As an employer, we take seriously our responsibility to provide "reasonable accommodations" for consumer staff as needed, building in flexibility wherever possible around work hours, part-time positions, etc.

In addition, Vinfen provides extensive training for all of its employees. For example, all employees in Vinfen's mental health residential programs receive eleven full days of training during their initial 60 days of employment. This intensive inservice, coupled with strong and individualized staff supervision and ongoing training opportunities, has helped the organization to integrate and support employees with varied backgrounds and abilities.

The Consumer-Staff Project

In 1991, Vinfen developed a contract proposal for a large and complex residential services project. The project included hiring 45 staff to serve 34 consumers being discharged from a state hospital. Within the project was an array of services, including a small day program, a four-bed crisis respite program, and integral case management services.

Vinfen already had in place an array of service components in its residential programs designed to support the empowerment of mental health consumers. These included direct involvement of consumers in the hiring of staff, performance evaluations on all staff which were conducted by consumers, and so on. As we looked for opportunities to extend our commitment to consumer empowerment, we decided to make a contractual commitment to hiring consumers as staff for this project. In our proposal, we obligated Vinfen to have at least one consumer staff member in each of the four sites included in this project, a minimum obligation of about 9% consumer staff.

Vinfen's commitment in this area generated significant interest on the part of the Department of Mental Health and local advocacy groups. However, as we began to recruit consumers as staff, we encountered a surprising level of suspicion on the part of advocacy groups. There appeared to be a great deal of concern about the degree to which people would be placed in "real jobs" and supported in making meaningful contributions to the organization. By working assertively with advocacy groups and vocational service providers, we found a number of individuals with psychiatric disabilities who were interested in working for Vinfen.

Central to operationalizing the concept of the consumer as provider is an awareness of the difference between the consumer as staff member and the creation of "consumer slots." The project rejected the notion of specialized or protected positions designated for consumers. Instead, job descriptions, training, expectations and accountability are the same for all staff, regardless of their history or background. Accommodation, when necessary, is an integral part of the supervision process and is negotiated with staff members on an individual basis. For example: our initial experience with consumers who had been hired to fill vacant full-time residential counselor positions indicated the need for more flexibility and a broader range of options. By creatively using job-sharing and part-time possibilities, we were able to hire seven consumers as staff with real responsibilities and accountability within the initial project.

It is interesting to note that the success of this practice over time has enabled a number of heretofore "anonymous" staff to disclose the fact that they, too, had a history of psychiatric difficulties. While the percentage of project staff that identify themselves as consumers generally floats at 18%, at times it has been as high as 23% of the staff.

In 1992, Vinfen was awarded another large contract which involved five sites and fifty-six staff. Again, we renewed our commitment to hiring a minimum of one consumer for each of the sites. Based on the experiences which consumers had with Vinfen during the previous year, we found that it was much easier to recruit consumers for this second project. In the initial months of this contract, we hired nine individuals with significant psychiatric histories.

As these two projects proceeded, program managers from across Vinfen's Mental Health Division began to take notice of the successes. We began to discuss a division level commitment to a goal of at least one consumer-staff member for each program site. In addition, we began to discuss the need to expand the range of positions for which we were hiring consumers. In the original two projects, the majority of consumers were hired as residential counselors. As a part of this process, we developed a division level commitment to a minimum of 10% consumer staff.

During the past few years, we have continued our commitment and currently employ between 50 and 60 mental health consumers as staff. This is very close to our goal of 10% consumer staff and we are beginning to discuss increasing our commitment to 15%. In addition, we have been relatively successful in recruiting consumers into a broader range of positions within the organization. Consumers currently hold jobs as residential counselors, program managers, and professional staff.

It is important to note that none of these positions are specialized consumer positions—that is, positions which are created for, or only available to, consumers of mental health services. Instead, we are committed to hiring significant numbers of consumers into all categories and positions. We believe that this increases the integration of consumers within the organization and creates more accessible career ladders for employees with disabilities. It also begins to counteract some of the stereotypes and/or stigma which may be present in the workplace itself, by providing mental health consumers with the chance to be seen as competent, capable colleagues. In addition, it reflects Vinfen's commitment to high levels of diversity within its overall workforce.

One important result of our commitment to hiring consumers into regular mainstream positions is the high level of participation which consumer staff have in program planning and development within the organization. Vinfen maintains a variety of standing committees which guide corporate policy in the areas such as training, quality management, human rights, research, and human resources. These committees draw membership from across the organization and participation is open to all staff, including consumer staff. As a result, the voices of consumer staff are increasingly heard in areas that affect overall organizational function, policies, and procedures related to service delivery, staff development, and so on.

Vinfen also has explored other creative avenues to provide work opportunities for mental health consumers. In 1994, we submitted a concept paper to the committee developing the state's application for funding under AmeriCorps, the program created by the Clinton Administration to promote community service. The project proposed by Vinfen, a partnership between disabled and non-disabled citizens to assist homeless individuals, would have provided mental health consumers with the chance to participate meaningfully and contribute as citizens through a community service project. It also would have provided consumers with the chance to gain valuable experience that could be applied to potential employment, receive a stipend, and earn money for education or further training. Although the project was not funded, the feedback Vinfen received was extremely positive and has encouraged us to look for similar opportunities to promote consumer contributions as staff, volunteers, and citizens.

Challenges and Learnings

While Vinfen's effort to recruit and retain consumers as staff has been quite successful, it has not been without difficulty. Over the past four years, we have had to grapple with issues in seven key areas that have been particularly challenging. We offer the following suggestions to assist those seeking to hire consumers as staff in their organizations.

1. Focus on Recruitment

Recruiting consumers who are interested in and capable of doing the job can be difficult. This is especially true in the initial months of an organization's commitment to hiring consumers. Consumers may be suspicious of the organization's motivations or level of commitment. In addition, consumers may have few role models which demonstrate to them that employment as a mental health provider is both possible and rewarding. Some consumers may have little or no work experience of any kind; thus, the very idea of employment may be intimidating.

In addition, there are some traditional aspects of hiring which many applicants find stressful, but may be especially difficult for some consumers. As a matter of policy, Vinfen requires Criminal Offense Record Information (CORI) reports on all prospective employees. As stated, this process can provoke anxiety for many applicants who may have gotten into trouble in the past. A significant number of mental health consumers have had some contact with the criminal justice system, often because of incidents that occurred while the consumers was not receiving services and/or during acute exacerbations of their illness. For some of these consumers, fears regarding how their history will be perceived, compounded by the stigma of mental illness, can become powerful barriers to pursuing employment. It is important to recognize this fact and help educate consumers about the CORI process and its impact on hiring. All positive CORI reports are thoroughly evaluated and judgments are made on the basis of the actual offense, how long ago it occurred, the circumstances, and an assessment of the applicant's current status/likelihood to pose a risk to others. Successful recruitment of consumers must be sensitive to these potential barriers.

Our programs developed a plan for recruitment of consumer applicants with help from Vinfen's Director of Consumer & Family Affairs. He recommended that we turn to groups which have high levels of credibility in the consumer community to help with recruitment. We found two kinds of groups particularly helpful. First, consumer self-help groups are a great source of employee referrals. Consumer self-help groups usually have a well-developed network of consumers who are active, confident and committed to improving the lives of their peers. Local projects such as Impact '94, Empowerment Inc., as well as chapters of the Alliance for the Mentally Ill often are looking for employment opportunities for consumers. We also contacted several agencies which assist homeless individuals (some of whom may be mental health consumers) in finding housing and employment. It is important to identify groups such as these and build relationships with them. These groups can use word of mouth and internal newsletters to let their members know that it is safe and beneficial for consumers to work for you.

A second category of groups which can be helpful in recruitment is vocational service providers. Vocational services providers share your goal of employing individuals with psychiatric disabilities. It must be noted that many employment specialists may also share the previously mentioned biases about consumers working in mental health. It is important to build relationships with one or more employment specialists who share your commitment to the importance of hiring consumers as staff and your belief that consumers are fully capable of doing the job.

In addition, recruitment must be seen as an ongoing process rather than a one-time or periodic undertaking. The key to successful recruitment over the long-run is building relationships with groups that will help you get the word out. It is helpful to have specific individuals within your organization who serve as a liaison to these groups. Take the time to build and maintain relationships with them and they will serve as significant supports to your efforts. Remember that the initial months of this process are the most difficult. As you establish a base of successful consumers who are employed in your organization, your ability to convince consumers of your commitment and ability to support them is greatly increased. However, strong relationships with advocacy groups and vocational providers will continue to be helpful even when your process is quite mature.

2. Train, Train, Train

Consumers coming into mental health organizations as providers may encounter further conflict regarding the value of their "experience" in mental health. On the one hand, they may have an enormous wealth of first-hand experience about mental health services, medications, providers, and so on. On the other hand, they may lack the critical knowledge which they need to be a successful employee and provider of services. There is no substitute for providing consumers with extensive training as they move into the role of providers. It is important to be aware that the training needs of the consumers are not significantly different from those of the general population. Often many employees coming into most positions in mental health organizations lack the skill and knowledge which the provider would like them to have. Orientation and training are essential, particularly in the more entry level positions which many consumers will assume for their first job in the field.

Some of Vinfen's consumer staff have pointed out that, due to the cruel timing of the onset of their illness, many consumers experience an interruption in their education and/or employment, such that critical basic skills may have been missed or need to be acquired. For example, some consumers may have difficulty reading and writing. Training programs need to address remedial education components and respond to consumer applicants/staff who may not have a high school degree or GED, but otherwise exhibit valuable skills (good interpersonal skills, sound judgment, etc.) pertinent to the job. Life experience, e.g., raising a family, also can indicate a level of responsibility, maturity, and caring, which are far more difficult to teach or train than the requirements of a GED. These statements also apply to non-consumer staff who have neither completed high school nor possess a GED.

Vinfen has a strong commitment to orientation and training for all of its employees, including consumers. Our orientation process consists of eleven days of inservice work covering basics such as crisis intervention, first aid, psychiatric medications, psychosocial rehabilitation, service planning and documentation, recovery and empowerment, overview of the mental health system, and so on. This orientation provides consumer staff with an opportunity to learn the values and culture of the organization. In addition, it is a useful jump start on the process of role transition. Finally, it introduces them to the organization on at least an equal level with their newly employed and non-disabled peers who are also in training. In fact, it is our experience that consumers play important leadership roles in these trainings. Their first-hand experience helps to illustrate key points in the orientation. Through this process, consumers may emerge as some of the most vocal and helpful trainees.

The orientation process is supported by ongoing inservice training opportunities. These include in-house workshops on a weekly basis as well as opportunities to attend outside workshops and conferences. These activities play a critical role in supporting the employee's efforts at role transition, by offering consumer-staff an opportunity to interact with the mental health world beyond the employer's organization, and by refining an understanding of the importance and generalizability of their role.

Finally, staff at Vinfen receive considerable training on site. For example, on site training for residential counselors usually takes place during the first six to eight weeks of employment. Program-specific training is conducted by the site's management team. When that phase is completed, new staff are assigned to seasoned workers and receive more in-depth training directly from that staff, or from other staff as appropriate. The house manager is directly involved in the training process, helping the new staff member understand his or her role within the residence and acting as a resource on policies and procedures. Gradually, the new team members are given their own assignments and usually are capable of working well independently after about eight weeks.

3. Take Steps to Reduce Role Conflict

One of the greatest challenges facing consumers who come to work as providers is the role conflict which they experience. For many consumers, it is difficult to move from a primary identity as a consumer of mental health services to that of a provider of mental health services. This tension can create difficulties. For example, as a consumer or an advocate, it may be appropriate to stop in the corner tavern with your peers for a beer. This same activity can create difficulties when it is done on company time with consumers being served by an organization. In addition, consumers who come from self-help and advocacy backgrounds may experience some role conflict as they move from being critics of the mental health system to members of it.

It is essential that providers develop mechanisms to support consumers in this role transition. We have found that in-house support groups are instrumental in helping consumers work through this role conflict. Consumer staff share their experiences with each other and the tensions which their role transition has created for them. This helps to normalize the experience and generates many useful ideas for coping with it. While it is important that these groups be peer-led, we have found it very useful to include one or two skilled facilitators who are long-time employees of the organization and who may or may not be consumers. These facilitators help to keep the group focused and serve as experts in the organization's culture. Questions about organizational norms and "the right thing to do" can often be answered by these long-time employees. In addition, they can serve as role models for newer employees, and help to sensitize other staff to the struggle their consumer colleagues experience.

Several of Vinfen's consumer staff have identified the "other side" of the role conflict or boundary issue: the difficulty some non-consumer staff experience in accepting a consumer as a colleague. As these staff have commented, consumers respect their peers for making something out of their lives and many consumer staff are excellent role models. The more difficult transition for consumer staff involves moving into a peer relationship with people who have had considerable power in their lives. They point out to us that consumers may find it much easier to imagine themselves as staff than for staff to imagine themselves as consumers. Perhaps an anecdote will help to illustrate this point.

Timothy had moved steadily up the residential ladder and was now living in a supported apartment. We had discussed the possibility of employment at a high intensity group home where he had once lived. It took about six months before he actually applied for a relief staff position. As a relief staff, Timothy could choose which shifts to work. His work was exemplary. Some of the residents knew Timothy from the time he had lived at the house, and none of them expressed any concerns regarding his presence as a staff member. However, staff had some difficulty seeing Timothy as a peer. One staff member consistently referred to him as "Timmy." Timothy made a salient observation to the house manager when they rode to a conference together. He wondered why they both went all the way to the program to meet when their houses were a block away from each other!

It is important to recognize that, in spite of an organization's best efforts, some level of role conflict will undoubtedly persist for a protracted period of time. For consumer-staff, changing identities is a long and complicated process. Employers should be ready to support consumer staff on an individual and group basis over the months or even years that this process may take. This is a significant commitment but one which we believe is required as a reasonable accommodation. Giving consumers an opportunity to get comfortable in their new identity and with the norms of a new organization is critical to the success of this initiative and well worth the effort. In addition, it is clear that more needs to be done to address the attitudes and expectations of non-consumer staff toward their consumer colleagues. First, we need to acknowledge that such conflict is possible, perhaps even likely to occur, and address it directly during orientation and training of new employees. As employers, our expectations of acceptance and respect for all individuals should be clearly stated and reinforced. Secondly, nonconsumer staff need to feel comfortable discussing with their supervisor any discomfort or difficulty they may have viewing consumers as colleagues. Effective supervision can help employees explore these feelings and change their behaviors (if not their attitudes) on the job. Finally, we should work with consumer staff to design an approach which educates and increases acceptance without breaching individual privacy, perhaps as part of a larger effort to teach tolerance for and appreciation of diversity in the workplace.

4. Develop Skilled Supervisory Staff

Good supervision is essential to the success of any employee in a mental health organization. This is particularly true for employees who have significant histories as mental health consumers. As we have suggested, consumer staff have considerable support needs, particularly in the initial months of their employment. It is important that supervisors have an appreciation for the challenges which these employees face and a commitment to providing them with the support and supervision which they need to succeed. Access to internal resources, such as Vinfen's Director of Consumer & Family Affairs and our consumer staff peer support group, can provide supervisory staff with an effective sounding board and/or forum to explore solutions to common problems.

Reasonable accommodation is at the core of appropriate supervision of and support for consumer-staff. Employers are obligated to provide accommodation and, in the world of human services, this means providing good supervision and support. Supervisors in organizations need to receive training themselves on the meaning and importance of accommodation as well as the organization's commitment in this area. It is important to recognize that interventions which constitute reasonable accommodation may be less clear in the area of psychiatric disability than in some other areas. It is easier to recognize what is a "reasonable" accommodation for someone in a wheelchair who requires an accessible building than for an employee who may have a bipolar disorder and be occasionally hypomanic. This means that accommodations are often highly individualized and require a high level of interpersonal skill in their delivery.

At Vinfen, we have found that developing a strong organizational commitment in all parts of the organization is essential to this process. We problem-solve on a regular basis through the chain of command and use this to provide support to supervisors. In addition, our human resource department is frequently called upon to provide technical assistance and support for supervisors who face these issues.

5. Emphasize Supervision and Support

Supervision and support of employees is critical to their success. When employing individuals with psychiatric disabilities, it is important to recognize that the employer must provide reasonable accommodation for them. As noted earlier, reasonable accommodation for individuals with psychiatric disabilities is a highly individualized process. The following example illustrates one approach taken by Vinfen to provide accommodation to employees.

Part-time employment: Full-time positions typically put staff under pressure to arrive on time and assume a great deal of responsibility very quickly. Consumers who have been out of the workforce for some time have had difficulty shouldering so much responsibility so soon. The only part-time position offered by one of our programs was a 30-hour overnight position that tended to leave consumer staff isolated and without much direction or support. The program managers explored ways to incorporate a part-time position into the staffing pattern so that more support was available to the staff member. The only salary money in the budget with sufficient flexibility was in the relief line.

The program often needed relief staff on Thursday, Friday and Saturday nights — nights that the program supervisor was scheduled to work and could be available to supervise and support a consumer staff member. Program staff determined that a total of 12 hours per week would meet the need for relief coverage and also provide a reasonable part-time schedule for a new consumer staff member. Vinfen's Director of Consumer & Family Affairs helped to recruit a consumer who was interested in working the described schedule and in possibly easing into a permanent part-time or full-time position. Weekly evaluation of this staff member's progress was a priority, with a full review of the position after six weeks. This review included feedback from the consumer to help the program assess the need for support and readiness to expand responsibilities.

It also is important to note that the provision of reasonable accommodation can be complicated by reluctance on the part of consumer staff to disclose his or her disability to other staff (see next item). It can be difficult to balance the consumer staff's concerns regarding privacy with the effect that "accommodation" can have on other staff when the disability is unknown to them. Without the proper context, accommodation can raise questions regarding favoritism, inconsistent expectations or standards, etc., which can damage overall morale.

6. Respect Privacy and Confidentiality

There are a range of issues related to privacy and confidentiality on hiring consumers to work in your programs. For example, there is a considerable stigma attached to psychiatric disability. Consumers may experience significant conflict about the degree to which they are willing to share their mental health history. We have found that some consumers are very open about sharing information about their disability, while others may only share this with a select few. While this is a highly individualized decision, we believe that it is useful for both the employee and the organization to share this kind of information. Supervisors work hard to respect people's decisions but also let people know that there may be unrecognized advantages to disclosing.

Many mental illnesses are cyclical in nature. It is not unusual for consumer staff to experience exacerbations in their illness during the course of their employment. This is particularly true during the initial months of employment which may be stressful. If the illness of a consumer staff member becomes severe enough to require hospitalization or a leave of absence, the supervisor may be faced with many questions from other staff members and consumers in the organization about the employee's whereabouts. It is important to work closely with employees and respect their preferences regarding how much information is shared about such situations. Again, Vinfen believes there is no shame in having a mental illness. We respect consumers' rights to confidentiality and their preferences for how much information is shared. However, we also take time to explain to them that it is safe to disclose the reasons for their absence.

Confidentiality becomes a particularly difficult issue when an employer hires individuals who are also consumers in that same organization's programs. As an example, an individual who lives in one of the organization's residential programs is becoming increasingly symptomatic and is quite open about this with staff. During the day, he serves as a job coach and drives the van for the same organization. To what degree are the residential staff allowed to share information with the vocational services staff about the individual's psychiatric condition? There are no simple answers to these kinds of questions. At Vinfen, we have worked hard to keep lines of communication open, which include first and foremost, the consumer staff member. In addition, our human resource department plays a key role in these situations. All questions and concerns are shared at a very early stage with the Human Resources Department, which serves as a decision-maker and controller around the flow of information.

While some organizations may be very intimidated with the prospect of grappling with these kinds of problems, hospitals and health maintenance organizations (HMOs) face them every day. It is very common for employees of HMOs or hospitals to also be patients in these same organizations. These organization have developed the ability to manage these "dual role" situations and mental health organizations can certainly do the same. It is our belief that facing these challenges around privacy and confidentiality is an aspect of reasonable accommodation and that providers who refuse to hire categories of employees because of their concerns related to privacy and confidentiality may be in violation of the Americans with Disabilities Act.

Conclusions

While the preceding sections have covered many of the major issues and shared some of our strategies for facing them, there other situations which can occur. Funding sources such as departments of mental health, vocational rehabilitation, public health, managed care organizations and so on may share some of the societal biases about mental illness. These funding sources may express concern about funding or referring consumers to organizations which have employees with histories of mental illness. It is important to take the time to educate these organizations about the relevance of federal law to this topic as well as the value of having consumers as staff members in programs. Funding sources can change this perceived problem into a competitive advantage.

Many consumers (like many of us) start their careers in mental health at relatively entry level positions. Consumers may face particular obstacles in developing a career track in mental health. Mental illnesses which strike in young adulthood may have interrupted educational experiences and employment. It is important to provide consumers with opportunities to develop a strong employment history as well as formal academic credentials. Again, this is not a situation which is unique to consumer staff. However, principles of reasonable accommodation need to be applied to this situation as well. The mental health system has made enormous progress in the last twenty-five years. There is a greatly reduced reliance on long-term inpatient services and there are many integrated and community-based options available. Many systems have moved from a focus on symptom management to a recovery and rehabilitation paradigm. We have begun to listen to consumers in advocacy roles and are slowly learning from the wisdom they share with us. We believe that hiring significant numbers of individuals with psychiatric disabilities to work as employees in provider organizations is an important next step in this set of system changes. Just as African Americans and other minority groups have discovered the importance of having services delivered by peers, the mental health system is beginning to recognize the value of having consumers of services play important roles as deliverers of services.

As this process moves along, it is important for consumers themselves to be involved in shaping and supporting the process. At the very least, providers need to support full compliance with federal requirements under the Americans with Disabilities Act and offer reasonable accommodations to individuals with psychiatric disabilities who want to be employed as providers. In Vinfen, however, we believe that it is important for providers to move beyond simple compliance with ADA. We believe that mental health providers should assume an affirmative obligation to recruit, support and retain consumers as employees in their organizations. This can be extraordinarily challenging work, but it is also extraordinarily important to the consumers that we serve as a provider — and an employer.

Anthony M. Zipple, Sc.D., is the senior vice president for mental health services at Vinfen Corporation in Cambridge, Massachusetts, and an adjunct assistant professor at Boston University.

Maureen Drouin, M.S.W., M.A.P.A., is a director of mental health services at Vinfen Corporation.

Moe Armstrong, M.B.A., M.A., is the director of consumer and family relations at Vinfen Corporation.

Melissa Brooks, B.A., is an assistant program director at Vinfen Corporation.

Joan Flynn, B.A., is a senior program director at Vinfen Corporation.

Will Buckley, M.A., M.Ed., is a program director at Vinfen Corporation.

Chapter 40
An Inclusion Framework: Preparing Psychosocial Rehabilitation Programs and Staff for the Consumer Hiring Initiative

Jessica A. Jonikas
Mardi L. Solomon
Judith A. Cook

Although mental health consumer hiring has been gaining increasing momentum in psychosocial rehabilitation settings, to date little attention has been given to strategies for preparing the existing workforce to accept the inclusion of consumer/survivor staff members. Typically, literature regarding preparations for consumer hiring has focused more on the potential training needs of peer providers themselves than on the staff development needs of existing personnel and necessary organizational modifications to ensure inclusion. In so doing, many consumers and nonconsumers have been indirectly or directly encouraged to view the changes required to truly include consumers in all levels of service delivery as something that is solely up to consumers themselves. Indeed, many organizations have begun hiring peer providers without full consideration of how this movement fits into their overall missions, the changes in organizational structures and practices necessary to ensure success, and existing staff members' perspectives and knowledge about consumer hiring. This lack of advance preparation has left many staff members (nonconsumer and consumer) with the feeling that they are dangling over an abyss of the confusion and chaos that often accompanies major organizational change. Even staff members who are dedicated to the consumer hiring initiative can become overburdened and resentful when left with the impression that their agencies did not adequately prepare for consumer hiring and that they are shouldering the burden of major change alone. Clearly advance preparation is no longer possible for the many agencies which are well-underway in implementing peer provider initiatives; however, there are strategies that administrators, practitioners, and clients can utilize in order to achieve full inclusion of peer providers, regardless of how long they have been *knowingly* hiring consumers. This chapter outlines several such strategies which can be utilized by agencies no matter where they are on the continuum of organizational development with respect to consumer hiring.[1]

---

[1] Much of the material in this chapter is discussed in greater detail in a manual by M. Solomon, J. Cook, J. Jonikas, and J. Kerouac, *Positive Partnerships: How Consumers and Nonconsumers Can Work Together as Service Providers, 2nd edition*. Chicago, IL: UIC National Research and Training Center on Psychiatric Disability, 1997.

It is important to point out that we believe that agencies will not be successful in their efforts to fully include consumer providers if only consumers themselves are expected to change or grow. We believe that the consumer hiring initiative in traditional rehabilitation programs is best viewed as a *partnership* between consumers and nonconsumers, which inherently requires that *nonconsumers* also receive training and support in their efforts to accept consumer providers as equals. To this end, this chapter focuses primarily on the staff development needs of *nonconsumer staff* members, and thus, fills a major gap in the current literature about the consumer hiring initiative. (Readers who are interested in the job development needs of consumer providers themselves are encouraged to reference Harp, 1991; Lavin & Everett, 1995; Shepherd, 1992; Sherman & Porter, 1991; Solomon & Draine, 1995a; 1995b.) Specifically, this chapter addresses ways in which traditional psychosocial rehabilitation programs can work with nonconsumer staff in order to refine organizational structures and practices in an effort to better accommodate peer providers. We introduce the concept of an *Organizational Inclusion Framework*, which agencies can use both to develop and evaluate organizational changes over time with regard to consumer hiring. Developing such a framework includes appointing an "Internal Change Team" to guide the process, conduct agency assessments, and create agency action plans for change based on the results of the assessments. In what follows, we will describe the steps involved in developing an Organizational Inclusion Framework.

An Organizational Inclusion Framework

An Organizational Inclusion Framework can be thought of as a conceptual paradigm delineating active consumer involvement in all levels of an organization's practices, particularly in the form of paid and/or volunteer service delivery positions. This type of consumer involvement requires acceptance of consumers/survivors in a variety of organizational realms in which they may not have been accepted in the past. Further, it requires that all existing (and new) staff members endorse the idea that peer providers have unique perspectives and skills to bring to bear on the process of rehabilitation and treatment (Cook, Jonikas, & Solomon, 1992; McGill & Patterson, 1990; Mowbray & Tan, 1992; Nikkel, Smith, & Edwards, 1992; Van Tosh, 1993). The development of this framework often requires restructuring of an agency's culture or climate, mission statement, values and goals, composition of personnel and leadership, as well as management practices (Jackson & Hardiman, 1994). Ultimately, an Organizational Inclusion Framework can be utilized as a standard against which agencies evaluate their progress towards, and outcomes of, full inclusion.

Although there should be common elements in all Organizational Inclusion Frameworks (e.g., inclusion of consumers/survivors on the Board of Directors, peer providers on the staff, periodic surveys of clients/staff for their suggestions for change, etc.), it is important that each agency develop a framework that also meets its own unique management needs. As individuals within different agencies work through the process of implementing change, they will adapt models and recommendations in different ways and will generate new ideas that work best within the particular context of their agencies (Martinez-Brawley, 1995). To facilitate this process, we recommend that agencies appoint a "Peer Provider Internal Change Team," which will serve as a catalyst for ongoing organizational change regarding consumer hiring (Jackson & Hardiman, 1994). This team will be responsible for developing and translating organizational innovation surrounding this initiative into a familiar and non-threatening message that can be persistently and clearly delivered to all staff (Martinez-Brawley, 1995). Such a change team must be representative of the diverse social groups and different job positions in the organization. The individual members must be able to make a significant time commitment to this work, have personal and professional competence in dealing with oppression and empowerment in the workplace, and be respected by peers, subordinates, and superiors in the organization. It is best to rotate membership at least every two years to ensure that new ideas are continually represented in the work of the team; this also can be accomplished with periodic formal or informal surveys of the agency's staff members and clients to assess the relevance and effectiveness of the team's efforts. Ongoing evaluation of organizational change, conducted on at least an annual basis, is a key strategy for ensuring that momentum is maintained and proceeds in the desired direction.

The work of the change team should be initiated with an all-agency assessment, as described below. This type of assessment measures both attitudes and knowledge about the consumer hiring initiative in order to identify barriers to and supports for full inclusion of consumers. The change team can utilize the information gathered through the assessment to develop the unique and individualized aspects of its agency's Organizational Inclusion Framework.

Agency Assessments

One of the first steps for successful consumer hiring within traditionally nonconsumer-run psychosocial rehabilitation agencies is an analysis of the agency's work environment in order to identify obstacles to and support for the integration of peer providers. Typically, full integration of consumer service providers in community-based rehabilitation settings is the end result of a lengthy process, with many complex stages. In thinking about either where to begin or how to improve this process, it is helpful to conduct a comprehensive agency assessment that addresses four major questions: 1) What are the agency's ultimate goals regarding the inclusion of consumers as service providers?; 2) How do the organization's procedures and practices support or inhibit full inclusion of consumers?; 3) How far along is the agency in attaining its goals?; and 4) How do existing staff members perceive the consumer hiring initiative and how well do they understand it? An assessment of this type requires involvement of *everyone* who has a role within the agency, including the clients, clinical and administrative personnel, and the Board of Directors. This is particularly important because an all-agency assessment of this sort typically reveals necessary changes at individual and organizational levels that will not be possible without profound commitment from all members of the organization.

Assessment Methods

There are many ways to proceed with an agency assessment. The types of questions asked will depend on the format chosen for conducting an assessment. Some useful methods include paper-and-pencil questionnaires/surveys, in-person interviews with as many staff members and clients as is possible, small focus groups with different contingents within the agency, and a series of meetings where everyone comes together to discuss their ideas/feelings about the direction of the agency and consumer hiring (meetings may be facilitated by an outside moderator, if necessary). It is best to employ more than one of these methods of assessment since they most likely will result in different types of information. Also, some individuals may find one method easier to respond to than another. Given the broad scope of the questions to be addressed, it is likely that the assessment will necessarily be conducted in stages, addressing one or, at most, two of the major questions at a time. Particular assessment methods may be best suited for particular questions, just as the most appropriate respondent groups may vary depending on the assessment topic.

In the following sections, we will discuss in detail each of the four previously described questions to be addressed in an all-agency assessment. We will consider each question in turn, discussing the purpose and content of the assessment and methods that will best address each topic. Additionally, we will present strategies for applying knowledge gained from each aspect of the assessment to begin to effect organizational change.

Step One: Envisioning the Ultimate Goal

Agency Mission, Values, and Culture

When seeking to evaluate an organization's mission, values, and culture, it is best to begin with a clear image of the goal that the agency is trying to accomplish or, in this case, a clear definition of what an agency is striving to achieve in terms of the peer provider initiative (Besancon & Zipple, 1995). Depending upon the agency's level of organizational development in this process, this may be as specific as "to have five consumer case managers on staff within two years," or as general as "to work with staff members to help them understand and value the peer provider initiative within the next year." In general, the vision of the end goal will evolve over time as members of the organization change and grow. Further, agencies may very well have two or three goals on which they are working that are related to hiring peer providers in general and to empowerment of consumers overall.

Ideally, the change team should use its all-agency assessment to determine the ways in which staff members view the ultimate goal(s) of the organization. As further detailed below, the data they collect should be compared to the agency's existing program mission, values, and culture to determine areas that need immediate attention. In this way, everyone in the agency is involved in the creation of a common vision or set of goals, especially those related to consumer hiring, toward which all will strive and which eventually will become the basis of the program mission, values, and culture. Further, by envisioning the end goals together, a group of individuals, who play different roles in creating the whole of the organization, is able to share its perceptions about what is happening at the group level. They are thinking beyond their particular roles to how the whole organization functions, both ideally and in actuality. By involving all personnel in the assessment process, the change team and/or agency administrators increase the likelihood that most staff members will become committed to growth and change.

Questions to elicit ideas about the future direction of the agency include what staff members believe the current agency mission is and what they think it *should* be. The assessment also determines barriers staff members encounter in trying to fulfill the agency's mission. In other words, as discussed below, staff members should be able to directly tie the program mission to their daily work. Additionally, it is useful to ask staff members what they *themselves* would like to see changed in the program mission and goals at this time, in order to determine not only the priority they assign to consumer hiring, but also other changes that they would like the team to recommend. Consideration of the complexity of staff needs in this manner may help reluctant individuals to feel more amenable to the changes suggested by the team that are specific to the peer provider initiative. Ultimately, however, the desired outcome of this part of the assessment is to reach a consensus regarding the agency's mission and its goals with respect to consumer hiring.

It is likely that the assessment will reveal needed changes in organizational mission, values, and culture in order to support full inclusion of consumer providers. In all probability, many agencies will find that there are some major discrepancies between their ideal and actual program missions of empowering mental health clients by helping them to become self-determining agents of their own change. Recognizing this discrepancy when it exists, and working to reconcile the real and the ideal, may be the greatest challenge posed by the consumer hiring initiative since it will require agency stakeholders to be absolutely honest in acknowledging their biases and failings with respect to consumer empowerment. To bring the agency's mission, values, and culture in line with its goals regarding consumer hiring is to establish the structural integrity of the Organization Inclusion Framework.

Organizational Development Strategies

Program Mission and Culture. Based on the findings of the assessment, the change team most likely will find that the best first step in their work is to rewrite or refine the program's mission statement. There are many variables which differentiate mental health agencies, for example, size, population being served, and type of services provided. Even programs within the same agency may differ in many ways. However, the thing that holds an agency together, the "cohesion factor" so to speak, is the program mission. Through it, insiders and outsiders to the agency should be able to determine what an agency does and why it functions as it does. In a well-run agency, everyone involved in the organization is able to articulate the mission of the program. This does not necessarily mean that everyone agrees about the nature of psychiatric disability and its treatment (although this would certainly help), but that the objectives of the agency are clearly defined. This cohesion creates a reference point for all interactions. While practices will change over time as knowledge of disability expands and new technologies evolve, the mission of the agency should remain a solid foundation permitting growth and change without chaos and upheaval.

The change team should work to create an organizational mission that describes not only the target population to be served and program goals, but the agency's values and beliefs about the rights of people with psychiatric disabilities. The team should ensure that a fundamental belief in equality and self-determination for people with psychiatric disabilities, which includes their right to hold paid and/or volunteer positions in service delivery programs, is clearly conveyed in its mission statement. Once developed, the new mission should be reviewed by all staff members and clients and, to the degree possible, refined based on their feedback. If an agency has a large staff, serving numerous clients, it may be best to gather feedback about the new mission in staff and team meetings, individual staff supervision sessions, and/or client skills training or support groups. The agency mission then must be conveyed to everyone participating at every level of the program including clients, service delivery staff, administrative personnel, and all individuals representing the agency to the community (e.g., development department staff, members of the Board of Directors, etc.). The mission also should be articulated in all written materials describing the program, including personnel handbooks, client handbooks, training materials for new staff members, agency brochures, and other important documents that are disseminated among all members of the staff and the public. Additionally, the team should recommend an orientation period for consumers and personnel new to the agency that helps to socialize them to this new organizational culture as well.

It is important for the change team to discuss with agency administrators what supervisors will do to help develop staff who are having difficulty accepting the refined mission, values, and culture of full inclusion. New staff and younger staff *may* have an easier time accepting an organizational mission that emphasizes active consumer involvement in all levels of programming than those who have worked within a more traditional mental health setting for a long time. In general, it will probably take some staff (whether new or tenured) a good deal of time to adjust to new ways of thinking about consumers and their roles within the system. These staff may need some extra support from their supervisors and coworkers to understand the agency's mission and incorporate new values and practices into their work. The more inclusive the change team is in involving everyone in the process of change from the very first goal-setting stage, the more people will feel a part of the process rather than that change is being imposed on them. It is important to give these staff the time and support they need while, at the same time, recognizing that for some of them the transition may be too uncomfortable, causing them to eventually leave the agency. Some staff turnover during times of significant change within an agency is to be expected, but proceeding sensitively and encouraging staff involvement from the initial assessment process onward should prevent total upheaval within the organization (this issue is discussed further below, in the section regarding individuals' perceptions and levels of knowledge).

Step Two: Connecting Program Mission and Culture to Practices and Procedures

Reevaluating and refining the work environment is a necessary first step to achieve full inclusion of peer providers, but is not sufficient to create lasting change in and of itself. An agency must then move to reviewing and modifying its organizational procedures and practices. With new goals established through the first part of the assessment process, followed by an effort to reconcile the agency's stated mission with these new goals, the next step is to move beyond the *ideology* of the consumer empowerment movement to the *practice* of full inclusion of consumers.

The question that must be asked within each agency at this second stage of the assessment process is whether the organization's procedures and practices support or inhibit progress toward the agency's goals. In honestly considering this question, individuals at many organizations would have to admit that although consumer self-determination is identified among their most important goals, they often do not truly integrate the *self-identified* needs of consumers into their organizational mission or daily activities. For example, while most organizations emphasize moving at the consumers' own pace, clients who choose to work towards maintaining community living, creating social networks, and/or becoming employed tend to attract more agency resources — such as staff approval and time — than do clients who do not or cannot work towards these goals. Again, a major purpose of conducting an agency assessment is to make such discrepancies apparent so that they may be addressed.

Probably the best source of information about practical barriers to full inclusion of consumer staff are peer providers themselves. If there are consumers/survivors currently on staff who have made their experiences within the mental health system publicly known, every effort should be made to create a forum in which they feel comfortable discussing ways that the structure of the work environment enhances or detracts from their ability to participate fully in the functioning of the agency. If there are no identified consumers on staff, it may be possible to interview consumer professionals in neighboring mental health agencies. Former clients who have gone on to work in mental health or a related field should be interviewed as they may provide particularly valuable feedback given their knowledge of the agency. Current clients, especially those who are interested in working in the field and are taking leadership roles within the agency, also will have important information regarding ways in which the agency encourages or discourages their movement into positions of power within the organization.

Conducting an assessment regarding agency procedures and practices with consumers and consumer professionals may involve no more than asking the questions, "Are there things that we do at this agency that make it difficult/easier for you to feel comfortable working here?" If these general questions do not elicit the desired information, there are many specific topics that may be raised to elicit more detail. For example, there are many questions the team could ask around the issue of disclosing one's disability to supervisors, coworkers, and clients (e.g., who to tell, how much to tell, when to tell, etc.). In fact, this issue may serve as a "barometer of inclusion" since it is likely that the decision to disclose one's disability will be less of a concern in a work environment that is truly accepting of consumer professionals than in one that is not. Another important topic for discussion in this area is formal and informal practices that are supportive of consumers and those that are stigmatizing or discriminatory. Examples of practices which may be raised for examination are: the allocation of various resources such as space or funds for special activities; the language and attitudes used when discussing clients/consumers (even when they are not present); and the dynamics of established decision-making processes (e.g., who gets power, what happens when consumers challenge decisions of nonconsumers, etc.).

Procedures for recruiting consumer job applicants, hiring new staff, and providing job training and continuing education should be reviewed in light of the consumer hiring initiative. Related to this is the agency's response to the Americans with Disabilities Act (ADA). All agencies should have some established procedures for ensuring that job applicants with disabilities are not discriminated against and that reasonable accommodations are made for employees with disabilities. Conducting the proposed assessment provides a good opportunity to gain respondents' perceptions of how well the agency has responded to the ADA and how receptive it is to requests for reasonable accommodations. Not only is this information an indication of how well the organizations' procedures meet the needs of its consumer staff, but it is also valuable in light of the potential legal ramifications of inadequate policies.

These are just some of the practices and procedures that may be addressed in this part of the assessment. Each agency will have specific practices which should be analyzed with respect to whether they help to facilitate full inclusion of consumer providers and further the agency's overall mission. This part of the assessment also should provide insight into whether established organizational practices help all staff members to experience their work as meaningful and to feel invested in their work (Hackman & Oldham, 1980). Such feedback will point the direction for revisions to existing practices and procedures that not only will foster inclusion of consumers/survivors at all levels of the organization, but will improve the work environment for everyone.

Organizational Development Strategies

There are some general strategies that agencies may find helpful in responding to the need to alter procedures and practices to be more inclusive of consumers. We assume an initial goal of most agencies will be to get more consumers on staff. Depending upon the results of the assessment, recruitment and hiring practices for staff positions may need to be revised in order to accomplish this goal. We suggest that the change team should first review the agency's organizational chart in order to determine the representation of consumers/survivors at all levels of the organization (if they do not know already) and to identify particular areas in which consumer involvement is lacking. The change team might then recommend the creation of a Personnel Committee, at least half of which is consumers/survivors. All job applicants would be interviewed by this committee to ascertain the applicant's commitment to client self-determination, promoting consumers as colleagues, and her/his ability to help clients realize their full potential. This committee also would be responsible for reviewing (and rewriting, if necessary) all job descriptions, so that they are reflective of the agency's commitment to equality and self-determination, as well as accommodating to the needs of people with psychiatric disabilities. This committee would be involved in ensuring reasonable accommodations for employees, upon request. Finally, the committee would develop specific recruitment strategies to reach out to potential applicants who have personal experience in the mental heatlh system. Appointment of consumers to the agency's Board of Directors is another strategy that will ensure that consumer perspectives are represented when important decisions are made regarding the agency's policies, future goals, and methods for achieving them.

On a daily basis, strategies should be implemented to foster open communication between staff members so that an environment in which people trust one another and feel free to discuss personal matters with each other is encouraged. Relationships between staff members and their supervisors are of primary importance, and thus, should be strengthened and nurtured, so that staff feel free to discuss work-related problems and personal problems which are interfering with work. If time for regular (weekly or biweekly) supervision is not already provided at the agency, making this time will be critical for developing supportive relationships between staff and their supervisors which are crucial in times of major organizational change. Creating time and structure in which to foster other supportive relationships between staff members will increase the likelihood that open communication will occur. Establishing a mentorship arrangement in which new staff members (consumers and nonconsumers) are paired with senior staff persons (who are not their supervisors) to whom they can go for advice and support is one way to encourage the development of supportive relationships. A consumer provider support group also might be started. Social gatherings and team meetings, as well all-staff and all-agency retreats, are other settings in which relationships may develop.

Encouraging open discussion of agency practices and policies that inhibit full inclusion of peer providers also means that all staff persons must learn to feel comfortable with conflict, criticism, and change. These are certainly good topics for inservice staff training, and local and national experts could be brought into the agency to share their advice for coping with conflict and change. Another suggestion is to create a Mediation Committee, again including adequate representation of consumers/survivors, which would be called upon to negotiate disagreements or difficulties between peer providers, consumer and nonconsumer providers, and supervisors and consumer staff.

Many of the suggestions we have made may be procedures and practices that already exist in the current organizational structure. For example, the agency may have in place a well-established support system for staff which includes regular clinical supervision, mentorship arrangements, and many opportunities for staff to interact and develop their relationships. Any features of the organizational environment that enhance feelings of community, general morale, dedication to the agency and its mission, and a sense of participating in an important process will be significant advantages for agencies that desire to promote consumer hiring. These assets should be identified through the assessment process and nurtured, while other areas that are not as conducive to promoting inclusiveness are changed.

Step Three: Determining Readiness for Change

Readiness for Change

A critical part of an initial assessment of an agency will be determining the agency's readiness for making the changes that will be needed to accomplish the organization's newly established goals. As discussed above, clarifying the relationship between existing procedures and practices and the agency mission should reveal many of the strengths and challenges the organization brings to the change process. It also is helpful to ask members of the agency *directly* about their feelings regarding the agency, how it functions currently, and what they would like to see changed. For instance, a survey might ask what individuals admire most and least about the agency; what they see as the organization's greatest strengths and weaknesses; and how optimistic or pessimistic they are about the chances for positive change to occur within the agency. This part of the assessment should ascertain whether there is general support for change at all levels of the agency (e.g., clients, staff, administration, etc.). Additionally, it is important to gather not only people's opinions, but also some tangible evidence of support for this change from all levels of the organization. To this end, it may be helpful to review the agency's "track record" in terms of introducing innovative ideas that have led to lasting changes within the agency's mission, structure, policies, and procedures. Being able to remind staff members of similar major changes in the past and the success with which they were implemented may help them to envision and have faith in the current process and its eventual outcomes.

Realistically, making the types of changes in a traditional mental health setting that may be needed to create an organizational climate that is truly inclusive is a major challenge that will require a lot of time, work, and additional resources. The intent of this part of the assessment is to determine how easily organizational change will unfold. This stage of the assessment allows the change team the opportunity to identify resources that are available to assist in accomplishing the organization's desired goals. These resources might be current procedures and practices that promote consumer empowerment (as previously described), a supportive administration, the physical layout of the agency (e.g. one in which consumers are forbidden to go into certain areas, offices, washrooms, etc.), or any other features of the organization that may reduce the amount of upheaval involved in hiring consumers on staff.

Organizational Development Strategies

Given the scarcity of time and money — key resources in the change process — in most psychiatric rehabilitation settings, it is especially important to accurately identify during the assessment existing resources that can be used to facilitate the change process in order to streamline the work involved. As an example, many of the strategies that we have outlined thus far require meetings to be held and committees to be formed. In all likelihood, individuals at the agency may feel that they attend more than enough meetings already. Few people will feel that they truly have the time to sit on committees, given all of their other responsibilities. Therefore, as much as possible, the change team should seek to utilize existing meetings for conducting assessments and utilize existing groups to form committees. Furthermore, while the work involved in preparing the organizational environment for peer providers will take time, there most likely are a number of other tasks each day on which individuals are spending time unnecessarily. The assessment can be a tool for determining what these tasks are and ways to phase them out. Staff trainings regarding the principles of "total quality management" would be useful in this area, since one of its major tenets is reducing tasks that staff cannot clearly identify as efficient and effective in fulfilling their agency's missions and goals. Similarly, the change team also should analyze whether daily operations and external regulations have become the *end* of programmatic activities rather than the *means*. They should recommend that any activities that staff members and clients cannot directly tie to fulfilling the program mission be dropped or refined accordingly.

Along these lines, financial resources may be needed in order to make some types of changes possible (e.g., money to hire consumers into newly created job positions, money to bring in experts for staff training, etc.). Whether such funds are allocated may very well be the primary test of the organization's commitment to change from the top administrative levels on down. In other words, in most cases, there must be a willingness to allocate resources (financial and otherwise) to this initiative for it to succeed. Again, however, the demand for financial resources may be minimized by evaluating whether there are current drains on agency funds that can be reduced or eliminated, given the agency's desire to succeed at consumer hiring and full inclusion.

Beyond the immediate commitments of time and money to initiate changes in the organization, there must be a long-term commitment made to the process since it will undoubtedly happen slowly. Assessing an agency's readiness for change means assessing individuals' readiness to make a major commitment to work for many years in order to substantially improve the organizational environment in particular and the mental health system in general. The logical next question, then, is whether or not individuals are able and/or ready to take on such a commitment. This is the next area for assessment.

Step Four: Improving Individuals' Perceptions and Understanding of Consumer Hiring

Staff Perspectives and Knowledge

An agency is made up of individuals, each with her or his own set of values, beliefs, levels of knowledge, and ways of doing things. Thus, it is important to understand how each individual sees herself or himself as related to the whole and how each person feels about hiring consumers as service providers.

In order to assess individuals' goals and perspectives regarding their roles within the agency, the change team would request that staff members share their ideas about what motivates them to be involved in service delivery, how they feel about mental health consumers working as service providers, and ways in which they think their jobs might be enhanced and/or made more difficult by working with peer providers. It also is important to ascertain the level of knowledge among the staff about the peer provider initiative. To this end, the change team would assess what staff members know about the philosophy and history of the consumer hiring initiative, the various models of consumer service provision, and the advantages of utilizing peers in paid and/ or volunteer staff positions. Evaluating levels of knowledge is done with the belief that most people find it hard to accept that which they do not understand or about which they are misinformed.

This part of the assessment is likely to reveal attitudinal and structural barriers that may impede the agency's ability to move toward full integration of peer providers. In our discussions with staff members from mental health programs across the country, we have identified a number of common barriers to consumer hiring that agencies confront at the staff level including: cultural attitudes and myths, power dynamics, and changing relationships between consumer and nonconsumer staff persons (Solomon, Cook, Jonikas, & Kerouac, 1997). Confronting these issues is bound to introduce a high level of complexity, uncertainty, and even distress into the change process. However, it is our view that unless these issues are directly addressed, full inclusion and empowerment of consumers/survivors is seriously compromised. As detailed below, there are a number of strategies at both the individual and group levels that can be utilized to begin to address these sociopolitical barriers to full inclusion.

Organizational Development Strategies

Consciousness-Raising. One of the first steps to overcoming issues of stigma, discrimination, and fear is *consciousness-raising* about these issues. Individual assessments, journal writing, and similar exercises that staff members complete on their own are good ways to raise awareness about consumer empowerment and hiring. Such exercises allow deeper and more profound exploration of personal feelings and issues than might be possible in a group setting. They also may be viewed as safer assessment methods by staff members who have serious reservations about treating consumers as equals, but are anxious about being criticized in a group or being viewed as recalcitrant. Individual exercises might ask members of the staff to commit to several months of exploring a variety of issues in a journal and/or in supervision. Topics for staff to focus on in such an exploration include their value systems and biases, their beliefs about social roles and power, how they would feel if one of their treatment decisions were challenged by a consumer, issues they worry about or have encountered when supervising consumers, and how they would feel about being supervised by a consumer/survivor.

Scheduling *group discussions* among personnel, administrators, and clients is another way to raise awareness about these issues and the need to confront them. Time could be set aside during regularly scheduled meetings (e.g., staff meetings, team meetings, board meetings, community meetings, etc.) for such discussions or special meetings could be called. A professional group facilitator may be brought in for one or more special sessions to assist those within the agency to work through their feelings about the changes they are making.

Because service recipients and providers are likely to have different concerns, they may choose to meet separately for some of these discussions. Similarly, nonconsumer and consumer staff persons also may wish to meet in separate groups to discuss these issues. Although some may worry about the ethics of separate meetings, this may be necessary at first so that nonconsumers and consumers feel safe in airing their concerns, personal biases, and fears. If separate meetings are held, however, they always must be facilitated by a person who, although sensitive to people's hesitations, is a staunch supporter of the consumer hiring initiative. At some point, all parties also should meet *together* since it is important for everyone at the agency to be aware of how others are feeling and the impact that consumer hiring has on them.

Inservice Training. It can be helpful for agencies to bring in someone from the outside to mediate dialogues with agency staff members about the many factors that may have an impact upon successful consumer hiring, including but not limited to attitudes about mental illness, stigma, and power dynamics, as well as cultural beliefs and value systems (Dan Fisher, personal communication, 10-01-93). When addressing the issues that arise from consumer hiring, agencies also would benefit from staff trainings regarding conflict resolution, team building, job satisfaction and burnout, successful clinical supervision, managing change, and working with persons from a variety of cultures and/or oppressed communities.

In general, staff training will be needed at every stage of the process of consumer hiring. For example, inservice training for all staff about the issues that arise when consumers transition from the role of client to coworker may help this process to go more smoothly for everyone. Even when peer providers are well-integrated and things seem to be running smoothly, additional training may be needed to help co-workers make reasonable accommodations when necessary, to assist supervisors in working well with consumer staff, to help peer providers recognize situations in which they need to ask for support and to feel comfortable doing so, to explore areas in which stigma or inequality is a problem, and other similar issues. Time also should be set aside for reading literature specific to the agency, articles describing the treatment model(s) on which services are based, and research studies regarding the efficacy of various services. Opportunities for personal development and to learn new skills (within and outside of the agency) should be provided in order to help increase job satisfaction and reduce burnout.

Policies Regarding Interpersonal Relationships. As previously mentioned, a significant barrier to consumer hiring is negotiating the changing boundaries of relationships between nonconsumer staff persons, consumer staff persons, and clients. Clearly, then, it will be important for the change team to address issues such as stigma and power dynamics in order to pave the way for satisfactory relationships between nonconsumer and consumer staff members. Keeping open lines of communication will be particularly important when it comes to relationships because these issues can be very sensitive.

It is important to note that relationship issues are of particular concern when consumers make the transition to staff positions within the same agency in which they received, or still receive, services. Role confusion and power dynamics can be especially problematic in this situation. Further, sexual relationships that predate the transition to member of the staff also can present difficulties for all parties. To deal with these concerns, some agencies have developed policies stating that relationships which existed before a consumer became part of the staff team are allowed to continue, but that staff person is prohibited from providing any services or being in any kind of supervisory position over the other person (Harp, 1991). Another common policy is to require that the peer-providers agree to limit or cease social relationships with current clients. This type of policy can contribute to the reluctance among some consumers to shift to provider positions because they must then give up many peer supports. Whether or not agencies choose to establish written rules regulating staff/client interactions, this issue must be discussed and some type of policy or guideline developed. Without some regulations in place indicating the types of interactions that are appropriate or inappropriate, agencies can make their clients vulnerable to potential abuses and are themselves vulnerable to lawsuits.

These are many of the possible steps that an agency can take to facilitate needed change in each of the four areas highlighted in an agency assessment. Because resources to implement programmatic transformation often are scarce, agencies should use their assessments to determine where efforts are most needed.

Organizational Action Plan

As is always true of assessments of this type, it is crucial that the change team provide information as soon as possible to everyone involved about the assessment results and subsequent action steps. It is desirable to start by developing a concise and easily understood *Organizational Action Plan* that addresses each of the four areas of the agency assessment, since attention or change is likely to be needed in each of these areas. The team should create one-year, three-year, and five-year plans based on the results of the assessment, clearly outlining both the findings and recommendations for organizational changes. This document could then be read and discussed in a variety of team meetings and/or individual supervision sessions. A yearly re-assessment also will help to ensure that the change process is on track and will identify areas in which new issues have arisen.

It is important to point out the need for individuals to strive to remain flexible and realistic about what an agency can accomplish and how long it will take. Certainly, it is very difficult to anticipate in advance every issue that hiring consumer providers will create because many of the norms within a work environment are unspoken or informal practices that are generally taken for granted. Only when a change occurs within the existing system are these subtle patterns apparent and called into question. It may be that nonconsumer staff persons are not consciously aware they are doing something that is seen as problematic or, even, discriminatory. It is likely that few staff persons are aware of the double standards which exist within their agencies until someone appears to have violated the established norm. When this occurs, the staff is forced to consider unspoken rules regarding agency etiquette and whether these are appropriate given the goals of hiring former or current clients and creating a workplace that is comfortable for everyone. This is why it is imperative for staff and consumers to reassess the program's missions and goals to ensure that these remain comfortable, fair, and empowering to all involved. Nevertheless, no matter how much an agency prepares in advance for a consumer to join the staff, some issues will arise which no one had anticipated. Part of the preparation process, therefore, should involve creating forums to address ongoing issues and fostering open communication so that new issues are discussed as they arise.

There is no doubt that trying to change an organization and its staff is a very difficult process. Anyone who has undergone a major life change (e.g., getting married, moving to a new city, changing jobs, etc.) can understand how difficult it can be to adapt to a new situation. "Change is a developmental process that requires personal adjustment" (Spaniol, Zipple, & Cohen, 1991).

People naturally resist change because it is challenging, if not downright difficult, and raises many complex issues. In making both personal and organizational changes, one must question her or his basic values, beliefs, and habitual ways of doing things. Just asking the questions can be distressing because one must consider the possibility that the way things have been done may not be the best way. There may be a great deal of investment in the status quo and to ask oneself and others to give that up may meet with significant resistance. It is important for all involved in implementing organizational changes to understand that resistance to change is natural, to recognize the stress and fear that change provokes for many people, and to respond in an empathic manner (Spaniol, Zipple, & Cohen, 1991).

Finally, it is helpful to remember that our conceptions of what is possible for ourselves and others change and expand all the time. As little as ten years ago, the very thought of knowingly hiring consumers/survivors as service providers in mental health agencies would have been unheard of, and consumers expressing such desires likely would have been told that they were being unrealistic or "grandiose." Today, many more agencies are willing to see this goal as not only realistic, but desirable. Expressions of human potential vary widely with cultural norms and beliefs, sometimes changing quite significantly even from one decade to the next. Therefore, it is very important for staff members and consumers *together* to question periodically all programmatic activities and philosophies, critically analyzing whether or not each one is truly beneficial to consumers — as *consumers* define beneficial — or is based on traditional cultural attitudes/myths that may be limiting to persons with psychiatric disabilities.

Conclusion

In this chapter, we have focused on ways in which individuals can restructure their programs to fully integrate consumer providers. Much of this process involves serious questioning about the goals, mission, and daily practices of one's organization, as well as the values and biases of individual staff members. Thus, strategies for assessing an agency's ultimate goals and how far along it is in attaining these goals were presented in order to initiate this questioning process. We recognize that agencies are likely to confront many barriers to the full inclusion of consumers/survivors on both the individual staff and organizational levels, and thus, have presented various strategies for overcoming these difficulties.

This is a unique time in the history of the mental health system. If viewed as an opportunity rather than a burden, the paradigm shifts needed to assimilate consumer hiring practices can be used to improve the whole of community-based mental health programs rather than just one aspect of hiring policies and program development. Ultimately, it is *consumers* who have much to teach the mental health field about both how power can be shared and how true equality finally might be realized.

References

Besancon, V. & Zipple, A.M. (1995). From day program to clubhouse: Practical strategies for supporting the transformation. *Psychosocial Rehabilitation Journal*, 18(3), 7-15.

Cook, J.A., Jonikas, J.A. & Solomon, M.L. (1992). Models of vocational rehabilitation for youths and adults with severe mental illness. *American Rehabilitation*, 18(3), 6-11.

Curtis, L.C. (1993). *Consumers as colleagues: Partnership in the workforce. In Practice*. Newsletter by the Center for Community Change through Housing and Support, Institute for Program Development, Trinity College of Vermont, Burlington, Vermont.

Hackman, J.R. & Oldham, C.B. (1980). *Work redesign*. Reading, MA: Addison-Wesley.

Harp, H. (1991). *A crazy folks guide to reasonable accommodation and "psychiatric disability."* Burlington, VT: The Center for Community Change through Housing and Support.

Jackson, B. & Hardiman, R. (1994). Multicultural organizational development. In E.Y. Cross, J.H. Katz, F.A. Miller, & E.W. Seashore (Eds.), *The promise of diversity: Over 40 voices discuss strategies for eliminating discrimination in organizations* (pp. 231-239). New York: Irwin Professional Publishing.

Lavin, D. & Everett, A. (1995). In B. DePoint (Ed.), *Working on the dream: A guide to career planning and job success*. Spring Lake Park, MN: Rise, Inc.

Martinez-Brawley, E.E. (1995). Knowledge diffusion and transfer of technology: Conceptual premises and concrete steps for human service innovators. *Social Work*, 40(5), 670-682.

McGill, C.W. & Patterson, C.J. (1990). Former patients as peer counselors on locked psychiatric inpatient units. *Hospital and Community Psychiatry*, 41(9), 1017-1019.

Mowbray, C.T. & Tan, C. (1992). Evaluation of an innovative consumer-run service model: The drop-in center. *Innovations and Research*, 1(2), 19-23.

Nikkel, R.E., Smith, G., & Edwards, D. (1992). A consumer-operated case management project. *Hospital and Community Psychiatry*, 43(6), 577-579.

Shepherd, L. (1992). *So you want to hire a consumer? Employing people with psychiatric disabilities as staff members in mental health agencies*. Burlington, VT: The Center for Community Change through Housing and Support.

Sherman, P.S. & Porter, R. (1991). Mental health consumers as case management aides. *Hospital and Community Psychiatry*, 42(5), 494-498.

Solomon, M.L., Cook, J.A., Jonikas, J.A., & Kerouac, J. (1997). *Positive partnerships: How consumers and nonconsumers can work together as service providers* (2nd Edition). Chicago, IL: UIC National Research and Training Center on Psychiatric Disability.

Solomon, P. & Draine, J. (1995a). One-year outcomes of a randomized trial of consumer case management. *Evaluation and Program Planning*, 18(2), 117-127.

Solomon, P. & Draine, J. (1995b). The efficacy of a consumer case-management team: 2-year outcomes of a randomized trial. *The Journal of Mental Health Administration, 22*(2), 135-146.

Spaniol, L., Zipple, A. & Cohen, B. (1991). Managing innovation and change in psychosocial rehabilitation: Key principles and guidelines. *Psychosocial Rehabilitation Journal, 14*(3), 27-38.

Van Tosh, L. (1993). *Working for a change: Employment of consumers/survivors in the design and provision of services for persons who are homeless and mentally disabled.* Rockville, MD: Center for Mental Health Services.

Jessica A. Jonikas, M.A., is managing director of the National Research and Training Center on Psychiatric Disability at the University of Illinois at Chicago (UIC). She is also a research specialist in health systems research in psychiatry at UIC.

Mardi L. Solomon, M.A., is a research consultant to the National Research and Training Center on Psychiatric Disability at the University of Illinois at Chicago.

Judith A. Cook, Ph.D., is director of the National Research and Training Center on Psychiatric Disability at the University of Illinois at Chicago (UIC). She is also professor of sociology in psychiatry at UIC.

Chapter 41
Integrating Prosumers into Clinical Settings

Larry Davidson
Richard Weingarten
Jeanne Steiner
David Stayner
Michael A. Hoge[1]

Most often in the brief history of the consumer-as-provider initiative (Stephens & Belisle, 1993), consumer providers have worked in self-help, peer support and consumer-run programs that provided alternatives to the formal mental health system. More recently, they also have been hired to develop and staff psychiatric rehabilitation and community support programs which — while situated within the mental health system *per se* — also remain outside of the purview and scope of more conventionally defined "clinical" programs such as community mental health center outpatient clinics, day hospitals, and inpatient units. Early success in the deployment of consumer providers within non-clinical settings has provided enthusiasm and support for the contributions they can make to engagement and recovery on the individual client level, and in shaping programs to be more responsive to client needs (Besio & Mahler, 1993; Dixon, Krauss & Lehman, 1994; Van Tosh, 1993). Restricting consumer employment to these settings, however, will limit its potential impact on the equally important levels of mental health systems and broader cultural change. For the consumer provider initiative to fulfill its promise on these levels, inroads will need to be made into the mainstay of the current treatment system, the clinical programs described above, that continue to provide the majority of care for clients with serious mental illness.

This chapter describes the efforts made at a large, urban community mental health center to integrate consumer providers into a number of different programs that span the clinical/non-clinical spectrum. These programs range from conventional clinical settings, such as an acute day hospital and outpatient clinic; to progressive, community-based, clinical modalities such as assertive community treatment and homeless outreach teams; to more rehabilitative interventions such as supported socialization programs. By reflecting on our experiences of integrating consumer providers into these diverse settings, we hope to identify the challenges this initiative may pose, particularly to clinical settings. We also hope to identify challenges common to both clinical and non-clinical settings, and suggest strategies that may be useful in addressing and overcoming challenges, as consumers become increasingly involved in the provision of mental health services.

[1] Work on this chapter was supported in part by Public Health Service Grant #R18SM47644 from the Substance Abuse and Mental Health Services Administration.

First, we provide a brief overview of the consumer provider initiative as it has been implemented at our own mental health center. Next, we focus on the issues that arise in the integration of consumer providers across the array of settings within the mental health center, and describe the variety of strategies we have employed to address and overcome these issues. We conclude with a discussion of the unresolved issues and open questions which remain with us as we move toward the next stage in the evolution of this initiative, involving changes in our models of clinical care and service delivery and changes in the social context of our treatment efforts.

Program Description

This chapter is drawn primarily from the experiences of administrative and supervisory staff, program directors, and front line consumer and nonconsumer staff at a large, urban community mental health center in the Northeast. We reflect on our own involvement in the introduction, development, and implementation of the consumer provider initiative at this center. We have also conducted open-ended, exploratory interviews with consumer providers, their supervisors, and their nonconsumer colleagues to obtain a variety of perspectives on the experience of integrating consumer providers and consumer-run services into a range of settings.

The first step in the process of introducing consumer-run services into the mental health center was the development of a peer education and support training program, modeled after earlier efforts in Colorado (Sherman & Porter, 1991) and Oregon (Nikkel, Smith & Edwards, 1992), to train and employ mental health consumers as case managers. This program, funded by a small grant from the state mental health authority, led to the creation of part-time volunteer positions for the consumer graduates; and eventually to a number of part-time paid positions as peer counselors, first within an acute day hospital and then within an outpatient clinic. These positions were created largely because a few middle managers were convinced of the therapeutic potential offered by consumers as providers—and because of their ability to capture small amounts of internal funds and external grant support to introduce this initiative during a time of resource constriction. Concurrent with these local developments, the state mental health authority was embarking upon a planning effort to increase the availability and visibility of consumer-provider positions within the state system. As part of this effort, a new position, Director of Peer Support, was created at the mental health center to stimulate and facilitate additional consumer employment. Through the combination of hospital downsizing efforts that moved state positions to community-based programs, and new grant developments at the mental health center, a number of additional full and part-time consumer provider positions were developed on an assertive community treatment team, a homeless outreach team, and a peer support research demonstration project.

In addition to working within their own programs, consumer providers have joined work groups and committees within the mental health center, given presentations to clients and family members, offered workshops and in-service training for staff, and participated in a state-wide consumer provider network established by a newly created Office of Consumer Resources within the state mental health authority. This state-wide organization currently has a membership exceeding 120 staff, and has come to be called the "Prosumer Network," adopting the term "prosumer" to denote the dual status of its members (Manos, 1992). The term "prosumer" will be used for the remainder of this chapter as a condensed term for consumer provider, following the lead and preference of those prosumers who established and maintain this network.

Issues and Strategies

Defining Roles

The first issue to be addressed in the hiring of prosumers is clarification of the roles they may play within the respective settings in which they will work. This question can be phrased most succinctly as: "What kinds of mental health services can prosumers provide?"

As has been suggested by Curtis (1993), it is important first to recognize that prosumers are able to provide the same range of services that can be provided by nonconsumers, assuming they have the requisite training, education and credentials to do so. There are now enough visible examples of consumer psychiatrists, psychologists, nurses, social workers, program managers, and administrators to persuade skeptics to at least consider the possibility of filling such positions with qualified and credentialed individuals who, in addition to their education, training and expertise, also happen to have a history of serious mental illness. Insofar as such individuals function in these roles, however, it remains unclear in what ways and to what extent their own personal history of disability informs their work; and therefore in what ways and to what extent they may differ from their nonconsumer colleagues. Hiring prosumers into existing, conventional roles certainly may further all of the agendas outlined above, from enhancing the care of individual clients to "busting" social stigma. However, new challenges will be encountered and new benefits will be reaped, only to the degree that the person's history of disability enters into his or her work. For the sake of this discussion, we would suggest that to the extent to which this occurs, whether as an asset or as a liability, the prosumer is no longer functioning soley as a psychiatrist or psychologist, but also as a peer of his or her clients. Given this understanding, we can reframe our original question as: "What are the particular services, and dimensions of service provision, that prosumers are uniquely qualified to offer by virtue of their personal history of disability and recovery?"

To this question, a number of answers have been offered in the literature, including advocacy and mediation; mentoring and role modeling; support, education and counseling; and assistance with meeting needs of daily living, such as housing and work (Besio & Mahler, 1993; Curtis, 1993; Shepard, 1992; Van Tosh, 1993). In addition to these specific services, prosumers have been described as performing their work with increased empathy for the day-to-day struggles of their clients; a higher tolerance of deviance; insider knowledge ("street smarts") of how to access resources and navigate the mental health and social service systems; a greater sensitivity to client competencies and strengths; a greater flexibility, patience, and persistence in exploring alternative approaches; and a greater awareness of, and responsiveness to, the basic needs and preferences of their clients (Besio & Mahler, 1993; Solomon et al., 1994; Van Tosh, 1993).

Our own experience thus far has reflected these findings in the literature, and also has suggested a number of contrasts in introducing such elements into different settings. We have found, for example, that "street smarts," advocacy, and a focus on assistance with meeting basic needs fit very well with the mission and culture of our homeless outreach team—so much so, in fact, that we were told consistently by program supervisors and staff that the full-time prosumer peer counselor was the most effective member of the team. He has been so successful in engaging clients that he has since been promoted to outreach worker, the same designation as his non-consumer colleagues, and has been asked to train other members of the team. We have had similar success in the staffing of our peer support research project, in which the elements of peer support, mentoring, and a focus on client strengths and competences are in the foreground. Community integration, overcoming stigma, and the cultivation of friendships are defining factors in the culture of the project; we have been able to make productive use of the perspectives and contributions of the prosumers who recruit clients into the study, recruit volunteers to befriend these clients, and initiate and facilitate friendships between clients and volunteers.

Our experience has been significantly different, however, within the context of an acute day hospital in which we created a part-time position for a peer counselor. While the culture of the day hospital included an emphasis on normalization and the fostering of adaptive coping in a community context, we nonetheless faced several issues in introducing consumer-provided services into this program. These issues stemmed, in part, from the ad hoc nature of this position (Curtis, 1993); that is, from the fact that we added a peer counselor position to an existing program in which there had not been a clear role for the prosumer elements described above. This created a good deal of initial confusion and awkwardness in integrating the prosumer into the staff and program milieu. We will return to some of the staff concerns; for this section, what is important are the ways in which the prosumer's role needed to be adapted in order to fit within the program model, and the ways in which the program also changed as a result of this process.

The programmatic challenges raised by introducing a prosumer into this conventional day hospital primarily concerned the functions of peer support and peer counseling within an acute clinical setting. No difficulties were encountered in having the prosumer participate in the life skills component of the day hospital. Teaching clients how to shop for groceries, cook, and structure their leisure time around social and recreational activities fits well with attention to the needs of daily living. The development of a peer support group, on the contrary, posed several dilemmas. Outside of the formal mental health system, and more recently within the scope of clubhouses, peer support groups have provided an on-going, natural support system. In this support system, consumers have assisted each other, shared survival tips and strategies, and been encouraged to advocate for themselves with the mental health system and the larger community. Leadership has emerged spontaneously within the context of these groups, whose membership has been open, and there has been a strong commitment to confidentiality among the members. All of these aspects of naturally occurring peer support groups are challenged by the mission and structure of an acute clinical program. Most importantly, the leader of the group is a paid employee who has allegiances and obligations to the program as well as to the other members of the group. This has created tensions between the prosumer's need to maintain the confidentiality of the group and to communicate freely with his or her colleagues; and the prosumer's at times conflicting roles as representative of the program (and thereby of the mental health system), and as advocate for individual clients. The acute nature of the program, and acute levels of distress and disorganization experienced by clients, have required prosumers to learn and apply clinical management skills that are more directive than those usually operating within the culture of a peer support group. In addition, rapid turnover of group membership has precluded natural leaders from emerging who could take over leadership of the group. With discharge from the program involving the end of a client's association with the group, the support provided by the group could not be ongoing.

Many of these issues were resolved over a two year period, during which changes were made in the peer support group to adapt it to the particular nature of an acute clinical setting, and in the nature of the program itself to make better use of the new peer support resources. Changes introduced into the peer support group were similar to those of AA and NA meetings when they were introduced into inpatient psychiatric units (Galanter, Castaneda & Salamon, 1987). The peer support group, however, adopted a more structured format. In addition to its goal of providing an avenue for mutual support and assistance between consumers, the group focused on enhancing clients' engagement in on-going peer support activites and more conventional mental health services. In line with this focus on engagement, education took on more of an emphasis than did advocacy, as prosumers began to feel more allied and affiliated with staff than clients. In becoming more accepted as part of the staff, prosumers began to have a subtle yet increasing influence on the overall program milieu. As the peer support group became a twice-weekly fixture of the clinical program, dimensions of the group culture and the prosumers' relationships with their clients naturally began to spread to other elements of the program milieu as well (see "Breaking Boundaries" below).

These contrasting experiences suggest that prosumers will be more easily integrated into programs that operate on the basis of the consumer-oriented values described above, and that prosumers will be able to influence programs to the extent that they are making valuable contributions to the programs' missions. We have developed a number of strategies to facilitate an on-going dialogue between administrators, program staff and prosumers to clarify roles, values and policies regarding such issues as confidentiality, advocacy, and the management of acute distress and disruptive behavior. Structures have been established to span day hospital and outpatient division boundaries so that prosumers can engage clients in on-going peer support groups held in community locations, where membership is open and there is more opportunity for natural leaders to emerge who are not paid employees of the mental health center. Consolidating all consumer-run services under the director of peer support has facilitated this spanning of program boundaries, and allowed us to generate recommendations for program and policy changes at the center-wide level that will provide more recognition and credibility for consumer values in shaping treatment philosophy. There have been prosumer representatives on work groups to revise principles of care, and to develop a self-help oriented relapse prevention program and a collaborative treatment planning process. There has also been a seminar co-led by a consumer-nonconsumer team; and prosumer presentations to staff groups under the aegis of in-service training to introduce concepts of self-help, recovery, and empowerment, and to initiate discussions of their relevance for the on-going clinical work of the center. As the mental health center is also an academic research center, we have been able to heighten the visibility of this initiative, and secure a formal sanction for it, by undertaking research projects to evaluate methods for incorporating consumer feedback and perspectives into program and policy development (Davidson et al., in press; Davidson et al., 1995).

Valuing Recovery

One of the core elements of change in treatment philosophy, is the transformation from seeing a person's history of disability as a liability to seeing recovery from a disability as a resource and potential strength. We have found that this transformation can at times be as difficult for prosumers and their clients as it is for their non-consumer colleagues (Solomon et al., 1994). We thus identify the facilitation of this transformation as the second major issue we have confronted in integrating prosumers into the mental health center, framing this question as: "What value does the prosumer's personal history of disability and recovery add to his or her work as a mental health provider?"

This question draws our attention to staff and client perceptions of the unique qualifications and experiences of prosumers, in the settings in which they work; on the ways in which they and their work are or are not valued in these settings; and on such tangible and institutional embodiments of value as discrimination and parity in remuneration, status, and opportunities for career advancement. Decisions about these specific dimensions, which publicly acknowledge value in each of the mental health center settings, arose from the evolution of the prosumer initiative as a whole. We begin this section, then, with a brief discussion of this process before turning to the more specific concerns described above.

In developing our initial consumer training program and a related initiative of inviting consumers to perform a few hours a week of volunteer service within the center, we received mostly unqualified enthusiasm and support from the staff. The only concerns aired at the time had to do with delimiting the role of consumer volunteers to ancillary and supportive functions, that did not encroach on the clinical functions and identity of the existing staff. Volunteers could accompany clients to AA and NA meetings or to the local consumer social club, lead recreational and social activities at the day hospital, and give invited presentations to clients and their families. These services and roles were seen as supplemental to the ongoing clinical work, and were welcomed as needed resources during a time of staff downsizing. Much more controversy and concern was raised, however, when we began the process of converting one of these volunteer positions into a paid part-time position, with an accompanying increase in the prosumer's responsibility and status within the program in which he had been volunteering. Staff greeted the news that their consumer volunteer was to become a paid employee of the mental health system, and thus a colleague, with very mixed feelings and reviews. While most people saw this as a good thing for the prosumer, as a step forward for him, they were concerned about the impact of this precedent both on themselves and on their clients. Some did not see him as qualified for the work he would be asked to do, worried about the implications of his self-disclosure as a consumer on the maintenance of appropriate therapeutic boundaries within the program, and also felt that his promotion in some way undermined their own status. Concerns were raised about how other paraprofessional staff would feel about him being considered their "equal," due to perceptions that he had less training and experience than they did (although in reality he had more specialized training in mental health care than some staff had when first hired into the system). Many of these concerns crystalized in staff discussions of whether or not the prosumer should be given access to clients' medical records, and allowed to eat lunch in the staff lounge, the concern being that staff would not be able to talk freely about their clients if he were in the room.

Extensive discussions with staff and program administration led to agreement that prosumers would be treated as full members of the staff, with access both to the staff lounge and to clients' medical records. The metaphor of being included in the staff lunch (or in other cases being given their own set of keys) continues to capture aspects of the integration process for prosumers, at different levels of subtlety, in different settings. It was in fact these lunch room discussions which first suggested the notion of "integration" as a way of understanding the process in which we were involved, drawing on experiences of integrating people of color at lunch counters in North Carolina during the Civil Rights Movement. In this case, the challenge presented by the stigma is to persuade people that having had a history of serious mental illness should not relegate someone to second class citizenship. While most everyone would agree with this statement in principle, it is the process of identifying and changing all of the subtle and not so subtle ways in which stigma has become operationalized that is difficult (Reidy, 1994; Solomon et al., 1994).

We have found it most fruitful to adopt a disability framework for these discussions, and to engage our staff in both structured and open explorations of whether or not it is possible for people with serious mental illness to overcome disabilities and recover their lives as fully functioning citizens. Longitudinal research on course and outcome of severe mental illness (e.g., Carpenter & Kirkpatrick, 1988; Harding, Zubin & Strauss, 1987), as well as analogies of discrimination drawn from the Civil Rights Movement, have been included in a series of "stigma-busting" workshops for staff. In these workshops, prosumer leaders have made a point of using their own success stories as visible evidence of the possibility of recovery. Recognizing that stigma is primarily a socio-cultural, rather than a personal phenomenon, these workshops have not blamed or attacked individual providers, nor have they focused primarily on examples of stigma and prejudice toward mental health consumers, but have invited staff into a dialogue about how to cultivate a more inclusive environment for people with disabilities. The positive and constructive tone of these prosumer-led workshops has gone a long way toward heightening staff sensitivity, allowing us to move beyond this level of conflict to a more accepting posture in which having prosumers sitting in treatment planning meetings and at the lunch table has now become commonplace.

We have learned that this was only the first and most obvious level of discrimination to be faced in the process of integration. The further we have progressed in the evolution of this initiative, the more we have encountered subtler levels of stigma and segregation, at least as defined by the prosumers themselves. On the emotional and personal level, being allowed into the lunch room does not guarantee that a person will feel that he or she actually belongs there, as opposed to being merely tolerated (Griffith, 1995). Prosumers have described experiences of continuing to be treated "different" from their nonconsumer colleagues, of being viewed as fragile and likely to relapse or become symptomatic at any moment, and of having colleagues question and be unsure of their competence and judgment. Several prosumers who were hired into part-time positions felt that they were being limited in the amount of money, security and status they could achieve, and felt held back from full-time employment (with its associated benefits) by what they perceived as discriminatory hiring practices. Those who performed tasks similar to their nonconsumer colleagues wondered about parity in salary, and began to question the monetary worth we were willing to accord their history of disability as a job qualification. Even when assured of parities in wage, they remained unsure of opportunities for career advancement given what they saw as their "token" position as prosumer. They were uncertain of how far "the system" would allow them to move up the career ladder given their consumer designation and their often limited education, training, and credentials. A prosumer peer support group, started by the director of peer support, had difficulty retaining its membership when several prosumers began to feel that this group was in itself a vehicle of segregration and a way of continuing to make them feel "different" from their nonconsumer colleagues. As might be expected from this discussion, we continue to address new instances of discrimination as they arise in the course of the further unfolding of this initiative.

In response to these concerns, we have found it useful to frame the prosumer initiative within the context of a broader affirmative action plan, one that views a history of disability as only one of many sources of sensitivity and competence upon which to draw, in composing a culturally diverse and representative work force (Stephens & Belisle, 1993). In addition, it has been important for us to make sure that we are providing parity in salary for similar work, that we are hiring prosumers into meaningful roles at a variety of levels of authority and status within the center, and that we are creating opportunities for career advancement for prosumers who may lack the conventional credentials that allow others to pursue promotions. Hiring and promoting prosumers into middle management and leadership positions has allowed us to provide role models for other prosumers and visible evidence that it is possible for people with psychiatric disabilities to assume responsible (non-"token") roles within the mental health system.

Breaking Boundaries

Assuming that a person's history of disability and recovery has a value and that it equips him or her for providing particular services, the next issue to be addressed is how best to use this history in working with clients. In other words: "What functions are performed by the prosumers' disclosure of their personal histories of disability and recovery to their clients and colleagues?" Answering this question should then allow us to begin to resolve complexities involved in questions of *to whom* a prosumer should disclose what information, under which circumstances, *when*, and to *what end*.

One of the core goals of the consumer provider initiative is to provide visible role models of recovery for clients who might otherwise believe that having a mental illness equals a death sentence. In order to achieve this goal, the fact that a prosumer has had a history of disability and is now in recovery needs to be communicated to clients in some way so that they can identify the prosumer as a role model. The most straightforward way for this fact to be communicated is for the prosumer to disclose this history, or some elements of it, to his or her clients in the context of their working relationship. Can such personal disclosure be made a formal and expected part of a person's job description, however? Would not such an expectation be a further example of discrimination on the job? What about the prosumer's need for, and right to, confidentiality? And may there not be instances in which clients need to be protected from indiscriminate, inappropriate, or unhelpful self-disclosure?

We continue to struggle to achieve clarity on these complicated and conflicting questions. Rather than trying to establish a delicate balance between the evolving needs of an individual prosumer and the diverse needs of his or her many clients, we have tried to reach increasing clarity about a number of distinctions that divide this vast territory into more manageable domains. In keeping with the tone and comments of the previous two sections, we first established a policy (following the ADA) that people with disabilities should have equal opportunities to seek, obtain and maintain any positions for which they are qualified and competent to perform. In cases where prosumers are applying for existing positions as nurses or psychologists, for example, they are entitled to maintain confidentiality regarding their history of disability and to have that fact in no way enter into the hiring decision or their job description unless they choose to do so. Many such "closet consumers" already exist within the mental health system, and continue to choose, for a variety of personal and professional reasons, not to disclose their personal history nor to make an issue of it in their work with clients.

Next, we distinguish this practice of non-discriminatory hiring into conventional positions, from the creation of new prosumer positions through the adoption of an affirmative action plan targeted to increase the visibility and availability of consumer role models within the mental health system. To the extent that these positions build explicitly on dimensions of service provision that stem from a person's history of disability and recovery, we conceptualize them as peer counselor roles and articulate clearly both how the person's history qualifies him or her for the role and in what ways disclosure of that history is expected to be a part of the role. Once these distinctions have been drawn and we are in agreement that self-disclosure of a prosumer's history can and should be an important part of his or her peer counselor role, we can then begin to explore when, under which circumstances, to whom, what information should be disclosed, and to what ends. Only a few general rules of thumb have been generated thus far to simplify this complex series of questions, beyond the basic principle that disclosures should always be made in the interest of the client rather than in the interest of the prosumer. We have found that disclosures about a prosumer's history of illness and hospitalization have limited utility, and are primarily useful in establishing an initial relationship and rapport built upon shared experiences. Disclosures related to coping and survival strategies and skills (e.g., how I've dealt with my voices or depression, or how I negotiated medications and dosages with my doctor) have been received better by clients and seem to have a more beneficial effect on their engagement in, and use of services. We have been led to wonder if the act of self-disclosure is as important as the enhanced sensitivity to a client's situation that a prosumer may have, based on his or her first-person experiences and familiarity. We have also noticed that there is less concern about maintaining boundaries in rehabilitative, as opposed to clinical settings, and that this question becomes moot in the context of ongoing peer support groups. Within clinical settings, however, it has become a fruitful and challenging issue for supervision, both for prosumers and their nonconsumer supervisors and colleagues. The process of figuring out when clients will be able to make productive use of personal information, how personal the information needs to be, and how best to communicate this information, has been very useful in challenging prosumers to think in more sophisticated ways about their clients. This same process has challenged the conventional, more rigidly boundaried practice of nonconsumer staff, raising questions about whether or not it is always helpful to clients for staff to keep their personal experiences hidden behind a stance of therapeutic neutrality (Curtis & Hodge, 1994; Kupers, 1993). Several nonconsumer staff have described how they no longer maintain rigid boundaries with their clients, following the lead of their prosumer colleagues in using aspects of their shared humanness to connect and enliven these relationships. We are currently involved in an attempt to rethink our models of group and individual treatment to incorporate some elements of peer support and counseling, and a more reciprocal appreciation of the real relationship between clinician and client (regardless of the former's consumer/non-consumer status).

Acculturating versus Co-opting

In all three of the previous sections we have suggested that there is a possibility for consumer-run services to be modified as they are introduced into clinical settings, and for the settings themselves also to be influenced through the integration of consumers as staff. In this section we focus explicitly on the bi-directional nature of this process, and take up the issue of to what degree prosumers are being acculturated to these settings, and to what degree they may be getting co-opted by these settings (Broadhurst, 1993; Klossner & McDowell, 1993). This question also can be framed as: "How can prosumers be oriented to their new roles without losing the unique perspective they bring to their work?"

For many prosumers, their first job within the mental health system may be their first job of any kind in many years; for some, their first "real" job since becoming disabled, or even their first "real" job ever. For example, one of our prosumers had already resigned himself to being on disability benefits for the rest of his life prior to participating in our consumer training program. His current job as a peer counselor is the first full-time position he has held since being diagnosed with schizophrenia over 25 years ago. When a person has not worked in over 25 years, and in some cases ever, there are many job skills that will need to be learned in becoming oriented to a new role. These skills range from the basics—such as being able to get up in the morning and get to work on time—to the more personal and challenging, such as learning how to subordinate one's autonomy and creativity to that of one's supervisor, without losing one's own integrity. On the more mundane side, the phenomenon of meetings provides a good example of the kind of unfamiliar territory which some prosumers will need to learn to navigate early in their mental health careers. At least in some settings, mental health providers spend a good deal of their time in meetings. These meetings typically have set agendas and fairly clear ground rules and expectations about who is to attend, how they are to behave, and how business is to be conducted. The act of attending such meetings, not to mention the art of figuring out when it is okay to talk and what it is okay to say, can be the source of great initial anxiety and fear on the part of some prosumers; they may seldom have had the experience of sitting in a room with eight to 12 providers in other than a treatment context, in which they were the focus. In such cases, prosumers need to become acculturated to the language and protocols that structure conventional ways of doing business in mental health settings, in order to become part of the provider team. The question for this section is, "When does this kind of acculturation to the way of conducting business become co-optation by 'the system'"?

The phenomenon of meetings continues to provide a good illustration of this issue. One of the concerns which staff have raised about hiring consumers is that the consumers will attend treatment team meetings and rounds, and that staff will feel uncomfortable talking about clients in the same way they usually do. This has been one of our goals in hiring consumers: that their visible presence in these meetings will indeed change the way staff typically talk about, and in turn think about, clients. Such changes will only occur, however, to the extent to which prosumers are not acculturated to the traditional way of talking about clients, but rather staff's way of talking about clients is changed by the presence of prosumers in meetings. The challenge is one of orienting prosumers to the necessary and essential functions of their work and the work environment without robbing them of the unique perspective they bring to the work (and for which they are, in part, being hired). While prosumers need to learn the functions of meetings, the organizational structure and the chain of command, they also need to be encouraged to object to the usual and expedient way of doing business should they feel, based on their first-hand knowledge, that it is not respectful or in the best interest of the client. Our prosumer peer support group, as well as individual supervision, have been used to reinforce with prosumers the point that learning what to say in which meetings need not entail learning to keep quiet about matters of significant concern.

Competing with the need for prosumers to speak up, is the natural tendency for a new employee to adopt the existing culture of the work place and work hard to "fit in" among his or her colleagues and supervisors. First, there is the fact that many prosumers obtaining employment within the mental health system do not necessarily perceive themselves to be agents of systems change, nor do they necessarily want such responsibility. In addition, the desire to be accepted may be particularly acute and pressing for individuals who have not held many or any jobs in the past, and who have serious doubts about their own abilities and self-worth. We have been both impressed and distressed by how profound this need has been for several prosumers, and how quickly they seemed to adopt some of the stigmatizing attitudes and language of their nonconsumer colleagues. As a case in point, an early newspaper article on our local prosumer initiative quoted one peer counselor as describing his clients as "impossible to reach." As mentioned earlier, the push to fit in and not remain different from nonconsumer colleagues was given as justification for dissolving the prosumer peer support group. We have kept this group alive, however, out of a concern that we were beginning to lose all sense of difference between consumer and nonconsumer staff, and that we perhaps had moved too quickly, and been too effective, in acculturating prosumers to the *status quo*.

In addition to sponsoring a prosumer peer support group within our center, we have developed a formal vehicle for systems change to take the burden for consumer advocacy off of individual prosumers. This structure serves the function of embedding a broad consumer-oriented agenda within our system, in a visible way that provides prosumers (and their like-minded nonconsumer colleagues) with a collective voice. This structure is a Consumer Involvement Committee composed of a mixed group of consumers, family members, and providers. This committee predated our consumer provider initiative and sponsored the consumer training program, which served as our system's first step toward consumer employment. Our experience with the evolution of this committee suggests one last dimension of the acculturation vs. co-optation debate. While membership on the committee began as volunteer service for all of the consumer members, a number of these members have since gone on to acquire positions as providers within the center. This has been the source of considerable tension and conflict on the committee, as members have taken opposing positions on this issue: prosumers typically viewing the process of integration as one of acculturation, and unemployed consumers criticizing them for allowing themselves to be co-opted. At times these arguments have become confrontational and unpleasant, with particularly empassioned advocates comparing prosumers to "Nazi collaborators." In addition to striving to achieve an open dialogue about these contentious and deeply personal issues, we have derived at least two lessons from these experiences.

First, it is crucial to provide formal channels for consumer feedback and input regarding policy and program development, that are separate from the work of individual prosumers, and on the basis of which ongoing and objective assessments can be conducted (e.g., through continuous quality improvement indicators). Such activities have included hosting an annual Consumer Town Meeting to generate an agenda for systems change, and the development and distribution of a consumer satisfaction survey to provide regular feedback at the program and agency level. Second, since these efforts will inevitably be limited in their impact on the system as a whole, it is equally crucial for there to be consumer advocates and "watchdogs," who remain independent of the system and who can continue to call for more radical changes without concern for personal repercussions (Stephens & Belisle, 1993).

Providing Supports and Accommodations

The last issue we shall discuss has already been the topic of some interest in the literature (Deegan, 1991; Fabian, Waterworth & Ripke, 1993; Howie the Harp, 1991; Mancuso, 1991, 1993; Parrish, 1991; Solomon et al., 1994) it is the question "What accommodations and supervisory resources and skills are required to support prosumers in these roles?" Should a system choose, on the basis of the foregoing considerations, to proceed in the employment of consumers as providers, what structures and supports will it need to provide in order for this initiative to be successful?

As we have noted already in the earlier discussion, there are many ways in which consumer and nonconsumer providers of mental health services are similar vis a vis their roles and needs. This has been a particularly challenging, but also promising, aspect of the discussions stimulated by the ADA concerning the provision of "reasonable accommodations" for consumer providers. The literature thus far has suggested a number of possible accommodations that can be provided to support consumers on the job, including such things as flexible hours, the ability to make phone calls to friends, leave time for treatment appointments and relapses, a supportive supervisor, and a less stressful work environment (Deegan, 1991; Howie the Harp, 1991; Mancuso, 1991, 1993; Solomon et al, 1994). It should be obvious from this list that at least some accommodations provided for prosumers will also benefit nonconsumer staff as well. While it may be important to provide these accommodations to prosumers, it would seem to be a more promising idea to attempt to make work environments more supportive and flexible for all employees, rather than to tie such changes specifically to the consumer status of an individual employee or group of employees (Bonnie & Monahan, in press). In addition to these more general accommodations that speak to the general nature of the work environment, there are more specific accommodations that may need to be provided to meet the special needs of individual prosumers. These accommodations address specific issues presented by a prosumer's disability, such as the need for environmental modifications to decrease stimulation and lessen distractions for an employee who hears voices, or the need for a quiet space and couch to provide periodic respite.

In addition to accommodations that are specific to an individual's needs and those that are equally appropriate for everyone, we have identified two major issues that speak to the particular needs of prosumers as they first acquire positions within the mental health system. The first issue is the need for intensive and ongoing supervision in the context of a supportive and respectful relationship. Due to the fact that many prosumers will not have held jobs for several years prior to becoming employed by the mental health system, there is a pressing need early in a prosumer's career for mentoring in job skills and professional development. Particularly if concerns about co-optation exist, prosumers will need a forum to sort out what they need to learn, in order to be effective in their new roles, and what they need to challenge, in the way business is done, in order to have a positive impact on organizational culture. We have found that there can be a considerable amount of conflict early on between maintaining an "outsider" status and an attitude of challenging authority out of principle; and the development of a collegial but assertive stance in picking one's battles and going through appropriate channels. Prosumers may initially identify so strongly with their clients that it impedes acceptance of their new roles within the system, as exemplified by the prosumer who declared that he "worked for the people, not for the system." We have also found the supervisor's role to be crucial in mediating between the needs and concerns of an individual prosumer, and the needs of the program in which he or she works. Mediation can work in both directions: either as a support to a prosumer who is advocating for a client or a cause, in the face of bureaucratic resistance, or as a buffer for a program that becomes concerned about the relapse or deterioration in functioning of a prosumer. It is crucial for the success of the supervisory relationship that the prosumers are valued for what they bring to the work, that the supervisor has a clear commitment to the success of the employee, and that the supervisor is experienced and skilled in the work and credible with the staff within the program.

While the value of these elements of supervision may seem obvious, we did not fully appreciate the importance of this relationship, and the time and energy it takes to foster it until we were well into this initiative. We now recognize charging and supporting supervisors with this responsibility as a major factor in the success or failure of the initiative, and as presenting a significant resource issue for our organization, as the addition of these tasks reduces the amount of time supervisors have to devote to their other responsibilities.

The second major issue encountered in supporting prosumers is their personal investment in the work and their lack of conventional defenses against the stresses and strains involved in providing mental health services to people in distress. Because they have themselves been in similar situations, and dealt with similar issues to those of their clients, prosumers may become personally invested in the work to a degree greater than their nonconsumer colleagues, and to an extent that they have a hard time leaving their work "at the office." This degree of investment can be further enhanced when prosumers have had relationships with some of their clients prior to assuming a provider role, and may continue to have such relationships outside of this role. The degree of attachment prosumers develop or maintain with their clients increases their vulnerability to the distress encountered as part of the work.

While prosumers may bring this vulnerability with them into the work based on their personal history, it may also be more difficult for them, for the same reasons, to develop the conventional defenses against this vulnerability that most providers adopt during their training and early in their careers. Particularly within the context of clinical programs, these defenses involve the objectification of clients into disease entities and the transformation of the person with the disorder into such constructs as "a schizophrenic" and "a borderline." This process of objectification involves a gradual loss of the shared humanity of the person with the disorder and the drawing of a distinction between those of "us" who are normal and "them": the abnormal, disordered and disabled (Main, 1977). Prosumers may understandably be suspect of the usefulness of this distinction, and may be much less trusting and accepting of the conventional strategies employed by their nonconsumer colleagues for keeping the pain of the work at a reasonable distance.

We have found the need for ways to manage clients' distress to be a highly challenging but promising issue for supervision, and to have as many implications for nonconsumer staff and organizational culture as for the prosumers themselves. Rather than encouraging prosumers to adopt a clinical stance toward their clients, we have begun a dialogue with staff about the functions and limitations of our conventional strategies, and an exploration of alternative ways of leaving the work "at the office," which can still allow us to recognize and value the shared humanity of our clients. These efforts are in their early stages, but are generating several implications for bringing about substantive changes in our treatment models and standards of practice that go beyond mere changes in terminology. These changes are being incorporated into the new models of individual and group treatment and into the collaborative treatment planning process alluded to earlier, all of which are based on a more active and goal-directed role for clients in determining and being responsible for their own treatment and recovery (Davidson & Strauss, 1992; 1995).

Discussion

Overall, we have been pleased with the progress we have been able to make in hiring and deploying consumers as providers in a range of settings within our mental health center. One major obstacle to success that we have encountered, in addition to those already described, can be viewed as an indicator of our success as well. This has been the dissolution alluded to earlier of the distinction between consumer and nonconsumer providers. We view the collapse of this distinction as a barrier, to the extent that we had hoped for our consumer provider initiative to have more of a direct and immediate impact upon the culture and practice of our conventional clinical programs. We have been surprised by how readily and amicably many of our prosumers have been accepted into these programs as people, while the program milieu and standards of practice remained relatively unchanged.

This same collapse of the consumer/nonconsumer distinction can also be viewed as an indicator of our success, however, to the extent that it demonstrates an acceptance of consumers as colleagues and a broadening of the diversity of the mental health work force. We have been encouraged by the willingness of providers, whose consumer status had not been known at the time of their employment, to come "out of the attic" and openly discuss their histories of disability and recovery. We have witnessed nonconsumer staff become more willing to do things with and for their clients related to real life concerns (such as host birthday parties, praise successes, and accompany clients to community activities); and we've been surprised by their reports that they now felt that they had "permission" to do things that they had always thought would have been helpful, but would have been seen in the past as "acting out" or "breaking boundaries." In these two ways, having consumers as colleagues and friends seems to have undermined stigma, and enhanced providers' appreciation of their commonalties with consumers on the personal level. Other indicators of success have been the transformation of what may have started out as "token" positions into meaningful roles, and a service delivery innovation into a standard practice. As we now move to deploy prosumers on our inpatient units (the last program within the center to do so), it is no longer considered a new or risky idea, but rather an important dimension in providing comprehensive care. Such positive signs have alerted us to the need to be cautious about pushing more rapidly for further, substantive changes in our system, as all of us struggle to make sense of the long-term implications of the steps we have already taken.

Our experience to date has confirmed Stephens & Belisle's (1993) contention that the act of hiring consumers as providers cannot by itself bring about major changes in the mental health system or larger culture. We have described earlier, however, some of the ways in which we have tried to build on this base to bring about such changes, by situating our consumer-provider initiative within broader consumer-oriented and affirmative action agendas. We also have pointed out some of the ways in which the consumer-provider initiative runs into difficulties and may need to be modified to fit the particular needs of clinical sites. Clarifying the roles of peer counseling, self-disclosure, therapeutic boundaries, and providing adequate supervision, appear to be the most pressing issues for clinical programs looking to incorporate consumer-run services; while issues of stigma, co-optation and accommodation appear to exist for most settings in which prosumers might work. Our experience also has confirmed our initial suspicion that while changes in paradigm may be more difficult to achieve within the purview of conventional clinical programs, such changes hold more promise and long-term implications for revising our system of care than those confined within the purview of community support and rehabilitative programs which have, from their origins, been more consumer-oriented. We are now faced with the difficult and complex task of integrating various sources of improvement in serious mental illness, from medications to empowerment, into one model of care. Such integration requires an extension of our paradigm, beyond a biopsychosocial model of disorder and its treatment, to a model that focuses on the restoration of the person's life in both illness and health (Davidson et al., in press; Davidson & Strauss, 1995). To the extent that we are successful in this task, we will continue to face uncertainty as we explore ways to bring together what were previously distinct and even opposing elements of persons, their disorders, and the contexts in which they live.

References

Besio, S.W. & Mahler, J. (1993). Benefits and challenges of using consumer staff in supported housing services. *Hospital and Community Psychiatry*, 44, 490-1.

Bonnie, R.J. & Monahan, J. (Eds.) (in press). *Mental disorders, work disability and the law*. Chicago, IL: University of Chicago Press.

Broadhurst, S. (1993). Co-optation—it's all too common. *Resources*, 5, 16-7.

Carpenter, W.T. & Kirkpatrick, B. (1988). The heterogeneity of the long-term course of schizophrenia. *Schizophrenia Bulletin*, 14, 645-52.

Curtis, L.C. (1993). Consumers as colleagues: Partnership in the workforce. *In Practice*, 4-5.

Curtis, L.C. & Hodge, M. (1994). Old standards, new dilemmas: Ethics and boundaries in community support services. *Psychosocial Rehabilitation Journal*, 18, 13-33.

Davidson, L., Hoge, M.A., Godleski, L., Rakfeldt, J., & Griffith, E.E.H. (in press). Hospital or Community Living? Examining consumer perspectives on deinstitutionalization. *Psychiatric Rehabilitation Journal*.

Davidson, L., Hoge, M.A., Merrill, M.E., Rakfeldt, J., & Griffith, E.E.H. (1995). Experiences of long-stay inpatients returning to the community. *Psychiatry: Interpersonal and Biological Processes*, 58, 44-55.

Davidson, L. & Strauss, J.S. (1992). Sense of self in recovery from severe mental illness. *British Journal of Medical Psychology*, 65, 131-45.

Davidson, L. & Strauss, J.S. (1995). Beyond the biopsychosocial model: Integrating disorder, health and recovery. *Psychiatry: Interpersonal and Biological Processes*, 58, 44-55.

Deegan, P.E. (1991). Support and accommodation strategies in a consumer-run and consumer- controlled program. *Community Support Network News*, 8, 9.

Dixon, L., Krauss, N., & Lehman, A. (1994). Consumers as service providers: The promise and challenge. *Community Mental Health Journal*, 30, 615-25.

Fabian, E.S., Waterworth, A., & Ripke, B. (1993). Reasonable accommodations for workers with serious mental illness: Type, frequency, and associated outcomes. *Psychosocial Rehabilitation Journal*, 17, 163-72.

Galanter, M., Castaneda, R., & Salamon, I. (1987). Institutional self-help for alcoholism: Clinical outcome. *Alcoholism: Clinical and Experimental Research*, 11, 424-9.

Griffith, E.E.H. (1995). Personal storytelling and the metaphor of belonging. *Cultural Diversity and Mental Health*, 1, 29-37.

Harding, C.M., Zubin J., & Strauss, J.S. (1987). Chronicity in schizophrenia: Fact, partial fact, or artifact? *Hospital and Community Psychiatry*, 38, 477-86.

Howie the Harp. (1991). *A crazy folks guide to reasonable accommodation and psychiatric disability*. Burlington, VT: Center for Community Change through Housing and Support.

Klossner, N.L. & McDowell, P.E. (1993). Guidelines for avoiding co-optation of consumers-employees. *Resources*, 5, 14-5.

Kupers, T.A. (1993). Psychotherapy, neutrality, and the role of activism. *Community Mental Health Journal*, 29, 523-33.

Main, T.F. (1977). Traditional psychiatric defenses against close encounter with patients. *Canadian Psychiatric Association Journal*, 22, 457-66.

Mancuso, L.L. (1991). Questions frequently asked about the ADA by workers with psychiatric disabilities. *Community Support Network News*, 8, 4-5, 13.

Mancuso, L.L. (1993). *Case studies on reasonable accommodations for workers with psychiatric disabilities.* Sacramento, CA: California Department of Mental Health and the Center for Mental Health Services.

Nikkel, R.E., Smith, G,. & Edwards, D. (1992). A consumer-operated case management project. *Hospital and Community Psychiatry, 43,* 577-9.

Parrish, J. (1991). Reasonable accommodation for people with psychiatric disabilities. *Community Support Network News, 8,* 8.

Reidy, D.E. (1994). Recovering from treatment: The mental health system as an agent of stigma. *Resources, 6,* 3-10.

Shepard, L. (1992). *So you want to hire a consumer? Employing people with psychiatric disabilities as staff members in mental health agencies.* Burlington, VT: The Center for Community Change through Housing and Support.

Sherman, P.S. & Porter, R. (1991). Mental health consumers as case management aides. *Hospital and Community Psychiatry, 42,* 494-8.

Solomon, M.L., Cook, J.A., Jonikas, J.A., & Kerouac, J. (1994). *Positive partnerships: How consumers and non-consumers can work together as service providers.* Chicago, IL: Thresholds National Research and Training Center on Rehabilitation and Mental Illness.

Stephens, C.L. & Belisle, K.C. (1993). The 'consumer-as-provider' initiative. *Journal of Mental Health Administration, 20,* 178-82.

Van Tosh, L. (1993). *Working for a change: employment of consumers/survivors in the design and provision of services for persons who are homeless and mentally disabled.* Rockville, MD: Center for Mental Health Services.

Larry Davidson, Ph.D., is assistant professor in the Department of Psychiatry of the Yale University School of Medicine and assistant director for program development and research of the Outpatient Division of the Connecticut Mental Health Center.

Richard Weingarten, M.A., is director of peer support at the Connecticut Mental Health Center and chair of the Consumer Involvement Committee for the Mental Health Network of South Central Connecticut.

Jeanne Steiner, D.O., is associate professor in the Department of Psychiatry of the Yale Unviersity School of Medicine and director of outpatient services at the Connecticut Mental Health Center.

David Stayner, Ph.D., is an instructor of psychology in the Department of Psychiatry of the Yale University School of Medicine.

Michael A. Hoge, Ph.D., is associate professor in the Department of Psychiatry and director of managed behavioral health services development of the Yale University School of Medicine.

Section 9

Perspectives on Consumers as Providers

Introduction to Section 9: Perspectives on Consumers as Providers

This section offers four system-level perspectives on consumers as providers: the first from a state-level mental health agency, the second by a family advocate, the third by a consumer advocate and the fourth by an evaluation organization. Despite quite different positions of their authors, all these chapters share some common themes.

The first theme is most clearly articulated by Granger: "We are all different. We are all the same." Any initiative involving consumers as providers is founded on the latter belief. Granger points out the importance of a social group or culture in the lives of all individuals: it is one way we are similar, one way we all belong. Consumer service provision builds on the similarity shared among individuals experiencing mental illness and how the shared experience can produce competence, development, and healing. This, of course, reflects conclusions stated in many other chapters relating to the benefits of having consumers provide services. In her chapter, Francell also endorses this conclusion, drawing similarities between the effectiveness of consumer-providers and of family members who have served as providers for ill relatives; for both, their personal experiences make their assistance more motivated and therefore more effective.

But at the same time, Granger admonishes, "We are all different"; consumer initiatives will not succeed unless there is recognition that consumers are themselves distinct. "The alignment of the needs of individual participants...with the goals of the organization requires structures that allow...[responsiveness] to individual participants." Congruent with this statement by Granger is the perspective offered by Francell that consumer-providers themselves need individualized training, proactive supervision, and supportive work settings. Similarly, among the South Carolina reforms described by Bevilacqua and colleague are efforts to survey consumers about individual housing preferences and to use this information to build additional housing units, rather than relying on professional opinions about what is clinically or therapeutically indicated for all consumers. And, finally, in their proposed evaluation model, Leff and colleague warn that the "consumer perspective" is not singular. There are multiple operational aspects to consumer service involvement which need to be assessed and monitored in any effort to evaluate consumer service provision. Similarly, there are multiple outcomes to this involvement which also need to be identified and measured.

The model developed by Leff, et al., not only identifies the need to examine multiple processes and indicators, but also indicates that the constructs of the model interact and that relationship paths can provide important understandings; for example, the understanding that the roles and functions available to consumers as providers are significantly affected by the type of program or agency in which the provider is employed; such as whether it is supportive or not, hierarchical or horizontal. This concept of interaction and inter-relationships is fully explicated on the administrative level in the chapter by Bevilacqua, et al. They describe the overall movement in South Carolina toward a community-based system of care and the view that reform could not take place without consumers as partners in system change. Interdependency was recognized as desirable and, thus, consumer-involvement was a necessity. But achieving consumer involvement required ownership in the ongoing process: "nothing about us without us." Full involvement meant commitment to consumer involvement in service delivery, not just planning and monitoring.

In another chapter, highlighting the need for meaningful consumer involvement, Francell warns us of "tokenism" as a real threat. We need to guard against agencies hiring "a consumer" simply to say they have one on staff. Job descriptions are needed, including activities that are significant, worthwhile, and purposeful to the organizational function and mission. The evaluation chapter by Leff, et al., also contains this integration and interdependency theme. For evaluation results to be meaningful, evaluators and evaluation must meaningfully involve consumers. Through participatory approaches, consumers can be empowered and their voices amplified, thus strengthening the validity of evaluative conclusions.

In the past, organizations delivering mental health and rehabilitation services have been marked by a sameness — often excluding diverse perspectives reflecting differences based on gender, race, culture, sexual orientation—and almost uniformly excluding the diverse perspective reflective of the consumers/clients/patients themselves. This has led to certain narrow conceptions of mission, means, and goals as well as of the way that resources are directed. The authors in this section argue that to be more effective, organizations should move toward inclusion of participants, expanding their conceptions and returning ability to people who are labeled as disabled. Inclusion needs to reflect true partnership, adequate supports, acceptance of diversity, and full participation in meaningful roles.

Chapter 42
Mental Health Systems Development: Benefits Created by Consumer Engagement

Joseph J. Bevilacqua
David Gettys
Vicki Cousins

This article will represent three different role perspectives: the state commissioner of mental health; the director of the statewide consumer organization; and the director of consumer affairs in the central office of the Department of Mental Health. These roles each have their own job descriptions and authority and though they complement each other in important ways, the struggle for identity and autonomy is a challenge to the consumer movement in South Carolina.

There is the curious paradox of desiring independence for our consumers and yet recognizing the need for an interdependence that is both accommodating to consumer needs as well as to the state organization which provides the auspices of service. The outcomes of these differing roles are similar but the process of operations and administration differ widely.

The initial push for developing greater consumer participation within the state of South Carolina, and more specifically, within the Department of Mental Health, came from different sources: national encouragement from NIMH and the reorganized Center for Mental Health services, and from non-governmental organizations like the SC Mental Health Association and the SC Alliance for the Mentally Ill. Individuals with vision and commitment within these advocacy groups were vocal and supportive. Our experience in South Carolina provides a good example of the value and, indeed, the need for national policy direction, state leadership, and strong grass-roots interest at the community level.

The Commissioner's Perspective, Joesph J. Bevilacqua

I believe very strongly in leadership coming from the top if change is to happen and be meaningful. My first challenge when I arrived in South Carolina in December 1985 was a pending law suit that had been initiated by the Department of Justice in 1983. Using the Civil Rights of Institutionalized Persons Act (CRIPA 1980) as the authorizing authority, the Department of Justice had charged that our main state mental hospital for persons with serious mental illness was neither providing a safe environment for our patients nor offering adequate therapeutic treatment by appropriate numbers of credentialed professionals.

The state response had been focused essentially on fixing the hospital. The role of the community had been largely ignored. My first policy decision was to broaden the state's response and address not only the hospital deficiencies but how and why patients entered the hospital and what plans were used for discharges and community placement.

A four year consent decree was agreed upon in June 1986 and it was successfully completed in June 1990. Over that four year period, the General Assembly provided 20 million dollars, of which 30% was for hospital improvements and 70% was retained for building community capacity.

This process of integrating the community and inpatient systems through the consent agreement, became the framework through which the consumer was increasingly viewed as a partner who shared with administration, providers, families and other advocacy organizations, important decisions to communitize our system and make it consumer friendly. It is important to note that the initial complaint to the Justice Department was made by the SC Protection and Advocacy organization. At that time, they were the lone voice complaining about the poor care being provided by the hospital.

During the period of the law suit and until I left the agency nearly ten years later, no major activity occurred without the full participation of consumers, families, the Mental Health Association, and other advocacy organizations. For example, Regional Planning Councils, Conference Planning committees, Budget Appropriation preparations, and legislative activity all engaged our consumers and other constituents. I believe this climate of open engagement served us well in fostering ideas and programs that came from outside the agency. External involvement provided important support during the period of transition from a centralized to a decentralized system.

Another example concerned Mr. Billy Brown, a consumer activist, who first raised the idea of consumers working in each of our 17 community mental health centers including the central office. It was not an easy idea to sell, but when it was picked up by the Planning Council (a function required by the Mental Health Block grant) and made part of the Block Grant application to the federal government, its legitimacy was obvious and persuasive.

Sections of this chapter written by Mr. David Gettys, the state director of SHARE (Self-Help Association Regarding Emotions), and Ms. Vicki Counsins, the director of the Consumer Affairs Office, will speak more directly to the consequences and implications of this important move. I would like to reflect on why I felt it was critical to have consumer engagement as an administrative goal and what issues emerged as this policy was pursued.

A major issue that surfaced early in my administration was the fragmentation of the community system from the inpatient system. In South Carolina, the state operates both the hospitals and the community centers; but in daily practice, they performed as two separate systems. This separation was facilitated by the central location of all inpatient services in the capital city of Columbia. And, although an acute care hospital was developed outside Columbia in 1987, the primary traffic for persons with serious mental illness was to the state hospital in Columbia. Continuity of care and community screening before admissions to inpatient services did not occur on a carefully planned basis. This began to change as we emphasized and developed alternative programs to hospitalization. In these endeavors, the planning and negotiations that took place assumed a very visible and inclusive process.

We developed community forums across the state emphasizing "Toward Local Care" policies. We created a Quality Assurance system that provided for advocacy representation from outside the agency to sit in on the abuse and incident review committee of the Department of Mental Health (Evans, Faulkner, Hodo, Mahrer, and Bevilacqua; 1992). A major effort to reduce the inpatient population was part of the "Toward Local Care" initiative (Deci, in press). This downsizing included an extensive protocol focused on quality of life measures. Follow up of patients occurred at six month intervals and a data base was established which now tracks discharged clients.

Two other actions were developed that, from a systems perspective, highlighted the changing environment within the agency as well as the mental health community.

The first was an action reaching out to the state's university and college system to establish the South Carolina Mental Health Public Academic Consortium (Bray & Bevilacqua, 1993). The consortium focused on involving traditional mental health disciplines and fostered active exchange and "focused learning" experiences between the world of practice and the schools of Nursing, Social Work, Psychology, and Psychiatry. This effort highlighted important work force issues such as psychosocial rehabilitation and co-occurring mental illness and addictive disorders. Reports were prepared that included joint efforts of academicians, practitioners, and consumers. Several of these reports are now focusing on curricula as a way to improve and impact the training content within academia.

The other action addressed the important issues of minorities within our system. South Carolina's population is roughly one-third African American. There is a greater proportion of African American representation in both the work force (primarily at the lower level) and patient population. We have developed plans and training programs across the department to highlight some of the racial disparities that exist. This is now a part and parcel of our developing an open system and acknowledging the necessary changes that have to take place.

The response to these activities has generally been positive. It has allowed us to see how fragile our system is. As we have moved consumers into paying positions we have begun to uncover some of the tensions and dysfunctions that exist between practitioners and consumers. Some obvious conclusions include:

1) Professionals are not comfortable sharing work space with consumers.

2) Decision making opportunities by staff are closely guarded.

3) The relationship between Supplemental Security Income payments and earned income through employment is often used as an

excuse to inhibit more independent behavior on the part of consumers. The uncertainty exists for both the consumer and the employer. 4) Respect for consumers as co-workers is difficult for professional staff to accept.

Recognizing these tensions, why then is consumer representation so important? One reason is to keep the system honest. We can't do the job that must be done without consumers at the table. Their unique point of view and their experience provides an opportunity for raising issues that professionals, bureaucrats, and administrators can address.

Consumer involvement helps to change the stereotype that we have about the people served by the mental health system, and acknowledges that professionals often have a greater problem with this stereotype than do ordinary citizens.

I believe it is important for consumers to help the agency open doors to improve the quality of life of all consumers.

Finally, I think it is important for consumers to build a network within the agency, and between that agency and the community. These networks must include both public and private systems of care. Networks cannot be successful without the contribution and the energy of consumers.

SHARE's Perspective, David Gettys

Mental health consumer and ex-patient organizations have sprouted up across the United States. During the early 1980's, the Federal Government began to supplement the funding for consumer/ex-patient groups in several states across America.

By 1985, a statewide consumer group had begun in South Carolina known as SHARE (Self-Help Association Regarding Emotions), whose mission was to empower mental health consumers and ex-patients by building and maintaining a statewide network of consumer-run self-help SHARE groups. They began collaborations with the University of South Carolina to design a process of organizing local self-help groups that were consumer-run and controlled. The process born out of the collaboration is today known as LEAD (Leadership Education and Development). It has since provided not only a resource for organizing locally, but has also given local groups the capacity to have continued input into state level activities.

Statewide consumer/ex-patient groups provided an opportunity for people to join at the local level and to speak out. Leadership conferences were held with wide ranging topics from how to start a self-help group, to protecting consumer rights, public speaking and fundraising. The momentum of these organizing efforts produced continuous ferment. People began to assert notions based on their former experiences as mental patients. Where they once were relegated to a life of disability and dependence, now they were saying "Let us do for ourselves." This period in time was viewed with much optimism by the consumers involved in this process. They had established a viable platform of reform and they were never going back.

The leadership of Billy Brown (the first person to become a Consumer Affairs Coordinator at a local mental health center) had in many ways led the statewide consumer organization toward empowerment. His leadership, vision, and desire to make South Carolina active in consumerism was a pivotal point in consumer development. Mr. Brown was at that time (1992) chair of the Consumer Employment Committee, of the SC Mental Health Planning Council as well as serving as President of the Board of Directors of SC SHARE (the statewide self-help consumer organization).

The planning council in South Carolina had aligned itself with the consumer organization. With the recommendations of the consumers, they put into place a local requirement of mental health centers to employ a consumer affairs coordinator in each community mental health center. This was a pioneering effort, and resistance was heard from some of the local mental health centers. Some directors voiced concerns of potential conflict of interest. Others placed blame on the State mental health director for "shoving this idea down their throats."

It was believed that with consumer participation on these planning councils, recommendations on how to deliver "comprehensive" community based mental health services could be realized. South Carolina had already begun to empty its state hospitals at a very rapid pace. These ex-patients needed community based services and they helped establish policies and procedures to fit their individual needs.

The notion was so completely foreign up to that point, that it took several years to implement the system. The goal of placing consumer affairs coordinators in management level positions as advocates for the consumers added an important dimension to policy operational activity and included assistance in grievance resolution. These developments slowly became a reality. Opponents were still asking, "How can consumer affairs coordinators be effective as internal employees and still maintain the ability to confront the local system in times of trouble?" But as time has gone by, we see that it is working.

Each consumer affairs coordinator works under the supervision of center directors, not for the state's Director of the Office of Consumer Affairs. Many consumers think this mission could have been better achieved if the latter had been true.

How then do these pieces fit into current practices and policies of the state mental health system as a whole? The first outcome is shared ownership in the ongoing process. The philosophy from a consumer's perspective is "nothing about us without us." How policies are developed in future years will now occur through the participation of those the policy is intended to serve.

It is no longer just the role of those delivering services. Today it is seen as a two-way street. Policy development is no longer viewed as power from the top to the bottom. Rather it is the sharing of power vertically and horizontally. Agreements are reached through consensus, not just from directives or one way orders via memoranda.

The result of consumer participation in regard to the design, delivery and evaluation of the ever changing public mental health system can be viewed as the foundation for current policy and practice. It will formulate the flow for a continuum that will include consumers as providers.

Two significant activities undertaken in the early 1990's by South Carolina SHARE helped facilitate more active participation of consumers of mental health services and are examples of good consumer engagement. The first was a statewide consumer preference housing and services survey. Participants from local SHARE groups across South Carolina were trained in survey administration and then conducted face-to-face interviews with peers. The premise of this study was to ask consumers where they would choose to live if they had a choice, and could remain in that housing for as long as they wanted. The second part of the study, entitled "Real Homes for Real People," became a boilerplate for improving housing conditions for consumers of mental health in South Carolina. The South Carolina Department of Mental Health, among others, used the data collected and have since created or built more than 500 additional units of housing. Other non-profit groups have also used the data as a baseline in designing new housing programs for consumers in South Carolina.

The second activity was a collaboration with the US Dept. of Justice, the Bazelon Center for Mental Health Law, the SC Department of Mental Health and SC SHARE. The project examined Title II of the Americans With Disabilities Act. Our charge at SHARE was to use a four-pronged approach in looking at the accessibility of public services for mental health consumers, and to measure to what extent they were discriminated against because they have a mental health diagnosis. The four processes that occurred over the 18-month project were: (a) convening four focus groups, (b) a questionnaire based on information elicited by focus groups, (c) tracking the ability of seven ex-hospital patients to access public services over time, and (d) a survey of 314 SHARE members statewide.

The final document produced is entitled *Opening Public Agency Doors*, (Rinere, 1995). The major outcome of this study was the need to educate workers in the public agencies to be more informed regarding the needs of people with mental illness.

Activities which grew out of this project involved training on the Americans with Disabilities Act, Title II, for workers in public agencies, and the changing of a discriminatory state driver's license application form that was in non-compliance with the ADA.

Today there is a true spirit of collaboration with consumers and providers. A viable system of consumerism is working in South Carolina. There continues to be collaborative efforts shown by the consumer affairs director, the 17 local consumer affairs coordinators, the state-wide mental health consumer organization, and the mental health system itself. Our state mental health system has seen a tremendous transformation in the last decade. This change can only be attributed to the efforts of the Department of Mental Health, and the consumers of service in South Carolina who were willing to step out, explore, and identify the elements and requirements of participation, which today we know as consumerism.

Office of Consumer Affairs' Perspective, Vicki Cousins

At the present time, hiring consumers is probably the most innovative and cost-effective initiative that a state director can take within a public mental health system.

Self-identified consumer employees in positions of respectability—if not authority—in a state agency might seem, to detractors, like inmates running the asylum. That's okay with me because it's part of my job description to be labeled; I get paid to do something with this inhumanity. Revenge is sweet: I'm working hard to make lasting places for self-identified consumer providers in our organization and to make consumer satisfaction our system's ultimate operational goal.

Citizens get a lot of bang for their buck when they decide to get behind the idea of hiring self-identified consumer employees in key positions throughout a public mental health system. Citizens made it happen in South Carolina. My best guess at a start-date was the late 1980s, when community advocacy groups co-sponsored a conference. I wasn't on the scene yet.

At that conference, Joel Slack spoke about the potential role of consumers in state agencies. By 1991, Billy Brown got himself hired by the Catawba Community Mental Health Center. With a supportive supervisor, (Sam Reynolds) and an alliance with SC SHARE (then director, Pam Goodman) and the other advocacy groups, Billy Brown motivated our State Planning Council to hire at all 17 community mental health centers, self-identified consumers as consumer affairs coordinators and to write this into their annual plan.

Given three years of this kind of blood, sweat, and tears, how could the state mental health director not mandate that all center directors comply with the request of the State Planning Council?

The process was completed and the Center positions were established by June 1995. The State Plan also called for a state director of the Office of Consumer Affairs to be hired. That happened in June 1994.

From start to finish, it took four years for consumers to be positioned throughout the state mental health system. It involved at least one person from every angle of the debate to take ownership of the initiative. And, it took Dr. Bevilacqua's administrative support.

Undercurrents of hostility between people working in large organizations will always flare and fade, especially during times of reform. Everyone is stressed, and there are turf issues! Somebody is bound to feel invaded or short-changed by our presence, at least until we've had enough time on the job to get some authentic successes under our belts. Unfortunately, academic credentials, not life experiences, are the great equalizers of employees who work for a state agency.

It's not easy to be associated with anything "new." "New" is not easily accepted in a large state agency. As the state director of the Office of Consumer Affairs, I spend a fair amount of energy stifling my newness, which helps to numb me a bit so I can then appear nice. Numbness and niceness have been helpful in keeping my former and present state director smiling about where the Office of Consumer Affairs is headed. But, most importantly, it has given me courage to set valuable, often unpopular, goals for my office.

I serve no less than thousands of internal and external customers. Some days it seems that they are all at my door. Numbness helps then, but a paid personal assistant (blessed are my four wonderful, voluntary interns) would work even better.

I'm afraid after a year and a half working as the first state director of the Office of Consumer Affairs, I'm getting used to aspects of the self-protective rules and regulations in state government. Is this an early warning sign of becoming co-opted by the system? Probably. Rules and regs have become like a daily dose of lithium for me—an administrative anvil over my head to keep my actions in check and to make sure I feel fellowship in bondage with other employees.

At one point my supervisor, former state mental health director Dr. Joseph Bevilacqua, asked me if I might be better off as a contracted employee, as a way to have more freedom and far less aggravation. I'm sure I would, but the job is too important; it has to be permanent and it has to be full-time. Detractors would love to see the position diminished. I'm still idealistic enough, and now close enough to key decision-makers in this agency, to think I'll have a hand someday in changing a few rules of doing business with self-identified consumers in a state agency.

In the purest, most beautiful sense, self-identified consumer-providers and administrators are change agents. Simply by virtue of surviving our jobs (and the hideously impractical, torturous one-year probationary period), we have succeeded. We do, however, have to be bigger, better, and braver than average. And our PDs (position descriptions) never come close to mentioning that.

In a thick, Southern accent, a fun-loving consumer recently said to me after a bizarre joke (which we both found hilariously funny), "Ya know, we just ain't right." And though I tend to agree with him, most "right" people I know are pretty uncomfortable with the feelings of being an outsider. Career-bound state employees are insiders. Most politicians are insiders. Consumer employees are still outsiders, but we're in.

It takes an outsider in a public mental health system to care less and less about finding answers to the environmental-psycho-social-genetic chicken and egg questions concerning consumers' psychiatric profiles. It takes an outsider to poke productive holes in the system's driving medical models. It takes an outsider to get the system to see what it really takes to support consumers to make it confidently through life with the agency's unobtrusive assistance and without it. It's our system's greatest challenge not only to learn how to do this, but to do it.

My family has always found me to be a little off the mark when it comes to my personal life choices, but they did not question my taking this job, primarily because I was to be well paid. I make at least twice what I made working for nonprofits in Missouri and Minnesota, and two-thirds of my top earnings in another career.

I believe my former supervisor would say that I was initially paid well because of the need to show parity with the salaries of other senior managers, thus empowering the position. The Division of Human Resources would probably say that I am paid well because of my work history, especially for my sales and marketing skills, and the earning power I had in that field. I say I am paid well because of my life experience as a consumer of mental health services, and because of the risk involved in self-identifying as having a mental illness. Unfortunately, my spin is not yet accepted systemically by the South Carolina Department of Mental Health.

I now regret not making a bigger issue of why I am paid what I am, at the time I was hired. If I had set a precedent then, perhaps I would be more successful now getting our 17 consumer affairs coordinator positions (at least the five slots which are full-time) up to an empowered, liveable income level. I'll just keep plugging away at it.

I feel strongly that, at least in South Carolina, for a chronic outsider, the State Office of Consumer Affairs position presents an amazing opportunity to learn much about the business of running a huge public agency. My work is mentored by the highest ranking agency official. The position at any level would not work in a state agency without the power, protection, and patience of its highest ranking official.

From my earlier comments, you can tell that the first year in this position was difficult. I know the consumer affairs coordinators (CACs) in the community positions had their share of obstacles to overcome as well. In my first year, we managed to fulfill the goal of establishing positions through attrition. We lost an incredibly productive CAC for two reasons: (1) the conflict created by not being allowed to do projects of her own creation and choosing, and (2) she gave up her power and protection when she insisted upon being supervised by someone other than the center director. Consequently, she couldn't get her projects through or compromise in any real way, and the frustration just wasn't worth it for her. Although her position may have resulted from a top-down mandate, day-to-day operations are controlled from the ground-up. I lost her, they lost her, consumers lost her, but the system was the biggest loser.

My first task when I came on board in June 1994 was to start working on a personal request for accommodations under the Americans with Disabilities Act of 1990. It took until November, five months later, to get a signature on a form which you couldn't even tell I had a hand in writing up. It made me numb.

I now know that requests for accommodations should not be systematized. They are clear, personal communications to a supervisor about what supports or accommodations a person with a disability needs to fulfill the essential functions of their jobs. Dr. Bevilacqua and I both got lost in the "big picture." I worried about having a tailored piece which I could share with the other CACs, and he worried about how accommodations would affect a state agency's thousands of employees. This continues to be an important issue for me and my new supervisor, John Morris, interim state mental health director.

We'll get it right, eventually, even if we "ain't right."

Conclusion

It is imperative for the public mental health system to be fully integrated with consumer participation. Our experiences in South Carolina have clearly demonstrated a strong need for a consumer role both within the provider system as well as outside the normal services organizations.

The increasing pressures for operating efficiently, through privatization and managed care, will require a response capacity that can use the ex-patient, survivor, consumer experiences as a challenge to the market-driven system that is being created by political and economic forces in our country. The necessary balance and reality check that consumers provide is essential if the needs of people with serious mental illness are to be adequately met.

There is a real danger that through the major shifts that are occurring through devolution and downsizing of our federal and state governments, we will lose the benefits we have attained for treating and caring for persons with serious mental illness. The communication, self-help, and psychosocial dimensions of our public mental health systems will atrophy without the strong and persistent presence of the consumer as a colleague, partner, and advocate.

References

Bazelon Center for Mental Health Law (1995, August). *Opening public agency doors: Title II of the Americans with Disabilities Act & People with Mental Illnesses: A collaborative approach for ensuring equal access to state benefit & service programs.* Washington, DC.: Victoria L. Rinere.CRIPA, Civil Rights of Institutionalized Persons Act 42. USC Sec. 1997. (1980).

Bray, J.D. & Bevilacqua, J.J. A multidisciplinary public—Academic liaison to improve public mental health services in South Carolina. *Hospital & Community Psychiatry,* 44. 985-999.

Deci, P., (in press) The forgotten alternatives. In S.H. Henggeler & A. Santos (Eds.), *Innovative services for difficult to treat populations.* Washington, DC: American Psychiatric Press ` `c.

Deci, P., (in press) Downsizing state operational psychiatric facilities: Three new research efforts to examine the quality of community care for persons with severe mental illness. In S.H. Henggeler & A. Santos (Eds.). *Innovative services for difficult to treat populations.* Washington, DC: American Psychiatric Press Inc.

Evans, O. N., Faulkner, L., Hodo, G., Mahrer, D., & Bevilacqua, J. A Quality Improvement Process for State Mental Health Systems. *Hospital & Community Psychiatry,* 43, 465-469.

Joseph J. Bevilacqua is currently director, Office of State Initiatives, Bazelon Center for Mental Health Law, Washington, D.C. He was professor of social work at the University of South Carolina. He served as commissioner of mental health from 1975 to 1995 in Rhode Island, Virginia and South Carolina. He has been active with the National Association of State Mental Health Program Directors, serving as their president for two terms.

David Gettys is the executive director of SC SHARE (Self-Help Association Regarding Emotions), a statewide consumer/ex-patient self-help organization. He has held this position for two years. SC SHARE is comprised of 63 self-help consumer-run groups throughout South Carolina, and has a growing membership of 3000 people. SHARE's mission is to empower consumers by building a self-help group network statewide. Mr. Getty has been a consumer of mental health services for 21 years, is married with 2 children, and resides with his family in Columbia, SC.

Victoria C. Cousins is employed full-time as the director of the Office of Consumer Affairs for the South Carolina Department of Mental Health. Ms. Cousins is the first self-identified consumer of mental health services to hold a planning and policy-making position in South Carolina at the Department's senior management level. She reports to the agency director. Born and raised in Maine, Ms. Cousins earned a B.A. in english literature from Bowdoin College in 1979. She is a member of NAC/SMHA, the National Association of Consumer/Survivor Mental Health Administrators.

Chapter 43
Consumers as Providers of Psychiatric Rehabilitation: Reflections by a Family Member

Claire Griffin-Francell

Family members understand and support the need for psychiatric rehabilitation. In the past, family members have undertaken the roles and functions now offered by professionals in the field of psychiatric rehabilitation. Indeed, many family members became the first case managers, psychiatric rehabilitation counselors, and primary support people for their loved ones because these options were not available, and the need was great. Many family members have been very concerned about employment opportunities and have taken on roles as mentors, job coaches, and rehabilitation counselors to guide their loved ones through the often confusing array of rehabilitation services, and to assist their loved ones in getting and keeping jobs.

In 1979 when the National Alliance for the Mentally Ill formed to advocate for better and more accessible supports, it was because these alternatives—many of the ones we now take for granted—did not exist. They were not available to our loved ones in adequate or sufficient quantity, and as family members saw these needs go unfulfilled, we acted to step in—to undertake the provision of this support and to advocate for its expansion.

Psychiatric rehabilitation did respond to these needs. And there emerged more supports and more diverse alternatives to meet these needs. Although there is still a need for family advocacy and supports offered by family members, there are more paid positions to supplement the support offered by families, and to remove the excessive burdens families face in caring for a loved one who experiences serious mental illness.

It seems natural now to talk about the involvement of consumers as providers of psychiatric rehabilitation. Family members have been involved in these activities for some time now. And consumers have demonstrated that they too are critical in the provision of community and rehabilitative supports. Family members, consumers, and professionals all have something of value to contribute to addressing serious mental illness as a neurobiological disorder. Making consumer service provision an actual aspect of mental health service delivery seems timely as we broaden our understanding of effective support, and as we appreciate the commitment family members and consumers have made in the past to the provision of support to their loved ones and to their peers.

A Personal Perspective

My son, who has struggled with serious mental illness, is a very good example. His own journey offers hope to people who have experienced serious mental illness and who, as a result of this background, can become more understanding and sensitive mental health practitioners. It took three years of struggle, several hospitalizations, an accurate diagnosis, and correct medication to set my son on the road to recovery. How he subsequently made his way back to health and recovery is a testimony to his courage and to the value of a family consumer partnership (Francell, 1994; Sullivan, 1994). When our son embarked on a career in social work with people coping with serious mental illness, my husband and I encouraged him to learn social work content to supplement the valuable experience he had obtained as a primary consumer of mental health services. Insights gained from a consumer perspective can make an employee a better agent for change, and a more effective force in systems reform.

Presently, in his role as director of research and development for the Cobb County Mental Health Services Board, our son has brought energy and passion to the agency in his commitment to serving the most in need. One year out of graduate school, he wrote and obtained a $750,000 grant for a program serving the homeless mentally ill population in his county. He was not able to do this just because of his background as a consumer. Rather, he was able to do this because he had technical writing skills developed from a baccalaureate degree in English, and social work expertise from graduate school. His background as a consumer provided him with empathy, sensitivity, and concern for the plight of the individuals for whom he now serves as an advocate. Much of what I include in this paper is informed by this personal experience. Much of what I discuss is a product of what my son has learned, what I have learned from his experience, and what our family has learned together.

The Ingredients of Success

Consumers may not necessarily have the educational background possessed by my son. Nonetheless, serving as a provider is a demanding role for anyone. Training and development are essential for all consumers who enter roles as providers so, like my son, they can put their passion and positive energy to work in effective and meaningful ways. A hopefulness about success on the part of the agency is also critical. Failure to put these supports in place will doom to failure an initiative devoted to consumer service provision.

In the field's eagerness to help create job opportunities for recovering persons, many families advocate for the development of new positions within the mental health field. They are thrilled when the family member is employed. They are thrilled when their family member receives a pay check. But we need to be wary here. There are two separate issues that need to be addressed to assure the success of consumers as providers: (1) on the job stressors; and (2) tokenism.

Buffering on the Job Stress

What happens when the stressors on the job start to negatively impact the health of the consumer-employee? There is a double-edged sword here.

The recipients of the care given by the consumer employee have a right to excellent service and they have a right to receive these services from care providers who are not impaired. The consumer employee has the right to reasonable accommodations. And, the mental health system needs to be vigilant about providing accommodations. Supports must be offered on the job. These supports must be designed to reduce work related stressors, or to help consumer employees to master these stressors. The mastery of stress will not only assure the effective performance of the consumer-employee but will also increase the likelihood that consumers will not receive services the quality of which is badly compromised.

The job cannot set the person up for failure, or for more and more stress. Responsible program development, and responsible human resource management, requires the field to enter this emergent area with a clear head and with clear vision. The design of the job, the preparation of the individual, ongoing supervision, skill development, peer support, and integration into the organization as a regular employee must be given consideration as important issues to resolve in order to assure that consumer-employees are and will be successful. Without this thoughtfulness and commitment by organizational leaders, people with serious mental illness may likely fail as employees. Their failure may reinforce for them personal inadequacies, and harden self doubt. Failure may lead to self-fulfilling prophecies on the part of the organization: "See they can't do it; we should not try." The agency may engage in victim blaming. The risks here are very high. But so are the payoffs—if it is done right.

Family advocates may want to monitor organizational initiatives and programs designed to help consumers to become employees or to otherwise serve as primary care providers. Supervisors must be carefully screened. In my family's own situation, I was amazed to discover the high number of mental health professionals who do not possess good management skills. I found incomprehensible the number of mental health professionals who cannot relate well to people who are recovering from an episode of serious mental illness. I found that they just did not understand how to relate to people as fellow human beings who were coming back from frightening personal experiences— ones that reduced their self-esteem, their feelings of competence, and their feelings of self-confidence.

Consumer-employees need the very best in supervision. Support, coaching, and guidance from a caring and skilled supervisor can provide an important and nurturant interpersonal context within which a person can thrive. This context can allow the consumer employee to learn new skills, reduce personal expectancies of failure that too often accompany new challenges and new situations, and develop on-the-job essential skills that are important to mastery of the work and to future progress.

I cannot emphasize enough the importance of good, proactive, and nurturant supervision. Both the consumer-employee and his/her family members may be struggling with expectancies for failure in the new role. Good supervisors will reframe these expectancies and will listen closely to the

employees and their family members about what supports are needed in order
to master the new employment situation. Many families share the disappointment of their family member who started a new job with high expectations
only to withdraw because of day to day stress and lack of employment supports. These experiences can inhibit motivation to reenter the work world at a
later time.

What are some of these supervisory supports? Learning about new employees' expectations for the job is critical. They may have some very unrealistic expectations about what they will be doing, and the need to undertake these
responsibilities in a flawless manner. These expectations can be clarified between supervisors, the new employees, and work associates. The new employees can be offered reassurance that they can make mistakes, and that they
may make these mistakes when they feel under pressure. The offer of consistent supervision, both individually and in groups, in which consumer employees are provided opportunities to discuss their concerns, to identify the stressors they experience, and to identify ways to reduce or eliminate stressors will
be an invaluable support.

Supervisors and work associates can reframe failure expectancies. Gen-
tly assuring consumer-employees that they will be successful is a powerful
tool. Helping consumer-employees to identify those supports they need to be
successful is another powerful tool. And, giving the consistent message that
we are here to help you will provide reassurance. Of course, the provision of
supports assumes that the program itself is committed to a humanistic work
culture. Placing consumer-employees under the supervision of an authoritar-
ian, perfectionistic, or unrealistic person is a recipe for failure.

Making a Real Commitment to Consumer Employment Versus Tokenism

As more and more recovered persons allow themselves to be identified
as having a mental disorder, we may see the stigma in societal institutions diminish. But until the time when people are considered for their value as persons with experience and skills rather than as disordered individuals, there is a
real threat that people may be hired as tokens to fill slots on an organizational
chart in a mental health agency. The agency may want to say that it is employing a consumer. After all, this can make the agency look informed, progressive, and committed to proactive work opportunities. But, many agencies do
not know what to do with the consumers that they have employed.

Agencies engaging consumers as employees must create work roles that
are meaningful. They cannot merely be marginal roles or functions but must
contribute to the fulfillment of an agency's mission and purpose. Consumer
employees in ancillary roles, like case management assistants, or program aides,
may be suitable for an initial effort. But an agency needs to answer important
questions about career and professional development. Like other employees,
people with serious mental illness will want to know their future possibilities

and their potential for continuing employment with the organization. How will people progress? Will they get opportunities for training and skill development? Will they be confined to employment tracks reserved only for consumers? Or, will they have opportunities to move through regular career paths to assume more and more responsibility as they themselves demonstrate more expertise and skill? To fail to answer these questions at the beginning may indicate that the agency is engaging in tokenism. To answer them, and to have a plan, means that the agency will be planning for the permanent and progressive involvement of people with serious mental illness as employees.

Being a pioneer carries its own burdens. The first African American in a white company, or the first woman in the corporate board room, if asked, may tell you that being the first and only can get quite lonely. A single consumer-employee may experience a need for peers. Peer support and validation may be indispensable in enabling consumer-employees to reduce stress, to learn about the organization, and to master new work roles.

Advocates may recommend the need to hire several consumers at once. Movement into the organization as a small cohort may offer the opportunity for supportive group development and for the formation of interpersonal ties with others who understand the personal issues involved in working as a consumer-employee. The offer of this form of support should not, however, reduce the integration and participation of consumer-employees into the mainstream life of the agency. Good support systems allow people to receive support from a range of sources, and to offer support in return.

The support group may be a place for reflection, problem solving, information sharing, and networking. After all, it is not unusual for members of groups who have a minority status to create their own organizational support groups and communities. But, consumer-employees need relationships with other workers, and they need to be encouraged to forge friendships that can serve as supports on and off the job. Most families will be encouraged to see their members participate in the normalizing aspects of work, and to shed their identity as mental health consumers.

I do not want to sound like I am suggesting a contradiction here. People with serious mental illness become employees because of their personal and first hand perspective with mental illness. And then I am suggesting that they shed this identity. Perhaps this is the outcome we should expect with a proactive effort at consumer employment. People enter the organization as consumer-employees, but they progressively integrate these perspectives and experiences into many other perspectives and experiences as they grow and develop in their work. By supporting this development, the agency helps people to create new identities and new self concepts. However, this will be most successful if people get the support they need and want.

Conclusion

As a family member of a son with serious mental illness, as an advocate for people and families coping with serious mental illness, and as a professional in the field of psychiatry, I view the involvement of consumers as providers as a very promising development within psychiatric rehabilitation. Not only does it expand the range of supports available to people, but it also enables people with serious mental illness to put their unique and important knowledge concerning mental health care and psychiatric rehabilitation to work on behalf of people coping with this issue.

Yet, I do not believe that merely having the status as a consumer makes one a good provider of services. Experience with mental health systems can offer some insights into the flaws and the omissions of the system, but it cannot alone replace the body of knowledge and skills that need to be acquired in order to do a good job. The perspective of a consumer is very important to sensitizing a person who serves in the role of the provider to the needs and issues faced by people with serious mental illness; yet individuals filling these roles need much more. They need skills to serve in critical roles within mental health and rehabilitation systems. They need organizational support and understanding to undertake their work well and effectively. And, they need professional development that will support their occupational and professional mobility. "Consumers as providers" cannot be a nominal effort. Any commitment to offering services to people with serious mental illness by other people who face these same concerns must reflect a commitment to support, skill enhancement, and professional development of the people who fill the roles of providers.

Individual families and organized families can serve as advocates for the achievement of effective service provision by consumer-providers. Families themselves often understand the barriers to employment their members have faced. And they have witnessed first hand the struggles their members have faced in the achievement of a place for themselves. They can be important sources of recommendations, information, and know-how regarding how to make consumer service provision work in practice. In their roles as primary care givers, family members understand how established mental health systems can ignore the skills, abilities, and capacities that consumers—both primary and secondary—can bring to these systems and the services that compose them.

Family members served as the first care managers and psychiatric rehabilitation practitioners. They had to. The personal experience of my own family is testimony to the truth that many families are caught off guard, often with systems of service that are not knowledgeable, responsive, or proactive to the needs faced during periods of tumult and crisis. The family movement expressed through the work of the National Alliance for the Mentally Ill emerged because professionals did not have the answers when it came to psychiatric rehabilitation. Increasingly more and more of us—professionals, consumers, and family members—are becoming enlightened about the important role partnership serves in promoting effective provision of psychiatric rehabilitation. The involvement of consumers as providers is an indicator of the potential legitimacy of this partnership. Consumers serving and supporting consumers is a very positive development. It complements families supporting families, and families supporting consumers. When we realize that progressive mental health systems are really composed of these partnerships—ones that bring together into caring networks professionals, consumers, and family members—we will have made more progress toward making recovery a reality.

Claire Griffin-Francell, A.P.R.N., is president of Southeast Nurse Consultants, Inc. located in Dunwoody, Georgia. She is active in the family movement and consults nationwide in the improvement of mental health and community support systems.

Chapter 44
Thinking About Diversity
David Granger

"Success comes out of fellowship that is controlled by organizations within its diversity. One must learn how to interlock the gears of individual desires so that they productively supplement the movement of each other."

— I Ching

"Gravity separates the primordial matter into distinct centers: First into galaxies, then into stars. It would be impossible to develop human entities without first dividing the cosmos into manageable hunks. But having made this separation, gravity compresses each star-to-be so that it begins to complexify matter into the full range of chemical elements."

— John L. Hitchcock (Atoms, Snowflakes & God)

"Shu and Tefnut engendered Geb and Nut [Earth and Sky]. Geb and Nut gave birth to Osirus, Horus-Khenty-irty, Seth, then Isis and Nepthys, of their bodies, one after the other... and they gave birth to the multitudes of this world."

— Rhind Papyrus

"Oddua and Yembo gave the beautiful Oshosi the task of hunting in order to feed the people. With him some good and bad was also brought into the world as he was a sorcerer. The birth of Oshosi brought the Yoruban refrain IN ORDER FOR THE WORLD TO BE A WORLD THERE MUST BE A LITTLE OF EVERYTHING."

— ITA Mythology of the Yoruba Religion

Thinking about Diversity

Diversity is a way of thinking about differences, the innumerable differences responsible for variety, uniqueness, and individuality at any and every level. But like so many other concepts, the concept of diversity is meaningless without some concept for its opposite. Similarity, sameness, commonality reciprocate with ideas of difference to create the dance of diversity. We are all the same, we are all different. We are diverse.

Diversity and similarity are intimately involved in our way of thinking about everything. Living things are similar, but different from non-living things. Shrubs are more like trees but different from grasses. All plants share certain commonalities that make them different from animals. Yet we all understand that no two leaves on a single tree are identical. Diversity is a matter of degree.

Health and illness are matters of degree. Health and illness are also matters of diversity. This is particularly true of what we call psychiatric illness and the many methods used to heal and restore individuals considered mentally ill. When we say someone has a mental illness, we are saying they are different. When we say we are consumer-survivors, we are essentially saying how we are the same as some, but different from others. As conscious human beings, we are perhaps the most complex systems we encounter. We can therefore exhibit diversity in any and all of the numberless ways in which we can create categories. We are male. We are female. We are young, old and middle aged. We are Hindu, Christian, Muslim, Sheik, Rastafarian, Jew, Taoist, and Branch Davidian. We are democrats, republicans, anarchists, libertarians, and theocrats. Our families come from England, Palestine, Hindu Kush, Black Mesa, Acadia, Alabama, and Eritrea. *The Diagnostic and Statistical Manual* of the American Psychiatric Association is just another catalogue of diversities.

Are the issues of diversity relevant to psychiatric rehabilitation? Are the issues of diversity relevant to the ways in which consumer-survivors participate in the healing and recovery process? Are issues of diversity relevant to the organization and operation of our social systems that are expected to assist persons considered mentally ill? In this author's view, few issues are more relevant to these endeavors than issues of diversity.

Understanding Culture as a Way of Understanding Diversity

The moment one forms an idea of a thing and successfully catches one of its aspects, one invariably succumbs to the illusion of having caught the whole. One never considers that a total apprehension is right out of the question. Not even an idea posited as total is total, for it is still an entity on its own with unpredictable qualities...the very fact of grasping the object conceptually gives it the golden opportunity to display all those qualities which would never have made their appearance had it not been imprisoned in a concept (Jung, 1969 p.168).

One way in which we are all different and unique is in our physical bodies. We all know that even identical twins have different patterns of ridges on their hands and fingers. Another way in which we are all unique has to do with our experiences. We have all had different experiences in our growth, development, and becoming. Through these experiences, we have learned different things.

Humans, like a number of other species, live, work, play, and grow in groups. The forms and functions of various human groupings are as diverse as the hues, sizes, and shapes of the individual members of the human family. Groups are a universal constant in human life and no consideration of the human condition is complete without attention to the roles and operations of the various groups of humans. Culture refers to what groups have learned and what they teach to members of the group. Most of this learning and teaching is not intentional, but occurs naturally as we develop and grow as individual members of various groups.

Our way of knowing and understanding is intimately a part of our culture; the common understanding prevalent in our groups is built upon assumptions that reflect the history of learning in our "groups." Schein gives the following definition of culture:

A pattern of shared basic assumptions that the group learned as it solved problems of external adaption and internal integration, that has worked well enough to be considered valid, and therefore, to be taught to new members as the correct way to perceive, think, and feel in relation to those problems (Schien, 1992 p. 12).

In Schein's model of culture, the basic underlying assumptions, the taken-for-granted beliefs, perceptions, thoughts, and feelings represent the deepest level of culture and the ultimate source of values and action.

The recovery and rehabilitation of persons considered to be mentally ill (by the group) has everything to do with the reciprocal relationship of the person to various groups. Individuals are parts of families, live in neighborhoods, are employees of corporations, are citizens or subjects of governments, and depend on a number of agencies, bureaus and organizations to carry out the tasks of daily life.

The forms and types of groups that affect individuals' lives are formal, informal, and at times even nebulous. The human condition is in large part determined by the status of people and the functions of their groups. We all live as members of a number of groups. Groups vary in terms of the power members of the group may have to control the conditions that affect their lives. The interest of groups vary, and the conflict or consensus within groups vary. Groups interrelate to numerous other groups in the complex web of modern society. As we attempt to live and thrive as members of various groups, we are confronted with the ideologies representing various cultural assumptions. Schein says of ideology:

Ideology can be seen as a set of overarching values that can serve as a prescription for action vis-a-vis other groups and the broader environment, especially in areas that are difficult to explain and manage. (Schein, 1992 p. 89)

Ideological content is concerned with "the nature of the self, the interaction between the self and the collectivity, the relation of the person to the physical environment, the nature of society, and the view of history" (Groliers, 1992).

The Group, the Individual, and Understanding Health and Illness

The ideology of individualism contains implicit content regarding the nature of the self, the relation of the individual to the collective, and the relation of the person to the physical environment. Individualistic ideology conceives the individual as separate and distinct from the collective and from the physical environment.

Objectivity and individualism are features of certain culturally based constructions and belief systems. Other cultures have developed other assumptive and explanatory systems that do not utilize or emphasize the concept of the self as separate from the collective and the environment.

> The spiritual life of the Indian was an integral part of his technology and basis of his entire framework of understanding...The Indian looked at a mountain and felt its presence. The white man looked and saw a pretty pile of rocks. The essence of the Indian's framework of understanding was integration with his environment. The essence of the white man's framework was separation from it. The white strove to conquer nature, the Indian sought nature for an ally (Campbell, 1985).

A number of cultures developed assumptive/explanatory systems that do not utilize the conception of the separate self at all.

> Dixon (1976) argues that the sense of the self in the African world view is intrinsically connected with both the community and nature; the individual is defined by his or her relationship within the community, and not as in the West by contrast to the collectivity. Just as the individual can only exist only in relationship to the community, so too can he or she exist only in relationship to nature (Fee, 1986).

The characterization of Chinese science by Joseph Needham as cited in Fee (1986), describes an assumptive/ explanatory system that was:

> profoundly non-Cartesian, refusing to make any sharp dichotomy between spirit and matter or between mind and body. Similarly, Chinese traditional medicine integrated spirit, mind body, diet and dreams, energy flows and physical sensations, and remains highly successful at an empirical level, while resisting all efforts to define it within the categories of physiological reductionism. Chinese physics also remained impervious to mechanical, atomism and physical reductionism. Abstract knowledge of the either A or not-A variety was avoided in Chinese science in favor of nonexclusive relationships of forces (Fee, 1986).

Fee (1986) identifies at least three separate literatures that critically address these forms of science:

> In the literature of black and Indian liberation, it is addressed as white or European science; in the literature of feminism, it is addressed as male science; in at least some of the literature of Marxism, it is addressed as bourgeois science (Lecourt, 1976; Navarro, 1981). Each of these critiques addresses one set of dominant/dominated power relations articulated and reproduced within scientific knowledge, reflecting the unequal power relations in the social world;

the critiques thus undermine the scientific legitimation of those dominant/dominated relations. In this view, scientific knowledge is a synthesis and reflection of dominant/dominated relations in the "natural"(human) world. The idea of a pure knowing mind outside history is simply an epistemological conceit (Fee, 1986).

The method by which a society relates the possession of knowledge and expertise to sanctioned social roles can provide justification for enormous inequalities within the society. The exclusion of certain ideologies from the sanctioned information creation process has the effect of validating the experience of certain individuals and invalidating the experience of others.

According to Warren (1963), each society must provide for five essential social functions: (1) production, distribution, consumption, (2) socialization, (3) social control, (4) social participation, and (5) mutual support. The ability of any individual or group to benefit from, or participate in, any of these functions depends upon the validation, by society, of the knowledge and expertise possessed by the individual or group. Inequity is created and perpetuated when certain experiences are recognized as resulting in the possession of knowledge and other experiences are excluded from the possibility of generating knowledge. This crucial inequity holds the entire society hostage to the dominant ideologies and the institutions empowered by those ideologies.

The cross cultural model of healing described by Brown (1991) considers three variables in the cultural constructions of illness. The three variables identified are: (1) conceptions of illness, (2) methods of assessment or diagnosis, and (3) role and function of the healer (Brown, 1991). Conceptions of illness in different cultures can be described as related to: (1) disturbance of the ethical ecological order, (2) disturbances of the social order, (3) normal condition of everyday life, (4) disturbance of normal development and regulation, and (5) disturbance of normal function (Brown, 1991).

American and western ideologies of individualism and objectivity have supported only conceptions (4) and (5) listed above. Our society's current inability to validate alternate conceptions of illness, diagnosis, and healing prevents persons with differing cultural (or personal) constructions of reality from pursuing healing interventions that reconcile the person to his or her conception of health.

Understanding Similarity and Self-Help

A visit to almost any bookstore can demonstrate the growing importance of a healing paradigm known generally as "self-help." The concept of self-help can refer to individuals using their own knowledge and experience to solve their problems. Self-help can also refer to groups of persons who share a particular problem using their collective knowledge and experience to help themselves and other members of groups. Self-help groups generally focus on a common problem (implicitly or explicitly defined by someone).

The role and function of self-help in psychiatric rehabilitation is explored in some depth elsewhere in this volume. It is important to keep in mind that cultural dynamics are an essential mechanism of the interaction of the individual and the self-help group. The defined "problem" implies a similarity for members of the group, but as I hope we have all discovered, we are much more complex than a single problem, however defined. We are diverse. We are all the same, we are all different. We are members of many groups, and as members of different groups we experience even similar or common problems differently.

The challenge of diversity is to begin to recognize, respect and value these differences and the knowledge represented by our different experiences. As consumer-survivors we are just as vulnerable as formal help organizations to being blinded by our own unquestioned assumptions and biases. Many of us have been told that we were, or are, out of touch with reality. Can we afford not to question every belief, value, perception and construct, no matter how cherished, in our endeavor to help ourselves? Can we afford not to give serious consideration to other's beliefs, values, perceptions and constructs, no matter how alien, in our endeavor to help each other?

Our experience of having our beliefs, perceptions and constructs invalidated should give us some advantage in dealing with the complex issue of diversity. We are all the same, we are all different. We all need to be a part of groups in which we are valued. We all need to be a part of groups in which we can participate, and hopefully through which we can affect the events which will impact our lives.

Any concept of healing or rehabilitation that does not enhance our ability to meaningfully participate in all the groups of which we are a part is failing us. Efforts at rehabilitation must begin to recognize the diversity of all the groups of which we are members. We separate ourselves and are separated into distinct groups to heal the problem that is the focus of our similarity. We must at the same time engage and embrace the diverse experiences of our members, who have identities as parts of other groups, in which they hurt and heal. We are all the same, we are all different. We are similar, we are diverse. Similarity, diversity, separation, unity. The beautiful and complex dance of diversity is the same dance as the dance of life and of mind by which we individually and collectively experience life.

Creating User Friendly Healing Systems

Just as individuals with a common problem can come together for the common purpose of helping themselves, our society has evolved more formal groups that exist (at least in theory) for the purpose of helping persons to have ability again (rehabilitate). These groups usually exist as formally defined organizations and institutions. These organizations enjoy the sanction of society in pursuing their mission. Providers, administrators, and support staff are parts of (roles within) these organizations. Customers or consumers of an organization's efforts are also vital participants in an organization's functioning and survival. The issue of whether the customer or consumer is inside or outside the organization is a distinction that depends on the cultural assumptions and common understandings of group members.

One representation of an organization is reflected in how that organization participates in transforming the environment. The idea of organizations emerges from the background of human history and work. There are certain other attributes that are conventionally taken to be essential qualities of an organization.

Bernard (1938) itemized three elements of an organization: (1) communication, (2) willingness to serve, and (3) a common purpose. Cooperative systems require a purpose that is generally accepted by the members of the organization. One must know what the purpose is before it can be accepted...the organizational purpose is distinct from individual motives, but the two are closely linked and necessarily reinforcing if satisfaction on the part of the individual and the organization is to result (Grundstein, 1981). However, Bernard added another important element to the organizational purpose. He believed the purpose is essential to add meaning to the environment. If an organization's environment is to make sense, it must be looked at from some perspective (Duncan, 1989 p. 117-118).

As organizations work at transforming environment, organizational purpose and goals become essential for the coordination of the activities of individual departments, units or persons. Internal integration is achieved and maintained by communication and the creation of a common understanding and alignment of purpose. To the extent that there exists a common understanding of the mutuality of individual and organizational goals, the attainment of organizational goals will provide reinforcement for individual activities.

Are issues of diversity relevant to creating an effective common understanding of organization goals? Are issues of diversity relevant to creating an effective and meaningful perspective of the organization's environment? Are issues of diversity relevant to creating an effective common understanding of what it means to have ability again? Are issues of diversity relevant to creating an effective understanding of who has ability and who does not?

It would seem that formally sanctioned institutions and organizations within our society might be more burdened by ideological biases that reflect the experience and learning of narrow select groups. Organizational assumptions regarding the distinction between physical and social reality, assumptions about human nature, the nature of human activity, and the nature of human relationships are particularly relevant to organizations operating in the area of human and public service and care.

Shared assumptions about mission, strategy, means, and goals, as well as assumptions about criteria for measuring results, will be profoundly affected by members' views of reality, human nature, human activity, and human relations. These assumptions will also inform the way in which demands and resources will be directed to systems within the organizations and systems in the environment. The culture of a group reflects the shared learning of the group. The group culture evolves in relation to the two sets of problems that any group must solve.

All group and organizational theories distinguish two major sets of problems that all groups, no matter what their size, must deal with: (1) survival, growth, and adaption in their environment and (2) internal integration that permits daily functioning and the ability to adapt (Schein, 1992 p. 11.).

One important construct that is essential to an effective shared self image of an organization has to do with the distinction of the organization from the environment. This distinction is of particular significance for public or non-profit organizations operating for the benefit of the community.

Concepts of organizational boundaries affect the development of assumptions regarding internal integration of the group (organizational participants). Organizational concepts regarding boundaries also frame questions and decisions regarding demands of environmental adaption.

The internal integration and external adaption issues are thus interdependent. The environment sets limits on what the organization can do, but within those limits not all solutions will work equally well. Feasible solutions are also limited by the characteristics of the members of the group (Schein, 1992 p. 93).

Who has ability? Who needs to have ability again? Who are members of the group (organization)? Who are part of the organization? Who are participants? Who has power? Who benefits from the organization's existence? How do participants benefit? How can the optimal alignment of individual and group motives be achieved? If the purpose of the organization is to return ability to the disabled, what is the role of the disabled in participating with the organization? Are the disabled participants in this endeavor part of the environment that is known and acted upon, or are the disabled knowers that act by their participation? If there is a group with a common purpose how are effective boundaries drawn?

The alignment of the needs of individual participants in organization with the goals of the organization require structures that allow the organization to respond to individual participants. Wages and pay are basic ways in which the organization responds to participants needs. It is also important to recognize that the organization is a significant social system in the life of the participant. As Duncan reports of Roethlisberger's finding at Hawthorne:

people are motivated more by sentiments than by money and that groups influence the behavior of individuals in such significant ways as to make it essential that managers recognize that business firms are more than mere economic institutions—they are social organizations composed of human beings and should be managed accordingly (Duncan, 1988 p.161).

Structuring responses of an organization to the activities of the participants depends on: (1) how individual activity contributes to the achievement of
the organizational goals; (2) what are the needs and desires of the participants;
and, (3) what means are available to the organization to respond to participants needs and desires.

Issues of boundaries, diversity, and inclusion are important for formal
rehabilitation organizations precisely because these groups have socially sanctioned access to the economic and social opportunities important to becoming
"able again." Organizational behavior has all the complexity of human behavior, and alignment of organizational purpose and individual need must involve
attending to all participants' need for growth, relatedness, self-actualization,
achievement, and expectancy.

This view conceives of the rehabilitation organization as a kind of self-
help group. All participants have individual needs. All participants have knowledge based on individual experience. All have ability. All are involved in
creating a common understanding of mission, goals, vision, strategies, and criteria for measuring success.

Shared assumptions concerning these important factors will ultimately
determine how the organization conceives itself, and how it conceives the
boundary between the organization and its environment. These assumptions
will also inform the way in which demands and resources will be directed to
systems within the organizations and systems in the environment.

The human family is beginning to understand the important role of biological diversity in the survival of individual species and entire ecosystems.
Diversity in living systems allows those systems to adapt and survive changes
in the physical environment. We now live in a rapidly changing social, economic, and physical environment. Our cultural diversity represents a vast resource of often untapped knowledge about adapting to and surviving change.
The survivors of any holocaust possess valuable knowledge about political institutions. Survivors of less than effective social systems possess valuable knowledge about our social institutions.

If we are to survive as individuals, or as a society, we must begin to embrace diversity in order to benefit from the diverse cultural learning that is our
human heritage. If we are to survive as groups, families, neighborhoods, or
organizations we must also embrace the vast diversity that is our current environment. We hear that communication and transportation technology are
shrinking our world. But as the world seems to shrink in terms of time and
space, it is expanding in terms of the diverse assumptions, beliefs, and values
with which we are in contact.

For humans, learning has been essential to adapting and surviving. At
the very least we can expand our methods of creating and evaluating information to legitimize and use the knowledge possessed by the diversity with which
we are now in contact. Groups, organizations, institutions can revisit assumptions regarding purpose, boundaries, roles, and activities. When we are a group
with a common purpose, we can attend to creating and evaluating information

regarding roles as well as activities that allow individuals to participate and identify with the group or organization through being a part of the group, as well as through acting for, or being acted upon, by the group.

The dance of diversity is a dance of complementarity. We are diverse. We are similar. There is no escape. If we would be "E Pluribus Unum," out of many one, then we must also be "E Unus Plurimum," out of one many.

References

Brown, D. (Speaker). (1991). *Theory And practice of cross-cultural counseling* (Cassette Recording No. ICC-03). Washington DC: International Counseling Center Cross Cultural Conference.

Campbell, R. (1985). *Fisher's guide: A systems approach to creativity and organization.* Boston, MA & New York, NY: Shambala.

Duncan, J. (1989). *Great ideas in management,* San Francisco, CA: Jossey-Bass Publishing.

Fee, E.(1986). Critiques of modern science: The relationship of feminism to other radical epistomologies. In Bleier, R. (Ed), *Feminist approaches to science.* New York, NY: Pergamon Press.

Groliers Academic American Encyclopedia (1992). Grolier Electronic Publishers, Inc.

Jung, C.G. (1969). *The structure and dynamics of the psyche, Volume 8 Collected works,* translated by R.F.C. Hull. Princeton, NJ: Princeton University Press.

Schein, E.H. (1992). Organizational culture and leadership. San Francisco, CA: Jossey-Bass Publishing.

Warren, R. (1963) *The community in America.* Chicago, IL: Rand McNally.

David A. Granger, M.S.S.A. is currently employed as manager of evaluation and quality outcome monitoring for the Cuyahoga County Community Mental Health Board, past president and board member of the National Mental Health Consumers Association, board member for the Ohio Multiethnic Mental Health Consortium and founding co-convener of The American Association of People of Color Mental Health Consumers.

Chapter 45
Evaluating Peer Providers

H. Stephen Leff
Jean Campbell
Cheryl Gagne
Lawrence S. Woocher

> *"Nothing about me, without me."*
>
> — South African disability movement slogan

The growing tide of health consumerism, which is rooted in legal issues (malpractice litigation and consumer rights protections) and total quality management (TQM, with its focus on customer satisfaction), has compelled the healthcare field to grapple with the need to be customer-driven. As opposed to the traditional view that "the expert knows best," consumerism is based on the assumption that principles of good healthcare must reflect consumer understandings, values, and desires. In the field of mental health, consumerism also holds that peer providers[1] (i.e., providers who have been labeled with a severe psychiatric illness and have received services), will translate consumer perspectives into systems of care that are more effective for service recipients, i.e., consistent with recipient understandings (Blanch, 1992).

It is to the issue of evaluating peer providers that we now turn. We define evaluation as activities, grounded in social and behavioral science methods, to judge interventions and outcomes and to determine the relationship between the two for the purposes of establishing, maintaining or improving the quality, effectiveness and efficiency of services (Rossi & Freeman, 1993). In this paper, we suggest that future evaluations of peer providers should couple traditional evaluation methods with participatory approaches to evaluation that include peer providers and the consumers they serve in the evaluation process. There has already been substantial interest and involvement of consumer-survivors in evaluation and research and their presence has proven to make evaluations more meaningful, useful for improving service delivery, and scientifically convincing (Campbell, Ralph, & Glover, 1993; Tanzman, 1993; Campbell & Schraiber, 1989; Fricks, 1995). Using this approach, we believe, will also result in evaluations that empower peer providers and consumers, and overcome peer provider and consumer resistance to evaluation. The remainder of this chapter is divided into two parts. In the first we discuss a *desired evaluation process*, combining participatory approaches and traditional

---

[1] We believe the term "peer provider" is the most accurate description and carries little or no stigmatizing effect. It is understood that this term may be used synonymously with "consumer provider," "service provider," and others.

evaluation methods. In the second, we present a *conceptual model of evaluation content* for guiding future study of the effectiveness of peer providers. The most successful evaluations use conceptual models to identify important variables to study so that significant influences on program effectiveness are not overlooked (Brekke, 1987). In describing this model, we also present some studies from relevant evaluation literature to support how constructs in the model could be operationalized and to suggest useful starting points for future evaluation research on consumer-provider initiatives.

Participatory Approaches to Evaluation

Advocates of peer-provided services believe that peer providers and consumers have a "first-hand" or "insider's" understanding of the expectations that recipients have of services and the ways in which traditional providers meet and fail to meet these expectations. Likewise, evaluation research with peer provider participation takes advantage of this unique understanding to increase the meaningfulness and usefulness of investigations. Utilizing a participatory process can reach beyond traditional research and evaluation which has often ignored the perspective of the service recipients or the peer providers because their definitions of the experience of mental illness are missing from the general culture. For example, much of the existing research in the field of mental health reflects a "blaming the victim" ideology. Problems are defined as person-centered and studies are done to measure deficits. Consequently, only one version of a set of events has been studied. This alienates consumers by disregarding their experiences and viewing them as the problem rather than suggesting that problems encountered by people with psychiatric diagnoses are social phenomena. Therefore, the perspectives of the mental health consumers and the expertise of mental health consumer-survivor researchers must be proactively sought out rather than ignored or silenced in the conduct of scientific inquiry because the inclusion of their voices enriches and validates the process of evaluation itself (Consumer-Survivor Mental Health Research and Policy Work Group, 1993; Rogers & Palmer-Erbs, 1994).

We believe that involving consumers in evaluations will empower their perspective and amplify their voices. This will strengthen the validity of our evaluations since the voices of consumers deserve amplification. Furthermore, for many traditionally disempowered groups, a grassroots-based, scholarly articulation of the value of "native" knowledge and practice has served to improve their quality of life and illuminate issues of social science. Its methods utilize a more participatory style of research where the groups being studied are consulted at every stage of the process, and assisted and encouraged to carry out research and evaluation themselves. Participatory research supports a coherent and mutually supportive pattern of concepts, values, methods, and actions that has wide applications.

Participatory approaches can also foster cooperation with evaluations, particularly those which are externally mandated, by addressing the most common reasons why peer providers and consumers might be reluctant to cooperate. In some cases, peer providers and consumers may associate feelings of powerlessness with evaluations if they had previously been treated as "objects." Participatory approaches to evaluations should share control of the evaluation process with peer providers and consumers by means of steering committees and more direct involvement. Peer providers and consumers may disagree with the outcomes proposed for measurement. They may believe, for example, that services should be evaluated in terms of their impact on empowerment when others have elected to measure functional change. Participatory approaches should enable peer providers and consumers to incorporate evaluation measures that reflect their understandings and values. Peer providers and consumers may also fail to see the need for adhering to time consuming and tedious protocols. The reasons for these protocols should be explained and reviewed in the participatory process. Finally, peer providers and consumers may feel that evaluations drain scarce resources from direct care. A participatory process should consider how resources allocated to evaluation can be used to improve services. It should be noted that the concerns of peer providers and consumers are often the concerns of other, non-evaluator stakeholders in mental health systems. These concerns may be particularly pronounced among persons in the organizations that employ peer providers, since persons in these organizations, whether traditional mental health agencies, consumer initiatives, self-help programs, or consumer-controlled alternatives, are likely to be particularly sensitive to the alienating aspects of traditional evaluations.

In recommending participatory approaches to evaluation, we believe we are subscribing to a process that has already demonstrated its worth. The last decade has witnessed the blossoming of a vibrant consumer-survivor research and evaluation agenda and the growing belief that consumer involvement in evaluation holds great promise for both system reform and continuous quality improvement of services (Campbell, Ralph, & Glover, 1993). As a result, new questions, methods and ways of interpreting data have emerged in the margins of traditional services research. Consumers are now participating in growing numbers in research and evaluation (Campbell, Ralph, & Glover, 1993) and have led recent efforts to determine needs and preferences for services and supports (Tanzman, 1993), to define outcome measures (Campbell & Schraiber, 1989; Consumer/Survivor Mental Health Research and Policy Work Group, 1992; Trochim, Dumont, & Campbell, 1993), and to develop and conduct consumer satisfaction assessments (Fricks, 1995).

More specifically, participatory models have the capacity to critically examine the context in which evaluation occurs to assure that it reflects the processes and outcomes of services as consumers know them. Such evaluation can go beyond statistics that record numbers of service recipients to include the meaningful interactions of those living with a psychiatric diagnosis. It can flesh out descriptions of gendered and racial experiences rather than just analyzing variables of sex and race. It can examine not only the differences between peer providers and those professionals without a diagnosis, but can explore what it means to be a person with mental illness working or receiving services within a program or agency.

The role of professional evaluator under a participatory approach is one of educator, consultant, learner and mediator (Rogers & Palmer-Erbs, 1994). It is the function of the professional evaluator to educate the evaluation team about methods, data collection and data analysis. The professional evaluator, in turn, learns about the "local culture" from other members of the team. Elden and Levin (1991) describe the role of the evaluator as a "colearner" rather than that of the "expert in charge" and state that it is critical that the evaluator must know how and when to step aside and allow the participatory evaluation team to take charge of its own investigation.

The major hypothesis of participatory models is that "insiders" have ready access to information that outside professional evaluators can only access with great difficulty if at all. The involvement of insiders in combination with the overall inclusion of many stakeholder groups is likely to improve the accuracy of the evaluation's depiction of the organization, the service delivery system, and a broad range of outcomes. Thus, not only does a participatory approach lend a voice to traditionally muted groups, but it provides the means for a more comprehensive, meaningful, and accurate evaluation of peer provided services.

The process of a participatory evaluation is also powerful in its potential to develop collaborative relationships between mental health consumers (including peer providers) and mental health service providers that extend beyond the evaluation effort. The dialogue necessary to cooperatively undertake an evaluation project has the potential to foster relationships between team members and contribute to future success in working together.

It is important to note that we do not consider participatory approaches as alternatives to existing evaluation methods, but rather as a means of enhancing evaluation methods through the participation of underrepresented individuals. Combining inclusive approaches with experiments, quasi-experiments and qualitative methods (Campbell & Stanley, 1966; Miles & Huberman, 1994) has the potential to result in evaluations that are meaningful and empowering as well as scientifically convincing. Traditional evaluation can be construed as a process in which evaluators educate each other as to theoretical, methodological, and utilization options and negotiate the trade-offs required by resource constraints and other practical limitations (e.g., the amount of time persons will set aside for interviews, the time administrators have to "process" evaluation results). In this construction of the evaluation process, participatory approaches highlight the importance of including a wide range of stakeholders in the process and devoting the time and resources necessary to allow for mutual education and negotiation (Rogers & Palmer-Erbs, 1994). It seems to us, that there is nothing inherent in such a more inclusive evaluation process that necessarily compromises the scientific validity of evaluation designs. We assume that such processes will consider the merits and feasibility of relevant design options. We further assume that design compromises will be made, as they usually must be, because of resource and other practical constraints (Campbell & Stanley, 1966), rather than due solely to stakeholder inclusion.

Obstacles to, and Resource Requirements for, Evaluations Combining Participatory Approaches and Traditional Evaluation Methods

It should be emphasized that to gain the benefits of participatory approaches coupled with more traditional methods requires overcoming some professional obstacles as well as investing significant resources. Consumer participation in evaluation, alone, does not necessarily guarantee success. Without constructive ways for dialogue to occur and shared decision-making to take place, participatory methods can reinforce a kind of turf war over controlling human beings. Legitimate decision-making power and the power to impact the policies and practices of the agencies they evaluate is essential to the success of consumer evaluators.

Important factors such as remuneration and other resource requirements also need to be addressed. Including a variety of stakeholders will almost certainly require additional resources (Rogers & Palmer-Erbs, 1994). Capturing more diverse perspectives can require more data collection and will likely mean more honoraria, consulting fees, and travel expenses than might be the case in a more traditional evaluation. Adequate pay and reimbursement of expenses for peer providers and consumers participating in evaluation is essential for trust, cooperation, and sustained commitment. Mowbray, Chamberlain, Jennings, and Reed (1988) conclude that consumer turnover for volunteer work in a peer-support project could be attributed to the fact that they were not paid.

Stigmatizing attitudes of some professionals working in the mental health field present another challenge to consumer participation in evaluation (Reidy, 1993). Professionals are often unwilling to give up power and control they have traditionally possessed, and consumers may hesitate to express their ideas (Curtis, 1993). Lord (1989) observes that the combination of traditional professional power and control, and consumer vulnerability, can stand in the way of true partnership. Other factors that cross-cut the preceding observations arise from the "anynee, menee, mynee, moe" approach by professionals that assumes any and all consumers are the same and will offer the same skills and experiences to evaluation. They consider "the consumer perspective" a homogeneous knowledge set without deference to skills, scholarship, or cultural diversity. This form of tokenism sets consumers up for failure to provide meaningful input at all levels of involvement.

Finally, as in any internal evaluation, the involvement of peer providers and consumers from within an agency poses problems of objectivity, coercion, privacy, and confidentiality. Considerable attention should be given to minimizing bias and coercion and maximizing privacy and confidentiality through careful training. In the consent process, persons being studied should be informed that their peers and/or caregivers will be involved in the conduct of an evaluation. Threats of bias or violations of confidentiality and privacy are more easily minimized if "outside" data collectors are used. Given this, we recommend that outside persons be used to collect data. The knowledge that insiders have can be incorporated into the data collection instruments and the training of data collectors. If the experience of being a consumer or a peer provider is deemed crucial to the data collection, consumers or peer providers might be recruited from organizations other than the one being evaluated. In those cases where this is not possible, we recommend careful training of internal data collectors that explicitly instructs persons how to avoid interjecting their biases into the data collection process. We also recommend a validation strategy in which external data collectors obtain data from a random sample of persons seen by inside collectors to estimate the degree and direction of any differences in data obtained by insiders and outsiders. If such differences are found, it may not be clear whether they reflect bias or differential disclosure to the two types of data collectors. However, the differences found can be reported so that evaluation users can take account of these findings in interpreting evaluation results.

Having discussed a suggested evaluation process, we now turn our attention to the content of evaluations of peer provided services. The development and explication of a conceptual model of peer provided services and the variables which influence process and outcomes should serve as a guide for future evaluation questions. A review of the literature to date will further provide a basis for evaluation questions posed in future studies.

Towards a Conceptual Model for Evaluating Peer Providers

To fully understand and evaluate peer providers, a conceptual model of how peer providers impact on the process of service delivery and outcomes is necessary. This model should describe the different types of outcomes peer providers might affect and the variables that might mediate these impacts. At this time we can present only a very preliminary version of such a model and data from only a small number of evaluations. Future evaluations and additional conceptualization, ideally involving participatory action approaches, will be necessary for model testing and elaboration.

The model we propose is presented in Figure 1. This model postulates that characteristics of providers influence the service delivery process, which in turn, influences outcomes for recipients, peer providers, organizations/agencies, and systems. It further postulates that the service delivery process is also influenced by program, agency, and system variables. Below, we discuss the specific components of the model and review evaluation literature vis a vis the extent to which it addresses these components. While Lovell, Stastny, and Katz (1992) and Kaufmann, Ward-Colasante, and Farmer (1993) used collaborative, consumer-oriented approaches reflecting the principles of stakeholder inclusion, the remaining studies reviewed did not appear to involve participatory approaches.

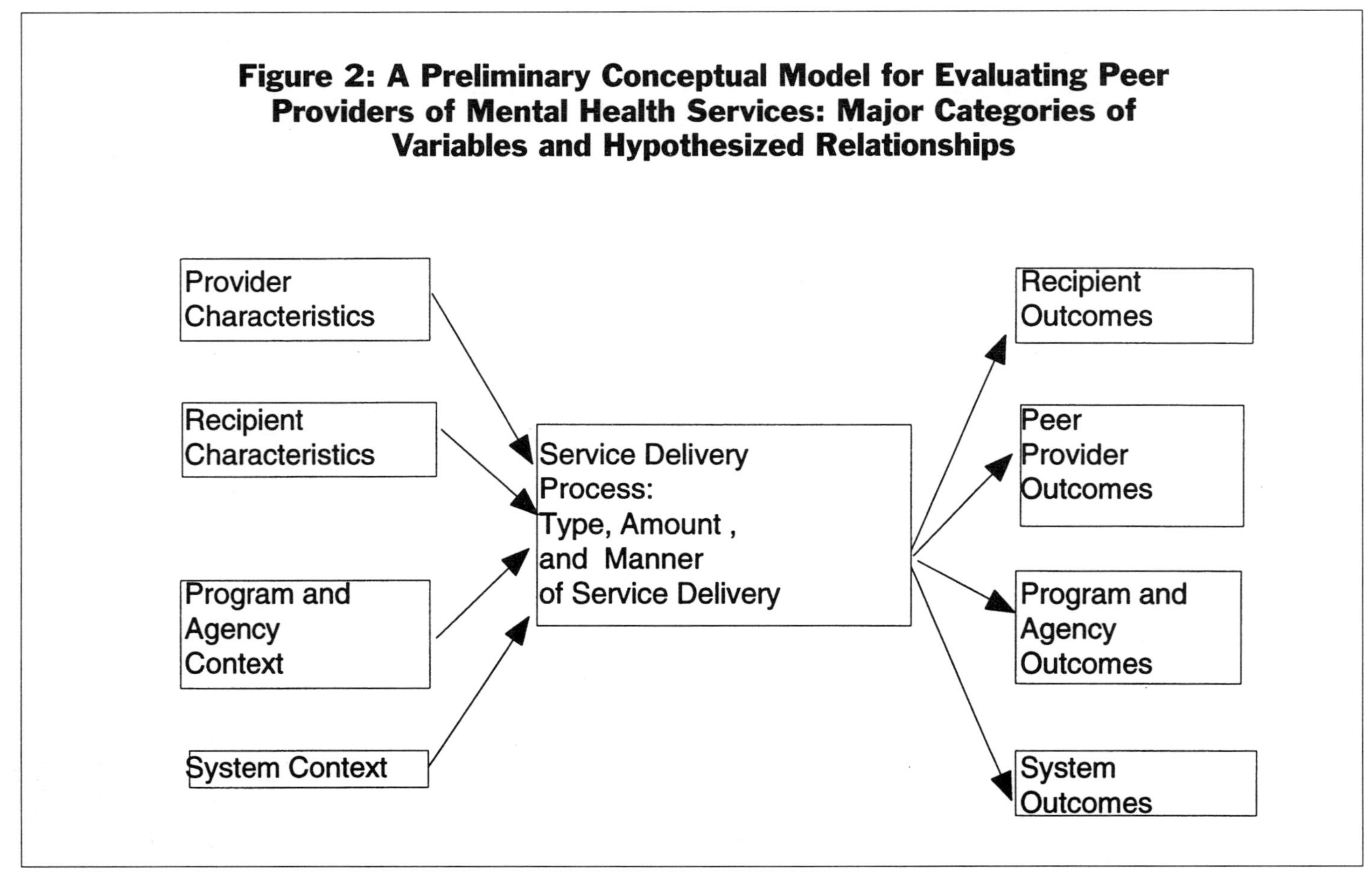

Figure 2: A Preliminary Conceptual Model for Evaluating Peer Providers of Mental Health Services: Major Categories of Variables and Hypothesized Relationships
Provider Characteristics
Recipient Characteristics
Program and Agency Context
System Context
Service Delivery Process: Type, Amount , and Manner of Service Delivery
Recipient Outcomes
Peer Provider Outcomes
Program and Agency Outcomes
System Outcomes

Provider Characteristics

Provider characteristics refer both to whether a provider is a consumer-survivor as well as sociodemographic and clinical characteristics on which providers might vary. We conceptualize these characteristics as independent variables. The impact of any type of provider might be influenced by other variables such as their age, gender, training, and experience. In the case of peer providers, where an insider's knowledge of mental illness is postulated to be important, the particular diagnoses, treatments, and treatment settings peer providers have experienced may affect their impacts. In the materials we reviewed, sociodemographic variables explicitly studied included sex, race, employment status, benefits (Sherman & Porter, 1991), age, education, and marital status (Solomon & Draine, 1995). Clinical variables included in evaluations were DSM III-R diagnosis, physical disability (Sherman & Porter, 1991), and number of psychiatric hospitalizations (Solomon & Draine, 1995).

Recipient Characteristics

Recipient characteristics describe the population being served. Variation in recipient characteristics can have a pronounced influence on how types of providers will affect service delivery and outcomes. Typical measures of recipient characteristics include age, sex, race, psychiatric diagnosis, level of functioning, and marital status. The literature reviewed examines a wide range of recipient characteristics including homelessness, living arrangement, drug and alcohol use, attitudes towards medication compliance (Solomon & Draine, 1995), benefits received (SSI and/or Medicaid), duration of disability (Heine, Hasemann, Mangine, Dearborn-Morris, & Royse, 1993), and employment status (Felton, 1992). An example of the utility of recipient characteristic data is provided by Mowbray, Wellwood, and Chamberlain (1988) who used an analysis of recipient demographics and global assessment scores (GAS) to conclude that the population studied was very similar to a population from a psychiatric inpatient unit. This enabled the researchers to infer with some confidence that the peer-provided service was effectively preventing hospitalizations in a population at-risk.

Program and Agency Context

Program and agency context refers to the nature of the programs and agencies in which providers work. As an example, programs may be classified into mental health agencies, consumer initiatives, self help programs, and consumer-controlled initiatives. We assume that provider functions, roles, and effects are influenced by the type of program or agency in which the provider is employed. For example, it is likely that the roles that peer providers play in agencies may differ with differing types and amounts of training prior to service provision. The effects of peer providers on professional providers should also be different when both types of providers are employed by the same agency. Additional questions can be raised about the differences in peer provider roles and functioning in programs that receive public funds as opposed to ones that are financially independent. Finally, programs and agencies may differ in the degree to which they are stigmatizing and present barriers to peer provider effectiveness, or provide training and other support. The literature we reviewed indicates that peer providers have worked in several types of agencies and organizations. Traditional mental health service agencies like state departments of mental health (Sherman & Porter, 1991), as well as consumer-controlled alternatives such as consumer-run advocacy and service agencies (Solomon, Draine, & Delaney, 1995), self-help groups, drop-in centers (Kaufmann et. al., 1993; Mowbray, Chamberlain, et al., 1988), and consumer owned and operated businesses (Mowbray, Chamberlain, et al., 1988) have utilized service recipients as providers of mental health services.

System Context

System context refers to the nature of the system in which the particular agency or program exists. For example, a program may be in the public mental health system, the private mental health system, part of a managed care network, or in the more general social service system. We would also expect that peer providers and their programs will function differently and have different impacts depending on wider system characteristics. For example, the roles of peers may vary as a function of the degree to which systems use hospitalization. In systems that use relatively more hospitalization, peer providers may play more of an advocacy role, whereas in ones that use less, peer providers may engage in more community support activities. The foregoing example involving advocacy highlights how peer providers might have impacts on systems as well as service recipients and programs. System context is largely absent in the literature that was reviewed. However, we believe it remains an important variable to consider when evaluating peer provider service programs.

Program and system variables can be independent variables when the dependent variables are peer provider roles and functioning. They can be mediating variables when the independent variables are peer provider roles and functioning and the dependent variables are service recipient, program related, or system related outcomes. It will be the rare evaluation that can systematically vary program or system context. However, we recommend that in all cases evaluations provide detailed descriptions of program and system contexts so that their impacts can be considered as evaluation studies accumulate.

Service Delivery Process: Type, Amount, Cost and Manner of Service Delivery

By process variables we mean variables related to the types of service delivered, the amounts of service, or the manner of service delivery. These variables are most often treated as mediating or as dependent variables. Studying these variables may elucidate the most efficacious and efficient way in which peer provided services can translate into positive outcomes. Examples of specific process variables in the literature reviewed include community resources used, units of service provided, in vivo versus office based services (Solomon & Draine, 1995), particular service activities and percent of time devoted to them (Mowbray, Wellwood, & Chamberlain, 1988), and pounds of food distributed by a consumer-run food bank (Lovell et al., 1992).

Recipient Outcomes

Recipient outcomes refer to the impact of service on the service recipients. These are critical measures in the evaluation of peer provider service programs. Recipient outcomes can include a wide range of variables such as level of functioning, quality of life, and empowerment. It should be noted that empowerment may refer to gaining power within the traditional mental health system as well as power to seek alternatives outside of it (McLean, 1995). Recipient outcomes studied in the literature reviewed were quality of life (Felton, 1992; Heine et al., 1993), income, social network size, interpersonal contact, satisfaction with the mental health system (Solomon & Draine, 1995), and working alliance (Solomon et al., 1995). There is evidence to suggest that positive effects were experienced when consumer-survivors were employed as providers in the recipient outcomes studies reviewed. In one of the few true experimental designs in the literature, Solomon and Draine (1995) report the results of a two-year outcome study using a randomized trial to compare a consumer case management team with a non-consumer team. Data from this study indicate that case management services delivered by consumers were as effective as those provided by non-consumers. Several other studies support the association of peer providers in case management roles with positive outcomes. Felton (1992) and Stastny et al. (1992) present both quantitative and qualitative evidence that peer providers acting as "peer specialists" on an intensive case management team were associated with beneficial client outcomes. The outcome measures in this evaluation included quality of life, social networks, self-esteem, mastery, psychiatric symptomatology, optimism about recovery, and program engagement (Felton, 1992). In addition to case management roles, studies indicate that peer providers were associated with positive outcomes in various service provider roles. Heine et al. (1993) report positive recipient outcomes as measured by symptom severity and quality of life when peer providers were part of a crisis response team. Service recipients also had positive attitudes towards peer counselors in hospitals as measured by a questionnaire assessing attitudes toward the project (McGill & Patterson, 1990). In addition, the use of peer providers in various social support roles was also associated with positive outcomes as measured by client re-hospitalizations (Mowbray, Chamberlain, et al., 1988).

Peer Provider Outcomes

Peer provider outcomes refer to the impact that taking on the role of service provider has on peer providers themselves. Peer provider outcome variables may include empowerment, employment success, job satisfaction, level of functioning, and role strain (Zander, Cohen, & Statland, 1957). The literature reviewed reports evidence for positive peer provider outcomes. McGill and Patterson (1990) report that consumer/survivors who served as peer counselors for hospitalized persons identified increased self-confidence, heightened empathy, and feelings of usefulness and responsibility after serving in the program. In a study of persons with mental illness serving as case management aides, Sherman and Porter (1991) report that a majority of peer providers successfully completed training and reported positive employment experiences. The study also suggests that peer provider roles may have a direct ameliorative effect on peer providers' mental health. The fifteen peer providers who were continuously employed as case management aides required only a combined two bed-days of psychiatric hospitalization over the course of more than two years.

Program and Agency Outcomes

Program and agency outcomes refer to the changes which may take place in a program or agency during the course of a peer-provided service. Programs may grow, downsize, or change form in some other way. These outcomes are one way to measure the impact of a particular service delivery program. Ways of measuring program and agency outcomes found in the literature include tracking number of clients served (Mowbray, Wellwood, & Chamberlain, 1988), number of peer providers employed or volunteering (Lovell et al., 1992), and continuation of public funding (Mowbray, Chamberlain, et al., 1988) The literature reviewed indicate that program and agency outcomes tend to support peer provider programs. A number of studies examined temporary or pilot peer provider programs, which, due to their success were extended and/or expanded by the sponsoring organizations (Sherman & Porter, 1991; Mowbray, Chamberlain, et al., 1988). There is also qualitative evidence which suggests that programs employing peer providers have become more respected in the mental health community or accepted as viable alternatives to traditional mental health service provision (Nikkel, Smith, & Edwards, 1992; Sherman & Porter, 1991; McGill & Patterson, 1990). In one dissenting report, McLean (1995) documents the failure of a peer provider project which she attributes to an organizational focus on advocacy and neglect of direct support.

System Outcomes

System outcomes refer to the effects which peer provider service delivery have on the system in which the agency or program functions. These types of measures may include a shift towards partnership between professionals and peer providers on case management teams, expansion of public funding for self-help groups and independently operated support groups, and greater emphasis on community based programs. The literature reviewed for the most part lacks data on system outcomes. There are some qualitative reports of an increasing acceptance of peer providers in the traditional mental health system (Sherman & Porter, 1991). Peer provider programs may have far-reaching effects and so system outcomes should not be neglected in future evaluations.

Summary and Conclusions

In this chapter, we recommend that evaluations of peer providers employ a strategy combining participatory action research with traditional evaluation methods. We believe this will overcome obstacles to evaluation and will make evaluations more meaningful and empowering. However, partnership with consumers and consumer organizations is only a first step. Participatory evaluation which begins to involve peers in meaningful roles is a prerequisite for more empowering research and service provision relationships in the sense that traditional mental health professionals can learn from consumers and vice-versa. Simply increasing participation and involvement will never by itself empower consumer-survivor evaluators or peer providers unless and until peers themselves control some services and evaluations. French (1992) writes, "Disabled people are now being empowered by the disability movement; the question is, can research become part of that empowerment?" (p. 186). It is our hope that additional evaluation research using participatory approaches will help clarify the preliminary conceptual model presented in this chapter and will help make the goals of scientific knowledge, improved services, and consumer empowerment realities.

References

Blanch, A. (1992). *Importance of research on the involvement of consumers in services*. Proceedings of the 3rd Annual NASMHPD Research Institute, Inc. Conference on State Mental Health Agency Services Research.

Brekke, J. (1988). The model-guided method of monitoring program implementation. *Evaluation Review*, 11, 281-300.

Campbell, D.T., and Stanley, J.C. (1966). *Experimental and quasi-experimental designs for research*. Chicago, IL: Rand McNally and Company.

Campbell, J. & Schraiber, R. (1989). *In pursuit of wellness: The well-being project*. Sacramento, CA: The California Department of Mental Health.

Campbell, J., and Ralph, R.O. (1993). From lab rat to researcher: The history, models, and policy implications of consumer/survivor involvement in research. Proceedings of the 4th Annual NASMHPD Research Institute, Inc. Conference on State Mental Health Agency Services Research and Program Evaluation.

Consumer/Survivor Mental Health Research and Policy Work Group (1992). Focus Group Meeting on Client Outcomes. Washington, DC.

Consumer/Survivor Mental Health Research and Policy Work Group. (1993). Consumer/Survivor Recommendations to the Mental Health Research Community.

Curtis, L.C. (1993). Consumers as colleagues: Partnership in the workforce. *In Practice*. Burlington, VT: Center for Community Change through Housing and Support, Institute for Program Development, Trinity College of Vermont.

Elden, M. and Levin, M. (1991). Cogenerative learning: Bringing participation into action research. In W.F. Whyte (Ed.) *Participatory Action Research*. Newbury Park, CA: Sage Publications.

Felton, H. (1992). Peer specialists as members of intensive case management teams: Longitudinal analysis of client outcomes. *Proceedings of the 3rd Annual NASMHPD Research Institute, Inc. Conference on State Mental Health Agency Services Research.*

Fetterman, D.M. (1994). Steps of empowerment evaluation: From California to Cape Town. *Evaluation and Program Planning, 17, 305-313.*

French, S. (1992). Researching disability: The way forward. *Disability and Rehabilitation, 14(4).*

Fricks, L. (1995). *Georgia evaluation and satisfaction team (GEST) handbook.* Atlanta: Georgia Division of Mental Health, Mental Retardation and Substance Abuse.

Heine, R., Hasemann, D., Mangine, S., Dearborn-Morris, E., and Royse, D. (1993). Consumer providers in crisis response systems. *Proceedings of the 4th Annual NASMHPD Research Institute, Inc. Conference on State Mental Health Agency Services Research and Program Evaluation.*

Kaufmann, C.L., Ward-Colasante, C., Farmer, J. (1993). Development and evaluation of drop-in centers operated by mental health consumers. *Hospital and Community Psychiatry, 44, 675-678.*

Lord, J. (1989). The potential of consumer participation: Sources of understanding. *Canada's Mental Health, 37(2).*

Lovell, A., Stastny, P., and Katz, G. (1992). The development of a consumer-run food bank and outreach program. *Proceedings of the 3rd Annual NASMHPD Research Institute, Inc. Conference on State Mental Health Agency Services Research.*

McGill, C.W., & Patterson, C.J. (1990). Former patients as peer counselors on locked psychiatric inpatient units. *Hospital and Community Psychiatry, 41, 1017-1019.*

McLean, A. (1995). Empowerment and the psychiatric consumer/ex-patient movement in the United States: Contradictions, crisis and change. *Social Science and Medicine, 40, 1053-1071.*

Miles, M.B., & Huberman, A.M. (1994). *Qualitative data analysis: An expanded sourcebook.* Thousand Oaks, CA: SAGE Publications, Inc.

Mowbray, C.T., Chamberlain, P., Jennings, M., and Reed, C. (1988). Consumer-run mental health services: Results from five demonstration projects. *Community Mental Health Journal, 24, 151-156.*

Mowbray, C.T., Wellwood, R.. and Chamberlain, P. (1988). Project Stay: A consumer-run support service. *Psychosocial Rehabilitation Journal, 12, 33-42.*

Nikkel, R.E., Smith, G., and Edwards, D. (1992). A consumer-operated case management project. *Hospital and Community Psychiatry, 43, 577-579.*

Reidy, D. (1993). *Stigma is social death: Mental health consumers/survivors talk about stigma in their lives.* (unpublished manuscript).

Rogers, E.S. & Palmer-Erbs, V. (1994). Participatory action research: Implications for research and evaluation in psychiatric rehabilitation. *Psychosocial Rehabilitation Journal*, 18(2), 3-12.

Rossi, P.H., & Freeman, H.E. (1993). *Evaluation: A systematic approach.* Newbury Park, CA: SAGE Publications, Inc.

Sherman, P.S., & Porter, R. (1991). Mental health consumers as case management aides. *Hospital and Community Psychiatry*, 42, 494-498.

Solomon, P., & Draine, J. (1995). The efficacy of a consumer case management team: Two-year outcomes of a randomized trial. *The Journal of Mental Health Administration*, 22, 135-146.

Solomon, P., Draine, J., & Delaney, M.A. (1995). The working alliance and consumer case management. *The Journal of Mental Health Administration*, 22, 126-134.

Stastny, P., Welle, D., Brown, C., Gelman, R., Shern, D., & Blanch, A. (1992). Peer specialists as members of intensive case management teams: Qualitative findings. *Proceedings of the 3rd Annual NASMHPD Research Institute, Inc. Conference on State Mental Health Agency Services Research.*

Tanzman, B. (1993). An overview of mental health consumers' preferences for housing and support services. *Hospital and Community Psychiatry*, 44(5).

Trochim, W., Dumont, J., & Campbell, J. (1993). *A report for the state mental health agency profiling system: Mapping mental health outcomes from the perspective of consumers/survivors.* Alexandria, VA: NASMHPD Research Institute, Inc.

Whyte, W.F. (1989). Advancing scientific knowledge through participatory action research. *Sociological Forum*, 4, 367-385.

Whyte, W.F. (1991). *Participatory action research.* Newbury Park, CA: Sage Publications.

Zander, A., Cohen, A., and Statland, E. (1957). Average attitudes of one professional group toward another. In *Role relations in the mental health professions.* Ann Arbor, MI: Research Center for Group Dynamics, Institute for Social Research. pp.133-141.

Dr. H. Stephen Leff, senior vice president at the Human Services Research Insitute and instructor in psychology at the Harvard Medical School, is director of The Evaluation Center @ HSRI, a program funded by the Center for Mental Health Services to provide evaluation technical assistance.

Dr. Jean Campbell is a consumer researcher at the Missouri Institute of Mental Health in St. Louis. Her work includes defining outcomes valued by service recipients.

Ms. Cheryl Gagne is a research and training associate at the Center for Psychiatric Rehabilitation and a doctoral candidate at Boston University. She is a psychiatric survivor.

Mr. Lawrence Woocher is a research assistant with The Evaluation Center@HSRI. His work has focused on the impact of managed care on persons with mental illness and others.

Section 10

Conclusions

Chapter 46
Consumers as Providers: Themes and Success Factors

Carol T. Mowbray
David P. Moxley

We started this volume with an overview of "where we came from", linking the development of the consumer-provider initiative to consumerism, mental health systems reform, civil rights, the disability movement, and so on. Many of the chapter authors traced the roots of their own programs back to small groups of mental health consumers, federal and state program development initiatives, market forces supporting less costly services, the vision or inspiration of a particular individual, organizational drives to improve efficiency or effectiveness, among other sources.

There are a variety of themes driving the development of these consumer-provider innovations. Their development is not merely the product of efforts by enlightened professionals. Indeed, many of these innovations emerged through the leadership of consumers themselves. The many chapters composing this volume suggest the motivation of consumers and ex-patients to create these service alternatives. Simply put, many mental health systems fail to provide supports and opportunities consumers need or want to improve the quality of their daily lives.

The creation of consumer service provision as an alternative illustrates the important role consumerism plays in the formation of responsive systems of community support; that mental health systems reform can occur through grassroots efforts and through the efforts of users themselves.

The collection of programs, personal accounts, and analyses represented in the chapters of this book present a description of "where we are now." While we make no claim to scientific validity, or the comprehensiveness of our program representation, this collection does include a wide array of geographical locations, program types, and provider roles. The contributors to the book were selected from among abstracts solicited through newsletters of advocacy and professional associations, and through letters to conference presenters, and personal and professional contacts. Thus, we should have some confidence in the veridicality of the representations. The themes represented in this volume are congruent with other literature that has gone before (although we believe our coverage expands upon it in key areas). We now present an editorial perspective on these themes. Following this, we look forward to "where we are going."

Where We Are Now: Themes from Consumers as Providers

The Origin of Consumer Service-Provision
The first major theme that seems to arise across models, geography and program types is that people have developed, sought out, and become involved in consumer-provider services because of dissatisfactions with the existing mental health system of care. These dissatisfactions subsume a number of major experiences reported by consumer-providers and recipients of their services:

(a) Catch 22 or *falling through the cracks*. Complaints voiced include services not being available when needed, not being readily accessible, not appropriate, not flexible or individually tailored. Per Scott's chapter, "if it couldn't be billed, it doesn't need to exist." Even when there are what appear to be appropriate services, clients report finding that they can't meet eligibility requirements.

Recycling through the system can turn into a vicious cycle. Some professionals may see this recycling as normal and indicative of a reality that not all people can be served by a particular system. However, as articulated by several personal accounts, this recycling may be more reflective of system failure as opposed to the failure of selected individuals to fit in.

Consumer service provision, as identified in the early chapters of this book, can represent dissent: People are looking for more sensitive service alternatives when formal systems are not responsive. Obviously, as demonstrated by many of the accounts in this book, dissent results from dissatisfaction and can lead to service innovation.

(b) With or without services, individuals with psychiatric disabilities commonly report lacking motivation and focus, and being *stuck in an illness role*. This circumstance may reflect demoralization or symptoms of the illness; most likely, it also reflects lack of opportunities presented by mental health programs and by society in general for people with mental illness to demonstrate or develop competencies or autonomy.

The absence of opportunities that help people to achieve integration in their communities is a very real threat to the effectiveness of community mental health systems and of community support. The absence of these opportunities suggests that many service systems face consumer relevance issues and if they fail to resolve these, consumers may create their own alternatives within the system or they may take the ultimate step in the expression of dissent by withdrawing from any involvement in formal services.

What is the nature of the opportunities that are lacking? Certainly they are very practical ones that fulfill people's desires for *involvement* and *relatedness* with other people coping with serious mental illness. *Control* of the opportunities may be another important feature. Support opportunities under the control of consumers themselves may foster stronger community than ones under exclusive direction of mental health professionals.

These opportunities, as identified by consumers themselves, help support productivity in everyday life. This may include work, career development, education, or recreation. Simply put, medically and clinically trained professionals may not see the creation of these opportunities as a legitimate function of their roles. Consumer service provision may offer these opportunities to fill existing vacuums created by limitations in professional role performance.

(c) To move out of the illness role, people felt that they needed *supports for rehabilitation.* Instead, they found relationships with mental health professionals to be hierarchical, impersonal, and/or judgmental. Consequently, consumers are afraid to talk openly about their problems and their feelings because this will be seen as further evidence of what's wrong with them, or it will cause other anticipated negative consequences. Thus, their emotional needs either go unmet or are exacerbated through professional relationships. What they need is support from others in order to pursue and follow through on rehabilitation options.

It appears from first person accounts and programmatic descriptions that client-professional relationships are not the preferred form of helping, perhaps because for many, professional services have not been very effective. Serious mental illness, with its significant social consequences, may demand a stronger and more pervasive form of helping. This may explain why many strategies of consumer service provision incorporate a membership model of helping and support. Membership promotes belonging, reciprocity, acceptance, and participation, among other outcomes. Membership offers flexibility in helping roles, loose boundaries between the helper and helpee, and mutual support. Service by professionals with limitations introduced by time, place, and hierarchy simply may not have the capacity to address the depth of need created by the social reaction to serious mental illness.

(d) Finally, consumers report that on their own, or being "treated" by professionals, they *lack knowledge, theory and/or techniques relevant to the recovery process.* They need other consumers to share personal experiences vis a vis their own recovery.

Recovery is receiving considerable attention by progressive rehabilitation systems. The concept of recovery focuses on the subjective experience of consumers themselves and the importance of consumers defining what recovery means in terms of its emotional, psychological, and interpersonal dimensions. The complexity and personal richness of recovery will be lost if left to professionals to define in isolation from consumers.

Consumer service provision may be an essential feature of a support system devoted to recovery. The poet Robert Frost would ask people: "What do you know?" By this he was referring to those life and personal experiences that lead to an in-depth understanding of oneself. Consumers know firsthand about illness, disability, and handicaps and how to cope and how to "spring back." Making this knowledge accessible to other consumers may encourage recovery. Consumer service provision brings consumers together in novel ways of support. These ways can liberate the tacit knowledge that consumers often keep to themselves. The "externalization" of recovery knowledge may be one of the most important outcomes produced by consumer service provision.

Benefits from Consumer Service Provision

The second theme that emerges, which resonates with other literature on consumers as providers, is that there have been substantial benefits experienced from consumer-provider services: for consumer-providers as well as for individual recipients, nonconsumer staff, and for improved services and systems of care.

For *service recipients*, these benefits directly address many of the dissatisfactions over and complaints about traditional services. That is, consumer-provided services, be they through settings outside of, or part of the usual mental health/rehabilitation system, *provide social support and nurturance.* Consumers feel that they are connected to a more supportive network, that fulfills their emotional and social needs, and that provides empathy by having individuals available who better understand their history and their current situation. Having such positive connections can serve as an *early warning system* for interventions; that is, consumers have more frequent contacts with providers who are more accessible and who, therefore, may be more sensitive to symptoms and changes in functioning before crises erupt.

Consumer-provided services also afford more *opportunities for decision-making and choice, and promote more independence.* There are more opportunities for problem-solving because relationships are less hierarchical and because peers offer examples of coping mechanisms and suggest strategies for change. Through other consumers, recipients are provided with more informational assistance; for example, education about their rights, their illness, treatment options, etc. These knowledge and decision-making opportunities can also contribute to promotion of insight and, thus, self-directed steps towards recovery.

In particular, the incorporation of a membership model can lead to the inculcation of new expectations about performance and follow through. Membership can offset the illness role by demonstrating to consumers that they are needed and that their contributions are critical to the success of a consumer service or support alternative.

A major result of consumer-provided services is the *increased sense of hope* that consumers report feeling vis a vis their own recovery. Consumer-providers act as role models and provide inspiration to others that rehabilitation is a real possibility. This addresses motivational issues and helps recipients move forward in their own process of recovery. Consumers report feeling a sense of personal empowerment, knowing that others can and do succeed, even with symptoms. Authors of first person accounts in this book reflect on the positive personal impact created by seeing others take on helping and leadership roles while coping with their illnesses.

Personal rehabilitation through involvement in consumer service provision (whether as participant, helper, or both) invokes an important recovery theme for some authors. Achieving a balance in providing support and receiving support is important to effective coping. Some authors talked about over-extension, giving too much of themselves, and failing to protect themselves. On a more positive note, authors also talked about setting expectations, establishing boundaries, and understanding their own strengths in roles as consumer service providers as essential to achieving their own recovery.

A final benefit theme is that services delivered by other consumers also contribute to the *empowerment* of recipients. This occurs through the increased sense of personal agency, described above. It also occurs through individuals feeling wanted, intellectually, emotionally, and physically. Particularly in self-help, but even in traditional mental health settings, consumers receiving services often have opportunities to be helpers themselves, when the services are consumer-provided. Consumer-provided services also effect changes for groups of consumers, by increasing their sense of community. And seeing consumers in provider roles expands the group's sense that they are able to ask for and gain greater power and control over services and outcomes. Consumer-provided services have also often directly produced expanded opportunities in traditional settings for consumers to assume new roles as activists—as members of boards, planning committees, etc.; or through initiating other services.

As many or more benefits have been cited for *consumers providing these services.* As for recipients, consumer-providers report the *acquisition of many new skills:* concrete skills vis a vis business practices, planning, organizing, empathic listening, etc. They also report gaining *strategies for life changes* to assist with recovery and improved coping mechanisms. Many consumer-providers have experienced *increased independence* and also report gaining a *supportive network* of friends and acquaintances themselves.

Besides such concrete benefits, individuals involved in consumer-service provision report *finding a new focus, inspiration and meaning* in helping others. They feel rewarded by the fact that they are providing assistance, and through the respect they receive from recipients, other peers, and sometimes from nonconsumer service providers. Many report that giving help to others increased their own motivation, gave their lives a new focus, and enhanced their level of aspiration about the future. These enhancements occurred for many because they saw themselves in a new light—not just as an illness, but as a person.

Overall, many consumers who were service providers report an *improved self-perception,* produced through an interplay of the benefits already described: that is, through an improved sense of competence, achievement, ownership and confidence, as well as through experiencing feelings of being needed and responsible.

Improved self-perception may be one of the most important benefits or outcomes of consumer service provision. A number of authors discuss a personal awakening — a realization that they have much to offer and that their journey through serious mental illness resulted in knowledge useful to others. This improved self-perception can help sustain consumer service providers and expand their roles and functioning as effective and potent helpers. They have something unique to offer — something that is very much needed within many contemporary mental health systems.

Probably of greater variation, but still cited in many reports, are *benefits to mental health and rehabilitation programs* themselves. *Nonconsumer service-providers* can benefit — cognitively by having an increased awareness of the recovery process, which can assist them in work with other clients. They can also gain a more accurate view of traditional services from the consumer's perspective, vis a vis what is helpful and what is not—to improve their own practice. Nonconsumer-providers can also experience attitudinal changes: seeing consumers in a new light, altering long-standing beliefs about the negative long-term course of schizophrenia and other major mental illnesses.

Consumer-based service provision can also contribute directly to *improvements in mental health and/or psychiatric rehabilitation services:* Peer counselors often promote improved dialogue between consumers and staff. By increasing rapport and a sense of understanding, consumer-providers may help their clients be more receptive to services offered that they might otherwise reject, based on their own negative attitudes or past service failures. By changing attitudes, as described above, consumer service providers interacting with staff and administrators can make them more open to the roles that other consumers can play in their own rehabilitation and in agency operations. In some programs, chapter authors have reported that consumer employment caused agency directors to reconsider entire models of group and individual treatment vis a vis their hierarchical and/or inflexible nature.

On a grander scale, consumer-service provision can *expand consumer involvement* in agency operations, overall. Thus, some chapter authors report that consumer positions have moved to permanent funding or been expanded, and that consumerism has become a part of inservice training for all staff. Perhaps more importantly, a cadre of knowledgeable consumers with activist orientations can be created — individuals who then desire to affect more and more aspects of services and move to address larger issues of dissatisfaction. Overall, as consumer service activities are seen as more successful, the consumer perspective should have greater impacts on planning service delivery, on other treatment models, and perhaps on overall standards of practice—for example, moving service relationships away from hierarchy and towards laterality; promoting the appropriate use of disclosure by consumer and nonconsumer service providers alike; mandating not just consumer sign-off on treatment plans, but genuine assimilation of consumer preference and choice in what and how services are delivered.

Consumer service provision can help an organization and/or system realize *quality improvement outcomes*. The success of this innovation requires some introspection on and analysis of service delivery arrangements, the roles of consumers, and the norms governing provider-user relationships. Consumer service provision requires a logic that is somewhat different from (and perhaps conflictual with) traditional thinking about professionalism and professional roles as prescribed by the cultures of many mental health systems.

Quality improvement assumes that professionals do not have all the answers and that their approach to practice is flawed. (If it wasn't, then there would not be the extent of dissatisfaction articulated by consumers.) Quality improvement requires a sensitivity to the perspectives of users and requires service providers to respond to their issues in a manner that increases satisfaction. Quality improvement in psychiatric rehabilitation can close the gap between consumer expectations of support and what they actually get in practice.

The path of quality improvement will likely lead to reconsideration of consumer roles. Assertive consumers will most likely seek to improve their status while they seek to make services more responsive to resolving consumer-defined issues. A quality improvement agenda in psychiatric rehabilitation will undoubtedly embrace consumer service provision.

The Cost of Innovation

Unfortunately, the outcomes associated with the consumer-provider innovation have been negative as well as positive. Reports in this volume have involved costs in terms of administration, nonconsumer staff, service recipients themselves, and personal issues for consumer-providers. *Administrative costs* entail increased *training needs, higher supervisory levels, and accommodation requests* vis a vis flexible hours, leave time, scheduling, etc. The administrative issues mentioned in this volume, however, do not appear to be extensive. In fact, mentioned more often are anticipated burdens that are not realized: e.g., fears that consumer employees will violate confidentiality when they become involved in staff treatment planning meetings. In fact, no reports in this volume or in the literature reviewed produced even one concrete instance where such violations occurred. Indeed, this issue can be addressed by making standards of ethical conduct understood by everyone involved in rehabilitation — providers, consumers, and supporters. There is no good reason to believe that consumer service providers will violate these standards any more than other actors in the rehabilitation process. Thus, administrative concerns appear to be of a minor nature.

Also minor in magnitude are "costs" experienced by service recipients. These entail allusions to some clients feeling resentful over their peers rising to provider status, of these consumer providers being seen as "uppity." Of greater magnitude are reports of resentment and hostility from *nonconsumer staff.* Most commonly reported are instances wherein the performance problems of consumer employees are attributed to their symptomatology, relapse, etc., rather than, as would be the case with others, to a lack of role clarity, need for training in a new function, etc. Oursler comments, "staff interpret behavior through the lens of illness when the lens of new worker would have been a better fit." Often this *'symptom' orientation* produces negative performance assessments; sometimes it results in consumer-providers being inappropriately excused, rather than challenged. In some instances, staff resentment of consumers acting as providers may represent a *desire to maintain the status quo,* or fears of competition and/or inequitable treatment—that individuals who lack their professional training will receive comparable compensation or even be able to replace them. In all these situations, it becomes clear that the stigma and discrimination associated with mental illness are not necessarily reduced among professionals providing mental health and rehabilitation services.

Competition among providers has always existed. Role conflict often emerges among physicians, nurses, social workers, and counselors as they compete for status, functions, and importance in rehabilitation settings. This competition may exacerbate as professionals compete for clients and define certain functions as the exclusive responsibility of their particular discipline. The incorporation of an interdisciplinary practice model can help reduce interprofessional competition. There is no reason why consumer service providers cannot be elements of this service matrix. Perhaps "ugly" competition will rear its head, but this negative outcome can be reduced or even eliminated through progressive leadership, supervision, and training.

The largest set of costs associated with consumer service provision appears to be in terms of *negative effects on consumer-providers* themselves. Some of these ill effects are directly attributed to treatment from nonconsumer professionals and administrators. Other problems are more subtle—i.e., what appear to be "set-ups" for failure due to consumer-provided services being given *too few resources, or accorded too much responsibility* without the augmentation of supports. (For example, hiring a consumer to do a job formerly assigned to a professional, but with no pre-service or in-service training to compensate, as in the employment situation reported by Weklar.) These stresses are often combined with, and perhaps exacerbated by the stress for many consumers brought on by working in general or by work in a mental health service setting, in particular. Examples of the former include fears about job performance or about over-working producing a relapse; fears about the unknown; fears of losing disability benefits, especially when pay rates, levels of employment, and job tenure are all unstable. Examples of particular stresses associated with working in a mental health setting are the fact that this work (particularly in an inpatient, crisis or residential unit) can trigger consumers' recall of their own traumatic experiences, and brings to the fore many of their own issues regarding competency, character, etc., which were never resolved. Also related to this type of work are the *boundary issues* which arise; for example, over-identifying with the service recipient, being unable to separate out one's own anger with the mental health system or with issues that particular clients are struggling with, extreme levels of disappointment when clients fail to follow through on agreed-upon plans, etc. External and internal issues have created *burnout, feelings of rejection, drop-out and even relapse* for some consumer-providers. Of course, such problems are often seen in nonconsumer staff. However, in consumer staff, they may be exacerbated, especially when staff lack training to deal with them. Some chapter authors report seeking out professional roles in human service systems other than mental health as a coping strategy.

But burnout, feelings of rejection, drop-out, and relapse should not be seen as rationalizations for the elimination of consumer service provision. Given the novelty of the roles created, some negative outcomes may be "normal" and perhaps expected. They are probably, however, not ones that are "caused" by consumers. Rather they must be seen as products of a system that is failing to offer appropriate supports and roles for good practice. We should expect that these negative outcomes have a probability of occurrence and take steps to prevent them. When they occur as a pattern within a service system, they should be analyzed as part of a quality improvement program that focuses on changes in systems and processes.

External Factors Contributing to Costs

The "costs" associated with the consumer-provider innovation appear to reflect a number of external realities. First, the fact that *stigma and discrimination towards mental illness are pervasive*—to the extent that they are practiced seemingly as much by mental health professionals as by the "uneducated" lay community. As mentioned previously, there are direct negative effects on consumers: ostracism produced from disclosure of past psychiatric histories, lowered staff expectations for performance, and/or denigrated assessments of competency. Other examples from the chapters include consumer-providers feeling co-opted and pushed towards acculturation to the extent that they give up an identification with other consumers and advocacy for consumer issues in order to "fit in." Particularly problematic is the "gallows humor" existent in mental health organizations—wherein consumer-focused jokes are accepted as the norm and staff insensitivity is so high that consumer providers accept this as a legitimate coping strategy by their nonconsumer staff peers.

Lack of acceptance of consumer service provision is undoubtedly also exacerbated by a *long-standing tension or even competition between professionals in traditional mental health services versus consumerism.* This tension is reflected in previous literature on consumer service provision and may reflect economic fears or threats to professional competency. In this volume, this tension emerges in many chapters; for example, in the skepticism expressed by professionals concerning referrals to consumer-providers, concerns about whether recipients served by other consumers will actually benefit and may even be harmed. Through an analysis of the chapters in this book, it might appear that the more consumers compete with and/or offer direct alternatives to mental health programs and non-consumer professionals, the more challenges and difficulties they experience. That is, self-help groups are less threatening than consumer-run programs, which are also less threatening than consumer employment. Furthermore, it appears that consumers in slots created for them may experience less difficulties than consumers who function in professional positions and happen to disclose their psychiatric histories.

Reflecting the previous two societal realities, but also contributing to the costs is the fact that *consumers themselves don't feel secure in their own worth.* They may be disempowered by their illnesses. Oftentimes they have suffered directly by losing opportunities for education and work experiences available to others—sometimes due to stigma and sometimes due to the unpredictable course of mental illness. Thus they have a lot of personal fears and self-doubt. This can expand to a lack of confidence concerning how to deal with the psychiatric crises and disturbed states of others. Personal issues aside, for persons without training, this is certainly understandable. Even many individuals who have professional certifications in human service specialities, like social work, psychology, nursing, etc., avoid work with those who have long-term mental illness because of their own fears and sense of discomfort. Many consumers need support, development, encouragement, and training for any vocational activity. In the past, mental health systems have had difficulties doing this at all, because of negative attitudes towards the capabilities of "chronic" clients. If this is true for positions involving routine, blue-collar work (like benchwork, assembly line, maintenance), why should we expect support and encouragement for consumers in provider roles—which are bound to be seen as requiring more competency, as well as being directly threatening to nonconsumer providers?

Finally, we should point out that service provider roles filled by consumers are likely to carry an *inherent tension and conflict*. That is, people with a mental illness label often experience stigma and discrimination, but peer provider roles are premised on staff in these positions having to disclose their psychiatric histories. Furthermore, functioning effectively in their positions requires these staff to continuously reveal their most painful experiences on an ongoing basis — for other people's benefit. This "requirement" can be contrasted with the expectation that professionally trained providers keep personal experiences and history to themselves. Professionals think selectively about self-disclosure and use it sparingly and with some caution. In contrast, self-disclosure as a norm of practice can increase the stress of a role that already constitutes difficult emotional labor.

While the self-disclosures of consumer-providers seem to help service recipients, this is also the kind of behavior most likely to produce ostracism from other (nonconsumer) staff, i.e., the people at an agency with much higher status than peers. Furthermore, consumer service provision inherently increases problems with boundary issues. Dual relationships may be good for the service recipient, but we need to ask, how much benefit are they for the consumer service-provider? Furthermore, we need to keep in mind that such stressful demands are often made in the context of paid employment that is minimum wage, without benefits, without tenure, without a career ladder, etc. Consumer service providers clearly need more support (social, emotional, and financial) than what they have been given through many psychiatric rehabilitation and mental health agencies.

Additional Barriers

Besides affecting the operation of consumer-provider innovations, the realities of stigma, discrimination, consumer-provider tensions, etc. can also contribute to other barriers which additionally weaken the prospects for the long-term success of this innovation. The *funding support* for many consumer-provider initiatives is minimal and/or ephemeral, leading to ongoing concerns about their economic survival. For instance, consumer-controlled programs often enjoy an initial period of flourish, but with success comes concern rather than stability. So, beyond initial "seed" funding, consumer programs lack a stable basis of support, and find themselves going from grant to grant, perhaps driven more by survival needs than by their own philosophy or by the unmet needs of prospective consumer service recipients. What appears to be needed is the ongoing commitment of a sponsoring organization, especially regarding administrative and fiscal issues. Sponsors need to provide a stable backing, address the needs, and promote growth of fledgling groups and initiatives, without controlling or co-opting them into the status quo of traditional services.

A second external barrier to consumer service provision is the *lack of meaningful involvement of consumers in planning* and/or implementing these initiatives. In some reports in this volume as well as in the existing literature, consumer service innovations have been initiated almost unilaterally by nonconsumer staff or administrators. External grant funds were made available, someone in the agency thought that this was a good idea, and an application was submitted on behalf of agency consumers. However, as Miya and colleagues point out, agency administrators need to "walk the talk", by fully involving consumers in the planning process for a consumer employment initiative. The chapter by Hilderbrand and colleagues demonstrates that when consumers were not part of the planning process, consumer employees did not feel empowered; they were just employees and dissatisfactions with the employment situation mounted.

A final impediment to success concerns *human resource issues.* Several of the chapters report that self-help groups and consumer-controlled programs have suffered from not having enough stable workers or leadership to maintain organizational survival. Turnover of consumer-providers is oftentimes high. In her chapter, Paynter comments on the "leadership challenge" experienced by Shining Reflections—i.e., the need to constantly encourage and groom new leaders. This can be due to positive forces (rehabilitation and recovery for work in more normalized settings), neutral forces (exercising choices that work in mental health/psychiatric rehabilitation settings are not for them), or negative forces (burnout, ostracism, inadequate resources, discrimination from mental health systems). Whatever the basis for consumers leaving service positions, there needs to be ongoing development, support, and training of individuals who are interested and capable of filling provider roles. It would appear that identification and recruitment of these new providers would most optimally occur from within the mental health system; therefore, the system should play a critical role with consumer groups/programs in making this happen.

No Road Map

While the needs, problems and barriers associated with consumer-provider innovations may be clear, the answers for how to carry out consumer-involvement in services and make it work are not. We do not yet have an established wisdom about how many of these issues can be resolved or avoided. Nor do we necessarily have a format or mechanism through which this wisdom may be accumulated and shared. However, through the production of volumes like this one, perhaps IAPSRS can incorporate this need into its mission. From several chapter authors, we have examples of some of the groundwork that agencies and consumer groups have had to lay. Their decisions and choices, documented in this volume, will hopefully contribute to a roadmap which can make explorations of consumer service provision easier for other consumer groups and/or mental health and psychiatric rehabilitation agencies.

One developmental issue concerns the *relationship between consumer-provided services and the rest of the mental health/psychiatric rehabilitation establishment.* Are these services an extension of and complementary to traditional mental health services or an alternative, a substitution? The answer probably depends on the nature of the other components in the mental health system, their adaptability, and their willingness to accommodate to change. Integration is usually a better solution than separation. However, integration is not always possible. Whatever the situation, solutions will require planning, training, and supports.

Another issue concerns the *structure and formalization.* For example, consumer-controlled services usually start with peer support and then evolve into many different services, programs, and businesses in response to opportunities and to meet the needs of members (which change over time). However, the direction and specifics of evolution are unpredictable. How do consumer organizations take advantage of opportunities, yet still assure that important needs of their constituencies are being met? The answer for "on our own" was to develop a mission statement, with strong member involvement, and to use it to guide future choices.

A third issue involves the *extent of formalization* for consumer innovations. Consumer service initiatives often start with no formal policies or procedures. But many find that they need some policies and develop them in response to needs. They have also found that they have to formalize structures and become more business-like—to get and keep funding. But how much is too much? How much formalization and search for available funds takes them away from their mission? The chapters in this volume can be helpful to other emerging consumer initiatives, by sharing information about the kinds of rules that have worked, how these rules have been enforced, and what the responses have been.

A final issue concerns consumers hired by mental health agencies. This has usually represented an exploratory activity, founded on good intentions, or in response to external funding opportunities (i.e., a demonstration project, as described by Solomon and colleagues). Consumers are hired because they are consumers, not in response to a program need identified. Consequently, their *job functions may lack clarity*, with neither consumer, supervisors or peers being clear about what roles consumers play: participant, advocate, leader, to name a few. Lack of role clarity causes stress for consumer-providers and may increase the resentment of other staff. In the case described by Hilderbrand

and colleagues, lack of role clarity caused stress and contributed to poor work performance. In Weklar's case, having no rules or guidelines concerning whether a consumer employee should be treated the same as or different from others caused consumer stress and seemed to contribute to negative evaluations. While administrators and/or consumer advocates probably thought that role clarification and employment guidelines could evolve over time, such a strategy does not seem to have optimized outcomes for those involved.

Ingredients for Success

For the current consumer-provider initiative to succeed, a number of concrete suggestions can be garnered from chapters in this volume. These are not necessarily comprehensive; nor will they work in every situation; nor guarantee the success of any initiative. However, they have enough examples from experience to justify their presentation and endorsement here.

1. Consumer-controlled programs and consumer-provider staff need physical and economic assistance that is adequate and stable. Self-help programs need consistent sponsors; consumer-controlled alternatives may often need start-up assistance with book-keeping, billing, personnel, space issues, etc., from mental health programs; consumer employees must be given stable employment and a decent wage—enough to enable them to get off SSI/SSDI if this is appropriate. Without such minimal economic adequacy, it is impossible to think that consumers and/or consumer groups can continue to cope with larger interpersonal and societal challenges which they face.

2. We need to recognize that "consumers" are not all the same, and respond to their heterogeneity and diversity. That is, it is not appropriate to expect that a single consumer in a provider or advocacy role will be able to "speak for" or otherwise adequately represent the interests of all service recipients. To adequately infuse consumerism into existing systems requires substantial investments, not just tokenism. For example, Zipple and colleagues suggest that 20% of an agency workforce be comprised of individuals with psychiatric disabilities.

3. Attention must be paid to the needs of individual consumers in provider roles and to the "meaning" their dual role has for them. This may involve attention from administrative staff as to what accommodations are necessary and how they may best be implemented (e.g., two part-time positions instead of one full-time, job-sharing for coverage during absences, alterations in work space assignments, etc.). Also necessary is the availability of enhanced supervision at

times to help consumer-providers deal with special issues (for example, experiences which trigger symptoms and how to handle these, boundary issues, etc.). Finally, mutual help on a group basis from peers should also be made available to consumer-providers.

4. We need to minimize rather than reify differences between consumers and "professionals." Consumer staff should be treated like any other employee with similar roles or responsibilities, having the same rights and responsibilities. Neither substandard expectations nor separation are appropriate, nor are they called for based on the experiences reported in this volume. When consumers are first involved as providers in agency operations, there may need to be an "integration" process to address issues and concerns for both consumer and nonconsumer staff. Jonikas and colleagues suggest the process through which agencies can address this. To overcome stigma, a first important step is to overcome an "us versus them" attitude on either side — consumers or nonconsumers.

5. To successfully negotiate the difficult issues involved, partnerships are needed between consumers, consumer groups and mental health/psychiatric rehabilitation agencies. Relationships are needed for concrete tasks like recruitment of consumers into self-help or applicant pools for employment. Individual consumers will often find it helpful to have mentorship and personal support from established professionals, whether or not they have a consumer background. For psychiatric rehabilitation to survive in the reduced funding climate of human services today, combined advocacy rather than hostility and back-biting are critical.

6. Finally, and perhaps of greatest importance, organizations which pursue consumer-provider service provision need to have a vision, mission, and values that are shared by all members. Once these are in place, operational issues can be more easily resolved by returning to the mission statement as a cross-check on what's appropriate and what's a priority.

Chapter 47
Futures for Empowerment of Consumer Role Innovation
Carol T. Mowbray
David P. Moxley

The previous chapter presented suggestions concerning what's needed for current consumer-provider initiatives to succeed. However, promoting further expansion and ensuring a significant impact in the future are different issues. We turn now to the question of where consumer service provision is headed. The longitudinal perspective from "where we have come from" (Chapter 1) to "where we are now" should give us some better understanding of where we are going. The importance of history should be, in part, to better predict the future. Yet these are turbulent times. We would like to be able to give our readers a forecast for the future of consumer-provider initiatives, or at least our best estimate. But the crystal ball is too dim, and software for computer-generated predictive analyses remains in *The Twilight Zone*. We had considered painting alternative scenarios for several possible futures. But the future in question doesn't depend on the shoot of a die, or even the spin of a roulette wheel—the numbers of possibilities are too high. The future for mental health and human service delivery is affected by too many forces which are themselves unpredictable. To name a few:

- market forces for profit and increased impotency of government control, contrasted with expanded consumer advocacy, consumer involvement in mental health systems operations, and demands for choice and satisfaction;
- conservative forces which minimize the individual's voice and amplify forces for profitability, contrasted with increased attention to disability rights and protection;
- demands and needs for human services, contrasted with a public that is increasingly unwilling to pay for assistance to anyone but "their own."

Not only are these forces unstable and unpredictable, but they are also likely to be interactive in unknown ways. Any statements that are made to foresee the status, operation, success, or even the existence of consumer-provider initiatives, will probably be simplistic, naive, or simply wrong! Thus, we have prudently avoided the temptation to end this volume by characterizing the expected future of consumer-providers.

While we have little confidence in our ability to prognosticate the future, we do have confidence in our ability to analyze the experiences represented through the programs and personal accounts depicted and to characterize those forces, settings and policies which are most or least likely to improve and/or expand the consumer-provider initiative.

Consumer-provider initiatives clearly work better in some environments and under some circumstances than others. For example, consumer-provider initiatives seem to have faced particular challenges operating in inpatient or residential programs; that is, settings where roles are rigid and relationships strictly hierarchical. In contrast, organizations that promote diversity on all fronts may be more supporting of, and also more likely to benefit positively from, consumer-provider initiatives. Also, programs that fully endorse a consumer-as-member orientation and promote consumer involvement in planning, governance, and other aspects of agency operations seem to have been more positive hosts for consumer-provider activities. Consumer-provided services also appear to fare better when they involve a group of consumers (as opposed to one or two tokens) who are sharing responsibility and leadership and appropriately dividing up needed roles, while recognizing individual strengths and limitations to make differential assignments. Finally, consumer-provided services seem to produce more positive impacts when they are fully integrated with other programs for mental health treatment and rehabilitation into a comprehensive system of care.

An Empowerment Framework

We believe that the environments and circumstances where the consumer-provider enterprise is more likely to flourish can be best characterized as "empowering." While we would acknowledge that the term is currently overused in mental health verbiage, this may be with justification, since the concept does fill many gaps. To avoid misunderstanding of our use of the term (another problem with current verbiage), by empowerment, we mean the process and the outcome associated with individuals (who are disenfranchised) gaining control over their lives and their environments. The empowerment goes beyond individual gains in self-efficacy, competency, etc., to encompass gains for the group. Furthermore, these gains are achieved through participation with others and collective action to produce access to and acquisition of resources, understanding of and involvement in sociopolitical processes, and overall improved consciousness and skill in methods of obtaining and maintaining personal and group power. Several of the chapters in this volume address empowerment. For example, Bledsoe talks about her experience with consumer service provision as "empowerment in action," establishing a "power base of mutual support."

This chapter presents a portrayal of environments and circumstances that are "empowering" for persons with psychiatric disabilities. We have adopted a framework presented by Maton and Salem (1995). Using a multiple case study methodology, they studied as research sites three diverse organizations which have produced empowerment in members individually and as a group.

They found that these empowering settings were characterized by the following: (1) a common belief system premised on the expectation of individual and group growth and development; (2) an opportunity role structure which provides "meaningful opportunities for individuals to develop, grow, and participate" (p. 643); (3) a support system that includes a wide variety of supports that are peer-based and produce a sense of community; and (4) leadership which is motivational, talented, shared, and committed. We will now elaborate on these characteristics, providing some positive and negative examples from current mental health settings and policy.

Belief Systems

Empowering settings and circumstances for individuals with psychiatric disabilities value growth and change, and build on member strengths to support beliefs that all members have the capacity to achieve personal growth towards salient goals. Such a set of beliefs is, of course, completely congruent with psychosocial rehabilitation principles. However, many traditional mental health agencies and programs do not include an orientation towards service recipients that is strengths-based, that helps them identify personal goals, and/or that incorporates their goals in service plans. For consumer-provider initiatives to be successful, the organizational climate of these mental health programs would have to change. Anti-stigma training for staff and for consumers themselves would also be necessary, along with strong messages that are proconsumerism and antidiscrimination from organizational leadership. At a systems level, policies also need to change so that, for example, assessments are comprehensive and contextualized, and individuals have control over their community service plans, not just involvement or mere "sign-off." Where these strengths-based and anti-stigma practices and policies do not exist, consumer service initiatives may face extreme challenges.

An Opportunity Role Structure

A second criteria for empowering environments is that they provide a full range of opportunities for individuals which are acceptable and appropriate to needs for growth and development. This means that service recipients should have available to them a wide array of rehabilitation options, from traditional vocational training and placements, to supported educational programs, to career counseling and guidance. Such an opportunity structure which is comprehensive, flexible, and individualized is in sharp contrast to the existing, ever more restrictive description of mental health programs. Even community-based agencies have been described as endorsing goals of merely "stabilization and medication" for clients (Harding, 1996), dictated by managed care systems whose major aims are often to minimize short-term costs and avoid long-term implications. In terms of consumer-providers, an opportunity role structure would include clear role definitions and provide many movement opportunities. Thus consumer-providers may enter a service delivery system through employment slots designated as "for consumers" or through organizations that are consumer-controlled. (These opportunities may offer protection and special supports initially.) However, beyond this system entry, consumer service provision in an empowering system must include opportunities for continued upward career mobility and expansion of consumer control into governance, planning, and systems operations. To be specific, a mental health program that designates one or two paraprofessional positions to employ consumers, but no more is not empowering; a mental health agency that puts in place a referral agreement with a self-help group, but no more, is not empowering; a mental health system that supports and contracts with a consumer-controlled agency for specified services, but no more, is not empowering. Such initiatives may represent good starts, but a program, agency, or system must also recognize that a fuller opportunity structure is necessary for the future.

At the policy level, much has been achieved to promote supports for individuals with disabilities through passage of the Americans with Disabilities Act. However, continued attention is required vis a vis knowledge dissemination and application of provisions of the Act. This has been recognized by many advocacy groups. However, beyond the ADA, other critical policy changes are also needed to promote an opportunity structure for individuals with psychiatric disabilities. Most problematic are policies associated with SSI/SSDI eligibility and receipt. While offering a critical safety net for disabled individuals unable to work to fully sustain themselves, the all-or-none definition of disability of SSI/SSDI exists as a significant disincentive for consumers to pursue vocational opportunities and to determine how much or how long they can work.

Our country's model of disability harkens back to the American Revolutionary War, as returning wounded veterans received payments for the loss of an ability to work. Since then, disability in the United States has been viewed in dichotomous terms: One is either "able" or "unable" to work; one is either "disabled" or "nondisabled." Progress achieved in the fields of psychiatric rehabilitation, developmental disabilities, aging, and physical and cognitive rehabilitation seriously questions the legitimacy of this dichotomy. Both research and experience have demonstrated that disability is best conceived as a continuum from high to nonexistent. The placement of a person on this continuum is greatly influenced by norms, values, and the availability of supports, assistive technologies, and environmental change.

The disability rights movement underscores the constructed nature of disability. As a social construction, disability and its conception can be radically altered through changes in attitudes, images, opportunities, and rights.

Disability policy needs revision to reflect current technologies promoting return to work as a goal—in any capacity, at any level, for any duration, with guaranteed disability payments and benefit availability as backups, perhaps for an indefinite duration. A more flexible disability payment system based on a continuum model of disability would allow consumers to start employment at the level reflecting their abilities and capacity and to move up in responsibility, pay rate, extent and duration of their employment at a pace appropriate for themselves and their employment situation. Currently these determinations are constrained by actual and perceived policies and also by consumer fears about permanently losing this safety net.

Support System

However beneficial they may be, the belief and opportunity structures in place can be setups for failure unless supports are available to enable actualization. For empowering environments, the supports need to be peer-based and thus nonhierarchical; they need to be acceptable to the consumers receiving them; and they need to be naturalistic, promoting the sense of community. Otherwise supports can become assistance that is not wanted and not helpful. Supportive service across an entire mental health agency does not mean that all services are delivered by peers. Rather, it could mean that in many ways those delivering services and receiving services are on a more equal basis—for example, as in a clubhouse model where the traditional distinction between staff and members vis a vis who's in charge are eliminated; in some forms of therapy wherein therapist/client distance is minimized and personal disclosures by the therapist are viewed as helpful and necessary, as long as they address client (and not therapist) needs.

However, the provision of support by a service provider (rather than control, guidance, direction, transference, etc.) produces much more complexity in terms of boundary issues. That is, providers are no longer guided by arbitrary distancing and noninvolvement rules, but must make such determinations on an individual basis, using their own good judgement. Empowering organizations need to set some standards or a framework for what individual support needs may be beyond particular providers, or inappropriate for them to address so that neither consumer or nonconsumer providers become overwhelmed.

In providing supports, empowering organizations will also need to address choice. Along with opportunities, supports offered must be multiple so that individuals may choose a support structure most compatible with their own style and needs. Real choices must be in place, along with the expectation that these choices will be exercised not just nominally offered. Within a choice framework, it should be expected that even with system encouragement for consumerism and anti-stigma campaigns, some individual service recipients will reject consumer-provided services in favor of medicalized or other more traditional models.

For consumers who provide services, this characteristic of empowering organizations means that specialized supports need to be available. Some chapter authors have offered suggestions for many of the modes through which such assistance could be delivered: e.g., specialized job coaches; supervisors with more specialized training and fewer staff to oversee; well-informed therapists for consumer-provider clients who can address needs at their mental health or psychiatric rehabilitation jobs as well as the usual areas of symptoms, medication, interpersonal relations, etc.; support groups for prosumers offered with or without disclosure; training for nonconsumer staff to address acceptance and promotion of all types of diversity; agency leadership which willingly negotiates accommodations under ADA and promotes employee relations that are equitable and that address individualized needs as much as possible.

We can no longer characterize contemporary systems serving people with serious mental illness along one dimension. Consumer service provision illustrates the growing complexity of these systems along the dimensions of: medical care; social services; rehabilitation; and social supports. The growth of consumer service provision introduces a fifth inescable dimension: that of consumerism in which systems are responsible for helping consumers to assist themselves and their peers to control their lives and living situations.

Leadership

The final characteristic of an empowering organization is leadership; it is described as inspirational, talented, shared, and committed. Such leaders can directly affect members, by acting as role models and by reinforcing the program's mission and philosophy. They can also foster empowerment by motivating members and staff and by establishing a model of empowerment for the organization through full member participation in decision-making and action. For the consumer-provider initiative, these leadership qualities should ideally apply to the mental health/psychiatric rehabilitation organization which relates to consumer service provision, as well as to the group of consumers providing the service.

In terms of mental health/psychiatric rehabilitation organizations, we have already identified aspects of operations for which leadership is critical—for example: in providing clear messages to staff that are proconsumerism and anti-stigma; in requiring strengths-based approaches that view clients in context; in setting standards for consumers to be in control of their community service plans; in expanding program offerings to develop the opportunity role structure to its full extent; in ensuring that consumers are given real choices among these program components, and so on.

Attracting and recruiting individuals with these leadership qualities to mental health/psychiatric rehabilitation organizations is a formidable task. Professional training which supports this leadership approach and encourages individuals to work with those who have psychiatric disabilities is still uncommon in social work, psychology, and other academic programs. Interdisciplinary, specialized training in psychiatric rehabilitation is rare. Clearly, more advocacy is needed in academic settings and professional associations to expand relevant training. Supporting and retaining talented, inspirational leaders within mental health/psychiatric rehabilitation organizations is perhaps an even more formidable task than their recruitment. Intrinsic rewards are, no doubt, experienced from interpersonal interactions based on this leadership style. However, it is oftentimes doubtful whether these benefits can outweigh the stresses associated with constant demands for paperwork, documentation, efficiency, downsizing, short-term performance expectations, threats of litigation, employment relations negotiations, etc. The need for advocacy and institutional support to identify, encourage, and reward outstanding leaders in mental health/ rehabilitation organizations is high, but not often recognized or fulfilled.

Concerning consumer leadership, needs and problems are also high, but probably somewhat different. As indicated in the literature review, many consumers may need training, support, and development vis a vis their willingness to take on leadership roles. Past stigma and discrimination, reduced educational and vocational opportunities, negative self-concepts, and symptoms of the illness itself all play a part. Furthermore, leadership needs to be shared, to help diffuse the stresses inherent in these positions, combat burnout, and counteract high turnover rates. Thus ongoing development of consumer leadership potential is a critical activity for the future expansion of consumer as provider innovations. Chapters in this volume by Jasper and by Zipple and colleagues describe successful efforts in this regard. However, what's clear from these descriptions is that this leadership development *requires* combined efforts and energy of consumer groups and established agencies.

Conclusion

From our identification of the major themes that emerged from contributors to this volume, we see a story of why and how consumer service provision arose and the benefits it has produced for recipients, for consumer-providers, and for mental health staff, programs, and systems of care. However, we also see a competing set of costs—especially to the personal well-being and outcomes of consumers providing services. These costs appear to be greater to the extent that consumer service provision actually competes with traditional providers. We suggested that these costs reflect some major external realities vis a vis stigma and discrimination towards mental illness (so pervasive that even mental health providers are perpetrators), the long-standing tension between professionals and consumerism, the fact that consumers themselves do not feel secure in their own worth, and the conflict inherent in consumer-provider roles. We concluded that an additional current problem inhibiting success is the lack of a road map, a shared knowledge base concerning how to prevent or ameliorate problems associated with consumer-provider innovations. We presented several examples of difficult situations and how their resolution evolved over time and was individualized to particular agencies and circumstances. We then made overall suggestions concerning what needs to be done at present to maintain consumer-provider efforts and to help ensure their success.

But the story wasn't over. We addressed concerns about where we are going from here in the further development, expansion, and impact of consumers as providers. We pointed out that predicting the future amidst numerous unstable forces, interacting in unknown ways was a task beyond the capabilities of our efforts and abilities. Instead, we suggested that consumer service provision would be more likely to flourish and exert significant impact when developed within empowering organizations and circumstances. We utilized an existing framework (Maton & Salem, 1995) and applied it to describe the characteristics of organizations that would likely be empowering vis a vis psychiatric disabilities and consumer-provider efforts.

The story has a few final details. Returning to the idea of a road map, expansions and continued innovations in consumer-provider services will be improved, and more likely to succeed overall, if they have available knowledge about others' trials, failures, and strategies. This is particularly true for small organizations, rural geographic areas, low income locations, and minority populations. Resources need to be expended on a priority basis to help ensure this information dissemination. This should be done in multiple formats (written, verbal, etc.) and to as many different audiences as possible at national, regional, state and local levels.

Secondly, we need to emphasize the importance of systematic, comprehensive evaluations of processes and outcomes associated with consumer service provision. This is an innovation which has multiple bases for expectations of success. However, to encourage further and further expansion based on expectation alone would certainly be unwise as well as unfair to consumers who provide and/or receive services. Thus, now and in the future, all organizations pursuing consumer-provider initiatives need to be guided by the evaluation suggestions in the chapter by Leff and colleagues. The impact of this innovation needs to be established, and its limitations known. Even maximally successful models have rarely been found to work for all people, in all situations, in all circumstances. Consumer service provision has a promising future; but hope and beliefs without knowledge can take us only so far in a market economy of practical realities.

Our mission in assembling this volume has been to present a realistic picture of the complexity and the heterogeneity of consumer service provision, so that organizations and individuals will have a more adequate knowledge base on which to assess this innovation. Our aims have not been to glorify or overstate its value, nor have they been to denigrate or pessimistically describe the barriers. Hopefully, the knowledge and ideas presented here will inform the field, so that the future and outcomes of consumer service provision proceed on a more enlightened basis.

References

Harding, C. (1996). Some things we've learned about vocational rehabilitation of the seriously and persistently mentally ill. Boston University Research Colloquium, Boston, April 17.

Maton, K.I. & Salem, D.A. (1995). Organizational characteristics of empowering community settings: A multiple case study approach. *American Journal of Community Psychology*, 23(5), 631-656.